How to Live with God

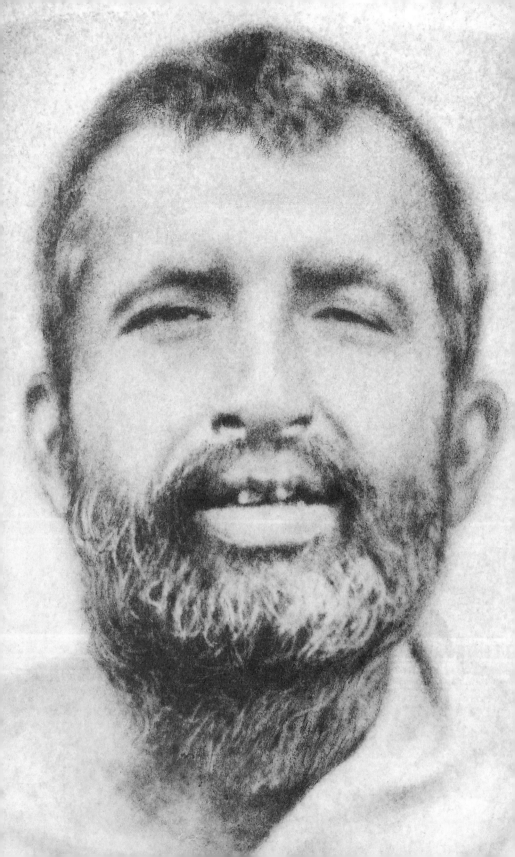

How to Live with God

In the Company
of Ramakrishna

Swami Chetanananda

Vedanta Society of St. Louis

Copyright © 2008 Vedanta Society of St. Louis

Library of Congress Cataloging-in-Publication Data

Chetanananda, Swami.
  How to live with God : in the company of Ramakrishna / Swami Chetanananda. — 1st ed.
     p. cm.
  Includes bibliographical references and index.
  ISBN 978-0-916356-85-9 (hardcover : alk. paper) -- ISBN 978-0-916356-86-6
(pbk. : alk. paper)
  1. Ramakrishna, 1836-1886--Influence. 2. Ramakrishna Mission. 3. Religious life--Hinduism. I. Title.
    BL1280.292.R36C45 2008
    294.5'44--dc22
                                        2007045545

FIRST EDITION 2008

Cover design by Diane Marshall

Printed in the United States of America

Those who wish to learn in greater detail about the teachings contained in this book may write to:
Vedanta Society of St. Louis
205 S. Skinker Blvd.
St. Louis, MO 63105, U.S.A.

www.vedantastl.org

Contents

List of Illustrations

Preface

Sometimes we imagine how wonderful it would have been if we could have lived with Buddha, Christ, or Ramakrishna. Blessed are those who lived with them on this earth; blessed are the few who saw and heard them; and thrice blessed are those who served them. These great ones are now beyond our sight, but they are not dead. Mystics and devotees still feel their presence and see their luminous forms in meditation. Some even speak with them. The *Chaitanya Charitamrita* says: "Gaur [Chaitanya] is still enacting his divine play; only a fortunate few can see it."

Relationships are very important in human life. A person who has no friends or relatives is lonely and sometimes feels helpless. In contrast, a person who has many friends and relatives feels strong and happy, and that person can depend on their help during critical moments in life. This is why human beings always seek companions.

The Sanskrit word *ātmiyatā, or relationship,* comes from the root word for Atman, the Self. The Brihadaranyaka Upanishad says: "Verily, not for the sake of the husband is the husband loved, but he is loved for the sake of the Self." Similarly, a spouse, children, wealth, worlds, gods, and everything else are loved for the sake of the Self. This Self is the substratum of the universe and all the beings within It. We are interrelated with all beings, and are always connected with God. But, because of maya we are unaware of this. The cause of our misery is that we have divorced ourselves from God, who is the only source of peace and bliss. If we can establish a strong relationship with God, our lives will be free from anxiety, uncertainty, and fear.

The main theme of this book is: How can we love God or an avatar? How can we live with Him? How can we establish a relationship with Him?

How can we love God?

Love and knowledge go together. We cannot love a man or a woman without knowing him or her. Again, we cannot know a person fully without having love for and interest in that person. The more we know someone, the more our love increases. A woman saw a handsome man in a gathering and fell in love with him. Then she heard from his friends that he was from a wealthy family and would inherit a fortune; this news increased her love immensely. Later she heard that he was a brilliant writer, an artist, a musician, and endowed with a noble character. The more she learned about the good qualities of that man, the more her love increased. A true lover wants to know every minute detail about the beloved.

How can we live with God?

A blacksmith puts an iron rod into the fire with his right hand and works the bellows with his left. After 15 or 20 minutes the iron rod becomes red. Then he grabs it with tongs and hammers it on his anvil to give it shape. Thus a cold, black iron rod becomes red hot and generates light and heat because of its association with the fire. Similarly if we can connect the mind with God every day for 15 or 20 minutes uninterruptedly, it will become luminous and spiritual.

In fact, one lives where one's mind is. When someone asks me how to live with God, I recall the three verses of the Bhagavad Gita in which Krishna succinctly says what devotees are supposed to do and what he will do for them: "Those whose minds are fixed on me, and whose lives are absorbed in me, derive satisfaction and delight from enlightening one another and always speaking of me. To those who are constantly devoted, who worship me with love, I give the power of discrimination by which they come to me. Solely out of compassion for them, I, dwelling within their hearts, dispel the darkness born of ignorance with the effulgent lamp of wisdom." (10:9-11)

How can we establish a relationship with God?

We establish a relationship with God in the same way we establish human relationships. There is a saying: "Relationships develop through frequent visits." Human relationships become established through frequent contact — otherwise, "out of sight, out of mind."

The vision of God depends on longing, but longing does not arise until the desire for worldly enjoyment comes to an end. How can we cultivate this longing for God and establish a relationship with Him? M., the recorder of *The Gospel of Sri Ramakrishna*, used an example from everyday life to explain this to devotees:

> One should have the company of holy people; that gradually develops longing. When the bride sees the bridegroom for the first time during the wedding ceremony, she is not very attracted to her husband. [In India at that time parents generally arranged their daughter's marriage while she was young.] When the ceremony is over, she does not want to leave her parents and relatives to go with her new husband. She cries and clings to her loving parents whom she has lived with all her life. This is natural. But it is not proper for her to live with her parents throughout her life. Her parents console her, saying: "Our sweet child, don't cry. He is your husband. His house is your real home and you will have to set up your own household there." Finally, encouraged by her friends and relatives, she leaves her parents and moves in with her husband. Years go by. Suddenly her mother becomes very sick, and her father writes to her: "My dear daughter, please come home immediately. Your mother is very sick." She replies: "Father, it is difficult for me to come just now. My son is taking his examination. My husband is busy in his office. If I leave, who will cook for them and manage this household? I am sorry that I can't come now. I shall try to visit you in the fall."

The bride in M.'s story establishes a relationship with the husband she barely knows by surrendering to him and making him her own through love and service. Likewise, a spiritual aspirant establishes a relationship with the unknown, unseen Lord through self-surrender, devotion, and service. The more those devotees learn about the glory and power of their beloved God, the more their love increases. The more those devotees meditate on God's beautiful form and divine qualities, the more their minds are soaked in God-consciousness. This is how a spiritual aspirant becomes intoxicated with love of God.

This book has its roots in my 35 years of in-depth study, research, and meditation on Ramakrishna. It reveals various facets of Ramakrishna's god-intoxicated life. Many materials concerning Ramakrishna were written in Bengali, Ramakrishna's mother tongue, but this literature is inaccessible to readers who do not know that language. For this book I have translated and edited articles that I previously wrote on Ramakrishna in Bengali; I have also included a few that originally appeared in

English. Fifteen chapters in this book were taken from my Bengali book, *Sri Ramakrishner Sannidhey* [*In the Company of Sri Ramakrishna*], (Udbodhan Office, Calcutta). Another article, "Dhyanabhumi Dakshineswar" [Dakshineswar: An Object of Meditation], was published in *Nibodhata* magazine (Sarada Math, Dakshineswar). A few articles appeared in the *Prabuddha Bharata* and *Vedanta Kesari* in English. The rest of the chapters in this book are based on lectures that I gave at the Vedanta Society of St. Louis. Five of them were from a series entitled "The Gospels of Sri Ramakrishna"; one discussed Swami Saradananda's *Sri Sri Ramakrishna Lilaprasanga*; the last was based on Swami Vivekananda's *My Master*.

Truly, I have no words to express my gratitude to my editors, proofreaders, typesetter, designer, and those who corrected the manuscript on the computer. This book was produced through teamwork, and I would like to express my indebtedness to my editors: Kim Saccio-Kent (a freelance editor in San Francisco), Linda Prugh (an English teacher in Kansas City), Pravrajika Shuddhatmaprana (a nun of Hollywood Vedanta Centre), Janice Thorup (a former adjunct professor of writing at Washington University, Saint Louis). Ralph Hile also edited the manuscript and prepared the index. I must inform the reader that there are some incidents and quotes that have been cited more than once in this book. I could not avoid these repetitions because removing them would disrupt the flow of thought in each context, and the ideas they illustrate would not be fully presented. I should also note that while quoting from *The Gospel of Sri Ramakrishna* I replaced "woman and gold" with "lust and gold."

Once Ramakrishna said to a devotee: "Look here. Just repeating the word 'siddhi' will not produce intoxication. You must actually get some hemp, rub it in water, and then drink the solution. Since you are going to lead a householder's life, create a roseate intoxication in your mind with the thought of God. You will be doing your duties, but let that pleasant intoxication remain with you."

The goal of this book is to create god-intoxication in the mind of the reader. When a drunkard removes the cork of his wine bottle, the very fragrance of the wine makes him happy even before he drinks it. In this book I have tried to create that "roseate intoxication" and bring joy to the reader by presenting the divine fragrance of Ramakrishna. When we enter a perfume shop, like it or not, the fragrance penetrates our nostrils. We cannot stop it. Ramakrishna's holy company is like this. He is lively, inspiring, joyful, and full of fun. With a glance he removes delusion and infatuation, and transforms us. Through Ramakrishna's life and his message we find that God is not a myth; He is within us and around us. Ramakrishna makes God-realization simple and easily accessible.

Finally I want to remind the reader that without samadhi, spiritual vision, or divine inebriation, spiritual life remains in an initial state — that is, it does not develop. It sometimes becomes dull and dreary, mechanical and superficial. The aim of this book is to remove spiritual boredom and despondency, and to create excitement and inspiration, hope and imagination, love and devotion in the minds of spiritual aspirants. Ramakrishna's visions and his samadhi are so vivid that when we see the photo of his smiling face in samadhi, our hearts are filled with hope and joy, peace and tranquility. Ramakrishna's descriptions of his own spiritual experiences penetrate our hearts, clear up the doubts and confusion in our minds, and create hunger for God.

There is no end to human imagination. When imagination becomes deep and concentrated, it becomes realization. Let us imagine we are in Ramakrishna's room in Dakshineswar. We see his cot and bed and his pictures of gods, goddesses, and saints on the walls. We do not see the Master's physical form, but we try to visualize his divine form there. We imagine that perhaps the Master has gone to the Panchavati or to the Mother's temple. He will be back soon. Let us wait.

Chetanananda

Kalpataru Day
1 January 2008
St. Louis, U.S.A.

An artist's imagination: Ramakrishna in the form of Rama with bow and arrow, of Krishna with a flute, and of Chaitanya with a water pot

1

Various Forms
of Ramakrishna

nnumerable people now regard Ramakrishna as their Chosen Deity
and object of meditation. There are many different ways to meditate: One can meditate on a divine form, divine qualities, divine
actions or events, messages of world teachers, a passage from the
scriptures, and so on. Devotees generally meditate on divine forms,
because when they repeat a mantra or the divine name of a particular
deity, that form appears in their minds. Due to impurities in the mind,
when we close our eyes to meditate we see darkness, or something like
mist, or perhaps some part of our Chosen Deity's form. But people whose
minds are pure and free from worldly desires see the luminous blissful
form of their Chosen Deity in its entirety. Swami Brahmananda used to
say: "When you practise meditation, first think of the blissful form of your
Chosen Deity. That will soothe your nerves. Think that He is looking at
you with a smiling face and with joy. Otherwise your meditation will be
dry and tedious."[1]

Once a Canadian woman said to me, "I like Vivekananda better than
Ramakrishna."

"Why?" I asked.

She replied, "Because Vivekananda is handsome."

I laughed and said: "Once a devotee said to Swami Vijnanananda:
'Swami, when we see Ramakrishna's picture, we don't perceive an
outstanding personality. But in Swami Vivekananda's picture there is a

great personality manifested.' Swami Vijnanananda responded: 'That is not true. The Master was an extraordinary and wonderful person. His picture shows a person who has passed through all six centres of the kundalini. Seeing his god-intoxicated form, we feel that he is absorbed in the ocean of bliss having transcended all centres. I see many divine forms in that picture of the Master. What great power he had! He would travel in the realms of the sun, moon, stars, and Brahma, just as he wished. Once the Master showed me his picture and said: "Look, I dwell in this. Meditate on me." One can find everything in the Master's picture.'"[2]

When the great sage Vivekananda composed the vesper song of the Master he wrote: "Your pure eyes are tinged with the collyrium of knowledge and your glance removes delusion instantly." In this modern age, just as a laser beam can very quickly remove cataracts from the eyes, so the Master's divine glance can wipe out all worldly attachments and delusions in the human mind.

Is God with form or without form, with qualities or without qualities? When someone asked the Master this question, he told the following story: "A man entered a forest and saw a chameleon on a tree. He reported to his friends, 'I have seen a red lizard.' He was firmly convinced that it was nothing but red. Another person, after visiting the tree, said, 'I have seen a green lizard.' He was firmly convinced that it was nothing but green. But the man who lived under the tree said: 'What both of you have said is true. But the fact is that the creature is sometimes red, sometimes green, sometimes yellow, and sometimes has no colour at all.'"[3]

By telling this story, Ramakrishna indicated that he was like that chameleon and that people of all religious paths would come to him and attain spiritual fulfillment. There was no limit to the Master's spiritual moods. Swami Vivekananda remarked: "The Master was an embodiment of infinite spirituality." Swami Saradananda wrote: "The Master used to say that God is limitless. Similarly, we saw that the Master's spiritual mood was also limitless." It is impossible to fully describe who Ramakrishna was. In this connection Girish Chandra Ghosh said: "Even after seeing Sri Ramakrishna so much, I am unable to say definitely what he really is or what his distinctive aspects are. I have seen him manifest himself differently at different times. During the festival at Panihati, for instance, I saw the Master in various spiritual moods. Since that time, I cannot say whether he is Purusha or Prakriti. He told me that even he did not know whether he was Purusha or Prakriti."[4]

Once Swami Saradananda asked Swami Brahmananda to approve a clay model for the Master's marble image. Brahmananda replied: "Which figure of the Master should I base my approval on? Even on the same day I saw him assume many forms. Sometimes one would find him lean and emaciated with disheveled hair; sometimes he was immersed in samadhi and his body was luminous; again sometimes he would be found to possess a stature much taller and stronger than his usual form, and he would pace from one end of the veranda to the other with big, long strides."[5] Those who lived with the Master day and night saw that he was polymorphic: He could change his form at will.

The scriptures say that a divine form does not cast a shadow. Nistarini Ghosh told her son Swami Ambikananda: "Once the Master saw that his body looked like crystal. His body did not cast a shadow. Observing this, the Master prayed: 'Mother, what is this? Please turn this divine beauty within. Suppress it, or fear will keep people from coming here. I want to mix with everyone, like other human beings.'"[6]

Ramakrishna's Physical Appearance

There are two important records of Ramakrishna as a divine incarnation: First, *The Gospel of Sri Ramakrishna*; second, the photographs taken of him. In his diary, M. recorded the daily life and messages of the Master in minute detail. This type of documentation does not exist for other incarnations. The Master's photographs give us his exact physical appearance, but one has to use one's imagination to visualize the forms of other avatars. The Master worshipped his own picture, and said: "In the course of time this picture will be worshipped in many homes."[7]

Once a monk asked the Holy Mother: "Does the Master dwell in the picture?" She replied: "Of course he does. The body and its shadow are the same. And what is this picture but a shadow of his body."[8]

Some people practise *Trataka* to intensify their meditation. In this technique, one gazes at the Master's picture or another object of meditation without blinking the eyes. When the eyes become strained, tears trickle down; then one meditates in the heart, closing the eyes. Ramakrishna's description of his own physical beauty also helps an aspirant to become absorbed in meditation: "At that time my beauty became manifest in such a way that people would stare at me," said the Master. "My face and chest were always crimson, and a lustre would emanate from my body. Because people stared at me, I would cover myself with a thick *chadar*. I would pray to the Divine Mother, 'Take away my external beauty, O Mother, and give me inner beauty.' I used to pass my hand over this body and slap it again and again, saying, 'Go within, go within.' After some days my skin turned pale, as you see it now."[9]

Once in the course of conversation, the Holy Mother described the Master's physical appearance, saying:

> His complexion was the colour of gold. His complexion blended with the colour of the golden amulet he wore on his arm. When I used to rub him with oil, I could clearly see a lustre emanating from his entire body. When he would come out of his room in the temple garden, people used to stand in line and say to one another, "Ah, there he goes!" He was fairly stout. Mathur Babu gave him a low wooden seat to sit on. It was rather a wide seat, but it was not quite big enough to hold him comfortably when he sat cross-legged to eat his meals. People would look at him, wonderstruck, when he went with slow, steady steps to the Ganges to take his bath. When he visited Kamarpukur, all the men and women would stare at him as soon as he left the house. One day he was going towards Bhuti's Canal, and some women saw him while fetching water. Agape, they looked at the Master and remarked, "There he goes!" I never saw the Master sad.[10]

Someone asked the Master's niece Lakshmi: "What was the condition of the Master's body during samadhi?"

She answered: "During samadhi, the Master's body became motionless. Tears trickled from his eyes, and sometimes both sides of his abdomen would tremble a little. His appearance was then extremely beautiful and one could see a halo around him."[11]

Once Swami Adbhutananda said to a devotee: "Look, some days you see something and it instantly penetrates the mind. I saw the Master in samadhi many times, but one day I saw him in a beautiful and unique form. His complexion had changed and his face radiated fearlessness and compassion. Even now I cannot forget that form of the Master."[12]

Akshay Kumar Sen wrote in his book *Sri Sri Ramakrishna Mahima*: "He had a broad forehead and his lips were beautifully curved and slightly reddish in colour. As a gentle breeze creates ripples on the surface of the river Yamuna, so his sweet smile was like a ripple on a river, catching the serene moonlight. His neck was well proportioned and his voice was like the sound of a flute. He had a large chest and arms reaching to the knees; his legs were graceful, and the soles of his feet were softer than oranges. His touch transformed a worldly person into a spiritual one. His entire form was endowed with divine qualities.

"It is extremely difficult to recognize God in human form. In whatever way and in whatever form He may appear, none can recognize Him if He does not empower that person to do so. One can realize Him only through divine consciousness. As clearly as I see an object in broad daylight, I saw that the Master's body was solidified pure consciousness. As excessive cold turns water into ice, so the Master's intense devotion transformed his body into pure consciousness."[13]

Mahendra Nath Datta, Swami Vivekananda's brother, gave the following description of the Master in his book *Sri Ramakrishner Anudhyan*:

> I first saw Ramakrishna Paramahamsa of Dakshineswar in Calcutta. I did not see any special characteristics in his form. He looked like a villager. His complexion was not dark, but it was no lighter than that of average Calcutta people. He had a trimmed beard. His eyes were normal, except that his eyelids blinked rapidly. His lips were not thin; rather, his lower lip was a little thick. A few of his upper teeth were visible between his lips. He wore a shirt with the sleeves rolled up to his elbows. After a while he removed his shirt and kept it by his side; he placed part of his cloth over his left shoulder. The room was quite hot and a man was fanning him with a long palm-leaf fan. His language was not like that of educated people in Calcutta; rather, it was rural. He stammered a little when he talked. His pronunciation was like the people of the western part of West Bengal. He said "L" in place of "N." For example, 'I said to Laren' instead of 'Naren.' At times he took a few spices from the spice bag that was in front of him.[14]

Swami Nirlepananda collected various descriptions of the Master from different people who met him.

> From Swami Saradananda: "The Master's head was well shaped and his back like a straight wall — in other words, without any curves or twists. His face and chest were smooth, fully developed. (One can ascertain the nature of a person by examining the formation of the head and the body.) When I saw the Master, his complexion was fair, a little lighter than that of Swami Brahmananda. He had some hair on his chest, but (smilingly) not as much as mine. His arms were a little longer than the average person, but they did not reach his knees. Otherwise he would have looked abnormal."
>
> From Tamu Datta, Vivekananda's cousin: "The Master's ears were below the eye lines. One can see it by studying the pictures of him. His eyes were broad and beautiful. His soles were convex."[15]

We have already mentioned that Swami Saradananda asked Swami Brahmananda to examine and approve a clay model for the Master's marble image. Maharaj went to the studio, studied the model for some time, and then asked the sculptor: "Why did you make this image with the back bent? He never bent his backbone when he sat."

The sculptor said: "According to anatomical measurement, if a man sits like that, he is supposed to be a little bent." Swami Brahmananda replied: "The Master's arms were quite long, which is very uncommon among people." About the Master's ears, the swami said: "The tops of ordinary people's ears are at about the level of their eyebrows, but the tops of the Master's ears were below the level of the eyes." Later, when the sculptor had corrected the model accordingly, the swami returned to the studio and gave his approval.[16]

Vaikuntha Nath Sanyal described the Master's physical beauty in a poetic way:

When I first saw the Master, his figure was neither short nor tall; his stature was medium, but his arms were a little longer than average. His hands were clasped, as if he were absorbed in worshipping an invisible deity. He chest was wide and crimson; his complexion was fair, like a mixture of turmeric and red paint, but with a shade of tan. His lips were reddish like vermilion. His eyes were large and remained closed as he listened to the glory of God's name. To come down from samadhi, he would repeat 'Govinda, Govinda,' and rub his eyes. His hair and beard were of medium length but dishevelled. He wore a thin red-bordered cloth and draped part of it over his shoulder. There were some round marks on his abdomen, which had been caused by a village doctor who branded him to cure his enlarged spleen. His figure had been strong and stout, but later became loose-limbed and tender.

As moonlight makes the inside of a room a bit luminous, so the Master's room was illumined by his physical beauty. His face was gracious and loving. He humbly sat on the same carpet with the devotees and charmed them by talking about God. His words were sweet and inspiring. Although there were no flowers or incense in the room, I sensed a sweet fragrance coming from his body, like that of a lotus. Ishan Mukhopadhyay, a great devotee of the Mother, remarked: "I get the same kind of divine fragrance here that I get in the Mother's temple at Kalighat." As soon as I saw the Master, I felt that he was my own eternally. I was so charmed and attracted that my head automatically bent down to the Master's feet. He also accepted me as his own and joyfully said: "You have come. Please sit down."

While meditating on Satchidananda, the Master's body would become so tender that his finger would be cut just by breaking a crisp *luchi* [fried bread]. In fact, the Master's body was as soft as butter. Out of mercy, the Master allowed me to massage his feet; but I was scared that I might injure him by rubbing them with my strong hands.

When the Master was intoxicated with the joy of kirtan, we felt that his divine body was as bright as molten gold and as soft as cream; it was as if he were distributing among his devotees the nectar that he had brought from heaven. We were dumbfounded when we saw him dancing in a semi-ecstatic state slowly and rhythmically. While he was pacing back and forth, his left hand would be held slightly up and his right hand extended below, his left foot forward and the right one backward. It was really unbelievable that such a body, as tender as a flower, could dance so madly and sweetly! We then felt that his over-flowing divine beauty had melted and was spreading over the devotees. Language is inadequate to describe the beauty of Sri Ramakrishna; one can only realize it through meditation.[17]

What Do You Think of Me?

The omniscient Ramakrishna knew others' thoughts and moods. Like an ordinary person, however, he would ask newcomers during their first meeting or after getting acquainted with them a little, "Well, what do you think of me?" Of course, he did not ask this of everyone. He used this question to evaluate the understanding of devotees whom he had already seen in a yogic vision. Different people answered differently: "Someone said, 'You are a real sadhu.' Others said: 'A true devotee of God'; 'A Mahapurusha — a great soul'; 'A Siddhapurusha — a perfect soul'; 'An incarnation of God'; 'Sri Chaitanya himself'; 'Lord Shiva himself'; 'You are God,' and so on. Some who belonged to the Brahmo Samaj and did not believe in divine incarnations, said, 'You are a lover of God, of the same rank as Krishna, Buddha, Jesus, and Chaitanya.'"[18]

One day the Master said to M: "Let me ask you something. What do you think of me? How many annas of knowledge of God have I?"

M. replied: "I don't understand what you mean by 'annas.' But of this I am sure: I have never before seen such knowledge, ecstatic love, faith in God, renunciation, and catholicity anywhere."

Another day, M. said: "God has created you with His own hands, whereas He has made others by machine. All others He has created according to law."

The Master said with a laugh: "Listen to what he is saying!" And finally he said: "Really and truly, I have no pride — no, not even the slightest bit."[19]

Ramakrishna's "I," his ego, had died forever. The fire of knowledge burnt his ego and it remained like a burnt rope, which has a form but cannot bind anything. This is called a "ripe ego." Human beings cannot function without an ego. However, the Master enacted his divine play using this ripe ego. One day he was having some fun with Hazra. The Master later described their conversation. "I asked Hazra: 'Tell me what you think of the people that come here. How much sattva does each one possess?' He said, 'Narendra has one hundred percent and I have one hundred and ten percent.' 'What about me?' I asked. And he said: 'You still have a trace of pink [rajas]. You have only seventy-five percent, I should say.'"[20]

Once in the course of conversation with another devotee M. said: "One day the Master asked Keshab Sen, 'Tell me, how many annas of knowledge of God do I have?' Keshab was reluctant to say anything. At last he said: 'Sir, shall I sell a needle to a blacksmith? What can I say about you?' When the Master insisted, Keshab said, 'You have sixteen annas' [one hundred percent] worth of knowledge.' To this, the Master said: 'I don't believe you. If Narada and Sukadeva had said that, I would believe it.' Did the Master insult Keshab? No, he did not. He only let Keshab know that those who are busy with name, fame, power, position, and worldly enjoyment cannot understand the Truth. He was just indicating his spiritual position."[21]

The Master had thrashed out the desire for name and fame so severely that it never dared to come back. According to the Catholic tradition, if a person performs three miracles during or after his or her lifetime, that person might be declared a saint. Of course, there are some other conditions that must be met also. Nowadays it is easy to become an avatar or divine incarnation. A teacher needs only a few fanatic disciples who will declare their teacher to be an avatar. The Master once jokingly said, "Chewing a betel roll and holding a cane, a dandy comes and calls me an avatar. Should I feel gratified at such a comment?"[22]

Only a jeweller knows the value of a jewel; an eggplant seller does not. One needs to practise tremendous spiritual discipline before one is able to recognize an avatar. When some devotees, overwhelmed by devotion, declared the Master to be an avatar, he said: "One practises medicine [Ram Chandra Datta] and another is the manager of a theatre [Girish Chandra Ghosh]. They tell me that I am an avatar. Thus calling me an avatar, they think that they have made me great and famous. But what do they know about an avatar?"[23]

It is extremely difficult to recognize an avatar. In the Gita, Krishna explains why: "Veiled by My maya born of the gunas, I am not revealed to all." (7:25) "Fools disregard Me when I assume a human form." (9:11)

Ramakrishna also made statements about the concept of the avatar: "He is an unknown tree"; "He is a king in disguise"; "He is infinite but enters into a three-and-a-half cubit human body"; "If He does not want to be captured, none can capture Him." The Katha Upanishad (1:2:23) says: "The Atman is attained by him alone whom It chooses." Ramakrishna said: "The police sergeant walks his rounds in the dark of night with a lantern in his hand. No one sees his face. If you want to see the sergeant, you must pray to him: 'Sir, please turn the light on your own face. Let me see you.'" Similarly, one should pray to God for His vision. As we see the sun by the light of the sun, so we see God by His grace. Ramakrishna appeared in various forms to different devotees at different times. Their visions prove that Ramakrishna was God with multiple forms.

Ramakrishna as a Cosmic Being

Swami Saradananda wrote in *Sri Ramakrishna and His Divine Play*:

One morning when Gadadhar [Ramakrishna's childhood nickname] was seven or eight months old, he fell asleep while Chandra was breast-feeding him. Seeing that her son was asleep, Chandra put him to bed, dropping the mosquito curtain to protect him. She then left the room and began her housework. Shortly afterwards, she returned to the room for something and found a tall, strange man lying in place of her child, covering the whole bed. She cried out in panic and hurriedly left the room, calling for her husband. When Kshudiram arrived, Chandra told him what had happened. They entered the room, but found no stranger; the child was sleeping as before. Even then, Chandra's fear did not subside. She said repeatedly: "An evil spirit must have possessed him. I clearly saw a large person lying in place of my son. In no way was it a delusion — there is no possibility that it was. Please bring an experienced exorcist to examine the child soon; otherwise, who knows what harm will befall him."

Kshudiram reassured her, saying, "We were blessed with divine visions before the birth of our son. It is no wonder that you have seen that person. Please don't harbour the notion that the child is possessed by an evil spirit. As Raghuvir Himself dwells in our house, no spirit can come here to do any harm to the child. Therefore, rest assured and do not divulge this to anyone. Know for certain that Raghuvir is always protecting the child."[24]

Ramakrishna Possessed by Gods and Goddesses

Prasanna, a devout daughter of Dharmadas Laha of Kamarpukur, considered Gadadhar to be the real Gadadhar, or Lord Vishnu. The simple-hearted Prasanna was captivated when she heard the young boy recount the sacred stories of gods and goddesses and sing devotional songs. She often asked him: "Look, Gadai, why is it that you sometimes seem to me to be God? Yes, I truly feel that you are God." At this the boy would smile sweetly and make no reply; or he would change the subject. Not deterred by his words, Prasanna would nod and say gravely, "Whatever you may say, you are not an ordinary human being."

Once the boy Gadadhar went with some village women including Prasanna to visit the goddess Vishalakshi at Anur. But as Gadadhar was crossing a field, singing of the glory of the goddess Vishalakshi, an extraordinary incident took place: suddenly, he was struck dumb, and his body stiffened and became numb. Tears poured from his eyes. He did not respond when the women asked if he felt ill. As they knew the boy was unaccustomed to making such a journey, the women were alarmed by the thought that he might have had sunstroke. They brought water from a nearby pond and splashed it over his head and eyes. But Gadadhar did not regain consciousness. Helpless, the women began to lament: "What is the way out of this predicament? How can we offer our promised worship to the goddess? How can we take Gadai, another's darling, home safely? There is no one here to help us. What do we do now?" The women were terribly worried and forgot all about gods and goddesses. Encircling the boy they fanned him, splashed water on him, and called his name repeatedly.

After a short while, the thought occurred to Prasanna that perhaps the goddess Vishalakshi had possessed the simple, trusting boy. She told her companions, "I have heard that the gods and goddesses possess simple and pure children, men, and women." She then suggested, "Instead of calling 'Gadai,' let us call 'Mother Vishalakshi' wholeheartedly." The women had deep respect for Prasanna because of her noble character, so they readily accepted her advice and began to address Gadai as though he were indeed the goddess: "O Mother Vishalakshi, be pleased with us. Protect us. Look upon us with compassion. Mother, save us from this great danger."

Amazingly, no sooner had the women called upon the goddess a few times than Gadadhar's face glowed with a sweet smile, and slight signs of consciousness became visible. They were now convinced that the goddess truly had possessed the boy. They bowed down to him again and again; and addressing him as Mother, they prayed to him.[25]

Once the Master went to visit Bamandas at the Biswases' house.

While returning the Master overheard him say: "Goodness gracious! The Divine Mother has caught hold of him, like a tiger seizing a man."[26]

Reverend Joseph Cook once accompanied Keshab Sen and Pratap Majumdar on a boat trip to visit Ramakrishna. While travelling with them on the Ganges, the Master went into samadhi. Observing the Master in samadhi, Pratap Majumdar remarked: "Good heavens! It is as if he were possessed by a ghost!"[27]

It was written in Mathur's horoscope that his Chosen Deity would always be gracious to him — nay, would even accompany him wherever he went and would assume a human form to protect him. He followed the Master like a shadow. One day Mathur said to him: "Father, there is nothing inside you but God. Your body is like an empty shell. It may look from outside like a pumpkin, but inside there is nothing — neither flesh nor seed. Once I saw you as someone moving with a veil on."[28]

Ramakrishna's cousin Haladhari was a pandit. He looked down upon the Master, and he did not understand the latter's divine madness. Sometimes, however, he was overwhelmed by the Master's ecstasy. Confused, Haladhari one day said to Hriday: "Hriday, you must have seen some divine presence in Ramakrishna; you would not serve him so faithfully otherwise."

About Haladhari's attitude, the Master said:

Many times Haladhari would be charmed by my devout worship in the temple, and he'd say to me, "Ramakrishna, now I know what your real nature is!" So I'd tell him jokingly, "Then don't get confused anymore!" Then he'd say: "You can't deceive me again. The Lord is definitely within you. This time I'm quite certain." So I'd reply: "All right. Let me see how long your conviction lasts." Then after finishing the temple service, he would take some snuff and begin to give a discourse on the Bhagavata, the Gita, the Adhyatma Ramayana, and other scriptures. He would then become puffed up with egotism and become quite a different person. Sometimes I would attend his discourses and would say to him, "I've realized all those spiritual states you've been reading about; I can understand everything that's in the scriptures." Immediately he would say indignantly: "You idiot! You think you can understand the scriptures?" "Believe me," I'd say, "the One who is within this body of mine teaches me everything. A little while ago you said that there was a divine presence in me. He tells me everything." Then he'd become frantic with rage and tell me: "Get out of here, you crazy fool! Are you claiming to be an incarnation of God? The scriptures say there'll be only one avatar in this age, and that's Kalki. You must be out of your mind to think such things!" So I would laugh and ask, "Didn't you tell me you'd never get confused again?" But of course he wouldn't listen to me when he was in that mood. We had the same scene over and over again. One day he saw me in an ecstatic mood sitting naked on a branch of the banyan tree of the Panchavati and passing water like a boy. From that day on he was thoroughly convinced that I had been possessed by a ghost."[29]

Haladhari was a devotee of Krishna and he was repulsed by the terrible aspect of the Divine Mother. Swami Saradananda wrote:

> One day he [Haladhari] even questioned the Master: "Can a person make any spiritual progress worshipping Kali, the embodiment of *tamas*? Why do you worship that goddess?" The Master did not answer him, but he was deeply hurt by this slander of his Chosen Deity. He hurried into the Kali temple and tearfully said: "Mother! Haladhari, who's a great scholar and knows the scriptures, says You're nothing but wrath and destruction. Is that really true?" At once he was reassured: Mother Kali revealed her complete nature to him. Wild with joy and relief, the Master ran to the Radhakanta temple, where Haladhari was seated at worship, and climbed on his shoulders. Excited, he told Haladhari again and again: "How dare you say that Mother is wrathful and full of tamas. She is everything. She is the embodiment of the three *gunas* and again She is pure love and goodness." The Master's words and divine touch illumined Haladhari's heart. As he sat there on the worshipper's seat he accepted the Master's words wholeheartedly. He saw the manifestation of the Divine Mother within the Master; filled with devotion, he offered flowers and sandal paste at his feet. Hriday soon came to Haladhari and asked him: "Uncle, you have said that Ramakrishna is possessed by a ghost. What made you worship him?" Haladhari replied: "I don't know. When he came in from the Kali temple, he simply overwhelmed me. I forgot everything. I clearly saw the Divine manifest Itself in him. He affects me like that whenever I am with him in the Kali temple. It is amazing! I don't understand it at all."[30]

Ramakrishna as Kali

Narendra did not believe in God with form, so at first he rejected Kali. Regarding this concept, he struggled for several years with his guru Sri Ramakrishna. But the Master told him, "You will be a servant of the Divine Mother." And finally, he dedicated Narendra to Mother Kali. One day many years later, Vivekananda discussed this with his Irish disciple, Sister Nivedita. She asked: "In the future, you say, many will call Ramakrishna Paramahamsa an Incarnation of Kali?" Swamiji replied: "Yes, I think there's no doubt that She worked up the body of Ramakrishna for Her own ends."[31]

One midnight in Dakshineswar the Master was walking in an ecstatic mood. As Golap-ma watched him, she saw Kali walking in his place. She was overwhelmed and it gave her goose bumps.[32]

Once Swami Brahmananda described the following incident:

I was then living on Baranasi Ghosh Street in Calcutta and visiting the Master regularly. One day I went to Dakshineswar in the early afternoon. The Kali temple was closed and the Master was resting after lunch. As soon as I entered his room, he asked me to sit on his bed. He talked for a while and then asked me to massage his feet. I replied: "Sir, excuse me. I can't do that. You were telling me wonderful stories; please continue." Regardless, he asked again: "Look, give me a little massage. You will benefit by serving a holy man." After he had asked me to do this two or three times, I finally touched his feet. Suddenly something miraculous happened that left me dumbfounded. I saw with my open eyes that Mother Kali quickly entered the room in the form of a young girl, seven or eight years old. She encircled the Master's bed a few times, Her anklets making jingling sounds. Then She merged into the Master's body. The Master smiled a little and then said, "You see, you have instantly received the result of serving a holy man."[33]

In September 1885 Ramakrishna moved to Shyampukur in Calcutta to be treated for cancer. The day before Kali Puja, he told some devotees: "Collect everything that is needed for worship just on a small scale. Tomorrow we shall have Kali Puja."

Swami Saradananda wrote:

Evening arrived with the sunset. At 7:00 p.m. the devotees found the Master seated silently on his bed, as on other days. He said nothing further about the worship. They cleared some space on his right and placed the worship articles there. Some devotees had seen the Master occasionally worship his own form with sandal paste and flowers when he lived in Dakshineswar. Today they had come to the conclusion that the Master intended to worship himself as a symbol of Universal Consciousness and the embodiment of Divine Power, or to perform the worship of his own Self as identified with the Divine Mother according to the scriptures. It is therefore not surprising that they placed the worship articles next to his bed. The Master watched them do that, but raised no objection.

When everything had been brought to his room, someone lit the lamps and burnt some incense, filling the whole room with light and fragrance. Seeing the Master still sitting quietly, the devotees sat near him. Some looked at him intently, awaiting his direction; some began to meditate on the Divine Mother. Time passed, and the Master remained silent. He neither came forward to perform the worship himself, nor did he ask any of us to do it.

The young devotees were present, along with Mahendra, Ram, Devendra, Girish, and some senior devotees. The Master sometimes said that of his devotees Girish had "one hundred and twenty-five percent" faith. Most of the devotees were puzzled by the Master's silence about the worship. But because Girish had such abundant faith in the Master, he was suddenly struck by this idea: "The Master does not need to worship the Divine Mother for his own sake. If his pure love has inspired him to perform the worship, why would he sit there quietly, doing nothing? That does not seem right. Were these arrangements made for the devotees to worship the Divine Mother in the Master's living form and be blessed? It must be so." He was overwhelmed with joy at that thought and immediately took flowers and sandal paste from a tray and offered them at the feet of the Master, saying, "Victory to the Mother." A thrill passed through the Master's body, and he went into deep samadhi. His face became luminous and a divine smile played upon it. His hands assumed the gestures symbolizing fearlessness and the bestowal of boons that are seen in images of Kali, thus indicating that the Mother was revealing Herself within him. These events happened so quickly that the devotees seated nearby thought Girish had offered flowers after seeing the Master in samadhi. To those who were a little farther away it appeared as if a luminous form of the Devi had suddenly appeared before them, taking possession of the Master's body.[34]

When Sri Ramakrishna was gravely ill at the Cossipore garden house, the Holy Mother was stricken with grief. One day, in a vision, a girl with long black hair and a dark complexion appeared and sat near her. Realizing that it was Mother Kali, she exclaimed:

"Oh, you have come!"

Mother Kali: "Yes, I have come from Dakshineswar."

After further conversation, the Holy Mother observed that the girl bent her neck to one side. She asked: "What has happened to your neck?"

Mother Kali: "Well, I have a sore throat."

The Holy Mother: "My goodness! The Master has a sore throat and you also have it?"

Mother Kali: "That is true."

Thus, the Holy Mother was made to understand that the Divine Mother and Sri Ramakrishna were one and the same.

When Sri Ramakrishna passed away, the Holy Mother cried out, saying, "O Mother Kali, where have you gone, leaving us behind?"[35]

Ramakrishna as Shiva

During Ramakrishna's boyhood in Kamarpukur at the time of the Shivaratri festival, a dramatic performance had been arranged at the Pyne's household. A troupe from the neighbouring village was to perform a religious drama based on the glory of Shiva. The performance was to begin about half an hour after dusk. That evening, news reached the village that the boy who was to play Shiva had become seriously ill, so the performance would have to be cancelled. The senior members of the village asked Gadadhar if he would act in that role, and he agreed. Swami Saradananda described the events that followed:

Once Gadadhar was in costume, he sat in the dressing room and thought of Shiva. When he was called to appear on the stage, one of his friends led him there. He mounted the stage at his friend's request. Absentmindedly, without looking in any direction, he slowly walked to the middle of the stage and stood there motionless. The audience was overwhelmed with joy and awe upon seeing Gadadhar in that costume with matted hair, bedecked with rosaries, and smeared with ashes. He entered with slow and steady footsteps, and then stood motionless with a heavenly, indrawn, unblinking gaze, and a sweet smile on the corners of his lips. According to village custom, the audience suddenly cried out, chanting the name of Hari. Some women ululated auspiciously and some blew conches. To calm the audience during the pandemonium, the director began to sing a hymn to Shiva. At this the audience quieted slightly. But beckoning and nudging one another, they began to comment in hushed voices: "Bravo, Bravo!" "How beautiful Gadai looks!" "We never thought the boy could act in the role of Shiva so wonderfully!" "If we somehow secure this boy, we can form a *yatra* party of our own."

Gadadhar remained standing there all the while; moreover, tears continually trickled down onto his chest. Thus some time passed, and Gadadhar neither changed his position nor said anything. Then the director and a few elderly villagers went over to Gadadhar and found that his hands and feet were numb and that he seemed to have lost all external consciousness. At this point the commotion in the audience increased terribly. Some shouted, "Water! Splash water on his eyes and face!" Some said, "Fan him!" Some called out: "Lord Shiva has possessed him. Chant Shiva's name!" Again some grumbled: "This boy has spoiled everything. Now they will have to stop the play!"

After a long while, when all efforts had failed to bring him back to normal consciousness, the audience dispersed. Some men carried Gadadhar home on their shoulders. We have heard that his family wept because despite all their efforts Gadadhar could not be roused from his ecstatic state that night. He became normal again after sunrise the next day.[36]

On 18 August 1883, Ramakrishna said to Rakhal in an ecstatic mood: "This religious fervour (*referring to himself*) is not like rain in the rainy season, which comes in torrents and goes in torrents. It is like an image of Shiva that has not been set up by human hands but is a natural one that has sprung up, as it were, from the bowels of the earth."[37]

In *Sri Ramakrishna and His Divine Play* (see V.7), Swami Saradananda described how Vaikuntha Nath Sanyal saw Shiva in Sri Ramakrishna. Vaikuntha himself mentioned this incident in his book *Sri Ramakrishna Lilamrita*:

The Master said to Vaikuntha: "Look, the Bhairavi Brahmani, Vaishnavcharan, Pandit Gauri of Indesh, and Padmalochan, the court pandit of the Maharaja of Burdwan, declared me to be an avatar. Now Girish, Ram, and Manomohan also call me avatar; I am really disgusted hearing all these things. Well, what do you think of me?"

Vaikuntha: "Those who call you an avatar are low-class people."

Master (*smiling*): "What do you mean? They complimented me by saying I am an avatar, and you are calling them low-class people?"

Vaikuntha: "As I understand it, an avatar is not a full but a partial manifestation of God."

Master: "You are right. But what do you think of me?"

Vaikuntha: "You are Lord Shiva Himself, not a part. You asked me to meditate on Shiva. But though I try every day, I cannot do so. Whenever I sit for meditation, your loving and blissful face appears before me in a luminous form. I cannot replace it with the form of Shiva, nor do I want to. So I regard you as Shiva Himself."

Master (*smiling*): "Is that so? But I know I am as insignificant as a hair on your head." (*Both laughed.*)[38]

Ramakrishna as Shiva and Kali

Ramakrishna used to say: "Brahman and Shakti are identical." As fire and its power to burn are the same, so Shiva and Shakti are one and the same. Mathur saw how Shiva and Kali simultaneously manifested in Ramakrishna. Swami Saradananda described the circumstances:

One day the Master was pacing back and forth on the northeastern veranda of his room, which extended east to west. He was in a spiritual mood, completely oblivious to his surroundings. Mathur was then seated alone in a room in his bungalow, which was situated between the temple complex and the Panchavati. It was not far from Mathur's room to the veranda where the Master was pacing, so Mathur could see him through a window. Sometimes he thought of the Master as he watched him walking in what was obviously an indrawn mood, and again he thought about various worldly affairs and made plans for his own future. The Master was not at all aware that Mathur was watching him from time to time as he sat in his parlour.

All of a sudden Mathur hurriedly ran out of his bungalow, threw himself down at Sri Ramakrishna's feet, and began to cry profusely.

The Master later narrated: "I asked Mathur: 'What are you doing? You are an aristocrat and Rani Rasmani's son-in-law. What will people say if they see you behaving like this? Calm yourself. Please, get up!' But who would listen to this? Gradually Mathur got control of himself and described his wonderful vision. He said: 'Father, I was watching you just now as you walked back and forth. I saw it distinctly: as you walked towards me, you were no longer yourself. You were the Divine Mother Kali from the temple! Then, as you turned around and walked in the opposite direction, you became Lord Shiva! At first I thought it was some kind of optical illusion. I rubbed my eyes and looked again, but I saw the same thing. As often as I looked, I saw it!' He said this again and again, crying. I said, 'But I know nothing about this.' He ignored me. I became very nervous. I thought that if someone reported this to Rani Rasmani, she might misunderstand and think that I had put a spell on Mathur. I consoled him in various ways and finally calmed him down. Was it for nothing that Mathur served me and loved me so much? The Divine Mother granted him various visions and experiences on many occasions."[39]

Ramakrishna as Vishnu-Narayana

In 1835 Kshudiram, Ramakrishna's father, went to the Vishnu temple of Gaya to offer pinda (obsequial rice balls) at the feet of Gadadhar, or Vishnu, for his departed ancestors. One night after falling asleep, he started dreaming. As Swami Saradananda related:

He saw himself again offering pindas to his ancestors at the holy feet of Lord Gadadhar in the temple. He also saw his ancestors in their luminous celestial forms, joyfully accepting the offerings and blessing him. After gazing at them for a long time, he could not control himself. Overwhelmed with devotion, he began to weep and bowed down to them, touching their feet. In the next moment the temple was filled with a divine effulgence. He saw his ancestors standing on both sides of the shrine in a reverential attitude with folded hands, praying to a luminous Person seated graciously on a beautiful throne. He saw that the complexion of this Effulgent One was as green as a blade of new grass, and that He was looking at Kshudiram affectionately. Smiling, the Effulgent One beckoned Kshudiram to draw near. Like an automaton, he walked towards the Effulgent One, prostrated before Him with overwhelming devotion, and began to praise Him with various hymns. The Effulgent One was pleased and spoke the following words to him in a sweet, melodious voice: "Kshudiram, I am very pleased with your sincere devotion. I shall incarnate Myself as your son and accept the loving service you offer Me in your cottage."

Listening to these amazing words, Kshudiram's joy knew no bounds. But in the very next moment he wondered how such a poor man as himself could feed and shelter such an Exalted Being. Filled with sadness, Kshudiram sobbed: "No, no, my Lord, I am not deserving of this favour. It is more than enough that You have blessed me by graciously revealing Yourself and wishing to be born as my son. If You truly would be my son, how could I, a poor man, be able to serve You?" The Divine Being was even more pleased upon hearing Kshudiram's plaintive words, and said: "Don't be afraid, Kshudiram. Whatever you offer, I shall accept with satisfaction. Don't raise any objections to the fulfillment of My wish."[40]

This is the story of Ramakrishna's conception.

One day the Master asked Pandit Gauri a question to test his understanding:

"Well, Vaishnavcharan calls this (*pointing to himself*) an avatar. How can it be? Tell me what you think about it."

Gauri gravely replied: "Does Vaishnavcharan call you an avatar? I consider that an understatement! I believe you are He by a fraction of Whose power the avatars come forth to this world in every age and accomplish their mission."

The Master smiled and said: "Ah — so you outbid him! What do you find in me that leads you to entertain this idea?"

Gauri replied: "I am saying this based on my deep personal experience and the testimony of the scriptures. I am ready to prove my contention to anyone who challenges me in the matter."

"Well, it is you who say so," the Master said like a boy, "but I know nothing about it."

Gauri said: "That is as it should be. The scriptures agree on this point. Because you do not know yourself, how can others know you? Only one whom you have graciously allowed to know you can do so."[41]

Once Manomohan had a vision of a luminous form. At first he could not believe that it was a divine form, but his doubt was dispelled when he saw three marks resembling a flag, a thunderbolt, and a goad, imprinted on the soles of Vishnu's feet. He became convinced that He was Narayana, bearer of the conch, discus, mace, and lotus; and he bowed down to that divine form, saying, "Victory to Ramakrishna in the form of Narayana!"[42]

About his young devotee Purna, Ramakrishna said: "Purna is a part of Narayana and a spiritual aspirant endowed with a high degree of *sattva*. In this respect he may be said to occupy a place just below Narendra [Swami Vivekananda]." One day the Master asked Purna: "Tell me, what do you think of me?" Overcome with exuberant devotion, Purna replied without hesitation: "You are God Himself, incarnated in flesh and blood! You are Narayana."[43]

In that same period, Gauri-ma was living at Balaram's house in Calcutta. One morning she began her daily worship of Vishnu as usual, by bathing the stone image of the deity. She was about to place it on the altar when she saw two live human feet there, without a human body. At first she thought that it was an optical illusion, but upon observing the altar carefully again and again she saw only those two human feet. Gauri-ma was frightened. The hair of her body stood on end, and her hands started trembling so much that she dropped the image. She took the image from the floor and put it back on the altar. She repeated the mantra, and while offering tulsi leaves upon it, she again saw those two live feet. She lost outer consciousness and fell to the floor.

She remained in an ecstatic mood that day and the following night. The next morning, Balaram and his wife took her to meet the Master at Dakshineswar. When she bowed down to the Master, she saw the same two feet that she had seen on the altar the previous day. She was overwhelmed with joy and astonishment. Ramakrishna just smiled.[44]

Vaikuntha Nath Sanyal wrote: "Jogin Sen was from Krishnanagar in the Nadia district. He was an assistant treasurer of the Government printing press. I was present the day Jogin received the Master's grace. The Master asked Jogin: 'Which form of God gives you the most joy?' Jogin replied: 'I don't know. But during the public celebration I fainted for a while upon seeing the four-handed Narayana. Today I see the same form in you.'"[45]

Swami Abhedananda began to practise meditation as instructed by Sri Ramakrishna. In the beginning he saw his Chosen Deity in various ways during meditation. Quite often he would go to Dakshineswar and report his experiences to the Master. The Master would respond, "Very good," or "Do this next," and so on. Later, during meditation one day, Abhedananda saw various forms of gods and goddesses merge into a particular divine form. When he informed the Master of this, the latter said: "Ah, you have seen *Vaikuntha* [the abode of Vishnu]! Henceforth you won't have any other visions."[46]

Ramakrishna as Gadadhar

One day in Dakshineswar Yogin-ma picked some flowers; she used a corner of her sari to carry them. Ramakrishna was at that time standing on the northern veranda of his room and saw Yogin-ma coming, carrying something. He asked her, "What are you carrying?" Yogin-ma showed him the flowers and then bowed down and offered them at his feet. Immediately the Master went into an ecstatic mood and blessed her, touching his foot to her head. Then, following Gopal-ma's instructions, she touched the Master's feet to her chest. One day long after the Master passed away, Yogin-ma was repeating her mantra when she heard a divine voice say: "Your chest has been imprinted with auspicious marks from the lotus feet of Damodar [an epithet of Vishnu]."[47]

Just before his death in 1909, Swami Advaitananda saw the Master appear before him, bearing a mace on one shoulder. Advaitananda asked, "Master, why are you carrying a mace?" The Master replied: "I am Gadadhar [literally, "bearer of the mace," an epithet of Lord Vishnu]. In this age I shall destroy everything, then rebuild."[48]

Ramakrishna as Jagannath

On 15 July 1885, Ramakrishna said to M.: "I want to tell you something very secret. Once, in a spiritual mood, I felt intense love for Jagannath, love such as a woman feels for her sweetheart. In that mood I was about to embrace Him, when I broke my arm. It was then revealed to me: 'You have assumed this human body. Therefore establish with human beings the relationship of friend, father, mother, and son.'"[49]

M. said that the Master told his devotees many times: "I am Lord Jagannath of Puri." M. continued:

Once he sent me to Puri and instructed me as to what was to be done there. He told me that I should embrace Jagannath. I was anxious because it was almost impossible to do that. At last the Master created an idea in my mind. I carried quite a number of coins and bills in my pocket when I entered the inner sanctuary of the temple. The place was a little dark. I purposely scattered the coins and bills on the floor.

When they heard the jingle of the coins, the priests began to collect that money. In the meantime, I climbed onto the altar and embraced Lord Jagannath. Someone saw me and raised a hue and cry. I got down immediately and began to circumambulate the deity. In the darkness, none could recognize the person who did it.

It was the Master who instructed me; it was he who gave me the idea; and it was also he who diverted the attention of the priests by creating greed in their minds. Now I wonder how I did such a heroic deed!

During his lifetime, the Master sent me to Puri a few times. He did not go to Puri. He said: "If I go to Puri, my body will not last." So he did not go. When I returned from Puri, the Master embraced me and said, "Here I embrace Lord Jagannath."[50]

In 1900, Manomohan Mitra and his wife went to Puri after the death of their daughter. His wife died there from cholera. One day Manomohan entered the temple and saw Ramakrishna in place of Jagannath on the altar. When he repeatedly saw the Master, he shouted: "Victory to Lord Jagannath in the form of Ramakrishna!"[51]

In 1917, Swami Turiyananda went to Puri. One day he visited Lord Jagannath. As he was going up the stairs to the temple entrance, he suddenly saw Sri Ramakrishna, with a garland of flowers around his neck, coming down the steps towards him. Turiyananda rushed forward and prostrated. But when he stretched out his hands to touch the Master's feet, he could no longer see him. He suddenly came back to his senses. Turiyananda said: "It was Lord Jagannath who descended as Sri Ramakrishna. That is why the Master refused to visit Puri and said, 'If I go there, my body will not last.'"[52]

The Master's niece Lakshmi recalled: "Once Balaram brought some prasad of Jagannath and gave it to the Master. The Master touched the prasad with his head and then went into ecstasy. He said: 'It is as if I am in Puri. There everything is large — vast ocean, wide roads, and infinite Lord Jagannath! If I go there, this body will not last [meaning that he would merge into Jagannath].'"[53]

In the spring of 1925 Lakshmi went to visit Lord Jagannath with her devotee Bipin. She was deeply immersed in thoughts of the Master. Entering the temple, she saw the Master seated on a bench on the right side of the shrine. Lakshmi was delighted to see the Master and thought: "I am happy that the Master is able to see Lord Jagannath." The Master then said to Lakshmi: "I am close to Jagannath. Why are you so anxious? You were thinking of me, so here I am." On another occasion Lakshmi was a little sad because she could not see the Master in the temple. Then

Jagannath appeared before her and said: "Don't be sad. I and your Ramakrishna are the same."[54]

Ramakrishna as Krishna

Swami Ambikananda described how his father, Navagopal Ghosh, saw Krishna in the Master:

Our house was at Badurbagan in Calcutta. During this period, devotees often arranged to have festivals in their homes on Sundays and invited Sri Ramakrishna and other devotees. They would hire a singer and musicians to entertain the Master and would prepare a sumptuous feast. Girish, Ram, and Kalipada were the organizers. Once my father arranged for a festival in our worship hall and invited the Master and his devotees. A scholar was engaged to recite the Bhagavata. The Master had been seated in the worship hall, but suddenly he jumped up and rushed to the courtyard and stood near the singer and the musicians, in the pose of Krishna with a flute in his hand. It was a wonderful sight. The other devotees encircled the Master and sang kirtan in chorus. My father brought a long flower garland for the Master and he placed it around his neck. After the kirtan, the Master sat on his seat and gradually came down from his ecstatic mood. My father saw a glowing light on the Master's face. At first he thought it was an optical illusion, so he went to wash his eyes. But again he saw the same light. Amazed, he asked his brother Jaygopal whether he saw anything unusual in the Master. "No, he looks just as usual," replied his brother. At last, my father realized that the Master, out of mercy, had shown him his divine, luminous form.[55]

Nistarini, Navagopal's wife, recalled: "One day the Master came to our house. A number of devotees had gathered to see him. When he arrived, he came straight upstairs and remained for some time talking with me. At that time I had a picture of Krishna in my shrine and I told him I was eager to have a vision of Krishna. He went downstairs where all the devotees were singing kirtan. Around his neck they placed a heavy garland that reached to his feet. At once he assumed the exact posture of Krishna and went into samadhi. All the devotees also went into a higher state of consciousness upon seeing him. Later he asked me if I was now satisfied; I said I would like to see Radha by Krishna's side. He smiled and replied: 'Oh, you will have to wait awhile for that.'"[56]

Once Ramakrishna said to Swami Vijnanananda: "In the Krishna incarnation, I played with the cowherd boys and girls, the gopis, in Vrindaban."

Vijnanananda recalled:

I was then a college student and could not believe what the Master had said. Perceiving my doubt, the Master began to describe the gopis' love for Krishna: "The gopis' love was a genuine divine love. They were mad for Krishna. Hearing the flute of Krishna, they would leave their husbands and rush to him. Although Krishna was not wealthy, they loved him more than they did their own lives. They offered their bodies and minds — everything — to Krishna. It is written in the Bhagavata that Krishna played with the gopis during the full moon night of autumn. At the time of *rasalila*, Krishna was immersed in samadhi and the gopis were also in ecstasy."

Saying this, the Master lost outer consciousness and became immersed in samadhi. I was also absorbed in a divine mood thinking of Krishna's play with the gopis. At that time, being in the Master's field of influence was like being in the place where the rasa festival was enacted. While I was within those bounds, the veil of ignorance that covered my understanding of the rasalila disappeared. I had a wonderful experience about the rasalila. When the Master came down from samadhi, he looked at me and smiled. I was dumbfounded.[57]

One day at Dakshineswar the Master told his nephew Ramlal: "I want to wear a yellow cloth like Krishna's." Ramlal took a new cloth and soaked it in water that had been mixed with turmeric paste. When it was dry, the Master put on that cloth and a garland. Pointing to the cloth and garland, he said: "O Pitambara [one dressed in yellow cloth], Vanamali [wearer of a garland of wild flowers]." Repeating these epithets of Krishna, he went into ecstasy and began to roll on the ground. The cloth dropped from his body and the garland was torn to pieces. Ramlal then dressed the Master in a white cloth and began to praise Krishna. The Master sat there motionless.[58]

Ramakrishna as Radha

Swami Saradananda wrote: "When the Master started to practise *madhura bhava*, he was eager to wear women's clothing and jewellery. Knowing the Master's desire, the devoted Mathur provided him with a beautiful and expensive sari from Varanasi, a skirt, a bodice, and a scarf. To complete the transformation, Mathur brought him a wig with curly hair and a set of gold jewellery. . . . It is no wonder that under the influence of women's attire, his feminine traits were aroused. But no one could have ever imagined that while immersed in that mood, his movements, speech, smile, glance, gestures, and other actions, as well as his thoughts, would become completely feminine."

Hriday said: "During that period at Dakshineswar, every morning Uncle would take a basket and pick flowers from the garden. As we watched him, we noticed that he always stepped out with his left foot first, as a woman does. The Brahmani said, 'When I saw him picking flowers I often mistook him for Radha.' Every day after collecting flowers, he would make beautiful garlands and decorate the images of Radha and Krishna. Sometimes he adorned the image of the Divine Mother and prayed piteously to Her, as did the gopis to the goddess Katyayani, begging Her to give him Krishna as his spiritual husband."

Swami Saradananda continued: "Knowing that the vision of Krishna is not possible without Radha's grace, the Master began to worship her with his one-pointed mind. He remained absorbed in meditation on her loving form and prayed to her unceasingly with a longing heart. As a result he was soon blessed with the vision of Radha. Her form merged into him like the forms of other gods and goddesses whose visions he had previously realized. He said: 'It is impossible to describe the incomparable, pure, heavenly beauty and sweetness of Radha, who renounced everything out of her passionate love for Krishna. Her complexion was light yellow like the stamens of the nagakeshara [*mesua ferra*] flower.'

"For some time following that vision, the Master felt that he was Radha. This happened as a result of deep meditation on Radha's form and character. He completely lost his sense of a separate identity."[59]

Gangamata of Vrindaban also saw Radha's appearance in Ramakrishna. Swami Saradananda wrote: "Gangamata was then about sixty years old. After observing her exuberant love for Radha and Krishna over a long period of time, the local people had come to regard her as a reincarnation of Lalita, the main female confidante of Radha, who had descended to earth to teach people divine love. The Master told us that when she first saw him, she recognized the same manifestation of *mahabhava* in him that she saw in Radha. She understood him to be a reincarnation of Radha herself, and she addressed him as 'Dulali,' darling friend. Gangamata considered herself blessed to have met Dulali without any effort of her own, and realized that her lifelong service and love for the Lord had been fulfilled."[60]

Swami Vivekananda also saw Radha in the Master, as recorded in *The Life of Swami Vivekananda*: "One night he dreamt that Sri Ramakrishna came to him and said, 'Come! I will show you Gopi Radha.' Narendra [Vivekananda] followed him. After having gone some distance, the Master turned to him and said, 'Where else will you go?' Saying this, Sri

Ramakrishna transformed himself into the beautiful personality and exquisite form of Radha herself. This so affected the conscious mind of Narendra that whereas, formerly, he had only sung songs of the Brahmo Samaj relating to the formless Brahman, he now sang songs on the spiritual love of Radha. When he narrated this dream to his brother disciples, they were amazed. One asked him, 'Do you believe in the significance of this?' Narendra answered, 'Surely I do.'"[61]

There is a great mystery hidden in Vivekananda's vision of Radha. Vaikuntha Nath Sanyal wrote:

> One may be a great monk or a scholar, but one cannot ignore one's *samskaras* [tendencies]. They evolve and dissolve by God's will. Due to the influence of these samskaras, or moral codes, or western education, Narendra disregarded Radha, the blissful aspect of God. The Master thought: If Narendra does not respect Radha, the embodiment of love, he will forever be deprived of the sweet and joyful aspect of life. Moreover, if he were devoid of love, it would not be possible for him to guide the religious order inaugurated by him (Ramakrishna). Previously the Master had established Narendra in the *nirvikalpa* state by a mere wish. Now, to enrich Narendra with divine love, he wrote with his finger on the bed: '*Srimati Radhe! Narendrake daya karo* [O Srimati Radha, bless Narendra].' Immediately, like magic or the influence of a great power, Narendra was absorbed in the mood of Radha and prayed: "Where are you, O Radha, the embodiment of love?" Thus, after practising sadhana for three days, the dry philosopher Narendra became softhearted and exclaimed: "I have seen a new light by the grace of the Master. If I had not experienced this love, my life would have been dry and dreary."[62]

Suresh Chandra Datta recorded: "Once during the dol festival of Krishna, the Master went to the Radha-Krishna temple of Dakshineswar. He was then in the mood of Radha. He began to playfully spray coloured powder on the image of Krishna and sang: 'While fighting today with colour, let me see whether you win or I win.' Those who witnessed this sight were overwhelmed."[63]

Ramakrishna as the United Form of Radha-Krishna

Swami Saradananda wrote: "Every one of the Master's devotees has seen to a greater or lesser degree the coexistence of masculine and feminine moods in him. Once Girish experienced this and boldly asked, 'Sir, are you a man or a woman?' The Master replied with a smile, 'I don't know.'"[64]

During his sadhana of madhura bhava (in the attitude of a lover for the beloved) the Master dressed like a woman. Hriday said: "When the Master was surrounded by ladies, it was hard for even his closest relatives to recognize him immediately. One day during that time Mathur took me to the women's quarters at his Janbazar house and said, 'Can you tell me which of them is your uncle?' And although I had been living with him for so long and serving him daily, I could not recognize him at first."[65]

During the Durga Puja at Janbazar, the Master was fanning the Divine Mother and Mathur did not recognize him at all. When Mathur's wife later told him that that person was the Master, he was dumbfounded. He said: "This is why I say that even in trifling matters no one can know the Father if he doesn't allow himself to be known. Look, I live with the Father twenty-four hours a day, and still I did not recognize him!"[66]

Mahendra Datta wrote: "Once some actresses visited the Master at Dakshineswar. They entertained the Master by acting in the roles of Sita and Savitri. The Master also entertained them by acting as a woman kirtan singer in the role of an envoy between Radha and Krishna. He mimicked those woman singers: how they raise their big nose rings and spit after chewing betel leaves, how they move their hands, their necks, and their heads. Amazed, the actresses said: 'Being a monk, how does he know all these women's gestures!'"[67]

Later, the Master told the devotees about his experience of Purusha and Prakriti: "Oh, what a state I passed through! I passed some days absorbed in Shiva and Durga, some days absorbed in Radha and Krishna, and some days absorbed in Sita and Rama. Assuming Radha's attitude, I would cry for Krishna; and assuming Sita's attitude, I would cry for Rama."[68] "I would meditate day and night on Sita and Rama. At those times I would constantly behold the forms of Sita and Rama. Again I used to be absorbed in the ideal of Radha and Krishna — the harmonization of two ideals: the Purusha and Prakriti."[69]

Atul Chandra Ghosh saw the united form of Radha and Krishna in Sri Ramakrishna. Akshay Kumar Sen described this episode in his book *Sri Ramakrishna Punthi*. Swami Abhedananda wrote in his autobiography:

> Atul, Girish's brother, was a great devotee of the Master. He could ascertain the condition of a patient by checking his pulse. For that reason, the Master would sometimes call for him. Once at 10:00 p.m., he [Atul] came from Baghbazar and found that the gate of the Cossipore garden house was closed. He knocked at the gate many times but got no response. Still he continued knocking. At last Brother Gopal heard the sound and opened the gate. Atul went upstairs to see the Master.

There he saw that Shashi was fanning the Master and Latu was sleeping on the other side of the room. Seeing Atul, Shashi handed the fan to him and went downstairs to rest. The Master was then sleeping, covered by a shawl.

After a while, Atul had a wonderful vision: He saw Krishna on the right half of the Master's body and Radha on the left half. Seeing this united form in the Master, Atul thought that it was a hallucination. In the meantime, Sharat entered the room to serve the Master. Then the Master turned his face to Atul and asked: "Hello, how long have you been here? You go downstairs now and take some rest. Sharat will be with me." Amazed, Atul went downstairs. He never forgot that united form appearing in the Master.[70]

Ramakrishna as Gopala

Regarding the vision of God, Ramakrishna said: "The more you advance towards God, the less you will see of His glories and grandeur. The aspirant at first has a vision of the goddess with ten arms; there is a great display of power in that image. The next vision is that of the deity with two arms; there are no longer ten arms holding various weapons and missiles. Then the aspirant has a vision of Gopala, in which there is no trace of power. It is the form of a tender child."[71]

Ramakrishna appeared as the pure and loving form of Gopala to several of his devotees. Swami Saradananda wrote:

Following Vaishnava sadhanas, the Brahmani had some periods of bliss arising from the *sakhya* and *vatsalya* attitudes. While she was staying at the Devamandal ghat in Dakshineswar, she would become absorbed in the vatsalya mood. Shedding tears for the Master, she would hold butter in her hand and loudly call for him, "Gopala, Gopala." Meanwhile, at Dakshineswar the Master was extremely anxious to see the Brahmani. Like a boy pining for his mother, the Master would run a mile to see her, sit near her, and eat the butter. The Brahmani would sometimes dress herself in a red silk Varanasi sari and jewellery borrowed from some neighbours and visit the Master, accompanied by some village women. She would bring various delicacies to him and sing songs about Gopala on her way; after feeding the Master, she would return. The Master told us that when the Brahmani was in that state — with dishevelled hair and overwhelmed by her spiritual mood — it seemed that she was Nanda's queen Yashoda [the foster mother of Krishna] grieving because of her separation from Gopala.[72]

Swami Saradananda described Aghoremani's vision of Gopala:

It was three o'clock one spring morning when Aghoremani [Gopal--ma] started to practise her japa. After finishing, she began pranayama and was about to offer the result of her practices to her Chosen Deity when she noticed Sri Ramakrishna seated at her left, his right fist clenched. She saw the Master vividly — as alive as she saw him in Dakshineswar. She wondered: "What is this? How did he get here at such an odd hour?" Gopal-ma later described it thus: "I looked at him in amazement and thought, 'How did he get here?' Meanwhile, Gopala (as she called Sri Ramakrishna) kept smiling sweetly. I gathered my courage and grasped his left hand — and Sri Ramakrishna's form disappeared. In its place appeared the real Gopala — a large baby, ten months old. His beauty and appearance beggars description! He crawled towards me and, raising one hand, said, 'Mother, give me butter.' I was overwhelmed and bewildered by this amazing experience! I cried out so loudly that if there had been men around the house they would have rushed there. With tearful eyes, I said: 'My son, I am a poor, helpless widow. What shall I feed you? Where shall I get butter and cream, my child?' But that wonderful Gopala did not listen to me. 'Give me something to eat,' he kept saying. What could I do? Sobbing, I got up and took some dry coconut balls from a hanging basket. Placing them in his hand, I said, 'Gopala, my darling, I offer you these wretched things, but please don't give me such poor food in return.'

"I could not perform japa at all. Gopala sat on my lap, snatched away my rosary, jumped on my shoulders, and crawled around the room. At daybreak, I rushed to Dakshineswar on foot like a crazy woman. Gopala accompanied me. I held his buttocks with one hand and his back with the other while his head rested on my shoulder. I distinctly saw Gopala's two tiny, rosy feet dangling over my bosom."

After arriving at Dakshineswar that spring day, Aghoremani, gripped by that exuberant spiritual mood, shed tears and said many things to Sri Ramakrishna: "Here is Gopala in my arms. . . . Now he enters into you (*pointing to Sri Ramakrishna*). . . . There, he comes out again. . . . Come, my child, come to your wretched mother." While talking in this manner, she saw the naughty Gopala vanish into the Master's body and reappear before her in the form of a luminous boy. His extraordinary play and childish pranks overwhelmed her, making her forget the strict rules, rites, and routines of the external world. Who could control oneself after being caught by that mighty spiritual tidal wave?

On that day Aghoremani became Gopal-ma, and the Master began to call her by that name. Sri Ramakrishna expressed great delight as he observed her wonderful ecstasy. To calm her, he stroked her chest and fed her with delicacies from his room. Even as she ate, Gopal-ma remained in ecstasy, saying: "Gopala, my darling, your wretched mother has led a life of dire poverty. She has to make her living by spinning and selling sacred thread. Is that why you are taking special care of her today?"

The Master kept her at Dakshineswar that day. She took her bath and meals there. In the evening, when she had calmed a little, the Master sent her back to Kamarhati. The Gopala of her vision went with her, nestled in her arms.[73]

Later, during the Return Chariot Festival of Jagannath, the Master spent a few days at Balaram's house, and Gopal-ma came to see him. Swami Saradananda wrote: "Shortly before evening the Master went into ecstasy. We have seen the metal image of Gopala in a crawling posture: Its knees and left hand are on the ground, and it is looking joyfully and wistfully upward and asking for something with its right hand raised, palm up. The Master went into ecstasy and assumed that posture, except that his eyes remained half-closed, as if focussed on something within. Shortly after the Master's ecstasy began, Gopal-ma's carriage arrived at Balaram's gate. She went upstairs and found the Master in the posture of her Chosen Deity. The devotees present understood that it was Gopal-ma's intense devotion that had brought about this sudden manifestation of Gopala in the Master. They appreciated Gopal-ma and adored her, considering her to be most fortunate. They remarked: 'What wonderful devotion! The Master assumed the form of Gopala because of her intense devotion.' But Gopal-ma said: 'Truly speaking, I don't care for this stiff posture in ecstasy. My Gopala should laugh and play, walk and run. But what is this? He has become stiff like a log. I don't like to see this sort of Gopala!'"[74]

Ramakrishna as Ramachandra

One day Kshudiram, Ramakrishna's father, travelled to another village on an errand. On his way home he became exhausted, so he rested awhile under a tree by the side of the road. He felt an urge to lie down, and as soon as he did so, he fell asleep. After a while, he began to dream: His chosen deity, Ramachandra, with a complexion like that of a blade of young grass, appeared before him as a divine boy. Pointing to a particular spot, Ramachandra said: "Unnoticed and uncared for, I have been starving here for many days. Take me to your home. I am eager to accept your service."[75] Kshudiram went there and found a stone emblem of Vishnu; he carried it to his home and installed it in his shrine.

Kshudiram called that image Raghuvir (an epithet of Ramachandra) and worshipped him daily with great love. Once, when Gadadhar was a child, Kshudiram had a desire to make a garland for the Lord. He picked flowers, made a garland, and sat down to worship Raghuvir. Meanwhile, the little Gadadhar wanted to put on that garland. Kshudiram bathed the deity and then closed his eyes to meditate. Gadadhar took this opportunity to put on the garland. He then called to his father and said: "Look, Father, I am Raghuvir. See how I am dressed with a garland and sandal paste like him."[76]

It is difficult to say who the Chosen Deity of the Bhairavi Brahmani was. Before she met Ramakrishna, she had received a command from the Divine Mother; she had attained perfection in Shakti worship according to Tantra; she was a great aspirant of the devotional path of Vaishnavism; but while travelling she always carried her stone image of Raghuvir.

Swami Saradananda described the Brahmani's vision of Raghuvir when she was at Dakshineswar:

After she had her breakfast and visited the temple deities, the Brahmani collected rice, flour, and other food from the temple store. She then began cooking in the Panchavati, preparing her offering to a stone image of Raghuvir that she carried about with her, and which hung around her neck.

When she had finished cooking, she placed the food before Raghuvir, closed her eyes, and began to think of her Chosen Deity. Soon she entered deep meditation and had a wonderful vision. Plunged in samadhi, she lost outer consciousness, and tears of joy trickled down her cheeks. At that moment the Master was in an ecstatic mood and felt an urge to go to the Panchavati. He went there, and possessed by a divine power, began to eat the food that had been offered by the Brahmani. After a while the Brahmani regained outer consciousness and saw the Master there, in an ecstatic mood. Finding this scene to be similar to her vision, she was filled with delight, and her hair stood on end. When the Master returned to the normal plane he felt ashamed of what he had done. He apologized, saying, "Who knows, mother, why I lose control over myself and do such things?" The Brahmani lovingly reassured him: "You did well, my son. It is not really you who has done this, but He who dwells within you. In my meditation I clearly realized who did it and why. I have come to understand that I do not need to perform formal worship anymore: My worship has borne fruit at last." Then the Brahmani unhesitatingly took the Master's leftover food as prasad. She saw that her beloved Raghuvir was living in Sri Ramakrishna, and she was overwhelmed with happiness. With tears of joy, she consigned to the Ganges the stone image that she had so lovingly worshipped for many years."[77]

When Ramakrishna was practising *vatsalya bhava* (the affectionate attitude towards God), he took initiation from Jatadhari into a Rama mantra. It is really amazing how the metallic image of Ramlala (the child Ramachandra) ate, slept, bathed, ran, and jumped like a living human being with the Master. The Master served Ramlala with as much affection as Rama's mother, Kausalya, had felt when serving him. Seeing the Master's close relationship with Ramlala, one day Jatadhari came to the Master and said, crying with joy: "Ramlala has revealed himself to me in a way that I have never known before but have always longed for. Now the desire of my life is fulfilled. Ramlala says he won't go away from here; he doesn't want to leave you. But I'm not sad about it anymore. He lives happily with you and plays joyfully, and I am full of bliss when I see him this way. I have learned now to be happy simply in his happiness. So I can now leave him with you and go away. I will enjoy knowing that he is happy with you."[78] Then Jatadhari gave the Master the image of Ramlala and said good-bye.

Nistarini, the wife of Navagopal Ghosh, was a devout woman. After her marriage, she went with her husband to see the Master at Dakshineswar. A temple cat had some kittens. The guards had been hitting them and the mother cat had taken shelter in the Master's room with her kittens. One day the Master asked Nistarini to take them to her home. She agreed. Pleased, the Master blessed her, saying: "You saved me from a great responsibility. By Mother's grace, may all good attend you and may you have the vision of your Chosen Deity." Her Chosen Deity was Ramachandra. One day while repeating the mantra, she had a vision of Lord Rama. Immediately she bowed down. And when she was taking the dust of his feet, she saw the form of Ramakrishna in place of Ramachandra. The Master smiled and said: "Now you know who I am."[79]

The Master's nephew Ramlal told the following story:

A young Ramait monk in Ayodhya had a vision that Lord Rama had again incarnated on earth, somewhere in the East. In order to see him, the monk started on foot eastward from Ayodhya. When he reached Bengal he heard that there was a great saint named Sri Ramakrishna near Calcutta. He finally found Dakshineswar after a long search and asked someone, "Where is Ramakrishna Paramahamsa?" The people of the Kali temple told him that the Master had just passed away a few days before. Hearing this heartbreaking news, the monk exclaimed:

"What! He passed away? I have come from Ayodhya on foot [nearly 1000 miles] just to see him. I went through so much hardship to get here and he has left the body!" The young monk began to sob.

The manager of the Kali temple offered him some food from the temple store, but he refused it. He went to the Panchavati and stayed there for two or three days without eating. One night Sri Ramakrishna appeared before him and said: "You have not eaten anything for several days. I have brought this pudding for you. Please eat it." He fed the monk and disappeared.

The next morning I [Ramlal] went to the Panchavati and found the monk full of joy. I asked: "What happened?" Then he told me everything. He even showed me the clay bowl in which the Master had brought the pudding. [Ramlal preserved the bowl for a long time, but later on it was somehow destroyed.][80]

Ramakrishna as Sita

Swami Saradananda's description of Ramakrishna's vision of Sita is very poetic. He wrote:

It was during this period [of practising dasya bhava, the servant attitude to God] that the Master had an unprecedented vision. This spiritual experience was so different from his previous ones that it became deeply imprinted in his mind and remained vivid in his memory forever. He described the event as follows: "One day at that time I was seated under the Panchavati. I was in a state of ordinary consciousness, well aware of my surroundings. All of a sudden, a luminous female figure of exquisite grace appeared before me. Her radiance lit up everything around her. I could see her, and at the same time I could see the trees and plants of the Panchavati, the Ganges, everything. I saw that she was human, for she had no marks of a divine being upon her, such as a third eye. But the sublime qualities reflected in her face — love, sorrow, compassion, and fortitude — are seldom to be seen even among goddesses. Slowly she advanced towards me, from the direction of the north, all the while looking at me with gracious eyes. I was amazed. I was wondering who she might be when suddenly a monkey uttered a cry, fell at her feet, and rolled on the ground. Then it came to me in a flash that this must be Sita, the daughter of King Janaka, who had suffered so greatly all her life, and whose whole life had been devoted to her husband, Rama. Overcome by emotion, I cried out 'Mother' and was about to fall at her feet when she instantly passed into my body and became merged in it. Overwhelmed with joy and wonder, I fell unconscious on the ground. This was the first vision I ever had with my eyes wide open, and when I wasn't meditating. I believe it is because my first such vision was of Sita in her sorrowful aspect that, like her, I've had so much suffering in my life."[*81]

The Master had visions of Sita many times and he prayed to the Divine Mother: "O Mother, make me like Sita, completely forgetful of every-thing — body and limbs — totally unconscious of hands, feet, and sense organs — only one thought in her mind, 'Where is Rama?'"[82]

Swami Ramakrishnananda said: "When the Master talked about Sita, he would become Sita altogether, so that there would be absolutely no difference between him and Sita."[83]

We do not know how to see something with one hundred percent of our mind; that is why we see indistinctly. We may see something, but a little while later we don't remember it. The Holy Mother described the sharpness of the Master's vision: "The Master saw Sita in the Panchavati, wearing a bangle with an unusual design. He presented me with a bangle similar to Sita's."[84]

Swami Turiyananda once told Swami Shantananda this fascinating story about the Master:

> One day Mathur was returning to Janbazar in his deluxe phaeton and was bringing Sri Ramakrishna with him. When the carriage reached Chitpore Road, the Master had a wonderful vision. He felt that he had become Sita and that Ravana was kidnapping him. Seized by this idea, he merged into samadhi. Just then the horses, tearing loose from their reins, stumbled and fell. Mathur could not understand the reason for such a mishap. When Sri Ramakrishna came back to the normal plane of consciousness, Mathur told him about the accident. Sri Rama-krishna then said that while he was in ecstasy he had perceived that Ravana was kidnapping him and that Jatayu [the great bird who had attempted to rescue Sita] was attacking Ravana's chariot and was try-ing to destroy it. After hearing this story, Mathur said, "Father, how difficult it is even to go with you through the street!"[85]

Ramakrishna in the Mood of Mahavir Hanuman

Swami Saradananda wrote:

> The Master knew that if one had the one-pointed devotion that Hanu-man had for Rama, it would be possible to have the vision of Rama. The Master therefore set out to immerse himself in the servant attitude

*Swami Saradananda, the author, recalled: The Master also said that Sita had made a gift of her sweet smile to him during that vision. So those who saw the Master smile knew how she smiled. — *Swami Saradanander Jivani* by Akshay Chaitanya, p.152; and *Sri Ramakrishna and His Divine Play*, tr. by Swami Chetanananda, p. 229.

of Hanuman in every respect and began his sadhana to attain perfection in dasya bhava. During this period he constantly focussed his mind on Hanuman and was so absorbed in that ideal, he completely forgot his separate existence and individuality. He later recalled: "I had to eat and walk like Hanuman and perform every action as he would have done it. I didn't do this of my own accord; it happened of itself. I tied my dhoti around my waist to make it look like a tail, and I moved about by jumping. I ate nothing but fruit and roots, and I didn't like them when they were skinned or peeled. I spent a lot of my time in trees, and I kept crying out 'Rama!' in a deep voice. My eyes took on a restless look, like the eyes of a monkey. And the most marvellous thing was that the lower end of my spine [the coccyx] lengthened nearly an inch!" Upon hearing this, we inquired, "Sir, do you still have the same growth there?" The Master replied: "No. When I later withdrew my mind from that kind of devotion, it [the coccyx] gradually went back to its normal size."[86]

Hanuman Singh, a temple guard, was a devotee of Mahavir Hanuman. He had tremendous love and respect for the Master, as much as he had for his Chosen Deity, Hanuman. Once another wrestler came to Dakshineswar and challenged him: The winner would have Singh's job. On the day of competition, Hanuman Singh bowed down to the Master and asked for his blessing, saying, "Master, if you bestow your grace on me, I'll definitely win."[87] And he won the match.

Ramakrishna in the Mood of Durga

Once Swami Saradananda related the following incident: "One day the Master was seated in the Panchavati. At that time the Divine Mother Durga appeared from the Ganges, walked towards him, and merged into his body. Later, the Master told Hriday: 'Mother Durga came. Look, Her footprints are still on the ground.'"[88]

Ramlal described how the Master had a vision of Durga seated on a blue lotus: "Once the Master went by steamer with Keshab Sen to visit the Eden Garden in Calcutta. He saw many blue lotuses in a pond there. He saw Mother Durga seated on a large lotus. Her right foot was hanging down, the left one was on the lotus, and Ganesha was on Her lap. The lotus was gently moving. When he had that vision, the Master went into samadhi."[89]

Every year during Durga Puja, Mathur would invite the Master to his Calcutta residence at Janbazar. The Master passed those days joyfully with Mathur and his family. One day when the Master attended the worship service, the priest was offering food to the deity. At that time an unusual event took place. Akshay Sen wrote: "When the priest was offering the food, the Master took it in his hand and began to eat. The priest was startled. Immediately Mathur said to the priest and others: 'Now I understand that my worship of the Mother Durga is successful, because the Master has taken the food.'"[90]

As a guru, the Master bestowed his grace on Mathur. On the last day of Durga Puja that year, Mathur said to the Master: "Father, whatever others may say, I won't allow the Mother to be immersed in the Ganges. I have ordered the worship to be continued daily. How can I survive in this world without the Mother?"

The Master stroked Mathur's chest and said: "Oh, is this what makes you afraid? Who has told you that you will have to live without the Mother? And where will She go even if you immerse Her image in the Ganges? Can the Mother stay away from Her son? For the last three days She has accepted your worship in the worship hall, but from today She will accept your worship constantly, sitting in your heart."[91] And Mathur was mollified.

Once Hriday performed Durga Puja in Sihar but the Master could not go with him. There Hriday saw the Master beside the image of Durga during vespers and the *sandhi-puja*. Later, when he returned to Dakshineswar, he described his vision to the Master. The Master said: "It is true that I felt an intense longing to see your worship during vespers and the sandhi-puja. In ecstasy I felt that in a shining body I moved along a luminous path and entered your worship hall."[92]

When Ramakrishna was in Shyampukur being treated for cancer, while in samadhi he travelled in his subtle form to see the Durga Puja at Surendra Mitra's house. He told his devotees: "A luminous path opened from this place to Surendra's house. I saw the presence of the Divine Mother in the image; She had been evoked by Surendra's devotion. A ray of light beamed forth from Her third eye! Rows of lamps were lit before the goddess in the worship hall. In the courtyard Surendra was crying piteously 'Mother, Mother!' All of you go to his house right now. When he sees you he will regain his peace of mind."

Narendra and some others bowed down to the Master, then left for Surendra's house. When they asked Surendra, they learned that what the Master had seen in samadhi was correct. The Master had indeed gone there in his luminous body to bless Surendra.[93]

Ramakrishna as the Kundalini Power

Ramakrishna became established in the divine mood when he was twenty-two or twenty-three years old. Later, he told his devotees how he had transcended the six centres of the kundalini:

A man's spiritual consciousness is not awakened unless his kundalini is aroused.

The kundalini dwells in the Muladhara. When it is aroused, it passes along the Sushumna nerve, goes through the centres of Svadhisthana, Manipura, and so on, and at last reaches the head. This is called the movement of the Mahavayu, the Spiritual Current. It culminates in samadhi.

One's spiritual consciousness is not awakened by the mere reading of books. One should also pray to God. The kundalini is aroused if the aspirant feels restless for God. To talk of Knowledge from mere study and hearsay! What will that accomplish?

Just before I attained this state of mind, it had been revealed to me how the kundalini is aroused, how the lotuses of the different centres blossom forth, and how all this culminates in samadhi. This is a very secret experience. I saw a boy twenty-two or twenty-three years old, exactly resembling me, enter the Sushumna nerve and commune with the lotuses, touching them with his tongue. He began with the centre at the anus and passed through the centres at the sexual organ, navel, and so on. The different lotuses of those centres — four-petalled, six-petalled, ten-petalled, and so forth — had been drooping. At his touch they stood erect.

When he reached the heart — I distinctly remember it — and communed with the lotus there, touching it with his tongue, the twelve-petalled lotus, which was hanging down, stood erect and opened its petals. Then he came to the sixteen-petalled lotus in the throat and the two-petalled lotus in the forehead. And last of all, the thousand-petalled lotus in the head blossomed. Since then I have been in this state.[94]

The Master used to call the Kundalini Power "Chaitanya-vayu," "Hari-bai," "Mahavayu," "the Snake," and "Mother." This power was active within the Master at all times. Sometimes the Master would arouse this power within his devotees through singing. Swami Saradananda wrote:

The Master bowed down to the Mother. Then, in an ecstatic mood, he walked with his boy devotees to the natmandir. He sat down and began to sing in his sweet voice:

O Mother, Consort of Shiva, You have deluded this world.
You entertain Yourself by playing the vina in the great lotus of the muladhara.

Your music vibrates through the great mantra in three scales, taking the form of the three gunas.

Your music strikes the three chords — sushumna, ida, and pingala — of that musical instrument, the body.

You play with melody, rhythm, and tempo at the six centres of the kundalini: Bhairava-raga in the muladhara, Sri-raga in the swadhisthana, Mallara-raga in the manipura, Vasanta-raga in the anahata, Hindola-raga in the vishuddha, and Karnataka-raga in the ajna.

Again, O Mother, You transcend all sound by crossing the three octaves.

O Mother, Sri Nandakumar says that one cannot realize the Supreme Truth unless You remove the veil of Your three gunas, which covers the face of Brahman.

The Master was singing while seated in the northern part of the natmandir facing the Divine Mother. The devotees — some sitting and some standing — were overwhelmed as they listened to the song. While singing, the Master suddenly stood up and went into ecstasy. The singing stopped. His divine smile flooded the entire place with bliss. The devotees remained motionless as they gazed upon the beautiful form of the Master. In this condition the Master crawled down the steps of the northern side of the natmandir to the temple courtyard.

After crossing the courtyard, the Master reached his own room and went to the western semicircular veranda to sit. He was still in ecstasy; the mood possessed him. Sometimes it lessened a little, but would increase again and he would almost lose consciousness. After being in this condition for some time, the Master — still in that condition — said to the devotees: Have you seen the Snake? It is giving me so much trouble! Forgetting the devotees, he addressed the snake-like kundalini (for he was then experiencing the Serpent Power): "Please go now. Madam, move away. I shall smoke tobacco and wash my mouth. I have not yet brushed my teeth." Thus, he spoke with the devotees at times and sometimes addressed the divine form seen in ecstasy. Gradually he returned to the normal plane of consciousness.[95]

When the kundalini was aroused, the Master's body would expand. Sometimes he became ravenous with hunger. Once at midnight in Dakshineswar, the Master was very hungry. He asked Ramlal to give him some food. Swami Saradananda wrote:

There were usually some fruits and sweets in the Master's room, but when Ramlal searched he found nothing. So he went to the nahabat and informed the Holy Mother and other women devotees. They hurriedly made a fire with hay and wood and cooked about two pounds of farina pudding. A woman devotee [Golap-ma] carried it to the Master in a big stone bowl. Entering the room, she saw a dim oil lamp flickering in the corner. The Master was pacing in an ecstatic mood, and Ramlal was seated nearby. In that calm and silent night, she was startled to see the Master's solemn, luminous face and his unclothed god-intoxicated form. His large eyes — before which the whole universe merged into and emerged from samadhi at will — were focussed inward. Her heart was filled with joy as she watched the Master pace majestically, moving blissfully and without motive, his mind one-pointed. It seemed to her that the Master's body had become much larger, as if he were not a person of this world! A god had taken human form, descending from heaven to this earth full of misery. Prompted by his compassionate heart, he had disguised himself and was pacing fearlessly in that dark night, intently considering ways to transform this death-stricken world into an abode of gods. This was not the same Master whom she saw all the time. She shivered with an indescribable awe as she drew near him.

Ramlal had already brought a seat for the Master, and the woman devotee put the bowl of farina pudding in front of it. The Master sat down and, still in an ecstatic mood, gradually consumed all of it.[96]

Later, Golap-ma described her experience: "Once I saw that when the Master was eating, a serpent-like being was gulping the food from his throat. I was amazed. The Master asked me: 'Well, can you tell me whether I am eating or someone else?' I told him: 'It seems a snake is sitting in your throat and gulping the food.' The Master was pleased, and said: 'You are right. Blessed you are that you have seen it.' I really saw that the Master was offering food to the serpent-formed kundalini."[97]

Nistarini Ghosh also saw the kundalini in the form of a snake in the Master's throat, taking food. Her son Swami Ambikananda later described what happened: "When the Master came to our house in Calcutta, my mother took him to our inner apartment for some refreshment. The Master was fond of sandesh, so the best available sandesh was purchased. The Master was seated and my mother sat in front of him with folded hands. The Master: 'Well, what do you want? You want to feed me with your own hand? All right.' When the Master opened his mouth, she put a sandesh into it and saw that someone gulped the sandesh. My mother was frightened by this. After having his refreshment, the Master asked my mother to take a little prasad. It is not customary for a host to eat before the guests. When my mother hesitated, the Master insisted that she eat. So she did. When the remaining prasad was sent downstairs, the devotees consumed everything. Then the Master said: 'You see, it is for this reason that I asked you to take prasad earlier.'"[98]

Swami Vijnanananda described his second meeting with the Master, which took place in Belgharia:

> A young man [Narendra] was singing a devotional song, "Jai, Jai Dayamaya, Jai Dayamaya" [Victory to the compassionate Lord; Victory to the compassionate Lord]. Sri Ramakrishna was standing in the centre of the group, and another young man [Baburam] was holding him so that he would not fall. The Master was completely oblivious to his surroundings. He wore a white cloth. His face shone with a heavenly lustre and a smile played on his lips. His teeth were visible, and there was such a joyful expression on his face that it seemed as if it would crack — like a melon! His eyes seemed to be gazing at something, and he appeared to be immersed in an ocean of bliss.
>
> Another thing that struck me has remained imprinted in my memory forever. From the base of the Master's spine right up to his head, the whole column had become inflated like a thick rope. And the energy that rose upward towards the brain seemed to be spreading its hood and swaying its head like a snake dancing in joy.[99]

Ramakrishna in the Ocean of Satchidananda

Satchidananda is formless, actionless, and devoid of qualities. Sat (existence), chit (consciousness), and ananda (bliss) are the essence of Brahman. The vision of the formless Brahman is a mysterious thing. As no painter or sculptor of Ramprasad's Kali has ever been born, so there is no one to describe the visions of Ramakrishna. We must let Ramakrishna himself tell us about his experience of Brahman and his vision of Brahman in every being.

Master (to M.): "There is no outsider here. The other day, when Harish was with me, I saw Satchidananda come out of this sheath. It said, 'I incarnate Myself in every age.' I thought that I myself was saying these words out of mere fancy. I kept quiet and watched. Again Satchidananda Itself spoke, saying, 'Chaitanya, too, worshipped Shakti.' I saw that it is the fullest manifestation of Satchidananda; but this time the Divine Power is manifested through the glory of sattva."[100]

Master: "I have had many amazing visions. I had a vision of the Indivisible Satchidananda. Inside It I saw two groups with a fence between them. On one side were Kedar, Chuni, and other devotees who believe in the Personal God. On the other side was a luminous space like a heap of red brick-dust. Inside it was seated Narendra immersed in samadhi."[101]

Master: "The Indivisible Satchidananda — I see It both inside and outside. It has merely assumed this sheath [*meaning his body*] for a support and exists both inside and outside. I clearly perceive this."[102]

Girish Ghosh once said to Ramakrishna: "You alone are the Perfect Brahman! If that is not so, then everything is false."[103]

Ramakrishna once took M. to Mati Sil's lake to teach him how to meditate on the formless Brahman. There were tame fish in the lake. Nobody harmed them. Visitors threw puffed rice and other bits of food into the water and big fish came in swarms to eat the food. Fearlessly the fish swam in the water and joyfully sported there. The Master told M.: "Look at the fish. Meditating on the formless God is like swimming joyfully like these fish, in the Ocean of Bliss and Consciousness."[104]

In Kamarpukur the Master once had a vision in front of some women devotees. Swami Saradananda wrote:

> One day the Master was resting in his room after lunch. Some neighbour women came to see him. They sat near him and began discussing spiritual matters. All of a sudden he went into ecstasy. In that state he felt that he was joyfully swimming like a fish in the ocean of Satchidananda — sometimes sinking and sometimes floating. The Master would quite often go into ecstasy like this while talking with others, so without paying much attention to it, the women were noisily expressing their own opinions about his condition. Then one of them asked the others to keep quiet until the Master's ecstasy came to an end. She said: "He is now swimming like a fish in the ocean of Satchidananda. If you make noise, that will interrupt his bliss." Although many of them did not believe her, they became silent. Later, when the Master came down to the normal plane and heard what the woman had said about his experience, he remarked: "She is right. It is really amazing. How could she know about it?"[105]

Ramakrishna as Christ

After the Master had practised sadhanas from various paths of Hinduism, Shambhu Mallick read the Bible to him. He therefore felt a desire to learn about Jesus Christ. Swami Saradananda described how the Master's desire was fulfilled:

> Jadulal Mallick's garden house is situated at the south side of the Dakshineswar Kali temple. The Master occasionally went there for a walk. From their first meeting, Jadulal and his mother loved and

respected the Master greatly. If they were away when the Master went to Jadu's garden for his walk, the caretakers would open the parlour for him and ask him to sit and rest awhile. There were some magnificent pictures hanging on the walls of that room, and one of them depicted the child Jesus on his mother's lap. The Master said that one day he sat in that room and intently studied that image, thinking of the wonderful life of Jesus. Just then he saw the picture become animate and luminous. Rays of light emanated from the bodies of Mother Mary and the child Jesus, entering the Master's heart and revolutionizing his mental attitudes. When he observed that his inborn Hindu impressions were vanishing from his mind and that different ones were arising, he tried to control himself by resisting them in various ways. He entreated the Divine Mother, saying, "Mother, what are You doing to me?" But the onslaught continued. The waves of those impressions rose forcefully and completely submerged the Hindu bent of his mind. The Master's love and devotion for Hindu gods and goddesses disappeared and his heart was filled with faith in and reverence for Jesus and his religion. He then had a vision of Christian clergymen offering incense and lights in front of the image of Jesus in a church, expressing their inner longing through prayer.

After he returned to the Dakshineswar temple garden, the Master remained uninterruptedly absorbed in meditation on those experiences pertaining to Jesus. He completely forgot to visit the Divine Mother in the temple. The waves of Christian faith that swayed him lasted for three days. When the Master was walking in the Panchavati at the end of the third day, he saw a beautiful but unfamiliar godman with a fair complexion advancing towards him, gazing at him steadily. The Master immediately realized that he was a foreigner who belonged to a different race. He saw that his eyes were large and beautiful, and though his nose was a little flat at the tip, it in no way marred the handsomeness of his face. The Master was charmed by the unique divine expression on his serene face and wondered who he could be. Very soon after that the figure drew near, and a voice from within told him, "This is Jesus Christ, the great yogi, the loving Son of God who is one with his Father, who shed his heart's blood and suffered tortures for the salvation of humanity." Then the godman Jesus embraced the Master and merged into him. In ecstasy, the Master lost external consciousness and his mind remained united with Saguna Brahman for some time. With this vision, the Master became convinced that Jesus was truly a divine incarnation.[106]

Later, Ramakrishna attended a service in a Christian church in Calcutta. On another occasion, a Christian named Williams,* who visited the Master, expressed this opinion: "You are Jesus Christ, the Son of God, the embodiment of Eternal Consciousness."[107]

On 28 July 1885 M. had a long conversation about Jesus with the Master. When Ramakrishna wanted to know whether there were any similarities between himself and Jesus, M. replied: "I feel that Christ, Chaitanyadeva, and yourself — all three are one and the same. It is the same Person that has become all these three." Master: "Yes, yes! One! One! It is indeed one. Don't you see that it is He alone who dwells here in this way."[108]

Prabhudayal Mishra, a Christian who belonged to the Quaker denomination, came to see Ramakrishna at the Shyampukur house in Calcutta. Manindra Krishna Gupta recalled:

I saw a man come upstairs. He wore a black shirt and a black cap. It seemed to me that he was a native of Bihar. He asked me: "Sir, does Ramakrishna Paramahamsa live here? I have come to see him. Could I see him right away?" "Of course," I replied. "Please follow me." I took him to the Master's room.

After sitting there quietly for a while, he said to the Master: "Sir, I am a Christian, and for a long time I have meditated in solitude on Christ. Though I am a Christian and my Chosen Deity is Christ, my mode of worship is like the Hindus, and I believe in their yoga scriptures. Once I had a desire to find someone who had attained the highest spiritual realization while still in the world. One day in meditation, I saw two persons. I had the strong feeling that one of them had attained the highest, and that the other one, seated at his feet, though he had not yet reached the highest, was not an ordinary person.

"After this vision, I felt certain that such great souls must exist, but where were they, and how could I find them? I travelled to many places, especially in the western part of India, seeking the two I had seen in my vision. At last I heard of Pavhari Baba of Ghazipur, and I went to see him. But when I met him, I was greatly disappointed, because he bore no resemblance whatsoever to either of the two men I was seeking. But to my astonishment, I saw a picture of one of them hanging on the wall in his room. When I asked Pavhari Baba about it, he said it was a picture of Ramakrishna Paramahamsa. Eagerly I

---

*We are reliably informed that Williams, after he had seen the Master a few times, became convinced that he was a divine incarnation. He gave up the world at the Master's advice, went to the Himalayas to the north of the Punjab, and passed away there after practising difficult austerities.

asked, 'Where can I find him?' Then Pavhari Baba told me that for many years he had lived at Dakshineswar, but was now very ill and had been moved to Calcutta for treatment by his devotees. So I am here, having come to Calcutta at Pavhari Baba's suggestion."

Then the man went on to say: "These clothes in which you see me are not my usual dress." And as he spoke he stood up and removed his outer garments, revealing an ochre cloth. Instantly the Master also stood up and went into samadhi, raising his hand, as it is seen in the picture of Christ. At this, the monk knelt down before him with folded hands and looked intently at Sri Ramakrishna. The monk was shedding tears and was shaking. We were all amazed to see the spiritual moods of both. After some time the Master came back to normal consciousness and sat on his bed. The monk looked at us, his face beaming with joy, and exclaimed, "Today I am blessed."

Then we took him to an adjacent room, where Swami Vivekananda offered him prasad and food. Finally, we asked the monk to tell us the cause of his ecstasy. "Well," he replied, "today I saw the one on whom I have meditated for so many years. I saw Lord Jesus in him."[109]

M. once described a similar incident: "Mr. Missir was a devout Christian. The Master was very fond of him and talked to him about God. The Master showed him Christ: One day he took Mr. Missir to the Kali temple. When the latter bowed down to the Mother and raised his head, he saw Jesus Christ in place of Kali. He later realized that the Master was Christ."[110]

Ramakrishna's Experience of Islamic Truth

After practising Vedanta, Ramakrishna began to practise Islam. At that time, a Sufi named Govinda Roy came to Dakshineswar to practise sadhana. This spiritual seeker had previously been a Hindu, but had embraced Islam. He knew Farsi and Arabic, studied the Koran daily, and practised Islamic disciplines. Impressed by his faith and love, the Master was attracted to Islam.

Swami Saradananda wrote: "This thought was immediately followed by action. The Master expressed his wish to Govinda, received initiation from him, and began to practise Islam according to its traditions. The Master said: 'I then devoutly repeated the holy name of Allah, wore my cloth as the Muslims do, and said their prayers several times a day. Because the Hindu feeling had disappeared from my mind altogether, I felt disinclined to visit the Hindu deities, much less to bow down to them. I spent three days in that mood, and I had the full realization of the sadhana of that faith.' While practising Islam, the Master at first had a vision of a radiant Being who looked grave and had a long beard; then he experienced the cosmic Saguna Brahman; and finally his mind merged into the absolute Nirguna Brahman."[111]

Ramlal gave this account: "Once the Master had a desire to pray in a mosque. There was a mosque on the way from our house to the Dakshineswar temple. Early one morning the Master went to that mosque and stood near the gate. He wore his cloth in the Muslim style. Opening the door, the Muslims found him standing there. They asked: 'Who are you? Where do you come from?' One of them recognized the Master and said: 'He lives in the temple and worships there.' Then the Master went inside the mosque and prayed with them. Thus he prayed three days with the Muslims. One day in the mosque he saw an old fakir who had white hair, a mustache, and a beard. He wore a long cloak and had a glass rosary around his neck. He carried a stick in his hand. He came close to the Master and said: 'You have come. Very good!' He smiled and blessed the Master, moving his hand over him. I heard this story from the Master."[112]

Manmatha Nath Ghosh, an eyewitness, described how the Master entered the Geratala mosque in an ecstatic mood: "One evening as I was passing by the Geratala mosque, I heard the loud prayer of a Muslim fakir: 'O my Beloved, please come! Please come, O my Beloved!' He was repeating this prayer with love and longing as tears rolled down his cheeks.

"Suddenly I saw Sri Ramakrishna climb down from a hired carriage and rush up to the fakir. The two embraced each other. This incident happened when the Master was returning from Kalighat after visiting the Divine Mother there. What a wonderful sight it was! Two other people were in the carriage. One of them was Ramlal, a nephew of Sri Ramakrishna, who used to give me prasad at the Master's command at Dakshineswar."[113]

Ramakrishna as the Sikh Guru Nanak

Ramakrishna heard about Buddha, the Jain Mahavir, and Shankara and based some of his teachings upon their messages. The Master remarked about Buddha: "Buddha was definitely an incarnation of God. There is no difference between his religion and the Vedic path of knowledge."[114] In the Master's room at Dakshineswar there were a stone image of Mahavir Tirthankar and a portrait of Christ; the Master would wave incense before both of them. Although he adored and respected them, he never said that the tirthankaras in Jainism and the ten gurus in

Sikhism, from Nanak to Govinda, were incarnations of God. About the ten gurus of Sikhism, the Master said: "They are all incarnations of the sage Janaka. I heard from some Sikhs that the royal sage Janaka had a desire to do good to humanity before he attained liberation. That is why he was born ten times as ten gurus from Nanak to Govinda, established religion among the Sikhs, and then merged forever into the Supreme Brahman. There is no reason to disbelieve this statement of the Sikhs."[115]

It is mentioned in the Ramakrishna literature that Rama, Krishna, Jesus, Chaitanya and others merged into the Master's body. But there is no mention of Buddha, Mahavir, Muhammad, Nanak, or Shankaracharya merging into him.

During the Master's time, there was a government magazine at the north side of the Dakshineswar temple garden. A group of Sikh soldiers were stationed there to protect it. Sometimes they would come to the Master for spiritual advice, and at other times they would invite him to their quarters for food. Swami Ambikananda said: "The Sikh guards of the magazine first called the Master 'Paramahamsa.' The Master would joyfully move around the bel tree, naked. The people of the Punjab are very devoted to monks, and they serve holy people with great respect. Observing the Master's exalted state, they remarked, 'Look, this man is a Paramahamsa!' From that time on the Master had the name 'Ramakrishna Paramahamsa.'"[116]

Once the Master said: "I have practised all kinds of sadhana: jnana yoga, karma yoga, and bhakti yoga. I have even gone through the exercises of hatha yoga to increase longevity. There is another Person dwelling in this body. Otherwise, after attaining samadhi, how could I live with the devotees and enjoy the love of God? Koar Singh used to say to me: 'I have never before seen a person who has returned from the plane of samadhi. You are none other than Nanak.'"[117]

One day the Master went to the Sikhs' quarters with Narayana Shastri. The men were delighted to see that the Master had come of his own accord. They bowed down to him, and sat to hear him talk about spiritual matters. The Master spoke, and they listened. However, Narayana Shastri interjected some words about jnana (knowledge) into the Master's discourse. Akshay Sen wrote: "The soldiers were angered by this, and threatened Narayana Shastri with a sword. They told Shastri, 'You are a worldly householder — you have no right to talk about knowledge.' Then the Master calmed those angry Sikhs with sweet words."[118]

The following incident took place sometime earlier. The uniformed

Sikh regiment was marching to the Calcutta fort under the guidance of a British commander when the Master was passing by with Mathur in his horse carriage. Seeing the Master on the street, the soldiers dropped their guns on the ground and bowed down to the Master, saying, "Victory to the guru." Such actions were not acceptable under military rules and would be considered a grave offence. Akshay Sen wrote: "The commander asked the soldiers: 'Why have you dropped your arms without permission?' They replied: 'It is the custom of our religion to respect the guru. We don't care whether we lose our lives, but we must bow down to our guru when we see him.' The Master blessed those soldiers by raising his hand. It was by the Master's grace that the British commander did not say a single word more to them."[119]

Ramakrishna as Chaitanya

Swami Saradananda described the events that took place when the Master attended a meeting of the Harisabha:

The members of the Harisabha considered themselves to be ardent followers of Chaitanya. To remember this constantly, they put an *asana* on the altar and envisioned Chaitanya's presence there. They performed their worship, reading, and other functions of the congregation in front of that seat, which they called "Sri Chaitanya's Seat." Everyone bowed down to the seat with devotion, and no one was allowed to sit there. On this day, like any other, the reading was performed in front of the seat, which had been decorated with flowers and garlands. The reader was reading with devotion, believing himself to be reciting the glory of Hari to Chaitanya himself, and the devotees were excited to be drinking the nectar of the Lord's words while in Chaitanya's divine presence. The joy and devotion of the reader and the audience were enhanced a hundredfold by the Master's arrival.

While listening to the nectar-like words of the Bhagavata, the Master became overwhelmed and suddenly ran towards Sri Chaitanya's Seat. He stood upon it and went into such deep samadhi that there was not even the slightest sign of life in him. As they beheld the Master's wonderful and sweet smile, luminous face, and raised arms with fingers up as seen in the common images of Chaitanya, the prominent devotees were convinced that the Master had become completely identified with Chaitanya in bhavamukha [an exalted state]. Although there were external differences between his body and mind and those of Chaitanya with respect to time, place, and circumstance, the Master did not perceive these differences at all as he ascended to the plane of bhavamukha. The reader stopped his recitation and looked at the Master in wonder. Although most in the audience did not understand the Master's ecstasy, they were overpowered by an indescribable awe and wonder and remained calm. No one could say anything, positive or negative. As they experienced indescribable bliss, all felt as if they were carried away to an unknown realm by the powerful spiritual current caused by the Master. At first they were nonplussed but then were compelled by that indescribable phenomenon to burst forth in a loud voice with "Haribol!" and to begin singing kirtan.

Gradually, the news spread throughout the Vaishnava communities by word of mouth. Bhagavandas Babaji [the spiritual leader of the community] also heard about it.

The perfected Babaji was terribly annoyed when he heard that the seat of his Chosen Deity had been desecrated by a stranger named Ramakrishna. He was so enraged that he did not hesitate to bitterly reproach the Master and call him a hypocrite.

Some days after the incident, the Master went to Kalna [where the Babaji lived] of his own accord with Hriday and Mathur.[120]

Accompanied by Hriday, the Master went to visit Bhagavandas Babaji. He waited outside and sent Hriday to the Babaji with the message that he had come to see him. Meanwhile, the Master appeared before the Babaji when the latter was taking a disciplinary action against a Vaishnava monk. The Babaji said: "Confiscate his rosary and expel him from the Vaishnava community." Swami Saradananda described what then took place:

> The Master could no longer remain seated like a courteous and gentle guest. He rose to his feet, demanding: "Is that how you think of yourself even now? You think *you* teach people? You think *you'll* expel this man from your community? You think *you* can decide to give up telling your beads or not? Who made *you* a teacher? Do you think *you* can teach the world unless the Lord who made it allows you to?" The Master's cloth had fallen from his shoulders to the ground as had the cloth from around his loins. A wonderful radiance shone from his face. He was in such ecstasy that he was not aware of what he was saying and to whom he was speaking. After those few words he became overwhelmed with emotion and went into samadhi.
>
> Those powerful words of the Master awakened Babaji's keen insight, and he recognized his own shortcomings and became humble and modest. Moreover, the extraordinary manifestation of a spiritual mood in Sri Ramakrishna convinced Babaji that the Master was not an ordinary person.
>
> Bhagavandas bowed down to the Master and said: "By your grace I see that you are Chaitanya Mahaprabhu. So it is no wonder that you

sat on 'Sri Chaitanya's Seat.' When I sensed a divine fragrance upon
your arrival, I told the devotees that some divine being had come to us
today."[121]

During the Master's pilgrimage to Navadwip, he had a vision of
Chaitanya. Swami Saradananda wrote:

> Many among us were sceptical about Chaitanya's being an avatar, and
> some even believed that the word *Vaishnava* stood for "low-class peo-
> ple." To remove this doubt, some of us asked the Master about it. In
> reply, he said: "Previously I also thought that way. Chaitanya is not
> even alluded to in the Bhagavata and other Puranas, so how could he
> be an avatar? I thought the shaven-headed Vaishnavas had set him up
> as an avatar. At any rate, I did not believe it. Then I went to Navadwip
> with Mathur. I thought that if Chaitanya were an avatar, there must be
> some signs of his manifestation, and that I would recognize them. I
> moved around with a view to seeing his divine manifestation and vis-
> ited the deities in the houses of Senior Gosain and Junior Gosain, but
> found nothing.
>
> Everywhere I saw wooden images of Chaitanya standing with
> raised arms. I felt dejected and wondered why I had come. When I was
> about to board the boat to return, I had a wonderful vision of two
> beautiful teenaged boys. I had never seen such beauty before. Their
> complexions were as bright as molten gold and they had halos round
> their heads. Smiling, they rushed towards me through the air, their
> arms raised. Immediately I cried out: 'Here they come! Here they
> come!' No sooner had I uttered those words than they came near and
> entered here (*pointing to his body*), and I fell down unconscious. I would
> have fallen into the water, but Hriday was nearby and caught hold of
> me. Thus, I was shown many such things and became convinced that
> Chaitanya was a true avatar, a manifestation of divine power."[122]

The Master's niece Lakshmi, told this story: "Chinu Sankhari was our
neighbour in Kamarpukur. He was a close friend of the Master. He was a
devout Vaishnava, who practised sadhana and developed some occult
powers. Brother Chinu would sometimes embrace the Master with affection and say: 'Gadai, whenever I see you, I feel you are Gauranga.'"[123]

The Bhairavi Brahmani noticed the signs of *mahabhava* in the Master,
and he described his divine experiences to her. She then realized that
Chaitanya had again appeared, this time as Ramakrishna. Swami
Saradananda wrote:

> Towards the end of the first four years [of his sadhana], the Master had
> a wonderful vision when he was living at Kamarpukur. One day the

Master was travelling by palanquin from Kamarpukur to Hriday's house at Sihar. During that journey the Master enjoyed seeing the vast fields under the blue sky, the green rice fields, the rows of banyan trees providing cool shade along the path, and the creepers bedecked with sweet fragrant blossoms, and hearing the melodious singing of birds. Suddenly two beautiful adolescent boys emerged from his body. They wandered far into the field searching for wildflowers and then came back near the palanquin, laughing, joking, and talking playfully. Thus, they proceeded joyfully for a long time and then reentered the Master's body.

Nearly a year and a half after this vision, Bhairavi Brahmani arrived at Dakshineswar. One day in the course of conversation, the Master described this vision to her. She responded: "My child, your vision was true. This time Chaitanya has been manifested in Nityananda's body. Both Chaitanya and Nityananda have come and are dwelling inside you now. That is why you had that vision." When Hriday later described that conversation to us, he mentioned that the Brahmani then recited the following two verses from the *Chaitanya Bhagavata*: "Putting his arms around the neck of Advaitacharya, Chaitanya said repeatedly: 'I shall enact my wonderful divine play once more. My form will be manifested as bliss during *kirtan*.' Gaur [another name of Chaitanya] is still enacting his divine play; only a fortunate few can see it."[124]

Soon after Ram Chandra Datta met Sri Ramakrishna, he started to read *Sri Sri Chaitanya Charitamrita*, an authoritative biography of Sri Chaitanya, written in Bengali. The more Ram read about that god-intoxicated life, the more he felt that Sri Ramakrishna and Sri Chaitanya were the same person. But sometimes he had doubts. Once, at the Master's request, Ram spent a night at Dakshineswar. When he was alone with the Master, he started looking at him in wonder.

"What are you looking at?" asked Sri Ramakrishna.

"I am looking at you."

"What do you think of me?"

"I consider you to be Chaitanya."

Sri Ramakrishna was silent for a moment and then said, "Well, the Bhairavi Brahmani used to say the same thing."[125]

On another occasion, the Master asked Ram: "What do you want?" Overwhelmed with emotion, Ram replied: "Lord, I don't know what to ask for. You decide for me." "Give me back the mantra I gave you in the dream," said the Master as he entered into samadhi. Immediately Ram prostrated himself before the Master and offered the mantra mentally at his feet like a flower. Gradually the Master came back to the normal plane of consciousness. "If you wish to see anything," said the Master to Ram, "look at me." Ram looked and saw that Sri Ramakrishna had taken the form of his Chosen Deity, the form of God that was dearest to his heart. Then Sri Ramakrishna told him: "You do not need to practise any more spiritual disciplines. Just come here and see me now and then, and bring with you a pice worth of something as a present."[126]

Once, in Dakshineswar, the exuberant Ram expressed his belief to the great devotee, Girish Chandra Ghosh: "Do you understand, Brother Girish? This time all three — Sri Chaitanya, Nityananda, and Advaita — are united in the form of Sri Ramakrishna. Love, devotion, and knowledge are equally manifested in this present Incarnation."[127]

Shyamasundari, the mother of Manomohan Mitra, said of the Master: "The Master is not a sadhu or a mahatma; he is God Himself. He was born in Navadwip as Chaitanya, and now the same Mahaprabhu is living in the Dakshineswar temple as Sri Ramakrishna and saving souls through his divine play."[128]

Swami Saradananda wrote:

We remember that in the evening Narendra took us for a walk in Cornwallis Square [now Azadhind Bagh]. On the way he told us of divine experiences that he had experienced by the grace of the Master. He was absorbed within himself for a while and then finally expressed his inner bliss with his heavenly voice:

Gora* bestows the Nectar of love;
Jar after jar he pours it out,
And still there is no end!
Sweetest Nitai** is summoning all;
Beloved Gora bids them come;
Shantipur*** is almost drowned,
And Nadia is flooded with love!

When he had finished singing, Narendra gently soliloquized: "He is actually distributing love. Love, devotion, knowledge, liberation, and whatever one desires — Gora [Sri Ramakrishna] is bestowing upon us whatever he wishes. What wonderful power!" He was silent for a while and then continued. "One night, I was lying on my bed with the door bolted. Suddenly he attracted me — or rather the soul that lives in this body — and drew me to Dakshineswar. He talked with me about various

---

*Gora is the nickname of Gauranga, or Chaitanya. – *Translator.*
**Nitai was the main disciple of Chaitanya. – *Translator.*
***Shantipur and Nadia are places associated with Chaitanya. – *Translator.*

topics, gave me advice, and finally allowed me to return home. He can do anything — this Gora of Dakshineswar can do anything!"[129]

Once the Master said to Swami Vivekananda: "Have you not heard about Gauranga of Nadia? I am that Gauranga."[130]

The musician Nilkantha saw Gauranga in Ramakrishna. In *The Gospel of Sri Ramakrishna*, M. described this scene:

> Ramakrishna said to Nilkantha, "I should like to hear that song of yours I heard in Calcutta."
> M.: "About Sri Gauranga?"
> Master: "Yes, yes!"
> Nilkantha sang the song, "The beautiful Gauranga, the youthful dancer, fair as molten gold."
> Sri Ramakrishna sang again and again the line, "Everything is swept away by the onrush of love," and danced with Nilkantha and the other devotees. Those who saw that indescribable dancing were never to forget it. The room was filled with people, all intoxicated with divine joy. It seemed as if Chaitanya himself were dancing with his companions.
> Sri Ramakrishna sang again, this time about Gauranga and Nityananda:
>
> > Behold, the two brothers have come, who weep while chanting Hari's name. . . .
> > He danced with Nilkantha and other devotees, improvising the line:
> > Behold, the two brothers have come, they who are mad with love of Radha.
>
> Hearing the loud music, many people gathered about the room. The music was over. Sri Ramakrishna bowed to the Divine Mother and said: "Bhagavata — Bhakta — Bhagavan. My salutations to the jnanis, my salutations to the yogis, my salutations to the bhaktas."
> The Master was seated on the semicircular porch with Nilkantha and the other devotees. The autumn moon flooded all the quarters with light. Sri Ramakrishna and Nilkantha talked.
> Nilkantha: "You are none other than Gauranga."
> Master: "Why should you say such a thing? I am the servant of the servant of all."[131]

Ramakrishna as a Luminous Being

Swami Saradananda described a vision that Hriday had:

> One night Hriday saw the Master going towards the Panchavati. Thinking that he might need his water pot and towel, he obtained

them and followed the Master. While walking, Hriday had an extraordinary vision. He saw that the Master was not a human being made of flesh and blood. Light was emanating from his body and illumining the entire Panchavati. As he walked, his luminous feet moved through the air without touching the ground. Hriday repeatedly rubbed his eyes, thinking this must be an optical illusion. He looked at the other objects around him and then back at the luminous form of the Master. Although he perceived the trees, creepers, Ganges, hut, and so on as before, he saw the Master's shining form again and again. Amazed, Hriday thought, "Is there any change in me that I am seeing the Master this way?" Then he looked at himself and saw that his own body was also luminous. He felt that he was a veritable attendant of God, living with Him and serving Him eternally. He felt as if he were a part of that luminous form of God and had assumed a separate form in order to serve Him. With this vision Hriday realized the mystery of his own life, and a current of bliss flowed in his heart. He then forgot himself, forgot the world, and forgot to consider what others might think of him, calling him mad. In ecstasy, he shouted frantically again and again: "O Ramakrishna, O Ramakrishna, we are not human beings. Why are we here? Come, let us go from place to place and save human souls. You and I are the same."

The Master said later: "Hearing his loud cry, I said: 'Ah! Keep quiet, keep quiet. Why are you shouting like that? People will rush here thinking some calamity has happened.' But he paid no heed to my words. Then I hurried to him and said, touching his chest, 'Mother, make this rascal dull and stupid again.'"

Hriday said that as soon as the Master uttered those words, his vision and bliss vanished and he became the same as before. The sudden fall from that unique blissful state filled his mind with sorrow. Sobbing, he asked: "Uncle, why did you do that to me? Why did you say that I should be dull? Now I will not have that blissful vision again." The Master consoled him, saying: "I do not mean for you to be dull forever. I only wanted to calm you down. I had to say that because you were making such a commotion over that little vision of yours. I experience so many divine visions in a day, but do I raise such a racket? You are not yet ready for visions. Keep quiet now; you will have many more experiences when the right time comes."[132]

In the early 1900s Swami Vishuddhananda met a gardener in the Dakshineswar temple garden who had had a vision of the Master's luminous form. The swami wrote:

I met a gardener of seventy-six or seventy-seven years old who had worked in the temple garden during Mathur's time. I first saw him cleaning, very carefully, the path from the Master's room to the Panchavati with a spud [a spade-like instrument]. He was a little bent because of his age. I observed that he steadfastly cleaned that path up to the pine grove and the bel tree. I was a little curious because I saw him do the same work every day. One day I asked him, "Have you seen the Master?" He laid the spud on the ground, then looked at me in wonder and said: "I am following his order. The Master told me that many of his devotees would come. So I am cleaning this path for them." He was reluctant to say anything more. When I pressed him to say something more, he told me this wonderful story: "One summer night I could not sleep, so I went for a walk in the garden. I saw a light coming from the Panchamundi area. I went there and found the Master immersed in samadhi under the bel tree; a light emanated from his body. I was so scared, I could not stay there long. The next morning I went to him, fell at his feet, and burst into tears. He asked: 'What is the matter? Why do you have so much overflowing devotion today?' I only said, 'Master, please bless me.' He realized what was in my mind. He lifted me up and said: 'Meditate on the form that you saw last night. Clean the path to the Panchavati. Many devotees will come in the future.' I meditate on that luminous form of the Master and clean this path every day."[133]

Ramakrishna as an Avatar

There are many signs of an avatar. In the Gita, Krishna mentioned the sign given in the scriptures: When religion declines and irreligion prevails, God incarnates as an avatar. He protects the holy and punishes the evil.

There are other signs of an avatar: he is full of compassion for all beings; he is a saviour to sinners; he comes to fulfill, not to destroy; he is endowed with supernatural powers; he is the embodiment of purity and renunciation; he is totally unselfish and eradicates the bad karma of his devotees; he establishes a new religious path. Moreover, when God incarnates as a human being, he is very charismatic.

When we study Ramakrishna's life, we find that he enacted his divine play in three phases:

First phase: Suresh Chandra Datta wrote that the mother of Gaya-vishnu Laha was very fond of little Gadadhar. Whenever she cooked any special dishes, she would first offer him a taste. She remarked: "Gadai, it seems you are not a human being; you are God." Prasanna Laha also recognized Ramakrishna's divinity when he was young. In addition, an old shopkeeper in Kamarpukur saw the divine mood of Gadadhar and realized that he was not human; he had descended to earth to enact his divine play. One day he carried a basket of sweets with him and privately made an offering of them to Gadadhar in a field. Choked with emotion, the old shopkeeper said to him: "Gadai, I am too old. I shall not be able to see your future divine play."[134]

One day at Dakshineswar Ramakrishna said to M.: "It is God alone who incarnates Himself as man to teach people the ways of love and knowledge. Well, what do you think of me?

"Once my father went to Gaya. There Raghuvir said to him in a dream, 'I shall be born as your son.' Thereupon my father said to Him: 'O Lord, I am a poor brahmin. How shall I be able to serve You?' 'Don't worry about it,' Raghuvir replied. 'It will be taken care of.'

"My cousin, Hriday's mother, used to worship my feet with flowers and sandal paste. One day I placed my foot on her head and said to her, 'You will die in Varanasi.'"[135]

Second phase: During this period the Master was recognized as an avatar by great scholars and highly evolved spiritual aspirants. Swami Saradananda wrote:

> We heard that one day during this period the Master and Mathur were at the Panchavati, and Hriday was also present. In the course of conversation the Master told Mathur the Brahmani's findings about him. He said: "She says that all the signs of the avatars are in this body and mind (*pointing to himself*). She is well versed in the scriptures and she has many books with her." Mathur replied with a laugh: "Father, whatever she may say, according to the scriptures there are no more than ten avatars. So how can her words be true? But it is true that Mother Kali has bestowed Her grace on you."
>
> While they were talking, Mathur saw a nun approaching them. He asked the Master, "Is this the woman?" "Yes," replied the Master. Pointing to Mathur, the Master told the Brahmani: "Mother, I was just telling him what you say about me. But he says that the scriptures mention only ten avatars and no more than that." Mathur saluted the Brahmani and admitted that he had raised that objection. She immediately replied: "Bhagavan Vyasa mentioned twenty-four avatars in the Bhagavata and then indicated an infinite number of them. Moreover, the Vaishnava scriptures clearly indicated that Chaitanya would be incarnated again. In addition, there is a striking resemblance in many characteristics between him and Sri Ramakrishna." Unable to respond to the Brahmani, Mathur remained silent.[136]

Swami Saradananda continued:

> During three important periods of the Master's sadhana, three emi-

nent spiritual pandits who were well versed in the scriptures came to him, observed his spiritual condition, and had an opportunity to discuss their impressions. Pandit Padmalochan met the Master when he had become perfected in the Tantra sadhana; Pandit Vaishnavcharan met him when he had attained success in the Vaishnava Tantra; and Pandit Gauri was blessed to see the Master endowed with divine splendour at the completion of all his sadhanas. When Padmalochan saw the Master, he said, "I see God's presence and divine power in you." Vaishnavcharan, in ecstasy, composed a hymn to the Master in Sanskrit and sang it to him, declaring him to be an avatar. When Gauri met the Master, he concluded: "I see that everything I have read in the scriptures concerning high spiritual states is manifest in you. In addition, I see other exalted states that are not recorded in the scriptures. You have reached a spiritual plane that surpasses anything described in the Vedas, Vedanta, or other scriptures. You are not human. Ishwara, the source of all avatars, dwells in you."[137]

Although the Master had no formal education, he was not afraid to be challenged by his disciples. He told them: "Examine a holy man by day and by night before believing in him"; "Test me as a money-changer checks for a fake coin." The Master was established in truth, and he was not afraid to be challenged.

Third phase: A king visits his kingdom incognito. When people recognize him, he quickly returns to his palace. During the last years of his divine play, the Master revealed his divinity to his devotees, bestowed fearlessness upon them, and then was eager to return to his own abode. He said: "The same avatar rose here from the ocean of Satchidananda and declared himself as Krishna, and rose there and declared himself as Jesus Christ."[138]

Keshab Sen said to Ram Datta: "You do not know who Sri Ramakrishna is. That is why you people are touching him and making him sing and dance. Cover his body in a soft velvet cloth and place him in a glass case. Offer a few good flowers to him and salute him from a distance."[139]

Before Suresh Datta met the Master, he was a member of the Brahmo Samaj and was devoted to Keshab Sen. Suresh wrote: "I don't know whether my Brahmo friends know or not, but I heard from a reliable source that Keshab secretly worshipped the Master as an avatar towards the end of his life. One day when the Master went to Keshab's house, the latter asked the Master to visit his shrine to sanctify it. The Master went to the shrine. Keshab then worshipped the feet of the Master with flowers and asked him not to disclose it to anyone."[140]

Towards the end of the Master's divine play, Girish openly began to say that the Master was an avatar. On 1 March 1885, the Master asked Narendra: "Do you agree with Girish about me?"

Narendra: "He said he believed you to be an Incarnation of God. I didn't say anything in answer to his remarks."

Master: "But how great his faith is! Don't you think so?"

A few days later the Master asked Narendra: "Well, some people call me an avatar. What do you think of this?"

Narendra: "I won't form an opinion based on others' views. I will say so only when I can understand and believe it myself."[141]

At the Cossipore garden house the Master suffered excruciating pain from throat cancer. He could not even swallow gruel. One day Narendra was seated nearby. He thought to himself that if at this critical moment the Master said he was an avatar, he would believe it. Immediately the Master said: "He who was Rama and he who was Krishna is now Ramakrishna in this body." Narendra was dumbfounded.[142]

When Ramendrasundar Bhaktitirtha was a boy, he met Ramakrishna. He knew a Christian Bengali professor of Scottish Church College, who was one of Vivekananda's professors. That professor described for Ramendra the following conversation, and Ramendra later recorded it in his reminiscences:

Professor: "Well, Narendra, what have you done? At last you have surrendered yourself to a mad priest! I also hear you think that priest is God and that he has come to the world as a saviour. Do you believe all these cock-and-bull stories?"

Vivekananda calmly replied: "Sir, you have heard the right thing. I believe that he is God and he has come to the world as a saviour. Previously, like you, I would have considered this to be a fairy tale. I said so to Sri Ramakrishna himself many times. To that, he would smile like a child, and say, 'Do I ask you to believe in me?' But, sir, I had to believe it at last. He showed me one day that God Himself had descended in that Ramakrishna-body. He who was Rama and he who was Krishna, he has become Ramakrishna. He first showed me the form of Rama and Krishna separately and then he showed me that both had merged into the Ramakrishna-body. It was not a hallucination. I saw it clearly with open eyes. Apart from this vision, I understood, realized, and saw in many ways that Ramakrishna was God Himself."[143]

Ramakrishna as The Kalpataru (The Wish-Fulfilling Tree)

On 1 January 1886, at the Cossipore garden house, Ramakrishna became the Kalpataru and blessed his devotees, saying, "Be illumined."

It was a memorable day. Akshay Sen wrote: "The Master promised that before leaving the world he would break the earthen pot in a market-place; in other words, he would make his divinity public."[144]

The Master entered the garden, followed by his devotees. Akshay, who was seated with a few others on the low bough of a tree, saw him. He rushed to where Sri Ramakrishna was standing and found him absorbed in samadhi, in the middle of his devotees. Akshay picked two champaka (*Michelia Champaka*) flowers and offered them at the feet of Sri Ramakrishna.

After a while the Master came down to the normal plane of consciousness and touched the devotees one by one. This act created great emotional fervour and excitement among the devotees. Some received the vision of their Chosen Deity; some experienced the awakening of the kundalini; some felt unspeakable bliss; and others went into ecstasy and began to laugh, cry, and shout. Akshay watched the entire scene from a distance. Then suddenly the Master's eyes fell on him, and he called to Akshay: "Hello!" Akshay ran to the Master, who touched his chest and whispered a mantra in his ear. At once Akshay experienced the effect of the Master's blessing. He could not contain the onrush of bliss, and unable to withstand such an upsurge of emotion, he fell to the ground. His limbs twisted as if he were deformed, and he burst into tears.[145]

The ocean of love was overflowing that day as Ramakrishna distributed love, devotion, spiritual visions, and samadhi among his devotees. When Harish Mustaphi later went to the Master's room, the Master blessed him. He was mad with joy, and tears flowed from his eyes. He came downstairs and told the disciples: "Brothers, I can't contain this bliss. What is this? I have never experienced such a thing in my life. It is the Master's infinite glory!"

Then the Master called Devendra Majumdar to his room and said to him: "Ram has declared me to be an avatar. Can all of you verify Ram's statement? Keshab's disciples also called him an avatar." Devendra later said: "How can we understand the mystery of the avatar? The Master himself cleared up the meaning. On the afternoon when he became the Kalpataru, he first called some to his upstairs room and blessed them; but he was not happy with that. He then came downstairs, went to the garden, and began to distribute spiritual illumination. He touched someone's chest or someone's head, and he said something in someone's ear."[146]

Swami Saradananda also described the events of that day:

At 3:00 p.m. the Master put on a red-bordered cloth, a shirt, a thick, red-bordered wrapper, a cap covering his ears, and a pair of slippers, and then descended the stairs slowly with Swami Adbhutananda. He closely examined the main hall, went out through the western door, and began to walk along the garden path. Seeing the Master walking, some householder devotees followed him joyfully.

When he was halfway along the path, he noticed Ram and Girish sitting in the shade of the mango tree. Addressing Girish, the Master said, "Girish, what have you found [in me] that makes you say all these things [I am an avatar, and so on] to everyone, wherever you go?"

Girish's faith remained unshaken although he had been asked this question so abruptly. Hurriedly he got up, went to the path, and knelt down at the feet of the Master. Saluting him with folded hands, Girish responded in a voice choking with emotion: "What more can I say of Him? Even the sages Vyasa and Valmiki could find no words to measure His glory!"

As the Master listened to those wonderful words of faith, the hairs on his body stood on end, his mind ascended to a higher plane, and he went into samadhi. Seeing the Master's face radiant with divine ecstasy, Girish joyfully shouted, "Jai (Victory to) Ramakrishna! Jai Ramakrishna!" and took the dust of his feet again and again. Meanwhile, the Master came down to a semiecstatic state, looked at the assembled devotees with a smile, and said: "What more need I tell you? May you all be illumined!"[147]

This infallible blessing of the Master opened the doors of spiritual experience for his devotees. Some began to laugh, some cried, some became absorbed in meditation, and some began to call others loudly to receive the Master's blessing.

When Haran Das took the dust of the Master's feet, he put his foot on Haran's head. He touched Akshay Sen's chest and gave him a mantra. He asked Navagopal Ghosh to practise japa and meditation; but Navagopal said that he had no time to do so. Then the Master asked him, "Can you repeat my name a few times?" "Yes, that I can do," replied Navagopal. Then the Master said: "That will do. You will not have to do anything else." He then blessed Upendra Majumdar, and the latter went into ecstasy. He blessed Brother Bhupati, saying, "You will attain samadhi." When Upendra Mukhopadhyay prayed for money, the Master said, "You will get plenty of money."

Ramlal was then standing behind the Master at that time. He thought to himself: "All these devotees have got some spritual experiences, but what have I achieved? I only carried the Master's water pot and towel.

As soon as this thought crossed my mind, he looked at me and said: 'Ramlal, what are you thinking? Come here.' He pushed aside my shawl and touched my chest, saying, 'Now see.' It is hard for me to describe that wonderful luminous form. Before that, during my meditation I could see with my mind's eye only a part of my Chosen Deity. When I saw his feet I could not see his face; and again, when I saw his form from the face to the waist, I could not see his feet. Moreover, whatever I saw never seemed to be alive. But no sooner had the Master touched me that day than the whole form of my Chosen Deity appeared in my heart as a living presence, looking benign and effulgent."[148]

Swami Saradananda wrote: "After the Master had blessed two or three devotees with his powerful divine touch, Vaikuntha went before him, reverently bowed down to him, and implored, 'Sir, please bestow your grace on me.' The Master answered, 'You have achieved everything.' Vaikuntha said: 'Sir, when you say that I have achieved everything, it must be so. Kindly help me so that I can understand it a little.' The Master said, 'All right,' and gently touched his chest for a moment. Vaikuntha described it thus: 'Consequently, a wonderful change came across my mind. I began to see the Master's gracious, smiling, and luminous form in the sky, the houses, the trees, all human beings, and in everything else I saw in all directions. I was overwhelmed with extreme bliss.'"[149]

The Master then bestowed his grace on Atul Ghosh and Kishori Roy. Girish checked to see if anyone was left to receive the Master's grace. He went to the kitchen and found the cook making chapatis. He brought him to the Master, and he was blessed.

On that day the Master did not touch two persons (one was Haramohan Mitra). Instead, he told them "Not now." They were very disappointed on that blissful occasion. Later, on another day, the Master blessed them. Haramohan revealed afterwards that the Master's divine touch allowed him to see gods and goddesses between his eyebrows.[150]

At last the Master returned to his room with Ramlal and said: "My body is burning because I took the sins of these people. Bring some Ganges water and sprinkle it all over my body."[151] In the evening Swami Vivekananda took Hazra to the Master and requested that he bless him. The Master said: "It is not the right time. He will see me at the end of his life."[152] Finally, Chunilal Basu came and Vivekananda sent him to the Master. "What do you want?" asked the Master. But Chunilal remained silent. Pointing to his body, the Master said: "Have love and faith in this place. You will also achieve everything."[153]

Devotees' Visions of the Master

Ramakrishna appeared before his devotees in a spiritual form during his lifetime. Once, in Dhaka, Vijay Krishna Goswami was meditating in his shrine. All of a sudden he saw the Master, even though he was actually at Dakshineswar. To determine whether it was a hallucination, he touched the Master's body and found it to be real. After returning to Calcutta Vijay went to Shyampukur, and in front of the devotees, he told the Master his experience:

Vijay: "I have seen him [meaning the Master] in Dhaka. I even touched his body."

Master (with a smile): "It must have been someone else."

Narendra: "I too have seen him many times. (To Vijay) How can I say I do not believe your words?"[154]

Nrityagopal Goswami also saw Ramakrishna in Dhaka. He described the event: "While I was in Dhaka, I was feeling extremely unhappy. There was a wooded area on the outskirts of the city that was often used as a graveyard. To my surprise at a distance I saw someone seated on the ground. I went up to him and asked, 'What are you doing here?' He said he wished to talk to me. Though he said very little, his words dispelled all my depression and doubts. He got up and started to walk away. Then he turned to me affectionately and said, 'Nrityagopal, my dear, do not let go of what you are holding on to.' After that I didn't see him anymore. I related all this to Vijay. He said he too had seen the same person in the woods. That night I had a remarkable dream in which I saw myself talking with that divine-looking person and listening to his wonderful words. My joy was beyond description."[155]

Swami Advaitananda wrote: "When I first met the Master, I could not understand him at all. I wondered why people call him a great soul!" He had the same experience during his second visit as well, and he decided not to visit the Master again. Finally, at a friend's request, he went to the Master a third time. This time the Master possessed him and he could not escape. About this, he said: "The Master possessed me. I would think of him day and night. The pang of separation from the Master gave me chest pain. No matter how hard I tried, I couldn't forget his face."[156]

Surendra Mitra practised meditation in his shrine every day. One day he had a desire to test the Master's divinity. He resolved that if the Master appeared in his shrine during meditation, then he would consider him to be an avatar. What a wonderful phenomenon! After a while he saw the Master in his shrine. After thus testing the Master, Surendra took refuge in him.[157]

Surendra had been an alcoholic and debauchee, but his life was changed by the grace of the Master. Swami Turiyananda said: "There is a story of Surendra, long after he had met Sri Ramakrishna, being tempted to visit a public woman one evening on his way home from the office. He went upstairs to the woman's apartment and entered her room. But lo, there was no woman, but Sri Ramakrishna himself standing there! In great shame, Surendra fled from the place."[158]

Once Devendra came to Dakshineswar and had an attack of malarial fever. The Master sent him back to Calcutta by boat and asked Baburam to accompany him. Devendra reached a relative's house and fell unconscious. For forty-one days he lay in a state of torpor and delirium. Often he uttered Sri Ramakrishna's name, thinking that he was still at Dakshineswar. Curiously, whenever extreme pain made him open his eyes, he would see Sri Ramakrishna sitting by his bed.[159]

Devendra described what happened after he received initiation from the Master: "At that time I would see the Master everywhere. While walking through the street, I would see the Master walking in front of me and sometimes looking at me. If I would stand, sit, or lie down, I saw the Master accordingly. He would always move around me. One day when I bowed down to Kali I saw that he was standing before me. It seems that the Master always stayed with me to make me understand that he was my all in all and my protector."[160]

Ramakrishna's Appearance after His Passing Away

After he passed away, Ramakrishna first appeared before the Holy Mother. On 16 August 1886, the Master's body was cremated and his ashes were brought in an urn to the Cossipore garden house. That evening the Holy Mother began to remove her jewellery, following the custom of Hindu widows. As she was about to take off her bracelets, Ramakrishna appeared before her, looking as he did before he was stricken with cancer. Pressing her hand, he said: "Am I dead, that you are acting like a widow? I have just moved from one room to another." She did not take off the bracelets, and instead wore them as long as she lived.[161]

The Holy Mother saw the Master many times after his passing away. On her way to Vrindaban for pilgrimage, she had a vision of the Master. She was in the habit of wearing Sri Ramakrishna's gold amulet on her arm. This amulet had been given to him to allay the burning sensation of his body when he practised intense spiritual disciplines at Dakshineswar.

In her train compartment she lay down with her arm on the windowsill, leaving the amulet exposed. The Master suddenly appeared and, looking at her through the window, said: "Why are you keeping the amulet that way? You may lose it." After that vision she took it off and kept it in a tin box with the Master's photograph.[162] It was in Vrindaban that the Master appeared to the Holy Mother, asking her to initiate Swami Yogananda.

When the Holy Mother was living at Kamarpukur, the narrow-minded and fanatical villagers criticized her because she wore a red-bordered sari and gold bracelets, and she did not live like an orthodox Hindu widow. In distress, she took off her bracelets. Again the Master appeared and said to her: "Do not discard your bracelets. Do you know the Vaishnava scriptures?" She said that she knew nothing about them. The Master told her that Gauri-ma would come there in the afternoon and explain the scriptures of the Vaishnavas to her. Gauri-ma arrived as he had promised and told her that she could not be a widow since her husband was none other than the Lord Himself. This reassured her. She put her bracelets on again and turned a deaf ear to people's criticism.[163]

One evening at about 8:00, within a week of the Master's passing away, Narendra and Harish were standing beside the little pond at the Cossipore garden house and talking about the Master. Suddenly, Narendra saw a shining form covered with a cloth coming slowly towards them. He thought: "Can it be the Master?" He kept quiet, fearing that he was a victim of a hallucination. But Harish saw it as well and whispered to Narendra, "Look, what is that?" At this, Narendra said loudly, "Who is there?" Hearing his voice, others came hurriedly from the house to see what was happening. That luminous form vanished in the jasmine bushes five yards from where they stood. This vision made a deep impression on Narendra's mind, and he believed that the Master still existed in his subtle body.[164]

Later, Swami Vivekananda wrote in the *Rule Book of Belur Monastery*: "The Lord has not yet given up the Ramakrishna form. Some see Him in that form even now and receive instructions from Him, and all can see Him if they so desire. This form will last until He comes again in another gross body. Though He is not visible to all, that He is in this Order and guiding it is a fact of everybody's experience."[165]

Someone asked Swami Brahmananda, "Can one see Ramakrishna even now?" The swami replied: "Yes, Swamiji saw the Master many times. We also see him from time to time."

Brahmananda collected some teachings of Sri Ramakrishna in

Bengali that were first serially published in *Udbodhan* and later translated into English under the title *Words of the Master*. He completed the book during a visit to Varanasi. When he was working on the manuscript of those teachings he would not allow anybody to stay in his room. Sometimes Maharaj would get up at midnight and ask his attendant to bring the manuscript to him. Once, after correcting it, he said: "The Master came and told me: 'I didn't say that. I said this.'"[166]

Ramakrishna appeared not only to the Holy Mother and his monastic disciples but also to some of his householder devotees. After the Master passed away on 16 August 1886, at the Cossipore garden house, some of his young disciples had to return to their homes against their wishes, while others had no place to go. They were like orphans. One evening early in September, while Surendra was meditating in his shrine, Sri Ramakrishna appeared to him and said: "What are you doing here? My boys are roaming about without a place to live. Attend to that before anything else." Surendra immediately rushed to Swami Vivekananda's house and said to some of the disciples: "Brothers, where will you go? Let us rent a house. You will live there and make it our Master's shrine; and we householders will come there for consolation. How can we pass all our days and nights in this world, with our wives and children? I used to spend a sum of money for the Master at Cossipore. I shall gladly give it now for your expenses."[167]

Doubt is like a disease of the mind. It comes and goes. Although Yogin-ma was an intimate companion of the Holy Mother, at one time she doubted her divinity. She said to herself: "Sri Ramakrishna was the embodiment of renunciation, and Mother is engrossed in the world, preoccupied day and night with the thought of her brothers, sisters-in-law, nephews, and nieces." Soon after this she was seated on the bank of the Ganges, meditating, when Sri Ramakrishna appeared to her in a vision and said, "Do you see what is being carried by the water of the Ganges?" Yogin-ma looked and saw the corpse of a newborn baby. She also saw many people offering worship to Mother Ganges. The Master then said: "Can anything make the Ganges impure? Regard her [Holy Mother] in the same way. Never doubt her. Remember, she is not different from this [*meaning himself*]." Yogin-ma immediately rushed to the Holy Mother and, after telling her the whole story, apologized. The Holy Mother smiled and consoled her.[168]

The Holy Mother told this story: "He who eagerly prays to God will see Him. One of our devotees, Tejachandra Mitra, passed away. What a sincere soul he was! The Master used to frequent his house. Someone had deposited two hundred rupees with Tejachandra. One day he was robbed of that amount by a pickpocket in a tramcar. He discovered the loss after some time and suffered terrible mental agony. He went to the bank of the Ganges and prayed to the Master with tears in his eyes, 'O Lord, what have you done to me?' He was not rich enough to make up that amount from his own pocket. As he was thus weeping he saw the Master appear before him and heard him say: 'Why do you weep so bitterly? The money is there under a brick on the bank of the Ganges.' Tejachandra quickly located and removed the brick and really found there a bundle of banknotes. He narrated the incident to Sharat [Swami Saradananda]. Sharat said: 'You are lucky to get the vision of the Master even now.'"[169]

Purna Chandra Ghosh was suffering from tuberculosis and remained bedridden for about six months before passing away. He calmly endured his physical pain and suffering without any complaint. If anyone came to comfort him, he would cheerfully say: "My Master, Sri Ramakrishna, is always seated at my bedside. I have no fear or worry."

As the days passed, Purna's body became emaciated, and he was not allowed to leave his bed because of his extreme weakness. One night, finding that everyone was fast asleep, he went to the bathroom alone. It was his nature not to trouble anyone about himself. While returning to bed he became dizzy and nearly fell. The next day he told a close devotee: "Who says that the Master does not exist? He is still living, and I perceive him clearly. Last night, while returning from the bathroom, I was about to fall unconscious. The Master caught me in his arms and carried me to the bed. He is there, just as he was before, and I can see him."[170]

Ramakrishna appeared not only to his Indian devotees, but also to Western devotees. While in Dakshineswar, after coming out of samadhi the Master told Ramlal: "I went to a new place. People of that place are different. Their complexion is white and they have blue eyes. It is a new country."

Saradananda used to hold classes regularly in Montclair, New Jersey, where he stayed at the home of Mr. and Mrs. Wheeler. Swami Atulananda, a Western monk, wrote in his book *With the Swamis in America*:

> An interesting incident took place when Swami Saradananda was living in this happy home. The swami had often spoken about Sri Ramakrishna and one day he produced his Master's photograph and showed it to the lady of the house. "Oh, swami," she exclaimed, "it is the same face!" "What do you mean?" said the swami. And then she told him that long ago, in her youth, before she was married, she had

had a vision of a Hindu and that it was the same face that now she saw in the photograph. "It was Sri Ramakrishna," she said, "but I did not know it until now. I was so much impressed and charmed at the vision at the time, that I remember the face very distinctly, and I have been going about here and there ever since I had the vision, wherever I heard that a Hindu had come to America, but I was always disappointed, not finding the same face. And now at last I see that it was Sri Ramakrishna."[171]

It is really amazing how, without a physical body, Ramakrishna protected his disciples from terrible catastrophes. Some bigoted American Christians plotted to kill Swami Vivekananda in Detroit, Michigan. They invited Swamiji for dinner, and when he was about to sip coffee, Ramakrishna appeared before him and said: "Don't drink. It is poison." Thus Swamiji was saved from sure death.[172]

Swami Vireswarananda told this story about Swami Premananda: "On one occasion Premananda was ready to go to East Bengal, and the devotees were waiting for him in the boat at the Belur ghat. They were supposed to take a train from Calcutta, and then take a steamer. Premananda went to the shrine to get the Master's permission to leave. A monk who happened to be there heard Premananda talking to the Master, but he didn't hear the Master's response. At last Premananda said, 'All right, Master, I shall not go.' He then went downstairs and told the devotees that he would not go that day. The devotees were disappointed; but the newspaper later reported that the steamer he was supposed to take from Goalanda to Dhaka had been sunk by a cyclone."[173]

Swami Abhedananda told this story: "I was in London in 1915. On 6 May I went to the booking office to purchase a ticket from London to New York on the *S.S. Lusitania*. While I was in that office, a mysterious thing happened. I was about to buy the ticket, but immediately I heard a clear voice forbidding me. I was dumbfounded. I thought it might be a freak of my mind. I looked around but couldn't find anybody. So again I went to the counter and the same thing happened. Then I decided to return to the apartment without buying any ticket. However, I planned to buy the ticket the following day. The next morning I saw in the newspaper in big letters 'S.S. Lusitania Is No More.' I was overwhelmed. Tears rolled down my cheeks. I realized that the Master had saved my life."*[174]

*On 7 May 1915, during World War I, this British liner was destroyed by a German submarine in the Atlantic Ocean, near Cork on the western coast of Ireland, killing 1,198 passengers.

Some Devotees Saw Ramakrishna at Death

According to the Hindu scriptures, a man becomes in the next life what he thinks of at the time of death. Krishna said in the Gita (8:5): "Whoso at the time of death leaves his body remembering Me alone and goes forth — he attains My Being; concerning this there is no doubt." Ramakrishna said: "Those who are in their last life will come here [*meaning to him*]." The cause of reincarnation is desire. A desireless person will not be born again. The seeds of desire slowly dissolve for those who come in close contact with an avatar, and they attain Self-knowledge.

The death accounts of the Master's devotees are wonderful. He was not only their companion while he was living, but he also appeared at the time of their death and took them to their final abodes.

Swami Shivananda recorded the death account of Rasik, the sweeper of Dakshineswar temple: "Those who wholeheartedly have taken refuge in the Master and loved him, they will inevitably attain liberation. Have you not heard the story of Rasik, the sweeper of Dakshineswar? He used to call the Master, 'Father.' One day the Master was returning from the Panchavati in an ecstatic mood. Rasik knelt down in front of him with folded hands and begged for his blessings: 'Father, will you not bestow mercy on me? What will happen to my life?' The Master told him: 'Don't be afraid. You will succeed. You will see me at the time of death.' It happened exactly as he said. Rasik's family members carried him into the tulsi grove just before his death, and at the time of death Rasik said: 'Father, you have come. The Father has come.' Saying so, he passed away."[175]

On 13 April 1890 Balaram Basu died from influenza in his Calcutta home. Swami Shivananda recalled his death:

> The passing away of each of the devotees of the Master is a wonderful event in itself. The departure of Balaram Babu was equally wonderful. His disease had taken a serious turn, and all were anxious. One day he went on repeating, 'Well, where are my brothers?' When this news reached us we hurried to his house at Baghbazar [in Calcutta]. We ourselves stayed by him and nursed him. For about two or three days before his passing away he would not allow any of his relatives to come near him; he wanted only us to be near at hand. The few words that he spoke were about the Master alone. One day, before the final departure, the doctor came in and declared that he was beyond cure.
>
> At the last moment we were seated around him, while his wife, stricken with unspeakable grief, was in the inner apartment with

Golap-ma, Yogin-ma, and others. Just then she noticed something like a piece of black cloud in the sky, which became denser by stages and began to descend. Soon it assumed the shape of a chariot and alighted on the roof of Balaram Babu's house. The Master came out of that chariot and proceeded towards the room where Balaram Babu lay. Soon after, he issued forth, taking Balaram Babu by the hand, and entered the chariot again, which then ascended and vanished in the sky. This vision raised her mind to a very high plane where there could be no touch of grief or sorrow. When she returned to normal she related this to Golap-ma, who came to apprise us of the fact. Balaram Babu had passed away just a little while before.[176]

Sharat Chandra Chakrabarty wrote the death account of Durga Charan Nag. At two o'clock in the morning two days before he passed away, Durga Charan said to Sharat Babu: "Sri Ramakrishna has come here to show me the holy places. Please tell me the names of holy places you have seen, and I will visit them one after another." As Sharat Babu mentioned the name of each place — Hardwar, Prayag, Varanasi, and Puri — Nag Mahashay immediately had a vision of it and vividly described what he was seeing.[177]

Pratap Chandra Hazra had an important role in the divine drama of Ramakrishna. He had been hypocritical, spiteful, mercenary, untruthful, and egotistical, but Ramakrishna's infallible blessing transformed his life. The blessed death of Hazra proved that the grace of an avatar can eradicate a soul's bad karma.

Hazra's obituary, published in *Tattwamanjari*, stated:

Hazra had a minor fever for three days; except for that, he had no other disease. A village doctor looked after him. In the evening of the third day, Hazra said to his wife: "Look, you inform the villagers tomorrow morning that they should be present at our house before 9:00 as I am going to die at that time." His wife thought that it was because her husband was delirious with fever that he was talking like that. She did not take it seriously. However, early the next morning Hazra persuaded his wife to spread his death forecast among the villagers. Some ignored it, thinking Hazra was crazy, and some came to watch the fun.

At 8:30 a.m. Hazra took his rosary and started to practise his japa as usual. People knew that it was his nature to do so. All of a sudden they noticed a change coming over Hazra's face, as if he were intently watching somebody. After a while he burst forth with the words: "Welcome! Most welcome! Here comes the Master! Master, after such a long time you have remembered me." He then said to his wife: "Please bring a seat. Be quick! Don't you see that Paramahamsadeva has come?" His wife stood there idly. But when Hazra repeated his request, she reluctantly spread a carpet there.

Then, addressing Sri Ramakrishna, Hazra said, "Master, please sit on the asana and wait here till I die. Please be gracious unto me." Saying so, Hazra began to repeat his mantra again. After a short time he exclaimed: "Welcome! Welcome, Ramdada [Ram Chandra Datta, a devotee of the Master]! How fortunate I am!" He then requested his wife to give an asana to Ram Chandra, which she did. With folded hands, Hazra requested that Ram Chandra too sit near him till death. Then again he started to repeat his mantra. Again he exclaimed: "Welcome! Yogin Maharaj [Swami Yogananda, a disciple of the Master] has come! Oh, what a joyful day!" He then asked his wife to give an asana to Swami Yogananda and requested that he sit near him till death.

He then addressed Sri Ramakrishna with folded hands, saying:

"Master, you are so gracious unto me. Please do me another favour. Please come with me to the tulsi grove [an auspicious spot in the courtyard] where I want to give up my body." With Sri Ramakrishna's consent, Hazra asked his wife to carry those three asanas and his bed to the tulsi grove. Then going there, Hazra requested that they sit on their respective asanas, and he lay down on his bed. He continued his japa and then repeated thrice, "Hari, Hari, Hari." In this way Hazra passed away. The villagers were amazed. They moved his body and found that it was devoid of consciousness. They then arranged his funeral and glorified him as a great soul.[178]

The story of Kalipada Ghosh's death is also interesting. In November 1884 he went by boat from Calcutta to Dakshineswar. When the Master saw Kalipada he said that he had just been thinking of going to Calcutta. Kalipada told him that his boat was at the landing ghat and that he would be glad to take him there. Sri Ramakrishna immediately got ready and left with Latu [later Swami Adbhutananda] and Kalipada. As they got in the boat, however, Kalipada privately instructed the boatman to steer the boat to the middle of the river. Then Kalipada knelt down and clasped the Master's feet, saying: "Sir, you are a saviour. Please save my life." "Oh, no, no," said Sri Ramakrishna. "Chant the name of the Lord. You will get liberation." Kalipada then said: "Sir, I am a wicked man and a drunkard. I do not even have time to chant the Lord's name. You are an ocean of mercy. Kindly save a ruffian such as I, who is devoid of disciplines and righteousness."

Meanwhile, Kalipada held firmly on to the Master's feet. Sri Ramakrishna could not find any way out of this predicament, so he asked Kalipada to stick out his tongue. Then he wrote a mantra on it. The

Master said, "Henceforth your tongue will automatically repeat this mantra." But Kalipada was not happy. He said to the Master, "I don't want this." "Then what do you want?" asked Sri Ramakrishna. "When I leave this world," replied Kalipada, "I shall see darkness all around, and that terrible darkness will fill me with horror. My wife, children, and other relatives won't be able to help me then. At that terrible time you will be my only saviour. You will have to take me, holding a light with your left hand and me with your right hand. I shall always be with you then. You will have to fulfill this prayer of mine." With his heart full of compassion, the Master said: "All right, all right. Your prayer will be fulfilled. My goodness! You have brought me to the middle of the Ganges and have created such a scene!"

Sri Ramakrishna had promised thrice in Swami Adbhutananda's presence that at the time of Kalipada's death he would take him, holding him by his right hand. Just as Kalipada breathed his last, he raised his right hand. Swami Premananda was present then. Hearing the news of Kalipada's death from Swami Premananda, Swami Adbhutananda said to some devotees: "Look, the Master came to Kalipada at his last moment. Holding Kalipada's hand, the Master guided him away. Brother Baburam saw it clearly. Whatever the Master said to anyone is bound to be fulfilled."[179]

Ramakrishna as Omniscient

God is omniscient. He knows every thought: No one can hide anything from God. His eyes are everywhere. He knows each individual being as well as the whole cosmic universe. Many incidents can be cited to illustrate Ramakrishna's omniscience.

Once Rani Rasmani came to Dakshineswar and, after bathing in the Ganges, entered the shrine of the Divine Mother for japa and meditation. Sri Ramakrishna was also there at that time. Rasmani had heard his devotional singing many times and was very fond of it, so she asked him to sing. Sri Ramakrishna began singing, but all of a sudden he stopped and turned towards Rasmani, exclaiming: "What! Even here you think such thoughts!" As he said this, he struck the Rani with the palm of his hand.

Immediately there was a commotion in the temple. Rasmani's women attendants began to scream, and the temple guards and officials rushed to the shrine to drag Sri Ramakrishna away. They hesitated, waiting only for the Rani's order. But Rasmani was sitting calmly in an introspective mood. Instead of listening to the song, she had been thinking about a lawsuit. She marvelled that Sri Ramakrishna had known what she had been thinking. When she became aware of her surroundings she noticed that people were standing around them, ready to punish Sri Rama-krishna, who was sitting quietly and smiling. Rasmani then ordered: "The young priest is not to blame. Do not take any action against him."[180]

One day Balaram decided to test Sri Ramakrishna's power of omni-science. As he carried a tray of sweets to the Master, he mentally selected two of them for the Master to take. Balaram was amazed when the Master smiled at him and took those very two sweets.[181]

One day on the way to Dakshineswar, Ram Datta bought some *jilipis*, a sweet that the Master liked very much. While crossing a bridge, a little boy begged for one of them. Ram tried at first to ignore him, but then he thought that perhaps the boy was God in disguise and he gave him a piece. After arriving in Dakshineswar, Ram put the sweets in the Master's room and spent the day there. In the afternoon Sri Ramakrishna asked for some refreshments and Ram immediately placed the jilipis in front of him. Sri Ramakrishna touched them and looked up. He then broke a few and, shaking his head, expressed his unwillingness to eat them. After this he washed his hands. Ram was mortified. He could not understand why the Master had refused his sweets. He was so upset that he threw the jilipis away and returned home. After a few days Ram came to Dakshineswar again and the Master said to him: "When you bring something for me, don't give any of it to anyone else beforehand. I can't take anything without offering it to God, and I can't offer anything to Him that has been defiled by being offered to someone else first." This incident convinced Ram that the Master was omniscient.[182]

Nistarini Ghosh knew that the Master was omniscient and that he answered the sincere prayers of his devotees. She described the following incident to Sister Devamata [Laura Glenn, an American devotee]:

> One Sunday we were all at Dakshineswar. A poor woman came bring-ing four *rasagollas* [sweet, juicy cheese balls] for the Master, but his room was so full of devotees that she dared not enter and offer them to him. She went to Mother's veranda [nahabat] and began to weep bit-terly that she had come so far and now she must go away without seeing the Master. We knew too that to bring even these four rasagollas meant a great sacrifice for her. Suddenly while she was thus weeping, Gurumaharaj [Sri Ramakrishna] appeared on the round veranda overlooking the river. He stood for a few minutes gazing at the Ganges, then he came down the steps and walked quickly towards Mother's house. When he entered the veranda, he looked hither and

thither as if searching for someone. Then, seeing the poor woman, he went to her and said, "I am feeling very hungry; can you give me something to eat?" The woman in great joy offered him her rasogollas. He ate all the four with evident relish and returned to his room, while she went home with her heart full of happiness.[183]

Ramakrishna: The Embodiment of All Gods and Goddesses

The indivisible Satchidananda is beyond name and form, which are in the domain of maya. Satchidananda is the Absolute Reality. It is formless and devoid of qualities. But God has a name and form, and He is endowed with qualities. The formless Satchidananda and God with form are like water and ice. In one aspect Ramakrishna was the eternal Satchidananda; in another, he manifested as forms of various gods and goddesses. Romain Rolland wrote: "In the life of Ramakrishna, the Man-God, I am about to relate the life of this Jacob's ladder, whereon the twofold unbroken line of the Divine in man ascends and descends between heaven and earth."[184]

On 26 September 1883, Ramakrishna told M. (who was drawn to God without form): "If you ever see me instructing you [in a dream], then know that it is Satchidananda Himself that does so."[185] Recalling his sadhana, he said: "Sometimes I considered myself to be a pitcher immersed in the water of that indivisible Satchidananda, which pervaded me through and through."[186]

Again, Ramakrishna said to Yogin-ma (who was drawn to God with form): "Look, your Chosen Deity is in this place (*pointing to his body*). If you think of me, that will bring recollectedness of your Chosen Deity."[187] On another occasion he told his niece Lakshmi: "If you cannot remember God, think of me. That will do."[188] Once Swami Vijnanananda said to a woman devotee: "Kali, Krishna, Shiva, and other gods and goddesses exist in the Master."[189]

Ramakrishna once instructed Swami Abhedananda to meditate on his form. The Master said: "Mother Kali and all gods and goddesses dwell in my body. If you meditate on my form that will be meditation on all gods and goddesses."[190]

Swami Saradananda wrote: "When one reflects on the life and teachings of the Master, one understands that he was the embodiment of all spiritual moods. Such a great king in the realm of spirituality had never been seen before."[191]

Ramakrishna taught his disciples how to establish a relationship with God. He said: "Look, before you begin meditating, think of this (*pointing to himself*) for a while. Do you know why I say this? Because you have faith in this place (*me*). If you think of this place, that will remind you of God. It is like when one sees a herd of cows, one remembers a cowherd; seeing a son, the father; seeing a lawyer, the court. Do you understand? Look, your mind is scattered among various places. If you think of this (*me*), it will be gathered in one spot. And if you think of God with that concentrated mind you will truly get deep meditation. That is why I am telling you all this."

The Master continued: "Whatever form of God or spiritual mood you like, hold onto that firmly; only then will you get steadfast devotion. 'God can be reached through devotion. Can anyone attain Him without that?' One needs *bhava* [a spiritual mood]. One should adopt a particular attitude and call on Him. 'As is a man's meditation, so is his feeling of love. As is a man's feeling of love, so is his gain; and faith is the root of all.' One should cultivate a spiritual attitude and faith, and hold onto Him firmly. Only then can one succeed. Do you know what *bhava* means? It is to establish a relationship with God and then to remember it all the time: for example, I am a servant of God; I am a child of God; I am a part of God. This is the ripe ego, the ego of Knowledge. Always remember this — even while you are eating, sitting, and resting. One should practise the constant recollectedness of God. Part of the mind should be directed towards Him always. Only then will you succeed. Establish a particular spiritual relationship with God and make Him your own."[192]

Vijay Krishna Goswami said: "I have seen illumined souls who have attained perfection by following their respective paths, but I have never seen another *Siddhapurusha* like Ramakrishna Paramahamsa, who attained perfection in all attitudes and in all paths. He is unique in the religious history of the world."[193]

As rivers originate in different places and lose their name and form after meeting the ocean, so when different religious paths reach the nondual God, they become one and can no longer claim their separate identities. Ramakrishna used to say: "There all jackals howl in the same way."

Ramakrishna was completely established in the nondual state. In this connection, Ram Chandra Datta said:

> The goal of the Vedanta scriptures is nondual knowledge. A man attains the result of studying and practising Vedanta when he experiences this supreme knowledge. After attaining this nondual knowledge, if a man worships God as Kali, Durga, Shiva, Rama, Krishna, Gauranga, Buddha, Allah, Jesus, or any other form of God, he will attain fulfillment in that attitude. This was Ramakrishna's message.

Ramakrishna practised and attained perfection in different paths and left the above message of harmony as an ideal. One can see that all spiritual attitudes were fully manifested in his life. His life and message are the source of the nondual knowledge of Vedanta. That is why the Vedantins would call him 'Paramahamsa.' He was also a fountain of love and devotion and preached God with form, so the devotees call him an 'Avatar.' He was a great Tantric. He practised various esoteric disciplines of Tantra under the guidance of the Bhairavi Brahmani and attained perfection, so the followers of Tantra called him 'Kaula.' The Nava-rasik sect of Vaishnavas called him 'Rasik-chudamani.' He became 'Sain' to the Bauls, 'Gosain' to the Vaishnavas, 'Alekh' to the Kartabhajas. The Sikhs realized him as Nanak, the Muslims as Paigambar, the Christians as Jesus, and the Brahmos as a knower of Brahman.[194]

So far we have recorded various forms of Ramakrishna, but truly there is no end to his forms. He was God, ever-free. He could assume at will the form of any of his devotees' Chosen Deities. Regarding the Master, Mathur rightly said: "Father is the God of multiple forms. Whatever form he assumes, it becomes exact and beautiful."[195]

Name, form, and qualities are in the domain of God's *lila* (divine play). We live in the realm of lila or maya. So in our lives we swing between happiness and misery, good and evil, victory and defeat, praise and blame — all of which are created by maya. For this reason, we do not have abiding peace. In his life, Ramakrishna demonstrated how one can travel back and forth between the absolute and the relative. As one starts with the gross and moves towards the subtle, so one can start with the name, form, and qualities of God and reach Brahman, who is beyond name, form, and qualities. Ramakrishna taught us how to love God with form and then experience the wonderful beauty of God without form. When this state is attained, one can live without fear or anxiety.

Ramakrishna did not like one-sidedness. He was not a dry monk: He loved to eat various delicacies; he was fond of listening to a flute being played with different ragas and raginis. Ramakrishna sang the mantra of religious harmony and demonstrated that he was ever-present in each and every form. In this present age, Ramakrishna's life and message is a beacon to the world, which is devastated by religious conflict, sectarian violence, and hatred.

How to Meditate on the Form of Ramakrishna

After studying various forms of Ramakrishna we have come to this conclusion that he was the infinite Lord who took a human form so that we can attain him easily. He himself said: "Who can comprehend everything about God? It is not given to man to know any aspect of God, great or small. And what need is there to know everything about God? It is enough if we only realize Him. And we see God Himself if we but see His Incarnation. Suppose a person goes to the Ganges and touches its water. He will then say, 'Yes, I have seen and touched the Ganges.' To say this it is not necessary for him to touch the whole length of the river from Hardwar to Gangasagar."[196]

Similarly, if one's mind perceives any part of Ramakrishna's body, that is akin to perceiving an avatar, or an incarnation of the infinite Lord. According to one's preference, one can meditate on any form of Ramakrishna. Patanjali also mentioned: "One can meditate on anything that appeals to one as good." However, it is wise to practise meditation according to the instruction of one's guru. But what does one gain from meditation? Ramakrishna answered: "As the children inherit the wealth of their parents, so those who meditate on me will inherit my treasures."[197] His treasures are discrimination, renunciation, knowledge, devotion, unselfish love, and samadhi.

Sometimes we gaze at the picture of Ramakrishna and think: "Will our lives end having only seen the picture of the Master? Shall we have no realization?" But we must remember, we can bring the picture to life through our imagination, and this can lead to realization. One can meditate on the entire form of Ramakrishna or on various parts of his body, connecting them with various episodes of his life. This method generates more fervour and concentration in the mind of the meditator. Here are some examples:

Ramakrishna's feet: The Master's feet remind us of the feet of Vishnu that are worshipped in Gaya, where Kshudiram had the vision of the Lord telling him that He wanted to be born as his son. The infinite Lord took a finite form and entered the womb of Chandramani. We can imagine how Ramakrishna walked on the paths and in the meadows of Kamarpukur, travelled to Calcutta on foot, and strolled around in the temple garden of Dakshineswar.

One day Manomohan, a devotee, came to Dakshineswar. Seeing him, the Master drew his feet up and sat cross-legged. Manomohan was hurt. He said: "Sir, please extend them as before. If you don't I shall cut them off and carry them to my home so that the devotees may worship your blessed feet."[198] The Master smiled and allowed the devotee to touch his feet.

Once Kalipada, another devotee, accompanied the Master from

Dakshineswar to Calcutta by boat. In the middle of the Ganges, Kali-pada grabbed the Master's feet and said: "Sir, I am a wicked man and a drunkard. You are an ocean of mercy. Kindly save a ruffian such as I, who is devoid of disciplines and righteousness." The Master, "What do you want?" "When I leave this world," replied Kalipada, "I shall see darkness all around, and that terrible darkness will fill me with horror. My wife, children, and other relatives won't be able to help me then. At that terrible time you will be my only saviour. You will have to take me, holding a light with your left hand and me with your right hand. I shall always be with you then. You will have to fulfill this prayer of mine." With his heart full of compassion, the Master said: "All right, all right. Your prayer will be fulfilled. My goodness! You have brought me to the middle of the Ganges and have created such a scene!"[199]

One early afternoon Rakhal arrived from Calcutta and found the Master alone, resting on his bed. He asked Rakhal to sit on the bed and massage his feet. At first Rakhal was reluctant, but the Master insisted, saying: "Look, there is a tangible result from serving a holy man." Soon after he began massaging the Master's feet, he saw the Divine Mother, in the form of a girl of seven or eight, circle the Master's bed a few times and then enter into his body. This vision overwhelmed Rakhal. The Master then said to Rakhal with a smile: "Did you see the result of serving a holy man?"[200]

Ramakrishna's hands: We can visualize the Master inside the Kali temple waving the light and fanning the Divine Mother during the vesper service, or holding a bit of cotton near the nostrils of the Kali image to determine whether the Mother breathes. Some other extraordinary events also took place within the Kali temple. During Ramakrishna's sadhana his longing for vision of Kali became so unbearable that he took the sword that hung on the wall and tried to end his life with it. In another incident, the Master slapped Rani Rasmani when he discovered that she was thinking of a law suit.

The Master used to write a mantra on the tongues of his disciples with his middle finger. One day when Narendra came to Dakshineswar, the Master touched his chest with the palm of his hand and the world disappeared from his mind. When Chandramani was dying at the bakul-tala ghat the Master held her feet with his hands and said with tearful eyes, "Mother, you don't know whom you carried in your womb." Ramakrishna once had a vision of Jagannath in a state of ecstasy and tried to embrace Him, but just then he fell and broke his arm.

Ramakrishna's Chest: The Master described his phenomenal renunciation and how he felt a terrible pain in his chest when a devotee tried to give him money: "Mahendra Pal of Sinthi once gave Ramlal five rupees. Ramlal told me about it after he had gone. I asked him what the gift was for, and Ramlal said that it was meant for me. I thought it might enable me to pay off some of my debt for milk. That night I went to bed and, if you will believe me, I suddenly woke up with a pain. I felt as if a cat were scratching inside my chest. I at once went to Ramlal and asked him: 'For whom did Mahendra give this money? Was it for your aunt?' 'No,' said Ramlal, 'it is meant for you.' I said to him, 'Go and return the money at once, or I shall have no peace of mind.' Ramlal returned the money early in the morning and I felt relieved."[201]

Ramakrishna's Back: The Master's experience of oneness with all creation was made manifest on his back: "One day the Master was in an ecstatic mood as he stood on the spacious ghat of the main porch looking at the Ganges. Two boats were anchored there, and the boatmen were quarreling with each other. Gradually their quarrel grew intense, and the stronger man slapped the weaker one sharply on his back. At this the Master cried out loudly in pain. The sound of his distressed cry reached Hriday inside the Kali temple. He hurriedly ran to the ghat and saw that the Master's back was red and swollen. Impatient with anger, Hriday asked repeatedly: 'Uncle, show me the person who hit you. I will chop off his head.' When the Master regained his composure, he told Hriday what had happened. Hriday was dumbfounded by this and asked himself, 'How is this possible?'"[202]

Ramakrishna's collar bone: When the Master was suffering from cancer at Cossipore, his body became so emaciated that it was hard to recognize him. One day Niranjan was attending the Master and observing his sunken eyes and prominent collar bone. Realizing that he was sad, the Master told Niranjan: "Look, I am now in such a state that whoever sees me in this condition will attain liberation in this life by the grace of the Divine Mother. But know for certain that it will shorten my life." Upon hearing this, Niranjan became more vigilant about protecting the Master. He sat at the gate day and night with a turban on his head and a stick in his hand to keep outsiders from visiting the Master. Niranjan sometimes had to hurt people, but he accepted this as an unpleasant duty necessary to protect the Master's life.[203]

Ramakrishna's Throat: The Master had a wonderful musical voice, and many people were moved when they heard him sing. Yet it was his throat that became affected by cancer. "One day in Shyampukur he had an incredible vision. He saw his subtle body come out of his gross body and move around the room. He noticed some wounds on the back of its throat and was wondering how those wounds came to be, when the

Divine Mother explained it to him: People who had committed various sins had become pure by touching him, thereby transferring their sins to his body and causing those wounds. At Dakshineswar the Master sometimes told us that he would not hesitate to be born millions of times and suffer for the good of humanity."[204]

At Cossipore "Gopal used to wash the Master's cancerous sore daily with a special solution of margosa leaves boiled in water, which is considered to be antiseptic. One day when Gopal touched the sore, the Master cried out with pain. Gopal said sadly: 'Sir, what can I do? If I wash your throat, you will get pain, so let me not do it.' 'No, no, you go on washing it. Look, I have no more pain,' the Master replied. He then withdrew his mind from that spot, and Gopal was able to wash the area carefully. All the while the Master remained silent and cheerful as if Gopal were washing someone else's wound."[205]

Ramakrishna's face: One can meditate on every aspect of the Master's face. The Holy Mother said that she had never seen the Master's face gloomy. He was a man of bliss and he shared it with others. His skin was so soft and sensitive that he could not be shaved with a razor. The barber would simply trim his hair and beard with a pair of scissors.

Innumerable teachings, including those from *The Gospel of Sri Ramakrishna*, came from the lips of the Master. But he always said that it was the Divine Mother who spoke through his mouth. Not a single untruth ever came from those lips. Swami Vivekananda once said: "For the first time I found a man who dared to say that he saw God, that religion was a reality. He criticized no one. For years I lived with that man, but never did I hear those lips utter one word of condemnation for any sect."[206]

The Master would brush his teeth every morning with a twig and also scrape his tongue. One day while he was in samadhi he fell down and broke off a part of one of his upper front teeth.

Sometimes we wonder: Do our prayers reach the Master's ears? Once Hazra also asked, "Does God listen to our prayer?" The Master answered: "Certainly. I can assure you of that a hundred times. But the prayer must be genuine and earnest."[207]

The Master's eyes were extremely bright and penetrating, compassionate and loving. During his days of sadhana he would cry so intensely for the Divine Mother that the ground of the Panchavati would become soaked with his tears. In later days someone asked him, "How can we attain God?" Ramakrishna replied, "Can you weep for him every day?" His eyes saw God in every thing and every being. In spite of all our imperfections and shortcomings, we hope the Master will always cast his glance of grace on us so that we can see him and fulfill the goal of human life.

Long after the Master's passing away, a disciple asked the Holy Mother, "Does the Master really partake of the food that you offer him?" She replied: "Yes, he does. A light comes out of his eyes and draws up the articles of food. His ambrosial touch replenishes them again, so there is no decrease."[208]

We shall conclude our meditation with this prayer: "O Ramakrishna, sweet is thy life story! Sweet indeed is thy holy name! Sweet too are thy forms, thy talks, and thy songs! In fact, what concerning thee is devoid of sweetness?"[209]

2

Ramakrishna: His Name and the Science of Japa

Ramakrishna is a wonder in the religious world. Every day innumerable people worldwide chant his name. Some are repeating his name as japa; full of joy, some are talking and hearing about him; and some are trying to know the person behind that name. Romain Rolland concluded *The Life of Ramakrishna* with this beautiful statement: "The man himself [Ramakrishna] was no more. His spirit had departed to travel along the path of collective life in the veins of humanity."[1]

Ramakrishna abhorred name and fame and was reluctant to preach about himself. He was happy just leading his divine life. Manomohan Mitra, an eyewitness, said: "One day the Master was talking to the devotees in the Panchavati. Meanwhile, Keshab Sen arrived with some of his Brahmo followers. After various discussions, Keshab said to the Master: 'Sir, if you permit, I want to make your message known to the public. It will definitely benefit people and bring peace to the world.' Ramakrishna replied in an ecstatic mood: 'It is not the right time to spread the message of this place [*meaning his message*] through lecturing and newspapers. The power and ideas that are within this body will automatically spread all over in the course of time. Hundreds of Himalayas will not be able to suppress that power.'"[2]

Ramakrishna is an immortal and unfading flower, full of beauty, colour, fragrance, and nectar. People from remote places rushed to the temple garden of Dakshineswar to sip the nectar that was Ramakrishna. Aswini Datta recorded his own experience: "What I saw and received in those few days [with the Master] has sweetened my whole life. That Elysian smile of his, laden with nectar, I have locked up in the secret closet of my memory. A thrill of joy passes through my heart when I think how a grain of the bliss shed from that laughter has been sweetening the lives of millions, even in distant America."[3]

Drinking the nectar-like words of the Master, M., the recorder of *The Gospel of Sri Ramakrishna*, was absorbed in bliss. With great love and enthusiasm, M. distributed the Master's teachings among the devotees. His devotion for Sri Ramakrishna was so great that it spread to those who heard him speak. In an inspired mood, M. tried to describe his Master. He said:

"The Master was like a five-year-old boy always running to meet his Mother.

"The Master was like a beautiful flower whose nature was to bloom and spread its fragrance.

"The Master was like a bonfire from which other lamps were lighted.

"The Master was like a celestial vina always absorbed in singing the glory of the Divine Mother.

"The Master was like a big fish joyfully swimming in calm, clear, blue waters, the Ocean of Satchidananda.

"The Master was like a bird that had lost its nest in a storm and then, perched on the threshold of the Infinite, was joyfully moving between the two realms, singing the glory of the Infinite."[4]

The Meaning of Ramakrishna's Name

There is an eternal relationship between a word and its meaning. The meaning is of two kinds: the literal meaning and its inner significance. The word "Ramakrishna" literally refers to an embodied man of that name, a son of Kshudiram and Chandramani, a temple priest of Dakshineswar, and so on. The inner significance of the word "Ramakrishna" is that this being is Satchidananda, the ever-free God, and an avatar. When one repeats this mantra and understands its meaning, one experiences the power of the name and gets joy within.

Swami Bhagavatananda, a famous and learned monk of Varanasi, once explained the profound meaning behind Ramakrishna's name. He said:

From the ordinary standpoint, *Ramakrishna* is a mere name; but if one explores deeply, one will find that it is full of mystery. For example:

Ramante yoginah asmin iti Rama [He who bestows delight upon the yogis is Rama.] *Karshati bhaktanam dukham papam mano veti Krishna* [He who absorbs and destroys the sin and suffering of the devotees, or he who attracts the devotees' minds and dissolves them in his devotion, is Krishna.] Rama and Krishna were born in their respective ages to remove the sufferings of humanity. At present, they have been manifested jointly in the form of Ramakrishna.

There is mystery in the name Rama. When Rama was born, his father, Dasharatha, asked the sage Vashishtha to name his son. Vashishtha said, "The name of this child is Rama." King Dasharatha and his ministers said: "That is a very short name. This child will inherit the throne, so he should have a long, dignified name." Vashishtha said: "O King, you do not know the glory and greatness of the name *Rama*. Please listen: The letter *ra* of the name Rama comes from the mantra *Namo Nārāyanāya*, which is the essence of the famous Vaishnava mantra. If you remove *ra* from that mantra, it becomes *Namo Nāyanāya*, which means 'salutations to the sensual objects of the world' instead of 'salutations to Lord Narayana.' Similarly, the letter *ma* of the name Rama is the quintessence of the Shiva mantra *Namah Shivāya*. If *ma* is removed from this mantra, it becomes *Na Shivāya*, which means 'everything is inauspicious,' instead of 'salutations to the all-auspicious Shiva.'" When Vashishtha thus unveiled the mystery of the name Rama, Dasharatha was pleased. *Rama* is in the name of Ramakrishna.

The spiritual meaning of the name *Krishna* is this: The root meaning of the word *krish* is "the ever-existent Brahman," and *na* is "happiness" or "bliss." This *sat*, or existence, and *ananda*, or bliss, are the essence of Brahman. That is the meaning of the word *Krishna*. If *sat* is removed from Brahman, nothing can exist; and if *ananda* is removed, we will not seek anything in this world. So the meaning of the word *Krishna* is *sat* and *ananda*. *Krishna* is also included in the name of *Ramakrishna*. The greatness of this name is beyond description.[5]

Those who are initiated repeat the name of their Chosen Deity, so it is important for them to know the inner meaning of that name. It helps the aspirant to be close to God. We try to unite ourselves with God through karma, prayer, japa, and meditation. Our spiritual practices become smooth and joyful if we have clear knowledge of His real nature. Two days before his passing away, Ramakrishna said to Vivekananda: "He who was born as Rama and Krishna is now living in this very body as Ramakrishna — not from the standpoint of your Vedanta, but actually so."

Swami Turiyananda commented on the above statement: "The point stressed here is that the Advaita school of Vedanta holds jiva and

Brahman to be one. Some take this to mean that everyone is equal to Rama and Krishna, and that they have no distinctive qualities. Lest Swamiji misunderstand the saying, 'He who was Rama and Krishna is now Ramakrishna in this body,' Sri Ramakrishna qualified this statement with the words, 'not from the standpoint of your Vedanta.' That is to say, the consciousness of Sri Ramakrishna was the consciousness of Ishwara [God] and not of the jiva. According to Advaita Vedanta, the jiva can attain the knowledge of his or her identity with Brahman by removing his or her ignorance through spiritual practices culminating in samadhi. Yet, despite all imaginable efforts, the jiva can never become Ishwara. The One who is Ishwara is eternally Ishwara. Even when Ishwara assumes a human body and appears to be a jiva, that One remains the same Ishwara and does not become the jiva."[6]

Name and Form

According to the Vedanta philosophy: Brahman is *asti-bhati-priya* [existence, consciousness, and bliss] and the world is *nama-rupa* [name and form]. Brahman alone is real; It exists in the past, present, and future. The world is made of name and form and has no absolute reality. It is visible just as a mirage is visible but in fact does not exist. If that is true, then one may say that because Rama, Krishna, Ramakrishna, Shiva, and Kali have names and forms, they must not be real. So is it meaningless to follow them? We see in Ramakrishna's life that to attain nirvikalpa samadhi, he cut the form of the Divine Mother Kali in two with the sword of knowledge.

The Vedanta scriptures say that it is true that name and form do not have absolute reality; however, they have an apparent and pragmatic reality. From the absolute standpoint, the guru, the disciple, the mantra, and ignorance itself are not real: They do not really exist. But the unreal guru through an unreal mantra can remove the unreal ignorance of the unreal disciple. Similarly, an unreal doctor uses unreal medicine to remove the unreal disease of the unreal patient. In fact, Brahman alone exists and He has become everything. As a snake He bites, and as a doctor He cures. This is His play.

Name and form cannot exist without Brahman. It is Brahman who has become manifest as beings and the universe through space, time, and causation. The nondualist says: "All this is verily Brahman"; "All this — whatever exists in this changing universe — is covered by the Lord." The dualist says: "Wherever my eyes fall, there Krishna manifests."

We live in the domain of name and form, which is maya. We must cling to the name and form that will help us to transcend the realm of maya: Rama, Krishna, Buddha, Jesus, Ramakrishna, and other avatars are the means by which we can reach Brahman, who is devoid of name and form. Krishna said in the Gita (7:14): "Verily, this divine maya of Mine, consisting of the gunas, is hard to overcome. But those who take refuge in Me alone shall cross over this maya." According to the Amritabindu Upanishad, the Sound-Brahman is lower knowledge; after becoming an adept in this lower knowledge, one attains the Supreme Brahman. Swami Shivananda wrote: "If a man repeats Ramakrishna's name and meditates on his form, he can reach Ramakrishna's peaceful abode, which is beyond name and form."[7]

Name and Form are Identical

Ramakrishna said, "The name and the person named are identical." This statement is very important from a philosophical standpoint. The word and its meaning are always connected; so the name and the person who bears it cannot be separated. Name first manifests as Om, the "Sound-Brahman." This is the first vibration of creation. Name, or sound, is indestructible; sound evolves and dissolves like the waves of the ocean. Name makes the Nameless visible. Swami Brahmananda said: "Have firm faith in God and in His name. Unite God with His name. God dwells in the hearts of devotees as the mantra. Repeat God's name and listen to His praises. God and the name of God are identical. If you get involved in this world without repeating His name, you will be lost in a maze."[8]

When we utter a man's name, his face manifests in our minds. When we call on Rama, it is not Shyama who responds. Likewise, if we call upon a particular deity, he or she responds. Of course, one must call on the deity wholeheartedly: "A man sleeping in a room behind closed doors wakes up if anybody knocks and calls out his name, and responds by opening the door. In the same way, if anyone takes the name of God, repeating His holy mantra, and performs spiritual practices with simple faith and zealous devotion, the Lord who dwells in all beings awakens and opens the door to the temple in the aspirant's heart. He fulfills the aspirant's cherished desire and reveals Himself in the form of the Chosen Deity."[9]

The devotional scriptures have glorified the greatness of God's name. According to the *Chaitanya Charitamrita*: "Chant Krishna's name with steadfast devotion because the Lord responds when He is called. Chaitanya joyfully said to Swarup and Ramananda Roy that singing the

Lord's name is the supreme means to God-realization in this Kaliyuga." Once a goswami said to Ramakrishna: "Sir, the chanting of God's name is enough. The scriptures emphasize the sanctity of God's name for the Kaliyuga." Ramakrishna replied: "Yes, there is no doubt about the sanctity of God's name. But can a mere name achieve anything, without the yearning love of the devotee behind it? One should feel great restlessness of soul for the vision of God. Suppose a man repeats the name of God mechanically, while his mind is absorbed in 'lust and gold.' Can he achieve anything?"[10]

Some say: We are ordinary human beings. We have not seen God. We do not know His real nature, or even where He lives. How can we contact Him? The sage Patanjali answered: "Devotion to God leads to divine union, or samadhi." "The word that manifests God is Om." "The repetition of this [Om] and meditation on Its meaning [is the way]." The scriptures say: "Without making the mantra conscious, if a man repeats it a million times, he will not get the result." It will be the mere repetition of a word.

Sadhana Awakens the Mantra

Many people in this world repeat the name of Rama, Krishna, Kali, Jesus, Allah, Ramakrishna, and other deities. One should strictly follow the guru's instructions and practise japa and meditation. After receiving initiation, some think that it is enough to repeat the mantra a fixed number of times.

The Tantric scriptures prescribe many sadhanas to make the mantra conscious. Ramakrishna and his disciples practised those disciplines. While worshipping the Divine Mother, Ramakrishna would draw a line around himself while uttering the mantra "rang," and as he did so he would see a wall of fire surrounding him, protecting him. Swami Vivekananda would see the mantra written in golden letters. We, however, see darkness when we close our eyes to repeat the mantra and meditate. Sometimes we feel depressed. If one wants a taste of spirituality, one should first learn from the guru how to awaken the mantra, then faithfully practise the instructions given.

Swami Vivekananda said about awakening the mantra: "The mantra-shastris [upholders of the mantra theory] believe that some words have been handed down through a succession of teachers and disciples, and that the mere utterance of them will lead to some form of realization. There are two different meanings of the term mantra-chaitanya. According to some, if you practise the repetition of a certain mantra, you will see the Chosen Deity who is the object or deity of that mantra. But according to others, the word means that if you practise the repetition of a certain mantra received from a guru who is not competent, you will have to perform certain ceremonies by which that mantra will become *chetana* or living, and then its repetition will be successful. Different mantras, when they are thus 'living,' show different signs, but the general sign is that one will be able to repeat it for a long time without feeling any strain and that one's mind will very soon be concentrated."[11]

There are many ways to awaken the mantra. All mantras are a combination of letters. The combined letters make a word. And each word has a meaning; this meaning originates from the power of knowledge; and the power of knowledge comes from the guru. When we have the knowledge of the mantra, the object of the mantra becomes manifest in our minds. For example: When we hear the word "cow," we immediately visualize the form of a cow. This knowledge of cow came to us from our parents or teachers who showed us a cow when we were children. During initiation, the guru tells us our mantra, then explains its meaning. But our minds are so impure that we cannot understand if we hear it only once. So we should hear, repeat, and remember the mantra again and again; then only will it be awakened.

The awakening of the mantra is a difficult subject. Without sadhana, one cannot understand the mystery of the mantra. It is not possible to awaken the mantra by reading books or listening to lectures. Vijay Krishna Chattopadhyay said: "When one unites the mantra, the guru, and the deity, the mantra awakens. The mantra is a mystical sound. The guru is the giver of knowledge. And the deity is the experience of that knowledge. The guru leads the disciple from dark ignorance to luminous knowledge by means of the mantra.

"Here is an example: Suppose I tell you that there is a ghost in that banyan tree by the side of the road. After you hear this from me, you begin thinking about the ghost. You also know the meaning of the word *ghost*: a terrible, frightening spirit. One dark night you need to pass near that tree on an errand. All of a sudden, you remember the story of the ghost that I graphically described to you. As soon as you go under that banyan tree, your hair stands on end, your throat becomes dry, and you have terrible palpitations. As you look at the tree, a branch moves a little in the wind, and you either cry out 'Ghost! Ghost!' or fall unconscious. This is the experience of the ghost, which came from the awakening of the 'ghost' mantra. The word 'ghost' is like the mantra; I am the guru who described that word to you; and your experience that there is a ghost in that tree is the deity of that ghost mantra."[12]

The Method of Japa

During initiation the guru instructs the disciple in the method of japa. If the disciple does not believe in and follow the guru's instructions, he or she will make no progress in spiritual life. Meditation is not so easy. Various worldly thoughts create restlessness in the mind and do not allow it to concentrate on God. That is why in the beginning one should practise japa for some time. Japa is the repetition of the mantra or God's name with a corresponding effort to hold Him in the mind. Krishna said in the Gita: "Of sacrifices I am the sacrifice of japa."

Most people complain: "Our minds are restless. What shall we do?" The scriptures answer: "Control the mind by repeated practice and by detachment." The Holy Mother said that the mind could be controlled if one repeated one's mantra fifteen to twenty thousand times a day. Swami Shivananda wrote in a letter (16 June 1922):

"An important and yet easy way of concentrating the mind is this: Sit before Sri Ramakrishna's picture, keep your eyes fixed on him, and start repeating his name. While you do so, have the firm belief that Sri Ramakrishna is looking at you, that he is listening to you repeat his name, and that the only purpose of his sitting there is to help you. Do this, and you will see your mind becoming calm. You will find your trust in him growing, and you will also have peace of mind."[13]

One can practise japa in many ways. For example, one can utter the mantra with sound (*vachanik*), or with a gentle sound so that only the chanter can hear (*upangshu*), or mentally (*manasik*). Some repeat the mantra while counting with a rosary or between the joints of the fingers. Some people practise japa by focussing on each centre of the kundalini. Some connect their mantra with their breath. The scriptures say that human beings are continuously repeating a mantra as they breathe. When one inhales, it sounds like "so"; when one exhales, it sounds like "ham." These two words are combined to form "so-ham" (*Sah-aham*), which means "*That I am.*" Its reverse form is "ham-sa" (*Aham Sah*) "I am That." All human beings knowingly or unknowingly are always repeating "so-ham" and "ham-sa." This is called the Hamsa mantra; it is also called the Ajapa Gayatri.

Various spiritual aspirants experimented with methods of focussing on God. They recorded the results of their sadhanas in the scriptures. For example, one can turn the mind inward very quickly by repeating the mantra while focussing on the six centres of the kundalini. An aspirant should repeat the mantra a certain number of times on each centre beginning with the muladhara (at the base of the spine) and ending with the sahasrara (at the crown of the head) and then returning from there to the anahata (at the heart). Thus one should go on repeating the mantra while focussing the mind on the Chosen Deity. Shakti dwells at the muladhara, and Shiva at the sahasrara, so this method of japa unites Shiva and Shakti. It is called Brahma-tattwa, or true yoga.[14]

The Tantric scriptures mention another method: Hold the breath and imagine that your kundalini is rising from the muladhara to the sahasrara through the sushumna channel, then immediately bring it back to the muladhara. After practising this technique a few times, one will notice a light like a flash of lightning, or a flame, or a glowing tube in the sushumna channel. The technique of concentrating one's mind on this flame is called meditation on *mantra-shikha*. Pandit Jaganmohan Tarkalankar, a famous Tantric teacher, wrote: "One should meditate on the guru in the sahasrara, the mantra at the root of the tongue, and the Chosen Deity in the heart. And then think that the guru, mantra, and Chosen Deity are luminous and that their light makes you luminous. Now repeat the mantra while focussing on the luminous form of your Chosen Deity in the heart."[15]

When we study *Sri Ramakrishna and His Divine Play* and *The Gospel of Sri Ramakrishna*, we find that the Master practised various kinds of sadhana as described in various scriptures. He also practised some new disciplines that he invented himself. For example, he said to the devotees: "During meditation, think that your mind has been tied to the feet of your Chosen Deity with a silk thread, so that it cannot run away. Why do I say a silk thread? Because those feet are extremely soft and delicate. It would hurt the deity if a different type of string were used." Again, he said: "Should one think of the Chosen Deity during meditation only and then forget Him? Always try to keep part of your mind on the deity. You have seen how a vigil lamp is kept burning during Durga Puja. One should always keep a lamp near the deity; it should not be allowed to go out. It is inauspicious if a householder's lamp goes out. Likewise, after placing the Chosen Deity in the lotus of the heart, one's meditation should be like the flame of a vigil lamp. While performing household duties one should look inside from time to time to see if the lamp is still burning."[16]

Sri Ramakrishna once said: "During my sadhana, before starting meditation on the Chosen Deity I would first imagine that I was washing the mind thoroughly. You see, there are various kinds of dirt and dross [bad thoughts and desires] in the mind. I would imagine that I was flushing out all impurities and placing the Chosen Deity there. Adopt this method."[17]

The restless mind loves to play. One can use japa to entertain the mind. For example, Ramakrishna's devotees who have visited the places connected with Ramakrishna and Holy Mother can repeat the mantra one hundred times while focussing their minds on the following: Ramakrishna's image at Kamarpukur and the Holy Mother's image at Jayrambati; Kali, Krishna, Shiva, the Master's room, the Nahabat, and the Panchavati of Dakshineswar; the Master's room at Cossipore; and the image of the Master at Belur Math. Thus a devotee can repeat the mantram 1000 times in one sitting.

During initiation, the guru advises the disciple to practise japa and meditation in the morning and evening, because nature becomes calm at the junctions between night and day, and between day and night. It takes steadfast devotion and regularity to make the japa effective. It is very important to make a habit of sitting at the same times. Suppose that a man eats breakfast at 8:00 a.m., lunch at 1:00 p.m., and supper at 8:00 p.m. He has followed this routine for forty years. His stomach is ready for food at those times. Similarly, if an aspirant sits for meditation at the same time every day, his or her mind will be ready for the presence of God. Gopinath Kaviraj, a scholar and mystic, said: "Maintain an exact time period for meditation. If you have decided to sit for meditation at 4:00 a.m., you must sit at that time. If that costs you money it does not matter. If there is an emergency that keeps you from sitting at that time, close your eyes and say, 'Lord, I am unable to meditate on you at this moment.' Even this one minute of recollectedness will be sufficient. To maintain the exact moment is a difficult task; but this habit brings God close to us. You can sit for long hours at other times, but don't forget your exact moment. You have seen how the Muslims say their prayers five times a day; they always maintain their schedule. Even during a journey, they will stop by the side of the road and say their prayers at the right time; they don't need a mosque. There are so many obstacles in one's spiritual journey! Strictly adhere to the exact time for meditation."[18]

Patanjali said: "By making samyama [concentration, meditation, and absorption] on single moments and on their sequence in time, one gains discriminative knowledge." (3:53) Most people do not know the mystery of time. A person with a well-ordered life can accomplish more than someone without it.

When Swami Brahmananda was in Vrindaban, he took a vow that he would repeat his mantra at midnight. He later described how the spirit of a holy man awakened him from sleep: "At that time Turiyananda and I were living together and practising japa and meditation punctually. We did not talk to each other unless we needed to. At 8:00 p.m. we would eat some bread that we had gotten by begging, and then go to bed. Just at midnight we would get up, and after washing we would sit for meditation. One night while I was asleep, someone pushed me and said: 'It is twelve. Will you not sit for meditation?' I immediately got up. I was a little groggy. I thought that Turiyananda had broken my sleep, but he informed me that he had not. Quickly I finished washing and sat for meditation. I saw a Babaji [a Vaishnava saint] repeating his mantra silently in front of me. I was a little frightened when I saw him. As I repeated my mantra, I looked at him from time to time. As long as I was seated on my carpet, I saw him standing, repeating his mantra. Later I used to see him daily repeating his mantra in the same way."[19]

How to Cultivate Taste for Japa

We chant God's name, but we do not enjoy its taste, and it does not intoxicate us. We sit in our shrines in the morning and evening, mechanically repeating our mantra with a rosary, but do not get any joy. So we quickly leave the shrine and make ourselves busy with other activities. Patanjali said: "One becomes established in God-consciousness when practice has been cultivated for a long time, uninterruptedly, with faith and devotion." (1:14) Controlling the mind does not come in a day, but by long and sustained practice. One needs patience to enter the inner spiritual world by way of japa. Suppose that one afternoon a man enters a movie house after the film has started. He sees dark all around, except for the red emergency exit signs and the light from the screen. After staying a while, he slowly begins to see the rows of chairs and can find his seat. Similarly, the darkness of the heart is lighted by japa and meditation. Then one gets joy. The great saint Tulasidas said: "As a lamp placed at the threshold of a room lights both the inside and the outside of the room, so the chanted name of Rama illumines us inside and outside."

Spiritual disciplines without passion are as flavourless as curry without salt. As cows love fodder mixed with oil cakes, so people enjoy spiritual life if they chant God's name with devotion. The great sage Vyasa said: "When one has a bile secretion disorder, sugar does not taste good. But if one goes on taking sugar earnestly every day, one gradually begins to enjoy the taste of sugar and the disease goes away. Similarly, the name of God may not appeal to those who are in ignorance. But if one practises spiritual disciplines regularly, ignorance disappears and a taste for the Divine Name is acquired." Sometimes influenza weakens a person's sense of taste; but one can taste a little if some pickle is added to one's food. Love for God is like that pickle. A drunkard loves to hear about wine. His mind dances with joy when he sees a bottle of whisky or vodka. His roseate intoxication starts the moment the cork of the bottle is opened. He drinks the whole bottle with great joy. At last he forgets the world and falls down unconscious on the sidewalk. In fact, one can enjoy a similar roseate intoxication by chanting God's name. Ramakrishna used to say: "Just repeating the word 'siddhi' will not produce intoxication. You must actually get some hemp, rub it in water, and then drink the solution. Since you are going to lead a householder's life, create a roseate intoxication in your mind with the thought of God. You will be doing your duties, but let that pleasant intoxication remain with you."[20]

We do not like to hear the names of people whom we abhor, but we love to hear the names of our loved ones. Loving relationships bring the taste of joy to us. Rupa Goswami wrote in his *Vidagdha Madhav*: "I do not know how much nectar is in that two-syllable word, 'Krish-na.' I am not content chanting his name with one mouth; I wish I had a million mouths. I also want to have a million ears to hear his name. When this name vibrates in my mind, all my senses are overpowered."

The Vaishnava scriptures emphasize that one should chant God's name with passion: This is the main discipline of the Vaishnavas. The devotee passes through several stages before attaining divine love: first, having faith; then seeking holy company; constantly chanting God's name, which removes all obstacles; then having steadfast devotion; tasting or experiencing sweetness; having attachment for God; being established in a spiritual mood; and finally attaining divine love. Chaitanya said: "*Jive daya name ruchi vaishnav sevan, Iha vina dharma nai shuna Sanatan.* [Listen, O Sanatan, there is no other dharma than practising compassion for all living beings, love of God's name, and service to devotees.]

Ramakrishna and the Divine Name

Five hundred years ago Chaitanya taught people how to chant the name of God. Everyone has the right to chant His name. Among devotees, there is no difference between rich and poor, learned and illiterate, brahmin and *pariah*. One of the mantras Chaitanya repeated was:

Rama Raghava Rama Raghava Rama Raghava pahi mam,
Krishna Keshava Krishna Keshava Krishna Keshava raksha mam.
[O Rama, O Raghava, save me.
O Krishna, O Keshava, protect me.]

Moreover, he also recommended repeating this famous Vaishnava mantra with thirty-two syllables:

Hare Krishna Hare Krishna, Krishna Krishna Hare Hare,
Hare Rama Hare Rama, Rama Rama Hare Hare.

Akshay Sen wrote about Ramakrishna's instruction concerning the divine name: "The human mind is possessed by impure thoughts, as if by an evil spirit. To purify the mind, one should continually repeat God's name with simple faith. This is the easiest means. Ramakrishna said again and again: 'There is infinite glory in God's name. The name is the seed; the name is the tree; and the name is the fruit. God dwells in His own name.' People generally do not care for verbal instruction, so in order to teach people, Ramakrishna used to chant God's name and dance rhythmically, clapping his hands in the morning and evening. He would become so intoxicated that his chanting led him to samadhi. Although one can attain samadhi after practising severe austerities throughout many lives, the Master proved that it could also be attained by chanting God's name. According to Ramakrishna, Narada's way of devotion is to chant, sing, and hear God's name. In this Kaliyuga, Narada's way of devotion is the best means for God-realization."[21]

As loud music does not allow us to hear each other's conversation, so loud kirtan overpowers worldly desires. It is said that the Divine Name devours lust. Ramakrishna advised his disciple Yogananda to chant God's name as an antidote to lust.

Ramlal said that in the mornings and evenings Sri Ramakrishna used to dance, chanting the names of the Lord: "Jaya Govinda, Jaya Gopala" [Victory to Govinda, Victory to Gopala]; "Keshava Madhava Dina Dayala" [O Keshava, Madhava, the compassionate friend of the lowly]; "Hare Murare Govinda, Vasu-Daivaki Nandana Govinda" [O Hari, Murari, Govinda, O son of Vasudeva and Devaki]; "Hare Narayana Govinda He" [O Hari, Narayana, Govinda]; "Hare Krishna Vasudeva" [O Hari, Krishna, son of Vasudeva].[22]

M. said: "Late in the evening the Master would chant this mantra, 'Brahma-maya-jiva-jagat' [Brahman-maya-soul-world]. One can attain perfection or see God by repeating this mantra. The Master said, 'This is a mysterious mantra.'"[23]

When Ramakrishna visited Balaram's home or that of any other devotee, he would chant God's name. Visitors would later remark: "How this Paramahamsa chants the Divine Mother's name! It penetrates the heart."[24]

The Gospel of Sri Ramakrishna records the many ways in which the Master chanted the names of gods and goddesses:

Krishna he dinabandhu [friend of the lowly]! Prana-vallabh!
Govinda! Ha Krishna! He Krishna! Jnana [Knowledge] Krishna!
Prana [Life] Krishna! Buddhi [Intellect] Krishna! Mana [Mind] Krishna! Deha [Body] Krishna!
Prana he Govinda, mama jivana [my life].
Satchidananda! Satchidananda! Satchidananda!
Karanananda-dayini! Karananandamayi! [Brahman is the source and giver of bliss.]
Haribol, Haribol, Harimay Haribol, Hari Hari Haribol. [Chant Hari's name.]
Ram, Ram, Ram, Ram, Ram, Ram, Ram, Ram, Ram.
Jaya Jaya Durge, Jaya Jaya Durge. [Victory to Mother Durga.]
Sahajananda, Sahajananda. [Pure Bliss.]
Om Kali, Om Kali.
Kali Brahma, Brahma Kali.
Maha-Kali, Nitya-Kali, Smashan-Kali, Raksha-Kali, Shyama-Kali.
Brahma-Atma-Bhagavan, Bhagavat-Bhakta-Bhagavan, Guru-Krishna-Vaishnav, Brahma-Shakti, Shakti-Brahma.
Veda, Purana, Tantra, Gita, Gayatri.
Sharanagata, Sharanagata. [I take refuge in You.] Naham naham, tuhun tuhun. [Not I but You.] Ami yantra tumi yantri. [I am an instrument, You are the operator.]
Hari Om, Hari Om! Om, Om, Om, Om, Om, Om, Om, Om Kali!
Krishna, Krishna, Krishna! Krishna Satchidananda.
Om Satchidananda! Govinda, Govinda, Govinda! Yogamaya!
Krishna Krishna! Gopi-Krishna, Gopi, Gopi! Rakhal-Jivan Krishna.
Nanda-nandana Krishna, Govinda, Govinda!
Srimat Narayana, Srimat Narayana, Narayana, Narayana!
Jagannath, Dinabandhu, Jagabandhu.
O Ma, O Ma, Brahmamayi.
Ma, Ma, Rajeswari [Queen.]

Ramakrishna never cared for a monotonous life. His personal experience taught him that God has many names. One can reach God by following any one of those names. One day at Dakshineswar the Master was humming "Gaur, Gaur," a name for Gauranga. Someone asked:

"Sir, you repeat the Mother's name. Why are you chanting Gaur's name?" The Master replied: "What can I do? You people have a wife, son, daughter, money, but I have only God. So, sometimes I say, Gaur, sometimes Ma, and other times Rama, Krishna, Kali, or Shiva. Thus I spend my time."[25]

God's name is the medicine to cure the suffering from the disease of worldliness. To eradicate human suffering, the Master used to sing to his devotees:

> "O Mother, ever blissful as Thou art,
> Do not deprive Thy worthless child of bliss!"
>
>   *   *   *
>
> "O Shyama, my only hope is in Thy hallowed name!"
>
>   *   *   *
>
> "If only I can pass away repeating Durga's name,
> How canst Thou then, O Blessed One,
> Withhold from me deliverance,
> Wretched though I may be?"

Once a devotee asked for advice from M. concerning his lack of sincerity in spiritual life.

M.: "Pray to the Master for longing."

Devotee: "I don't feel any inclination to pray."

M.: "Well, if you cannot do that, repeat the mantra that you received from your guru. Your mind may not be concentrated, but go on repeating the mantra ten to fifteen thousand times a day. You will develop love for God by repeating the name. Then gradually you will feel detachment for worldly objects, and finally your kundalini will be awakened."

Devotee: "I don't feel any longing to repeat the mantra."

M.: "Then your case is serious and there is little hope for survival. Developing a taste for God's name is the last treatment for a dying person. If you have love for God's name, you will transcend fear. It comes in time."[26]

The Results of Chanting God's Name

Everyone in this world is looking for peace, bliss, and liberation. These three things are not different; they are one and the same. The minds of ordinary people are full of restlessness, worry, and anxiety. Chanting God's name restrains sense impulses, cleanses the mind of impurities, strengthens the intellect, and energizes the body. Swami

Shivananda said: "The name of Ramakrishna is the mantra for this age. Those who take refuge in his name will attain peace. Chant his name with devotion. Tremendous power is hidden in his name."[27]

God has incarnated in every age, taking different names. In this age He has appeared as Ramakrishna. Swami Basudevananda wrote: "There is wonderful glory in his name. This name offers assurance in bad times, joy in good times, medicine for disease, light in darkness. After death, this name leads a person to the realm of immortality. This name establishes peace during conflict and makes the mind one-pointed in meditation."[28]

The primary result of chanting God's name is to see God or to attain liberation; the secondary result is physical and mental peace. Ramakrishna said: "If a man repeats the name of God, his body, mind, and everything become pure."[29] "The name of God has very great sanctity. It may not produce an immediate result, but one day it must bear fruit."[30]

Again the Master said: "All the sins of the body fly away if one chants the name of God and sings His glories. The birds of sin dwell in the tree of the body. Singing the name of God is like clapping your hands. As, with just one clap of the hands, the birds in the tree fly away, so do our sins disappear at the chanting of God's name and glories."[31]

It is said that King Dasharatha went out to hunt and accidentally killed a brahmin. To expiate this great sin, he went to his guru, the sage Vashishtha, but he was not at home. The sage's son advised Dasharatha to repeat the name of Rama three times, and later informed his father. Vashishtha was angry at his son and said: "You will be born as a chandala [an untouchable]. If a man repeats Rama's name once, he becomes free from all sins of the world. You underestimated the glory of that name by advising Dasharatha to repeat it thrice."

Sometimes the Master humorously glorified God's name. On 1 January 1883, a devotee brought a basket of *jilipi* (a type of sweet) for the Master. Eating a bit, he said to the devotee with a smile: "You see, I chant the name of the Divine Mother, so I get all these good things to eat." All laughed. He continued: "But She doesn't give such fruits as gourds or pumpkins. She bestows the fruit of Amrita, Immortality — knowledge, love, discrimination, renunciation, and so forth."[32]

On 21 September 1884, the Master went to see *Chaitanya Lila* at the Star Theatre. M. describes the event:

> Girish Chandra Ghosh, the manager of the theatre, accompanied by several officials, came out to the carriage, greeted the Master, and took him and the party upstairs. The Master was conducted to one of the

boxes and M. sat next to him.

The hall was brilliantly lighted. The Master looked down at the pit and saw that it was crowded. The boxes also were full. For every box there was a man to fan those who occupied it. Sri Ramakrishna was filled with joy and said to M., with his childlike smile: "Ah, it is very nice here! I am glad to have come. I feel inspired when I see so many people together. Then I clearly perceive that God Himself has become everything."

M.: "It is true, sir."

Master: "How much will they charge us here?"

M.: "They won't take anything. They are very happy that you have come to the theatre."

Master: "It is all due to the grace of the Divine Mother."[33]

In this present age Ramakrishna demonstrated the result of chanting God's name. He did not touch money; he saved nothing; he built no home; but he joyfully spent his life chanting the Mother's name. Regarding the glory of the Master's name, the Holy Mother said: "The Master told me, 'Those who take my name, will not suffer.' 'Those who think of me, will never want for food.' 'For those who call on me, I shall be present at their last moment.'"[34] The Holy Mother said: "One will have to bear the result of one's action. But if you chant God's name, you will get the prick of a needle instead of a plough-deep cut. Japa and austerities eradicate a lot of bad karma."[35]

"Who are You?"

It is extremely difficult to recognize the person called Ramakrishna. Vivekananda, Girish, and many great scholars were puzzled by him. One day Girish asked the Master, "Sir, who are you?" Ramakrishna replied: "Some say I am Ramprasad; some say I am Raja Ramakrishna. I just live here."[36] Yogin-ma's grandmother read an article on Ramakrishna in Keshab Sen's magazine and came to Dakshineswar. Ramakrishna did not care for fancy clothing, and he did not wear an ochre cloth. He had no rosary nor any external marks on his body. The old grandmother asked the Master: "Hello, could you tell me where the Paramahamsa is?" The Master answered: "Who knows? Some call him 'Paramahamsa'; some call him 'young priest,' and others 'Gadadhar Chattopadhyay,' or 'crazy brahmin.' Ask someone else about him."[37]

Ramakrishna hid himself. He had no desire to make himself known to the general public. Sometimes he indirectly or directly revealed his real nature to devotees:

Master: "Well, do you find me to be like anybody else?"

M.: "No, sir. You can't be compared to anybody else."

Master: "Have you heard of a tree called the 'achina' [literally, unrecognizable]?"

M.: "No, sir."

Master: "There is a tree called by that name. But nobody knows what it is."[38]

Master: "Alas! To whom shall I say all this? Who will understand me? . . . God becomes man, an avatar, and comes to earth with His devotees. And the devotees leave the world with Him."

Rakhal: "Therefore we pray that you may not go away and leave us behind."

Master: "A band of minstrels suddenly appears, dances, and sings, and it departs in the same sudden manner. They come and they return, but none recognizes them."[39]

Master (to M.): "The other day when Harish was with me, I saw Satchidananda come out of this sheath [his own body]. It said, 'I incarnate Myself in every age.'"[40]

"It is the Divine Mother Herself who dwells in this body and plays with the devotees."[41]

The disciples never hesitated to test the Master. Each time they did so, the Master would pass the test effortlessly. With a smile, he would tell them playfully: "Still you doubt! Have firm faith and strong conviction. He who in the past was born as Rama and Krishna is now living in this very body (pointing to himself). But this time his advent is very secret, like a king who visits his own kingdom incognito! As soon as people recognize him and whisper, he immediately departs from that place. It is just like that."[42]

The Master revealed his identity at other times as well: "Wherever there is any trouble in the Divine Mother's empire, I shall have to rush there to stop it, like a government officer."[43] "One who is living his last birth will come here. A person who has sincerely called on God, even once, will definitely come here."[44]

"Look, before you begin meditating, think of this (pointing to himself) for a while. Do you know why I say this? Because you have faith in this place (me). If you think of this place, that will remind you of God."[45]

"Look, your Chosen Deity is in this place (pointing to his body). If you think of me, that will bring recollectedness of your Chosen Deity."[46]

"Just Mention My Name"

Ramakrishna seldom used the words "I" and "mine." In The Gospel of

Sri Ramakrishna and *Sri Ramakrishna and His Divine Play*, we find that he used the words "this," "in this," "here," and "in this place" to indicate himself. "I" and "mine" are the warp and woof of maya. This net of maya could not catch Ramakrishna; he had full control over it. While explaining the word *bhavamukha*, Swami Saradananda tried to unveil the mystery of Ramakrishna's "I." Saradananda described four stages of the ego:

1. When the Master was absorbed in nirvikalpa samadhi, his "I" or ego was dissolved in Nirguna Brahman.
2. When the Master came down one step from that exalted state, his feeling "I am a part of God" would gradually disappear and the Cosmic I or the Divine Mother's "I" would become manifest through him, and he would act as a guru. At that time the Master would not appear to be humbler than the humblest: His demeanour, and his behaviour with others and other actions took a different form. Becoming like the mythical wish-fulfilling tree, he would ask a devotee, "What do you want?" as if he were ready to use his superhuman power to fulfill the devotee's desire immediately.
3. After coming one step down from that state, the Master would say, "I am a child of the Mother," "I am a devotee," "I am a servant." Thus he would become humbler than the humblest and teach people by becoming an instrument of the Divine Mother. He used to call this "ripe I," the last stage of the "knowledge I."
4. The lowest state is the "unripe I," or "ignorant I." The Master gave examples of this ego: "I am a brahmin, I am a son of such and such, I am a pandit, I am rich," and so on. This "I" is the cause of bondage. Swami Saradananda wrote, "After the Master attained nirvikalpa samadhi, the Master's little, or unripe, 'I' completely disappeared."[47]

Ramakrishna said to Swami Turiyananda: "Nothing can be achieved — neither knowledge, nor devotion, nor vision — without God's grace." Then he sang a song in which Hanuman tells the sons of Rama:

"O Kusa and Lava, why are you so proud?
If I had not let myself be captured,
Could you have captured me?"[48]

One day Ramakrishna compassionately asked M.: "What do you think of me? How many annas of knowledge of God have I?" M. replied: "I don't understand what you mean by 'annas.' But of this I am sure: I have never before seen such knowledge, ecstatic love, faith in God, renunciation, and catholicity anywhere." The Master laughed. Then the

Master asked M. to visit him at Balaram Basu's house in Calcutta. M. bowed down and took his leave. When he returned, he found the Master pacing in the natmandir. Seeing him again, the Master asked the cause for his return. M. said: "Perhaps the house you asked me to go to belongs to a rich man. They may not let me in. I think I had better not go. I would rather meet you here." Master: "Oh, no! Why should you think that? Just mention my name. Say that you want to see me; then someone will take you to me."[49]

"Just mention my name — then someone will take you to me," is a significant, hopeful statement. He is telling not only M. but all lost and confused people of the world how to reach him. Doors will open in all directions for anyone who repeats his name — whether it is a wealthy man's mansion, or a poor man's cottage, or the labyrinth of the world. As a prince has free access to any room in the palace and gatekeepers open the door for him with a salute, so Mahamaya opens the door of liberation for the disciples and devotees of an avatar. The avatar is the ruler of maya.

On another occasion the Master said to M.: "The devotees who come here may be divided into two groups. One group says, 'O God, give me liberation.' Another group, belonging to the inner circle, doesn't talk that way. They are satisfied if they can know two things: first, who I am; second, who they are and what their relationship to me is. You belong to this second group."[50] If people can establish a relationship with an avatar, their lives will be successful and they will be able to overcome worldly suffering and the fear of death. "I am a devotee of Rama" — this faith and strong relationship empowered Mahavir Hanuman to win every battle and make the impossible possible.

On 1 January 1886 Ramakrishna became the Kalpataru [wish-fulfilling tree] and blessed his devotees, saying, "Be illumined." Navagopal Ghosh was not there at that time. When he came to Cossipore later, Ram Chandra Datta told him: "Hello, sir, what are you doing? The Master has become a Kalpataru today. Please go to him right now. If you have anything to ask for, this is the right time." Navagopal rushed to the Master and, bowing down to him, asked, "Master, what will happen to me?"

After a little pause, the Master asked, "Will you be able to practise a little japa and meditation?"

Navagopal replied: "I am a family man with several children. Moreover, I am very busy with my various household duties and taking care of my family members. Where is the time to practise spiritual disciplines?"

The Master kept quiet for a while and then said, "Can't you even repeat the Lord's name a few times regularly?"

"I don't have time, Master."

"All right! Will you be able to repeat my name a few times?" "Yes, that I can do."

Then the Master said: "That will do. You will not have to do anything else."[51]

The compassionate Master showed his devotees the easiest way to attain God. In the twelfth chapter of the Gita, Krishna told Arjuna about various methods of keeping the mind on God. He said: "Fix your mind on Me. If you are unable to do that, then seek to reach Me by the yoga of constant practice. If you are unable to do that, then devote yourself to My service. If you are unable to do even this, then be self-controlled, surrender the fruit of all action, and take refuge in Me." Similarly, Rama-krishna would advise some devotees: "Repeat the mantra for three days in the shrine of Mother Kali. If you cannot do that for three days, please do so for a day." He said to others: "If you cannot practise japa and medi-tation, think of me." "You will not have to do any spiritual disciplines; you visit me often. As you have come today, please come another couple of days." "Come on either Tuesday or Saturday; that will be enough." Sometimes the Master would say: "After coming here, those who pray with a simple heart, 'O Lord, how can I know You?' will definitely expe-rience Him."[52] Sometimes he would write something on a devotee's tongue, or say: "It will be enough to think of or meditate on me."[53]

Ramakrishna's Name is Spreading

It is said that there is always a shadow under the lamp, but its light shines all around. M. once went to Kamarpukur. When an old brahmin pandit of the village heard that M. was a school headmaster, he said: "Oh, you are a devotee of Gadai? Being a learned man, why did you become his devotee? He has not read any scriptures. He is illiterate." M. told him a few of the Master's teachings: "A mere pandit, without discrimination and renunciation, has his attention fixed on 'lust and gold.' The vulture soars very high but its eyes are fixed on the charnel-pit."[54] "It is true that many things are recorded in the scriptures; but all these are useless without the direct realization of God. The almanac forecasts the rainfall of the year. But not a drop of water will you get by squeezing the almanac."[55] Later, that pandit understood his mistake.[56]

People around a great soul do not understand his value, whereas people from afar become attracted to the great one. Akshay Sen wrote:

"One summer day some devotees were seated with the Master in the Panchavati. They were talking about God. In the course of conversation, someone referred to the people from Dakshineswar, Ariadaha, and Baranagore. Out of curiosity, he asked the Master: "People from distant places are coming to you and gaining peace. Why don't people from these nearby places come to you?" Without giving any direct reply, the Master pointed to a cow tied with a tether on the bank of the Ganges. She was obviously very thirsty but could not drink the sweet water nearby. In the meantime, some stray cows came from outside the temple garden and began to drink the Ganges water. Then the Master explained: "Look, this cow is tied with a rope; she is near the water but cannot drink it. On the other hand, those stray cows are free and they drink the water as soon as they are thirsty. People near the temple garden are bound, so they do not come here."[57]

Sound carries over a distance. The messages that were delivered by Ramakrishna in the temple garden of Dakshineswar are now crossing the oceans to spread all over the world. It is true: "The name does not make a man famous; it is the man who makes his name famous." Some time ago I read a book entitled *Thomas Merton, Monk*. Thomas Merton was a well-known writer and a Trappist monk, who died in 1968. This book is a compilation of reminiscences of Thomas Merton by some Catholic monks and nuns. One day there was a discussion about divine love among the monks:

Thomas Merton: "If you love another person, it's God's love being realized. One and the same love is reaching your friend through you, and you through your friend."

David: "But isn't there still an implicit dualism in all this?"

Thomas Merton: "Really there isn't, and yet there is. You have to see your will and God's will dualistically for a long time. You have to experience duality for a long time until you see it's not there. In this respect I am a Hindu. Ramakrishna has the solution."[58]

A few years ago in Kansas City I went with some American devotees to a Japanese restaurant. Seeing me, a waitress asked me, "Are you from India?" "Yes," I replied. That young Japanese woman joyfully exclaimed: "I know Ramakrishna." Amazed, I asked, "How do you know Ramakrishna?" She said that she had been a member of the Costa Mesa Yoga Centre in Southern California, where she had read about Ramakrishna. Still the voice of that young woman with her Japanese accent is ringing in my ears: "I know Ramakrishna."

3

How to Understand Ramakrishna

The vast ocean has a fixed depth and is bound by its shores. However extensive the earth may seem, it is nonetheless limited, a body in space. Even the seemingly limitless universe has boundaries. Only God is fathomless, limitless, boundless, infinite, indivisible, and formless — One without a second. Human beings cannot use their finite minds to understand the infinite God. In enigmatic language, the Kena Upanishad (1:3) hints at this: "He by whom Brahman is not known, knows It; he by whom It is known, knows It not. It is not known by those who know It; It is known by those who do not know It."

Ramakrishna told Pandit Ishwar Chandra Vidyasagar: "What Brahman is cannot be described. All things in the world — the Vedas, the Puranas, the Tantras, the six systems of philosophy — have been defiled, like food that has been touched by the tongue, for they have been read or uttered by the tongue. Only one thing has not been defiled in this way, and that is Brahman. No one has ever been able to say what Brahman is. . . . Men often think they have understood Brahman fully. Once an ant went to a hill of sugar. One grain filled its stomach. Taking another grain in its mouth it started homeward. On its way it thought, 'Next time I shall carry home the whole hill.' That is the way shallow minds think. They don't know that Brahman is beyond one's words and thoughts."[1]

Nevertheless, this Brahman, who is beyond mind and speech, is the real nature of human beings. And the goal of human life is to realize this true nature. Brahman, who is devoid of form and qualities, manifests as an avatar with form and qualities so that human beings can think of or meditate on Him. When the mind becomes pure and free from ignorance, the human being returns to his or her true abode, which is Brahman.

It is extremely difficult to recognize the avatar, or God in human form. He eats, sleeps, and performs all actions like an ordinary person, yet He is different, extraordinary, and unique. One day, Ramakrishna asked M.: "Well, do you find me to be like anybody else?"

M.: "No, sir."

Master: "Like any other paramahamsa?"

M.: "No, sir. You can't be compared to anybody else."

Master: "Have you heard of a tree called the 'achina' [literally, unrecognizable]?"

M.: "No, sir."

Master: "There is a tree called by that name. But nobody knows what it is."

M.: "Likewise it is not possible to recognize you. The more a man understands you, the more uplifted he will be."[2]

Ramakrishna Knew Who He Was

Ramakrishna knew that his nature was divine. He cloaked himself in his yogamaya to enact his divine play so that he could appear as a normal human being. Sometimes he disclosed his identity to his close devotees. Once he said: "There is no outsider here. The other day, when Harish was with me, I saw Satchidananda come out of this sheath. It said, 'I incarnate Myself in every age.' . . . I saw that it is the fullest manifestation of Satchidananda; but this time the Divine Power is manifested through the glory of sattva."[3]

When Ramakrishna's mother was dying at Dakshineswar, her body was carried to the bakul-tala ghat on the Ganges. The Master cried as he held his mother's feet, and exclaimed: "Mother, how fortunate you are that you carried me in your womb!" As a grief-stricken man, the Master mourned for his mother; but as a divine being, he told her that she was not an ordinary woman: she had carried Narayana, the Supreme Brahman, in her womb.

Two important words appear in the Vedanta scriptures: *sva-samvedya* and *para-samvedya*. Sva-samvedya indicates that a jnani, a knower of Brahman, knows his or her own true nature. Para-samvedya indicates that people evaluate the state of a jnani by looking for certain signs described in the scriptures. The Master sometimes became one with Brahman in nirvikalpa samadhi, but when he descended to the dualistic plane, he perceived the world as we do. He told his devotees: "There are two persons in this [his body]: One is the Divine Mother. And the other is Her devotee. It is the devotee who broke his arm, and it is the devotee who is now ill. . . . Do you understand? Alas! To whom shall I say all this? Who will understand me?"[4]

The Master would point to himself and say: "It is like an image of Shiva that has not been set up by human hands but is a natural one that has sprung up, as it were, from the bowels of the earth."[5] The Master would cry from the heart for the welfare of suffering humanity. On 15 March 1886 he said to M.: "If the body were to be preserved a few days more, many people would have their spirituality awakened. But this is not to be. Such is not the will of God. This time the body will not be preserved, lest, finding me guileless and foolish, people should take advantage of me, and lest I, guileless and foolish as I am, should give away everything to everybody. In this Kaliyuga, you see, people are averse to meditation and japa."[6]

The Master himself declared: "He who was Rama and he who was Krishna is now Ramakrishna in this body." This is a clear statement that needs no explanation. As the same moon rises again and again, so the same God descends to earth as an avatar at different times and at different places. After fulfilling the need of the age, the avatar returns to his or her own abode. Ramakrishna said: "Seeing an Incarnation of God is the same as seeing God Himself."[7] Jesus also said: "He that hath seen me, hath seen the Father. I and my Father are one."

Who Can Know God?

None can know God without His grace. The Katha Upanishad (1:2:23) says: "The Atman is attained by him alone whom It chooses." In this connection, Ramakrishna has given this example: "The police sergeant walks his rounds in the dark of night with a lantern in his hand. No one sees his face; but with the help of that light the sergeant sees everybody's face, and others, too, can see one another. If you want to see the sergeant, however, you must pray to him: 'Sir, please turn the light on your own face. Let me see you.' In the same way one must pray to God: 'O Lord, be gracious and turn the light of knowledge on Thyself, that I may see Thy face.'"[8]

One day, M. said: "Can we understand the avatar? Our intellects are very tiny and insignificant. Can ten litres of milk be put in a one-litre container? Even Arjuna, who was an aspirant of such a high calibre, could not understand Krishna. He exclaimed: 'All the sages have declared You to be the eternal, self-luminous Person, the first of the gods, unborn and all-pervading; likewise have the divine sages Narada, Asita, Devala, and Vyasa proclaimed. So, too, have You said unto me.'[9] If Arjuna speaks in this way, what can we say?

"No one can recognize the avatar if he does not want to be known. One can know him through his grace, otherwise not. The avatar is a mysterious phenomenon. How can a man with limitations — a conditioned being — comprehend the avatar?"[10]

The Vedanta scriptures say: *Tasya bhāsā sarvamidam vibhāti* (all are lighted by the light of the Atman). All beings in the world are conscious because the Atman is conscious. When the light of the Atman falls on the intellect, that reflected light is called *chidābhāsa*. As children hold mirrors and focus the reflected light of the sun onto various objects, so people acquire knowledge by using their intellects to focus the light of the Atman onto different objects. When people focus that reflected consciousness on God, they attain the knowledge of God. The intellects of ordinary people are covered by ignorance. If one yearns to know God, God is merciful and draws one's intellect towards Him.

Ramakrishna knew that M. would record his message. For that reason, the Master trained M. so that he could comprehend his message, and he sometimes evaluated M.'s power of understanding. First, the Master crushed M.'s ego (as M. recorded in the *Gospel*) because an egotistic person cannot understand God. The ego is like a thick wall that acts as a barrier to God-realization. The Master compassionately revealed his true nature to M. and made him his very own.

Master: "The jnanis think of God without form. They don't accept the Divine Incarnation. But I accept God with form when I am in the company of people who believe in that ideal, and I also agree with those who believe in the formless God."

M. (*smiling*): "You are as infinite as He of Whom we have been talking. Truly, no one can fathom your depth."

Master (*smiling*): "Ah! I see you have found it out. Let me tell you one thing. One should follow various paths. One should practise each creed for a time. I had to practise each religion for a time — Hinduism, Islam, Christianity. Furthermore, I followed the paths of the Saktas, Vaishnavas, and Vedantists. I realized that there is only one God towards whom all are travelling; but the paths are different."[11]

Master: "Do you ever dream of me?"

M.: "Yes, sir. Many times."

Master: "How? Did you dream of me as giving you instruction?"

M. remained silent.

Master: "If you ever see me instructing you, then know that it is Satchidananda Himself that does so."[12]

Master: "Brahman is beyond mind and speech. A salt doll entered the ocean to measure its depth; but it did not return to tell others how deep the ocean was. It melted in the ocean itself. It is God alone who incarnates Himself as man to teach people the ways of love and knowledge. Well, what do you think of me?

"Once my father went to Gaya. There Raghuvir said to him in a dream 'I shall be born as your son.' Thereupon my father said to him: 'O Lord, I am a poor brahmin. How shall I be able to serve You?' 'Don't worry about it,' Raghuvir replied. 'It will be taken care of.'

"Once Mathur said to me: 'Father, there is nothing inside you but God. Your body is like an empty shell. Once I saw you as someone moving with a veil on.'"[13]

Ramakrishna Cannot Be Known without Practising Austerities

One cannot enter the spiritual realm without practising spiritual disciplines, austerities, and renunciation. The scriptures say: *Devo bhutva devam yajet* (first be a god and then worship God). In other words, one must develop a divine nature in order to understand God. During the Vedic period, students would carry sacrificial wood to their teachers and inquire about Brahman. Varuna told his son Bhrigu: "Seek to know Brahman by means of austerities. For austerities are [the means of knowing] Brahman" (Taittiriya Upanishad 3:1:2). Pippalada said to his disciples: "Stay with me a year more, practising austerities, chastity, and faith. Then you may ask questions according to your desire" (Prashna Upanishad 1:2). In the Chandogya Upanishad, we find that Indra and Virochana went to Prajapati, practised brahmacharya for thirty-two years, and then inquired about the Atman. Even after thirty-two years of spiritual disciplines, Virochana still believed that the body is the Atman. It took 101 years for Indra to realize the nature of the Atman.

A pure mind is indispensable in spiritual life. One can purify the mind by performing unselfish actions, studying the scriptures, practising austerities, prayer, and meditation. These actions reduce worldly propensities and increase one's power of comprehension. M. used to say: "One cannot know God by reading books or listening to lectures.

One can understand a little by practising austerities and sadhana. Without having holy company, one cannot grasp the idea of Reality or God. Meditate on the life and message of Ramakrishna. Then one will be able to have some glimpses of the truth."[14]

To mark the centenary of Ramakrishna's birth it was decided that a commemorative volume would be published. A monk went to M. and asked for his suggestions. M. said: "The life-force of religion is austerity. The Master was the embodiment of that austerity. If you can travel all over India and collect the spiritual experiences of aspirants who have renounced everything for God, that will be an excellent and memorable volume as a tribute to the Master."[15]

The avatar makes it possible for human beings to comprehend the infinite God. The avatar is God in human form. The Bhagavata says: *Dehasto'api adehasthah* (although He lives in a body, actually He is bodiless). In other words, He is devoid of body-consciousness. It is truly a wonder that the infinite God can be contained in a human being, three-and-a-half cubits high. It is hard to believe that a huge banyan tree dwells in a tiny seed. One day the Master used an analogy to explain this mystery to M.:

M.: "You explained clearly, the other day, how God incarnates Himself on earth."

Master: "Tell me what I said."

M.: "You told us to imagine a field extending to the horizon and beyond. It extends without any obstruction; but we cannot see it on account of a wall in front of us. In that wall there is a round hole. Through the hole we see a part of that infinite field."

Master: "Tell me what that hole is."

M.: "You are that hole. Through you can be seen everything — that Infinite Meadow without any end."

Sri Ramakrishna was very much pleased. Patting M.'s back, he said: "I see you have understood that. That's fine!"[16]

Human beings can understand these subtle things by practising austerities, and with God's grace. Ramakrishna tried his utmost to hide himself in various ways. First, he was born into a very poor family, thinking that no one would be able to recognize him. Generally, people know the wealthy persons of society. Second, he avoided formal schooling: He thought that people would disregard him if he had no formal education. Learned people usually command love and respect from society. Third, he became a temple priest. He thought people would overlook him, saying: "He is an illiterate temple priest. He is expert in packing rice and plantain and knows nothing else." But all these means of hiding himself failed. One cannot suppress a blazing fire; its flames spread in all directions.

It was extremely difficult to grasp the self-effacing Master. Swami Saradananda wrote:

> When the small, selfish "I" is destroyed, the Cosmic I and its power as a guru appear in order to benefit humanity. Again, among illumined souls, some act in the role of gurus or rishis by God's will. To teach others, they demonstrate noble qualities: passion for truth, dispassion for untruth, good conduct, steadfastness, observance of rules, discrimination, scriptural knowledge, erudition, and so on, as circumstances dictate, like ordinary people. We have used the word *demonstrate* because, although these illumined souls are endowed with full knowledge of the absolute, nondual Brahman — in which there is no good and bad, virtue and vice, piety and sin, and the other objects and ideas that exist in the realm of maya — still they remain on the dualistic plane to show people the way to transcend the realm of maya. If ordinary gurus and rishis spend time benefiting humanity, what can we say of the avatars or the great teachers of the world? It is therefore difficult for ordinary people to comprehend what such great ones do and how they behave, especially in the case of Sri Ramakrishna, the avatar of this present age. The avatars' displays of splendour, vigour, and supernatural power are recorded in the scriptures, but these were so hidden in the Master that no one could discern a hint of them by seeing him superficially a few times. Only true spiritual seekers who received his grace and had a close relationship with him understood him.
>
> Ask yourself: What external quality of his could attract you to him? His learning? He was practically illiterate. How could you know that due to his prodigious memory he had complete mastery over the Vedas, Vedanta, and other scriptures after hearing them only once? Do you intend to understand him by measuring his intellect? He always said: "I am nobody. I don't know anything. My Mother knows everything." What counsel can you seek from such a person? If you insisted upon his guidance, he would respond: "Ask Mother. She will tell you." Could you then trust his words and act accordingly? You may think: "Ah, what advice he has given me! We have been hearing such things since we read children's books like *Kathamala* and *Bodhodaya*: God is omniscient, omnipotent, formless, and the embodiment of consciousness. If He wills, He can make us know and understand everything. But can we function according to this proposition?" Do you intend to evaluate the Master by means of wealth, name and fame? Good gracious! He had very little of those things. Yet he

would advise us to renounce all of them at the outset. Such was the case with every aspect of his life. The only way to comprehend him is to be drawn by his purity, his love of God, and his devotion. It is well and good if these attract you; otherwise, it will be impossible for you to understand or know him.[17]

Ramakrishna in the Eyes of His Relatives

As the saying goes: "There is always darkness below the oil lamp." Ramakrishna's friends and relatives who were always around him could not understand him. M. said:

The Master's relatives could not recognize his divinity. They would think of him as their brother or uncle, as family members do. The relatives of Jesus and Chaitanya could not understand them either. Sometimes the villagers of Kamarpukur would say to Ramlal: "We hear your uncle is very famous and he has many devotees. You now have a very nice time. You will be financially well off." Ramlal replied: "No, it is not like that. Everyone is busy in his own happiness. Our condition is the same as before." The villagers: "Why? So many rich people visit your uncle! Can he not ask them to donate some money to you?" Sometimes the villagers would say: "People of Calcutta are foolish! We have known Gadai from his childhood. Now they are making a fuss over him."

Seeing the Master always in samadhi, his mother said: "Look, Kesto, why do you become stiff like a log? Who will look after me if I die?" (His mother called him "Kesto" instead of Ramakrishna.) The Master replied: "Mother, I don't know what to do. You ask Ramlal and he will look after you." In other words, he was always absorbed in thoughts of the Divine Mother; he could not think of any worldly affairs.

One may live with an avatar, but one cannot necessarily know him if he does not want to be known. The temple authorities asked Hriday to leave the Dakshineswar temple. One day, later on, he came to see the Master. Standing outside the gate, he cried: "Uncle, take me back. I am deprived of your company and so I suffer." The Master replied: "Why, was it not you who said to me, 'You follow your ideal and let me follow mine?'" Hriday: "Yes, I did say that. But what did I know?" Tears also appeared in the Master's eyes. No one could recognize the Master if he did not want to be known. When Hriday lived with the Master, he did not know who the Master was. When he was separated from him, he realized the Master's greatness.[18]

Of all the Master's relatives, Hriday lived with him for the longest period (from 1855 to 1881). During the Master's sadhana, Hriday served and protected him. Hriday gave Swami Saradananda much information about the Master's life, which he recorded in *Sri Ramakrishna and His Divine Play*. Hriday was an eyewitness to the Master's divine and human aspects. He considered himself to be great after having imbibed the Master's greatness. He eventually became terribly egotistic. The Master said: "A man living on the plane of sattva cannot bear noise and uproar. That is why Hriday was sent away. It was the Divine Mother who sent him away. During the later part of his stay he went to extremes; he became very rough and abusive. . . . He tormented me as much as he served me. He said: 'You are a fool! If I weren't living with you, where would your profession of holiness be?' One day he tormented me so much that I stood on the embankment ready to give up my body by jumping into the Ganges, which was then at flood-tide. . . . Once, when Hriday tormented me, I thought of leaving this place and going to Benares."[19]

However, Hriday's mother did recognize the Master's divinity. The Master said: "My cousin, Hriday's mother, used to worship my feet with flowers and sandal paste. One day I placed my foot on her head and said to her, 'You will die in Benares.'"[20] This actually came to pass.

When the Master was in a divine mood, he transcended the rigid caste system and other social prejudices. But Rameswar, his next older brother, kept to the caste rules of their village. The Master said: "When I went to Kamarpukur, Ramlal's father was frightened. He thought I might eat at any and every house. He was frightened to think I might be expelled from the caste. I couldn't stay long. I came away."[21]

While the Master was in Kamarpukur, his mother, Chandramani, and Rameswar could not understand his divine state. They thought he was insane so they used various methods — performing rituals for peace, exorcising evil spirits by uttering charms and incantations, making sacrifices, fasting at the Shiva temple, and so on — to cure him. They thought that the Master was possessed by a ghost.

Haladhari, one of the Master's cousins, was a scholar and an orthodox brahmin, and was a priest at the Dakshineswar temple. He had a supernatural power, and whatever he said came to pass. Sometimes the Master would ask various questions of him. Once, on a full-moon night, the Master asked Haladhari, "Brother, is it the night of the new moon?" Later, the Master told his devotees: "Yes, it is true. Once I was told that a characteristic of a man of Perfect Knowledge is that he cannot distinguish between the full moon and the new moon. But how could one convince Haladhari of that? He said: 'This is certainly the dark Kaliyuga.

He cannot distinguish the full moon from the new moon! And people respect him!"[22]

Once the Master cautioned Haladhari because he was then practising some questionable esoteric sadhanas and people in the temple began spreading rumours about him. This enraged Haladhari, and he cursed the Master, saying that he would vomit blood. The curse took effect, but it became a boon for the Master. If he had not expelled the blood, he might well have died during jada samadhi.

The Master described what happened one day in Dakshineswar when he was in divine intoxication: "I touched my head and lips with the leaf-plates from which beggars had eaten their food in the guesthouse of the Kali temple. Thereupon Haladhari said to me: 'What have you done? You have taken the food left by beggars. How will you marry off your children?' These words aroused my anger. I said to him: 'You wretch! Isn't it you who takes pride in the study of the Gita and the Vedanta? Isn't it you who teaches people that Brahman alone is real and the world illusory? And yet you imagine that I shall beget children! May your mouth, which recites from the Gita, be blighted!'"[23]

Sometimes Haladhari was overwhelmed by seeing the Master's longing and divine intoxication, but his mind oscillated between reverence and doubt. Swami Saradananda recorded what the Master said about this:

Many times Haladhari would be charmed by my devout worship in the temple, and he'd say to me, "Ramakrishna, now I know what your real nature is!" So I'd tell him jokingly, "Then don't get confused anymore!" Then he'd say: "You can't deceive me again. The Lord is definitely within you. This time I'm quite certain." So I'd reply: "All right. Let me see how long your conviction lasts." Then after finishing the temple service, he would take some snuff and begin to give a discourse on the Bhagavata, the Gita, the Adhyatma Ramayana, and other scriptures. He would then become puffed up with egotism and become quite a different person. Sometimes I would attend his discourses and would say to him, "I've realized all those spiritual states you've been reading about; I can understand everything that's in the scriptures." Immediately he would say indignantly: "You idiot! You think you can understand the scriptures!" "Believe me," I'd say, "the One who is within this body of mine teaches me everything. A little while ago you said that there was a divine presence in me. He tells me everything." Then he'd become frantic with rage and tell me: "Get out of here, you crazy fool! Are you claiming to be an incarnation of God? The scriptures say there'll be only one avatar in this age, and that's

Kalki. You must be out of your mind to think such things!" So I would laugh and ask, "Didn't you tell me you'd never get confused about me again?" But of course he wouldn't listen to me when he was in that mood. We had the same scene over and over again. One day he saw me in an ecstatic mood sitting naked on a branch of the banyan tree in the Panchavati and passing water like a boy. From that day on he was thoroughly convinced that I had been possessed by a ghost.[24]

One day Haladhari remarked that Kali is the embodiment of tamas. This hurt the Master. He went to the Kali temple, and the Divine Mother reassured him by revealing Her true nature. The Master then went to the Krishna temple where Haladhari was worshipping the deity. The Master sat on his shoulders and said: "How dare you say that Mother is wrathful and full of tamas? She is everything. She is the embodiment of the three *gunas* and again She is pure love and goodness." The Master's words and divine touch illumined Haladhari's heart. As he sat there on the worshipper's seat he accepted the Master's words wholeheartedly. He saw the manifestation of the Divine Mother within the Master; filled with devotion, he offered flowers and sandal paste at his feet.[25]

Ramakrishna in the Eyes of the Temple Officials

According to the Gita, the avatar's "birth and actions are divine." Ramakrishna's divine birth and his actions were much misunderstood by ordinary people. At first, the owners of the Dakshineswar temple, Rani Rasmani and later Mathur Biswas, considered the Master to be a whimsical young man who was slightly mad. They thought this because his behaviour, demeanour, and speech were not like those of other people. The Master once slapped Rani Rasmani as she sat in the Kali temple; he knew that she was thinking about a lawsuit. The temple guards were ready to throw him out, but Rasmani stopped them. She realized that the Master was omniscient and that the punishment he had given her was justified. Nonetheless, Mathur took him to Ganga-prasad Sen, a well-known doctor of Calcutta, to determine whether the Master was insane. The doctor prescribed some medicines and ayurvedic oil. When the medications were ineffective, Mathur thought that the Master's unbroken chastity had affected his mind. He consulted with Hriday, and then sent a prostitute to the Master's room one evening.

Later, the Master told his devotees: "When I was passing through that exalted state, someone, in order to test me and also to cure my madness, brought a prostitute into my room. She was beautiful to look at, with pretty eyes. I cried, 'O Mother! O Mother!' and rushed out of the room. I ran to Haladhari and said to him, 'Brother, come and see who has entered my room!' I told Haladhari and everyone else about this woman."[26] Mathur did not stop there. On another occasion he tested the Master by taking him to Lakshmi Bai, a famous courtesan in Mechuabazar, Calcutta. The Master saw the Divine Mother in that woman and went into samadhi.

Mathur finally realized that the Master was God in human form when he saw both Shiva and Kali in him. Mathur had tested the Master by offering him his wealth and his estate, engaging beautiful courtesans, giving him power to rule over himself and the members of his family, and serving him as God; but the Master remained unperturbed. Mathur realized that the Master was above temptation and free from ego.

Some temple officials treated the Master poorly, but others respected him. The Master said: "I fed a cat with the food that was to be offered to the Divine Mother. I clearly perceived that the Divine Mother Herself had become everything — even the cat. The manager of the temple garden wrote to Mathur Babu saying that I was feeding the cat with the offering intended for the Divine Mother. But Mathur Babu had insight into the state of my mind. He wrote back to the manager: 'Let him do whatever he likes. You must not say anything to him.'"[27] On another occasion the manager used abusive language when referring to the Master's unconventional mode of worship. When the Master heard about this from others, he just smiled. It did not upset him at all.

The Master went to Calcutta to attend a service in a Christian church, but he stood outside on the street and watched the proceedings. He later said: "I didn't sit inside the church because I was afraid that the temple manager wouldn't allow me to enter the Kali temple anymore." When the Master entered the Shiva temple one day, he went into ecstasy and began to cry and to loudly chant a hymn to Shiva. The temple officials thought that the Master's insanity had gone too far, and they watched him closely. Mathur arrived on the scene. One of the officials seriously suggested that the Master be forcibly removed from the shrine because he was very close to the deity. "Touch him if you don't value your head!" cried Mathur furiously.

When they realized how devoted Mathur was to the Master, some temple officials became jealous. On one occasion, the manager asked the gatekeeper to prevent the Master from entering the Mother's temple. But the Master pushed the gatekeeper aside and performed the rituals as usual. The manager reported this to Mathur, but the latter sent orders that no one was to interfere with the Master's activities. The officials felt helpless and frustrated.

Ram Chandra Datta wrote: "One day the Master thought: 'People call me mad. But I see the Divine Mother and talk to Her. She also guides me. Is this false or a hallucination? Well, let me test it today.' He then went to take his bath in the Ganges. In the meantime, Ramdhan, one of Rasmani's favourite officers, went there. Ramdhan was so antagonistic to the Master that he would not even speak to him. When he saw Ramdhan, the Master mentally said to the Divine Mother, 'Mother, if You truly exist, make Ramdhan my friend. Only then shall I know that You are real and listen to my prayers.' As soon as this thought arose in the Master's mind, Ramdhan came to the Master and said gently, 'Sir, it is all right that you have the vision of Kali. But why do you have to go so far?' Saying so, Ramdhan left."[28]

Bholanath Mukhopadhyay was a clerk who became a temple manager after the death of Dinanath. He loved and respected the Master. Once there was litigation between the temple authorities and Jadu Mallick, whose garden house was next to the temple garden. Bholanath gave testimony against Jadu in this case and was very fearful because of this. He took refuge in the Master and asked him to consult with Adharlal Sen, a deputy magistrate and devotee of the Master. When the Master told everything to Adhar, he said: "It is not a serious case. There may be a little trouble but it will be fine." This alleviated the Master's worries.

The Master also sometimes consulted with Bholanath. One day the Master was anxious about Narendra, Rakhal, and other young devotees. Hazra remarked: "Why are you so worried about them? Please think of the Lord." Puzzled, the Master prayed to the Divine Mother, and then asked Bholanath about the situation. Bholanath said: "You will find the explanation in the Mahabharata. On coming down to the plane of ordinary consciousness, a man established in samadhi enjoys himself in the company of sattvic people. He feels peace of mind at the sight of such men."[29] When the Master heard this, his mind was set at ease.

When the Master was ill at the Cossipore garden house, he needed some rubbing oil. He told his devotees: "If some of you go to Dakshineswar and see Bholanath, he will give you a medicinal oil and will also tell you how to apply it."[30]

The Master had a childlike nature. M. wrote: "The Master had dinner at Keshab Sen's house. He then told us not to tell others that he had been there, or the temple officials wouldn't allow him to go inside the Kali temple. The next day he saw the manager nearby and told him: 'Look, yesterday I went to Keshab's house. He arranged a nice feast. I really don't know whether that food was touched by lower-caste people. Well, will it do any harm to me?' The manager smiled and replied: 'Sir, it does not matter. Nothing can pollute your mind.'"[31]

Swami Adbhutananda told this story: "One day a servant of the Kali temple smoked and left his hubble-bubble behind. Immediately, the Master took it and began to smoke. The brahmins of the temple saw him. They said that the young priest had lost his caste and that they wouldn't eat with him anymore. The Master remarked: 'How wonderful! I am relieved that I shall not have to eat with those rascals anymore.'"[32]

During the Master's time, there were various kinds of workers in the Kali temple: managers, clerks, brahmin cooks, servants, maidservants, gatekeepers, gardeners, sweepers, and so on. The Master mixed with everyone freely, listened to their stories of weal and woe, and gave them advice. A maidservant named Brinde used to clean the Master's room. On 26 February 1882, M. first visited the Master. He asked Brinde: "Is the holy man in?"

Brinde: "Yes, he's in the room."

M.: "How long has he lived here?"

Brinde: "Oh, he has been here a long time."

M.: "Does he read many books?"

Brinde: "Books? Oh, dear no! They're all on his tongue."

M.: "Perhaps it is time for his evening worship. May we go into the room? Will you tell him we are anxious to see him?"

Brinde: "Go right in, children. Go in and sit down."[33]

This illiterate woman understood a little of the Master's greatness.

The Master saw the Divine Mother in all women. He said: "All the women you see are only She, the Divine Mother. That is why I cannot rebuke even Brinde, the maidservant."[34] The Master would save some luchi and sweets from the night's prasad for Brinde's breakfast. If there were too many Calcutta devotees, however, he gave the prasad to them instead. When this happened, Brinde would become very upset that there was no prasad left for her. The Holy Mother said: "The Master was very fearful lest the Calcutta devotees come to know about it. Early one morning he came to me in the nahabat and said: 'Hello, I used the prasad meant for Brinde. Please make some chapati or luchi for her; otherwise she will quarrel with me. One should always avoid troublesome people.'"[35]

In *The Gospel of Sri Ramakrishna*, M. recorded a touching incident concerning a maidservant who knew that the Master was a saviour of the fallen:

Bhagavati, an old maidservant of the temple proprietor, entered the room and saluted the Master from a distance. Sri Ramakrishna bade her sit down. The Master had known her for many years. In her younger days she had lived a rather immoral life; but the Master's compassion was great. Soon he began to converse with her.
Master: "Now you are pretty old. Have you been feeding the Vaishnavas and holy men, and thus spending your money in a noble way?"
Bhagavati (*smiling*): "How can I say that?"
Master: "Have you been to Vrindaban, Benares, and the other holy places?"
Bhagavati: "How can I say that? I have built a bathing-place, and my name is inscribed there on a slab."
Master: "Indeed!"
Bhagavati: "Yes, sir. My name, 'Srimati Bhagavati Dasi,' is written there."
Master (*with a smile*): "How nice!"
Emboldened by the Master's words, Bhagavati approached and saluted him, touching his feet. Like a man stung by a scorpion, Sri Ramakrishna stood up and cried out, "Govinda! Govinda!" A big jar of Ganges water stood in a corner of the room. He hurried there, panting, and washed with the holy water the spot the maidservant had touched. The devotees in the room were amazed to see this incident. Bhagavati sat as if struck dead.
Sri Ramakrishna consoled her and said in a very kindly tone, "You should salute me from a distance." In order to relieve her mind of all embarrassment, the Master said tenderly, "Listen to a few songs."[36]

Bhartabhari was a gardener in the temple garden. He was very devoted to the Master and helped him put a fence around the tulsi grove. The Master said: "In those days whatever desire arose in my mind would come to pass. I planted a tulsi-grove in the Panchavati in order to practise japa and meditation. I wanted very much to fence it around with bamboo sticks. Soon afterwards a bundle of bamboo sticks and some string were carried by the flood-tide of the Ganges right in front of the Panchavati. A temple gardener [Bhartabhari] noticed them and joyfully told me."[37]
Swami Vishuddhananda talked about an elderly gardener of Dakshineswar whom he met in the early 1900s. [We don't know if this

man was Bhartabhari.] This illiterate gardener recognized the Master's divinity. One night he saw the Master meditating under the bel tree; a light was emanating from his body. The gardener was so frightened that he could not stay there long. The next morning he fell at the Master's feet in tears, and said, "Master, please bless me." The Master saw what was in his mind. He lifted the gardener up and said: "Meditate on the form that you saw last night. Clean this path that leads to the Panchavati. Many devotees will come here in the future."[38]

Only one who is simple can understand another simple person. Rasik, one of the sweepers at the temple garden, was extremely guileless; but he understood the Master's greatness and took refuge in him. At the time of his death, Ramakrishna appeared before him. (See the chapter entitled "The Story of Rasik.")

Some gatekeepers and night guards were also devoted to the Master. Sometimes the Master would go to Calcutta and return late at night. The gatekeeper on duty would wait for him near the gate. The Master would take him to his room and feed him luchi and sweets that had been kept for his supper. Sometimes if he could not sleep at night, he would go to the gatekeepers and ask, "Hello, could you chant Rama's name for a little while?"

There was a guard named Hanuman Singh. The Master was very fond of him because he was not only a wrestler but also a steadfast devotee of Mahavir Hanuman. Another wrestler came and wanted to take over Singh's job by defeating him at wrestling. Singh began to eat one meal a day and to practise japa and meditation. On the day of the competition, Hanuman Singh bowed down to the Master and asked his blessing, saying, "Master, if you bestow your grace on me, I'll definitely win."[39] He won the match.

God is attained by devotion. M. wrote: "When the Master visited Jadu Mallick's garden house, the caretaker would fan the Master. The Master was very pleased with his loving service and sometimes went into samadhi. That caretaker invited the Master to dine with him. The Master accepted his invitation and asked me to go with him. If some wealthy man had invited the Master to dine, he might not have accepted."[40]

It is impossible for an egotistic person to understand the Master. M. wrote: "Rani Rasmani and Mathur recognized the Master's divinity. But Trailokya, Mathur's son, and others could not understand him. Once at the Dakshineswar kuthi [mansion], Trailokya arranged a party and some women singers were also invited. He invited the Master and requested him to sing a song. The Master said: 'I have come here to listen to their songs. It is not necessary for me to sing at this party.' However, the Master sang and those women sang also. When the Master was about to leave, they offered him some refreshments but he refused. Trailokya, however, sent some food to the Master's room through a servant."[41]

Ramakrishna in the Eyes of His Gurus and the Pandits

The Bhairavi Brahmani, the Tantric nun who was one of the Master's teachers, was an aspirant of a high calibre. She learned about the Master through the grace of the Divine Mother. The Master used to address her as "Mother," and told her about his divine visions, loss of outer consciousness, sleeplessness, burning sensation, and other physical changes that had happened to him.

He asked repeatedly: "Mother, what are these things that keep happening to me? Am I mad, really? Have I developed a terrible disease by wholeheartedly calling on the Divine Mother?" While listening to the Master, the Bhairavi became excited and elated. Like a compassionate mother, she repeatedly reassured him, saying: "Who calls you mad, my son? This is not insanity. You have achieved *mahabhava*; that is why you are having all these experiences. How can ordinary people understand your condition? They cannot — so they call you mad. Sri Radha experienced this state and so did Sri Chaitanya. All this is recorded in the bhakti scriptures. I have all these books with me. I will read them to you and prove that whoever has sincerely yearned for God has experienced these states, and everyone doing so must pass through them."[42]

Vaishnavcharan was a great scholar and Vaishnava spiritual leader. He had developed a subtle insight from sadhana and at first glance recognized the Master as a great soul. Vaishnavcharan listened to the Brahmani's opinion and heartily approved of what she said about the Master's condition. Not only that, but Vaishnavcharan remarked with amazement that according to the devotional scriptures, mahabhava consists of nineteen main spiritual moods, which so far had been manifested only in Radha and Chaitanya. Now all those signs were visible in the Master.

Pandit Gauri was a Tantric scholar and aspirant. He also was invited to Dakshineswar to evaluate the Master's condition. The Master asked Gauri a question to test his understanding: "Well, Vaishnavcharan calls this (*pointing to himself*) an avatar. How can it be? Tell me what you think about it."

Gauri gravely replied: "Does Vaishnavcharan call you an avatar? I consider that an understatement! I believe you are He, by a fraction of

Whose power, the avatars come forth to this world in every age and accomplish their mission."

The Master smiled and said: "Ah — so you outbid him! What do you find in me that leads you to entertain this idea?"

Gauri replied: "I am saying this based on my deep personal experience and the testimony of the scriptures. I am ready to prove my contention to anyone who challenges me in the matter."[43]

Tota Puri was an illumined soul who had attained nirvikalpa samadhi after practising sadhana for forty years. He considered the Master to be a devotee of Mother Kali, but nonetheless initiated him into sannyasa. When the Master attained samadhi quite soon after initiation, Tota was amazed. He exclaimed: "Ah! What a display of divine maya! This is real samadhi — nirvikalpa samadhi — the ultimate result of the path of knowledge according to Vedanta. He has achieved it in three days! How miraculous is God's power!"[44]

Bhagavandas Babaji of Kalna criticized the Master because he stood in ecstasy on the seat of Chaitanya in Colootola, Calcutta. Later the Master went to Kalna and met the Babaji. Swami Saradananda wrote: "Babaji was moved by seeing Sri Ramakrishna's repeated ecstasy and overflowing bliss during their discussion; furthermore, he saw in Sri Ramakrishna the vivid manifestation of mahabhava that he had been struggling to understand for a long time by studying the scriptures. So he felt a deep love and respect for Sri Ramakrishna. When he heard that this was the Paramahamsa of Dakshineswar who out of ecstasy had occupied Sri Chaitanya's seat at the Harisabha congregation in Colootola, there was no limit to his sorrow and repentance for the bitter reproaches he had levelled against the Master. Humbly, he bowed down to Sri Ramakrishna and begged for his forgiveness."[45]

Ramakrishna told Pandit Shashadhar Tarkachudamani, the great Hindu evangelist, that one cannot teach people until one receives a command from God. Shashadhar was overwhelmed by the Master's renunciation, purity, longing, and ecstasy. He went to Balaram's house and prayed to the Master with folded hands and tearful eyes: "Sir, philosophy has dried up my heart. Please bestow upon me a drop of devotion." The Master went into ecstasy and touched the pandit's heart on that day.[46]

Pandit Padmalochan was a great Vedanta scholar and court pandit of the Maharaja of Burdwan. The Master met him a few times. Padmalochan was deeply spiritual and recognized the Master's exalted state. He considered the Master to be an incarnation of God and offered his devotion accordingly. The Master said: "Padmalochan was such a great pandit, but he still had so much faith in and devotion for me! He said: 'As soon as I recover [he was ill], I shall have all the pandits summoned to a meeting where I shall declare you to be an avatar. I'll see who can refute my pronouncement.'"[47] But soon after, Padmalochan moved to Varanasi, where he passed away before he could arrange such a meeting.

The Master evaluated the understanding of people he met by asking questions. He paid no heed to pandits who lacked renunciation and purity. He considered them mean-minded if they were attached to sex and money, or hankered after name and fame.

As a blazing fire cannot be suppressed, so at that time the Master's greatness spread all over. Many distinguished pandits and people came to evaluate the Master. Some egotistic pandits tried to argue with him by quoting the scriptures. When this happened, the Master would leave the room, saying, "I am going to the bathroom." The egotistic pandits apparently thought that the Master had been defeated; thus the Master, as a Kalpataru, fulfilled their desire for victory. Shortly afterwards, the Master would return in an ecstatic mood. He would touch the debaters and ask, "Hello, what do you say?" The Master's magic touch would overwhelm such pandits; their condition would become like that of a charmed snake with its hood down. Some of them would then humbly pray to the Master and ask for spiritual help.[48]

Once when a famous pandit from Uttarpara came to visit the Master at Dakshineswar he saw that the Master was seated on his bed while some of his devotees sat on the floor. The pandit sarcastically asked the Master: "Are you a paramahamsa? Very good! Wonderful! I see you have a nice bolster and mosquito curtain." The Master pointed out to the pandit his fine shoes and the other fancy things in his room. The pandit then sat on the Master's bed and exclaimed: "What a paramahamsa I have seen today!" He then quoted a passage from the scriptures and said to the visitors: "You are all simple folk. You have come from Calcutta to see this paramahamsa! In fact, you are all deceived. He is not a real paramahamsa." He then described the signs of a paramahamsa by explaining that Sanskrit verse. It was evening. The pandit left the room and went to practise his sadhana on the bank of the Ganges. He closed his eyes and began to meditate on his Chosen Deity. All of a sudden, he got up and ran back to the Master's room. He saw that the Master was in samadhi. With folded hands, the pandit stood in front of him, addressed him as God, and began to recite hymns praising him.[49]

Ramakrishna in the Eyes of the Brahmos

One day Ramakrishna went with Mathur to see Devendra Nath Tagore, the leader of the Adi Brahmo Samaj, at Jorasanko, Calcutta. The Master examined his physical characteristics and found that he had very fair skin tinted red. His hair had not yet turned grey. Through his yogic vision the Master saw Devendra's inner life. He later related: "I found that Devendra had combined both yoga and bhoga in his life. He had a number of children, all young. Though he was a jnani, yet he was preoccupied with worldly life. I said to him: 'You are the King Janaka of this Kaliyuga. I have heard that you live in the world and think of God; so I have come to see you. Please tell me something about God.'

"He recited some texts from the Vedas. He said, 'This universe is like a chandelier and each living being is a light in it.'

"We talked a long time. Devendra was pleased and said to me, 'You must come to our Brahmo Samaj festival.' I said that depends on the will of God. Devendra insisted: 'No, you must come. But put on your cloth and wear a shawl over your body. Someone might say something unkind about your untidiness, and that would hurt me.' 'No,' I replied, 'I cannot promise that. I cannot be a babu.' Devendra and Mathur laughed.

"The very next day Mathur received a letter from Devendra forbidding me to go to the festival. He wrote that it would be ungentlemanly of me not to cover my body with a shawl."[50]

The Master met Keshab Chandra Sen, the leader of the Navavidhan Brahmo Samaj, in 1875 at the Belgharia garden house of Jaygopal Sen. They became very close. Keshab was not only a great orator and writer, but also deeply spiritual — a true seeker of God. The Master held Keshab in high esteem. On 1 January 1881, Keshab came to visit the Master at the Dakshineswar garden with his followers. M. included a record of their conversation in the *Gospel*:

Master: "You, Keshab, want me; but your disciples don't. . . . Well, Keshab, say something! They are eager to hear your words."

Keshab (*humbly, with a smile*): "To open my lips here would be like trying to 'sell needles to a blacksmith.'"

It was about four o'clock in the afternoon. They heard the music from the nahabat in the temple garden.

Master (*to Keshab and the others*): "Do you hear how melodious that music is? One player is producing only a monotone on his flute, while another is creating waves of melodies in different *ragas* and *raginis*. That is my attitude. Why should I produce only a monotone when I have an instrument with seven holes? Why should I say nothing but 'I am He, I am He?' I want to play various melodies on my instrument with seven holes. Why should I say only 'Brahma! Brahma?' I want to call on God through all the moods — through shanta, dasya, sakhya, vatsalya, and madhura. I want to make merry with God, I want to sport with God."

Keshab listened to these words with wonder in his eyes and said to the Brahmo devotees, "I have never before heard such a wonderful and beautiful interpretation of jnana and bhakti."

Keshab (*to the Master*): "How long will you hide yourself in this way? I dare say people will be thronging here by and by in great crowds."

Master: "What are you talking of? I only eat and drink and sing God's name. I know nothing about gathering crowds."

Keshab: "All right, sir, I shall gather the crowd. But they all must come to your place."

Master: "I am the dust of everybody's feet. If anyone is gracious enough to come here, he is welcome."

Keshab: "Whatever you may say, sir, your advent cannot be in vain."[51]

Keshab understood the Master's greatness and his divinity. He began to write about the Master's life and teachings in the Brahmo journals — *Sulabh Samachar*, *Sunday Mirror*, and *Theistic Quarterly Review*. Many people of Calcutta, and especially the Young Bengal, began to visit the Master as a result.

Towards the end of his life, Keshab worshipped the Master as God. M. wrote: "The Master told us: 'One day I went to Keshab's house. He requested me to go with him into his private shrine. He said: "I worship God in that shrine. Please come and sanctify it." As soon as I entered the room, he closed the door and began to worship my feet with flowers and sandal paste. He then said, "Please don't tell anyone about this."' Why did he forbid the Master to do so? Because he [Keshab] was a guru and this might have caused some commotion among his disciples."[52]

Keshab's followers could not comprehend the Master's ideas and teachings because those devotees drank deeply of Western ideas. They might have understood some of what he said, but they did not want to accept all of it. Keeping this in mind, after giving them instructions, the Master would often say: "I have said whatever came into my head. Take as much of it as you wish. You may leave off the head and the tail."[53]

Trailokya Sanyal, a devotee of Keshab, wrote in his book *Keshab Charit* (Life of Keshab) that Ramakrishna had been disgusted by family life, but after meeting Keshab had changed his opinion about worldly life. M. recorded in the *Gospel*:

Girish (*to Trailokya*): "You have written that, after coming in contact with Keshab, Sri Ramakrishna changed his views about worldly life; but it isn't true."

Trailokya: "I referred to those who wanted to lead a worldly life. I didn't mean renouncers."

Master: "What are you talking about? People talk about leading a religious life in the world. But if they once taste the bliss of God they will not enjoy anything else. Their attachment to worldly duties declines. As their spiritual joy becomes deeper, they simply cannot perform their worldly duties. More and more they seek that joy. Can worldly pleasures and sex pleasures be compared to the bliss of God? When a man becomes mad for God, he doesn't enjoy money or such things."

Trailokya: "But, sir, if a man is to remain in the world, he needs money and must also save. He has to give in charity and — "

Master: "What? Do you mean that one must first save money and then seek God? And you talk about charity and kindness! A worldly man spends thousands of rupees for his daughter's marriage. Yet, all the while, his neighbours are dying of starvation; and he finds it hard to give them two morsels of rice. And they talk about doing good to others!"

Girish (*to Trailokya*): "Then what you have written is not true."

Trailokya: "Why so? Doesn't he [meaning Sri Ramakrishna] admit that a man can lead a spiritual life in the world?"

Master: "Yes, he can. But such a man should first of all attain Knowledge and then live in the world. First he should realize God. Then 'he can swim in a sea of slander and not be stained.' The world he lives in after attaining God is the world of vidya. In it he sees neither woman nor gold. He finds there only devotion, devotee, and God."[54]

Vijay Krishna Goswami, a Brahmo leader, recognized the Master's divinity to some extent. He had travelled to various sacred places of India and met many holy people. When the Master was suffering from cancer at the Shyampukur house in Calcutta, Vijay came to see him. Vijay remarked: "I realize that everything is here where we are sitting now. This roaming about is useless. At other places I have seen two, five, ten, or twenty-five percent of him [*meaning the Master*], at the most. Here alone I find the full one hundred percent manifestation of God."[55] Later, Vijay said: "I have seen some great souls who had achieved perfection in their respective paths and moods, but only in the Master have I seen one who has attained perfection in all paths and moods. It is new in the religious history of the world."[56]

The Master was fond of Shivanath Shastri, a leader of Sadharan Brahmo Samaj. Shivanath was impressed by the Master's devotion, faith, renunciation, and longing for God. But he stopped visiting the Master when he saw that Vijay's spiritual life had been affected by Sri Ramakrishna's advice, and that he had disconnected himself from the Brahmo Samaj. Shivanath told Vivekananda that the Master's bhava samadhi was a kind of nervous disorder and that he had become insane because he had practised excessive austerities. Shivanath also did not like it that drunkards and immoral actors and actresses visited the Master; moreover, the devotees had started to declare that Ramakrishna was an avatar.

Word travels from mouth to mouth. The Master soon heard everything. When he met Shivanath one day, he asked: "Well, Shivanath, I hear that you call my samadhi a disease and say that I become unconscious at that time. You think day and night of bricks, wood, earth, money, and all sorts of material things and yet consider yourself to be of sound mind, while I — who meditate day and night on God, whose consciousness makes the whole universe conscious — you consider to be ignorant and unconscious. A fine piece of reasoning! What sort of intellect do you have?" Shivanath was speechless.[57]

Most of the Westernized Brahmos could not understand the Master's greatness, but they observed his influence on the Brahmo Samaj. Previously they had conducted their services with meditation, reading from the Vedas, and lectures; but later they introduced kirtan, devotional songs, dancing, and prayers to the Divine Mother. Pratap Chandra Majumdar, a disciple of Keshab Sen, said: "Did we understand what true religion was before we met him [Sri Ramakrishna]? We had merely rebelled against orthodox Hinduism. But after we met him, we realized what true spiritual life is."[58]

Ramakrishna in the Eyes of Devotees and Visitors

Sri Ramakrishna said about himself: "There is no pretence [hypocrisy] here." True religion is a matter of experience; it is not show business. People observed that the Master was married but not a regular householder; he was a monk but did not wear an ochre cloth. Neither was he shaven-headed, nor had he any tuft of hair. His body was not besmeared with ashes, nor was he a hemp smoker like some other monks. What kind of sadhu was this? He did not sit on a tiger skin or cover his body with holy marks or use rudraksha beads while repeating the mantra or quote Sanskrit shlokas from the scriptures. He did not practise hatha yoga or give any medicines or amulets to cure diseases. He went to Calcutta by horse carriage and visited his devotees there. He talked about God and enjoyed good food. He lived in a beautiful room near the Ganges in Dakshineswar. His room was decorated with pictures and his bed was clean and tidy. While talking about God, he sang and danced. He laughed, made jokes, and had fun. He ate like other people, chewed betel rolls, and smoked a hubble-bubble. It is hard to recognize such a person to be an avatar. Yet there was such an attractive power in the Master that anyone who saw him could not forget him. Once he went to see a play in a Calcutta theatre. While there, he said to Baburam and M.: "Don't make a fuss if I fall into an ecstatic mood or go into samadhi. Then the worldly people will take me for a cheat."[59]

Devotees who were pure and simple and had spiritual insight recognized the Master's divinity. Durga Charan Nag said: "After visiting the Master a few times, I realized that he was Lord Narayana Himself; He was secretly enacting His divine play in Dakshineswar." Someone asked, "How did you know this?" Nag Mahashay replied: "The Master, out of his mercy, revealed to me his divine nature. Can anyone know him without his grace? A man can practise austerities for a thousand years, but without God's grace, no one can understand Him."

On another occasion, the Master asked Nag Mahashay: "What do you think of me?" He saluted the Master with folded hands and replied: "You cannot hoodwink me anymore. Through your grace I have come to know that you are that Supreme One." Immediately the Master went into ecstasy and touched Nag Mahashay's chest with his right foot. Suddenly, Nag Mahashay also went into ecstasy. He saw a divine light engulfing all the moving and unmoving objects of the world.[60]

Once the Master asked Ram Chandra Datta: "What do you think of me?" Ram replied: "Master, I read in the *Chaitanya Charitamrita* about the signs manifested in Gauranga. Now I see those signs in you, so I consider you to be Gauranga." Sri Ramakrishna was silent for a moment and then said, "Well, the Bhairavi Brahmani used to say the same thing." Ram later said: "From then on I knew that he was God." In the 1890s Ram gave a series of lectures on the life and teachings of Sri Ramakrishna; he presented the talks at the Star and Minerva theatres. In his lecture, "Is Ramakrishna Paramahamsa an Avatar?" he substantiated his opinion using scriptural quotations, reasoning, empirical evidence, and incidents from his own personal experience. He said: "Ramakrishna is lord of the lowly and helpless; he is the saviour of the fallen and deluded souls; he is the beacon light of ignorant people. Those who are helpless like us, tired of revolving continuously on the wheel of samsara [relative world], and those who perceive only emptiness in their lives — for them, Ramakrishna incarnated as an avatar."[61]

On 1 January 1886 at the Cossipore garden house the Master asked Girish, "Well, Girish, what have you found in me that you proclaim me before all as an incarnation?" Falling to his knees before the Master and saluting him with folded hands, Girish responded with great emotion: "What more can I say of Him? Even the sages Vyasa and Valmiki could find no words to measure His glory!"[62]

On 15 August 1897, during the weekly meeting of the Ramakrishna Mission, Girish was asked his opinion regarding the Master as an avatar. He replied: "I shall be disheartened if there is another kind of god. I went straight to the Master from a despicable house of ill fame, and he gave me a seat to sit on. He carried sweets for me from Dakshineswar to the theatre, a place that some people considered sinful. I have never received such love from anyone else. To me, the Master is God — an avatar. One word of his has transformed my life completely. It is not difficult to obey, to love, or to worship him; it is extremely difficult to forget him."[63]

The householder disciple Purna Chandra Ghosh was an *ishwarakoti* (a godlike soul). The Master remarked about Purna: "Purna is a part of Narayana — and a spiritual aspirant possessing a high degree of sattva." During Purna's second visit, the Master asked him: "What do you think of me?" Filled with devotion, Purna replied without hesitation, "You are God Himself, come to earth in flesh and blood."[64]

The woman devotee Gopal-ma saw her Chosen Deity, Gopala, in the Master. Another woman devotee, Yogin-ma, knew that the Master was omniscient. One day the Master said to Yogin-ma: "Your Chosen Deity is in this place (*pointing to his body*). If you think of me, that will bring recollectedness of your Chosen Deity."[65]

Shyamasundari, Manomohan Mitra's mother, recognized the Master as God. When Manomohan's eldest daughter, Manikprabha, was seriously ill, he decided not to go as usual to Dakshineswar. His mother insisted that he go, saying: "Please go to him right now and inform the Master of your daughter's illness. Bring a little dust from that place where the Master meditates." Manomohan said: "How can I discuss these mundane things with the Master?" Shyamasundari replied: "You won't have to tell him verbally. Go to him and mentally inform him. He is all-knowing. He will understand your pain and then everything will happen according to his will."[66]

Manomohan went to Dakshineswar with a heavy heart and bowed down to the Master. He had felt that his daughter would not live, but by the grace of the Master she recovered.

Once Golap-ma saw the kundalini power as a snake within the Master's throat, swallowing the food that he ate. On another occasion, the Master was walking in Dakshineswar when Golap-ma saw him as Mother Kali.

Gauri-ma, another woman devotee, said of him: "My guru, Sri Ramakrishna and Mahaprabhu Chaitanya are identical."

Many people came to the Dakshineswar temple garden and asked the Master, "Where is the paramahamsa?" The Master would reply: "Who knows? Some call him the paramahamsa, some the young priest, and some the mad brahmin. Find out for yourself." Ramakrishna became a human being and demonstrated how to get rid of the ego and become humbler than the humblest.

Suresh Chandra Datta narrated this story: Once a slender and obviously poor man entered the Master's room. His feet were dirty. He addressed the Master, saying, "Hello, Ramakrishna," then sat on his bed. He patted the Master's shoulder and said, "Brother, prepare a smoke for me." The Master immediately rushed to prepare tobacco, but his devotees took the tobacco bowl from him and prepared the smoke. That man silently smoked for a while, then left, saying, "Brother, I am Ram." When he left, the devotees asked: "Master, why did you try to prepare tobacco for him? You could easily have asked us to do it."

The Master replied: "What is wrong with serving others?"

Once the Master was walking in the Dakshineswar garden when a doctor from Calcutta came to visit the Kali temple. He thought the Master was a gardener and ordered him to collect some jasmine flowers for him. The Master immediately obeyed the doctor. This doctor later came to treat the Master when he had cancer. He now realized the mistake he had made and regretfully said: "My goodness! What have I done? I asked this person to pick flowers for me."[67]

The Master wore a red-bordered cloth. Most of the time his upper body was bare, but sometimes he would cover it with half of his dhoti. Again, sometimes he put on a cheap shirt of coarse fabric. Newcomers sometimes thought he was a simple temple priest or even a gardener.

Swami Vishuddhananda told this story: "Once a friend of Mathur came to visit Dakshineswar and noticed that the garden was full of flowers. He saw the Master nearby and thought he was a gardener. He asked the Master to make a bouquet for him. The Master immediately made a beautiful bouquet and presented it to the gentleman. He was very pleased and told Mathur: 'Look, your gardener made this bouquet for me. Where did you get this wonderful gardener?'

"Mathur: 'Let us go and see the gardener.' Both went and found the Master. Mathur said to his friend: 'He is not a gardener. He is the paramahamsa.'"[68]

Later, many people lamented that they had missed the opportunity to meet Sri Ramakrishna. An engineer went with Swami Yogananda's father to see Swami Vivekananda. They had previously visited Dakshineswar but had not seen the Master. Swamiji asked the engineer, "Why did you not meet Sri Ramakrishna Paramahamsa?" The man replied: "I went with this gentleman up to the door of Sri Ramakrishna's room, but he said to me: 'This paramahamsa is mad. Don't go to him. Let us go to the sadhu in the Panchavati,' so we went there. Without his grace and good fortune, one cannot see him. Now I feel sad that I did not see him because of what someone said."[69]

Durgacharan Bandyopadhyay of Taltala, Calcutta, was a famous physician. He was an alcoholic, but he treated the Master with great care. The Master said: "Durgacharan would come to Dakshineswar at 10:00 at night and call 'Hriday, Hriday.' As soon as I heard his voice, I would say to Hriday, 'Please open the door for him.' When Hriday opened the door, Durgacharan would come into my room and sit there without saying a word. Only the doctor knew how he had regarded me."[70] It is divine grace — hard to explain.

Later the Master was at the Cossipore garden house, suffering from cancer. Ram Datta knew Dr. Kailash Chandra Basu, a well-known physician in Calcutta. Ram went to Dr. Basu to discuss the Master's illness. Dr. Basu had heard Ram describe the greatness of his guru, and he said: "Look, Ram, you people try to make a mountain out of a molehill. If you find a little goodness in a man, you won't rest until you have given him a big title such as 'paramahamsa' or 'avatar.' And at the same time you want to show that you are great devotees and important people. On the one hand, you say that Paramahamsadeva is an avatar, and on the other, you are asking me to check his throat cancer. How can a paramahamsa have cancer? I wouldn't mind humiliating this kind of paramahamsa or avatar by twisting his ears."

Ram felt dejected hearing that comment. He said to Dr. Basu: "Listen, don't speak such disrespectful words about that great soul. That brings harm both to the speaker and the listener." Dr. Basu apologized to Ram and both took a carriage to Cossipore. When they arrived near the pond of the garden house, the Master sent his attendant to the doctor and asked him to come to his room. No sooner had Ram and Dr. Basu entered, than the Master saluted the doctor and asked: "Hello, doctor, will you examine my disease first or twist my ears?" Dr. Basu was startled. He realized that this paramahamsa was the all-knowing God. No one else had been present when he talked with Ram. How did Ramakrishna know what he had said? Dr. Kailash Basu humbly said to the Master: "Sir, please forgive the offence of this wretched person. I made a mistake uttering slurs about you without knowing you. Please don't embarrass me further." He examined the Master with love and respect and became his lifelong devotee. His ego had been crushed. Later, he would never leave home without bowing down to the picture of the Master. After the Master's passing, he donated 2,500 rupees to Kankurgachi Yogodyana, where a part of Sri Ramakrishna's relics were installed.[71]

Ramakrishna in the Eyes of His Intimate Disciples

Ramakrishna divided his disciples into two groups: the inner circle and the outer circle. He talked about God with the outer circle and guided their minds towards Him. He enjoyed his divine play with the inner circle and trained them to carry his message. M. said: "The Master told us, 'It will be enough if you know who am I and who you are. Nothing else is necessary.' In other words, He is God and has come as an avatar; and the devotees are his parts or companions. If the devotees know this, they will never be entrapped by maya."[72]

Girish Ghosh, Ram Chandra Datta, and some other devotees, out of their exuberant devotion, began to proclaim publicly that the Master was an avatar. The Master forbade them to do so when he heard about it. Irritated, he said: "One is a doctor and the other is the manager of a theatre — and they come here and call me an avatar! They think that by doing that they add to my prestige and make me appear great in the eyes of the world. But do they understand what it means to be an avatar?"[73] It is true that only an avatar knows his real nature. Only Shankara knew his philosophy fully. Swamiji said: "If there were another Vivekananda, then he would have understood what this Vivekananda has done!" Ordinary people evaluate a saint or an avatar through their own mental capacity and understanding. There is a saying, "One attains success according to one's thinking."

Ramakrishna's householder disciples understood the Master in one way, and his monastic disciples in quite another. Whatever the Master made them understand, they understood accordingly. Swami Adbhutananda humorously recalled: "After the Master's passing away, sometimes we would talk about the Master's transcendent love. If one person said, 'The Master loved me the most,' another would at once contradict him and say, 'No, he loved me the most.' One day during such a discussion I told them: 'The Master did not leave any property behind and still your squabbling seems unending. The Lord alone knows whether you would have gone to court if he had left us any property.' There was an outburst of laughter at my remark."[74]

Among the disciples of Sri Ramakrishna, some were *ishwarakotis*, some were *nityamuktas* or ever-free souls, and some were companions of previous avatars. They understood more or less that their guru was God in human form, a great soul, or their very own. Someone asked Swami Adbhutananda, "Swami, did you feel that the Master was God?" He replied: "Is it possible to serve him or live near him if one feels that he is God? I would think of him as my own father. . . . It is Swamiji who said that the Master was an avatar. What more shall I say? He is my guru, my father. How can I know or understand him?"[75]

Swami Turiyananda used tremendous self-effort to realize God. He practised Vedanta without compromise and even stopped visiting the Master for a period of time. One day the Master saw him in a gathering and said to his devotees: "Nothing can be achieved — neither knowledge, nor devotion, nor vision — without God's grace. Well, is it an easy matter to realize that lust and gold are unreal and to have the firm conviction that the world is eternally nonexistent? Is it possible without His compassion? Can a man have that conviction through his own effort? A man is after all a tiny creature, with very limited powers. What an infinitesimal part of truth can he grasp by himself!"[76]

Swami Saradananda wrote the comprehensive biography of Sri Ramakrishna. Towards the end of his life he said: "When I began to write the *Lilaprasanga* I thought I understood the Master. But now I clearly see that the life of the Master is very deep. I was merely hovering over the top branches; the root is far beneath the ground."[77]

The Master always encouraged his disciples to test him as "a money-changer checks a coin." He said: "See a holy man by day and by night. Then only should you trust him." The Master knew that Swamiji would be the main carrier of his message, so it was important for him to know the Master well. If he did not, the Master's message would not reach people properly.

In the beginning, Swamiji considered the Master to be mad. His speech, behaviour, and deportment were not like those of ordinary people. Swamiji argued with the Master, tested him for six years without any compromise, and at last recognized his divinity. Swamiji had a deep spiritual experience when the Master touched him. He later said: "How can I consider this person mad when he was able to destroy the strong structure of my mind at will — a mind that is endowed with tremendous willpower — and reshape it as if it were a lump of clay, making it think as he wished?"[78] Christopher Isherwood wrote: "Among Vivekananda's many tremendous qualities, one of the greatest that he had, for us, was his capacity to be a doubter. . . . When a being like Vivekananda is converted, then the whole of the nineteenth century is altered."[79]

Swamiji expressed his feelings for and recognition of Sri Ramakrishna in his poems and hymns, letters and lectures, actions and conversations. He wrote in his hymn to Sri Ramakrishna:

"O Ramakrishna, establisher of righteousness, embodiment of all religions, best of avatars, salutations to thee. . . .

"O breaker of the world's bondage, adored by the world, I worship thee; Stainless, yet assuming human form; attributeless, yet full of attributes. . . .

"I am Your servant, birth after birth, O Ocean of Mercy! Your ways are unknown to me, as are my own — but who cares to know?"

One day Swamiji said to Sharat Chakrabarty: "Is it possible that one would enjoy lust and gold and understand Sri Ramakrishna aright at the same time? Or will it ever be possible? Never put your faith in such words. Many among the devotees of Sri Ramakrishna are now proclaiming themselves as *ishwarakotis* (godlike souls), *antaranga* (of inner circle), and so on. They could not imbibe his great renunciation or dispassion, yet they say they are his intimate devotees! Sweep away all such words. He was a prince of *tyagis* (renunciants), and obtaining his grace can anybody spend his life in the enjoyment of lust and gold?"

Disciple: "Is it then, sir, that those who came to him at Dakshineswar were not his devotees?"

Swamiji: "Who says that? Everybody who has gone to Sri Ramakrishna has advanced in spirituality, is advancing, and will advance. Sri Ramakrishna used to say that the perfected rishis of a previous *kalpa* (cycle) take human bodies and come to earth with the avatars. They are the associates of the Lord. God works through them and propagates His religion. Know this for a truth that they alone are the associates of the avatar who have renounced everything for the sake of others, who, giving up all sense enjoyments with repugnance, spend their lives for the good of the world, for the welfare of all."

Disciple: "Then is it not true — what the householder devotees of Sri Ramakrishna are preaching about him in diverse ways?"

Swamiji: "It can't be said that they are altogether false; but what they are saying about Sri Ramakrishna is only partial truth. According to one's own capacity, one has understood Sri Ramakrishna and so is talking about him. It is not bad to do so. But if any of his devotees has concluded that what he has understood of him is the only truth, then he is an object of pity. Some are saying that Sri Ramakrishna was a *Tantrik kaula* (monk), some that he was Sri Chaitanya born on earth to preach *Naradiya bhakti* (bhakti as taught by Narada); some again that to undertake spiritual practices is opposed to faith in him as an avatar; while some are opining that it is not agreeable to his teachings to take to sannyasa. You will hear such words from the householder devotees, but do not listen to such one-sided estimates. He was the concentrated embodiment of how many previous avatars! Even spending the whole life in religious austerity, we could not understand it. Therefore one has to speak about him with caution and restraint. He bestowed spirituality according to the capacity of each individual. If one realizes a spray from the ocean of his spirituality, one instantly becomes a god. Such a synthesis of universal ideas you will not find in the history of the world again. Understand from this who was born in the person of Sri Ramakrishna."[80]

God's Play Is Inscrutable

God's play as a human being is sweet and wonderful, but inscrutable. The Cosmic God acts out His divine play in this world as son, brother, husband, uncle, and friend. Suppressing His infinite power and hiding His real nature, God teaches His devotees, makes jokes with them, joins them in their happiness and misery, sings and dances, smiles and cries; and sometimes out of mercy, He reveals His true nature. The Master said: "Not everyone can recognize an Incarnation of God. Some take Him for an ordinary man, some for a holy person; only a few recognize Him as an Incarnation." In this connection the Master told the following parable: A man evaluated his diamond first through an eggplant seller, who offered nine seers of eggplant; and then through a cloth merchant, who offered 900 rupees; and finally through a jeweler, who offered 100,000 rupees.

The doctor Ram Chandra Datta was proud of his devotion. He began to declare that the Master was an avatar. While in ecstasy, the Master once fell down and injured his arm. When Ram came to see the Master, the latter teased him, saying: "Ram, tell me why I had this accident. Now give me a lecture on that."

Another day the Master told Ram: "Look, the shad fish swims about 15 feet under cold water, but it is very rich and hard to digest. The green coconut, however, is heated by the sun 30 feet above the ground, but its milk is very cool and soothing. The blacksmith who sits near the fire to pump the bellows suffers from cold and sneezing. A diver who is always in the cool water drinks rock candy syrup to cool his system. People say that if you think of Krishna, all your problems will go away. But you can see that Krishna was always with the Pandavas, serving them, and those Pandavas had unending problems and misery. Look, Ram, whatever you may say, one cannot limit God or understand His inscrutable play."[81]

How can we recognize the avatar? How can we establish a relationship with him? How can we love him whom we have not seen? Many such questions arise in our minds. The gopis of Vrindaban tied Krishna with the cord of love. The Bhagavata says: "The unconquerable God becomes conquered by the devotees' love. Although He is independent, He becomes dependent because He is extremely compassionate and loving to His devotees. When unselfish devotees dedicate themselves in the service of God, He also distributes Himself among them to repay the debt." (6:16:34) Ramakrishna also said: "God becomes tender for the sake of His devotees. He appears before them, setting aside His powers."[82]

One cannot grasp God through money, learning, intellect, or psychic powers. One needs love, devotion, detachment, humility, and self-surrender. One has to offer the body, senses, and mind to God and establish a relationship with Him through meditation on His name, form, qualities, action, and lila. About such devotees, Krishna says in the Gita: "I bestow the yoga of understanding by means of which they come to Me." (10:10)

M. established such a firm relationship with the Master that his mind was absorbed forever in Ramakrishna. M. said: "Previously I would think that the Master was my very own. My goodness! The more I thought of him, the more I found that he was infinite — infinite! When he associated with us, he became truly like one of our own, like father and mother. After a while that relationship would disappear and he would become the infinite, limitless consciousness — an ocean of knowledge, love, peace, and bliss!

"It is in the Bhagavata: The moonlight reflects on the water. The fish think that the moon is one of them. They play with the moon and when the moon sets, they become miserable. The moon is not in the water; it is in infinite space. The Master was like that. Some would think of him as guru, father, mother, and so on. He behaved with them according to their attitude; and again from time to time he would assume his infinite form. Those who can grasp his infinite nature, they fully surrender to him. Trials and tribulations cannot perturb them."[83]

The nature of a lover is to know, recognize, and unite with the beloved. There is joy in union. One cannot love a stranger. Sri Rama-krishna is our beloved. The more we try to know and love him, the closer we move to him. It is true that we are ordinary human beings, so we shall never be able to understand the infinite Ramakrishna. But if our efforts are sincere and forthright, out of mercy he will reveal his true nature to us. There is no other way to understand him.

4

Ramakrishna's Desires

This beautiful universe is created by desire. Everything in this world exists because of desire. When desire comes to an end, the world dissolves. Desire is a mysterious phenomenon. According to the Upanishads: "In the beginning of creation, a desire arose in the mind of God, the Creator, that He would be many. He created these worlds and the world-guardians. Having created all this, He entered into it."[1] Thus God's desire to create entered into every human being, and this desire bound each soul. Bondage brings misery; liberation brings joy. The ever-free God began to play hide-and-seek with His created beings. This world, the product of maya, or ignorance, is His playground. God is the master of maya and individual beings are its slaves. Human beings become free when they transcend ignorance and desire, and thereby see God.

According to Vedanta the wheel of *avidya-kama-karma* (ignorance-desire-action) is continuously rotating. Desire does not arise without ignorance, and an incentive to perform action is not possible without desire. In the *Yogavashistha Ramayana* the sage Vashistha defined desire in this manner: "The instinct that gives no opportunity to consider the result of action, but suddenly arises in the mind and induces a person to act, is called desire."[2] The scriptures compare desire to intoxicants. As a drunkard loses all power of discrimination, so does a man with innumerable desires created by maya. He becomes confused and cannot distinguish good from bad. The Brihadaranyaka Upanishad says: "The self [individual being] is identified with desire alone. As is its desire, so is

146

its resolution; and as is its resolution, so is its deed; and whatever deed it does, that it reaps."[3]

According to the sage Vashistha, there are two kinds of desire: pure and impure. A person incarnates because of impure desires and attains liberation through pure desires. Impure desires are of three kinds: desire for name and fame, desire to become a scholar by studying the scriptures, and desire for physical pleasure. A person possessed by the desire for name and fame always expects glory and praise from others. Regarding the desire for scriptural knowledge, there is a beautiful story about the sage Bharadwaj. Through his yogic power, this sage had lived for the equivalent of three lifetimes in one life. During that period, he practised brahmacharya and studied the scriptures. Finally he became old and bedridden. Indra, the king of gods, appeared before him and asked, "Bharadwaj, what would you do if you could live for another lifetime?" The sage replied: "I would practise brahmacharya and continue studying the scriptures." Indra then showed him three mountain-high heaps of unread scriptures, gave him a handful of those books, and said, "Bharadwaj, these are all the Vedas." Indra explained to him the futility of studying the scriptures and then gave him the knowledge of Brahman. The Amritabindu Upanishad says: "After studying the Vedas, the intelligent one who is solely intent on acquiring knowledge and realization, should discard the Vedas altogether, as the man who seeks to obtain rice discards the husk."[4] There is another story in this vein: The sage Durvasa went to bow down to Shiva. He was carrying a heavy load of books on his back. The sage Narada compared Durvasa to an ass, a beast of burden. In a rage Durvasa threw his books into the ocean; Shiva then instructed him in the knowledge of Brahman.

One should use higher intellectual desires to counteract gross worldly desires, and pure spiritual desires to counteract intellectual desires. Impure desires have been compared to iron chains and pure desires to gold chains. Both are chains, and both bind a person equally well. According to the *Yogavashistha Ramayana*, when desires cease, the mind dissolves; then comes illumination. Although it is the nature of desire to bind, desire for God releases a soul. The scriptures say, "*Akāmo Vishnu-kāmo vā*": the desire for Vishnu, or God, is not considered a desire, because it brings liberation instead of bondage. Ramakrishna used to say: "*Hinche* is not an ordinary green. One generally becomes indisposed by eating greens. But hinche removes excessive bile; it does one good. Sugar candy is not an ordinary sweet. Sweets are generally harmful, but sugar candy removes acidity."[5]

There is no end to human desires. According to the Brihadaranyaka Upanishad, all desires are divided into three groups: the desire for progeny or sex, the desire for wealth or money, and the desire for name and fame. Liberation is possible only when one becomes free from these three desires.

Desire is very subtle, but is powerful in its manifestations. It makes people restless and creates all sorts of trouble. The real nature of human beings is the infinite Brahman, but their desires make them weak. Where there is desire, there is imperfection. Shankara said: "Who is poor? The person who has many desires."[6] Desire is a dynamic phenomenon. "*Vāsanā pushyati vapuh*": It is desire that holds the body. Without desire the human body would fall to the ground like a ripe fruit. Knowing this, avatars or *jivanmuktas* (those who are liberated in life) cherish some harmless desires so that their bodies will continue to exist, allowing them to serve humanity. Their desires, however, are like a burnt rope that keeps its shape but cannot bind.

Ramakrishna's Fancies

Ramakrishna had various trivial desires and wishes. But his desires and expectations were not like those of ordinary human beings. Desires arise in the mind of a jiva who has samskaras, or past impressions; but an avatar is free from samskaras. The natural trend of an avatar's mind is upward. And because the egos of avatars are ripe, their wishes are united with God. God plays His divine lila through them. There is a difference between a fancy and a desire: If one fancies a thing, it is all right if it is available, or if not, it does not matter. But desire is real and deep-rooted: One feels that he or she must have that object.

Ramakrishna expressed his fancies in various ways on different occasions. Once he explained:

It is not good to cherish desires and hankerings. For that reason I used to fulfill whatever desires came to my mind. Once I saw some coloured sweetmeats at Barabazar and wanted to eat them. They [his devotees] brought me the sweets and I ate a great many. The result was that I fell ill.

In my boyhood days, while bathing in the Ganges, I saw a boy with a gold ornament around his waist. During my state of divine intoxication I felt a desire to have a similar ornament myself. I was given one, but I couldn't keep it on very long. When I put it on, I felt within my body the painful uprush of a current of air. It was because I had touched gold to my skin. I wore the ornament a few moments and then had to put it aside. Otherwise, I should have had to tear it off.

I once felt a desire to eat the famous sweetmeats of different cities. I had a desire to hear Shambhu's musical recital of the Chandi. After fulfilling that desire I wanted to hear the same thing by Rajnarayan. That desire also was satisfied.

At that time many holy men used to visit the temple garden. A desire arose in my mind that there should be a separate storeroom to supply them with their provisions. Mathur Babu arranged for one. The sadhus were given foodstuffs, fuel, and the like from that storeroom.

Once the idea came to me to put on a very expensive robe embroidered with gold and to smoke a silver hubble-bubble. Mathur Babu sent me the new robe and the hubble-bubble. I put on the robe. I also smoked the hubble-bubble in various fashions. Sometimes I smoked it reclining this way, and sometimes that way, sometimes with head up, and sometimes with head down. Then I said to myself, "O mind, this is what they call smoking a silver hubble-bubble." Immediately I renounced it. I kept the robe on my body a few minutes longer and then took it off. I began to trample it underfoot and spit on it, saying: "So this is an expensive robe! But it only increases man's rajas."[7]

Once I ate some onion.* While eating it I examined it: "O mind, this is onion." Then I moved it to different places in my mouth, and at last spat it out.[8]

Once I had a desire to eat dal cooked in a blacksmith's house. From my childhood I had heard the blacksmiths say, "Do the brahmins know how to cook?" I ate the dal, but it smelt of the blacksmith.[9]

Desire for Devotees

Ramakrishna was always involved with God. He was not satisfied with merely seeing God. He said: "One who lives near the sea sometimes has a desire to find out how many pearls are hidden in the ocean depths. Similarly, after realizing the Divine Mother and being constantly near Her, I thought that I should see Her multiple forms. If I had a desire to see Her in a particular way, I would importune Her with a longing heart. Then the gracious Mother would supply whatever was necessary to experience that form, make me practise that sadhana, and reveal Herself to me accordingly. Thus I practised sadhanas belonging to various paths."[10]

Ordinary people spend their days with their families and friends, money and property, possessions and activities. These bound souls are entangled by their worldly desires. They are so deluded and infatuated that they are unaware of their divine nature; they live like slaves of

*Onions are considered rajasic, not conducive to spiritual life.

maya. Every person in this world passes his or her days somehow or other. Ramakrishna spent his days with God, devotees, and devotion. He said: "You busy yourself with five different things, but I have only one ideal: I do not enjoy anything but God. This is what God has ordained for me."[11] Ordinary people experience momentary pleasure from worldly objects, but Ramakrishna was carried away by a permanent current of divine bliss. He said: "Once, in a spiritual mood, I felt intense love for Jagannath, love such as a woman feels for her sweetheart. In that mood I was about to embrace Him, when I broke my arm."[12] But even then, this acute physical pain could not distract his mind from God.

In front of the Krishna temple at Dakshineswar, Ramakrishna once had a vision: He saw a light emanating from the image of Krishna. The light first touched him, then moved to a copy of the Bhagavata. This convinced him that "God, the devotee, and the scripture are one." He said: "I cherished a desire. I said to the Mother, 'O Mother, I shall be the king of the devotees.'"[13] The Divine Mother fulfilled his desire. When God incarnates as a human being, He plays with devotion and devotees. The Master searched for devotees. He said: "I have been seeking a companion, a sympathetic soul who will understand my feelings. When I see a great devotee, I say to myself, 'Perhaps he will accept my ideal.' But later on I find that he behaves in a different way.

"A ghost sought a companion. One becomes a ghost if one dies in an accident on a Saturday or a Tuesday. So whenever the ghost found someone who seemed to be dying from an accident on either of these days, he would run to him. He would say to himself that at last he had found his companion. But no sooner would he run to the man than he would see the man getting up. The man, perhaps, had fallen from a roof and after a few moments regained consciousness."[14]

God takes a human form for the sake of the devotees, and He enacts His divine drama with them. The Master said: "The whole thing is to love God and taste His sweetness. He is sweetness and the devotee is its enjoyer. The devotee drinks the sweet Bliss of God. Further, God is the lotus and the devotee the bee. The devotee sips the honey of the lotus."[15] If there were no devotees, who would know of the glory of God? As devotees seek God, God looks for devotees.

Later, the Master described the mental anguish he had gone through before the arrival of the devotees. "In those days," he told them, "there was no limit to my yearning to see you all. My heart was wrung like a wet towel, and I was restless with pain. I wanted to weep aloud, but I couldn't cry in public or people would misunderstand me. I could just manage to keep my grief under control during the day. But when evening came and the vesper music resounded from the temples of the Mother and of Vishnu, I could master my feelings no longer; I was overcome by the thought that another day had gone and still you were not here. I would climb onto the roof of the kuthi and cry out at the top of my voice: 'Come to me, my boys! Where are you? I can't bear to live without you!' I thought that I would go mad. Then after some days, you began to come, one after another, and I calmed down. As I had seen you all earlier in my visions, I immediately recognized you when you came, one by one. After Purna came, the Mother said: 'You had visions about those who were to come. It is now complete with Purna's arrival. No others belonging to this class of devotee will come in the future.' The Mother showed you all to me and said, 'These devotees are your inner circle.'"[16]

Ramakrishna's lips would burn when he talked to worldly people. So he searched out spiritual companions with whom he could talk about God. He prayed to the Divine Mother: "Certainly I shall not have any children, Mother. But it is my desire that a boy with sincere love for God should always remain with me. Give me such a boy."[17] That is the reason Rakhal (later Swami Brahmananda) came to Dakshineswar.

Ramakrishna had such an intense desire to meet devotees of God that he did not wait for an invitation to meet those people. When the Master heard that Devendra Nath Tagore was a spiritual person who chanted God's name, he went with Mathur to see him. Devendra invited the Master to attend the Brahmo festival, but he later withdrew his invitation because the Master did not wish to dress like the Brahmos. On another occasion, the Master and Mathur went to Baghbazar to see Dina Mukherjee, a great devotee. The Master later described the scene: "It was a small place. The arrival of a rich man in a big carriage embarrassed the inhabitants. We too were embarrassed. That day Dina's son was being invested with the sacred thread. The house was crowded, and there was hardly any place for Dina to receive us. We were about to enter a side room, when someone cried out: 'Please don't go into that room. There are ladies there.' It was really a distressing situation. Returning, Mathur Babu said, 'Father, I shall never listen to you again.' I laughed."[18]

The devotees could not fathom why, when, where, or how desires would crop up in the Master's mind. And he did not hide those desires; rather, he expressed them as a child would. He once said: "Four desires have come into my mind: I shall eat fish soup cooked with eggplant. I shall visit Shivanath. The devotees will repeat the name of Hari over their beads, and I shall watch them. And the Tantric devotees will drink consecrated wine, eight annas' worth, on the *ashtami* day, and I shall watch them and salute them."[19] It is difficult to explain these mysterious desires. Many good dishes were available. Why did he want to eat fish soup with eggplant? It seems that when he was a little boy, his mother had cooked that dish, so that desire suddenly cropped up in his mind. Why did he want to see Shivanath? In that connection the Master said: "There is substance in that person who thinks of God for a long time. That person develops the power of God within. . . . I feel happy when I see Shivanath. He always seems to be absorbed in the bliss of Brahman."[20]

After expressing those four desires, Ramakrishna went into samadhi. After coming down to the relative plane of consciousness, he said: "Satchidananda! Satchidananda! Satchidananda! Shall I repeat that? No, it is the day of the Divine Mother, the Giver of the bliss of divine inebriation. O Mother, full of the bliss of divine inebriation! Sa, re, ga, ma, pa, dha, ni. It is not good to keep the voice on 'ni.' It is not possible to keep it there very long. I shall keep it on the next lower note.

"There are different planes of consciousness: the gross, the subtle, the causal, and the Great Cause. Entering the Great Cause, one becomes silent; one cannot utter a word. But an ishwarakoti, after attaining the Great Cause, can come down again to the lower planes."[21] This kind of statement unveils the mystery of the Master's trivial desires, such as fish soup with eggplant or meeting with Shivanath. The desireless mind merges into samadhi, so he had to create some desires to keep his mind at a lower level in order to teach human beings.

As an avatar, Ramakrishna demonstrated how to serve a holy person. In this connection, M. wrote: "The Master was then twenty-five or twenty-six. Many monks would then visit Dakshineswar. We heard this story from the Master. Prior to Tota Puri's arrival, a monk lived in the Panchavati and worshipped Gopala [the child Krishna]. The Master visited him and listened to him talk. He served that monk, carrying water and food. After three days he stopped visiting the monk. Then the monk asked, 'Why are you not visiting me anymore?' The Master replied: 'I decided to serve you for three days, and I did.' He served the monk as a guru. He did not go to him any longer because that monk had a narrow outlook."[22]

When we think of the Master's wonderful desires, we sincerely believe that he would play with desires; he was not a slave to them as we are. We suffer terribly from the horrible disease of desire. Its symptoms are greed, fear, anxiety, restlessness, and lack of peace.

God assumes the responsibilities of those fortunate ones who surrender to Him. Krishna declared in the Gita (9:22): "Those persons who worship Me, meditating on their identity with Me and ever devoted to Me — to them I carry what they lack and for them I preserve what they already have." The Master once described his intense desire to help the spiritual aspirants who came to Dakshineswar:

> Once, a desire arose in my mind to supply the aspirants of all sects with whatever they needed for their sadhanas. If all their needs were met, they could then practise sadhana without anxiety, and I would watch them joyfully. When I told this to Mathur, he said: "That's no problem, Father. I'll arrange everything right away. You distribute everything just as you wish." Arrangements had already been made to regularly give rice, lentils, flour, and so on to mendicants from the temple store. Now Mathur made additional provisions for water pots, blankets, seats for meditation, and even marijuana and hemp for those who used them and wine for Tantric aspirants.
>
> At that time many Tantric aspirants who came would arrange a Chakra, a holy circle in which they would perform rituals as a group. I supplied them with peeled ginger, onion, puffed rice, and fried gram — ingredients used in their rituals — and observed how they used these articles in their worship and prayers to the Divine Mother. On many occasions they made me join their holy circle, and sometimes invited me to lead the group. They would always ask me to drink the consecrated wine, but when they found that I was incapable of taking it because I got intoxicated while merely chanting the Mother's name, they did not ask me anymore. However, because it was the custom to drink wine in the holy circle, I would put a drop on my finger and mark my forehead with it, or smell it, or at the most sprinkle a drop on my tongue, then pour the wine in their glasses. I noticed that after drinking wine, some of them would concentrate on the Divine Mother and call on Her passionately. Some of them, however, would drink greedily and become drunk instead of calling on the Divine Mother. One day I saw them become excessively drunk, so I stopped supplying wine to them.[23]

Desire to Decorate His Room and Place of Sadhana

Undoubtedly, one's environment has a great impact on the human mind. The temple garden of Dakshineswar created a favourable atmosphere for Ramakrishna's spiritual journey. The pinnacles of the Kali temple, the Natmandir, the Vishnu temple, the twelve Shiva temples, the spacious courtyard surrounded by buildings, the beautiful flower gardens, the quiet and densely wooded areas, the Panchavati, the murmuring sound of the Ganges, the songs of the birds, and the melo-dious music from the nahabat created a mystical abode where Ramakrishna lived for thirty years and practised his sadhana.

Although Ramakrishna was in an ecstatic mood most of the time, he kept his room in a beautiful and orderly way. Every morning Golap-ma or someone else would dust and mop his room. He had two wooden cots, one for sleeping and another for sitting. These cots, plus a stool and a shelf for sweets and fruits, were the only furniture in his room. The devotees would sit upon carpets or mats on the floor. His bed was clean, as were his clothes. He always kept his things in their proper places and advised his devotees to do the same. He ate his meals in his room, sitting on a low wooden seat. In the evening a temple maidservant would light the oil lamp in his room and burn incense.

On the walls of his room hung pictures of many gods, goddesses, and saints, including images of Kali, Saraswati, Krishna, Rama, Chaitanya with his singing group, Dhruva, Prahlada, a white marble statue of Buddha, Jesus rescuing the drowning Peter, and so on. The Master enjoyed displaying many holy pictures in his room.

Ramlal said: "One day, the Master asked Beni Madhav of Sinthi: 'Could you bring me some good holy pictures for my room?' Sometime later Beni Madhav asked me to collect them from him. I brought the Master five pictures — Dhruva, Prahlada, Gauranga, Jagannath, and Kamale Kamini [a goddess standing on a lotus]."[24] Once Ramakrishna showed Aswini Kumar Datta the pictures in his room and asked him whether a picture of Buddha could be had. "Very likely," answered Aswini. The Master said, "Please get one for me."[25]

Viewing pictures of gods, goddesses, and holy people awakens a divine feeling. The Master always encouraged his devotees to keep holy pictures in their homes. On 9 March 1884, the Master said: "I should like to have two pictures, one of a yogi seated before a lighted log, and another of a yogi smoking hemp and the charcoal blazing up as he pulls. Such pictures kindle my spiritual consciousness, as an imitation fruit awakens the idea of a real one."[26]

On 24 August 1882, the Master said to M.: "The mind of the yogi is always fixed on God, always absorbed in the Self. You can recognize such a man by merely looking at him. His eyes are wide open, with an aimless look, like the eyes of the mother bird hatching her eggs. Her entire mind is fixed on the eggs, and there is a vacant look in her eyes. Can you show me such a picture?"[27] M. could not find such a picture during the Master's lifetime, but later he had an artist paint one.

Ramakrishna's first job in the Kali temple of Dakshineswar was as a dresser of the Divine Mother Kali. In the *Gospel* M. described various ornaments of Mother Bhavatarini. The Master saw the anklets of the women of western India, and immediately he had a desire that the Mother wear that kind of anklet. Mathur had them made and the Master put them on Her feet and fulfilled his desire. It is natural that the lover loves to adorn his or her beloved. Later the Master arranged to have ornaments made for the Holy Mother and remarked: "She is Sarada — the goddess Saraswati — she loves to adorn herself."

The Master was keenly interested in keeping his place of sadhana clean and tidy. Before he began to practise austerities in Dakshineswar, he felt the necessity of planting the Panchavati, a grove held to be a favourable atmosphere for spiritual sadhana. Previously he had meditated under the amalaki tree near the goose pond, but it later died. Then he planted an ashwatha tree on the west side of the sadhan-kutir and asked Hriday to plant the saplings of banyan, ashoka, bel, and amalaki. These five trees, which are called a Panchavati, were surrounded by tulsi and aparajita plants. The Master said: "I planted a tulsi-grove in the Panchavati in order to practise japa and meditation. I wanted very much to fence it around with bamboo sticks. Soon afterwards a bundle of bamboo sticks and some string were carried by the flood-tide of the Ganges right in front of the Panchavati. A temple servant noticed them and joyfully told me."[28]

Pilgrims make a place holy through their prayers and tears, love and devotion, japa and meditation, chanting and vigil. Dakshineswar has become a great holy place through Ramakrishna's phenomenal sadhana and the visits of many holy people and spiritual aspirants. In 1868 the Master went to Vrindaban. He brought back some dust from that holy place associated with Krishna and scattered it around the Panchavati. M. recorded: "The Master had brought a madhavi creeper from Vrindaban in the year 1868 and had planted it in the Panchavati. The creeper had grown big and strong. Some children were jumping and swinging from it. The Master observed them and laughed. He said: 'They are like young monkeys. They will not give up swinging even though they sometimes fall to the ground.'"[29]

"I Bring My Mind Down for You"

If one analyzes the human mind, one will find that it has many layers. One may transcend gross desires, but there will still be subtle desires in the mind. Transcending the most subtle desires, one finally becomes devoid of desires and realizes God. There is even a competition among the desires: Suppose one subdues the desire for sex by the desire for money, and then the desire for sex and money by the desire for name and fame. It is really difficult to get rid of this mesh of desires. The Master used to say: "One cannot realize God so long as one has a little desire. Therefore, try to fulfill the small harmless desires, but get rid of big harmful desires through discrimination."[30]

The mind is really mischievous. It is hard to control. Peace and happiness depend solely on attaining a calm state of mind. Whereas we struggle hard trying to cut through the meshes of maya and to raise the mind upward, the Master would cultivate some small desires, so that he could keep his mind on the earthly plane and help the devotees. The natural tendency of his mind was to merge with the nondual reality and to remain there.

Desires are mysterious and they love to play with human minds. The Master unveiled the mystery of desire through spiritual experiences. He said: "The minds of ordinary people dwell in the subtle nerve centres near the anus, the sex organ, and the navel. When a person's mind is purified to some extent, it sometimes rises to the heart centre, has a vision of light or of luminous divine forms, and experiences a little bliss. When the mind is accustomed to remaining in this place, it ascends to the throat centre. At that time, it is almost impossible for that person to talk about anything other than the ideal on which the mind has been concentrated. Although it has reached this height, the mind can descend to the lower centres and completely forget that high ideal. But if through steadfast devotion the mind transcends the throat centre and reaches the centre between the eyebrows, that person experiences supreme bliss in samadhi. Compared to that state, the enjoyment of sense objects in the lower centres seems insipid. There is no fear of falling from this centre. Here the light of the Supreme Self is visible behind a thin veil. Although a little separation from the Supreme Self remains, one gets clear glimpses of nondual knowledge when the mind reaches that point. No sooner does the mind pass beyond this centre than the knowledge of difference and sameness vanishes and that person becomes established in complete nondual knowledge.

"My mind descends to the throat centre so that I can teach all of you, but it is a struggle to keep it down there. Because I dwelt continually in the realm of complete nondual knowledge for a period of six months, my mind is naturally inclined in that direction. It is difficult for me to bring my mind down without nurturing some little desires such as, 'I shall do this,' 'I shall eat that,' 'I shall see this person,' 'I shall go there,' and so on. And if my mind does not come down, it is impossible for me to perform functions, such as talking, moving, eating, protecting the body, and the like. So when I merge into samadhi, I entertain a small desire such as 'I shall smoke tobacco,' or 'I shall go there'; but even then I have to express that desire again and again so my mind will come down a little."[31]

Ramakrishna's Desire for Food

One day the Master was eating in his room at Dakshineswar. There was rice on his plate and other dishes were in small bowls around his plate. The Master had been a light eater all through his life. Swami Turiyananda was there and watching the Master eating. Seeing those various dishes, Turiyananda was thinking that the Master loved to eat in a rajasic way. The Master immediately read his mind and said: "Well, the tendency of my mind is always towards the Infinite. I eat very little. I take food from different bowls and savour them on my tongue. It is by such rajasic [luxurious] devices that I hold the mind down to the lower planes. Otherwise I could not talk with you."[32]

During sadhana the Master suffered from various physical problems, such as a burning sensation, sleeplessness, excessive hunger, and so on. He later described what happened in vivid detail, saying: "I was seized with a ravenous appetite that no amount of food could satisfy. No sooner had I eaten something than I would feel hungry again. Day and night my mind was possessed by one thought alone: what to eat. I pondered, 'What kind of disease is this?' When I described it to the Brahmani, she replied: 'My son, don't worry. The scriptures explain that those who advance on the path of spirituality pass through such abnormal states. Wait, I shall cure it.' She asked Mathur to supply all kinds of food — from flattened rice and sugarcoated parched rice to sandesh, rasagolla, luchi, and other delicacies — and stack it all in a room. She then told me, 'My son, stay in this room day and night and eat whenever and whatever you like.' I remained in that room and walked around, touching various foods. Every now and then I would taste one item or another, according to my fancy. In this way three days passed, that strange hunger and desire for food left me, and I was relieved."[33]

Ramakrishna's stomach was not strong; he suffered various stomach problems. His mother, Chandramani, would advise him: "Don't eat the prasad of the Kali temple [which was very hot and spicy]. As long as your stomach is bad, I shall ask your wife to cook rice and fish soup on the wood-burning stove. Please eat that." When the Master was tired of eating that bland diet, he would ask his mother: "Mother, why don't you cook one or two vegetables for me with special seasonings as you used to in Kamarpukur? I love to eat your cooking. I am tired of eating the vegetables cooked here." Chandramani then cooked some dishes for her son.[34]

The Master enjoyed food cooked with the kind of seasoning his mother had used during his childhood. One day at Kamarpukur he said to his niece Lakshmi, "Go to the shop and buy one anna's worth of flavouring spices." And then he said to the Holy Mother, "Please cook a soup of mixed lentils and season it with the spices in such a way that its aroma would cause a pig to grunt." Another day he overheard his sister-in-law say to the Holy Mother, "There is no *panchphoran* (cumin, fennel, caraway, fenugreek, and black cumin) in the kitchen, so cook without it." Immediately the Master said: "What is this? If you run short of those spices, why don't you get a pice worth of them? One should not eliminate a thing which is necessary. I left the fish curry, rice pudding, and other fancy dishes of Dakshineswar and came here to eat your cooking, expecting it to be flavoured with wonderful seasonings. How can you think of cooking without it?" The Master's sister-in-law was embarrassed and she immediately arranged to get those spices.[35]

Ramakrishna did not care for monotony in his sadhana nor did he care for monotony in his food. He prayed to the Divine Mother: "Mother, keep me in this world so that I may enjoy it." The Master did not like dogmatic views at all. He said: "Hindus, Muslims, Christians, Saktas, Saivas, Vaishnavas, the Brahmajnanis of the time of the rishis, and the Brahmajnanis of modern times, all seek the same object. A mother prepares dishes to suit the stomachs of her children.

"Do you know my attitude? I love all the preparations of fish. I have a womanly nature. I feel myself at home with every dish — fried fish, fish cooked with turmeric powder, pickled fish. And further, I equally relish rich preparations like fish-head, kalia, and pilau."[36]

Generally the Master would visit Kamarpukur during the rainy season. One morning after waking up, he said to the Holy Mother: "Today I shall eat this spinach dish. Please cook it for me." And it was cooked and served to him. A few days later he said: "What is this? As soon as I get up in the morning, I think about what I shall eat today! Shame! Shame!" Then he said to the Holy Mother: "I have no more desire to eat any particular dish; I shall eat whatever you cook and serve."[37]

Sometimes in an ecstatic mood the Master would eat a large amount of food but that would not upset his stomach. Once in Kamarpukur at night he went to bed after supper; then he immediately got up and said: "What is the matter? You are all going to bed without giving me any food." Ramlal's mother replied: "My goodness! You just now finished your supper!" The Master: "When did you feed me?" The ladies understood that the Master was in ecstasy. They offered some puffed rice to him but he refused to eat only puffed rice. Later Ramlal went to a shop and bought some sweets. The Master then went to bed after eating that puffed rice and the sweets.

Once also in Jayrambati the Master demanded food at midnight. The Holy Mother told him that there was only rice soaked in water and nothing else. But the Master asked her to see whether there was any left-over fish in the pantry. She went to the kitchen and found a tiny maurala fish and a little gravy in a bowl. She then served the Master a large amount of soaked rice and the fish dish which appeased his inordinate hunger.

Similar situations would sometimes occur at Dakshineswar. One midnight the Master got up, called Ramlal, and said: "I am very hungry. Find some food for me." Ramlal searched the room but could not find any sweets or fruits, so he went to the nahabat and informed the Holy Mother. She immediately made a fire with some straw and wood and began to cook farina pudding. Golap-ma carried the bowl, containing two pounds of pudding, to the Master. He sat down and began to eat. The Master then asked her, "Well, can you tell me who is eating — myself — or someone else?" Golap-ma replied: "It seems to me that there is someone else inside you who is eating."The Master was pleased to hear this and said with a smile, "You are right."[38] Golap-ma later described her vision of the kundalini power within the Master's body that was accepting oblations: "It seemed to me that as soon as the Master put food in his mouth the snake-shaped Kundalini Shakti within him was aroused and snatched at the food and devoured it."[39]

The scriptures say: "One should not visit a deity or a monk empty-handed." Gopal-ma of Kamarhati went to see Ramakrishna at Dakshineswar and carried some stale sandesh to give him. As soon as the Master saw her, he asked: "Oh, you have come! Please give me what you brought for me." Gopal-ma later said: "I was terribly embarrassed. How could I give him that stale sandesh? So many people brought so many fancy dishes to feed him. But as soon as I arrived, he asked for that bad sandesh." She was speechless with fear and shame, but she reluctantly handed those stale sweets to him. The Master immediately started to eat them with great relish and said to her: "Why do you spend money on sweets? Prepare some sweet coconut balls, and when you visit this place bring one or two of them with you. Or you may bring a little of the ordinary dishes that you cook yourself — a hodge-podge curry with pumpkin leaves or a preparation with potatoes, eggplants, drumsticks [an Indian vegetable], and little balls of mashed legumes. I want to eat your cooking."

A few days later, Gopal-ma again walked the three miles to see Ramakrishna, this time carrying a hodge-podge curry for him. As soon as she arrived, the Master demanded food as before and after relishing it, said: "What a delicacy! It is like nectar."[40]

During the period of his sadhana the Master was in a mood of divine madness, and so he was quite incapable of discriminating in respect of caste or food — he ate food offered by one and all. While practising Islam, the Master expressed a wish to eat Muslim food. Mathur hired a Hindu cook to prepare Muslim food for the Master under the guidance of a Muslim chef.

The Master described his divine madness: "Once, for a few days, I was out on an excursion with Mathur Babu on his house-boat. We took the trip for a change of air. During that trip we visited Navadwip. One day I saw the boatmen cooking their meal and stood and watched them. Mathur said to me, 'What are you doing there?' I replied with a smile, 'The boatmen are cooking, and their food looks very good.' Mathur felt that I might ask the boatmen to give me a portion of their food; so he said: 'Come away! Come away!'"[41]

There was no end to the Master's childlike curiosity. He used to narrate his strange desires to the devotees and make them laugh. On one occasion he told them: "Once I saw Krishnakishore eating luchi and curry on an ekadashi day [the eleventh day after the new or full moon.] I said to Hriday, 'Hridu, I want to observe Krishnakishore's ekadashi!' And so I did one day. I ate my fill. The next day I had to fast."[42]

Once while returning from Calcutta by carriage, the Master told Ramlal at the junction of Baranagore road: "Ramlal, I am extremely hungry. Go to Fagu's shop and buy some *kachuri* (spicy fried bread)." Fagu was devoted to the Master. He also would serve the Master a glass of water and a betel roll along with the food. Ramlal brought *kachuri*, but found the Master was not in the carriage. The coachman informed him that the Master had gotten down from the carriage and had walked toward the north. Ramlal left the food in the carriage, ran, and held the hand of the Master, who was walking in a god-intoxicated mood. Finally he was able to bring him back to the carriage.[43]

The Master was very fond of *jilipis* and ice cream. Girish Chandra Sen, a Brahmo devotee, wrote: "Whenever we visited Dakshineswar, Sri Ramakrishna always served some refreshments. And when he went to Keshab's house he was also served with luchis and vegetable curries. He was very fond of ice cream. Keshab would always try to get some ice cream for him, and sometimes he would send it to Dakshineswar. Sri Ramakrishna was also fond of jilipis [a sweet]. Once after dinner someone asked him to eat some more. He said, 'My stomach is full, but if you give me a jilipi I shall eat it.' Then he explained: 'During the fair the roads are jammed and overcrowded. At that time it is difficult for a man to pass through the street. But if the Viceroy's carriage comes along, all other carriages make room for his to pass. Similarly, the stomach makes room for jilipis.'"[44]

Sarada Sundari Devi, Keshab Sen's mother, mentioned: "Sri Ramakrishna visited our house quite often, and I first met him in our hall on the third floor. Once during the winter festival of the Brahmo Samaj, he came to the Lily Cottage [Keshab's home]. When the kirtan [singing] was over I said to him, 'Sir, please have some refreshments.' He thought a while and said, 'Yes, the Divine Mother told me to eat a jilipi at Keshab's house.' I gave him a jilipi, which he took in his hand and ate. Then while leaving, he said to Keshab, 'The Divine Mother also told me to eat an ice-cream cone at Keshab's house.' Keshab was wondering where he could get an ice-cream cone, as there was no shop nearby. Just then, however, an ice-cream vendor came by. Keshab bought an ice-cream cone, and Sri Ramakrishna ate it joyfully."[45]

Aswini Kumar Datta wrote in his reminiscences:

I visited him. When I bowed down to him and took a seat, he said, "Can you bring me some of that stuff — a little sour, a little sweet — that begins to fizz when you push down the cork?"
Myself: "Lemonade?"
Master: "Why don't you bring a bottle for me?"
I think I brought him a bottle. I asked him a few questions.
Myself: "Do you observe caste?"
Master: "How can I say yes? I ate curry at Keshab Sen's house. Let me tell you what once happened to me. A man with a long beard [a Muslim] brought some ice here, but I didn't feel like eating it. A little later someone brought me a piece of ice from the same man, and I ate it with great relish. You see, caste restrictions fall away of themselves."[46]

The Master used to chew betel rolls and smoke tobacco. There was a hubble-bubble, earthen cup for tobacco, and other things in the corner of his room. He would tell his nephew Ramlal, "Prepare tobacco for me." Later Ramlal explained the secret of the Master's smoking habit: "The Master often suffered from gas. Vishwanath Kaviraj of Agarpara was treating the Master. The Master asked him, 'Well what is the effect of smoking?' Kaviraj replied: 'It reduces gas in the system. When you smoke, please add some coriander and fennel to the tobacco. You will get good results.' I saw the Master smoke according to the direction of that ayurvedic doctor."[47]

After his meals, the Master would chew a betel roll or some spices from his spice bag. His spice bag contained betel nut, *joan* (ptychotis), fennel seed, cardamom, cubeb, cloves, and so on. He chewed these and shared them with his disciples. One day he gave a betel roll to Gangadhar (later Swami Akhandananda) and said: "Please chew it. It is good to chew it after meals; it removes bad breath." Previously the Master would chew a lot of betel nut, but later he gave it up when he was told by an exorcist that it would make a person more lustful.

In the Brihadaranyaka Upanishad (3:5:1), Yajnavalkya raised this question, "How does the knower of Brahman behave?" Then he answered his own question, saying, "Howsoever he may behave, he is such indeed." The scriptures say: The person who travels in the path of Nirguna Brahman, that person is beyond the injunction and prohibition of the scriptures. The following statement of the Master justifies the scripture: "I used to go to Krishnakishore's house. Once, when I was there, he said to me, 'Why do you chew betel-leaf?' I said: 'It is my sweet pleasure. I shall chew betel-leaf, look at my face in the mirror, and dance naked among a thousand girls. [Because the Master was a vijnani, a man of realization.] Krishnakishore's wife scolded him and said: 'What have you said to Ramakrishna? You don't know how to talk to people.'

"In this state, passions like lust and anger are burnt up, though nothing happens to the physical body. It looks just like any other body; but the inside is all hollow and pure."[48]

At breakfast the Master would take some fruits and sweets; during lunch he would take cooked food that had been offered to the Divine Mother, and at supper a couple of luchis and farina pudding which had also been offered to the Mother. His Calcutta devotees would bring for him various fruits — oranges, mangoes, pomegranates, jamrul, and dried fruits; and various kinds of sweets — sandesh, rasagolla, mihidana, jilipi, sar, curd, kshir, and so on. He enjoyed food and shared it with the devotees. The Master would tell the devotees humorously: "Look, I chant the Mother's name, so I get all kinds of good food."

Towards the end of his life when the Master had cancer, the Holy Mother would prepare various kinds of pudding for him. Because of his throat pain, he could not eat it properly. His taste buds were dulled, so sometimes he would chew amalaki. One day he said to his attendants: "I feel terribly hungry. I would like to eat potfuls of *khichuri* (rice and lentil). But the Divine Mother won't let me eat."

Vaikuntha Nath Sanyal wrote about the Master's desire for eating khichuri: "There was always something new appearing in each of the Master's actions, and so it was with his desire to eat khichuri. When we study the lives of the avatars, we find that each one of them had some liking for a particular food. Ramachandra's favourite dish was *rajbhog* (a sweet); Krishna's, butter and kshir; Buddha's, *phanita* (a sweet); Chaitanya's, flattened rice mixed with sweet curd and fruits. Perhaps the Master expressed a desire to eat khichuri, foreseeing that in the future it could be distributed among all people in the head monastery of his Order, like the prasad of Jagannath in Puri. Swami Vivekananda, the main disciple of the Master, introduced this khichuri offering to the cosmic form of the Master, which was something new in India."[49]

Ramakrishna's Desire to Wear Unusual Clothing

It was hard for Ramakrishna to keep clothes on his body because he was so absorbed in samadhi or in a god-intoxicated state most of the time. After separating the Atman from the body, he lived in the Atman. He had almost no body-consciousness. He was oblivious to his clothes and his surroundings. Aswini Datta wrote:

When the samadhi was over, he began to pace the room and with both hands pulled up the cloth he was wearing, till it reached his waist. One end of it was trailing on the floor and the other was hanging loose.

Nudging my companion, I whispered, "See how nicely he wears his cloth!"

A moment later he threw away the cloth with the words: "Ugh! What a nuisance! Off with it!"

He began to pace up and down the room naked. A few minutes later he sat down, still naked, on the northern end of his cot, facing the west, and asked me, "Well, do you consider me ungentlemanly?"

Myself: "Of course not. You are a perfect gentleman. But why do you ask me that?"

Master: "You see, Shivanath and others don't think I am a gentleman. When they come I have to wrap a cloth or something around me."[50]

The Master was not an austere, dry monk — he was full of fun. One day he put on a red-bordered cloth and went to see Keshab Sen at Jaygopal Sen's garden house. Looking at the red borders, Keshab said: "What's this? Such a flash of colour today! Such a display of red borders!" The Master said, "I have to cast a spell on Keshab; hence this display."[51] (*All laughed.*)

When the Master started to practise madhura bhava in the early days of his sadhana, he was eager to wear women's clothing and ornaments like Radha. Upon learning this, the devoted Mathur provided him with a beautiful and expensive sari from Varanasi, a skirt, a bodice, and a scarf. To complete the transformation, Mathur brought him a wig with curly hair and a set of gold jewellery. When the Master visited Mathur's Calcutta residence, Mathur served food to the Master on a gold plate with a silver cup and glass. Once Mathur bought him a shawl that was worth one thousand rupees — a lot of money at the time. Like a jubilant boy, the Master showed it to people around the temple. But then he examined the shawl: "What is there in this shawl? Nothing but sheep's wool. Like everything else, it is a modification of the five elements. It protects one from cold, no doubt, but that can be done with a blanket or a quilt just as well. And like other material things it does not help one to realize God. Rather, it makes the owner assume an air of superiority and enhances his vanity and egotism. So it takes a man away from God. Such are its defects!" With that thought he threw the shawl on the ground, exclaiming: "It cannot help one to realize God!" He began to spit on it and trample it into the dusty ground. Then he got a match and tried to burn it, but someone grabbed it away from him. When he heard of the shawl's sad fate, Mathur was not at all offended. He only remarked: "Father did the right thing!"[52]

On 13 July 1885, a devotee asked the Master, "What are the desires of those who are incarnations of God?"

Master (*smiling*): "I find that I have not got rid of all my desires. Once I saw a holy man with a shawl, and I too wanted to put on one like it. Even now I have that desire. I don't know whether I shall have to be born again for it."

Balaram (*smiling*): "Then you will be born again just for a shawl?"

The Master remarked: "One has to keep a good desire so that one may give up the body meditating on it."[53]

Although Ramakrishna prayed to the Divine Mother not to give him physical beauty, people nonetheless flocked to see his divine form. In *Sri Ramakrishna and His Divine Play*, Swami Saradananda described a wonderful scene:

> Once while the Master was in Kamarpukur, arrangements were made for his visits to Jayrambati and Sihar. Because the Master was constantly in bhava samadhi, his limbs were as delicate as those of a boy or a woman. He could not walk even a short distance and needed a palanquin or a carriage to convey him. A palanquin had been brought for the trip to Sihar via Jayrambati. Hriday was also ready to go. After lunch the Master put on a scarlet silk cloth and fastened his gold amulet around his arm. His lips were crimson from chewing betel. As he was about to get into the palanquin, he noticed that a large crowd had gathered on the street nearby. Seeing so many men and women around, the Master asked Hriday in wonder, "Hriday, what is the reason for this crowd?"
>
> Hriday: "For what else? You are going away, and they (*pointing to the crowd*) won't see you for some days. So they have come to have a parting look at you."
>
> Master: "But they see me every day. What new feature has attracted them in such large numbers today?"
>
> Hriday: "You look so handsome in that silken cloth, and your lips shine with crimson colour. That is why they want to see you."
>
> As soon as the Master heard that those people were attracted to his physical beauty, an unusual mood filled his mind. He thought: "Alas! These people are preoccupied by this external, ephemeral, physical beauty. No one wants to see God, who is within."
>
> He had abhorred physical beauty beforehand, but this incident increased that aversion a thousandfold. "What?" he exclaimed. "People are gathering just to look at a man! I won't go. Wherever I go, people will crowd about like this!" In utter disgust the Master returned to his room and took off the silk cloth. Filled with humility, the Master did not go to Jayrambati and Sihar that day. In spite of the entreaties of Hriday and others, he did not go out at all. Just imagine, O reader, how this unique person was repelled by his body and felt it to be insignificant. And then consider ourselves: How crazy we are for physical beauty! How busy we are in meticulously grooming and dressing the body![54]

The cloth, shirt, shawl, coat, slippers and other things that Ramakrishna wore are preserved in the museum at Belur Math. The Master used to wear a thin red-bordered cloth and a shirt made from cheap fabric. In winter, he wore a black coat, a muffler, socks, and a cap that covered his ears. When the Master was sick in the Cossipore garden house, Hirananda came from Sindh to see him. He suggested that the Master would be more comfortable if he wore pajamas made in Sindh. The Master agreed and reminded him, "Please don't forget to send the pajamas."[55] One winter, M. brought a denim shirt, but the Master did not accept it. M. usually supplied the Master with the things he needed every day, such as a towel, a small cloth for his oil bath, a stool, a stone bowl, a knife, a clay bowl used for preparing tobacco, and so forth.

The Master's Desire to Travel

Because the Master stayed mainly in a divine mood, his limbs were as tender as butter. Once he cut his finger while breaking a luchi. It hurt him if the barber shaved him with a razor, so he trimmed the Master's beard with scissors instead. It was hard for the Master to walk bare-footed. When he travelled even a short distance, he would go by palanquin, horse carriage, or boat. Once he lamented: "Gauranga and Nityananda walked door to door with the message of God, and I can't go anyplace without a carriage." Of course, the Master had walked when he first arrived in Calcutta from Kamarpukur. When he visited Kamarpukur later, he crossed some of the distance by boat, some by train, and some by bullock cart.

On three occasions Ramakrishna travelled with Keshab Chandra Sen by steamer. The first trip was on 15 July 1881. Nagendra Nath Gupta recorded the event: "In 1881 Keshab Chandra Sen, accompanied by a fairly large party, went on board a steam yacht belonging to his son-in-law, Maharaja Nripendra Narayan Bhup of Coochbehar, to Dakshineswar to meet Ramakrishna Paramahamsa. I had the good fortune to be included in that party. We did not land, but Ramakrishna, accompanied by his nephew Hriday, who brought a basket of puffed rice and some sandesh for us, boarded the steamer, which steamed up the river towards Somra."[56]

Girish Chandra Sen also describes this outing in his reminiscences: "He was like a simple child. The examples he used in his teachings he wanted to see with his own eyes. For that reason he expressed a desire to ride a steamer. Once Keshab picked Sri Ramakrishna up from Dakshineswar in a steamer. Some Brahmo followers were with them. Sri Ramakrishna was pleased to hear the *jhak-jhak* sound of the steamer. One of our friends requested him to look through the telescope of the steamer, but he replied: 'My mind is now attached to God. How can I withdraw it from Him and put it on this telescope?'"[57]

His second trip with Keshab took place on 22 February 1882. The Master's nephew Ramlal Chattopadhyay wrote about this:

One day Keshab Sen came to Dakshineswar with his followers and asked the Master: "Sir, Mr. Cook is a pandit and devotee, and he is waiting in the boat. Would you like to go on a boat ride with us?" The Master agreed and said to me, "O Ramlal, you come with me." When we reached the boat, Keshab introduced the Master to Mr. Cook, who was very happy.

After a while the steamboat came near the Barabazar bridge, and the Master said to Keshab: "Keshab, I am hungry. Could you give me something to eat?"

Keshab: "Tell me, sir, what you would like to eat. I shall get it for you."

Master: "Let Ramlal go and get some jilipi."

I came back with jilipi, a betel roll, and tobacco for the Master. Then the Master asked me to clean a place on the steamer with Ganges water, and he ate the refreshments there. After he had finished eating, he smoked tobacco. It was evening and he was in an ecstatic mood. We helped him get down from the steamer, and he was staggering as we put him in the carriage. The Europeans laughed and whispered to Keshab. I asked Keshab why they were laughing, and he replied: "They said that the Master has drunk too much wine, so he is staggering. I told them that he did not drink any wine. He is in a divine mood, and that is why he is intoxicated." Those people were amazed, seeing the Master in samadhi.[58]

On 27 October 1882 M. recorded the details of the Master's third trip with Keshab in *The Gospel of Sri Ramakrishna*: "It was Friday, the day of the Lakshmi Puja. Keshab Chandra Sen had arranged a boat trip on the Ganges for Sri Ramakrishna. About four o'clock in the afternoon the steamboat with Keshab and his Brahmo followers cast anchor in the Ganges alongside the Kali temple at Dakshineswar.

"Sri Ramakrishna was in his room talking with Vijay and Haralal. Some disciples of Keshab entered. Bowing before the Master, they said to him: 'Sir, the steamer has arrived. Keshab Babu has asked us to take you there.' A small boat was to carry the Master to the steamer. No sooner did he get into the boat than he lost outer consciousness in samadhi."[59]

While Mathur was alive, the Master used his gorgeous phaeton to visit places in Calcutta. After Mathur's death, the Master used a carriage rented from Beni Saha. The Master enjoyed indulging his fancies and satisfying his curiosity; he did not care for monotony. His life was firmly grounded in God. Nonetheless, he would go to Calcutta to see the glamour of the city. He went to the Bengal Photographer's studio to see how photos were taken; he saw the Ochterloney Monument, Fort William, the Governor's Palace, Calcutta's Maidan (large park), the zoo, the museum, the circus, the Kali temple of South Calcutta, and so on. He saw plays at the theatres in Calcutta, including *Nava Vrindaban*, *Chaitanya-lila*, *Nimai Sannyas*, *Brishaketu*, *Prahlad-charitra*, *Daksha-yajna*, and so on. He went to see the picture gallery of gods and goddesses at Nandalal Basu's house in Baghbazar. The Master accompanied Mathur on pilgrimage and visited Vaidyanath, Varanasi, Mathura, Vrindaban, Prayag, and Navadwip. Mountains and oceans are the largest things in the world. The Master had a desire to see them. When M. returned after a visit to Darjeeling, the Master asked him whether he had experienced any awakening of consciousness upon seeing the vast Himalayas. The Master also wanted to see the Padma River in East Bengal.

Ramakrishna's Wishful Thinking

According to Vedanta, the mind creates the body. Through intense desire and will power, the human mind can change the body. Ordinary people cannot understand this phenomenon. St. Francis of Assisi meditated on Christ so intensely that stigmata manifested in his body. When Ramakrishna practised dasya sadhana, the attitude of a servant towards God as exemplified by Hanuman, the monkey devotee of Rama, his tailbone became slightly elongated like a monkey's tail. And when he practised madhura bhava, the romantic love of God that is epitomized by the gopis of Vrindaban, he actually began to resemble a woman.

Whenever the Master practised any sadhana, he put his whole heart and soul into it and remained absorbed in the mood associated with it day and night. He never gave up a sadhana until he had succeeded in it. Swami Saradananda described an interesting desire of the Master:

> At the threshold of his youth a kind of fancy arose in the Master's mind, prompted by the influence of his inner feminine nature. Because they were born as women, the gopis of Vrindaban attained Satchidananda Krishna through love. This led him to think that if he had been born as a woman, he could worship and attain Krishna like the gopis. Thus, viewing the male body as an obstacle to attaining Krishna, he imagined that if he were to be born again he would be a beautiful young widow with long hair, born in a brahmin family, knowing none other than Krishna as her husband. There would be provision for plain food and clothes and a small plot of land next to his hut, where he would grow a few vegetables. There would be an

elderly woman with him who served as a guardian, a cow that he would milk himself, and a spinning wheel. His boyish imagination went further. After finishing the household work for the day, he would sing songs about Krishna while spinning the cotton. Then in the evening he would make sweets from the milk of that cow and cry piteously that he might feed the sweets to Krishna with his own hands. Pleased, Krishna would suddenly appear as a cowherd boy and eat them; thus he would visit daily without anyone knowing. Although the Master's fantasy was not fulfilled in that particular manner, it was accomplished in a modified form when he practised madhura bhava."[60]

What an incredible desire the Master had! In the Bhagavata, Uddhava carried a message from Krishna to the gopis of Vrindaban. When he observed their devotion, he was overwhelmed. He bowed down to those milkmaids and prayed: "May I be born as a tree or a creeper of Vrindaban that grows from the dust touched by the feet of the gopis."

The Master prayed to his beloved Divine Mother for his necessities, saying: "Mother, who will look after me? I haven't the power to take care of myself. I want to listen only to talk about Thee. I want to feed Thy devotees. I want to give a little help to those whom I chance to meet. How will all that be possible, Mother? Give me a rich man to stand by me."[61] In answer to that prayer, Mathur served the Master for fourteen years. Later, the Divine Mother engaged Shambhu Mallick, Surendra Mitra, Balaram Basu, and others to look after the Master.

On 2 March 1884 Ramakrishna told the devotees:

"The body has, indeed, only a momentary existence. God alone is real. Years ago, when I had been suffering terribly from indigestion, Hriday said to me, 'Do ask the Mother to cure you.' I felt ashamed to speak to Her about my illness. I said to Her: 'Mother, I saw a skeleton in the Asiatic Society Museum. It was pieced together with wires into a human form. O Mother, please keep my body together a little, like that, so that I may sing Thy name and glories.'

"Without desires the body cannot live. (*Smiling*) I had one or two desires. I prayed to the Mother, 'O Mother, give me the company of those who have renounced lust and gold. I should like to enjoy the society of Thy jnanis and bhaktas. So give me a little strength that I may walk hither and thither and visit those people.' But she did not give me the strength to walk."

Trailokya (*smiling*): "Have all the desires been fulfilled?"

Master (*smiling*): "No, there are still a few left. The body is really impermanent. When my arm was broken I said to the Mother, 'Mother, it hurts me very much.' At once She revealed to me a carriage and its driver. Here and there a few screws were loose. The carriage moved as the driver directed it. It had no power of its own. Why then do I take care of the body? It is to enjoy God, to sing His name and glories, and to go about visiting His jnanis and bhaktas."[62]

Krishna said in the Gita that four kinds of people worship God: those who are distressed, those who seek knowledge, those who seek wealth, and those who are spiritually wise. Although the Master suffered from terminal cancer, he was ashamed to ask the Divine Mother to cure it. Swami Saradananda recorded a conversation that illustrates this:

> Pandit Shashadhar told the Master: "Sir, we have read in the scriptures that a great soul like yourself can cure his own physical illness by mere will power. If you but concentrate your mind on the affected part of the body for a while with the resolve that it be healed, you will be cured. Why don't you try it, sir?"
>
> The Master replied: "As a pandit, how can you make such a suggestion? This mind has been given up to God once and for all. How can I withdraw it from Him and make it dwell on this cage of flesh and bone?"
>
> Pandit Shashadhar was silenced. But Swami Vivekananda and other devotees pressed the issue further. As soon as the pandit left, Swamiji fervently begged the Master to follow the pandit's advice. He said, "Sir, you must cure yourself, at least for our sake."
>
> Master: "Do you think I'm suffering like this because I want to? Of course I want to get better, but does that desire cure my disease? It all depends on Mother."
>
> Swamiji: "Then please pray to Her for your recovery. She will definitely listen to you."
>
> Master: "It is easy for you to say that, but I could never utter such words."
>
> Swamiji: "No, sir, that won't do. You must tell the Mother about it, at least for our sake."
>
> Master: "All right, let me see if I can ask Her."
>
> After a few hours Swamiji returned to the Master and asked: "Sir, did you ask the Mother? What did She say?"
>
> Master: "I said to the Mother, 'I can't eat anything because of this pain (*pointing to the sore in the throat*) — please let me eat a little.' But She pointed to all of you and said: 'Why, you are eating through so many mouths already!' I then felt ashamed and couldn't utter another word."[63]

According to the Yoga scriptures, yogis attain various occult powers by *samyama* which comes from concentration, meditation, and samadhi.

Thus yogis can perform miracles. The Master did not care for such powers because they develop the ego and distract the mind from God. He said: "People of small intellect seek occult powers — powers to cure disease, win a lawsuit, walk on water, and such things. But the genuine devotees of God don't want anything except His lotus feet. One day Hriday said to me, 'Uncle, please ask the Mother for some powers, some occult powers.' I have the nature of a child. While I was practising japa in the Kali temple, I said to Kali, 'Mother, Hriday asked me to pray to You for some occult powers.' The Divine Mother at once showed me a vision. A middle-aged prostitute, about forty years old, appeared and was covered with filth. The Mother showed me that occult powers are as abominable as the filth of that prostitute. Thereupon I went to Hriday and scolded him, saying: 'Why did you teach me such a prayer? It is because of you that I had such an experience.'"[64]

People are eager to become famous through scholarship. The Divine Mother taught the Master everything. He said: "Weeping, I prayed to the Mother: 'O Mother, reveal to me what is contained in the Vedas and the Vedanta. Reveal to me what is in the Purana and the Tantra.' One by one She has revealed all these to me."[65]

Set Fire to Desires

As day and night never appear at the same time, so desire for God and desire for the world cannot coexist. The scriptures therefore advise seekers of God to be desireless. The Kaivalya Upanishad says: "Not by work, not by progeny, or wealth; only by renunciation does one attain immortality." Desires bind human beings — and a bound person is miserable. No one wants misery; people want bliss. Ramakrishna was free from desires himself, and he taught his disciples how to be rid of desires. He said: "Mental renunciation is the essential thing. One must set fire to one's desires. Then alone can one succeed."[66]

"Subtle are the ways of dharma. One cannot realize God if one has even the least trace of desire. A thread cannot pass through the eye of a needle if it has the smallest fibre sticking out."[67]

"No spiritual progress is possible without the renunciation of lust and gold. I renounced these three: land, wife, and wealth."[68]

M. heard the Master say: "Desires are hidden like ghee clinging to the sides of an empty jar. A man had a ghee jar and it was empty. His neighbour came and asked for a little ghee. The man said that he had no ghee. The neighbour said: 'Why don't you put the jar in the sun?' Shortly a cup of melted ghee appeared inside the jar. Thus desires remain hidden in the mind in a dry form. When they get the heat of the sun — in other words, when they come in contact with sense objects — they manifest. If a person practises austerity and develops the fire of knowledge, all desires are burnt to ashes."[69]

At first, when one sits for meditation, sense objects appear in the mind. But when meditation becomes deep, they no longer bother the aspirant. It is not unusual for bad thoughts to appear in our minds when we sit for meditation; they also appeared in the Master's mind. He recalled: "How many things I saw during meditation! I vividly perceived before me a heap of rupees, a shawl, a plate of sweets, and two women with rings in their noses. 'What do you want?' I asked my mind. 'Do you want to enjoy any of these things?' 'No,' replied the mind, 'I don't want any of them. I don't want anything but the lotus feet of God.'"[70]

Worldly desire is the greatest enemy of spiritual life. The scriptures describe many ways to kill this enemy. The fire of renunciation, the fire of knowledge, discrimination, unselfish action, and devotion to God, are just a few of those methods. The Master cautioned his devotees, saying: "During meditation if you find any worldly desire in your mind, know that a great obstacle has cropped up. At that time please stop your meditation and pray wholeheartedly to God, 'O Lord, don't fulfill this desire of mine.'"[71] The desire of a true devotee is always fulfilled. An aspirant gets what he or she wants if the desire is sincere. Fulfillment of desire depends on a person's sincerity.

Ramakrishna was without desire. He was free from desire because his only object of desire was the Self, and that desire had been satisfied. His life was untouched by karma and its consequences, and free from ignorance and afflictions. He was not an ordinary jiva, who is born with ignorance and the drive to fulfill his or her desires. He was an avatar, an extraordinary Supreme Being.

Ramakrishna's life and speech were established in truth, and so his fancies and desires were always fulfilled. One day he said to M.: "Through faith alone one attains everything. I used to say, 'I shall take all this [his spiritual experience] to be true if I meet a certain person or if a certain officer of the temple garden talks to me.' What I would think of would invariably come to pass."

M.: "Was there never any exception?"

Master: "No. At that time everything happened that way. I would repeat the name of God and believe that a certain thing would happen, and it would invariably come to pass."[72]

Ramakrishna taught how to play with desires. He showed how one can transform worldly desires into spiritual desires and become free from bondage.

5

Ramakrishna and the People of Calcutta

Everything created in this world is subject to change. This is the law. Ayodhya, the birthplace of Ramachandra, and Mathura, the birthplace of Krishna, have changed over time but they still exist. Poets, artists, writers, playwrights, and historians of different ages have used their imagination to describe those places, narrating the lives and messages of the ancient teachers, composing songs, writing stories and dramas, creating paintings, and making sculptures. Their descriptions and writings have kept the great teachers' lives vivid in the minds of innumerable people and they continue to inspire them.

How different are present-day Calcutta and Kamarpukur from what they were in the nineteenth century! Then, one could reach Kamarpukur from Calcutta only by crossing the Ganges, Damodar, Mundeswari, and Dwarakeswar rivers with great difficulty; whereas now there are bridges. In the course of time, our modern technological civilization has completely transformed the unpolluted, virgin village such as Kamarpukur. One now finds electricity and paved roads in Kamarpukur. There are cinemas, restaurants, hotels, hospitals, schools, and colleges. People have telephones, computers, television, and cars. Everything available in the city of Calcutta has reached the village of Kamarpukur. People in Calcutta live like prisoners in their brick buildings. There is little opportunity for the people of Calcutta to relax for a few days in a remote village like Kamarpukur and breathe a little fresh air. When we go to Kamarpukur now, we have to imagine the rural and unpolluted atmosphere of Ramakrishna's Kamarpukur.

Imagine Kamarpukur one hundred and seventy years ago. She was like the village queen of Bengal, full of green trees, vast meadows, lakes and ponds, fruits and flowers, huts and temples. The villagers were simple and unsophisticated. Blue sky above, green paddy field below, bright sunshine all around, wild monsoon clouds during the rainy season, colourful roads of red dust, the sound of birdsong, the gentle and cool breeze blowing over the meadow — these scenes spontaneously transport the mind to an ethereal plane. They are not mere imagination; they did in fact exist in Kamarpukur — the Bengal Bethlehem — Ramakrishna's birthplace.

Look at this pond: It belongs to the *kamars*, or blacksmiths. The village of Kamarpukur got its name from this pond. As the village women sit on its ghat and clean their utensils, pots, and pans, they share their stories of joy and sorrow. The pond is covered with a layer of green scum. The women push this scum aside by splashing the water before they fill their pitchers. One can hear a *bhak-bhak* sound as the water enters the pitchers, but there is no sound once they are full. Similarly, after God-realization one becomes silent. When the pitchers are removed, the algae flows gently back to cover the clean water. It is like a game between maya and Satchidananda — veiling and unveiling.

Every morning the farmers walk through the zigzag paths of the village with their ploughs and bullocks as they make their way to the fields. They tie puffed rice in the corner of a piece of cloth and carry it with them for breakfast. There is a grocer's shop under a banyan tree at a corner where two paths meet. Here the villagers can buy everything they need: rice and lentils, oil and spices, sago and barley, candy and biscuits, matches and kerosene oil. This is also where they hear the village news: who was born, who has died, who is engaged, and other gossip. The village market takes place twice a week, in the afternoon. People from neighbouring villages come to shop as well as to sell their merchandize. One can hear their *ho-ho* calls from a distance. Unlike in the city, here there is no rush. Elevated blood pressure, diabetes, stress, heart problems, and other such conditions are unknown to the villagers. They are simple, gentle, honest, and religious.

Blessed is this village of Kamarpukur! It has many places of worship: The Yogi Shiva temple, the Gopeswar Shiva temple, the Pyne Shiva temple, the Lahas' Durga temple. Nearby are the Shiva temple of Mukundapur and the Vishalakshi temple of Anur. The whole village resounds with religious festivals throughout the year: Shiva's gajan, Krishna-lila, Ram-lila, Durga Puja, Dharma festival, and other festivals celebrated with singing, dancing, fasting, vigils, and so on.

There are two cremation grounds located at opposite ends of the village. Bhuti's cremation ground is near Bhuti's Canal; Budhui Moral's cremation ground is near a large pond. There are two big banyan trees on the east side of that pond. It is eerie there in the evening. The two cremation grounds remind people that the human body is destructible and this world is impermanent.

Palm trees line both sides of the main road to Puri, which skirts the south side of the village. At twilight the boys return home with their cows, hooves churning up red dust against the reddish sunset. The lively boys shout "hei-hei" as they chase the cows, and some play bamboo flutes. It is a sight to see.

In the evening one can hear the auspicious sounds of conch shells and bells during the vesper services held in the temples and homes of the village. The chandelier in the temple of the wealthy Lahas and the oil lamp in Ramakrishna's poor cottage are both lit. The dark night descends on Kamarpukur. Mothers and grandmothers begin to tell their children the immortal stories from the Ramayana and the Mahabharata. The flickering flames of the oil lamps reflected on the mud walls of the thatched huts and the boundless imagination of the children create a mysterious world.

Ramakrishna was born in this atmosphere. Like the ancient yogis, he learned from nature. Barefoot, he walked in pastures with the other village boys without caring about the sun or rain, cold or heat. Beauty and serenity, love and peace nourished the mind of the young Ramakrishna for seventeen years. From his birth he was endowed with purity and simplicity, love and devotion, truthfulness and nonattachment. He learned how with love for God one can overcome grief and misery, pain and poverty.

Vaikuntha Nath Sanyal wrote: "It seems Goddess Nature gave birth to this ever-pure child [Ramakrishna] by churning up all of Her divine qualities. Because of this, and because She imparted Her scientific wisdom to him, he found unity in diversity. He saw God manifested in fields and lakes, fruits and flowers, birds and beasts, temples and cremation grounds, men and women. Thus he enjoyed unspeakable bliss at all times."[1]

Kamarpukur 1930s

Calcutta mid-19th century

Calcutta in the Nineteenth Century

Ramakrishna left Kamarpukur for Calcutta in 1853, when he was seventeen. Despite his elder brother's request, the young Ramakrishna refused to acquire a mere bread-winning education. He said: "I want to have that education which gives a person true knowledge of God and makes life blessed." Ramakrishna observed how people in Calcutta thought; and he saw how they ran after sense enjoyments and roamed the city in search of money and name and fame. With his sharp discriminating intellect he understood that a life predicated on worldly enjoyment cannot bring permanent peace and bliss. Even at his tender age, he realized that these people would not be freed from misery, grief, and the bondage of maya; and he was concerned for them. During Ramakrishna's time, the people of Calcutta, in general, considered the world alone to be worthy of their attention; God was not worthy of their time. Though these people were educated, they were ignorant.

The city of Calcutta was the capital of the British government in India, and the city had been carried away by the current of Western culture. The people there were argumentative and sceptical, and they put their faith in science and reasoning. After observing the lifestyle of these Calcutta people, Ramakrishna took shelter at the temple garden of Dakshineswar. There he began his spiritual journey in order to prepare himself for confronting those Westernized hedonists.

If one does not know the background of nineteenth-century Calcutta, one will not understand how Ramakrishna reacted to the Westernized people he found there. The nineteenth century was a revolutionary time for Bengal and for India as a whole. There was a renaissance in religion, literature, education, social movements, and politics. British rule brought Western civilization and the Christian religion to India. Like a great flood, these forces began sweeping aside the customs of traditional Hindu society, Hindu civilization, and Hindu religion. Indians were dazzled by Western science, philosophy, literature, and materialism. The Christian missionaries took advantage of the people's blind and helpless condition to attack the indigenous society, customs, literature, scriptures, and religion. Thus the people of Calcutta lost confidence in themselves and began imitating the West. In desperation, they cried out for help.

The Bible came to supplant the Vedas, Vedanta, and the Gita. The stories of the Ramayana, Mahabharata, and Puranas were considered unsophisticated folktales and were replaced with Maria Edgeworth's tales. The works of Shakespeare replaced the works of Kalidasa and Bhavabhuti. Most of the young people of Calcutta took initiation, so to speak, from three gurus: David Hare, Henry Vivian Derozio, and Thomas Babington Macaulay. These men taught the Calcutta populace that everything of the West was good, and everything of the East was bad.

Derozio was born in Calcutta in 1809 and died in 1831 when he was only twenty-two. At the age of eighteen he became a professor in the Hindu College, where, through the force of his personality and brilliance he formed two groups known as "Young Bengal" and "Young Calcutta." His biographer, Thomas Edwards, wrote about him: "Neither before nor since his day has any teacher, within the walls of any native educational establishment in India, ever exercised such an influence over his pupils." The students of Calcutta began to learn from this young Eurasian poet, philosopher, and teacher the thought of Francis Bacon, John Locke, George Berkeley, Charles Reade, Thomas Paine, Dugald Stewart, and other Western savants. A great revolution was raising a ferment in their minds; they began to use reason in evaluating everything. Their motto was: "Don't accept anything without evidence." They demanded to know *why, when, how, where,* and *what* for everything, and they questioned ancient religious traditions and social customs. They gave free rein to these rebellious views in their meetings, lectures, debates, newspapers, and magazines. The youth of Calcutta shouted in schools and colleges: "Destroy Hindu dharma!" and "Wipe out superstition!" When young people on the street saw brahmin pandits wearing traditional religious marks, they would yell at them, "Hey there, we eat beef! We eat beef!" The most extreme actions that the students of Hindu college carried out were to eat bread and meat bought from a Muslim shop, or else to drink alcohol. A Christian missionary named Reverend Hough used to live in Howrah. During a youth convention at his home, his young daughter served wine to Ramtanu Lahiri, one of the movement's leaders. Thus the custom of drinking was introduced among students.

Binay Ghosh wrote in his famous book, *Calcutta Culture*: "The culture of Calcutta is a distinct entity; it is neither Bengali nor British. The 'Calcutta Culture' originated from the polarity between the Bengali and British cultures." Observing the Bengalis' keen desire to imitate Westerners at that time, Dwijendralal Roy wrote a parody:

We gave up the dhoti and the chadar;
We put on pants, coat, hat, and boots;
We're dressed like a British monkey.

We laugh like the British,
We cough like the French,
And we love to smoke cigarettes,
Extending our legs as they do.

Calcutta was in deep turmoil. The *Purani Roshni*, or the School of Old Light, came forward to counteract the *Nayi Roshni*, or the School of New Light. On 7 March 1835, Lord William Bentinck, the governor general of India, made English the official language of India. Language is the carrier of ideas, and the dominant idea at this time was pure materialism. However, some of the new social movements did benefit society: For example, the Nayi Roshni abolished the custom of widow burning, and established the Calcutta Medical College and Calcutta University.

Raja Ram Mohan Roy, Devendra Nath Tagore, Keshab Chandra Sen, Shashadhar Tarkachudamani, Ishwar Chandra Vidyasagar, Bankim Chandra Chattopadhyay, and other leaders tried to stop the Western influence from spreading, sometimes through compromise and sometimes through obstruction. Ram Mohan Roy established the Brahmo Samaj; Devendra Nath Tagore started the Tattwabodhini Sabha and the Tattwabodhini Pathshala; orthodox Vaishnavas opened Hari Sabha centres in an attempt to preserve their own traditions.

While Calcutta was shaking from a veritable storm of lectures, social reforms, educational reforms, religious movements, political struggles, and so forth, Ramakrishna was at Dakshineswar deeply immersed in meditation in the Panchavati. In 1856 the Widow Marriage Bill was passed through the efforts of Ishwar Chandra Vidyasagar, who also started a crusade against polygamy and child marriage. In 1857 the Sepoy Mutiny broke out, heralding the beginning of the uprising against the British. That same year, Calcutta University was inaugurated. It was also the year that Keshab Chandra Sen joined the Brahmo Samaj of Devendra Nath Tagore. Later, however, conflict arose from their difference of opinion: Devendra's religious views were based on Vedanta, whereas the source of Keshab's inspiration was Christ's life and message. In 1863 Keshab established the Brahmo Samaj of India. It is amazing to think of the condition of Calcutta during that period. On one side there was orthodox Hindu society, and on the other Derozio's radical youth; in-between were moderate groups such as the Brahmo Samaj. Calcutta was then like a place devastated by a tornado: Its religious life and society were unsettled, and people were fearful, confused, and disoriented. Now the question arose: Who would show the way out of this chaotic labyrinth?

A Great Weapon for Destroying the Demon of Doubt

In 1836, Ramakrishna was born in Kamarpukur to counteract Western materialism. In ancient times, Ramachandra killed the demon Ravana; Krishna killed the demons Kamsa and Shishupala. In this age, as Swami Vivekananda said, Ramakrishna used his spiritual power to destroy the subtle, invisible, and demoniacal doubts that poisoned the minds of the people of Calcutta. Narendranath Datta (later Swami Vivekananda), a product of the Young Bengal Movement, went to Dakshineswar to ask Ramakrishna this question: "Does God exist?" Ramakrishna, the temple priest of Dakshineswar, gave a convincing answer: "Yes, I have seen God. I see Him as I see you here, only more clearly. God can be seen. One can talk to Him. But who cares for God? People shed torrents of tears for their wives, children, wealth, and property, but who weeps for the vision of God? If one cries sincerely for God, one can surely see Him."

Swami Saradananda wrote: "Mathur had a fair knowledge of English. When Western thought and culture enter the mind through English education, a person develops self-esteem and feels equal to all. Mathur had this kind of independent attitude. That is why we find him trying to use reasoning to dissuade the Master from losing control in ecstatic love of God. As an example we will describe here the conversation between the Master and Mathur on whether God is bound to abide by His own laws regarding worldly matters. The Master said: 'Mathur told me: "Even God has to obey His own laws. Once God establishes a law, not even He can overrule it." I said: "What do you mean? He who makes a law can unmake it if he so desires, or he can replace it with another law." Mathur refused to accept this view. He said: "It is God who made the law that a red flowering tree will produce only red flowers and never white ones. Let me see if He can produce a white blossom on a red flowering tree." I replied: "If He wills, He can do anything — even that." Still he refused to accept my words.

"'The next day when I went towards the pine grove to answer the call of nature, I saw two flowers on the same branch of a red hibiscus tree, one red and the other dazzling white without any red stain. I broke off the branch, took it to Mathur, and said, "Look." Mathur then said, "Yes, Father, I am defeated!"'"[2] Thus the Master removed Mathur's doubt.

There was no end to the tests that Ramakrishna had to undergo from the youth of Bengal. Narendra tested him by putting money underneath his mattress to verify any physical reaction to the touch of money. One night when Jogin did not see the Master in his room, he thought that the Master had secretly gone to the nahabat to see his wife. He was embarrassed when he found the Master returning from the Panchavati, but the Master reassured him and was pleased that his disciple had tested him.

Once the Master said to Mahendralal Sarkar: "My hand gets all twisted up if I hold money in it; my breathing stops."[3] And when Dr. Bhagavan Rudra, came to see Ramakrishna, the Master said to him: "Do you see what has happened to me? I cannot touch money." Saying so he extended his hand to the doctor and said: "Put some money in my hand to test me." As soon as the doctor placed money in the palm of the Master's hand, his breath stopped and his hand became numb. The doctor was dumbfounded; such an experience had never been recorded in the annals of science.[4]

Who Were the People of Calcutta?

Ramakrishna saw three kinds of people in Calcutta: yogis (spiritual aspirants), bhogis (enjoyers of sense objects), and yogi-bhogis. But most of the people he met were bhogis. When the Master first met Narendra and saw prodigious spiritual signs on his body, he marvelled: "Is it possible that such a great person endowed with sattva guna can be found in Calcutta?" Most of the disciples of Ramakrishna came from Calcutta and the surrounding areas.

When the Master said "Calcutta people," he meant the city's Westernized and worldly inhabitants. They were beggars in search of name and fame, and their main goal was the enjoyment of lust and gold. They were bound souls and atheistic. By referring to "Calcutta people," the Master was indicating all the sceptical hedonists of the world. One should not conclude that the Master held a low opinion of everyone who lived in Calcutta at that time; if this had been true, he would not have sacrificed his life for the spiritual welfare of those people. "Calcutta people" can be found in Europe, America, and other parts of the globe. He remarked: "It is not in England alone that one sees attachment to worldly things. You see it everywhere."[5]

The Master made some strong remarks about the bound souls of Calcutta so that they might be awakened. He did not hate anybody. Even his strongest criticisms were sweet, vivid, and poetic. For example: "Bound souls never think of God. If they get any leisure they indulge in idle gossip and foolish talk, or they engage in fruitless work. Those who are in bondage are sunk in worldliness and forgetful of God. Not even by mistake do they think of God. Bound souls are tied to the world by the fetters of 'lust and gold.' They are bound hand and foot."[6]

The Master continued: "The souls that are entangled, involved in worldliness, never come to their senses. They lie in the net but are not even conscious that they are entangled. If you speak of God before them they at once leave the place. The entangled souls repeat those very actions that make them suffer so much. They are like the camel, which eats thorny bushes till the blood streams from its mouth, but still will not give them up. Such a man may have lost his son and be stricken with grief, but still he will have children year after year. He may ruin himself by his daughter's marriage, but still he will go on having daughters every year. And he says: 'What can I do? It's just my luck!' When he goes to a holy place he doesn't have any time to think of God. He almost kills himself carrying bundles for his wife."[7] Comparing bound souls to worms, the Master said: "The worm thrives in filth; it is happy there. It dies if put in a pot of rice." Bound souls are like "pecked fruits." They prefer the odour of "fish baskets" to flowers. He also commented: "There are people whose spiritual consciousness is not at all awakened even though they hear about God a thousand times. They are like a crocodile, on whose hide you cannot make any impression with a sword."[8]

An Expedition to Calcutta

Ramakrishna attained perfection after twelve years of strenuous sadhana. He travelled along various religious paths and finally discovered that they all lead to one and the same goal. He then declared: "As many faiths, so many paths." Then he went on to confront the materialistic milieu of Calcutta, the capital of the British empire in India. However, his health was very delicate. Once he tearfully lamented: "Gaur and Nitai carried the message of God from door to door, and I cannot go anyplace without a carriage." The Master used hired horse carriages to visit the homes of devotees who lived in Calcutta.

The road between Cossipore and Baranagore was extremely rough as it was made of brick and stone. The jerking of the carriage would even speed up the digestion of food in the stomach. Generally, Latu, Baburam, or Ramlal accompanied the Master and would carry the Master's towel and his spice bag, which contained fennel seed, cubeb, and cloves. The Master would chew these spices on his expeditions to Calcutta. Seated in the carriage, he would make jokes and look out the door.

Upon arriving at the Brahmo Samaj in Calcutta, he would hurl his powerful weapon — humility — at the Brahmos. He would enter the

Brahmo temple and bow down, touching his head to the ground; then addressing the audience, he would say, "Salutations to the modern Brahma-jnanis." The Master recalled: "I visited Keshab at his house in Coolootola Street. Hriday was with me. We were shown into the room where Keshab was working. He was writing something. After a long while he put aside his pen, got off his chair, and sat on the floor with us. But he didn't salute us or show us respect in any other way.

"He used to come here now and then. One day in a spiritual mood I said to him: 'One should not sit before a sadhu with one leg over the other. That increases one's rajas.' As soon as he and his friends would arrive, I would salute them before they bowed to me. Thus they gradually learnt to salute a holy man, touching the ground with their foreheads."[9] Thus Ramakrishna bent the heads of the Brahmos to the ground by his humility.

Once Dr. Abdul Wajij, a Muslim, went with Ram Chandra Datta to see Ramakrishna in Dakshineswar. He described the event in his reminiscences: "When we arrived, Sri Ramakrishna was not in his room. We waited for him at the Panchavati. When Sri Ramakrishna came there, Ram Babu bowed down to him. We decided not to bow down, as according to our religious tradition, we are not supposed to bow down to anyone other than Allah. We were, however, willing to pay proper respect to him. But as soon as he came near he bowed down to us. We were puzzled and were compelled to bow down to him."[10]

In the 1880s the Young Bengal began to visit Ramakrishna. Girish Chandra Ghosh described the atmosphere at that time:

> I must tell you the condition of religion that prevailed in the country at that time. During my school days those who were called "Young Bengal" were the people who were recognized in society as respectable and learned. They were the first products of Western education in Bengal. The majority of them were materialists. A small minority had been converted to Christianity. Some of them accepted the creed of the Brahmo Samaj, but few of them had any respect for Hinduism. Orthodox Hindus were bitterly torn by sectarianism. Conflict between Shaktas and Vaishnavas was very strong. And Vaishnavism too was divided into many sects, each contending for supremacy over the other. Rivalry was growing fast between one sect and another. Moreover there were other faiths prevalent at the time. Each faith condemned the followers of the other faiths to the darkness of hell. Added to this, many brahmin priests were degenerate. They were completely ignorant of their own scriptures and were not even famil-

iar with the formalities of religion, and yet they acted as priests and preachers. In a word, they lived a most hypocritical life.

On the other hand, the youths of the day, having studied a few pages of English, became iconoclasts at heart. The materialists were considered the most enlightened people on earth because of their erudition and scholarship, and so their words were accepted as the supreme authority. The sign of scholarship was not to believe in God. Under such circumstances, the young educated people lost all faith in their own religion. But there would be discussion now and then among ourselves about the existence of God. Occasionally I would attend the services of the Brahmo Samaj, and would sometimes visit the one in our neighbourhood, but I arrived at no conclusion. Whether God existed or not I was doubtful. If He existed, which religion should I follow? I argued much, deliberated much, but could not find any solution.[11]

Girish was a bohemian, one of the products of the "Young Bengal". Swami Adbhutananda wrote about how the Master conquered the "Young Bengal": "One day Girish Ghosh saluted the Master by raising his folded hands to his forehead. The Master immediately returned the salutation by bowing from the waist. Girish saluted the Master again. The Master saluted Girish Babu with an even deeper bow. At last, when Girish Babu prostrated flat on the ground before him, the Master blessed him. Later Girish Babu would say: 'This time the Lord has come to conquer the world through prostrations. In His incarnation as Ramachandra it was the bow and arrow, and as Krishna it was the flute; as Chaitanya, the Name. But the weapon of His powerful Incarnation this time is the salutation.'"[12]

Yogin-ma's brother was displeased by his sister's devotion to Ramakrishna, so he hired a powerful ruffian from Baghbazar named Manmatha to intimidate him. When the Master visited their house, Manmatha was near the gate. The Master said, "Hello," and touched him. Immediately Manmatha knelt down before him and begged forgiveness. Later, Manmatha became a great devotee of the Master and would cry, saying, "Priyanath, Priyanath — O my Beloved!"

On one occasion the Master went to Calcutta with Hriday, and the latter showed him the Viceroy's palace with its big columns. Just then the Divine Mother revealed to him that they were merely clay bricks laid one on top of another. In those days the people looked at the Viceroy's palace in awe, because it represented the glory and grandeur of the British rulers. Ramakrishna, however, saw it as merely clay. He said:

"God and His splendour. God alone is real; the splendour has but a two-days existence."[13] He did not even leave the carriage to see that beautiful building.

The Master also went to see Fort William, the British fort in Calcutta. The Sikh regiment was marching there when he arrived by carriage, and when the soldiers saw him, they dropped their rifles on the ground and bowed down to him, saying, "Victory to the guru!" The British commander-in-chief was nonplussed. When he asked the Sikh soldiers about their unusual behaviour, they replied that it was the custom of their religion to show respect for their guru in that manner. Thus Ramakrishna conquered the British fort by merely sitting in his carriage; it was not even necessary for him to step out of the vehicle. This is truly amazing! The Master later compared the road to Fort William with the path to perdition. He said: "Men do not realize how far they are dragged down by women. Once I went to the Fort in a carriage, feeling all the while that I was going along a level road. At last I found that I had gone four storeys down. It was a sloping road. A man possessed by a ghost does not know he is under the ghost's control. He thinks he is quite normal."[14]

People of Calcutta endowed with learning, intelligence, wealth, and power would go to Ramakrishna and argue with him. When he realized that they were not accepting what he said, he would move closer and touch them. That magic touch would immediately deflate their egos. One day the Master said: "Do you know why I touch a man while talking to him? My touch reduces the power of his obstinacy, and he understands the truth correctly."[15]

Adharlal Sen, a deputy magistrate of the British government, was a devotee of the Master and visited the Master faithfully every evening after his office hours. However, he was often tired, and would fall asleep on the carpet in the Master's room. One day when Adhar inquired about the Master's powers, he laughed and said: "A Deputy magistrate frightens people; but by the grace of the Mother, I put this deputy magistrate to sleep on the floor."[16]

The Low-Mindedness of Calcutta People

When Ramakrishna visited Calcutta by carriage, he would look out the window and observe people on the street. With his subtle insight he could see what was in their minds. On 7 September 1883, the Master said to M.: "The other day I went to Calcutta. As I drove along the streets in the carriage, I observed that everyone's attention was fixed on low things. Everyone was brooding over his stomach and running after nothing but food. Everyone's mind was turned to lust and gold. I saw only one or two with their attention fixed on higher things, with their minds turned to God."

M.: "The present age has aggravated this stomach-worry. Trying to imitate the English, people have turned their attention to more luxuries; therefore their wants have also increased."[17]

The Master noticed that most people's minds were focussed below the navel. He always tried to move their thoughts to a higher plane. Sometimes he would quarrel with his beloved Divine Mother: "Why do You bring all these worthless people here? They are like milk diluted with water five times over. My eyes are burning from smoke as I continually blow on the wet fuel to evaporate the water. I am reduced to a skeleton. It is beyond my strength; do it Yourself if You want it done. Bring some good people here who can become spiritually awakened with one or two words."[18]

As he continued to talk to the people who visited him, Ramakrishna gradually developed cancer in his throat. A few days after his throat began to hurt he noticed that the crowd of spiritual aspirants at Dakshineswar was growing daily. In an ecstatic mood, he then told the Divine Mother: "Why do You bring so many people here? You have created a huge crowd! I have no time even to bathe and to eat. This (*pointing to his own body*) is a perforated drum. How long will it last if You go on beating it day in and day out?"[19]

When Buddha was on his deathbed, his disciple and attendant Ananda tearfully asked him, "Master, who will teach us when you depart?" Buddha replied, "My message." Similarly, Ramakrishna left his divine life and immortal message, which will transport humanity to higher and higher realms age after age.

Renunciation Is Not for Everyone

Ramakrishna was extremely careful while giving advice to the people who visited from Calcutta. Tormented by worldly suffering, they came to him for peace and bliss. He never hurt their feelings or disparaged them. Just as an expert and experienced doctor can quickly diagnose a patient's disease, so the Master knew the problems of those who came to him for help. He advised people according to their capabilities and level of tolerance. He generally advised householders, for example, to renounce mentally and not outwardly.

Master: "It is not good to force oneself into renunciation."

Ram: "Keshab Sen used to say: 'Why do people go to him [Ramakrishna] so much? One day he will sting them and they will flee from him.'"

Master: "Why should I sting people? Do I ask everyone to renounce the world? I say: Live in this world and also love God. Have yoga and bhoga. My goodness, if I tell them to renounce everything, they will not come here anymore. . . . It is impossible to ask the people of Calcutta to renounce all for the sake of God. One has to tell them to renounce mentally. . . . I tell them to hold God in one hand and do their duty with the other. After visiting this place a few times they will realize that their relationship with their wives, children, and relatives are only for a few days, and they will automatically develop nonattachment."[20]

The Master worked very hard to give the people of Calcutta a small taste of real spirituality and a chance to attain immortality in this life. He taught them ways to attain peace. It was impossible for the Master to compromise truth. Sometimes he told them: "'Lust and gold' alone is the world; that alone is maya. Because of it you cannot see God or think of God. After the birth of one or two children, husband and wife should live as brother and sister and talk only of God. Then both their minds will be drawn to God, and the wife will be a help to the husband on the path of spirituality. None can taste divine bliss without giving up animal feeling. A devotee should pray to God to help him get rid of this feeling. It must be a sincere prayer. God is our Inner Controller; He will certainly listen to our prayer if it is sincere."[21]

Worldly people feel uncomfortable when they see an all-renoucing monk, because they love sense enjoyment. The bliss of Brahman is beyond their reach. Ishan Mukhopadhyay of Calcutta asked Ramakrishna:

"Sir, why have you renounced the world? The scriptures extol the householder's life as the best."

Master: "I don't know much about what is good and what is bad. I do what God makes me do and speak what He makes me speak."

Ishan: "If everybody renounced the world, they would be acting against God's will."

Master: "Why should everybody renounce? On the other hand, can it be the will of God that all should revel in 'lust and gold' like dogs and jackals? Has He no other wish? Do you know what accords with His will and what is against it? You say that God wants everybody to lead a worldly life. But why don't you see it as God's will when your wife and children die? Why don't you see His will in poverty, when you haven't a morsel to eat? . . . Why should everybody renounce? Is renunciation possible except in the fullness of time? The time for renunciation comes when one reaches the limit of enjoyment. Can anybody force himself into renunciation? There is a kind of renunciation known as 'monkey renunciation.' Only small-minded people cultivate it."[22]

The People of Calcutta Loved Lectures

In the nineteenth century a storm of lectures blew over the city of Calcutta. Religious and social reformers — the leaders of the Navavidhan, the Nava Hullol, the Hari Sabha, and other societies — created a tremendous commotion with their lectures, contradicting and refuting each other's opinions. There were many arguments among the leaders as they tried to convert each other to their own views through their learning, intelligence, and reasoning. The Master observed what was going on in Calcutta.

M. had been influenced by his Western education. During his second visit, he argued with Ramakrishna about the worship of clay images.

Master: "But why clay? It is an image of Spirit."

M.: "But, sir, one should explain to those who worship the clay image that it is not God, and that, while worshipping it, they should have God in view and not the clay image. One should not worship clay."

Master (*sharply*): "That's the one hobby of you Calcutta people — giving lectures and bringing others to the light! Nobody ever stops to consider how to get the light himself. Who are you to teach others? He who is the Lord of the Universe will teach everyone.

"He is our Inner Guide. Suppose there is an error in worshipping the clay image; doesn't God know that through it He alone is being invoked? He will be pleased with that very worship. Why should you get a headache over it? You had better try for knowledge and devotion yourself."

M.'s ego was crushed. He wrote: "This was M.'s first argument with the Master, and happily his last."[23]

Krishna Prasanna Sen, Shashadhar Tarkachudamani, and other speakers advertised their lectures in the newspapers. When Ramakrishna went to meet Pandit Shashadhar, he learned that he had not received a commission from God. The Master said to him:

What will a man accomplish by mere lectures without the commission from God? A worthless man may talk his head off preaching, and yet he will produce no effect. But people will listen to him if he is armed with a badge of authority from God.

When the lamp is lighted the moths come in swarms. They don't have to be invited. In the same way, the preacher who has a commission from God need not invite people to hear him. He doesn't have to announce the time of his lectures. He possesses such irresistible attraction that people come to him of their own accord. People of all classes, even kings and aristocrats, gather around him.

You may deliver thousands of lectures, but they won't make the slightest impression on worldly people. Can one drive a nail into a stone wall? The point of the nail will sooner break than make a dent in the stone. What will you gain by striking the tough skin of the crocodile with a sword?

A pandit who doesn't know how to discriminate between the Real and the unreal is no pandit at all. You must have noticed kites and vultures soaring very high in the sky; but their eyes are always fixed on the charnel-pits. Do you know the meaning of "charnel-pits"? It is lust and gold.[24]

The Master remarked about the Brahmo Samaj: "Is the meeting of the Brahmos a real devotional gathering or a mere show? It is very good that the Brahmo Samaj holds regular devotions. But one must dive deep; mere ceremonial worship or lectures are of no avail."[25]

Swami Adbhutananda vividly described the commotion that was then going on in Calcutta:

Can one preach religion simply by beating a drum? Is religion something external to us, something one person speaks about and another person accepts? Religion is realization, and one cannot realize the truth through noise and fanfare. The more a preacher shouts, the more people's minds turn outward; and unless the mind is turned inward, God-realization is not possible.

What an upsurge of religion there was here in Calcutta a few years ago [1880s]! Preachers of the Salvation Army were found speaking on religion at almost every crossroads of the city. The Brahmo leaders used to preach their doctrines in their temples. The Vaishnavites would sing kirtan in their worship halls. Just think of all those meetings! One day Keshab Sen spoke on the New Dispensation in Beadon Square, the next day Reverend Kali Krishna Bandyopadhyay spoke on Christianity, and the third day Swami Krishnananda spoke on Hinduism. People would gather around them and listen. One preacher abused Hinduism and another defended it. What a storm of religious preaching! But what has come of all that? Where are they now? Those religious leaders tried to attract people through their preaching. Meanwhile, another group was devoting their time to silent meditation and prayer and directing their energies to the realization of God. And now don't you see multitudes gathering around this second group?

Inevitably, if there is no substance inside, a man's words are empty and carry no conviction. There must be renunciation, dispassion, and genuine love for God; only then will people believe you. The Lord's will works in this peculiar way. Look at Swami Vivekananda's life. After practising hard spiritual disciplines he got the command from the Master to preach, and people have accepted what he said. With one lecture Swamiji became world-famous.[26]

Calcutta People's Greed

During his sadhana Ramakrishna carefully considered a rupee and a clod of clay, saying "money is clay and clay is money." He then threw both into the Ganges. He lived for fifty-one years and proved that one can live in this world without touching any money. Mathur and Lakshmi Narayan Marwari offered money to the Master. Not only did he refuse it, but he also scolded them for trying to tempt him. Worldly people love money: They think it will bring them peace and joy. With money one can buy luxurious homes, expensive cars, fancy clothes, and other comforts — but not God.

Ramakrishna told the people of Calcutta: "Spiritual practices with a view to winning a lawsuit and earning money, or to helping others win in court and acquire property, shows a very mean understanding. Money enables a man to get food and drink, build a house, worship the Deity, serve devotees and holy men, and help the poor when he happens to meet them. These are the good uses of money. Money is not meant for luxuries or creature comforts or for buying a position in society."[27]

One day the Master jokingly told some Calcutta people: "You see, we don't take any collection during the performance at our place. Jadu's mother says to me, 'Other sadhus always ask for money, but you do not.' Worldly people feel annoyed if they have to spend money.

"A theatrical performance was being given at a certain place. A man felt a great desire to take a seat and see it. He peeped in and saw that a collection was being taken from the audience. Quietly he slipped away. Another performance was being given at some other place. He went there and, inquiring, found that no collection would be taken. There was a great rush of people. He elbowed his way through the crowd and reached the centre of the hall. There he picked out a nice seat for himself, twirled his moustache, and sat through the performance."[28]

Mahendra Pal of Sinthi gave to Ramlal five rupees for the Master without informing him. The Master described his reaction: "I asked Ramlal what the gift was for, and he said that it was meant for me. I thought it might enable me to pay off some of my debt for milk. That night I went to bed and, if you will believe me, I suddenly woke up with a pain. I felt as if a cat were scratching inside my chest. I at once went to Ramlal and said to him: 'Go and return the money at once, or I shall have no peace of mind.' Ramlal returned the money early in the morning and I felt relieved."[29]

Jadu Mallick was a multimillionaire in Calcutta and also a devotee of Ramakrishna. Swami Adbhutananda recalled:

One day the Master told Jadu Babu, "You have saved so much for this world; what have you acquired for the next?"

Jadu Babu replied: "Young priest, you are the one who will take care of the other world for me. You will save me at the moment of death, and I am waiting until then. If you don't grant me liberation, your name 'deliverer of the fallen,' will be marred, so you cannot forget me at my death."

You see, although Jadu Mallick had plenty of money, he couldn't give up the desire for more. Another time the Master told him, "Jadu, you have saved so much money, yet still you want more."

Jadu Babu replied: "That desire will not go. You cannot give up the desire for God; in the same way, we worldly people cannot give up our desire for money. Why should I renounce money? You renounce all the things of the world and yearn for God, while I am a beggar asking for more and more of His riches. Doesn't worldly wealth also belong to Him?"

The Master was very pleased to hear this line of argument. "If you maintain this attitude, you have no need to worry. But tell me, Jadu, are you saying this sincerely?"

Then Jadu Babu replied, "Young priest, you know that I cannot hide anything from you."[30]

Sometimes the Master made fun of the miserliness and calculating minds of people in Calcutta. He taught them how to get rid of their attachment for money and small-mindedness, and sometimes he told them unpleasant truths. He told Surendra, a wealthy man, about Jaygopal Sen who was also rich: "Those who have money should give it to the poor and needy. Jaygopal Sen is well-to-do. He should be charitable. That he is not so is to his discredit. There are some who are miserly even though they have money. There is no knowing who will enjoy their money afterwards.

"Jaygopal came here the other day. He drove over here in a carriage. The lamps were broken, the horse seemed to have been returned from the charnel-house, and the coachman looked as if he had just been discharged from the Medical College Hospital. And he brought me two rotten pomegranates!"[31]

Then came Surendra's turn. The Master bluntly told him: "You tell lies at the office. Then why do I eat the food you offer me? Because you give your money in charity; you give away more than you earn. I cannot eat anything offered by miserly people. Their wealth is squandered away in these ways: first, litigation; second, thieves and robbers; third, physicians; fourth, their wicked children's extravagance."

Then the Master affectionately said to Surendra: "Come here every now and then. Nangta [Tota Puri] used to say that a brass pot must be polished every day; otherwise it gets stained. One should constantly live in the company of holy men. The renunciation of 'lust and gold' is for sannyasins. It is not for you. Now and then you should go into solitude and call on God with a yearning heart. Your renunciation should be mental."[32]

Ramakrishna is the ideal for those who go on strike to force their demands on wealthy people. In 1868 the Master went on pilgrimage to Baidyanath with Mathur. Seeing the dire poverty of the local people, the Master asked Mathur to feed and clothe them. When Mathur expressed his reluctance, the Master said that he would not continue on the pilgrimage, but instead would stay with those poor people. At last Mathur fulfilled the Master's wish. Another time, the Master went with Mathur to Ranaghat where the latter had property. Seeing the pitiable condition of Mathur's tenants, the Master asked him to exempt them from taxes, which he did reluctantly. Ramakrishna was a paid temple priest who worked for Mathur, but he nonetheless told him: "You may be a rich man, but that does not mean I have to flatter you."

Ramakrishna said to Mani Mallick, another wealthy man of Calcutta: "Rakhal says that the people in his native village have been suffering seriously from a scarcity of water. Why don't you build a reservoir there? That will do the people good. You have so much money; what will you do with all your wealth? But they say that *telis* [the low oil-man caste] are very calculating." The Master's comment made the devotees smile, but it rent Mani Mallick's heart. As a surgeon cuts a tumour from a patient's body, so for their spiritual welfare, the Master tried to remove from the devotees' minds their attachment to worldly things. The Master's words had an effect, and Mani Mallick humbly said: "Sir, you referred to a reservoir. You might as well have confined yourself to that suggestion. Why allude to the 'oil-man caste' and all that?"[33]

Sometimes people from Calcutta would argue with the Master when their self-interest was challenged. The Master said that when a man becomes mad for God, he doesn't enjoy money or such things. Trailokya, a Brahmo devotee, remarked: "Sir, if a man is to remain in the world, he needs money and he must also save. He has to give in charity and —"

Master: "What? Do you mean that one must first save money and then seek God? And you talk about charity and kindness! A worldly man spends thousands of rupees for his daughter's marriage. Yet, all the while, his neighbours are dying of starvation; and he finds it hard to give them two morsels of rice; he calculates a thousand times before giving them even that much. And they talk about doing good to others!"[34]

Bankim Chattopadhyay, a famous novelist and deputy magistrate, heard that the Master had thrown money into the Ganges, saying, "Rupee is clay and clay is rupee."

Bankim: "Indeed! Money is clay! Sir, if you have a few pennies you can help the poor. If money is clay, then a man cannot give in charity or do good to others."

Master: "Charity! Doing good! How dare you say you can do good to others? Kindness belongs to God alone. A householder, of course, needs money, for he has a wife and children. He should save up to feed them. They say the bird and the sannyasin should not provide for the future."[35]

In this connection, the Master said to the wealthy Dr. Mahendralal Sarkar: "It is useless to try to hoard money. With great labour the bees build a hive; but a man breaks it and takes the honey away."

Doctor: "Whom shall we hoard for? — For a wicked son, perhaps."

Master: "It is not a wicked son alone. Perhaps the wife is unchaste. She may have a secret lover. Perhaps she will give him your watch and chain! It is not harmful for a householder to live with his wife. It is attachment to 'lust and gold' that begets pride of learning, pride of money, and pride of social position. One cannot attain divine knowledge till one gets rid of pride."[36]

Calcutta People Are Generally Sensual

Kamini-kanchan — lust and gold, or sex and money — are verily maya. This is a mantra uttered by Ramakrishna in this age. God-realization is possible when a person realizes this truth. The Master did not define maya as do other Vedanta teachers, with a long, complicated Sanskrit sentence such as *miyate anena iti maya* — "The thing that limits or covers the Infinite is maya." Most people in this world are running after lust and gold. The Master emphatically told the people of Calcutta: "What is there to enjoy in the world? Kamini-kanchan? That is only a momentary pleasure. One moment it exists and the next moment it disappears. The world is like an overcast sky that steadily pours down rain: The face of the sun is seldom seen. There is mostly suffering in the world. On account of the cloud of kamini-kanchan one cannot see the sun."[37]

"It is impossible to ask the people of Calcutta to renounce all for the sake of God. One has to tell them to renounce mentally."[38]

"Kamini-kanchan is the cause of bondage. Kamini-kanchan alone constitutes samsara, the world. It is kamini-kanchan that keeps one from seeing God."

Master (To Kedar, Vijay, and the other devotees): "He who has renounced the pleasure of a wife has verily renounced the pleasure of the world. It is kamini-kanchan that hides God. You people have such imposing moustaches, and yet you too are involved in kamini-kanchan. Tell me if it isn't true? Search your heart and answer me."

Vijay: "Yes, it is true."

Master: "I see that all are under the control of woman. One day I went to Captain's house. From there I was to go to Ram's house. So I said to Captain, 'Please give me my carriage hire.' He asked his wife about it. She too held back and said: 'What's the matter? What's the matter?' At last Captain said, 'Ram will take care of it.' You see, the Gita, the Bhagavata, and the Vedanta all bow before a woman.

"A man leaves his money, his property, and everything in the hands of his wife. But he says with affected simplicity, 'I have such a nature that I cannot keep even two rupees with me.'

"A man went to an office in search of a job. There were many vacancies, but the manager did not grant his request. A friend said to the applicant, 'Appeal to Golapi, and you will get the job.' Golapi was the manager's mistress."[39]

The Master said to his young disciples: "You see, the bigwigs — babus, judges, magistrates, and so on — may brag or talk big outside, but they are like earthworms and slaves to their wives. If an order, however unjustifiable, comes from the inner apartment [meaning from the wife], he has no power to overrule it."[40]

On 24 May 1884, the Master said to Adhar Sen: "You are a scholar and a deputy magistrate, but with all that you are hen-pecked."[41]

The Master continued: "One day Keshab came here with his followers.

They stayed till ten at night. We were all seated in the Panchavati. Pratap and several others said they would like to spend the night here. Keshab said: 'No, I must go. I have some work to do.' I laughed and said: 'Can't you sleep without the smell of your fish-basket? Once a fishwife was a guest in the house of a gardener who raised flowers. She came there with her empty basket after selling fish in the market and was asked to sleep in a room where flowers were kept. But because of the fragrance of the flowers, she couldn't get to sleep for a long time. Her hostess saw her condition and said, 'Hello! Why are you tossing from side to side so rest-lessly?' The fishwife said: 'I don't know, friend. Perhaps the smell of the flowers has been disturbing my sleep. Can you give me my fish-basket? Perhaps that will put me to sleep.' The basket was brought to her. She sprinkled water on it and set it near her nose. Then she fell sound asleep and snored all night.'"[42]

The people that the Master encountered lived worldly lives and were begetting children every year, yet they expected God-vision. Some women from Calcutta also visited Ramakrishna and asked: "Why can't we put our minds in God? Why are our minds so restless?" The Master told them: "Ah! How can that be now? There is still the smell of child-birth about you. Let that first leave you. It will come in the fullness of time. It is enough for this life that you have come to me. In the next life the spiritual path will be easy of attainment for you."[43]

Calcutta People Are Easily Excited

Some of the people from Calcutta that Ramakrishna encountered were easily excited by passing fads. They were gossipy, and believed any rumour they heard. They loved excitement and were easily carried away. They were fickle and changed their minds often. They made many promises, but they did not keep their word. Kaliprasanna Sinha wrote in his famous book *Hutum Panchar Naxa*: "Hysterical Calcutta! Here every day there is something exciting going on. It is an incredible wonderland."

In his book, Kaliprasanna vividly described how Krishna Mohan Bandyopadhyay, a leader of the Young Bengal, preached Christianity in Calcutta: "In some places the foreign missionaries are distributing a basketful of Bibles, and Brother Katikrishna [Reverend Bandyopadhyay] is with them. Dressed like a suburban policeman in pants, a long and loose robe, and a black conch-shaped hat, he is preaching the glory of Christianity, moving his hands and face as if to the tune of a court announcer. Watching his preaching, one would believe he was the announcer at a puppet-show. Some porters with baskets, some school children, and some hawkers listen attentively to Brother Katikrishna's talk but cannot understand it."

We find the attitude of Calcutta people towards Christianity in this humorous and sarcastic picture recorded in *Hutum Panchar Naxa*. Those who became Christians out of momentary excitement were in deep trouble when that frenzied emotion was over. They were totally isolated from society because they were neither welcomed by the Europeans nor accepted by Indians.

Kaliprasanna further wrote: "When any fad starts in the city, it does not end quickly. Out of passing popular excitement, a schoolteacher, a Haldar brahmin, a businessman, and a *kayastha* gentleman became Christians; a few aristocratic women also found light in Christianity. Later, many of them faced dire poverty. Some were deprived of their inheritance; some lamented as they faced their pitiable condition. The excitement of Christianity, like a passing flash of light on the street, momentarily illuminated everything all around and then disappeared, leaving everything in darkness."

Then the Brahmos instituted *Brahma-upasana* to replace the Hindu rituals and image worship. Disparaging this new fad, Kaliprasanna wrote: "When the Brahmos are following the ceremonies according to the Hindu fashion — such as the Brahmo funeral ceremony, the Brahmo rice-eating ceremony, the Brahmo birth ceremony, and the Brahmo sacred thread ceremony — then what is the objection to Saraswati and Durga worship according to the Brahmo way?"

After arriving in Calcutta, Ramakrishna understood the character of the people there. The Master told them: "The members of the Brahmo Samaj do not accept God with form. Narendra says that God with form is a mere idol. The modern Brahmajnanis have not tasted the sweet bliss of Brahman. Their eyes look dry and so do their faces. They won't achieve anything without ecstatic love of God.

"A fop, seated comfortably with one leg over the other, chewing betel-leaf and twirling his moustache — a carefree dandy —, cannot attain God."[44]

During a steamboat trip the Master said to Keshab Sen: "It is extremely difficult to teach others. A man can teach only if God reveals Himself to him and gives the command. Unless you have a command from God, who will listen to your words?

"Don't you know how easily the people of Calcutta get excited? The milk in the kettle puffs up and boils as long as the fire burns underneath. Take away the fuel and all becomes quiet. The people of Calcutta love sensations. You may see them digging a well at a certain place. They say they want water. But if they strike a stone they give up that place; they begin at another place. And there, perchance, they find sand; they give up the second place too. Next they begin at a third. And so it goes. But it won't do if a man only imagines that he has God's command."[45]

The Master sketched a picture of those excitable people with two analogies: first, their excitement is as momentary as the foam of hot milk; and second, their minds are always restless. Nothing could escape his keen sight. In Calcutta the Master saw the Baroari festival, a public worship ceremony, the cost of which is borne by the whole community.

He said: "They provide various images for the Baroari because people of different sects assemble there. You see there images of Radha-Krishna, Shiva-Durga, and Sita-Rama — different images in different places. A crowd gathers before each image. But it is quite different with those who are not spiritually minded at all. In the Baroari one sees another image also — a prostitute beating her paramour with a broomstick. Those people stand there with gaping mouths and cry to their friends: 'What are you looking at over there? Come here! Look at this!'"[46]

People who are easily carried away by passing fads always change their minds. Their characters are weak: They are not always truthful and do not always keep their promises. Pointing to the frenzied and imitative nature of the Young Bengal, Dwijendralal Roy wrote a hilarious parody:

At first I was indifferent to any religion,
But I fell in love with a Christian woman.
Thus I developed faith in Christianity;
I changed my mind and gave up my own faith.
Then I came in contact with the new Brahmo religion;
Its doctrine is easy: Meditate closing the eyes.
My sister and I planned to be initiated into it.
Meanwhile, I was married in the Hindu way.
Again I changed my mind and gave up that path.

This is how fickle people act. Ramakrishna observed all this and remarked: "Calcutta people are hysterical."

It upset the Master if someone did not keep his or her promise. A person who deviates from the truth cannot realize God. Jadu Mallick had promised the Master that he would arrange a recital of the Chandi in his house. Some time had elapsed, but he had not yet kept his promise.

Master: "Well, what about the recital of the Chandi?"

Jadu: "I have been busy with many things; I haven't been able to arrange it."

Master: "How is that? A man gives his word and doesn't take it back! 'The words of a man are like the tusks of the elephant: they come out but do not go back.' A man must be true to his word."[47]

The Master visited Pandit Ishwar Chandra Vidyasagar, a great educator, philanthropist, and social reformer. When the Master invited him to Dakshineswar, he agreed to visit — but he never came. Later the Master said to M.: "Why doesn't Vidyasagar keep his word? 'If one who holds to truth and looks on woman as his mother does not realize God, then Tulsi [a saint] is a liar.' If a man holds to truth he will certainly realize God. The other day Vidyasagar said he would come here and visit me. But he hasn't kept his word."[48]

The Master was also annoyed with the Brahmo leader Shivanath Shastri when he broke a promise. He remarked: "Shivanath has one great defect: he doesn't keep his word. Once he said to me that he would come to Dakshineswar, but he neither came nor sent me word. That is not good. It is said that truthfulness alone constitutes the spiritual discipline of the Kaliyuga. If a man clings tenaciously to truth he ultimately realizes God. Without this regard for truth, one gradually loses everything."[49]

The Master paid no attention to the criticism of Calcutta people. Like drunkards, they are drunk with worldliness; their words are like meaningless gibberish. The Master said: "Most of the people of Calcutta are worldly. They are respectful one moment and disrespectful the next. Some people criticize me because I wear a red-bordered cloth, black polished slippers, and recline on a bolster. I consider such comments of worldly people to be like the ebb and flood tides of the Ganges. I have seen how the water level of the Ganges may be full in the morning, but later it subsides. People say so many things. I spit on their good comments as well as their bad comments. But there are some people in Calcutta who are endowed with faith and devotion, and they do not forget to pay their respects to a holy man."[50]

How the Master Disciplined Calcutta People

Ramakrishna, the saviour of the fallen and lowly, was concerned for the ungodly people in Calcutta. There is a saying: "Only one who loves can discipline or punish appropriately." The Master was always eager to help those who were tormented by worldly life: the poor, afflicted, and fallen people of society. Sometimes the Master's divine behaviour appeared strange to others, and many misunderstood him.

The Master said:

In the state of God-intoxication I used to speak out my mind to all. I was no respecter of persons. Even to men of position I was not afraid to speak the truth.

One day Jatindra Tagore [an aristocrat] came to the garden of Jadu Mallick. I was there too. I asked him: "What is the duty of man? Isn't it our duty to think of God?" Jatindra replied: "We are worldly people. How is it possible for us to achieve liberation? Even King Yudhisthira had to have a vision of hell." This made me very angry. I said to him: "What sort of man are you? Of all the incidents of Yudhisthira's life, you remember only his seeing hell. You don't remember his truthfulness, his forbearance, his patience, his discrimination, his dispassion, his devotion to God."

Many days later I went with Captain to see Raja Sourindra Tagore. As soon as I met him, I said, "I can't address you as 'Raja,' or by any such title, for I should be telling a lie."

"One day, in that state of divine intoxication, I went to the bathing ghat on the Ganges at Baranagore. There I saw Jaya Mukhopadhyay repeating the name of God; but his mind was on something else. I went up and slapped him twice on the cheeks.

At one time Rani Rasmani was staying in the temple garden. She came to the shrine of the Divine Mother, as she frequently did when I worshipped Kali, and asked me to sing a song or two. On this occasion, while I was singing, I noticed she was sorting the flowers for worship absent-mindedly. At once I slapped her on the cheeks. She became quite embarrassed and sat there with folded hands.[51]

Blessed are Jaya Mukhopadhyay and Rani Rasmani, who were thus disciplined by the Master! Later on, when their minds were restless during meditation, the memory of Ramakrishna's harsh action probably helped them to be mindful. When our minds become restless during japa and meditation, we can focus on the Master if we think that he is seated in front of us and may slap us. Ramakrishna himself described his own experience: During meditation he would see a young monk holding a sharp trident emerge from his body and say to him, "If you do not meditate on your Chosen Deity, shunning other thoughts, I will pierce your chest with this trident!"[52] We too need someone to take a trident in hand and control our restless minds.

The scriptures say: "If you want liberation, shun sense objects like poison." We think about the things that we love. We think of sense objects because we love them. We do not realize that those thoughts bind us to this world and bring us much misery. With a view to protecting people from worldly thoughts, the Master would travel from door to door, visiting his Calcutta devotees. He talked to them about God and spiritual topics. Even when he was suffering from cancer, he told his physician Dr. Sarkar: "If you won't take offense, I shall tell you something. It is this: You have had enough of such things as money, honour, lecturing, and so on. Now for a few days direct your mind to God. And come here now and then. Your spiritual feeling will be kindled by hearing words about God."[53]

On another occasion, while in an ecstatic mood the Master said to Dr. Sarkar: "Mahindra Babu, what is this madness of yours about money? Why such attachment to wife? Why such longing for name and fame? Give up all these, now, and direct your mind to God with whole-souled devotion. Enjoy the bliss of God."[54]

The Master asked Bankim Chandra Chattopadhyay, a celebrated writer and deputy magistrate: "Well, what do you say about man's duties?"

Bankim (*smiling*): "If you ask me about them, I should say they are eating, sleeping, and sex-life."

Master (*sharply*): "Eh? You are very saucy! What you do day and night comes out through your mouth. A man belches what he eats. If he eats radish, he belches radish; if he eats green coconut, he belches green coconut. Day and night you live in the midst of lust and gold; so your mouth utters words about that alone."

Then the Master said tenderly: "Please don't take offence at my words."

Bankim replied: "Sir, I haven't come here to hear sweet things."[55]

Swami Vivekananda said that Ramakrishna was "Love Personified." His heart bled for the poor, the persecuted, and those who suffered. When people came from Calcutta to Dakshineswar, the Master would try to entertain them in many ways: He talked to them about God, told them about his sadhana, and sang and danced when in ecstasy. He would ask them: "Do you chew betel roll, or do you smoke tobacco?" At that time Dakshineswar was a small village; there were no sweet shops around. When devotees brought some sweets and fruits for him, he would keep some to share with other visitors. He would also save temple prasad to feed the devotees so that they would attain devotion. He always saved some prasad from his supper for Brinde, the temple maidservant. Sometimes he would give that prasad to the devotees the night before. When this happened, he would go to the Holy Mother early the next morning and ask her to prepare something for Brinde. He always served refreshments to the Calcutta devotees when they visited him. M. recorded in *The Gospel of Sri Ramakrishna*: "The devotees sat in silence, listening to the Master's words. When evening came, a lamp was lighted in the room. Preparations were being made for feeding Keshab and others. Keshab (*with a smile*): 'What? Puffed rice again today?' Master (*smiling*): 'Hriday knows.' The devotees were served first with puffed rice, and then with luchi and curries on leaf plates. All enjoyed the meal very much. It was about ten o'clock when supper was over."[56]

The Master had a vision: "The devotee, the scriptures, and God — all three are one." So serving devotees is equal to serving God. The Master demonstrated how to serve devotees. Once M. went to Dakshineswar to practise spiritual disciplines under the Master's guidance for a few days. The Master arranged for his stay, making sure that he had food and milk. Another time, the Master fed rice pudding to Girish with his own hand. And when the Master was sick in Cossipore, he crawled across the floor, poured water into a glass from a pitcher, and gave it to Girish after serving refreshments. He would pack the Divine Mother's prasad and carry it to Calcutta in his carriage. Sometimes he would wait on the sidewalk for his young devotee Purna so he could feed him. He also went to the theatres to bless the actors and actresses. He asked Adhar to come to Dakshineswar so that he could have the company of holy people. The Master talked to him about God, gave him refreshments, and arranged for him to rest on the floor. Then he sent Adhar back to his home in Calcutta.

"Look after Calcutta's People"

A few years before he developed cancer, Ramakrishna said to the Holy Mother: "When you find me accepting food from anyone and everyone, spending nights in Calcutta, and feeding a portion of food first to someone else and afterwards eating what is left — then you will know that the day is near when I will leave this body."[57] This unveils the hidden connection between the Master's stay in Calcutta and his giving up the body. Knowing what he did, why did he go to live at Shyampukur in Calcutta?

Swami Prabhananda mentioned the following reasons: "Everyone believed that everything the Master did, even his suffering from physical illness, was for the good of humankind. Some thought that the Master voluntarily embraced the disease so that his devotees could serve him and thus satisfy their unfulfilled desires. Some thought that the Master had moved to Shyampukur in Calcutta so that people would not have to go to Dakshineswar to see him and have his holy company. Some said that the Master came to Calcutta so that he could divert the materialistic outlook of Westernized Calcutta people to the path of spirituality."[58]

For thirty years, many people in Calcutta doubted Ramakrishna's divinity. Towards the end of his life, he finally revealed his true nature to them and then began the last act of his divine drama. While he was in Dakshineswar, the Master told his disciples repeatedly: "When many people regard this [me] as God, and love and respect me as such, it [this body] will soon disappear."[59] This actually happened. At the Shyampukur house, the Calcutta devotees worshipped the Master as the Divine Mother Kali.

One day at the Cossipore garden house shortly before his passing, the Master was gazing intently at the Holy Mother when she said: "Tell me what is in your mind."

He replied in a tone of complaint: "Look here, won't you do anything? Must this [pointing to his body] do everything?"

"But," she protested, "what can I do? I am a mere woman."

"No, no," the Master insisted. "You will have to do many things."

On another day at Cossipore, the Holy Mother carried the Master's food to his room and found him lying in bed with his eyes closed. She said aloud: "Please get up; it is your mealtime." When the Master opened his eyes, he appeared to have returned from a trip to a faraway realm. He said to her, in an abstracted mood: "Look at the people of Calcutta; they are like worms squirming in darkness. You must bring light to them. This is not my burden alone. You, too, shall have to share it."[60]

After absorbing the sins of Calcutta's people, the sinless Ramakrishna developed cancer and passed away. The Holy Mother conducted his spiritual ministry for the next thirty-four years. She suffered from poverty and illness, but she loved and served the people of Calcutta without complaint. It is amazing how the Holy Mother tackled the problems of worldly people. One person would cry and complain to her; another twisted her ankle so that she could remember him; and yet another would demand, "Mother, put your foot on my chest." People came to her to cure their diseases, or to be consoled. She had no rest. Her body burned if any impure person touched her feet.

One day she told a devotee: "Please fan me. My whole body is burning. I bow down to Calcutta! People come and complain about their problems and misery. I can't bear it anymore. Some have committed

204 • How to Live With God

many wrong things; some have many children and they cry if one or two die. They are not human beings; they are like animals and have no self-control. So the Master used to say: 'They are like milk diluted with water five times over. My eyes are burning from smoke as I continually blow on the wet fuel to evaporate the water. Where are my all-renouncing children? Please come so that I get relief talking to you about God.' The Master said the right thing. Please fan forcefully. Today people are coming continually from 4:00 p.m. on; I can't see their sufferings anymore."[61]

The Holy Mother was very shy. Most of the time she wore a veil when she was with the devotees. She could not move freely in her Calcutta residence, so sometimes she went to her parental home in Jayrambati. There she could move about in her village and meet her own kinfolk and neighbours. Once a monk thought that it would be difficult for the Mother to walk from a neighbour's house to Koalpara Ashrama, so he suggested that she ride in a palanquin. The Holy Mother told that monk: "This is our native village. I love to move freely here. In Calcutta I live in a cage. I stay there with great hesitance and restrictions. My son, don't try to take away my freedom."[62] That monk apologized immediately.

Truly speaking, the people of Calcutta did not allow her to rest even in that remote Jayrambati Village. People flocked there for initiation and spiritual guidance. She collected groceries and vegetables, cooked food for the devotees, and even made their beds. Beyond that, she looked after her niece Radhu and Radhu's mentally-ill mother, her demanding brothers, and the poor villagers. We do not yet understand the extent of what Ramakrishna and the Holy Mother did for the Calcutta people.

Ramakrishna felt deeply for the women of Calcutta. His heart cried for them. Once Gauri-ma, a woman devotee, was picking flowers near the nahabat in Dakshineswar when the Master appeared with a pot of water. He held on to a branch of the bakul tree with one hand and began pouring water with the other. As he did this, he said, "Gauri, let me pour water and you knead the mud." Surprised, Gauri-ma answered: "There is no clay here. How can I knead the mud? This place is full of stone chips." The Master smiled and said: "My goodness! What I meant and what you have understood! The condition of women in this country is very poor and painful. You will have to work for them." Gauri-ma did not like the idea. "It is hard for me to get along with worldly people," she told him. "I don't care for all the hustle and bustle. Give me a few girls, and I shall take them to the Himalayas and mould their character." But the Master shook his head and insisted: "No, no. You will have to work in the city. You have practised enough spiritual disciplines. Now you should serve the women with your spiritual energy."[63] To obey the Master's command, Gauri-ma established a school for girls in Calcutta and worked hard to educate and uplift Indian women.

Swami Vivekananda carried the message of Vedanta to the West and then returned to India. On 1 May 1897, he established the Ramakrishna Mission in Calcutta; and later he inaugurated the headquarters of the Ramakrishna Order in Belur, not far from Calcutta.

Blessed is Calcutta! This city was touched by the blessed feet of Ramakrishna, Holy Mother, and Swami Vivekananda. It is their playground and a place of pilgrimage.

6

The Stage for Ramakrishna's Divine Play

I t is extremely important for the reader to know the history of the surroundings in which Ramakrishna enacted his divine drama for thirty years. The Dakshineswar Kali temple was built by Rani Rasmani, a wealthy woman of Calcutta. In 1847 she had planned a pilgrimage to Varanasi. The night before her departure, the Divine Mother appeared to her in a dream and said: "You need not go to Varanasi. Install my image in a beautiful spot along the bank of the Ganges and arrange for my worship and offerings to Me. I will manifest Myself within that image and accept your worship every day."*[1]

Rani Rasmani bought a piece of land in Dakshineswar, a few miles north of Calcutta, and over the next eight years built a huge temple complex there. She spent an enormous amount of money to complete the temple and install its deities. Rasmani's design was unusual in that she included temples to Kali, Radha-Krishna, and Shiva all in the same compound. Generally, Kali and Shiva temples are built side by side but a temple to Krishna is traditionally not included in the same compound. Perhaps Rasmani was intuitively following a divine plan: In the future Ramakrishna would come to the temple complex and practise different religious paths, demonstrating the harmony of religions. On 31 May 1855

---

*In another version of this incident it is said that Rasmani started her journey, and on the first night her party halted near Dakshineswar, where she had the dream.

Ramkumar, Ramakrishna's elder brother, officiated over the dedication ceremony of the temple; Ramakrishna was also present on that occasion.

It is amazing that it was a woman who formed the main backdrop for the Master's divine play. Swami Vivekananda's disciple Sister Nivedita put it nicely: "Humanly speaking, without the Temple of Dakshineswar there [would have] been no Ramakrishna; without Ramakrishna, no Vivekananda; and without Vivekananda, no Western mission [of Vedanta]."[2]

In the eyes of devotees, Ramakrishna is still in Dakshineswar and Dakshineswar is still as it was in the 1880s. Of course, due to the passing of time some changes have taken place in the temple garden. The temples have deteriorated; most of the trees that grew during the Master's time are now dead; and crowds of pilgrims have overrun the formerly peaceful temple garden. Such changes are inevitable. We are thankful to M. (Mahendra Nath Gupta) for the vivid description of the temple garden that he included in the first part of *Sri Sri Ramakrishna Kathamrita* (*The Gospel of Sri Ramakrishna*). The description is in the Bengali version of the *Gospel*. I translated it in full in *Ramakrishna as We Saw Him* (Vedanta Society of St. Louis, 1990); in this chapter I shall present some excerpts from this description. M. begins:

> It is Sunday. The devotees have the day off, so they come in large numbers to the temple garden to visit Sri Ramakrishna. His door is open to everybody, and he talks freely with all, irrespective of caste or creed, sect or age. His visitors are monks, paramahamsas [illumined souls], Hindus, Christians, Brahmos, the followers of Shakti and Vishnu, men and women. Blessed was Rani Rasmani! She, out of her religious disposition, built this beautiful temple garden and brought Sri Ramakrishna, the embodiment of divinity, to this place. She made it possible for people to see and worship this God-man.[3]

With these words M. invites suffering humanity to relax in the blissful abode of the Dakshineswar temple garden and listen to the immortal message of Ramakrishna. His intention was to imprint the setting of the temple garden in the minds of the audience before he presented the drama.

When one visits a holy place and worships the deities there, one's mind is purified and one then develops longing to hear more about God. M. said:

> According to the scriptures, one should circumambulate a holy place at least three times because that makes an indelible impression on the

mind of the pilgrim. But once is enough for those who have a good memory and a strong power of observation.

What should one do in a holy place? First, drink a little of the deity's sanctified water. Second, sit in front of the deity for a while. Third, sing or chant the glories of God. Fourth, feed the holy people. Fifth, bring some fruits and sweets to offer. Sixth, don't be stingy or cheat anybody.[4]

In the sixteen volumes of *Srima Darshan*, Swami Nityatmananda recorded conversations with M. and many of his memories of the Master that are not in the *Gospel*. In this chapter, I shall translate some of this material into English for the first time.

We spend our money, time, and energy in order to visit a holy or historical place. We hire a guide who explains the importance of that place, for otherwise our trip would be meaningless. After Rama-krishna's passing away, M. took many people to Dakshineswar and acted as their guide.

In the eyes of a lover, everything related to the beloved is sweet and precious. M. tried to imprint his experiences with the Master on the minds of his visitors, thus giving them a taste of the divine bliss that M. had enjoyed.

The Chandni (Porch)

The Dakshineswar Kali temple is on the Ganges, five miles north of Calcutta. One can travel by boat to Dakshineswar and disembark at the chandni ghat to enter the temple complex. One is supposed to purify oneself with Ganges water before visiting the deities; it was here at the chandni ghat that Ramakrishna would bathe. After Ramakrishna's passing, when M. visited Dakshineswar, he would come to this ghat and soak a towel in the water of the Ganges. When he returned home he would squeeze the towel and sprinkle that water on his visitors, reminding them that this water came from the spot where the Master used to bathe. Swami Nityatmananda wrote: "M. reached the chandni ghat. He sat on the second step from the top and four yards from the north. He said: 'The Master sat here when Keshab Sen and his followers came.'"[5] The Master sat on this ghat as if he were a ferryman waiting for passengers who sincerely wanted to cross the turbulent ocean of maya.

Bhavatarini Kali

M. described the image in the Kali temple at Dakshineswar:

South of the Krishna temple is the Kali temple. The beautiful image of the Divine Mother is made out of black stone and her name is

Temple Garden of Dakshineswar from the Ganges

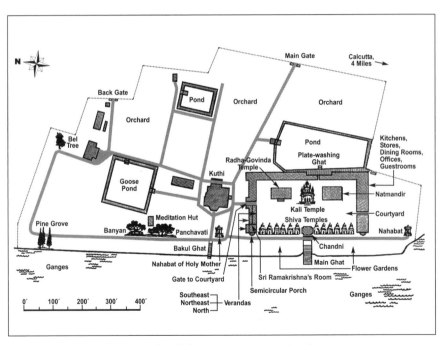

Map of Dakshineswar Temple Garden

"Bhavatarini," or the Saviour of the World. The floor of this temple is inlaid with white and black marble. A high altar, with steps to the south, is also made out of stone. Above this is a thousand-petalled lotus made of silver, on which Lord Shiva is lying, with his head to the south and feet to the north. The image of Shiva is made of white marble. On his chest stands the beautiful three-eyed image of Mother Kali, wearing a Varanasi silk sari and various ornaments.[6]

The height of the image is 33½ inches. M. later said about this image: "The Master told us that the sculptor of this image was Navin [Pal]. He would work on the image the whole day and eat one vegetarian meal at 3:00 p.m. He undertook severe austerities to make that image of Kali in Dakshineswar. That is the reason the image looks so alive. As the sculptor's heart was full of devotion, his hands transmitted that feeling to the stone image."[7] There are many Kali images in Bengal, but the image in Dakshineswar is special because the Master invoked the deity within it. He checked to see if the Mother was alive by holding cotton near Her nostrils; as he did this, he saw the Mother breathing.

The image of Kali is much misunderstood by Western people, who think She is terrible and frightening. Kali is the Shakti, or the power of Brahman by which He creates, preserves, and dissolves. She is the Cosmic Energy and manifests in both benign and destructive ways. She is the Divine Mother who loves all beings because all are Her children.

Kali's deep blue complexion represents the infinite; each hair is a jiva, or individual soul. Her three eyes symbolize her knowledge of past, present, and future. Her white teeth symbolize sattva (peace); Her red tongue, rajas (activity). Her protruding tongue between the teeth reminds the viewer that one controls restlessness with calmness. Her necklace consists of fifty skulls, symbolic of the fifty letters of the Sanskrit alphabet, the origin of sound. Her upper-right hand grants fearlessness as Her lower-right hand offers boons. She cuts human bondage with the sword in Her upper-left hand and imparts wisdom with the lower-left one, which holds a severed head. She is infinite, so she is naked, clad in space. Shiva is cosmic consciousness and Kali is cosmic energy; Shiva lies on His back beneath Kali's feet. No creation is possible without their union.

During his second visit to Dakshineswar, M. raised a question about the "clay" image of Kali, and Ramakrishna told him, "It is an image of Spirit." He further explained that God is both formless and with form, like water and ice.

The Terrace

There is a terrace between the steps of the Kali temple and the natmandir. "Sometimes the Master used to sit here alone or with the devotees facing the Mother not far from the edge of the natmandir," wrote M. One day Ramakrishna dedicated M. to the Mother by singing this song:

> Thy name, I have heard, O Consort of Shiva, is the destroyer of our fear,
> And so on Thee I cast my burden: Save me! Save me! O kindly Mother![8]

Another day the Master was seated on the terrace, close to the eastern column of the natmandir when he prayed:

> Mother, I don't want any physical enjoyment;
> Mother, I don't want name and fame;
> Mother, I don't want the eight occult powers;
> Mother, I don't want the other hundred powers;
> Mother, give me pure, unchanging, selfless devotion to you.
> Mother, may I never be deluded by your bewitching maya.[9]

Natmandir

M. described this building:

> In front of the Kali temple and just to the south is the spacious natmandir. It is rectangular and the terrace is supported by both inner and outer rows of columns. Theatrical performances take place here on special occasions, especially during the night of Kali Puja. On the front side of the roof of the natmandir there are images of Shiva and his followers, Nandi and Bhringi. Sri Ramakrishna used to salute Lord Shiva with folded hands before entering the Mother's temple, as if he were seeking his permission to enter the temple.[10]

One day M. went to the natmandir, where he embraced the left column of the inner row on the north side of the building. He remained for a while with closed eyes, then said to his companions: "This column has been touched by the Master. While listening to the *yatra* performance of Nilkantha, the Master embraced the column out of ecstasy."[11]

M. described a wonderful scene that he witnessed in the natmandir during his third visit to Dakshineswar: "It was now late in the evening and time for M.'s departure; but he felt reluctant to go and instead went in search of Sri Ramakrishna. At last he found the Master pacing alone in the natmandir in front of the Kali temple. A lamp was burning in the temple on either side of the image of the Divine Mother. The single lamp in the spacious natmandir blended light and darkness into a kind of mystic twilight, in which the figure of the Master could be dimly seen. In the dim light the Master, all alone, was pacing the hall rejoicing in the Self — as the lion lives and roams alone in the forest."[12]

Krishna Temple and the Courtyard

M. wrote:

East of the chandni and twelve temples is a large tiled courtyard. There are two temples in the middle of the courtyard — the Radhakanta [Krishna] temple on the north side and the Kali [Divine Mother] temple on the south side. In the Radhakanta temple there are two images on the altar — Radha and Krishna — standing and facing west. Steps lead from the courtyard into the sanctuary. The floor of this temple is inlaid with marble. Chandeliers hang from the ceiling of the veranda. They are usually covered with red linen and used only during festive occasions. In front of the veranda is a row of columns.[13]

Ramakrishna became the priest of the Krishna temple when the previous priest slipped, dropping Krishna's image and breaking the foot. The Master subsequently repaired this image.

While listening to the Bhagavata on the veranda of the Krishna temple, the Master had a vision: He saw a light emanate from the image, then touch him, and then touch the Bhagavata. He experienced the truth that the scripture, the devotee, and the deity are one. On another occasion, a photograph of Ramakrishna was taken as he sat in front of this temple. This photograph subsequently became the one most commonly worshipped by the devotees in the shrine.

The Brahmos did not believe in God with form. When Keshab Sen and the Brahmos came to Dakshineswar, the Master would escort them to the temples. When they reached the Krishna temple, Ramakrishna would wrap part of his wearing cloth around his neck and bow down to Krishna from the courtyard, touching his forehead to the lower step of the temple. This is how he taught them to respect the deity.[14]

Blessed are the tiles in that courtyard! They were touched by the Master's feet thousands of times. M. recalled:

Seven or eight days after my first meeting with the Master, as he was walking through the courtyard of the Kali temple I said to him, "It is better to take one's life than to suffer such terrible pain." At once he replied: "Why do you say so? You have a guru. Why do you worry?

Your guru is always behind you. He can remove your suffering by a mere wish. He makes everything favourable. A juggler threw a rope with many knots in it in front of a thousand people, and none could untie a single knot. But the juggler immediately removed all the knots just by a jerk of his hand. Don't worry. The guru will remove all your obstacles." What agony I was suffering, but I had found the Master. How he guided my life! Later my father came. We were reconciled with love and affection, and he took me back home. In retrospect we see that God is all-auspicious, but we judge things superficially. It was my family problems and my desire to commit suicide that led me to God.[15]

Twelve Shiva Temples

M. described them thus: The chandni is located at the centre of twelve Shiva temples — six of them on the north and six on the south. Seeing the twelve temples from a distance, passengers in boats on the Ganges point out to one another: "Look! There is the temple garden of Rani Rasmani."[16]

It is said that the Master embraced the northern-most image of Shiva, which is situated near his room. Swami Saradananda wrote: "One day the Master entered one of the Shiva temples of Dakshineswar and began to recite the *Shiva-mahimnah*, a hymn in praise of the deity. He was beside himself in ecstasy as he recited the following verse: 'O Lord, if the blue mountain be the ink, the ocean the ink pot, the biggest branch of the celestial tree the pen, and the earth the writing-leaf, and if by taking this, the goddess of learning writes forever, even then the limit of Your glory can never be reached.'"[17]

Ramakrishna's Room

Ramakrishna spent 14 years, from 1871 to 1885, in a room located at the northwest corner of the temple courtyard and immediately to the north of the Shiva temples.

After Ramakrishna's passing, M. would tell the devotees:

One should see everything connected with the Master in detail. For example, in the Master's room there are cots, a jar containing Ganges water, pictures of gods and goddesses — Kali, Krishna, Rama, Chaitanya and his kirtan party, Dhruva, Prahlad, Christ extending his hand to the drowning Peter, and a white marble image of Buddha, which was given to him by Rani Katyayani, the wife of Lalababu. There was a picture of the goddess of learning on the western wall. Whenever a new person would come, the Master would look at that picture and pray, "Mother, I am an unlettered person. Please sit on my tongue," and then he would speak to him. If a person can imprint these divine sights on his mind, he will have deep meditation, and even sitting at home he can live at Dakshineswar with the Master.[18]

One can feel the tangible spiritual atmosphere in this room. Here the Master had many visions, and he went into samadhi on numerous occasions. This is where he received his visitors and disciples and talked to them about God. Unfortunately during the centenary of the Dakshineswar temple garden in 1955, the Master's red cement floor was replaced with mosaic tile, so we can no longer walk on the same floor that he trod.

The Semicircular Porch

M. wrote:

To the west of this room is a semicircular veranda. Standing here facing west, Sri Ramakrishna would watch the holy river Ganges flow by. In front of the veranda is a narrow garden path running from north to south. On the other side of this path is the flower garden and then the embankment. From here, one can hear the sweet, melodious murmuring of the Ganges.[19]

M. later told Swami Nityatmananda: "Sometimes at 2:00 or 3:00 a.m., the Master would pace on the embankment. He said: 'At that time one can hear the *anahata* sound [music of the spheres]. Only the yogis can hear it.'"[20]

The Southeast Veranda

Ramakrishna would walk through the southeast veranda when he visited the temples. Ramlal recalled: "One day the Master was seated on the southeast veranda of his room. All of a sudden, he saw the Divine Mother standing on top of the temple, wearing Her anklets, extending one of Her legs towards the courtyard. Immediately he cried out and forbade Her, waving his hands: 'Don't — don't go farther! You will fall.' Saying so, the Master went into samadhi."

One day Ramakrishna was resting on his bed while Baburam (later Swami Premananda) fanned him. Narendra (later Swami Vivekananda) sat smoking with Hazra on the southeast veranda of the Master's room. Hazra said to Narendra: "You are all mere boys! You are visiting Sri Ramakrishna off and on, and he just keeps you satisfied with fruits and sweets. Hold him — press him — and get something [power, wealth, and so on] from him." As soon as the Master heard this from his room he jumped up from his bed, rushed to the veranda, and shouted: "Naren, come to my room right now. Don't listen to his calculating advice. The beggar pesters the rich man, saying, 'Sir, give me a pice! Give me a pice!' Being disgusted with the beggar, the rich man throws a small coin to him, saying, 'Take this and get out of here.' You are my very own. You will not have to ask for anything from me. Whatever I have, it is all yours."[21]

The Northern Veranda

M. described the importance of the northern veranda:

Here the devotees used to celebrate the Master's birthday. They would sing devotional songs in chorus and eat prasad with him. Keshab Chandra Sen and his followers often met with the Master here to talk about God. Afterwards the Master would feed them puffed rice, coconut, luchi [fried bread], and sweets. On this same spot Sri Ramakrishna, seeing Narendra [Swami Vivekananda], went into samadhi.[22]

During his third visit, M. heard Swami Vivekananda sing this song as he stood on the northern veranda:

Meditate, O my mind, on the Lord Hari,
The Stainless One, Pure Spirit through and through.
Ever more beauteous in fresh-blossoming love
That shames the splendour of a million moons,
Like lightning gleams the glory of His form,
Raising erect the hair for very joy.

M. described Ramakrishna's reaction:

The Master shuddered when this last line was sung. His hair stood on end, and tears of joy streamed down his cheeks. Now and then his lips parted in a smile. Was he seeing the peerless beauty of God, "that shames the splendour of a million moons?" Was this the vision of God, the Essence of Spirit? How much austerity and discipline, how much faith and devotion, must be necessary for such a vision![23]

Standing at the northeastern corner of this veranda, the Master would say good-bye to the Calcutta devotees. "One day," M. said, "I saw the Master sweeping the path next to the northern veranda with a broom. He told me, 'Mother walks here; that is why I am cleaning this path.'"[24]

The Northeastern Veranda

One day Ramakrishna was pacing back and forth on the northeastern veranda of his room in Dakshineswar. He was in a spiritual mood, completely oblivious of his surroundings. Mathur was then seated alone in a room of the kuthi (mansion) near the nahabat, and was watching him through a window. All of a sudden Mathur ran out of the house, threw himself down at Ramakrishna's feet, and began to cry profusely.

"What are you doing?" said Sri Ramakrishna in alarm. "You are an aristocrat and Rani Rasmani's son-in-law. What will people say if they see you acting like this? Calm yourself. Please, get up!"

Mathur gradually got control of himself and said: "Father [as he called Ramakrishna], I was watching you just now as you walked back and forth — I saw it distinctly: As you walked towards me you were no longer yourself. You were the Divine Mother Kali from the temple! Then, as you turned around and walked in the opposite direction, you became Lord Shiva! At first I thought it was some kind of optical illusion. I rubbed my eyes and looked again, but I saw the same thing. As often as I looked, I saw it!"[25]

The Nahabat (The Music Tower)

There are two nahabats in the temple garden, one on the south side and the other on the north side. M. described the music that came from one of these towers: "Early in the morning, before the eastern horizon becomes red, the *mangala-arati* [morning service] to the Divine Mother begins with the sweet sound of temple bells. In the nahabat, morning melodies are then played on the flageolet to the accompaniment of drums and cymbals. These are welcome sounds of love and joy to all, for the Mother of the Universe has awakened to bless Her beloved children."[26]

Ramakrishna's mother used to live in the upper room of the northern nahabat and the Holy Mother lived in the lower room. To protect her privacy, the veranda was screened with plaited bamboo mats, which cut off the sun and fresh air. The Holy Mother lived there like a caged bird. She would cook for the Master on the northern veranda of the nahabat. (*Pointing to the steps to the upper floor of the nahabat*) M. said: "The Holy Mother would sit here and repeat her mantra. As a result of her limited movement, she developed rheumatism that caused suffering all through her life. Her little room was filled with groceries and other things; and sometimes women devotees also stayed there. Oh, what superhuman patience, perseverance, and self-control! Her self-sacrifice and service are incomparable."[27]

The Flower Gardens

M. described the beautiful temple gardens:

On the bank of the Ganges and just to the west of the Panchavati are a bel tree and a sweet-scented, milk-white *gulchi* flower tree. Sri Ramakrishna was very fond of *mallika* [a type of jasmine], *madhavi*, and gulchi. He brought a madhavi plant [a flowering creeper which Radha liked] from Vrindaban and planted it in the Panchavati. East of the goose pond and the kuthi is another pond around which are many flowering plants such as the *champak*, the five-faced hibiscus, the pendant hibiscus [resembling earrings], roses, and the *kanchan* [gold]. On a fence there is an *aparajita* [a blue flower used in the worship of the Divine Mother], and nearby are jasmine and *shefalika*.

West of the twelve Shiva temples, there are many flowering trees such as the white oleander, red oleander, rose, jasmine, and double-petalled jasmine. Also growing there are *dhutura* flowers, which are used for the worship of Shiva. Tulsi [basil] plants grow in brick vases between these flowering trees.

South of the nahabat are more double-petalled jasmine as well as other varieties of jasmine, gardenias, and roses. Two more flowering trees grow near the chandni ghat: the lotus oleander and the *kokilaksha*, or cuckoo-eyed flower. The colour of the latter resembles that of the eyes of a cuckoo. West of the Master's room there are quite a few plants: *Krishna-chura*, double-petalled jasmine, jasmine, gardenia, mallika, roses, hibiscus, white oleander, red oleander, five-faced hibiscus, china-rose, and so on.

Formerly Sri Ramakrishna picked flowers for worship. One day when he was plucking bel leaves from a bel tree near the Panchavati, a layer of bark came off the tree. At that moment he experienced that God, who dwells in every being and everything, must have felt pain at this. He never again picked bel leaves for worship. Another day while picking flowers he had a vision: He saw that the flowers of each tree formed a bouquet and all those bouquets hung around the neck of the cosmic form of Shiva. Thus he experienced that the worship of God is going on day and night. After that experience he could no longer pick flowers.[28]

M.'s description of the flower gardens makes us feel that we are roaming in the gardens of heaven.

The Bakul-tala

M. wrote:

West of the nahabat are a bakul tree and a bathing ghat. The women of the neighbourhood bathe at this ghat. In 1877 Sri Ramakrishna's aged mother passed away there. Following the Hindu custom, the Master's dying mother was taken to this ghat and the lower half of her body was immersed in the holy water of the Ganges. She breathed her last in the presence of her weeping son.[29]

M. told Swami Nityatmananda: "Holding the feet of his mother, the Master said: 'Mother, who are you that carried me in your womb?' The Master knew that he was an avatar, so he exclaimed in joy: 'You are not an ordinary woman.'"[30]

The Panchavati

M. described the Panchavati as it appeared in Ramakrishna's time:

A little north of the bakul tree is the Panchavati. This is a grove of five trees — banyan, pipal, ashoka, amalaki, and bel — which were planted under Sri Ramakrishna's supervision. After returning from his pilgrimage [in 1868] he spread the holy dust of Vrindaban around this place. The Master practised various kinds of sadhana [disciplines] in the Panchavati grove, sometimes going there alone at night. Later he often accompanied the devotees as they walked around the holy spot. East of the Panchavati is a thatched hut [now, a brick room], in which Sri Ramakrishna practised meditation and austerities [Advaita sadhana under Tota Puri].

Next to the Panchavati is an old banyan tree which has grown around a pipal tree, both looking as if they were one tree. The banyan is an ancient tree, and as a result there are many holes in it which are the homes of birds and other animals. Around this tree is a circular brick platform with steps on two sides — north and south. The platform is used by people who visit the temple garden and especially by those who wish to sit in solitude and meditate on God with the holy Ganges flowing before them. Sri Ramakrishna used to sit on the northwest corner of the platform and practise various kinds of spiritual disciplines. He would cry to the Divine Mother with a longing heart, as the cow longs for her calf.[31]

M. told Swami Nityatmananda: "European indigo planters used to live here. This banyan tree and the platform existed during their time. This platform was the first place where the Master practised intense sadhana. Between the Panchavati and the old banyan tree was the madhavi creeper that the Master brought from Vrindaban. He planted it himself."[32]

Swami Subodhananda told M. the following incident: "The Master told me: 'I was then possessed by divine madness. One day I was weeding in the Panchavati. I was unaware that a beautiful young woman was standing behind me. Piqued, she said to me: "Hello, sadhu! I have been standing behind you for such a long time and you have not looked at me or talked to me! I have visited many ashramas and everywhere people are eager to talk to me and want me to live there. But you didn't even care to look at me. You are a real sadhu."'"[33]

M. described this particular scene many times:

Sri Ramakrishna was going to the pine grove. After a few minutes, M. and Latu, standing in the Panchavati, saw the Master coming back towards them. Behind him the sky was black with the rain-cloud. Its reflection in the Ganges made the water darker. The disciples felt that the Master was God Incarnate, a Divine Child five years old, radiant with the smile of innocence and purity. Around him were the sacred trees of the Panchavati under which he had practised spiritual disciplines and had beheld visions of God. At his feet flowed the sacred river Ganges, the destroyer of man's sins. The presence of this God-man charged the trees, shrubs, flowers, plants, and temples with spiritual fervour and divine joy.[34]

Sadhan Kutir (Meditation Hut)

The Sadhan Kutir is situated east of the Panchavati. It is here that Tota Puri initiated the Master into sannyasa, and here that he attained nirvikalpa samadhi. M. said: "It was a thatched hut with an earthen floor when the Master practised Vedanta sadhana there. Later it was rebuilt as a brick building and there was nothing inside. Now someone has installed a Shiva image there. So many things will crop up in the future; people will say that image was there during the Master's time. Thus it happens everywhere."[35]

Pine Grove and Bel-tala

M. described the pine grove and bel-tala:

Going a little north of the Panchavati one reaches a fence of iron wire. North of this fence is the pine grove — a collection of four pine trees. Sri Ramakrishna and the devotees would use this place to answer the call of nature.

East of the pine grove is the bel-tala. Sitting under this bel tree, Sri Ramakrishna practised many difficult disciplines [especially tantric sadhanas under the guidance of the Bhairavi Brahmani]. To the north of the pine grove and bel tree is the high boundary wall of the temple garden, and on the other side of the wall is a government magazine.[36]

Gazi-tala and the Main Gate

M. wrote:

There is a path running east to west between the northern portico of the courtyard and the kuthi. While walking east, one can see a beautiful pond with a concrete ghat on the right side. There is another ghat for this pond on the eastern side of the Kali temple, which is used to clean the sacred utensils and dishes. A pipal tree is next to the northern ghat. This place is called Gazi-tala. Long ago an old Muslim saint lived here, passing his days in the contemplation of God. His departed spirit is worshipped even today by Hindus and Muslims who live near the temple. [At the Gazi-tala Ramakrishna practised Islamic sadhana under the guidance of a Sufi named Govinda Roy.]

The main gate of the temple garden is a little east of the Gazi-tala. People who come from Alambazar or Calcutta enter the temple compound through this gate, and the people of Dakshineswar come through the northeastern gate, which is a little north of the main gate. A guard protects the main gate. When the Master would return late from Calcutta by carriage, sometimes even at midnight, the guard at the main gate would unlock the gate for him. Then the Master would invite the guard to his room and feed him fried bread and sweets which had been sent as prasad.[37]

Kuthi (Mansion)

M. described the mansion in which Ramakrishna lived for many years:

Coming out of the temple courtyard through the northern portico, one comes across a two-storeyed mansion called the kuthi. Whenever Rani Rasmani or her son-in-law Mathur and other relatives came to visit Dakshineswar, they stayed in this kuthi. During their lifetime Sri Ramakrishna lived [for 16 years] in a room on the west side of the ground floor of this mansion. From this room one can go to the bakul-tala ghat and have a very good view of the Ganges.[38]

Swami Saradananda described a touching incident that took place on the roof of the kuthi. It is amazing how Sri Ramakrishna prayed for the disciples who acted in his divine drama:

After the Master had attained all the spiritual experiences, divine inspiration prompted a new desire to arise intensely in the Master's mind. He became extremely anxious to meet the devotees he had seen previously in spiritual visions and to transmit his spiritual power into their hearts.

The Master said: "In those days there was no limit to my yearning. During the daytime I could just manage to keep it under control. Severely tormented by the worthless, mundane talk of worldly people, I would wistfully anticipate the day when my beloved companions would arrive. I hoped to find solace in conversing with them about God and to lighten my heart by relating to them my own spiritual experiences. Every little incident would remind me of them, and thoughts of them completely engrossed me. I kept planning what I should say to this one and what I should give to that one, and so forth. When evening came, I couldn't control my feelings any longer. I was tortured by the thought that another day had passed and they still hadn't arrived! When the vesper service started, and the temples resounded with the ringing of bells and the blowing of conch shells, I would climb up to the roof of the kuthi [mansion] and cry out at the top of my voice, with the anguish of my heart: 'Come to me, my children! Where are you? I can't bear to live without you!' A mother never longed so for the sight of her child, or a friend for a friend, or a lover for his sweetheart, as I did for them. Oh, it was beyond all describing! And soon after this, they did at last begin to come."[39]

M. made a wonderful comment about Dakshineswar: "The spiritual fire is blazing intensely there, and whoever goes there will be purified. The body does not burn, but mental impurities are consumed in no time. Then a man can attain immortality. God himself, in a physical form, lived there for thirty years! One can tangibly feel the spirituality at Dakshineswar."[40]

There is a beautiful verse in the Sri Sri Chaitanya Charitamrita: Adyapiha sei lila kare gora rai, kono kono bhagyavane dekhibare pai. "Chaitanya is still performing his divine play; only the fortunate ones can see it." Let us pray to Sri Ramakrishna to grant us the good fortune to be able to visualize his divine play.

7

Dakshineswar: An Object of Meditation

A Divine Plan

Providence may have decreed that the pilgrimage of a devout woman would not be successfully carried out, but this failed pilgrimage found fulfillment instead in the form of the Dakshineswar temple garden. This great woman, Rani Rasmani (1793-1861), had long desired to make a grand pilgrimage to Varanasi. Elaborate preparations had been made, but during the night before she was to embark, the Divine Mother appeared to her in a dream and said: "You need not go to Varanasi. Install my image in a beautiful spot along the bank of the Ganges and arrange for my worship and offerings there. In this image I shall be present constantly and shall ever accept your worship." (In another version of this incident it is said that Rasmani started her journey, and on the first night they halted near Dakshineswar, where she had that dream.)[1]

The construction of the Dakshineswar temple complex began in 1847 and required more than eight years to complete. In addition to the main temple, dedicated to the Divine Mother Kali, there are also twelve small temples dedicated to Shiva and a temple dedicated to Krishna. Rasmani spent 50,000 rupees for the land, 160,000 rupees to build an embankment along the river, and 900,000 rupees for the temple complex. In addition, she spent 226,000 rupees for some property that was meant to be used as an endowment for the maintenance of the temple.

Rani Rasmani was not an ordinary woman. Sri Ramakrishna said: "Rani Rasmani was one of the eight *nayikas* [attendant goddesses] of the Divine Mother. She came down to the world to spread the worship of the Divine Mother."[2] Before Ramakrishna's arrival in Calcutta, Rasmani began to set the stage for the coming avatar, where he would enact his divine play for thirty years. Shiva and Shakti traditionally remain side by side, so temples to Kali and Shiva are generally built close to one another. But Rani Rasmani included a Radha-Krishna temple in the same compound with her Kali temple and twelve shrines to Shiva. This was something new. Perhaps Rasmani was inspired by the Divine Mother to thus symbolize the harmony of faiths in concrete form for Ramakrishna, who was the embodiment of all religions.

My First Visit to Dakshineswar

It was probably in June 1950 that I made my first visit to Dakshineswar. I was fourteen years old. I vividly remember how I took the bus, route number 78, from Barrackpore to Dunlop Bridge; from there I took bus number 32B to Dakshineswar. When I arrived at about 2:30 p.m. the temples were closed, so my companion and I waited in the Panchavati until 4:00 p.m. My companion told me that Sri Ramakrishna used to sit under those trees and talk to the Divine Mother. My young mind began to picture this holy place as it must have looked during the time of Ramakrishna's austerities and divine play.

When I first visited Dakshineswar, there was no barbed-wire fence around the Panchavati. Between the Panchavati and the Panchamundi where Ramakrishna practised Tantra, there were some old pine trees and some mango, lichi, and other fruit trees. There was a bamboo fence around the Panchamundi, and anyone could sit on its circular cement platform. The Dakshineswar temple garden was like a beautiful ancient hermitage. When I visited Dakshineswar in 1997, I saw that a brick wall had been built between the Panchavati and the Panchamundi and that a meditation cottage had been constructed near the pine grove. These constructions have ruined the beautiful atmosphere of Rasmani's temple garden. But nonetheless, Dakshineswar still holds a powerful attraction for me.

From 1950 onward I visited Dakshineswar regularly. Almost every Sunday, I would go to Udbodhan, the Holy Mother's house, in North Calcutta. From there, I would go to Dakshineswar in the evening. First I would visit the temples, then I would go to Sri Ramakrishna's room and sit for meditation between the western wall and his bed. I would imagine that the Master was seated on his bed with his legs hanging over the side; I would touch my head to his feet. This was how I daydreamed as a boy. At that time there was no wooden fence around the Master's bed. Even though the caretaker burned a lot of incense, the room was infested with healthy mosquitoes that lived on the pure blood of the Master's devotees.

There was a red cement floor in the Master's room at that time, the same as in his time. Photos which the Master had collected — Jagannath, Dhruva, Prahlada, Chaitanya and the kirtan party, Jesus rescuing Peter, and so on — hung on the walls. In 1955, during the centenary of Dakshineswar, the temple authorities built a temple to Rani Rasmani between the Master's room and the nahabat, and they replaced the red cement floor of the Master's room with a mosaic. In India our sense of history is very poor. How wonderful it would have been if the temple authorities had installed a museum in the kuthi where Rasmani and Mathur lived, instead of building a temple obstructing the path to the *nahabat*. Ramakrishna lived in that kuthi for 16 years. A good museum would have tremendous educational value and would attract pilgrims and visitors. There is no shortage of Kali temples in Bengal, but the Dakshineswar Kali temple is unique because of Sri Ramakrishna.

M. has left us a vivid description of the Kali temple of Dakshineswar in the first part of *Sri Sri Ramakrishna Kathamrita*, which has been fully translated in the appendix of *Ramakrishna As We Saw Him*. This wonderful historical document will help future generations to visualize the playground of Sri Ramakrishna and meditate on his divine play. I have some pictures of old Dakshineswar in which one can see beautiful flower gardens on the bank of the Ganges, a dense forest in the Panchavati area, pilgrims bathing at the chandni and bakul-tala ghats, and the domed temples between the two nahabats. This panoramic view reflected on the Ganges makes us think that the heavenly palace of Indra has descended in Dakshineswar.

Every particle of dust at Dakshineswar is holy; every bit of ground there is precious to the devotees of Ramakrishna. Ramakrishna lived here for 30 years, practised various sadhanas, taught his devotees and disciples, and enacted his divine play. This temple garden of Dakshineswar is now an object of meditation for innumerable people from all over the world. There are many people who have never been to Dakshineswar, but they have read *The Gospel of Sri Ramakrishna* and *Sri Ramakrishna and His Divine Play*. They try to visualize the playground of Ramakrishna, imagining various scenes in the Master's life: how he tested the image of Kali by putting cotton near Her nostrils to see if She breathed; how Ramakrishna repaired the broken foot of Krishna; how he tearfully embraced the image of Shiva and glorified the Lord. They also picture in their minds the places where Ramakrishna practised Tantra, Vedanta, and Islam; the chandni ghat where Ramakrishna bathed; and the room in which he slept. These visualizations are helpful for meditation.

Two Sweet Memories

Ramlal, a nephew of Ramakrishna, recalled:

I was young at the time, and it was winter. The Master used to go for a walk in the morning, covering himself with a shawl and wearing a cap on his head. I used to cut a twig for the Master that he used as a toothbrush. We would go to the main road through the northeast gate of the temple garden and then walk up to Barrackpore Trunk Road, which was broad and straight. Standing on the road one day, the Master said: "Look, this broad and straight road is like the mind of a sadhu. It is not crooked." One could see the pinnacle of the temple from that road. As he looked at the curved structure of the temple's pinnacle one day, the Master said: "The temple is overflowing with joy because the Divine Mother is in its inner sanctuary. The temple is having goose bumps out of joy." The Master said so many wonderful things. On our way back, he would stop in our [Ramlal's] house near the temple garden to inquire about the family members and their welfare. Sometimes he would say: "Give me some puffed rice. Let me have my breakfast here." Afterwards, he would slowly return to the temple.

I remember another incident. Mathur presented a beautiful necklace to the Divine Mother. Later, Mathur's son Trailokya became the custodian of the Dakshineswar temple. The Master told him: "Your father gave a necklace to the Divine Mother. Will you not present anything to Her?" Trailokya had anklets made for the Divine Mother. She looked beautiful when She was dressed with those anklets. One day the Master was seated on the southeast veranda of his room. All of a sudden, he saw the Divine Mother standing on the top of the temple. She was wearing those anklets, and was about to step forward towards the courtyard. Immediately the Master cried out and waved for Her to stop, shouting: "Don't — don't go farther! You will fall." As he did this he went into samadhi.[3]

At Dakshineswar with Swami Subodhananda

The following account was recorded by Swami Subodhananda's attendant:

At 3:00 p.m. [in November 1929 (6 Paush 1336)] we left for Dakshineswar from Udbodhan House by car with Swami Subodhananda. As we passed Baranagore, the swami said: "When the Master was alive, I walked through this street many times to see him at Dakshineswar. The Master said to M. and other devotees, 'Please pay this boy's carriage fare or boat fare whenever he comes.' I was afraid to travel by boat because I did not know how to swim."

When the car reached Dakshineswar, the swami first took us to the bel-tala [the Panchamundi, where the Master had practised tantra]. Seeing the bamboo fence around the bel tree and its cement platform, the swami said: "This fence was not here during the Master's time. The place where the Master sat for sadhana is now within that fence."

When we arrived at the Panchavati, the swami bowed down to the platform. Pointing to the brick cottage where the Master had attained nirvikalpa samadhi, the swami said, "During the Master's time this room was a thatched hut with a mud floor."

While we were passing near the nahabat, the swami said, "The Holy Mother lived in the small room in the nahabat." Reaching the Master's room, the swami bowed down on the floor. We also bowed down. The swami recalled: "Oh, what a crowd was here during the Master's time!" The swami sat there for a while.

He then left the room to visit the Divine Mother in the temple. We followed him. He came down the steps of the southeastern veranda and walked through the courtyard. He stopped in front of the steps of the Shiva temples on the north side. He said: "One day I came to Dakshineswar and the Master's room was full of people. Meanwhile, the Master left his room accompanying me. We sat on the steps of these temples. The Master then gave me spiritual instructions and passed his hand over my head and body. Shortly something [the kundalini power] arose in my head and overwhelmed me and made me almost unconscious. After a while, the Master again passed his hand over my head and I became normal again."[4]

Ramakrishna's Divine Play

Ramakrishna enacted the first part of his divine play in Kamarpukur, the second part in Dakshineswar, and the last part in Shyampukur and

Cossipore. In an ecstatic mood, the Master once said to Mathur, "As long as you are alive, I shall be in Dakshineswar." This startled Mathur; he was apprehensive because he knew that the Divine Mother was protecting him and his family through the Master. So when he heard the Master's words, he thought that the Master would forsake his family after he died. He then humbly told the Master: "What are you saying, Father? My wife and son Dwaraka are very much devoted to you." Observing Mathur's distress, the Master replied, "All right, I shall remain as long as your wife and Dwaraka live." It indeed came to pass that the Master left Dakshineswar for good after both Jagadamba and Dwaraka had passed away. Dwaraka died in 1878, Jagadamba in 1881. The Master remained in Dakshineswar until September 1885.

Krishna left Vrindaban and went to Mathura which is only seven or eight miles away. He was so unattached that he never returned to see his dear ones in Vrindaban. The Master left for Calcutta and Cossipore to enact the last part of his divine play, and never returned to Dakshineswar. However, he sometimes sent his disciples to practise sadhana there. Swamiji would go to Dakshineswar with a few brother disciples and spend the whole night in the Panchavati in meditation. Later, Swamiji reminisced: "Oh, what weird scenes things bring before me, the weirdest scenes of my whole life! Perfect silence, broken only by the cries of the jackals, in the darkness under the great tree at Dakshineswar. Night after night we sat there, the whole night through, and He [Ramakrishna] talked to me, when I was a boy."[5] Later, M. took the devotees to Dakshineswar and pointed out the spots connected with various events of the Master's life.

In 1897, Swami Vivekananda returned to India from the West and celebrated the birth anniversary of Sri Ramakrishna at Dakshineswar. The monks of the Ramakrishna Order have a special affection for Dakshineswar, the playground of Ramakrishna. Swami Satprakashananda told me about a visit he paid to Dakshineswar on the Jagaddhatri Puja day in 1917. Swamis Brahmananda, Saradananda, and Akhandananda made the trip, along with many devotees. Swami Akhandananda loudly chanted various hymns in the Mother's temple in his melodious voice. In an ecstatic mood, Swami Brahmananda went to all the temples, the Master's room, the Panchavati, and the Panchamundi. The monks and devotees expected that Brahmananda would say something about the Master, but he remained silent. He was absorbed in the thought of his guru.

Swami Nirvanananda, an attendant of Brahmananda, recalled: "It was a hot summer day in June at 3:00 p.m. There was a flat roof adjacent to the room of Swami Brahmananda in Belur Math. The swami got up from his rest and walked barefoot to the northeast corner of the roof. Barefoot, I carried water for the swami so that he could rinse his mouth. The roof was so hot that it was very painful to stand there. I was continually shifting from foot to foot. I noticed that the swami was in an ecstatic mood gazing at Dakshineswar across the Ganges. His feet were very soft, but he stood motionless on that hot roof. After a while, he came back to the normal plane."[6]

Blessed is the holy land of Dakshineswar — an object of meditation for devotees of the Master.

8

Christmas Vacation with Ramakrishna

Roughly 120 years have passed since Ramakrishna lived in the temple garden of Dakshineswar. When we visit Dakshineswar even now we can see the same image of the Divine Mother Kali that Ramakrishna worshipped; the same image of Krishna that he worshipped, and which he repaired; the same image of Shiva that he embraced. We can enter Ramakrishna's room and see the cots on which he sat and slept; his collection of pictures still hangs on the walls. We can bathe at the chandni ghat where he used to bathe; we can sit in the Panchavati and under the bel tree where he practised severe disciplines. When we walk over the tiles of the courtyard, we think that God in human form once walked over them. How blessed are those tiles! Now we are trying to remember Ramakrishna through japa and meditation; how wonderful it would be if we could live with him for a few days!

When Ramakrishna lived in Dakshineswar, Calcutta was the capital of India (Delhi became the capital in 1912). Although Dakshineswar was only four or five miles away, very few people of Calcutta went to see him. It is said that there is always a shadow under a lamp. The nearest relatives may not understand the greatness of an illumined soul, but people far away recognize him and search him out. People in India go to the mountains and visit holy places while on vacation. They spend much money, time, and energy on these trips, but they are not interested in meeting a great soul who lives nearby.

Travel is very important in human life. Vacations relieve monotony and stress, reinvigorate us, and give us a break from our ordinary lifestyle. When we are away from home, we feel relaxed and at least temporarily experience freedom from our daily routine and worldly duties. The joy of this freedom refreshes our body and mind.

M., the recorder of *The Gospel of Sri Ramakrishna*, spent his Christmas vacation with Ramakrishna at Dakshineswar from 14 December 1883 to 5 January 1884. However, he recorded the events for only fourteen of the twenty-three days.

On 9 December 1883 M. was meditating on the western veranda of the nahabat. While returning from the pine grove, the Master saw M. and said: "Hello! You are here? You will get results very soon. If you practise a little, then someone will come forward to help you." M. looked up at the Master with joy and hope. The Master continued: "The time is ripe for you. The mother bird does not break the shell of the egg until the right time arrives."[1] M. had read many books on religion and philosophy, but had not found peace of mind. From this point on the Master's company brought a new turn to M.'s life.

The Master started walking towards the Panchavati, accompanied by M. No one else was with them. While listening to the Master's spiritual experiences, M. took a couple of leaves from a tree in the Panchavati and put them in his pocket.

Master: "See there — that branch has been broken. I used to sit under it."

M.: "I took a young twig from that tree — I have it at home."

Master (*with a smile*): "Why?"

M.: "I feel happy when I look at it. After all this is over, this place will be considered very holy."[2]

M. was inspired after talking to the Master. He decided to spend his Christmas vacation practising spiritual disciplines under the Master's guidance. On Friday, 14 December 1883, at 9:00 a.m., M. arrived at Dakshineswar and bowed down to the Master. "If an aspirant practises a little spiritual discipline, then someone comes forward to help him." These words of the Master had penetrated M.'s mind; later he repeated them to the devotees who came after the Master's passing.

Late that afternoon, M. and Ramakrishna stood on the south side of the nahabat, talking:

Master: "Where will you sleep? In the hut in the Panchavati?"

M.: "Won't they let me have the room on the upper floor of the nahabat?"

M. selected the nahabat because he had a poetic temperament. From there he could see the sky, the Ganges, the moonlight, and the flowers in the garden.

Master: "Oh, they'll let you have it. But I suggested the Panchavati because so much contemplation and meditation have been practised there and the name of God has been chanted there so often."[3]

Before M.'s vacation, the Master had told him: "You should not eat every day at the guesthouse of the Kali temple. The guesthouse is intended to supply free food to monks and the destitute. Bring your own cook with you." M. had accordingly done so. The Master arranged a place for the man to cook and he asked Ramlal to speak to the milkman about milk. The Master suggested that M. eat plain rice, vegetables, and milk. During sadhana one's mind should not dwell on rich and fancy food. The Bhagavata says: *Jitam sarvam, jite rase* — One who has controlled the tongue has controlled everything.

When a flower blooms, bees come of their own accord. People came to hear the Master talk about God, even though he did not advertise. A schoolteacher came one afternoon with a group of students. The Master glanced at M. and said: "One attains God when one feels yearning for Him. An intense restlessness is needed. Through it the whole mind goes to God.

"One must have childlike faith — and the intense yearning that a child feels to see his mother. That yearning is like the red sky in the east at dawn. After such a sky the sun must rise. Immediately after that yearning one sees God."[4]

He then told the story of Jatila, a little boy who was afraid to go to school through the forest. His mother asked him to call on his elder brother Madhusudana [Krishna] if he became afraid. The boy had complete faith in his mother's words. The next day, on his way to school, he cried out, "Brother Madhusudana." Krishna appeared and walked with him to school. After telling that story to the students, the Master said, "One must have this childlike faith, this yearning."

M. describes the first evening he spent at Dakshineswar:

Late at night M. sat alone in the nahabat. The sky, the river, the garden, the steeples of the temples, the trees, and the Panchavati were flooded with moonlight. Deep silence reigned everywhere, broken only by the melodious murmuring of the Ganges. M. was meditating on Sri Ramakrishna.

At three o'clock in the morning M. left his seat. He proceeded towards the Panchavati as Sri Ramakrishna had suggested. He did not care for the nahabat anymore and resolved to stay in the hut in the Panchavati.

Suddenly he heard a distant sound, as if someone were wailing piteously, "Oh, where art Thou, Brother Madhusudana?" The light of the full moon streamed through the thick foliage of the Panchavati, and as he proceeded he saw at a distance one of the Master's disciples [Latu] sitting alone in the grove, crying helplessly, "Oh, where art Thou, Brother Madhusudana?"

Silently M. watched him.[5]

When people go on pilgrimage during their vacations, they move around the whole day, eat at restaurants to enjoy good food, buy various souvenirs for friends and family, watch movies or plays, and sleep in comfortable beds at night. M.'s vacation was quite different: The Master had created a hunger for God in his mind, so he slept very little and he tried to be absorbed in God all the time.

Saturday, 15 December 1883

M. was absolutely honest and he did not hide anything. In the *Gospel* he even recorded the scoldings that he received from the Master. Ordinary people try to hide their shortcomings. The Master was all-knowing, so he knew what was good for his disciples. On the second morning of M.'s vacation, he bluntly scolded M.:

> Master: "Aren't you ashamed of yourself? You have children, and still you enjoy intercourse with your wife. Don't you hate yourself for thus leading an animal life? Don't you hate yourself for dallying with a body which contains only blood, phlegm, filth, and excreta? He who contemplates the Lotus Feet of God looks on even the most beautiful woman as mere ash from the cremation ground."
>
> M. sat there silently, hanging his head in shame.
>
> Master: "A man who has tasted even a drop of God's ecstatic love looks on 'lust and gold' as most insignificant. . . . One gradually obtains that love for God if one but prays to Him with a yearning heart and always chants His name and glories."[6]

Later, the Master remarked: "Those who are my own will not be angry even if scolded. They will come back again."

M.'s account continues:

> It was ten o'clock in the morning. . . . The Master went to the temple accompanied by M. Entering the shrine, the Master sat before the image. He offered a flower or two at the feet of the Divine Mother.

Then he put a flower on his own head and began to meditate. He sang a song to the Divine Mother:

Thy name, I have heard, O Consort of Shiva, is the destroyer of our fear,
And so on Thee I cast my burden: Save me! Save me, O kindly Mother![7]

M. later wrote that while singing that song the Master dedicated him to the Divine Mother.

Sunday, 16 December 1883

The image of Ramakrishna and his surroundings that M. presents in the *Gospel*, are so vivid that they can help us in our meditation. For example, here he writes of the events that took place on Sunday morning, 16 December 1883:

Sri Ramakrishna was seated with M. on the semicircular porch of his room at about ten o'clock in the morning. The fragrance of gardenias, jasmines, oleanders, roses, and other flowers filled the air. . . .

[The Master went into an ecstatic mood.] His body became motionless and his mind stopped functioning; tears streamed down his cheeks. After a while he said, "O Mother, make me like Sita, completely forgetful of everything — body and limbs —, totally unconscious of hands, feet, and sense organs — only the one thought in her mind, 'Where is Rama?'"

M. wondered: "Was the Master inspired by the ideal of Sita to teach M. the yearning that a devotee should feel for God?"[8]

In the afternoon the Master told some devotees:

"Maya is nothing but 'lust and gold.' A man attains yoga when he has freed his mind from these two. The Self — the Supreme Self — is the magnet; the individual self is the needle. But the magnet cannot attract the needle if the needle is covered with clay."

Mukherjee: "How can one remove it?"

Master: "Weep for God with a longing heart. Tears shed for Him will wash away the clay. When you have thus freed yourself from impurity, you will be attracted by the magnet. Only then will you attain yoga."[9]

During his sadhana, whenever the Master saw the sunset he would weep, saying, "Mother, another day is gone in vain; still Thou art not revealed unto me." The Master told M. many stories about how sunsets reminded him of his longing, so in the *Gospel* we find many descriptions of the sunset and evening hours.

It was evening. Sri Ramakrishna was meditating on the Divine Mother and chanting Her holy name. The devotees also went off to solitary places and meditated on their Chosen Ideals. Evening worship began at the temple garden in the shrines of Kali, Radha-Krishna, and Shiva.

It was the second day of the dark fortnight of the moon. Soon the moon rose in the sky, bathing temples, trees, flowers, and the rippling surface of the Ganges in its light. The Master was sitting on the couch and M. on the floor. The conversation turned to the Vedanta.

M.: "Is the world unreal?"

Master: "Why should the universe be unreal? That is a speculation of the philosophers. After realizing God, one sees that it is God Himself who has become the universe and all living beings.

"The Divine Mother revealed to me in the Kali temple that it was She who had become everything. She showed me that everything was full of Consciousness. The Image was Consciousness, the altar was Consciousness, the water-vessels were Consciousness, the doorsill was Consciousness, the marble floor was Consciousness — all was Consciousness.

"I found everything inside the room soaked, as it were, in Bliss — the Bliss of Satchidananda. I saw a wicked man in front of the Kali temple; but in him also I saw the Power of the Divine Mother vibrating.

"That was why I fed a cat with the food that was to be offered to the Divine Mother. I clearly perceived that the Divine Mother had become everything — even the cat."[10]

M. was dumbfounded; he had never heard such a thing. Earlier, M. had asked, "Is the world unreal?" The Master had not replied to M.'s question by quoting scriptures or explaining his answer with logic and philosophy. M.'s western education could not solve this riddle: Where does matter end and Consciousness begin? Sri Ramakrishna's experience of Oneness revealed the truth of the Chandogya Upanishad: *Sarvam khalu idam Brahma* — Verily, everything is Brahman.

Monday, 17 December 1883

It was about eight o'clock in the morning. Sri Ramakrishna was in his room with M. . . .

Master: "The whole thing in a nutshell is that one must develop ecstatic love for Satchidananda. . . . One must become mad with love in order to realize God. But that love is not possible if the mind dwells on 'lust and gold.' . . . Gauri used to say that when a man attains ecstatic love of God all the pores of the skin, even the roots of the hair, become like so many sexual organs, and in every pore the aspirant enjoys the happiness of communion with the Atman."[11]

M. felt intense renunciation and expressed his desire to become a monk. He described Ramakrishna's reaction: "The Master fixed his gaze on M. and said, 'By renouncing everything?' M., 'What can a man achieve unless he gets rid of maya?' . . . Both remained silent a few minutes."[12]

Tuesday, 18 December 1883

M. had tremendous powers of observation. Like a shadow he followed Sri Ramakrishna day and night. His overwhelming desire to experience samadhi impelled him to meticulously record the instances in which he saw the Master go into samadhi: "It was a winter morning, and the Master was sitting near the east door of his room, wrapped in his moleskin shawl. He looked at the sun and suddenly went into samadhi. His eyes stopped blinking and he lost all consciousness of the outer world. After a long time he came down to the plane of the sense world."[13]

The Master's samadhi reminded M. of this passage from the Gayatri mantra: *Om tat savitur varenyam bhargo devasya dhimahi* — I meditate on the luminous One who dwells in the solar region.

Later that day, the Master and some devotees went to Calcutta:

Sri Ramakrishna had vowed to offer green coconut and sugar to Siddheswari, the Divine Mother, for Rakhal's welfare. He asked M. to pay for the offerings.

That afternoon the Master, accompanied by M., Rakhal, and some other devotees, set out in a carriage for the temple of Siddheswari in Calcutta. On the way offerings were purchased. On reaching the temple, the Master asked the devotees to offer the fruit and sugar to the Divine Mother. They saw the priests and their friends playing cards in the temple. Sri Ramakrishna said: "To play cards in the temple! One should think of God here."[14]

We find in the Bible that Jesus went into the temple of God, cast out everyone who bought and sold in the temple, overthrew the tables of the moneychangers, and said: "It is written, 'My house shall be called the house of prayer.' But ye have made it a den of thieves."[15] Like Christ, Ramakrishna could not bear hypocrisy, and he was outspoken about it.

The Master left the temple and went to see his rich devotee Jadu Mallick. When they arrived, they found Jadu surrounded by his admirers, who were well-dressed dandies. Jadu welcomed the Master. M. describes their conversation:

Master (*with a smile*): "Why do you keep so many clowns and flatterers with you?"

Jadu (*smiling*): "That you may liberate them." (*Laughter.*)[16]

Wednesday, 19 December 1883

The places where Christ and Buddha lived have become holy. Even now people from all over the world visit those places and try to absorb their presence. Ramakrishna lived in the temple garden of Dakshineswar for thirty years. M. tried to preserve the Master's presence and the panoramic beauty of the temple garden through his powerful, photographic memory and his poetic imagination. After one hundred and twenty years, M.'s vivid descriptions still bring Ramakrishna and his surrounding to our minds:

> It was nine o'clock in the morning. Sri Ramakrishna was talking to M. near the bel tree at Dakshineswar. This tree, under which the Master had practised the most austere sadhana, stood in the northern end of the temple garden. Farther north ran a high wall, and just outside was the government magazine. West of the bel tree was a row of tall pines that rustled in the wind. Below the trees flowed the Ganges, and to the south could be seen the sacred grove of the Panchavati. The dense trees and underbrush hid the temples. No noise of the outside world reached the bel tree.[17]

Now that bel tree, the pine grove, and the big banyan that was in the Panchavati are gone. This wonderful place that had been made sacred by Ramakrishna's sadhana is full of vendors. A brick building has been built near the bel tree, and another wall has been built between the bel tree and the Panchavati. The entire area is filled with restaurants and shops. All this is very painful for devotees. Time — the devourer of all — has swallowed that beautiful environment. If God wills, someone may come forward to restore the temple garden according to M.'s description. We now return to M.'s narrative:

> Sri Ramakrishna went to the Panchavati on his way back to his room. M. accompanied him. It was about ten o'clock.
>
> M.: "Sir, is there no spiritual discipline leading to realization of the Impersonal God?"
>
> Master: "Yes, there is. But the path is extremely difficult. After intense austerities the rishis of olden times realized God as their

innermost consciousness and experienced the real nature of Brahman. But how hard they had to work! They went out of their dwellings in the early morning and all day practised austerities and meditation. Returning home at nightfall, they took a light supper of fruit and roots."[18]

M. had a busy life. He was the headmaster of a school; he had a wife and children and other family responsibilities. During this vacation he was trying his utmost to practise various sadhanas.

M. saluted the Master and went to a secluded place under the bel tree. He carried his prayer carpet and a jug of water with him. M. continues:

At midday, finding that M. had not yet returned, Sri Ramakrishna started towards the bel tree; but on reaching the Panchavati he met M. carrying his prayer carpet and water jug.

Sri Ramakrishna said to M.: "I was coming to look for you. Because of your delay I thought you might have scaled the wall and run away. I watched your eyes this morning and felt apprehensive lest you should go away like Narayana Shastri. Then I said to myself: 'No, he won't run away. He thinks a great deal before doing anything.'"[19]

Sometimes we wonder if God thinks of us. Ramakrishna's life shows how much love and concern he had for his devotees. He always thought of their welfare. As God attracts the devotees so also the devotees attract God. Love is reciprocal. If you love, you will be loved — this is the law. M. writes:

Following Sri Ramakrishna's direction, M. spent the night in the hut at the Panchavati. In the early hours of the morning he was singing alone:

I am without the least benefit of prayer and austerity, O Lord!
I am the lowliest of the lowly; make me pure with Thy hallowed touch.
One by one I pass my days in hope of reaching Thy Lotus Feet,
But Thee, alas, I have not found.

Suddenly M. glanced towards the window and saw the Master standing there. Sri Ramakrishna's eyes became heavy with tears as M. sang the line: "I am the lowliest of the lowly; make me pure with Thy hallowed touch."[20]

M. felt the Master's grace.

Friday, 21 December 1883

M. describes his morning with Ramakrishna: "In the morning the Master and M. were conversing alone under the bel tree. The Master told him many secrets of spiritual discipline, exhorting him to renounce 'lust and gold.' He further said that the mind at times becomes one's guru."[21]

In the afternoon the Master advised a monk who was a worshipper of the formless God: "Dive deep; one does not get the precious gems by merely floating on the surface. God is without form, no doubt; but He also has form. By meditating on God with form one speedily acquires devotion; then one can meditate on the formless God."[22]

Saturday, 22 December 1883

M.'s family life caused him much pain; he had even contemplated suicide. But he forgot all of his problems when he was with Ramakrishna: the Master's immortal words brought him peace.

M. records a conversation that took place in the morning:

A devotee: "Sir, how does one obtain love for God?"
Master: "Go forward. The king dwells beyond the seven gates. You can see him only after passing through all the gates.
"At the time of the installation of Annapurna at Chanak, I said to Dwarika Babu: 'Large fish live in the deep water of a big lake. Throw some spiced bait into the water; then the fish will come, attracted by its smell; now and then they will make the water splash.' Devotion and ecstatic love are like the spiced bait."[23]

Sometimes we ask ourselves: How can we love God if we have not seen Him?

The Master said: "God sports in the world as man. He incarnates Himself as man — as in the case of Krishna, Rama, and Chaitanya. . . . If you seek God, you must seek Him in the Incarnations. . . . One needs spiritual practice in order to know God and recognize Divine Incarnations."

That afternoon, the Master said: "To love an Incarnation of God — that is enough."[24]

Sunday, 23 December 1883

After the midday meal Sri Ramakrishna rested a few minutes in his room. M. was sitting on the floor. The Master was delighted to hear the music that was being played in the nahabat. He then explained to M. that Brahman alone has become the universe and all living beings.

Master: "I perceive that living beings are like different flowers with various petals. They are also revealed to me as bubbles, some big, some small."

While describing in this way the vision of different divine forms, the

Master went into an ecstatic state and said, "I have become! I am here!" Uttering these words he went into samadhi. His body was motionless. He remained in that state a long time and then gradually regained partial consciousness of the world. He began to laugh like a boy and pace the room. His eyes radiated bliss as if he had seen a wondrous vision. His gaze was not fixed on any particular object, and his face beamed with joy. Still pacing the room, the Master said: "I saw the paramahamsa who stayed under the banyan tree walking thus with just such a smile. Am I too in that state of mind?"

Master (*to M*): "One attains this state immediately after freeing oneself of all grief and desire."

(*To the Divine Mother*): "Mother, Thou hast done away with my worship. Please see, Mother, that I don't give up all desire."[25]

According to Vedanta, a person attains samadhi when the mind becomes free from desire. Cessation of desire, dissolution of the mind, and illumination: These three things happen simultaneously. We are always tormented with innumerable desires and cannot get rid of them. Ramakrishna, however, prayed to have some desires so that his mind would stay in the world so that he could teach and awaken the spiritual consciousness of earnest souls.

Monday, 24 December 1883

At eight o'clock in the morning Sri Ramakrishna and M. were talking together in the pine grove at the northern end of the temple garden. This was the eleventh day of M.'s stay with the Master.

It was winter. The sun had just risen. The river was flowing north with the tide. Not far off could be seen the bel tree where the Master had practised great spiritual austerities.

Master: "Not everyone can recognize an Incarnation. It is God alone who incarnates Himself as man to teach people the ways of love and knowledge. Well, what do you think of me?

"Once my father went to Gaya. There Raghuvir said to him in a dream, 'I shall be born as your son.' Thereupon my father said to Him: 'O Lord, I am a poor brahmin. How shall I be able to serve You?' 'Don't worry about it,' Raghuvir replied. 'It will be taken care of.'

"My sister, Hriday's mother, used to worship my feet with flowers and sandal paste. One day I placed my foot on her head and said to her, 'You will die in Benares [Varanasi].'

"Once Mathur Babu said to me: 'Father, there is nothing inside you but God. . . .'

"I am shown everything beforehand. Once I saw Gauranga and his devotees singing kirtan in the Panchavati. I think I saw Balaram there and you too. . . . I shall have to be born once more. Therefore I am not giving all knowledge to my companions. (*With a smile*) Suppose I give you all knowledge; will you then come to me again so willingly?"

"I recognized you on hearing you read the *Chaitanya Bhagavata*. You are my own. The same substance, like father and son.

"Before you came here, you didn't know who you were. Now you will know. It is God who, as the guru, makes one know."

Sri Ramakrishna stood up. There was silence all around, disturbed only by the gentle rustling of pine-needles and the murmuring of the Ganges. The Master went to the Panchavati and then to his room, talking all the while with M. The disciple followed him, fascinated. At the Panchavati Sri Ramakrishna touched with his forehead the raised platform around the banyan tree. This was the place of his intense spiritual discipline, where he had wept bitterly for the vision of the Divine Mother, where he had held intimate communion with Her, and where he had seen many divine forms.[26]

The Bhakti scriptures say: *Ādau shraddhā* — one first needs sincere faith in God. M. continually learned about spirituality from the Master's actions, talk, and behaviour. All this he related to the devotees who came after Ramakrishna's passing. The Master knew that M. was to be the recorder of his gospel, so he wanted M. to be present when he talked to others. We continue with M.'s narrative:

Sri Ramakrishna was resting after his midday meal when Surendra, Ram, and other devotees arrived from Calcutta. It was about one o'clock. While M. was strolling alone under the pine trees, Harish came there and told him that the Master wanted him in his room. Someone was going to read from the *Shiva Samhita*, a book containing instructions about yoga and the six centres.[27]

Everything cannot be learned from a book or a manual. We cannot even learn the alphabet by ourselves. Similarly, in spiritual life we need an experienced teacher who has realized the truth. Here we see Ramakrishna in his role as teacher:

It was evening. The Master was sitting on the floor of his room with the devotees. He was talking to them about yoga and the six centres, which are described in the *Shiva Samhita*.

Master: "Ida, Pingala, and Sushumna are the three principal nerves. All the lotuses are located in the Sushumna. They are formed of Consciousness, like a tree made of wax — the branches, twigs, fruits, and so forth all of wax. The Kundalini lies in the lotus of the Muladhara.

That lotus has four petals. The Primordial Energy resides in all bodies as the Kundalini. She is like a sleeping snake coiled up. . . . (*To M.*) The kundalini is speedily awakened if one follows the path of bhakti. God cannot be seen unless She is awakened. Sing earnestly and secretly in solitude:

> Waken, O Mother! O Kundalini, whose nature is Bliss Eternal!
> Thou art the serpent coiled in sleep, in the lotus of the Muladhara."[28]

Tuesday, 25 December 1883

Ramakrishna came to fulfill, not to destroy, so he observed ancient traditions. It was the day of ekadashi, when one is supposed to fast. The Master did not put too much emphasis on physical austerity. It is hard to think of God if one experiences hunger pangs.

Master (*to M.*): "One should fast on the eleventh day of the lunar fortnight. That purifies the mind and helps one to develop love of God. Isn't that so?"

M.: "Yes, sir."

Master: "But you may take milk and puffed rice."[29]

Wednesday, 26 December 1883

Sri Ramakrishna visited Ram Datta's Kankurgachi Yogodyana with M. and other devotees. Arriving at this retreat centre, the Master got out of the carriage. Ram received the Master. Standing near the tulsi grove, the Master said: "How nice! It is a fine place. You can easily meditate on God here."[30]

Thursday, 27 December 1883

We know very little about the day-to-day activities of Buddha, Christ, or Chaitanya. For Ramakrishna, however, we have the *Gospel*, in which M. meticulously recorded the Master's daily routine, engagements, visitors, and conversation. Details, like those given here in the *Gospel*, help the reader to clearly visualize the Master:

> The temple garden was filled with the sweet music of the dawn service, which mingled with the morning melody from the nahabat. Leaving his bed, Sri Ramakrishna chanted the names of God in sweet tones. Then he bowed before the pictures of the different deities in his room and went to the west porch to salute the Ganges.
>
> Some of the devotees who had spent the night at the temple garden came to the Master's room and bowed before him. M. had been staying there two weeks.

Sri Ramakrishna said to M.: "I have been invited to Ishan's this morning. Baburam will accompany me, and you too." M. made ready to go with the Master.[31]

It is not possible to describe Ramakrishna's philosophy: He accepted all philosophical paths and said that they were complementary, not contradictory. All paths lead to the same goal. Ramakrishna was the embodiment of all religions, and he harmonized all yogas and philosophical paths.

At Ishan's house the Master spoke on various topics. He explained the three main schools of Vedanta philosophy — dualism, qualified nondualism, and nondualism — by citing Hanuman's attitude: "O Rama, sometimes I feel that You are the Master and I am Your servant. Sometimes I meditate on You as the whole and on myself as the part. But when I have the Knowledge of Reality, I see that I am You and You are I."[32]

That evening, the Master visited Ram's house. He taught the devotees assembled there how to pray: "Listen, I prayed to the Divine Mother for pure love. I said to Her: 'Here is Thy righteousness, here is Thy unrighteousness. Take them both and give me pure love for Thee. Here is Thy purity, here is Thy impurity. Take them both and give me pure love for Thee. O Mother, here is Thy virtue, here is Thy vice. Take them both and give me pure love for Thee.'"[33]

Saturday, 29 December 1883

M.'s record continues:

It was the day of the new moon, auspicious for the worship of the Divine Mother. At one o'clock in the afternoon Sri Ramakrishna got into a carriage to visit the temple of Kali at Kalighat. . . . While the carriage was waiting near the north porch of the Master's room, M. went to the Master and said, "Sir, may I also go with you?"

Master: "Why?"

M.: "I should like to visit my home in Calcutta."

Sri Ramakrishna reflected a moment and said: "Must you go home? Why? You are quite all right here."

M. wanted to see his people a few hours, but evidently the Master did not approve.[34]

During M.'s second visit in March 1882, the Master had told him: "If you enter the world without first cultivating love for God, you will be entangled more and more. You will be overwhelmed with its danger, its grief, its sorrows. And the more you think of worldly things, the more you will be attached to them.

"One must go into solitude to attain this divine love. To get butter from milk you must let it set into curd in a secluded spot: if it is too much disturbed, milk won't turn into curd. Next, you must put aside all other duties, sit in a quiet spot, and churn the curd. Only then do you get butter."[35]

Sunday, 30 December 1883

At three o'clock in the afternoon, while M. was walking up and down under a tree, a devotee came to him and said that the Master had sent for him. M. went to Sri Ramakrishna's room and found a number of devotees there. . . . Ram, Kedar, and others had arrived from Calcutta. Ram had brought with him the Vedantist monk whom the Master had visited near his garden a few days earlier.[36]

While talking about Brahman with the monk, the Master went into samadhi. Kedar told the monk: "Look at him, sir. This is samadhi." The monk had read of samadhi but had never seen it before.[37]

Monday, 31 December 1883

M. was witness to Ramakrishna's divine play. Like a playwright, he set the stage and the scene, and made the characters living through their wonderful dialogue with the Master. Later, he would tell the devotees, "I have seen one person in my life who would talk with God in front of me." M. wrote:

In the evening . . . the Master remained in his room, absorbed in contemplation of the Divine Mother. After a while the sweet music of the evening worship in the temples was heard.

A little later the Master began to talk to the Mother in a tender voice that touched the heart of M., who was seated on the floor. After repeating, "Hari Om! Hari Om! Om!", the Master said: "Mother, I don't want Brahmajnana. I want to be merry. I want to play."[38]

Wednesday, 2 January 1884

Jaygopal Sen, a Brahmo devotee, asked the Master: "How does one receive the grace of God?"

Master: "Constantly you have to chant the name and glories of God and give up worldly thoughts as much as you can. . . . I used to cry for God all alone, with a longing heart. . . . The thing is that one must love God. The attraction of the husband for the chaste wife, the attraction of the child for its mother, the attraction of worldly possessions for the worldly man — when a man can blend these three into one, and direct it all to God, then he gets the vision of God."[39]

That evening, the Master sat in his room with Rakhal and M. Ramakrishna had forbidden M. to indulge in reasoning, and now he explained why:

Master: "It is not good to reason too much. First comes God, and then the world. Realize God first; then you will know all about His world. . . .

"Through too much reasoning your spiritual life will be injured; you will at last become like Hazra. I used to roam at night in the streets, all alone, and cry to the Divine Mother, 'O Mother, blight with Thy thunderbolt my desire to reason!' Tell me that you won't reason anymore."

M.: "Yes, sir. I won't reason anymore."

Master: "Everything can be achieved through bhakti alone.

"You will realize everything when God Himself teaches you. Then you will not lack any knowledge."[40]

Friday, 4 January 1884

Sri Ramakrishna was sitting in his room. M. was still staying with the Master, devoting his time to the practice of spiritual discipline. He had been spending a great part of each day in prayer and meditation under the bel tree, where the Master had performed great austerities and had seen many wonderful visions of God.

Master (to M.): "One should assume a particular attitude towards God while praying to Him — the attitude of a friend or servant or son. I assume the attitude of a child. To me every woman is my mother. The divine Maya, seeing this attitude in an aspirant, moves away from his path out of sheer shame."[41]

Saturday, 5 January 1884

It was the twenty-third day of M.'s stay with Sri Ramakrishna. M. had finished his midday meal about one o'clock and was resting in the nahabat when suddenly he heard someone call his name three or four times. Coming out, he saw Sri Ramakrishna calling him from the veranda north of his room.

M. saluted the Master and they conversed on the south veranda.

Master: "I want to know how you meditate. When I meditated under the bel tree I used to see various visions clearly. One day I saw in front of me money, a shawl, a tray of sandesh, and two women. I asked my mind, 'Mind, do you want any of these?' I saw the sandesh to be mere filth. One of the women had a big ring in her nose. I could see both their inside and outside — entrails, filth, bone, flesh, and blood. The mind did not want any of these — money, shawl, sweets, or women. It remained fixed at the Lotus Feet of God.

"No spiritual progress is possible without the renunciation of 'lust and gold.' I renounced these three: land, wife, and wealth. . . . How can one expect to attain God without renunciation? Suppose one thing is placed upon another; how can you get the second without removing the first?"[42]

At dusk Sri Ramakrishna went to the Kali temple; he was pleased to see M. meditating there. M. describes the scene:

The evening worship was over in the temples. The Master returned to his room and sat on the couch, absorbed in meditation on the Divine Mother. M. sat on the floor. There was no one else in the room.

The Master weeping and praying to the Mother with a voice choked with emotion: "Mother, may those who come to You have all their desires fulfilled! If you keep them in the world, Mother, then please reveal Yourself to them now and then. Otherwise, how will they live?"

Master (to M.): "Yes, I know everything: what your Ideal is, who you are, your inside and outside, the events of your past lives, and your future.

"I scolded you on learning that you had a son. Now go home and live there. Let them know that you belong to them. But you must remember in your heart of hearts that you do not belong to them nor they to you."

M. sat in silence.

Master (to M.): "The Nitya and Lila are the two aspects of the Reality. God plays in the world as man for the sake of His devotees. They can love God only if they see Him in a human form; only then can they show their affection for Him as their Brother, Sister, Father, Mother, or Child."[43]

During his vacation, M. had lived constantly with the Master and observed his divine and human aspects. He was a spectator to Ramakrishna's divine drama, and he sometimes acted in it as well. He loved the Master passionately, and his ego was completely absorbed in his beloved guru. That is why when he wrote the *Gospel* he tried to hide himself, referring to himself by various names, such as Mani, Mohinimohan, an English-educated man, a devotee, and so on. He knew how to drink the nectar of the divine words of the Master, so the *Gospel* is beautiful and sweet; it touches our inmost feelings. M. tried to preserve in the *Gospel* a record of the Master's meditation, samadhi, worship, prayers, dreams, visions, actions, devotion, purity, renunciation, singing, dancing, laughter, humour, sadhana, pilgrimage, dealings with human beings, psychology, philosophy, social and scientific outlook, and finally his message.

A painter puts several coats of paint on doors and window frames to protect the underlying wood from rain and sun. Similarly, during the twenty-three days of M.'s visit, Ramakrishna put a spiritual coating on M.'s mind so that it would not be polluted by the world.

On the last day of his vacation, M. received the Master's blessings and left for home.

9

Ramakrishna in the Streets and Meadows

We are accustomed to seeing images of Ramakrishna in the monastery temples, on the altars of shrines in private homes, hanging on the walls of our rooms, and on our desks. But is he limited to these places only? The Master said, "I will be worshipped from house to house"; but now his presence has spread everywhere. One can see him now in the thatched huts of village farmers, in the mansions of wealthy people in the cities, in the caves and cottages of the Himalayas, in shops, and in taxis. His image is even carried in travellers' purses and wallets.

Just as Ramakrishna loved to travel through the streets of Calcutta and along village roads, he also enjoyed travelling along various religious paths. He showed people how to move through this impermanent world. However, his body was very delicate, so he lamented: "Gaur and Nitai carried the message of God from door to door, and I cannot go anyplace without a carriage." Driven by his desire to rescue people from the whirlpool of maya, he visited his devotees, walking or travelling by palanquin, bullock cart, horse carriage, and train. Whenever he heard of anyone who had a sincere longing for God, he would rush to see that person. He did not care about formal invitations, and he disregarded social etiquette. His attitude was: "Hello! You are a devotee and think of God, so I have come to see you." He said: "If a man takes one step towards God, God comes a hundred steps towards him." A devotee once said: "I did not take even one step, but the Master took hundreds of steps and came to me."

Although Ramakrishna was mostly absorbed in a divine mood, he would move around to locate hungry souls. Once he said to M.: "You don't want anything from me, but you love to see me and hear my words. My mind also dwells on you. I wonder how you are and why you don't come. Could you give me your address?"[1] Thus collecting the devotees' addresses, the Master travelled through the streets of Calcutta to look after their welfare. Sometimes the devotees' intense longing pulled Ramakrishna from Dakshineswar to Calcutta at night. If someone found it difficult to see him in Dakshineswar, when visiting another devotee's home in Calcutta, he would send for that person.

Human beings live in their memories. Clinging to their memories, they smile and cry; they ruminate over the past and dream about the future. Some memories remain dormant, while others are vivid. We may not see the physical presence of Ramakrishna in Kamarpukur and Jayrambati, in Varanasi and Vrindaban, or in the lanes and streets of Calcutta, but those places, houses, and streets still exist. Every day we walk though those streets and see those places connected with Ramakrishna; but we are so overburdened with our family responsibilities, suffering from poverty and mental anguish, that we have no time to evoke the Master's presence in our memories. During our journey, if someone reminds us that the Master came to this house or walked through this street, then momentarily at least he manifests in our minds and we feel his presence.

M., the recorder of *The Gospel of Sri Ramakrishna*, lived on his memories of the Master. He would bow down to the place on Bechu Chatterjee Street where the Master's elder brother had once conducted a school. He also paid respects to the house of the Mitra family at Jhamapukur where the Master had once worked as a priest. Observing his companions' surprise, M. would say, "Do you know that anyone who walks through this street will become a yogi?"[2] People who did not understand M.'s divine madness thought he was merely unbalanced.

Not only did M. live on the memories of Ramakrishna, but he also recorded those vivid pictures of his guru's life in his immortal book, *The Gospel of Sri Ramakrishna*. In this chapter I shall help the reader visualize Ramakrishna's travels through the meadows, to holy places, and in the streets of Calcutta. Based on M.'s accounts and on the records that other eyewitnesses left, we shall follow the holy footprints of the Master. While mentally travelling with him, we shall listen to his fascinating conversation and learn many interesting things that his keen mind revealed. It will not always be pleasant to travel with him. Most of the time he was in a state of god-intoxication. While travelling, we will be anxious that the Master might have an accident at any moment.

This chapter is divided into three sections: Days in Kamarpukur, on pilgrimage, and travel in Calcutta.

Days in Kamarpukur

Ramakrishna lived in rural Kamarpukur until he was seventeen. He freely travelled through its roads, gardens, and meadows. He identified himself with the beautiful and unpolluted surroundings of his birth-place. Instead of studying in school, he intensely studied the nature of the universe as well as the nature of the human mind. Swami Vivekananda remarked: "The man at whose feet I sat all my life — and it is only a few ideas of his that I try to teach — could [hardly] write his name at all. All my life I have not seen another man like that, and I have travelled all over the world. When I think of that man, I feel like a fool, because I want to read books and he never did. He never wanted to lick the plates after other people had eaten. That is why he was his own book."[3]

The fun begins when one starts to study one's own mind. Rama-krishna read his own mind thoroughly. Most of the Master's teachings came from his study of nature and his observation of village life. For example, he was asked, "How should one live in this world?" He answered: "Perform your worldly duties keeping God in your mind, as a dancing girl dances while balancing jars or trays on her head." The Master told his devotees:

At Kamarpukur I have seen the women of the carpenter families sell-ing flattened rice. Let me tell you how alert they are while doing their business. The pestle of the husking machine that flattens the paddy constantly falls into the hole of the mortar. The woman turns the paddy in the hole with one hand and with the other holds her baby on her lap as she nurses it. In the meantime customers arrive. The machine goes on pounding the paddy, and she carries on her bargains with the customers. This is called the yoga of practice. Fifteen parts of her mind out of sixteen are fixed on the pestle of the husking machine, lest it should pound her hand. With only one part of her mind she nurses the baby and talks to the buyers. Likewise, a householder should devote fifteen parts of his mind to God . . . and perform the duties of the world with only one part.[4]

If you want to teach others, you must have a commission from God. In that connection, Ramakrishna gave an example from his village: "At Kamarpukur there is a small lake called the Haldarpukur. Certain people used to befoul its banks every day. Others who came there in the morning to bathe would abuse the offenders loudly. But the next morning they would find the same thing. The nuisance didn't stop. The villagers finally informed the authorities about it. A constable was sent, who put up a notice on the bank which read: 'Commit no nuisance.' This stopped the miscreants at once."[5]

Ramakrishna walked through the rice fields and in the mango orchards. Sometimes he went along when villagers went to visit the shrines in neighbouring areas. Ramakrishna's first experience of Cosmic Consciousness took place in a field near Kamarpukur. He later described that incident:

> In that part of the country children are given puffed rice to eat from small baskets. Those who are poor and have no baskets tie the puffed rice in the corner of their wearing cloth. Boys go out to play on the roads or in the fields carrying puffed rice either in a basket or in the corner of their cloth. It was June or July. I was then six or seven years old. One morning I took some puffed rice in a small basket and was eating it as I walked along the narrow ridges of the rice fields. In one part of the sky a beautiful black cloud appeared, heavy with rain. I was watching it and eating the puffed rice. Very soon, the cloud covered almost the whole sky. Then a flock of cranes came flying, white as milk against the black cloud. It was so beautiful that I became absorbed in the sight; I lost consciousness of everything outside of myself. I fell down, and the puffed rice was scattered over the ground. I cannot say how long I was in that state. Some people saw this and carried me home. That was the first time I lost external consciousness due to ecstasy.[6]

He also talked about his second spiritual experience, which took place on the way to Anur, a nearby village: "I experienced one of my first ecstasies when I was ten or eleven years old, as I was going through a meadow to the shrine of Vishalakshi. What a vision! I became completely unconscious of the outer world."[7]

Ramakrishna's neighbour Durgadas Pyne kept the women of his family in strict purdah* and did not allow them to listen to the Master's spiritual conversations. The Master told him: "Can women be protected

*Hindu and Muslim custom in which women are kept isolated from men, except for relatives.

by purdah? They can be protected only through moral education and devotion to God. If I wish, I can visit the women of your household and learn everything about them." Durgadas arrogantly challenged him, saying, "I'd like to see how you can do that." "All right, you will see," replied Ramakrishna. One evening sometime later he disguised himself as a weaver woman and, having passed inspection by Durgadas himself, entered the house and met with his family. This humbled Durgadas' arrogance.

When Ramakrishna was a young boy, he bathed with his friends at the women's ghat of Haldarpukur. An elderly woman once told him that it was bad for him to watch women when they were bathing, but she did not give any specific reason. She told him not to do this again. The young Ramakrishna, then called Gadadhar, was curious. For several days he hid in the trees near the ghat, and then told the woman: "The day before yesterday I saw four women bathing, yesterday six, and today eight. But nothing bad has happened to me." The woman then went to Chandradevi and laughingly told her what her son had said. Later, while they were resting, Chandra told Gadadhar gently, in a convincing way: "My son, it is true that nothing bad will happen to you if you watch the women bathing, but they will feel humiliated. They are like me. If you dishonour them, it is the same as dishonouring me. So in the future don't be disrespectful towards them. Is it good to hurt them as well as me?" Gadadhar understood, and he never did that again.[8]

Chinu Sankhari, an old bracelet maker, recognized Gadadhar's divinity. One day in a meadow near Kamarpukur, Chinu worshipped the young boy, putting a garland around his neck and feeding him with jilipi. Chinu tearfully said to him: "Gadai, I am old and will not live long. I shall not be able to see your divine play. I shall not complain about that, however. Please bestow your grace on me and fulfill the purpose of my life."[9]

It is true that every child loves to play; but seldom do we find a child who tears his clothing to make a loin cloth, puts religious marks on himself, and pretends to be a monk. Gadadhar regularly visited the itinerant monks who stayed in the roadside inn of Kamarpukur. And seldom do we see a child who puts on religious plays for fun. Gadadhar and his friends performed *Ram Lila* and *Krishna Lila* in the mango grove of Manikraja, under his direction. People marvelled when they saw his ingenuity and expert acting.

People generally love to ruminate about the sweet and sad stories of their childhood days. Ramakrishna recalled: "During my younger days the men and women of Kamarpukur were equally fond of me. They loved to hear me sing. I loved to visit the free eating-places maintained for holy men and the poor, and would watch them for hours. . . . I loved to hear the reading of sacred books such as the Ramayana and Bhagavata. If the readers had any affectations, I could easily imitate them and would entertain others with my mimicry. . . . I could reproduce the whole drama from memory. Some would say that I was connected with the Kaliyadaman-Yatra party."[10]

It would have been something to see Ramakrishna, dressed as a bridegroom and wearing a garland and sandal paste, walking from Kamarpukur to Jayrambati. Akshay Sen humorously described Ramakrishna's marriage procession in his famous book *Sri Ramakrishna Punthi*. He compared Ramakrishna's wedding to the marriage of Shiva accompanied by Nandi and Bhringi.

When the railway began to run between Burdwan and Calcutta, Ramakrishna would take a train to Burdwan and then proceed by bullock cart to his native village, Kamarpukur. He later told his devotees what would happen on these journeys: "Once I was going from Burdwan to Kamarpukur in a bullock cart when a great storm arose. Some people gathered near the cart. My companions said they were robbers. So I began to repeat the names of God, calling sometimes on Kali, sometimes on Rama, sometimes on Hanuman."[11]

Later, he told them another story: "Once I was on my way to Burdwan from Kamarpukur. At one place I ran to the meadow to see how living beings are sustained. I saw ants crawling there. It appeared to me that every place was filled with Consciousness. Again, I perceive that living beings are like different flowers with various layers of petals. They are also revealed to me as bubbles, some big, some small."[12]

Although Ramakrishna had disconnected himself from worldly affairs, he had to appear in court a couple of times: once to register land and another time as a witness in a case. The reader might wonder how it was possible for him to be involved with such things when he was in a god-intoxicated state most of the time. Ramakrishna said: "No spiritual progress is possible without the renunciation of lust and gold. I renounced these three: land, wife, and wealth. Once I went to the Registry Office to register some land, the title of which was in the name of Raghuvir. The officer asked me to sign my name; but I didn't do it, because I couldn't feel that it was 'my' land. I was shown much respect as the guru of Keshab Sen. They presented me with mangoes, but I couldn't carry them home. A sannyasin cannot lay things up."[13]

Once when Ramakrishna visited Sihar, his nephew Rajaram had a fight with a neighbour and injured him. The man sued Rajaram and called Ramakrishna to be a witness in the case. He knew that the Master was a man of truth. Ramakrishna could not ignore the summons, so he had to travel nearly thirty miles to Vishnupur from Sihar. He scolded Rajaram when he got there, telling him to settle the case out of court or face punishment. Frightened, Rajaram settled the case and the Master did not have to appear before the judge.

Sometimes we see Ramakrishna as a babysitter, looking after his nephews Akshay and Shivaram. He said: "The paramahamsa [an illumined soul] is like a five-year-old child. He sees everything filled with Consciousness. At one time I was staying at Kamarpukur when Shivaram was four or five years old. One day he was trying to catch grasshoppers near the pond. The leaves were moving. To stop their rustling, he said to the leaves: 'Hush! Hush! I want to catch a grasshopper.' Another day it was stormy. It rained hard. Shivaram was with me inside the house. There were flashes of lightning. He wanted to open the door and go out. I scolded him and stopped him, but still he peeped out now and then. When he saw the lightning he exclaimed, 'There, Uncle! They are striking matches again!'"[14]

Another time, he said: "When I lived at Kamarpukur, Hriday's son, a child four or five years old, used to spend the whole day with me. He played with his toys and almost forgot everything else. But no sooner did evening come than he would say, 'I want to go to my mother.' I would try to cajole him in various ways and would say, 'Here, I'll give you a pigeon.' But he wouldn't be consoled with such things; he would weep and cry, 'I want to go to my mother.' He didn't enjoy playing anymore. I myself wept to see his state. One should cry for God that way, like a child."[15]

Swami Saradananda wrote:

One day the Master was travelling by palanquin from Kamarpukur to Hriday's house at Sihar. During that journey the Master enjoyed seeing the vast fields under the blue sky, the green rice fields, the rows of banyan trees providing cool shade along the path, and the creepers bedecked with sweet fragrant blossoms, and hearing the melodious singing of birds. Suddenly two beautiful adolescent boys emerged from his body. They wandered far into the field searching for wildflowers and then came back near the palanquin, laughing, joking, and talking playfully. Thus, they proceeded joyfully for a long time and then reentered the Master's body. Later Bhairavi Brahmani explained the meaning of that vision: "My child, your vision was true. This time Chaitanya has been manifested in Nityananda's body. Both Chaitanya and Nityananda have come and are dwelling inside you now. That is why you had that vision."[16]

Ramakrishna was tremendously attractive, and many people flocked to him. They were eager to listen to his immortal words. As a result he had very little time to eat or sleep. He described an event that happened at this time: "Once I visited Hriday's house at Sihar. From there I was taken to Shyambazar. For seven days and nights I was surrounded by a huge crowd of people. Such attraction! Nothing but kirtan and dancing day and night. People stood in rows on the walls and even were in the trees. Hriday would drag me away from the crowd to a paddy-field for fear I might have an attack of heat apoplexy. At Shyambazar I learnt the meaning of divine attraction. When God incarnates Himself on earth He attracts people through the help of Yogamaya, His Divine Power."[17]

Swami Saradananda wrote:

Once while the Master was in Kamarpukur, arrangements were made for his visits to Jayrambati and Sihar. Because the Master was constantly in bhava samadhi, his limbs were as delicate as those of a boy or a woman. He could not walk even a short distance and needed a palanquin or a carriage to convey him. A palanquin had been brought for the trip to Sihar via Jayrambati. Hriday was also ready to go. After lunch the Master put on a scarlet silk cloth and fastened his gold amulet around his arm. His lips were crimson from chewing betel. As he was about to get into the palanquin, he noticed that a large crowd had gathered on the street nearby. Seeing so many men and women around, the Master asked Hriday in wonder, "Hriday, what is the reason for this crowd?"

Hriday: "You look so handsome in that silken cloth, and your lips shine with crimson colour. That is why they want to see you."

"What!" he exclaimed. "People are gathering just to look at a man! I won't go. Wherever I go, people will crowd about like this!" In utter disgust the Master returned to his room and took off the silk cloth. Filled with humility, the Master did not go to Jayrambati and Sihar that day.[18]

The Master's niece Lakshmi, recalled: "When the Master was in his village, every evening he sat by the door of his parental home, watching the people as they passed along the street. All the women had to go that way to bring water from the tank. They would come with their jugs. When they saw him at the door, they would sit down in the little yard in front, with their water jugs beside them, and forget everything in the joy of hearing him talk or sing of God. Fearing lest they might be neglecting their duties, he asked about them. One girl said: 'I have a cow. When I heard that you were coming, I cut straw enough to last a month and filled my room with it.' To another he said, 'How is your baby?' 'Oh! I forgot,' she exclaimed. 'I left it with a neighbour.' She had walked more than a mile to come and see him."[19]

One cannot realize God without guileless faith. The Master had such faith, as the following incidents indicate. He said:

One day something bit me while I was sitting in the grass at Kamarpukur. I was afraid it might have been a snake, and I didn't know what to do. I had heard that if a snake bites you again immediately after its first bite, it takes back its own venom. At once I set out to discover the hole so that I might let the snake bite me again. While I was searching, a man said to me, "What are you doing?" After listening to my story, he said, "But the snake must bite in the same place it has bitten before." Thereupon I went away. Perhaps I had been bitten by a scorpion or some other insect.

I had heard from Ramlal that the autumn chill was good for one's health. Ramlal had quoted a verse to support it. One day, as I was returning from Calcutta in a carriage, I stuck my head out of the window so that I might get all the chill. Then I fell ill.[20]

Sometimes the Master would relate stories from his village days to the people who visited him from Calcutta, so that they could develop faith. For example, the Master told them this folktale:

Ranjit Roy was the landlord of that part of the country. Through the power of his tapasya he obtained the Divine Mother as his daughter. One day he was engaged in the duties of his estate. The girl with her childlike nature, was constantly interrupting him, saying: 'Father, what is this? What is that?' Ranjit Roy tried, with sweet words, to persuade her not to disturb him. But the girl would not go away. At last, absent-mindedly, the father said, 'Get out of here!' On this pretext she left home. A peddlar of conch-shell articles was going along the road. From him she took a pair of bracelets for her wrists. When he asked for the price, she said that he could get the money from a certain box in her home. Then she disappeared. In the meantime the peddlar came to the house and asked for the price of his bracelets. The money owed to the peddlar was found in the box, as she had indicated. Ranjit Roy was weeping bitterly, when people came running to him and said that they had noticed something in the lake. They all ran there and saw an arm with conch-shell bracelets on the wrist, being waved above the water. A moment afterwards it disappeared. Even now people worship her as the Divine Mother at the time of the annual festival.[21]

Once a devotee asked Ramakrishna: "How does one receive the grace of God?" The Master answered his question by citing things he had seen on the streets of Calcutta and in the fields of his village. He said: "Constantly you have to chant the name and glories of God and give up worldly thoughts as much as you can. With the greatest effort you may try to bring water into your field for your crops, but it may all leak out through holes in the ridges. Then all your efforts to bring the water by digging a canal will be futile.

"You will feel restless for God when your heart becomes pure and your mind free from attachment to the things of the world. Then alone will your prayer reach God. A telegraph wire cannot carry messages if it has a break or some other defect."[22]

What happens to the ego of an illumined soul? To answer this question, Ramakrishna used an analogy taken from village life: "He who has seen God retains his 'I' only in name. No evil can be done by that 'I'. It is a mere appearance, like the mark left on the coconut tree by its branch. The branch has fallen off. Only the mark remains."[23]

If anyone sought help from the Master, or surrendered to him, he took responsibility for that person. Once there was a heavy rain at Kamarpukur and the roads were flooded. The Master was wading through the water to get somewhere when he saw a catfish moving near his feet. He picked it up and then released it in the Lahas' pond. When Hriday heard about this, he said: "Uncle, why did you let it go? We could have made a nice soup with that catfish." The Master replied: "No, Hriday, I could not kill it. That fish took refuge in me."[24]

On Pilgrimage

Pilgrims make a place holy. Spiritual people throughout the ages go to places of pilgrimage and create a tangible spiritual atmosphere through their worship and prayer, japa and meditation, longing and austerities. Even ordinary people can feel their spirituality awakening when they visit such places. Ramakrishna said: "Although God dwells everywhere equally, He manifests more in holy places. One can get water by digging in any spot, but one does not need to dig where there is a well, pool, pond, or lake. At those places one can get water whenever one needs it."

One should observe that Ramakrishna's knowledge did not come from studying books and scriptures, as ours does; his wisdom came from keen study and observation of nature, human beings, and whatever else he saw around him. We find in the Chandogya Upanishad that Satyakama got his knowledge of Brahman from a bull, fire, a swan, and a bird. Similar incidents occurred in the Master's life. He related: "The Mother reveals to me that She Herself has become everything. One day I was coming from the pine grove towards the Panchavati. A dog followed me. I stood still for a while near the Panchavati. The thought came to my mind that the Mother might say something to me through that dog."[25]

In this world one always encounters obstacles if one wants to do something good. There was a sweet but heated exchange between Mathur and his wife, Jagadamba, about going on a pilgrimage. Jagadamba: "Let us go on a pilgrimage."

Mathur: "What shall we gain from a pilgrimage? If you want to see God, see Father [Ramakrishna]. I don't want to go on a pilgrimage: Such a trip would be a misuse of money and torture to the body. The one whose glance bestows devotion and liberation, who grants the results of all pilgrimages — that Person is in our house. Where shall I go if I leave him? I am not going anywhere. If you wish, you go; but I am not going."

Jagadamba: "What do you mean? Why should we go without Father? Let us take Father with us."

Mathur: "Well, if Father goes with us, I shall go."

As a loving daughter runs to her father to fulfill her wishes, so Jagadamba rushed to the Master and said: "Father, please agree to go with us. Please don't refuse, Father." What could the Master do? Moved by Jagadamba's sincere appeal, the Master agreed to go on the pilgrimage with them.

Preparation for the pilgrimage began. Mathur's objections turned into enthusiasm. Three third-class railway cars were reserved for cooks, servants, maids, and guards; and one luxury car was for the Master, Hriday, and Mathur and his family. One hundred people in all went on that pilgrimage, and 100,000 rupees were spent.

The first stop was Vaidyanath in Bihar. The Master was making a pilgrimage with his wealthy devotee and should have been enjoying himself. But when he saw the poor, emaciated, and suffering people in a village near Vaidyanath, Ramakrishna told Mathur: "You are a steward of Mother's estate. Give each of these poor people one piece of cloth, and one good meal, and also some oil for their heads." Mathur was reluctant at first. He said: "Father, this pilgrimage is going to cost a great deal, and there are many people here. If I give them what you ask, I may find myself short of money later. What do you think I ought to do?" The Father paid no heed to that excuse. Overwhelmed with compassion, he shed tears at the sight of the villagers' abject misery and cried in anguish: "You wretch! I'm not going to Varanasi. I'm staying here with these people. They have no one to care for them. I won't leave them."[26] At last Mathur had to yield. Ramakrishna was a true friend of the poor and destitute.

When people travel, they sometimes miss their train or have similar mishaps. Ramakrishna was no exception. On the way to Varanasi, he and Hriday disembarked at the Mugalsarai railway station. The train left before they got back on board. Mathur tried to stop the train and asked the guard to disconnect his reserved cars, according to a previous contract, but his request was not granted. Mathur arrived in Varanasi with a heavy heart. He sent a wire to the Mugalsarai station master to send Ramakrishna and Hriday by the next train. The Master did not have to wait for the next train, however. Rajendralal Bandyopadhyay, a high-ranking railway officer from Calcutta, arrived in his special train and gave Ramakrishna and Hriday a ride to Varanasi.

There is a saying: As long as Varanasi exists, religion will remain established in India. While entering Varanasi, Ramakrishna saw with his divine eye that the abode of Shiva was made of gold. The luminous spiritual thoughts of monks and devotees throughout the ages had accumulated in this holy place and gilded the city. But Ramakrishna's glorious vision created a terrible problem for him. How could he pollute the holy land of Varanasi by answering the call of nature? He saw this divine luminosity in the paths, fields, gardens, wells, ponds, monasteries, and temples. He did not see Varanasi as made of brick, stone, and wood, as we do. The Master said that for some days Mathur arranged for a palanquin to carry him across the Asi (a stream located beyond Varanasi) to answer the call of nature. When that particular mood later came to an end, he no longer needed to do that.

During their stay in Varanasi, Ramakrishna and Hriday went by palanquin almost daily to visit the temple of Lord Vishwanath. Considering that the trip itself put the Master into ecstasy, what can we say of his visit to the deity? But although he went into ecstasy in all the temples, he experienced it most deeply in Kedarnath. Sometimes Mathur accompanied the Master, acting as his bodyguard. Swami Saradananda wrote:

One day Mathur took the Master on a boat trip. The main cremation ground of Varanasi is near Manikarnika. When Mathur's boat approached the Manikarnika ghat, the air of the cremation ground was full of smoke because many bodies were being cremated on the funeral pyres. The Master's face expressed ecstatic joy at the sight, and the hairs of his body stiffened. He emerged from the covered part of the boat and walked over to the bow, where he went into samadhi. Mathur's guide and the boatmen all ran to catch him, lest he fall into the water. But they did not need to do anything. The Master remained standing, calm and motionless, with a wonderful smile on his face. The whole place appeared to be serene and holy. Mathur and Hriday stood protectively nearby but did not touch the Master. In astonishment, the boatmen gazed at this extraordinary figure.

When the Master's ecstasy came to an end sometime later, everyone disembarked at the Manikarnika ghat, had their bath, performed rituals, and then returned to the boat to continue their journey. The Master then described his vision to Mathur and the others: "I saw a tall white figure with tawny matted hair steadily approach each funeral pyre in turn, carefully raise each individual soul from its cast-off body, and whisper into its ear the particular name of Brahman that liberates a soul. Seated on the opposite side of the pyre, the all-powerful Divine Mother Kali untied the gross, subtle, and causal knots of bondage created by each individual soul, thus sending the soul to the Absolute by opening the gate of liberation. Lord Vishwanath was blessing those souls by bestowing in an instant the experience of nondual, infinite bliss that people can attain only after ages of concentration and austerity."[27]

What a beautiful scene! The Master might have fallen into the Ganges, as he had no body-consciousness during samadhi. Mathur always kept a vigilant eye on him; Mathur's mind was focussed always on the welfare of the Master.

People usually approach wealthy benefactors with gratefulness and humility, and do not dare to say a harsh word to them. But it was not possible for Ramakrishna to compromise the truth. He did not care whether a person was rich or poor. He always told people what was good for them. One day during the pilgrimage Mathur was talking about business with a wealthy friend. The Master could not bear it. He later expressed his agony: "I used to weep when I heard people talk about worldly matters. When I accompanied Mathur Babu on a pilgrimage we spent a few days in Varanasi at Raja Babu's house. One day I was seated in the drawing room with Mathur Babu, Raja Babu, and others. Hearing them talk about various worldly things, such as their business losses and so forth, I wept bitterly and said to the Divine Mother: 'Mother, where have You brought me? I was much better off in the temple garden at Dakshineswar. Here I am in a place where I must hear about "lust and gold." But at Dakshineswar I could avoid it.'"[28]

Friends greet each other in many ways, such as hugging, shaking hands, offering flowers, or exchanging gifts. In Varanasi Ramakrishna greeted Trailanga Swami, an illumined soul, by offering some snuff, and he accepted it. The holy men met at the Manikarnika ghat, where Trailanga Swami was living. Although he was observing a vow of silence, he was trying to help with the construction of a new ghat on the Ganges. Seeing that Hriday was healthy, the swami indicated that he should shovel some earth for the ghat. Hriday refused at first, but he obeyed when the Master asked him to. Observing the swami's eyes, ears, other sense organs, and the conformation of his limbs, the Master told Hriday: "All the signs of a real paramahamsa exist in him. He is the veritable Vishwanath."[29]

Nothing significant happened when the pilgrims reached Prayag, the confluence of the Ganges and the Yamuna. Ramakrishna bathed in the confluence of the holy rivers, and the group stayed there for three nights. Following scriptural injunctions, Mathur and the other men shaved their heads, but the Master did not do so. He said, "It is not necessary for me to perform this rite."

The paths and ghats, fields and forests, hills and waterways of Vrindaban are associated with memories of Krishna. Ramakrishna loved this place, the playground of Krishna, because it was devoid of pomp and worldliness. He was overwhelmed with ecstasy when he saw the beauty of Vraja — its gardens bedecked with flowers and fruit trees, the deer and peacocks moving freely through the forest, the monks and devotees praying and chanting God's name, the simple and spiritual behaviour of its people, the vast and open sandy banks of the river Yamuna, and the zigzagging path for the pilgrims who circumambulate this holy place.

Ramakrishna recalled his visit to the area:

I went to Vrindaban with Mathur Babu. The moment I came to the Dhruva ghat at Mathura, in a flash I saw Vasudeva crossing the Yamuna with Krishna in his arms.

One evening I was taking a stroll on the beach of the river. There were small thatched huts on the beach and big plum trees. It was the "cow-dust" hour. The cows were returning from the pasture, raising dust with their hoofs. I saw them fording the river. Then came some cowherd boys crossing the river with their cows. No sooner did I behold this scene than I cried out, "O Krishna, where are You?" and became unconscious.

I wanted to visit Shyamkunda and Radhakunda; so Mathur Babu sent me there in a palanquin. We had a long way to go. Food was put in the palanquin. While going over the meadow I was overpowered with emotion and wept: "O Krishna, I find everything the same; only You are not here. This is the very meadow where You tended the cows." Hriday followed me on foot. I was bathed in tears. I couldn't ask the bearers to stop the palanquin.

At Shyamkunda and Radhakunda I saw the holy men living in small mud huts. Facing away from the road lest their eyes should fall on men, they were engaged in spiritual discipline. One should visit the "Twelve Grove."[30]

He continued: "At the very sight of Mount Govardhan I was overpowered with divine emotion and ran to the top. I lost all consciousness of the world around me. The residents of the place helped me to come down. When I saw the meadows, the trees, the shrubs, the birds, and the deer, I was overwhelmed with ecstasy."[31]

In Vrindaban, the Master wore the garb of Vaishnava ascetics for fifteen days and followed their traditions. Every day Hriday took the Master to the Kaliyadaman ghat for his bath. Ramakrishna wanted to circumambulate the holy ground of Vrindaban, but Hriday and Mathur stopped him, saying that it would be a tremendous hardship for him.

In Vrindaban, the Master met the ascetic Gangamayi. He recalled: "Gangamayi became very fond of me in Vrindaban. She was an old woman who lived all alone in a hut near the Nidhuban. Referring to my spiritual condition and ecstasy, she said, 'He is the embodiment of Radha.' She addressed me as 'Dulali.'

"I didn't want to leave her and return to Calcutta. As Hriday dragged me by one hand and she by the other, I remembered my mother, who was then living alone here in the nahabat of the temple garden. I found it impossible to stay away from her, and said to Gangamayi, 'No, I must go.' I loved the atmosphere of Vrindaban."[32] It is amusing to imagine that scene on a street in Vrindaban: Hriday is pulling one of the Master's hands and saying, "My uncle," while Gangamayi is pulling the other hand, saying, "My Dulali."

It was not easy to care for the god-intoxicated Ramakrishna during a journey. Mathur could take care of the Master because he had genuine love for him. He felt that without the Master his life would have been empty and joyless. At that time it was fashionable for rich people to travel by boat on the Ganges. Mathur took the Master with him on one of his trips. The Master later recalled: "Once, for a few days, I was out on an excursion with Mathur Babu in his house-boat. We took the trip for a change of air. During that trip we visited Navadwip. One day I saw the boatmen cooking their meal and stood and watched them. Mathur said to me, 'What are you doing there?' I replied with a smile, 'The boatmen are cooking, and their food looks very good.' Mathur felt that I might ask the boatmen to give me a portion of their food; so he said: 'Come away! Come away!'"[33]

As in Varanasi, in Navadwip the Master almost fell out of the boat. He later said: "When I was about to board the boat to return, I had a wonderful vision of two beautiful teenaged boys. I had never seen such beauty before. Their complexions were as bright as molten gold and they had halos round their heads. Smiling, they rushed towards me through the air, their arms raised. Immediately I cried out: 'Here they come! Here they come!' No sooner had I uttered those words than they came near and entered here (*pointing to his body*), and I fell down unconscious. I would have fallen into the water, but Hriday was nearby and caught hold of me. Thus, I was shown many such things and became convinced that Chaitanya was a true avatar, a manifestation of divine power."[34]

Mathur considered Ramakrishna to be a member of his family. He took the Master to his birthplace in Khulna (now in Bangladesh). During that journey Mathur hired a palanquin for the Master and an elephant for himself. But the childlike Master demanded to ride on the elephant, and Mathur made the necessary arrangements. A lover is always happy when he or she can bring joy to the beloved.

Mathur also took the Master to visit his estate at Ranaghat in the Nadia district. While visiting a village in Mathur's estate, the Master was deeply grieved upon seeing the residents' misery and poverty. He asked Mathur to give each of the villagers enough oil to bathe with, a new cloth to wear, and some food. Mathur fulfilled the Master's wishes. Ramakrishna even asked Mathur to exempt them from taxes for one year. It must be remembered that Mathur was the owner of the Kali temple, and Ramakrishna was a priest, an employee of the temple. It may seem strange that Ramakrishna gave orders to Mathur, as would an employer. But Ramakrishna truly believed that Mathur was the caretaker of the Divine Mother's temple and that he was Her son. As the son of the Divine Mother, Ramakrishna was able to understand the suffering of

Her children better than anyone else. Therefore, the Master had every right to tell Mathur how to satisfy the people's needs.

Travel in Calcutta

Human life is guided by social norms and customs, and controlled by injunctions and prohibitions. These rules and regulations make the journey of life mechanical and monotonous. Truly, life is dull and joyless without freedom. This is why our modern urban civilization seems superficial and artificial. Although Ramakrishna lived on the outskirts of Calcutta, the capital of British India, he was not affected by its materialistic civilization. His mind dwelt in God, so he walked his own path, without concern for public opinion.

At that time a tremendous commotion was going on in Calcutta, sparked by the materialism of the West. The trend of Western civilization was towards lust and gold, greed and sense enjoyment. Calcutta, the citadel of Indian culture, was in an uproar. Indian society was shaken because its national ideals, system of education, and religion were being attacked by Western civilization.

Ramakrishna observed that, in general, the worldly people of Calcutta had been hypnotized by the West. To break the spell they were under, Ramakrishna began travelling through the streets of Calcutta: he visited the Maidan (Central Park) and Fort William; he went to the theatres; he visited the houses of the rich as well as of the poor. If the mountain will not go to Muhammad, Muhammad must go to the mountain. So Ramakrishna went uninvited to the people of Calcutta and talked to them about God. He reminded them again and again of the goal of human life. He said: "Wherever there is any trouble in the Divine Mother's empire, I shall have to rush there to stop it, like a government officer."[35]

Swami Saradananda described the following journey that Ramakrishna took to Calcutta:

One day the Master decided to visit Jadu Mallick's house in Calcutta to see that devotee's mother, who was very devoted to the Master. The Master had not heard any news about the family for a long time. A carriage arrived after the Master had finished his lunch. Meanwhile, our friend A. had come to Dakshineswar by boat to see the Master. The Master inquired about A.'s welfare, then said: "It is nice that you have come. I am going to Jadu's house today. On the way I shall stop at your house and see G., whose work has kept him from coming here for many days. Let us go together." A. agreed. He was then newly acquainted with the Master and had seen him at only a few places. He did not yet know that the wonderful Master could experience bhava samadhi at any time, at any place, even at the sight of trivial, contemptible, or untouchable things or persons.

The Master got into the carriage. The young devotee Latu, now known as Swami Adbhutananda, took the Master's towel, spice bag, and other necessary articles and followed him into the carriage. A. also climbed in. The Master sat on one side and Latu and A. occupied the other. The carriage started and after crossing through the market at Baranagore it passed by Mati Lake. Nothing eventful happened. As the childlike Master saw the various sights along the way, he asked questions of Latu and A., or made jokes on different topics as he normally did.

There was a small market to the south of Mati Lake. To the south of that market were a tavern, a dispensary, a few rice warehouses with tiled roofs, and a stable. At this point, the same road went straight towards Calcutta, but another wide road extended right up to the Ganges, and one could take it to the well-known Sarvamangala and Chitreswari temples.

In the tavern some drunkards were noisily drinking and laughing. Some of them were singing out of joy and some were dancing and gesticulating. The owner of the tavern, having engaged his bartender in serving his customers, was standing absent-mindedly at the door of the shop. There was a large vermilion mark on his forehead. The Master's carriage passed in front of the tavern just then. Perhaps the owner knew the Master; when he saw him in the carriage, he saluted him with both hands.

The noise in the tavern attracted the Master's attention and he perceived the merry mood of the drinkers. The bliss of God arose in the Master's mind as he observed their intoxicated delight. But in addition to this bliss, he also experienced the state of drunkenness: He became deeply intoxicated and his speech became slurred. Suddenly he stood up, leaned out of the carriage, and stood with one foot on the footboard. Like a drunkard, he expressed his joy at seeing their pleasure, and waving his hand, addressed them loudly: "Wonderful! Have fun! Bravo! Bravo!"

A. said: "We had no warning that the Master would suddenly be in that ecstatic state. He had been talking like a normal human being. But his mood changed so abruptly when he saw those drunkards! I was scared to death. I was about to grab him and pull him back inside the carriage, but immediately Latu intervened, saying: 'You do not have to do anything. He will control himself and will not fall.' So I kept quiet, but my heart was palpitating. I thought that I had made a mistake by travelling in the same carriage with this mad Master. I told myself I would never do so again. Of course, describing these events takes more time than when they actually happened. The carriage continued past the tavern, and the Master returned to his seat. When the Master saw the Sarvamangala temple, he said: 'That goddess Sarvamangala is a living deity. Bow down to Her.' Saying so, he himself bowed down and we followed his example. When I looked at the Master then, I found him to be as usual, smiling gently. But my heart did not stop palpitating for a long time, as I kept remembering what a bloody accident could have happened if he had fallen from the carriage.

"When the carriage reached our house, the Master said to me, 'Go and find out whether G. is at home.' I went, came back, and reported, 'No, G. is not at home.' He then said: 'Well, I missed G. I thought that I would ask him to pay today's extra carriage fare. However, I am now acquainted with you. Could you pay one rupee today? You see, Jadu Mallick is a miserly man. He will not pay more than the fixed fare of two rupees and four annas. But after I've visited several devotees, who knows how late I shall return to Dakshineswar tonight? If it becomes too late, the driver pesters me to return. So it has been arranged with Beni that however late it may be, the driver will not disturb me if he is paid three rupees and four annas. I am asking you because Jadu will pay two rupees and four annas, and if you pay one rupee then there will be no problem for today's fare.' I gave one rupee to Latu and bowed down to the Master, who then left to see Jadu Mallick."[36]

Now we shall travel with Ramakrishna in our imagination. We shall listen to him talk while going by horse carriage or walking in the streets of Calcutta. We shall not enter anyone's house, because it is not proper to enter someone's home uninvited. We shall observe his movements and learn from him how to walk with God. We are indebted to M., the recorder of *The Gospel of Sri Ramakrishna*, who has left these wonderful street scenes and immortal words of the Master. We shall present to the reader excerpts from M.'s invaluable record, and occasionally, we shall add our own comments.

A Visit to Ishwar Chandra Vidyasagar

M. narrated the Master's visit to Ishwar Chandra Vidyasagar, which took place on 5 August 1882:

Ramakrishna had long wanted to visit Ishwar Chandra Vidyasagar, a great scholar, educator, writer, and philanthropist. Learning from M. that he was a teacher at Vidyasagar's school, the Master asked: "Can you take me to Vidyasagar? I should like very much to see him." M.

told Ishwar Chandra of Ramakrishna's wish, and the pandit gladly agreed that M. should bring the Master some Saturday afternoon at four o'clock.

On the afternoon of August 5 the Master left Dakshineswar in a hackney carriage, accompanied by Bhavanath, M., and Hazra. Vidyasagar lived in Badurbagan, in central Calcutta, about six miles from Dakshineswar. The carriage crossed the Baghbazar bridge and then reached Amherst street via Shyambazar. On the way the Master joyfully talked with his companions; but as the carriage neared Vidyasagar's house his mood suddenly changed. He was overpowered with divine ecstasy. Not noticing this, M. pointed out the garden house where Raja Rammohan Roy had lived. The Master was annoyed and said, "I don't care about such things now." He was going into an ecstatic state.

The carriage stopped in front of Vidyasagar's house. The Master alighted, supported by M., who then led the way. In the courtyard were many flowering plants. As the Master walked to the house he said to M., like a child, pointing to his shirt-button: "My shirt is unbuttoned. Will that offend Vidyasagar?" "Oh, no!" said M. "Don't be anxious about it. Nothing about you will be offensive. You don't have to button your shirt." He accepted the assurance simply, like a child.[37]

Ramakrishna had a prolonged conversation with Vidyasagar. While talking to Vidyasagar about Brahman, Ramakrishna said: "What Brahman is cannot be described. All things in the world — the Vedas, the Puranas, the Tantras, the six systems of philosophy — have been defiled, like food that has been touched by the tongue, for they have been read or uttered by tongue. Only one thing has not been defiled in this way, and that is Brahman." In this connection he cited the example of a salt doll that wanted to tell others how deep the ocean was. But no sooner did it get into the water, than it melted.

When one is illumined, one becomes silent. The Master gave examples from what he had seen around himself, such as, "The bee buzzes as long as it is not sitting on a flower. It becomes silent when it begins to sip honey. An empty pitcher makes a gurgling sound when it is dipped in water. When it fills up it becomes silent."

After leaving Vidyasagar, the Master met with one of his devotees, as M. narrated:

Ramakrishna then took leave of Vidyasagar, who with his friends escorted the Master to the main gate, leading the way with a lighted candle in his hand. Before leaving the room, the Master prayed for the family's welfare, going into an ecstatic mood as he did so.

As soon as the Master and the devotees reached the gate, they saw an unexpected sight and stood still. In front of them was a bearded gentleman of fair complexion. No sooner did he see the Master than he fell prostrate before him.

When he stood up the Master said: "Who is this? Balaram? Why so late in the evening?"

Balaram: "I have been waiting here a long time, sir."

Master: "Why didn't you come in?"

Balaram: "All were listening to you. I didn't like to disturb you."

The Master got into the carriage with his companions.

Vidyasagar (to M.): "Shall I pay the carriage hire?"

M.: "Oh, don't bother, please. It is taken care of."

Vidyasagar and his friends bowed to Ramakrishna, and the carriage started for Dakshineswar. But the little group, with the venerable Vidyasagar at their head holding the lighted candle, stood at the gate and gazed after the Master until he was out of sight.[38]

Boat Trips with Keshab Chandra Sen

Ramakrishna travelled by steamboat thrice with Keshab Chandra Sen. The first trip was on 15 July 1881 and Hriday was with him. The Master was pleased to hear the jhak-jhak sound of the steamer. Someone requested the Master to look through the telescope of the steamer, but he said, "My mind is now attached to God. How can I withdraw it from Him and put it on this telescope?" The second trip took place on 23 February 1882. On that day Keshab went to the Master with Reverend Joseph Cook, Miss Pigot (an American missionary), Nagendra Nath Gupta (the editor of the *Tribune*), Prince Gajendra-narayan of Coochbehar, Pratap Majumdar, and other Brahmo devotees. Observing the Master's unceasing samadhi and ecstatic mood Pratap remarked: "Good heavens! It is as if he were possessed by a ghost!"[39]

M. provided a detailed description of the third boat trip, which took place on 27 October 1882:

It was Friday, the day of the Lakshmi Puja. Keshab Chandra Sen had arranged a boat trip on the Ganges for Sri Ramakrishna.

About four o'clock in the afternoon the steamboat with Keshab and his Brahmo followers cast anchor in the Ganges alongside the Kali temple at Dakshineswar. . . . Some disciples of Keshab entered [the Master's room]. Bowing before the Master, they said to him: "Sir, the steamer has arrived. Keshab Babu asked us to take you there." A small boat was to carry the Master to the steamer. No sooner did he get into the boat than he lost outer consciousness in samadhi. Vijay was with him.

M. was among the passengers. As the boat came alongside the steamer, all rushed to the railing to have a view of Sri Ramakrishna. Keshab became anxious to get him safely on board. With great difficulty the Master was brought back to consciousness of the world and taken to a cabin in the steamer. . . . He said to himself in a whisper: "Mother, why have You brought me here? They are hedged around and not free. Can I free them?"[40]

On that day the Master described the mystery of Kali, sang many songs, and held the Brahmos spellbound with his illuminating talk and humour.

M.'s narrative continued:

The boat cast anchor at Kayalaghat [Calcutta] and the passengers prepared to disembark. On coming outside they noticed that the full moon was up. The trees, the buildings, and the boats on the Ganges were bathed in its mellow light. A carriage was hailed for the Master, and M. and a few devotees got in with him. The Master asked for Keshab. Presently the latter arrived and inquired about the arrangements made for the Master's return to Dakshineswar. Then he bowed low and took leave of Sri Ramakrishna.

The carriage drove through the European quarter of the city. The Master enjoyed the sight of the beautiful mansions on both sides of the well-lighted streets. Suddenly he said: "I am thirsty. What's to be done?" Nandalal, Keshab's nephew, stopped the carriage before the India Club and went upstairs to get some water. The Master inquired whether the glass had been well washed. On being assured that it had been, he drank the water.

As the carriage went along, the Master put his head out of the window and looked with childlike enjoyment at the people, the vehicles, the horses, and the streets, all flooded with moonlight. Now and then he heard European ladies singing at the piano. He was in a very happy mood.

The carriage arrived at the house of Suresh Mitra, who was a great devotee of the Master and whom he addressed affectionately as Surendra. He was not at home.

The members of the household opened a room on the ground floor for the Master and his party. The cab fare was to be paid; Surendra would have taken care of it had he been there. The Master said to a devotee: "Why don't you ask the ladies to pay the fare? They certainly know that their master visits us at Dakshineswar. I am not a stranger to them."[41]

If someone were to now follow the same route that Ramakrishna took 120 years ago, one would see many changes. The names of some streets are different; cars and buses have replaced the horse carriages, and electric lights have replaced gas lights; the British government in India is no more.

After Mathur's death, the Master's carriage fare was paid by some devotees who could afford the expense. The Master's funny remark asking for the fare at Surendra's house makes us laugh; and again we think how an avatar visited the houses of his devotees for their benefit.

Ramakrishna at the Circus

Ramakrishna prayed to the Divine Mother, "Mother, don't make me a dry monk." We are amazed when we find that the Master, who was mostly in a state of divine intoxication, went to Calcutta to see the circus on 15 November 1882. Sometimes we plan to meet our friends at a particular place and time and then go to a theatre or a movie house. The Master did the same thing, as M. recorded in the *Gospel*:

Sri Ramakrishna, accompanied by Rakhal and several other devotees, came to Calcutta in a carriage and called for M. at Vidyasagar's school where he was teaching. Then they all set out for the Maidan. Sri Ramakrishna wanted to see the Wilson Circus. As the carriage rolled along the crowded Chitpore Road, his joy was very great. Like a little child he leaned first out of one side of the carriage and then out of the other, talking to himself as if addressing the passers-by. To M. he said: "I find the attention of the people fixed on earthly things. They are all rushing about for the sake of their stomachs. No one is thinking of God."

They arrived at the circus. Tickets for the cheapest seats were purchased. The devotees took the Master to a high gallery, and they all sat on a bench. He said joyfully: "Ha! This is a good place. I can see the show well from here." There were exhibitions of various feats. A horse raced around a circular track over which large iron rings were hung at intervals. The circus rider, an Englishwoman, stood on one foot on the horse's back, and as the horse passed under the rings, she jumped through them, always alighting on one foot on the horse's back. The horse raced around the entire circle, and the woman never missed the horse or lost her balance.

When the circus was over, the Master and the devotees stood outside in the field, near the carriage. Since it was a cold night he covered his body with his green shawl.

Sri Ramakrishna said to M.: "Did you see how that Englishwoman stood on one foot on her horse, while it ran like lightning? How difficult a feat that must be! She must have practised a long time. The slightest carelessness and she would break her arms or legs; she might even be killed. One faces the same difficulty leading the life of a householder. A few succeed in it through the grace of God and as a result of their spiritual practice. But most people fail. Entering the world, they become more and more involved in it; they drown in worldliness and suffer the agonies of death. Therefore spiritual practice is extremely necessary; otherwise one cannot rightly live in the world."[42]

Every one of the Master's actions was meaningful. He went to see the circus and then used an example from it to tell his devotees how one could attain perfection through practice.

The Festival in Panihati

On 18 June 1883, the Master attended a Vaishnava festival with some of his disciples. M. described the event:

Sri Ramakrishna had been invited to the great religious festival at Panihati near Calcutta. This "Festival of the Flattened Rice" was inaugurated by Raghunath Das, a disciple of Chaitanya. It is said that Raghunath used to run away from home, secretly practise his devotions, and enjoy the bliss of spiritual ecstasy. One day Nityananda said to him: "Thief! You run away from home and enjoy the love of God all alone. You hide it from us. I shall punish you today. You must arrange a religious festival and entertain the devotees with flattened rice." Since then the festival has been annually celebrated at Panihati by the Vaishnavas.

The Master had been invited by Mani Sen who was the custodian of the [Radha-Krishna] temple. Ram, M., Rakhal, Bhavanath, and a few other disciples went with the Master in a carriage. On his way to Panihati Sri Ramakrishna was in a light mood and joked with the youngsters. But as soon as the carriage reached the place of the festival, the Master, to the utter amazement of the devotees, shot into the crowd. He joined the kirtan party and danced, totally forgetting the world. Every now and then he stood still in samadhi, carefully supported by Navadwip Goswami for fear he might fall to the ground. Thousands of devotees were gathered together for the festival. . . . The crowd seemed to become infected by the Master's divine fervour and swayed to and fro, chanting the name of God, until the very air seemed to reverberate with it. Drums, cymbals, and other instruments produced melodious sounds. . . . Flowers were showered from all sides on his feet and head. The shouting of the name of Hari was heard even at a distance, like the rumbling of the ocean.[43]

In the afternoon Ramakrishna returned to Dakshineswar, as M. narrates:

The Master, accompanied by the devotees, took a carriage to return to Dakshineswar. They were going to pass the temple garden of Mati Seal on the way. For a long time the Master had been asking M. to take him to the reservoir in the garden in order that he might teach him how to meditate on the formless God. There were tame fish in the reservoir. Nobody harmed them. Visitors threw puffed rice and other bits of food into the water, and the big fish came in swarms to eat the food. Fearlessly the fish swam in the water and sported there joyously.

Coming to the reservoir, the Master said to M.: "Look at the fish. Meditating on the formless God is like swimming joyfully like these fish, in the ocean of Bliss and Consciousness.[44]

Travelling by Carriage with the Master

On 21 July 1883, M. joined the Master as he travelled to Calcutta. He wrote:

It was about four o'clock in the afternoon when Sri Ramakrishna, with Ramlal and one or two other devotees, started from Dakshineswar for Calcutta in a carriage. As the carriage passed the gate of the Kali temple, they met M. coming on foot with four mangoes in his hand. The carriage stopped and M. saluted the Master. Sri Ramakrishna was going to visit some of his devotees in Calcutta.

Master (*to M., with a smile*): "Come with us. We are going to Adhar's house."

M. got joyfully into the carriage. Having received an English education he did not believe in the tendencies inherited from previous births. But he had admitted a few days before that it was on account of Adhar's good tendencies from past births that he showed such great devotion to the Master. Later on he had thought about this subject and had discovered that he was not yet completely convinced about inherited tendencies. He had come to Dakshineswar that day to discuss the matter with Sri Ramakrishna.

Master: "Well, what do you think of Adhar?"

M.: "He has great yearning for God."

Master: "Adhar, too, speaks very highly of you."

M.: "I haven't much faith in rebirth and inherited tendencies. Will that in any way injure my devotion to God?"

Master: "It is enough to believe that all is possible in God's creation. Never allow the thought to cross your mind that your ideas are the only true ones, and that those of others are false. Then God will explain everything.

"What can man understand of God's activities? . . . Once, when I was explaining God's actions to someone, God suddenly showed me the lake at Kamarpukur. I saw a man removing the green scum and drinking the water. The water was clear as crystal. God revealed to me that Satchidananda is covered by the scum of maya. He who puts the green scum aside can drink the water."

The carriage came to the crossing at Shobhabazar in Calcutta. The Master continued, saying: "Sometimes I find that the universe is saturated with the Consciousness of God, as the earth is soaked with water in the rainy season. Well, I see so many visions, but I never feel vain about them."

M. (*with a smile*): "That you should speak of vanity, sir!"

Master: "Upon my word, I don't feel vanity even in the slightest degree. . . . Have you found anyone else resembling me — any pandit or holy man?"

M.: "God has created you with His own hands, whereas He has made others by machine. All others He has created according to law."

Master (*laughing, to Ramlal and the other devotees*): "Listen to what he is saying!"

Sri Ramakrishna laughed for some time, and said at last, "Really and truly I have no pride — no, not even the slightest bit."[45]

Like a child, the Master laughed and his joy was contagious.

The Master had an open mind, and he always loved to learn new things. He said: "As long as I live so long do I learn." M.'s narrative shows this aspect of Ramakrishna, as the conversation continues on the way to Calcutta:

Master: "Do you believe in English astronomy?"

M.: "It is possible to make new discoveries by applying the laws of Western astronomy. Observing the irregular movement of Uranus, the astronomers looked through their telescopes and discovered Neptune shining in the sky. They can also foretell eclipses."

Master: "Yes, that is so."

The carriage drove on. They were approaching Adhar's house. Sri Ramakrishna said to M.: "Dwell in the truth and you will certainly realize God."

M.: "You said the other day to Navadwip Goswami: 'O God, I want Thee. Please do not delude me with Thy world-bewitching maya. I want to realize Thee."

Master: "Yes, one should be able to say that from one's innermost soul."[46]

After giving M. this valuable advice, the Master entered Adhar's parlour. Afterwards, the Master visited the houses of Jadu Mallick and Khelat Ghosh. In both homes he talked about God and sang devotional songs, then finally returned to Dakshineswar late at night.

The Master's Keen Power of Observation

When Ramakrishna travelled through the streets of Calcutta by horse carriage, he kept the doors open so he could observe the fashions and lifestyles of the people he saw. Nothing escaped his keen vision. On 7 September 1883 he said to M.:

> "The other day I went to Calcutta. As I drove along the streets in the carriage, I observed that everyone's attention was fixed on low things. Everyone was brooding over his stomach and running after nothing but food. Everyone's mind was turned to 'lust and gold.' I saw only one or two with their attention fixed on higher things, with their minds turned to God."
>
> M.: "The present age has aggravated this stomach-worry. Trying to imitate the English, people have turned their attention to more luxuries; therefore their wants have also increased."[47]

Ramakrishna felt terrible discomfort when he heard worldly conversation. On 9 September 1883 he said to M.:

> "I see people coming to the Ganges to bathe. They talk their heads off about everything under the sun. The widowed aunt says: 'Without me they cannot perform the Durga Puja. I have to look after even the smallest detail. Again, I have to supervise everything when there is a marriage festival in the family, even the bed of the bride and groom.'"
>
> M.: "Why should we blame them? How else will they pass the time?"
>
> Master (*with a smile*): "Some people have their shrine rooms in their attics. The women arrange the offerings and flowers and make the sandal paste. But, while doing so, they never say a word about God. The burden of the conversation is: 'What shall we cook today? I couldn't get good vegetables in the market. That curry was delicious yesterday. That boy is my cousin. Hello there! Have you that job still? Don't ask me how I am. My Hari is no more.' Just fancy! They talk of such things in the shrine room at the time of worship!"[48]

A Visit to Kankurgachi

People generally like to invite a holy person or a famous leader to inaugurate a new house or retreat quarters. Ram Datta bought a garden house retreat and wanted the Master to inaugurate it. M. described Ramakrishna's first visit to the garden, on 26 December 1883:

Sri Ramakrishna, accompanied by Mani Mallick, M., and several other devotees, was in a carriage on his way to Ram's new garden [Kankurgachi in Calcutta]. The garden, which Ram had recently purchased, was next to Surendra's. Ram adored the Master as an incarnation of God. Manilal was a member of the Brahmo Samaj. The Brahmos do not believe in Divine Incarnations.

Master (to Manilal): "In order to meditate on God, one should try at first to think of Him as free from upadhis, limitations. God is beyond upadhis. He is beyond speech and mind. But it is very difficult to achieve perfection in this form of meditation.

"But it is easy to meditate on an Incarnation — God born as man. Yes, God in man. The body is a mere covering. It is like a lantern with a light burning inside, or like a glass case in which one sees precious things."

Arriving at the garden, the Master got out of the carriage and accompanied Ram and the other devotees to the sacred tulsi-grove. Standing near it, he said: "How nice! It is a fine place. You can easily meditate on God here."

Sri Ramakrishna sat down in the house, which stood to the south of the lake. Ram offered him a plate of fruit and sweets, which he enjoyed with the devotees. After a short time he went around the garden.

Next Sri Ramakrishna proceeded towards Surendra's garden. He walked on foot a little distance and saw a sadhu sitting on a couch under a tree. At once he went up to the holy man and joyfully began a conversation with him.

Master: "To which order of monks do you belong? Have you any title — Giri, Puri, or the like?"

Sadhu: "People call me a paramahamsa."

Master: "That is good. 'I am Shiva' — that is a good attitude. But I must tell you something else. The process of creation, preservation, and destruction that is going on day and night is due to Shakti, the Power of God. This Primal Power and Brahman are one and the same. Shakti cannot exist without Brahman, just as waves cannot exist without water. There cannot be any instrumental music without an instrument."

After a pleasant conversation with the sadhu, the Master returned to the carriage, the holy man walking with him. Sri Ramakrishna looked upon him as a friend of long acquaintance, and they walked arm in arm.[49]

This amazing scene shows how simple and natural the Master's human aspect was. After the party reached Surendra's garden, the Master said to Ram: "Bring this sadhu to Dakshineswar when you come."

Visits to Ishan

M.'s poetic faculty was given free rein in his vivid descriptions of the Master's actions and his surroundings. Although these events are 120 years old, we still see them very clearly, as if they were happening in front of us.

On the morning of the Master's journey to Ishan's house in Calcutta on 27 December 1883, M. described a scene that has some similarities to Krishna's journey to Hastinapur with the proposal of avoiding war in the Mahabharata:

The temple garden was filled with the sweet music of the dawn service, which mingled with the morning melody from the nahabat. Leaving his bed, Sri Ramakrishna chanted the names of God in sweet tones. Then he bowed before the pictures of the different deities in his room and went to the west porch to salute the Ganges.

Some of the devotees who had spent the night at the temple garden came to the Master's room and bowed before him. M. had been staying there two weeks.

Sri Ramakrishna said to M.: "I have been invited to Ishan's this morning. Baburam will accompany me, and you too." M. made ready to go with the Master.

At eight o'clock the carriage hired for the Master stood waiting in front of the nahabat. On all sides plants and trees were in flower, and the river sparkled in the sunlight of the bright winter's day. The Master bowed once more before the pictures. Then, still chanting the name of the Divine Mother, he got into the carriage, followed by M. and Baburam. The devotees took with them Sri Ramakrishna's woolen shawl, woolen cap, and small bag of spices.

Sri Ramakrishna was very happy during the trip and enjoyed it like a child. About nine o'clock the carriage stopped at the door of Ishan's house. Ishan and his relatives greeted the Master and led him to the parlour on the first floor.[50]

M. describes the events of 25 June 1884:

It was the day of the Rathayatra, the Car Festival of the Hindus. At Ishan's invitation Sri Ramakrishna went to his house in Calcutta. For some time the Master had had a desire to meet Pandit Shashadhar Tarkachudamani, who had been staying with one of Ishan's neighbours. So it was decided that he would visit the pandit in the afternoon.[51]

M. continued:

276 • How to Live With God

About four o'clock in the afternoon the Master left in a carriage for the house where Pandit Shashadhar was staying. As soon as Sri Rama-krishna got into the carriage he went into samadhi. His physical frame was very tender as a result of the austerities he had undergone during the long years of his spiritual discipline and his constant absorption in God-consciousness. The Master would suffer from the slightest physical discomfort and even from the vibration of worldly thoughts around him. Once Keshab Chandra Sen had said that Sri Rama-krishna, Christ, and Sri Chaitanya belong to a delicate species of humanity that should be kept in a glass case and protected from the vulgar contact of the world.

It was the rainy season, and a fine drizzle of rain had made the road muddy. The sky was overcast. The devotees followed the carriage on foot. As the carriage stopped in front of the house, the host and his relatives welcomed the Master and took him upstairs to the drawing-room. There the Master met the pandit.[52]

Although the Master had not had any formal education, his words of wisdom would burst forth with similes like fireworks. The Master told the pandit: "When the fruit appears the blossom drops off. Love of God is the fruit, and rituals are the blossom." He also said, "When the lamp is lighted the moths come in swarms. They don't have to be invited. In the same way, the preacher who has a commission from God need not invite people to hear him. . . . At Kamarpukur I have seen people measuring grain. It lies in a heap. One man keeps pushing grain from the heap towards another man, who weighs it on a scales. So the man who weighs doesn't run short of grain. It is the same with the preacher who has received a commission from God. As he teaches people, the Divine Mother Herself supplies him with fresh knowledge from behind. That knowledge never comes to an end."[53]

After a long conversation with the pandit, the Master returned to Ishan's house before dusk. After a while, the Master was prepared to leave. M. described the scene:

Ishan and the other devotees stood by the Master. They were waiting to bid him good-bye. Sri Ramakrishna said to Ishan: "Live in the world like an ant. The world contains a mixture of truth and untruth, sugar and sand. Be an ant and take the sugar."

Again, "the world is mixture of milk and water, the bliss of God-consciousness and the pleasure of sense-enjoyment. Be a swan and drink the milk, leaving the water aside.

"Live in the world like a waterfowl. The water clings to the bird, but the bird shakes it off. Live in the world like a mudfish. The fish lives in the mud, but its skin is always bright and shiny.

"The world is indeed a mixture of truth and make-believe. Discard the make-believe and take the truth."

Sri Ramakrishna got into the carriage and left for Dakshineswar.[54]

Ramakrishna at the Theatre

Sri Ramakrishna was planning to go to a performance of *Chaitanyalila* (Life of Chaitanya) at the Star Theatre on 21 September 1884. Mahendra Mukherji was to take him to Calcutta in his carriage. They were talking about choosing good seats. Some suggested that one could see the performance well from the one-rupee gallery. Ram said: "Oh, no! I shall engage a box for him." The Master laughed. Some of the devotees said that public women took part in the play. They took the parts of Nimai, Nitai, and others.

Master (*to the devotees*): "I shall look upon them as the Blissful Mother Herself. What if one of them acts the part of Chaitanya? An imitation custard-apple reminds one of the real fruit. . . . I was once taken to the Maidan in Calcutta to see a balloon go up. There I noticed a young English boy leaning against a tree, with his body bent in three places. It at once brought before me the vision of Krishna and I went into samadhi."[55]

The Master later told M. privately: "What Ram says applies to rajasic people. What is the use of reserving an expensive seat?"

M. continued his description of that day:

About five o'clock that afternoon Sri Ramakrishna was on his way to Calcutta. M., Mahendra Mukherji, and a few other devotees accompanied him in Mahendra's carriage. Thinking of God, the Master soon went into an ecstatic mood. After a long time he regained consciousness of the world. He observed: "That fellow Hazra dares teach me! The rascal!" After a short pause he said, "I shall drink some water." He often made such remarks in order to bring his mind down to the sense plane.

Mahendra (*to M.*): "May I get some refreshments for him?"

M.: "No, he won't eat anything now."

Master (*still in ecstatic mood*): "I shall eat."

Mahendra took the Master to his flour-mill located at Hatibagan. After a little rest Sri Ramakrishna was to go to the theatre. . . . Sri Ramakrishna washed his face. A smoke was prepared for him. He said to M.: "Is it dusk now? If it is, I won't smoke. During the twilight hour of the dusk you should give up all other activities and remember God." Saying this he looked at the hairs of his arm. He wanted to see whether he could count them. If he could not, it would be dusk.[56]

Every one of the Master's words and actions have deep meaning. Muslims punctually pray five times a day. Orthodox Hindus repeat the Gayatri mantra three times a day. Some practise spiritual disciplines at sunrise and sunset, and some do *purascharan* from sunrise to sunset. Maintaining punctuality in spiritual disciplines is extremely important. It is called *kshana rahasya*, or to observe the mystery of time. For example, we have set times for breakfast, lunch, and dinner. As a result, our stomachs demand food at those times. Similarly, if we set aside time for meditation at 6:00 a.m. and 6:00 p.m., our minds will automatically demand spiritual food at those times. The Master did not have a watch. He saw how villagers determined morning by listening to the singing of the birds and evening by seeing whether one can still see the hairs on the arm.

Let us resume M.'s narrative:

About half past eight in the evening the carriage with the Master and the devotees drew up in front of the Star Theatre on Beadon Street. The Master was accompanied by M., Baburam, Mahendra, and two or three others. They were talking about engaging seats, when Girish Chandra Ghosh, the manager of the theatre, accompanied by several officials, came out to the carriage, greeted the Master, and took him and the party upstairs. Girish had heard of the Master and was very glad to see him at the theatre. The Master was conducted to one of the boxes. M. sat next to him; Baburam and one or two devotees sat behind.

The hall was brilliantly lighted. . . . Sri Ramakrishna was filled with joy and said to M., with his childlike smile: "Ah, it is very nice here! I am glad to have come. I feel inspired when I see so many people together. Then I clearly perceive that God Himself has become everything."

M.: "It is true, sir."

Master: "How much will they charge us here?"

M.: "They won't take anything. They are very happy that you have come to the theatre."

Master: "It is all due to the grace of the Divine Mother."

After the performance, a devotee stopped the Master as he was about to enter a carriage. He asked him how he had enjoyed the play. Smiling, the Master replied: "I found the representation the same as the real."

M.'s narrative continued:

The carriage proceeded towards Mahendra's mill. Suddenly Sri Ramakrishna went into an ecstatic mood and murmured to himself in loving tones: "O Krishna! O Krishna! Krishna is knowledge! Krishna is soul! Krishna is mind! Krishna is life! Krishna is body! O Govinda, Thou art my life! Thou art my soul!"

The carriage reached the mill. Mahendra fed the Master tenderly, with various dishes. With Mahendra and a few other devotees, Sri Ramakrishna left in the carriage for the Dakshineswar temple garden. The Master was in a happy mood. He sang a song about Gauranga and Nitai.

Mahendra: "Please bless me that I may have love for God."

Master: "You are generous and artless. One cannot realize God without sincerity and simplicity. God is far, far away from the crooked heart."

Near Shyambazar, Mahendra bade the Master good-bye, and the carriage continued on its way.[57]

The Annakuta Festival in Barabazar

Two days after the annual Kali puja, the Marwaris of the Barabazar section in Calcutta celebrated the Annakuta festival. (Annakuta means "hill of food.") During this festival a vast quantity of cooked food is offered to the deity and later distributed among devotees and the poor.

M. described how the Master took part in the festival, on 20 October 1884:

Sri Ramakrishna had been invited by the Marwari devotees to the ceremony at 12 Mallick Street. It was the second day of the bright fortnight of the moon. The festival connected with the worship of Kali, known as the "Festival of Light," was still going on at Barabazar.

About three o'clock in the afternoon M. and the younger Gopal came to Barabazar. M. had in his hand a bundle of cloths he had purchased for Sri Ramakrishna. Mallick Street was jammed with people, bullock-carts, and carriages. As M. and Gopal approached 12 Mallick Street they noticed Sri Ramakrishna in a carriage, which could hardly move because of the jam. Baburam and Ram Chattopadhyay were with the Master. He smiled at M. and Gopal.

Sri Ramakrishna alighted from the carriage. With Baburam he proceeded on foot to the house of his host, M. leading the way. They saw the courtyard of the house filled with big bales of clothes, which were being loaded into bullock-carts for shipment. The Marwari host greeted the Master and led him to the third floor of the house. A painting of Kali hung on the wall. Sri Ramakrishna bowed before it. He sat down and became engaged in conversation with the devotees. One of the Marwaris began to stroke his feet. The Master asked him to stop.

After reflecting a minute he said, "All right, you can stroke them a little." His words were full of compassion.[58]

The picture of Barabazar that M. painted is over 120 years old, but
anyone who visits that area of Barabazar now will see the same scene.
The streets are still jammed with traffic, only now horse carriages and
bullock-carts have been replaced by handcarts, jeeps, and trucks. And
visitors will see the angry and disgusted faces of the drivers of carts, cars,
and trucks instead of the smiling face of Ramakrishna.

We shall wait on the sidewalk of Mallick Street till the Master returns
from the house. M. continues:

> Sri Ramakrishna took leave of the host. It was evening and the street
> was jammed as before with people and vehicles. He said: "Let us get
> out of the carriage. It can go by a back street." Proceeding on foot, he
> found that a betel-leaf seller had opened his stall in front of a small
> room that looked like a hole. One could not possibly enter it without
> bending one's head. The Master said: "How painful it is to be shut in
> such a small space! That is the way of worldly people. And they are
> happy in such a life."
>
> The carriage came up after making the detour. The Master entered it
> with Baburam, M., and Ram Chattopadhyay. The younger Gopal sat
> on the roof of the carriage.
>
> A beggar woman with a baby on her arm stood in front of the car-
> riage waiting for alms. The Master said to M., "Have you any money?"
> Gopal gave her something.
>
> The carriage rolled along Barabazar. Everywhere there were signs
> of great festivity. The night was dark but illuminated with myriads of
> lights. The carriage came to the Chitpur Road, which was also brightly
> lighted. The people moved in lines like ants. The crowd looked at the
> gaily decorated stores and stalls on both sides of the road. There were
> sweetmeat stores and perfume stalls. Pictures, beautiful and gaudy,
> hung from the walls. Well-dressed shopkeepers sprayed the visitors
> with rose water. The carriage stopped in front of a perfume stall. The
> Master looked at the pictures and lights and felt happy as a child. Peo-
> ple were talking loudly. He cried out: "Go forward! Move on!" He
> laughed. He said to Baburam with a loud laugh: "Move on! What are
> you doing?" The devotees laughed too. They understood that the Mas-
> ter wanted them to move forward to God and not to be satisfied with
> their present state.
>
> The carriage drove on. The Master noticed that M. had brought
> some cloths for him. M. had with him two pieces of unbleached and
> two pieces of washed cloth. But the Master had asked him only for the

unbleached ones. He said to M.: "Give me the unbleached ones. You may keep the others. All right. You may give me one of them."

M.: "Then shall I take back one piece?"

Master: "Then take both."

M.: "As you please, sir."

Master: "You may give me those when I need them. You see, yesterday Beni Pal wanted me to carry away some food for Ramlal. I told him I couldn't. It is impossible for me to lay up for the future."

M.: "That's all right, sir. I shall take back the two pieces of washed cloth."

Referring to a devotee, Sri Ramakrishna said: "I said to him yesterday, 'Tomorrow I shall go to Barabazar; please meet me there.' Do you know what he said? He said: 'The tram fare will be one anna. Where shall I get it?' He had been to Beni Pal's garden yesterday and had officiated there as a priest. No one had asked him to do it. He had put on the show himself. He wanted people to know that he was a member of the Brahmo Samaj. (*To M.*) Can you tell me what he meant when he said that the tram would cost him one anna?"

The conversation turned to the Annakuta festival of the Marwaris.

Master (*to the devotees*): "What you have seen here one sees at Vrindaban too. . . . Did you notice the Marwaris' devotion? That is the real Hindu ideal. That is the Sanatana Dharma. Did you notice their joy when they carried the image in procession? They were happy to think that they bore the throne of God on their shoulders.

"The Hindu religion alone is the Sanatana Dharma. The various creeds you hear of nowadays have come into existence through the will of God and will disappear again through His will. They will not last forever."

M. was going home. He saluted the Master and got out of the carriage near Shobhabazar. Sri Ramakrishna proceeded to Dakshineswar in a happy mood.[59]

During this journey we heard the Master talk about his phenomenal renunciation. We feel sorry for that thrifty man who rejected an avatar's invitation because he did not want to spend one anna for tram fare. Some people consider a small donation to a charity for religious purposes to be a misuse of money, but they do not hesitate to spend a lot of money for a vacation, shopping, eating in a restaurant, going to the movies, and so on. This is the nature of worldly people.

At Balaram Bose's House

During Sri Ramakrishna's time, Dakshineswar was a village and there was no regular transport system between it and Calcutta. People had to travel there by foot, carriage, or boat. For this reason the Master needed a place in Calcutta so that he could meet with his devotees who lived in the city. Balaram Bose's house served that purpose.

M. described one meeting at Balaram's house, which took place on 11 March 1885:

Balaram was indeed blessed among the householder disciples of the Master. Sri Ramakrishna often described him as a *rasaddar*, or supplier of stores, appointed by the Divine Mother to take care of his physical needs. Balaram's house in Calcutta had been sanctified many times by the Master's presence. There he frequently lost himself in samadhi, dancing, singing, or talking about God. Those of the Master's disciples and devotees who could not go to Dakshineswar visited him there and received his instruction. And so it happened that whenever the Master was at Balaram's house, the devotees would gather there. It was the Master's chief vineyard in Calcutta. It was here that the devotees came to know each other intimately.

The shadow of evening fell on Calcutta. For the moment the noise of the busy metropolis was stilled. Gongs and conch-shells proclaimed the evening worship in many Hindu homes. Devotees of God set aside their worldly duties and turned their minds to prayer and meditation. This joining of day and night, this mystic twilight, always created an ecstatic mood in the Master.

The devotees seated in the room looked at Sri Ramakrishna as he began to chant the sweet name of the Divine Mother. After the chanting he began to pray. Every word of this prayer, uttered from the depths of his soul, stirred the minds of the devotees. The melody of his voice and the childlike simplicity of his face touched their hearts very deeply.

Girish invited the Master to his house, saying that he must go there that very night.

It was nine o'clock in the evening when the Master was ready to start for Girish's house. Since Balaram had prepared supper for him, Sri Ramakrishna said to Balaram: "Please send the food you have prepared for me to Girish's. I shall enjoy it there." He did not want to hurt Balaram's feelings.

As the Master was coming down from the second floor of Balaram's house, he became filled with divine ecstasy. He looked as if he were drunk. Narayan and M. were by his side; a little behind came Ram, Chuni, and the other devotees. No sooner did he reach the ground floor than he became totally overwhelmed. Narayan came forward to hold him by the hand lest he should miss his footing and fall. The Master expressed annoyance at this. A few minutes later he said to

Narayan affectionately: "If you hold me by the hand people may think I am drunk. I shall walk by myself."

Girish's house was not far away. The Master passed the crossing at Bosepara Lane. Suddenly he began to walk faster. The devotees were left behind. Presently Narendra was seen coming from a distance. At other times the Master's joy would have been unbounded at the thought of Narendra or at the mere mention of his name; but now he did not even exchange a word with his beloved disciple.

Girish stood at the door to welcome the Master. As Sri Ramakrishna entered the house, Girish fell at his feet and lay there on the floor like a rod. At the Master's bidding he stood up, touching the Master's feet with his forehead. Sri Ramakrishna was taken to the drawing-room on the second floor. The devotees followed him and sat down, eager to get a view of the Master and listen to every word that fell from his lips.

As Sri Ramakrishna was about to take the seat reserved for him, he saw a newspaper lying near it. He signed to someone to remove the paper. Since a newspaper contains worldly matters — gossip and scandal — he regarded it as unholy. After the paper was removed he took his seat.[60]

On 24 April 1885, the Master was going to Girish's house with some devotees when some people made a remark that he overheard. Laughing, he said to M.: "What are these people saying? 'There comes Paramahamsa's battalion!' What these fools say!"[61] Public opinion or criticism did not bother the Master: his mind was above the pairs of opposites, beyond praise or blame.

Ramakrishna's Compassion

Sri Ramakrishna had infinite love and compassion for everyone and everything, even animals. He would go to Calcutta by horse carriage, but he had deep feeling for those horses. The Master did not allow too many passengers in his carriage. The Master would tell devotees who asked for a ride, "No, there is no room in this carriage." He would ask them to hire a carriage for themselves or to come by boat. He felt that it would be hard for the horses to pull too many people.

Swami Akhandananda wrote in his reminiscences: "The Master would always visit Calcutta by the hired carriage of Beni Pal of Baranagore because his horses were strong and healthy. The Master felt pain if the coachman whipped the horses. He cried out, 'Uh! Someone is hitting me.' Beni Pal always supplied his best horses for the carriage that the Master would be riding in. The coachman did not whip the horses; he only made some noise and shook the reins."[62]

M. recorded the love and concern the Master had for his devotees, as this incident of 6 April 1885 shows:

Sri Ramakrishna was on his way in a carriage to Devendra's house in Nimu Goswami's Lane. The younger Naren, M., and one or two other devotees were with him. The Master felt great yearning for Purna. He began to talk of the young disciple.

Master (to M.): "A great soul! Or how could he make me do japa for his welfare? But Purna doesn't know anything about it."

M. and the other devotees were amazed at these words.

The carriage proceeded to Devendra's house. Once Sri Ramakrishna had said to Devendra at Dakshineswar, "I have been thinking of visiting your house one day." Devendra had replied: "The same idea came to my mind today, and I have come here to ask that favour of you. You must grace my house this Sunday." "But," the Master had said, "you have a small income. Don't invite many people. The carriage hire will also run to a big amount." Devendra had answered, laughing: "What if my income is small? 'One can run into debt to eat butter.'" At these words Sri Ramakrishna had laughed a long time.

Soon the carriage reached Devendra's house. Sri Ramakrishna said to him: "Devendra, don't make elaborate arrangements for my meal. Something very simple will do. I am not very well today."[63]

In the Bible we have read the parable of the ten virgins who were waiting for the bridegroom to appear. All of the women fell asleep while their lamps burnt on. At midnight when the bridegroom appeared, only the five virgins who had brought an extra supply of oil for their lamps were ready to attend the wedding feast. The five foolish virgins were excluded from the feast. We find a similar incident in *The Gospel of Sri Ramakrishna*. After a beautiful conversation about God at Devendra's house the Master was about to leave. M.'s record continues: "Devendra and the other devotees took the Master to his carriage. Seeing that one of his neighbours was sound asleep on a bench in the courtyard, Devendra woke him up. The neighbour rubbed his eyes and said, 'Has the Paramahamsa come?' All burst into laughter. The man had come a long time before Sri Ramakrishna's arrival, and because of the heat had spread a mat on the bench and lain down, and gone sound asleep.

"Sri Ramakrishna's carriage proceeded to Dakshineswar. He said to M. happily, 'I have eaten a good deal of ice-cream; bring four or five cones for me when you come to Dakshineswar.'"[64]

Visiting Devotees in Calcutta

M. continued his record:

It was about three o'clock in the afternoon. Sri Ramakrishna was sitting in Balaram's drawing-room with the devotees. . . . Narayan and certain other devotees had remarked to the Master that Nanda Bose, an aristocrat of Baghbazar, had many pictures of gods and goddesses in his house. Hence Sri Ramakrishna intended to pay a visit to Nanda's house in the afternoon [28 July 1885]. A brahmin woman [Golap-ma] devoted to the Master lived near by. She often came to see him at Dakshineswar. She was extremely sorrowful over the death of her only daughter, and the Master had agreed to go to her house. She had invited him with great earnestness. From her house the Master was to go to the house of Ganu's mother [Yogin-ma], another devotee. . . .

He was ready to go to Nanda Bose's house. A palanquin was brought for him, and he got into it repeating the name of God. He had put on a pair of black-varnished slippers and a red-bordered cloth. As Sri Ramakrishna sat down in the palanquin, M. put the slippers by his side. He accompanied the palanquin on foot. . . .

They entered the gate of Nanda's house, crossed the spacious square, and stopped in front of the building. The members of the family greeted the Master. He asked M. to hand him the slippers and then got out of the palanquin and entered the large hall. It was a very spacious room. Pictures of gods and goddesses were hanging on all sides. . . .

A picture of Keshab's Navavidhan hung on the wall. Suresh Mitra, a beloved householder disciple of the Master, had had it painted. In this picture Sri Ramakrishna was pointing out to Keshab that people of different religions proceed to the same goal by different paths.

Master: "That was painted for Surendra."

Prasanna's father (*smiling*): "You too are in that picture."

Master (*smiling*): "Yes, it contains everything. This is the ideal of modern times."

The master of the house had not yet shown any sign of serving Sri Ramakrishna with refreshments. Sri Ramakrishna himself said to Nanda: "You see, you should offer me something to eat. That is why the other day I said to Jadu's mother: 'Look here. Give me something to eat.' Otherwise it brings harm to the householder."[65] [It is a custom that if a holy man visits a home, the owner must offer him something to eat or at least a glass of water.]

Nanda ordered some sweets. After having refreshments the Master left for Golap-ma's house. M.'s narrative continues:

The Master arrived at the house of the brahmin lady who was grief-stricken on account of her daughter's death. It was an old brick house. Entering the house, the Master passed the cowshed on his left.

He and the devotees went to the roof, where they took seats. People were standing there in rows. Others were seated. They were all eager to get a glimpse of Sri Ramakrishna.

The brahmani had a sister; both of them were widows. . . . The brahmani had been busy all day making arrangements to receive Sri Ramakrishna. . . . The brahmani's sister came to the Master and saluted him. She said: "Sister has just gone to Nanda Bose's house to inquire the reason for your delay in coming here. She will return presently."

The brahmani came and saluted the Master. She was beside herself with joy. She did not know what to say. In a half-choked voice she said: "This joy is too much for me. Perhaps I shall die of it."

She was talking like this when her sister came up and said: "Come down, sister! How can I manage things if you stay here? Can I do it all by myself?"

But the brahmani was overwhelmed with joy. She could not take her eyes from the Master and the devotees.

After a while she very respectfully took Sri Ramakrishna to another room and offered him sweets and other refreshments. The devotees were entertained on the roof.

It was about eight o'clock in the evening. Sri Ramakrishna was ready to leave. . . . A man showed the way with a light. At places it was dark.[66]

After visiting the house of Ganu's mother, the Master returned to Balaram's house. M. describes the scene:

He [Ramakrishna] was resting in the small room to the west of the drawing-room. It was quite late, almost a quarter to eleven. . . . M. was stroking the Master's feet. They talked together.

Master (*referring to the brahmani and her relatives*): "Ah! How happy they were!"

M.: "How amazing! A similar thing happened with two women at the time of Jesus. They too were sisters, and devoted to Christ. Martha and Mary."

Master (*eagerly*): "Tell me the story."

M.: "Jesus Christ, like you, went to their house with his devotees. At the sight of him one of the sisters was filled with ecstatic happiness. . . . The other sister, all by herself, was arranging the food to entertain Jesus. She complained to the Master, saying: 'Lord, please judge for yourself — how wrong my sister is! She is sitting in your room and I am doing all these things by myself.' Jesus said: 'Your sister indeed is blessed. She has developed the only thing needful in human life: love of God.'"

Master: "Well, after seeing all this, what do you feel?"

M.: "I feel that Christ, Chaitanyadeva, and yourself — all three are one and the same. It is the same Person that has become all these three."

Master: "Yes, yes! One! One! It is indeed one. Don't you see that it is He alone who dwells here (*pointing to himself*) in this way."

M.: "You explained clearly, the other day, how God incarnates Himself on earth."

Master: "Tell me what I said."

M.: "You told us to imagine a field extending to the horizon and beyond. It extends without any obstruction; but we cannot see it on account of a wall in front of us. In that wall there is a round hole. Through the hole we see a part of that infinite field."

Master: "Tell me what that hole is."

M.: "You are that hole. Through you can be seen everything — that Infinite Meadow without any end."

Sri Ramakrishna was very much pleased. Patting M.'s back, he said: "I see you have understood that. That's fine!"

M.: "It is indeed difficult to understand that. One cannot quite grasp how God, Perfect Brahman that He is, can dwell in that small body."

The Master quoted from a song:

Oh, no one at all has found out who He is;
Like a madman from door to door He roams,
Like a poor beggar He roams from door to door.[67]

Sri Ramakrishna loved to travel to holy places, including the houses of his devotees in Calcutta. But it was not so easy to travel with him. Swami Turiyananda recalled:

One day Mathur Babu was returning to Janbazar in his deluxe phaeton,* bringing Sri Ramakrishna with him. When the carriage reached Chitpur Road the Master had a wonderful vision. He felt that he had become Sita, and that Ravana was kidnapping him. Seized by this idea, he merged into samadhi. Just then the horses tore loose from their reins and stumbled and fell. Mathur Babu could not understand the reason for such a mishap. When Sri Ramakrishna returned to normal consciousness, Mathur told him about the accident with the horses. Sri Ramakrishna then said that while in ecstasy he perceived that Ravana was kidnapping him, and that Jatayu** was attacking Ravana's chariot and trying to destroy it. After hearing this story,

---

*A light, four-wheeled carriage.
**The great bird who had attempted to rescue Sita.

Mathur Babu said, "Father, how difficult it is even to go with you through the street!"[68]

Sri Ramakrishna was not only a great teacher, but also a great learner. He went to visit the Calcutta Zoo. He said: "I went into samadhi at the sight of the lion, for the carrier of the Mother awakened in my mind the consciousness of the Mother Herself."[69]

After visiting the Calcutta Museum, he said: "I was shown fossils. A whole animal has become stone! Just see what an effect has been produced by company! Likewise, by constantly living in the company of a holy man one verily becomes holy."[70]

Ramakrishna described his visit to the studio of Bengal Photographers in Calcutta: "Today [10 December 1881] I enjoyed very much the machine by which a man's picture is taken. One thing I noticed was that the impression doesn't stay on a bare piece of glass, but it remains when the glass is stained with a black solution. In the same way, mere hearing of spiritual talk doesn't leave any impression. People forget it soon afterwards. But they can retain spiritual instruction if they are stained inside with earnestness and devotion."[71]

10

The Story of Rasik

R asik was a sweeper in the temple garden of Dakshineswar. Because he was poor and had been born into a low-caste family, he was almost unknown to the temple visitors of the area. Only a few of Ramakrishna's devotees noticed him. Rasik's job was to sweep the garden paths and courtyard, clean the privy, and so on. His lowly status barred him from entering the temple; he could not even touch the priests because of social restrictions. His part in the divine drama of Ramakrishna was enacted offstage. Pilgrims and visitors were not interested in meeting the sweeper of the temple garden. His monthly salary was probably not more than one or two rupees (as a priest, Ramakrishna earned only five rupees per month). In addition, Rasik was a private man: He did not know too many people other than Ramakrishna and the temple officials who had hired him.

We try to know or love God through japa, meditation, austerities, and studying the scriptures; but the Katha Upanishad tells us: "The Atman is attained by him alone whom It chooses." We realize God by His grace. Rasik was illiterate, so he could not use his intellect to understand Ramakrishna. But he was simple, guileless, and spiritual. The Master was also extremely simple, so he bestowed his grace on this sweeper of the temple garden.

Swami Vishuddhananda recalled:

I heard from Brother Ramlal [Ramakrishna's nephew] about how the Master's unconditional grace was bestowed on Rasik. He was the sweeper of the Dakshineswar temple garden. Every day he saw the Master from a distance. He observed that many people were visiting the Master in his room. He pondered: "I am so close to the Master; still I cannot go to his room and touch his feet. What kind of sin have I committed? The Master is saving so many souls — good and bad. How unfortunate I am! I see him from a distance but cannot go near him." Thus a storm was raging in his mind over a period of a few years. He had no peace.

One day a golden opportunity arrived. The Master went to the pine grove to answer the call of nature and Brother Ramlal was waiting near the Panchavati. Rasik hid himself behind a tree and thought: "I don't care what happens. I can't bear it anymore." When the Master came back towards the nahabat, Rasik hurriedly fell on the garden path, grabbed his feet, and exclaimed: "Father, what will happen to me?" This unexpected approach startled the Master a little, and then he went into samadhi. Thus some time passed. Rasik washed the Master's feet with his tears and so eased the pent-up pain of his heart. The Master returned to his normal state, touched Rasik's head, and said, "You have achieved everything."[1]

Kedarnath Bandyopadhyay of Dakshineswar wrote in his memoirs: "Rasik Hari of Dakshineswar Village belonged to the sweeper caste. I saw the Master talking to Rasik, standing in his courtyard, as if they were friends. Seeing Rasik a little tipsy, the Master said with a smile: 'I understand what happened. Don't drink too much.' Rasik fell at the Master's feet and said: 'Father, who will give me a little alcohol? I cannot afford to drink. Luckily, Natabar Panja's mother died, so I got some extra money for doing some cleaning. But whose mothers are going to die every day, Father? They will die after my death.'"[2]

Christopher Isherwood said, "A great guru is first and foremost a great disciple." Ramakrishna is an ideal example of this statement. He told his disciples: "As long as I live, so long do I learn." The Master learned continually; he never closed the door of his heart. He learned from sweepers, drunkards, and circus performers. That is why there is such a great variety in his teachings. The important role that Rasik played in Ramakrishna's life is not widely known.

While in meditation, Ramakrishna's mind once ran to Rasik's house. This may surprise the reader, but it actually happened. The Master described this incident, saying: "The Chitshakti, Mahamaya, has become the twenty-four cosmic principles. One day as I was meditating, my mind wandered away to Rashke's house. He is a scavenger. I said to my mind, 'Stay there, you rogue!' The Divine Mother revealed to me that the men and women in this house were mere masks; inside them was the same Divine Power, Kundalini, that rises up through the six spiritual centres of the body."[3]

Ramakrishna did not stop at visiting Rasik's house in his meditation; he actually went there in the dead hours of night and cleaned Rasik's privy. Ramakrishna was desperately trying to destroy the eight fetters that bind us: hatred, shame, lineage, pride of good conduct, fear, secretiveness, social status, and grief. The temple officials did not know about this secret sadhana of the Master. They would have made a commotion if they had heard about it, because Ramakrishna was an upper-class brahmin and the priest of the Kali temple. Swami Vivekananda mentioned this incident in his lecture "My Master":

> He set about to learn humility, because he had found that the common idea in all religions is "Not I, but Thou," and that the Lord fills the heart of him who says, "Not I." The less of this little "I," the more of God there is in him. This, he found, was taught by every religion in the world, and he set himself to realize it. Whenever he wanted to do anything he never confined himself to theories, but would enter into the practice immediately. Now, there was a family of pariahs living near the temple. The pariahs number several million in the whole of India, and are so low in society that some of our books say that if a brahmin, on coming out of his house, sees the face of a pariah, he has to fast that day and recite certain prayers before he becomes holy again. In the dead of night, when all were sleeping, my Master would enter the house of the pariahs and cleanse the dirty places there, saying, "O Mother, make me the servant of the pariah, make me feel that I am even lower than the pariah."[4]

This pariah was Rasik, a great devotee. Unknowingly he helped to fulfill the Master's sadhana of humility.

Ramakrishna swept the path of the temple garden and told the devotees that the Divine Mother walked there. A visitor once thought he was a gardener and asked the Master to pick flowers for him, which he did.

M. recorded a similar incident: A young disciple Latu used to live with the Master at Dakshineswar and serve him. Once a householder devotee presented Latu with a new pair of sandals. But because he was busy most of the time serving the Master, he had no time to wear them. One night a jackal carried one of them away. When the Master learned about this, he searched the garden. He finally found the sandal after an hour; he then returned it to his young disciple. Latu immediately exclaimed: "Sir, what have you done? I am supposed to serve you — not

Rasik fell at the feet of Ramakrishna near the Panchavati. (*painting*)

Tulsi grove (on pedestal) in Rasik's courtyard

the other way around!" Saying this, he took the sandal from the Master's hand. What affection the Master had for his devotees!

Ramakrishna's ego had died forever and his "I" was completely possessed by the Divine Mother. As a result, his will and Mother's will were one. He told his devotees: "You see, there is no show or deceit here. I just said to the Divine Mother in my ecstatic mood, 'O Mother, may those sincere seekers who come here [*referring to himself*] obtain perfection.'"[5] The simple-hearted Rasik recognized the Master's divinity by his grace. He was sincerely drawn to the Master and thus attained perfection.

Rasik's Passing Away

There are several death accounts of Rasik. Each one is a little different, but that is nothing to wonder at. When we read the Bible, we find the same stories of Jesus recorded differently by Matthew, Mark, Luke, and John.

M. told Rasik's story:

Rasik was a sweeper in the temple garden of Dakshineswar. The Master told us about him: One day Rasik asked him, "Master, what will happen to me?" The Master blessed him and said, "You will see me at the time of death."

Rasik built a tulsi grove in his courtyard where he would practise spiritual disciplines. Later he became ill, and at last one day at noon he asked his wife to call his sons and carry him to the tulsi grove. There, fully conscious, he gave up his body while chanting the Master's name.

Rasik was a great soul. He not only saw the Master over a long period of time, but he also recognized him as an Incarnation of God. Through the Master's grace he was prompted to ask that vital question, "What will happen to me?" Though Rasik was a sweeper, the Master gave him immortality. The Master himself told us that once he cleaned the open drain of Rasik's house with his own hair while praying with tears in his eyes, "Mother, destroy my pride of being a brahmin."[6]

Swami Shivananda said:

Anyone who takes shelter under the Master with all sincerity and with his whole being, anyone who loves the Master, will inevitably get liberation. Have you not heard the story of that sweeper named Rasik who lived at Dakshineswar? He used to call the Master "Father." One day the Master was returning from the direction of the Panchavati, absorbed in a spiritual mood. At that time, Rasik knelt down before him and prayed with folded hands: "Father, why don't you bless me? What will be in store for me?" The Master then assured him: "You need have no fear. You will have your wish fulfilled. You will see me at the time of death." And that's exactly what happened. A little while before his death, he was carried near the tulsi grove. And as the moment of death approached, Rasik cried out: "Here you are! You have come to me, Father! You have really come, Father!" And thus he breathed his last.[7]

Swami Sankarananda narrated:

Rasik was a great devotee. He had a tulsi grove at his house. As he belonged to the lowest caste, he would stay away from people. He would satisfy himself with seeing the Master from a distance. When the Master would go to the pine grove, Rasik would touch the Master's footprints with his forehead. Once the Master saw this and looked at him with compassion. Rasik asked: "Father, shall I not achieve anything in this life?" The Master replied: "Of course, you will achieve everything. So many devotees come here, and you serve them by cleaning this temple garden." After the Master's passing away, Rasik was grief-stricken. His health broke down also; he could not work anymore. Gradually he stopped coming to sweep the temple courtyard. His daughter started to sweep, taking the place of her father. Rasik was very sick. Before death, he asked his wife and others: "You all eat your lunch early today. Don't come near me until I call you." It was 10:00 a.m. All of a sudden, his face beamed with joy. He cried out: "Father, you have come! So you have not forgotten me."[8]

Kumudbandhu Sen recorded the following reminiscence of Ramlal, one of Ramakrishna's nephews:

Listen, Uncle was resting one afternoon in his room. He got up and then came to the veranda. Pointing to Rasik, the temple sweeper, he said to me, "Rasik is not an insignificant mortal but a denizen of heaven in human form." Another day the Master went to the pine grove and I carried the water pot and towel. Rasik was sweeping the Panchavati area. When the Master was returning to his room, Rasik prostrated at his feet. Smiling, the Master inquired about his welfare. Rasik got up and said that he could not avoid the accident of his lowly birth, which had condemned him to the despicable life of a sweeper. The Master quickly replied that he should not bemoan his social status, for he was after all born a human being, the highest of God's creation. The Supreme Spirit dwelt in him.

The Master reminded him that there was no employment so humble as to be incompatible with the highest spiritual aspiration. It was Rasik's good fortune to have been entrusted with the sacred task of sweeping the temple courtyard and temple steps, sanctified by the dust of the feet of thousands of devotees who came to worship at the shrines. With tearful eyes Rasik asked, "Father, shall I be saved?" With a gracious smile the Master asked him to raise a tulsi grove in a corner of his yard and chant the Lord's name there.

Two years after the demise of the Master, Brother Ramlal met Rasik's wife near the Panchavati. She was weeping inconsolably. Brother Ramlal asked her what had happened. How was Rasik? She replied that her husband was very ill. Her sons had called in a doctor but he refused to take any medicine. He insisted on being given *Charanamrita* (sanctified water). As Rasik was a devout Vaishnava, Brother Ramlal forthwith went to the Radhakanta temple, collected some sanctified water and some tulsi leaves, and gave them to Rasik's wife. Since Brother Ramlal did not see her again, he went to their hut a few days later. Rasik's wife and sons cried and said that he had passed away.

They narrated the last days of Rasik: The sanctified water of the Radhakanta temple seemed to have a stimulating effect on Rasik. He felt better. His fever abated and he spent his waking hours in chanting the Lord's name and fervent prayers. One day when they had returned home after their work at about midday, he insisted that they take their meal at once. After they had complied with his wish, he asked them to take him out to the tulsi grove. It was hot outside. They reluctantly obeyed his wish. He lay on a mat with his rosary in his hand and asked them to chant God's name. After half an hour his face brightened up. There was an ardent look in his eyes and a smile playing on his lips. He exclaimed: "Oh, Thou hast come at long last! How surpassingly beautiful and gloriously resplendent!" He then closed his eyes and it seemed to them that a halo played round his radiantly peaceful face as he fell into eternal sleep.[9]

Rasik was not a prominent actor in the divine drama of Ramakrishna. Although the audience did not see him onstage, he had the responsibility of keeping the stage — the temple garden of Dakshineswar — clean. He demonstrated in his life that work is worship and each person is great in his or her own place.

11

Ramakrishna and the Bohemians

According to the Bhagavad Gita, God incarnates as a human being in every age when religion declines and irreligion prevails. First, He reestablishes the eternal religion; second, He protects the good; and third, He destroys the evil. If Ramakrishna is an avatar, then he will have these characteristics.

Ramakrishna Reestablished Religion

The nineteenth century was a period of chaos in the religious history of India. So many religious movements evolved, dissolved, and passed into oblivion. India was then under the rule of the British, the French, and the Portuguese. Christian missionaries took this opportunity to convert Indians under the umbrella of the Christian rulers. Western scientists and philosophers vehemently attacked the traditional religious ideals of India and declared the supremacy of modern science. Some educated Indians espoused these ideals and accepted their premise: the goal of life is not God but sense enjoyment. Eat, drink, and be merry.

During this tumultuous period, Ramakrishna successfully reestablished India's eternal religion, using reasoning and experience. He practised Hinduism, and then Islam and Christianity. He realized the same Truth through every path and then declared: "As many faiths, so many paths." Thus Ramakrishna preached the harmony of religions in this modern age.

Ramakrishna Protected the Good

As an avatar, Ramakrishna protected good people from the trap of maya and also made bad people good. In truth, Ramakrishna protected everyone who sought refuge in him: good or bad, pious or sinful, rich or destitute, devout or drunkard. For this reason, some puritans and narrow-minded critics levelled charges against Ramakrishna, saying that he did not show sufficient moral abhorrence of prostitutes and immoral people. They also accused him of giving shelter to those who were intemperate in their habits. Max Müller, the famous German orientalist, gave a satisfactory explanation for Ramakrishna's tolerance in his book, *Ramakrishna: His Life and Sayings*: "If, as we are told, he did not show sufficient moral abhorrence of prostitutes, he does not stand quite alone in this among the founders of religion. If he did not 'honour the principle of teetotalism according to Western notions,' no one, as far as I know, has ever accused him of any excess in drinking."[1] Regarding the second accusation, Swami Vivekananda remarked: "Heaven save the mark! A formidable accusation, indeed! Why did not the Mahapurusha [Ramakrishna] kick away and drive off in disgust the drunkards, the prostitutes, the thieves, and all the sinners of the world?"[2] There is a saying: "A Church is not a museum for saints. It is a hospital for sinners."

Ramakrishna Destroyed the Evil

Some may say that although Rama killed Ravana and other demons, and Krishna killed Kamsa and others, Ramakrishna did not destroy anyone. That is true. We know from biographies of Ramakrishna that he never uttered a single harsh word to anyone, not to speak of punishing the wicked. His life was full of love and sublimity, and his body was extremely frail. He may not have destroyed any demon or vanquished any wicked person, but he had a wonderful ability to eradicate evil tendencies in others. The subtle is more powerful than the gross. It is easy to kill a man, but very difficult to kill his evil tendencies. Ramakrishna killed the greatest demon in this age: doubt. Through his divine life and spiritual experiences he removed all doubt from those who came to him. He realized God and imparted that realization to the Westernized disciples who challenged him.

Thus we find that all three characteristics of an avatar were present in Ramakrishna.

Ramakrishna and Girish Chandra Ghosh

It is really amazing how the sweet, soft-natured, fragile Ramakrishna tackled the bohemians. The famous actor and playwright Girish Chandra Ghosh was a rebel, drunkard, debauchee, atheist, and thorough bohemian. Girish introduced himself to Ramakrishna by saying, "I am a sinner."

Ramakrishna: "The wretch who constantly harps on sin becomes a sinner."

Girish: "Sir, the very ground where I used to sit would become unholy."

Ramakrishna: "How can you say that? Suppose a light is brought into a room that has been dark a thousand years. Does it illumine the room little by little, or all in a flash?"[3]

There were few sins in which Girish had not indulged. He once said: "I have drunk so much wine in my life that if the wine bottles were placed one upon another, they would stand as high as Mount Everest."[4]

"One night," said Girish, "in a euphoric and drunken mood, I was visiting a house of prostitution with two of my friends. But suddenly I felt an urge to visit Ramakrishna. My friends and I hired a carriage and drove out to Dakshineswar. It was late at night, and everyone was asleep. The three of us entered Ramakrishna's room, tipsy and reeling. Ramakrishna grasped both my hands and began to sing and dance in ecstasy. The thought flashed through my mind: 'Here is a man whose love embraces all — even a wicked man like me, whose own family would condemn me in this state. Surely this holy man, respected by the righteous, is also the saviour of the fallen.'"[5]

Girish surrendered and gave his power of attorney to Ramakrishna. He had "one hundred twenty-five percent faith" in the Master, and he knew the Master was an avatar and the saviour of the soul. Years later he would say, "Had I known that there was such a huge pit in which to throw one's sins, I would have committed many more."

Girish's transformation is now legendary. Ramakrishna told him: "Girish Ghosh, don't worry. People will be amazed at your transformation."[6]

Some people say that Ramakrishna developed cancer by absorbing the sins of Girish and others like him. Girish did not visit the Master very often at Cossipore because he could not bear to see the Master ill. One

Girish Chandra Ghosh
(1844-1912)

Kalipada Ghosh
(1849-1905)

day Girish went there after the Master had eaten some farina pudding. The unwashed cup with the remnant of the pudding, mixed with the discharge from the wound in his throat, was still on the floor, and some ants were eating it. Pointing to the cup, Ramakrishna said to Girish, "Look! And still people call me an avatar!" Girish immediately remarked: "Sir, now even those ants will get liberation. For what other reason should you have this disease?"[7]

Ramakrishna and Surendra Nath Mitra

Surendra Nath Mitra seemed to be a typical young man of his day — open-minded, carefree, and indifferent to religion. He was handsome and well built. As a commercial agent of the Dost Company, a large British firm in Calcutta, he had a well-paying job. He was married but had no children. Most of his friends were of the bohemian type, and like them, he often got drunk and was promiscuous. At the same time, however, he was frank, outspoken, large hearted, and extremely generous. When he was thirty years old, Surendra met Ramakrishna.

Although Surendra was quite affluent, his licentious conduct was ruining his mental peace. He even thought of killing himself. Ram Chandra Datta was a neighbour of Surendra's, and he knew about his anguish. Ram had been visiting Ramakrishna at Dakshineswar for some time. Wanting to help Surendra, Ram asked him many times to accompany him. But Surendra always refused. He said: "Look, it is very good that you respect him, but why should you take me there? I shall be a misfit there — like a crane among swans.* I have seen enough of that."[8] Ram was hurt by this sarcastic remark about his guru, but he did not give up. After much persuasion Surendra finally agreed: "All right, I shall go. But if that holy man of yours is a fake, I shall twist his ears."[9] Such was the attitude with which Surendra approached Ramakrishna.

Surendra's life gradually changed: He became a great devotee and a supplier of the Master's needs. He loved and served the Master wholeheartedly and later became the first patron of the Ramakrishna Monastery at Baranagore.

Ramakrishna and Kalipada Ghosh

Kalipada was one of those wayward souls who were saved by Ramakrishna. Like Girish, he was an out-and-out bohemian, a

---

*Surendra was making a pun on the word *hamsa*, which means either a swan or the soul. The word parama-hamsa, means a sannyasin of the highest order, or, sarcastically, a great swan.

debauchee, and a drunkard. Swami Adbhutananda related in his reminiscences how Ramakrishna transformed Kalipada's life:

Girish Babu arrived one night with Kalipada Ghosh. Kalipada was a terrible drunkard. He refused to give money to his family, spending it for wine instead. But his wife was very pure. I heard that many years earlier she had come to the Master, seeking some kind of medicine that would change her husband's tendencies. The Master sent her to Holy Mother. Holy Mother sent her back to the Master. He again sent her to Holy Mother, and this exchange went on three times. At last, Holy Mother wrote the Master's name on a bel leaf that had been offered to the Lord and gave it to Kalipada's wife, telling her to chant the Lord's name.

Kalipada's wife chanted the Lord's name for twelve years. When the Master first met Kalipada, he remarked, "This man has come here after tormenting his wife for twelve years." Kalipada was startled but said nothing.

Then the Master asked him, "What do you want?"

Kalipada asked shamelessly, "Can you give me a little wine?"

The Master smiled. "Yes, I can. But the wine I have is so intoxicating that you will not be able to bear it."

Kalipada took him literally and said: "Is it real British wine? Please give me a little to soak my throat."

"No, it is not British wine," said the Master, still smiling. "It is completely homemade. This wine cannot be given to just anyone, for not everyone can stand it. If a person tastes this wine even once, British wine will seem insipid to him ever after. Are you ready to drink my wine instead of the other?"

For a moment Kalipada was thoughtful, and then I heard him say, "Please give me that wine which will make me intoxicated my entire life." The Master touched him, and Kalipada started to weep. We tried to calm him, but he went on weeping in spite of our attempts.[10]

One day Ramakrishna asked Kalipada to open his mouth and stick out his tongue. Then the Master wrote a mantra on it with his finger. Thenceforth a curtain fell on the dark chapter of Kalipada's life. His whole personality changed, and people were amazed by his spiritual transformation. Later, he would cry as he chanted the name of Ramakrishna.

Ramakrishna and Manmatha

Swami Akhandananda, a monastic disciple of Ramakrishna, wrote the following story of Manmatha, who was hired to intimidate the Master.

Sri Ramakrishna often used to visit the devotees' houses in Calcutta. Once he went to Yogin-ma's house at Nebubagan, Baghbazar. Hiralal, Yogin-ma's brother, did not like his sister visiting the Master at Dakshineswar. We heard that when Yogin-ma invited the Master to her house, Hiralal hired Manmatha, a famous gymnast and wrestler of Gosainpara, to frighten him. Manmatha arrived and heard a few words of the Master. He immediately fell at the Master's feet and said with tears: "My Lord, I am guilty. Please forgive me."* The Master said: "All right. Come one day to Dakshineswar."

I had a close acquaintance with Manmatha. He requested me: "Please accompany me to Dakshineswar. The Master asked me to visit him." We then fixed a date and went by a carriage. We brought a jar of rasagollas [sweet juicy balls] from Navin Maira, a famous confectioner, for him.

It will not be irrelevant to say something about Manmatha. He was a great gymnast and he had such strength that he alone could face a hundred people. Every Saturday two groups of boys of Vidyasagar's School would compete to determine which was stronger. The Baghbazar group hired Manmatha. When the fight began between the Baghbazar group and Shyampukur group, the former ran away as the latter was stronger. Manmatha fought alone and then collapsed on the ground and the rival group hit him mercilessly with the poles of parallel bars. Pleased, the Shyampukur group said to Manmatha: "Bravo! You have defeated us by receiving such heavy blows. Perhaps no one else in Calcutta could have withstood such a beating."

There was an amateur theatre party in Baghbazar. In the drama *Sarat-Sarojini*, Manmatha acted in the role of a robber. When he would appear on the stage with a roar, dressed in a red silk cloth and a shaggy wig, the audience trembled with fear.

Manmatha also worked as a bodyguard for Priya Mitra, the only son of Kirti Mitra, a very wealthy man of Calcutta. Manmatha was a rank bohemian. He gave up his sacred thread and would eat forbidden food.

When I took Manmatha to the Master, he received him tenderly and talked to him. I said: "Sir, this fellow is a notorious ruffian and even the gangs of Calcutta are frightened of him. Sometimes he is hired by a gang. The Master poked his body with his finger and asked: "Hello, is it true? Oh, how hard your body is!"

The Master heard that Manmatha had given up the sacred thread, so he asked, "Why don't you wear the sacred thread?" Manmatha replied, "Sir, I feel uneasy, since it gets soaked with perspiration." The

*Another version: Manmatha was waiting near the entrance. The all-knowing Master knew Manmatha's intention. As he left, he touched Manmatha and said, "Hello!" and the latter fell at his feet.

Master asked him to wear it again. He then accompanied Manmatha to the Kali temple and blessed him there.

The next time we went to visit the Master, we went by boat and took rasagollas for him. This time the Master also gave some advice to Manmatha. Later, Manmatha did not speak openly to anyone about the grace he had received from the Master. Outwardly nobody could find any sign of his transformation.

Some years later when I was travelling in the Himalayas, Swami Shivananda told me the following about Manmatha's change: "Manmatha lives at his maternal uncle's house near the Siddheswari temple in Baghbazar. He is now a totally different man. His strong muscular body is now emaciated and his head is covered with bushy hair. He is completely indifferent to his body."

After some years of staying in Tibet, I returned to Baranagore Monastery in 1890. One afternoon Manmatha came. He was barefooted and wore only one piece of cloth. He was crying with folded hands, "Priyanath, Priyanath — O my beloved Lord!" Swami Vivekananda and other swamis were then at the monastery. We sang devotional songs and talked about the Master. Swamiji asked Manmatha to sit on our bed, but he sat on the floor. With folded hands he only repeated, "Priyanath, Priyanath," and nothing else. I took him to the shrine and gave him some prasad. He then left, repeating, "Priyanath, Priyanath."

After five years I went to see Manmatha and found that he was gazing towards the sun without blinking. He had no outward consciousness. He was wearing an ochre robe and had a sacred thread over his shoulder. His large body was emaciated owing to severe austerities. He was completely indifferent to the outside world. I was amazed observing Manmatha's transformation by the divine touch of Sri Ramakrishna. A few days later I heard that Manmatha had just died of cholera.[11]

Ramakrishna's Love and Acceptance

Ramakrishna's playmates in his divine play came from all levels of society. He welcomed saints and sinners, agnostics and atheists, devotees and jnanis, rich and poor, drunkards and prostitutes, critics and hypocrites, actors and singers, students and teachers, judges and lawyers, doctors and scholars, among others. His spiritual power, selfless love, liberal outlook, sweet and simple behaviour, purity and renunciation, and above all his magnetic personality attracted all sorts of people and they felt the Master to be their very own. Ramakrishna's life demonstrated how pure love, not force, can transform wayward souls.

12

The Mysterious Kalpataru

On 1 January 1886, in the garden of the Cossipore house where he lived his last days, Sri Ramakrishna became the Kalpataru, the wish-fulfilling tree. He blessed his devotees, saying, "Be illumined."

Now the Kalpataru Festival is celebrated every year in Cossipore. A large crowd assembles in the garden of the house where Ramakrishna had lived, rejoicing at the memory of this blessed event. People come from far and near to pray to Ramakrishna to fulfill their desires, for God is the Kalpataru.

Let us imagine ourselves in that garden during the festival. We see a large mango tree in the corner of the garden, and sitting under it an old man with a fair complexion is telling the story of the Kalpataru. With a sweet smile on his face, the storyteller begins his tale: "The mysterious Kalpataru is a celestial tree. No one has seen it, but everyone has heard about it. One gets whatever one wants from this wonderful tree, but the opportunity comes only once a year. People wait the whole year for this auspicious day.

"In the beginning of creation, a desire to become many arose in the Creator's mind. He played with desires in many ways and finally gave these restless desires to human beings. He Himself remained completely free from desire. He said to human beings: 'Now you may play with desires and enjoy yourselves. I have kept no desire for myself; I have given all of my desires to you. Although I am without desires, I rule over them. I am Kalpataru, the wish-fulfilling tree.'

Cossipore garden house. Ramakrishna became the Kalpataru (a wish-fulfilling tree) on 1 January 1886, near the curve of the mango tree.

"Desire is deceitful and enchanting. It has no beginning and no end. Human beings become old, but desire does not: It is eternally youthful. It loves to dance in people's minds, raising stormy waves. Drunk with desire, people constantly ask: Give us this; give us that. Give us youth and beauty. Give us money and property. Give us objects of enjoyment. Give us healthy bodies. Give us wonderful wives or handsome husbands. Give us nice children. Give us happiness.

"People go to temples with a list of desires. If you go to the Tarakeswar Shiva temple, you will see rocks tied with strings hanging around the railings of the temple. Those rocks are left to mark the prayers of the afflicted and the poor. You can hear people touching their heads to the marble floor of the temple. You hear the prayers mentioned in the Invocation to the Chandi: *Rupam dehi jayam dehi yasho dehi dwisho jahi* — O Mother, give me beauty, victory, and fame and destroy my enemy."

As he describes the mystery of desire, the storyteller glances at a pair of young girls. One of the girls, Kalpalata, says to her friend, Hemangini: "Let us leave. We have heard enough of that talk. We are ordinary human beings; moreover, human life is connected with desires. Our Ramakrishna said that God is the Kalpataru. One should ask Him for whatever one wants. He fulfills our desires. We must ask Him for what we want, not the people on the street. Let us go to the pandal and listen to the kirtan."

Hemangini responds: "Please wait a while. We have heard kirtan many times. Let us hear about the mysterious wish-fulfilling tree on this auspicious day."

The storyteller continues: "It is true, Ramakrishna said that God listens to our prayers and fulfills them a hundred times. But our prayers must be genuine and earnest. He also cautioned that one should be extremely careful when praying to the Kalpataru: Some prayers can be extremely dangerous. Listen to one of Ramakrishna's stories:

"Once a traveller came to a large plain. He had been walking in the sun for many hours, so he was thoroughly exhausted and perspiring heavily. He sat down in the shade of a tree to rest a little. He was not aware that he was sitting under the Kalpataru. He was extremely hungry and thirsty. When he thought about food and drink, instantly he found cold water and various kinds of delicious food before him. He at once began to eat and drink, enjoying himself immensely. He then began to think that it would be nice if he could have a soft bed to sleep on. No sooner had this thought appeared in his mind than he found a comfortable bed by his side. He was astonished, but he stretched out on it. He then thought to himself how pleasant it would be if a young woman could massage his aching body. Immediately a young woman appeared and gave him a massage. Excited by these amazing events, he pondered the events of the day. But then the thought occurred to him: 'What would happen if a tiger were to attack me now?' Then and there a tiger jumped upon him, broke his neck, and began to eat him. Thus the traveller lost his life.

"This is the play of the mysterious wish-fulfilling tree. Such is the fate of men in this world. If during meditation you pray for money, worldly things, or name and fame, your desires will be satisfied to some extent; but remember there is the dread of the tiger behind each gift you get. Those tigers — disease, bereavement, worry, loss of honour and wealth, and so on — are a thousand times more terrible than a live tiger."

A young man named Nikhil is listening to the storyteller absent-mindedly. He once read about the Kalpataru incident in a Bengali book. This thought arises in his mind: "On this auspicious day the Master blessed his devotees, saying: 'Be illumined.' As a result, some had ecstasy, samadhi, visions, awakening of the kundalini, and so on. I think I should ask the Kalpataru Ramakrishna for the bliss of Brahman."

The storyteller continues: "Ramakrishna was a magician of samadhi. Most of the time he was absorbed in samadhi; and if anyone wanted samadhi, he could transmit it with a touch or by writing a mantra on one's tongue. An ordinary aspirant can experience samadhi but cannot give it to others.

"Once Mathur asked the Master for bhava samadhi. The Master said: 'Why are you asking for samadhi? You are all right; you are enjoying both secular and spiritual joy. If you attain samadhi, your mind will be completely withdrawn from the world. Who will protect your wealth and property then? Everything you own will be looted indiscriminately. What will you do then?'

"But who would listen to this? Mathur was adamant: He insisted that the Father give him bhava samadhi. So the Master said: 'Very well, I'll ask Mother about it. She will do as She thinks best.' A few days later Mathur experienced bhava samadhi. The Master described what happened: 'Mathur sent for me. When I went to his place, I found him altogether changed. He wasn't the same man. While talking about God, he was shedding floods of tears. His eyes were red from weeping, and his heart was pounding. When he saw me, he fell down and clasped my feet. "Father," he said, "I admit it. I am beaten! I've been in this state for the past three days. Everything is going wrong. Please take back the ecstasy you gave me. I don't want it." "But you begged me for ecstasy," I said. He replied: "I know I did. And it is indeed a blissful state — but what is the use of bliss when all my worldly affairs are going to pieces? This ecstasy of yours, Father, suits only you. The rest of us don't really want it. Please take it back." Then I laughed and said, "That's what I told you all along." "I know you did, Father," replied Mathur. "But what I didn't understand was that this thing would possess me like a spirit, and that I'd have to take every step and do everything exactly as it told me to, twenty-four hours a day!" Then I rubbed Mathur's chest, and he was himself again."[1]

"Hriday also demanded samadhi from the Master, and then was in deep trouble. In ecstasy, he shouted frantically again and again: 'O Ramakrishna, O Ramakrishna, we are not human beings. Why are we here? Come, let us go from place to place and save human souls. You and I are the same.' The Master said later: 'Hearing his loud cry, I said: "Ah! Keep quiet, keep quiet. Why are you shouting like that? People will rush here thinking some calamity has happened." But he paid no heed to my words. Then I hurried to him and said, touching his chest, "Mother, make this rascal dull and stupid again.""[2]

"Another time, the Master wrote a mantra on the tongue of a devotee. Immediately the devotee went into ecstasy and began to chant, 'Mother, Mother.' The Master sent him back home with an escort. His wife was furious when she saw him, thinking to herself: 'What is this? He is drunk! Where did he go? He does not talk. He does not eat. Did someone put a spell on him? What will happen to me? How shall I take care of the children?'

"She heard that the Paramahamsa of Dakshineswar had done this to her husband. Immediately she took a companion and rushed to Dakshineswar. She inquired, 'Where is the Paramahamsa?' and reached the Master. She burst into tears and exclaimed: 'What did you do to my husband? How shall I handle my household and my children?' The Master was embarrassed. He said: 'Please bring your husband back to me.' She went home and then escorted her husband to Dakshineswar. 'It seems to be a heavy dose,' said the Master. 'Please stick out your tongue again.' Then the Master wrote something on his tongue and he became normal again.

"Who is capable of withstanding samadhi? On the Kalpataru day the Master touched a devotee whose body then became twisted; he fell down unconscious. Does anyone aspire for samadhi after listening to these stories?"

The young man, Nikhil, understands.

After a while, a Tantric aspirant named Swami Bhairavananda comes and sits under the mango tree. He is dressed in red. He has bushy hair and a black-and-gray beard and moustache. His eyes are reddish from smoking hemp. He lives in the Cossipore cremation ground and repeats his mantra at midnight. As he listens to the storyteller, he thinks to himself: "If I could have one of the eight occult powers, I would be famous. People would recognize me as a great soul."

The storyteller continues: "Our scriptures say: 'Shun ego like alcohol, fame like hell, power like pig's filth. Renounce these three and be happy.' Ramakrishna looked down upon occult powers and cautioned spiritual seekers that they were great obstacles to yoga. He compared occult powers to filth and said that they were not worth more than a penny.

"Perhaps you remember that Ramakrishna's tantric guru was the Bhairavi Brahmani. She had a disciple named Chandra who had achieved an occult power called *gutika-siddhi*. After sanctifying a *gutika* [a tiny ball] with a mantra and fastening it onto his arm, he could make himself invisible and thus gain access to even closely guarded places. If a person achieves occult powers before realizing God, he or she becomes egotistic. This enhancement of the ego traps the aspirant in a net of desires, preventing any further movement towards a higher spiritual ideal. It finally becomes the cause of his or her downfall.

"As time went on, Chandra became infatuated with the daughter of a rich man. He began to use his occult power to visit her secretly. However, he was eventually caught and humiliated, and he lost all his power.

"Ramakrishna taught us a wonderful prayer: 'Mother, I don't want any physical enjoyment. Mother, I don't want name and fame. Mother, I don't want the eight occult powers. Mother, I don't want the other hundred powers. Mother, give me pure, unchanging, selfless devotion to you. Mother, may I never be deluded by your bewitching maya.'"[3]

Bhairavananda listens to this very attentively, stroking his beard.

Mrinmay, a young man from Baranagore who recently earned his B.A. degree, has come to Cossipore to pray to Ramakrishna for a job. However, the garden house is overcrowded and the long line to enter the shrine reaches the main road. He decides to get out of the hot sun and sit a while under the mango tree. As he listens to the storyteller's talk, he remembers that Swami Saradananda had discussed the science of alchemy in his *Sri Ramakrishna Lilaprasanga* (*Sri Ramakrishna and His Divine Play*). Suddenly, the desire to make gold from baser metals arises in his mind.

The storyteller continues: "People come to the Kalpataru and pray for money, and for gold and silver. Those who have read the *Lilaprasanga* are aware that Ramakrishna's guru Tota Puri had the knowledge of alchemy. He told the Master that by means of that knowledge he had converted copper and other metals into gold on many occasions. He said that the senior paramahamsas of his community possessed this knowledge and that he had received it from his guru, and he explained their tradition: 'It is strictly forbidden to use this power for self-interest or enjoyment of luxury; the penalty for doing so is incurring the curse of one's guru. There are many monks in the community, and sometimes the head of the community has to travel with them from one place of pilgrimage to another. He also has to arrange for their food and other necessities. It is the command of the guru: "If there is any shortage of money at such a time, it is permissible for the head monk to use the knowledge of alchemy in order to serve the monks."'[4]

"We don't know if Tota taught alchemy to Ramakrishna, but the Master said to his nephew, 'Ramlal, if I believed that the world were real, I would cover Kamarpukur with gold.'[5]

"A greedy man thinks that if he could learn that knowledge from Ramakrishna, he could be rich overnight and would no longer struggle with poverty.

"This reminds me of a Greek story. There was a man named Midas who was extremely greedy. He believed that gold is the source of happiness. He always searched for gold, hoarded gold, and dreamt of gold. His mind was so absorbed with gold that the god of wealth appeared before him and offered him a boon. Midas prayed: 'Lord, please give me the boon that whatever I touch will turn to gold.' 'So be it,' said the god, and disappeared.

"The next morning Midas got up and went to the bathroom to brush his teeth. As soon as he touched his toothbrush, it turned into gold. He could not brush his teeth. Midas was excited. He walked about in his room and began to touch everything, turning it all into gold.

"He went to eat his breakfast. As he touched his grapes, toast, eggs, and coffee they all became gold. Now he became a little irritated: He was hungry but could not eat. He then went to his flower garden and touched his beautiful roses, and they all turned into gold, losing their beauty and fragrance. Soon after, his little daughter ran to him; forgetting everything, he affectionately took her in his arms. The girl immediately became lifeless gold. 'Enough!' Midas cried out and fell to the ground. He said: 'Lord, please take back your boon.'"

Mrinmay, the young man from Baranagore, now gets up and stands in line so that he can bow down to the Master in the shrine.

The storyteller continues: "God and His wealth: Those who want wealth, get it but don't get God. Those who seek God attain Him, and He supplies what they need. Krishna said in the Gita: 'Those who worship Me, meditating on their identity with Me and ever devoted to Me — to them I carry what they lack and for them I preserve what they already have.'

"Ramakrishna always emphasized that one should know God first and learn everything else afterwards. Jesus said something similar: 'First seek the kingdom of heaven and everything shall be added unto you.' Some people think that they must read books before they can know about God. In this respect, Ramakrishna said: 'If I want to know Jadu Mallick, must I first know the number of his houses and the amount of money he has in government securities? Do I really need all this information? Rather, I should somehow enter his house, be it by flattering his gatekeepers or by disregarding their rough treatment, and talk to Jadu Mallick himself. Then, if I want to know about his wealth or possessions, I shall only have to ask him about them. Then it will be a very easy matter for me. First comes Rama, then His riches, that is, the universe. This is why Valmiki repeated the mantra, "mara." *Ma* means God, and *ra* the world, that is to say, His riches.'"[6]

Gradually dusk falls over the Cossipore garden. The storyteller ends his talk by reciting a Hindi couplet for the audience: "O desire, you are like a low-caste cobbler. I was the Supreme Brahman, but your touch made me mean and miserable, a beggar."

An itinerant monk has been listening to the storyteller's talk. He has a dilemma: He is trying to decide what he should ask for from the Kalpataru. Searching for peace, he has travelled to the Himalayas, to caves and forests, to holy places, ashramas, and monasteries. Once he said to an old monk: "Swami, I left home, abandoned my family and friends, and renounced all my possessions; still I have not achieved anything tangible. Even now I feel restless." The old monk replied: "My son, you have come under the wish-fulfilling tree. Many fruits are hanging on that tree. One day some will definitely fall; you will get them if you stay under the tree. But if you want those fruits right now, please shake the tree — shake the tree." By this the itinerant monk understood that possessing the fruit, or liberation, is possible only through intense effort.

The evening lights go on and one can hear the vesper music throughout the garden. Standing under the mango tree, the itinerant monk is thinking about something the Master once said: "You have come to the garden to enjoy mangos. What need have you to calculate about the afterlife and what happens then, and things like that? Eat your mangoes. You need devotion to God. But you must remember this, that God is the Kalpataru.

Come, let us go for a walk, O mind, to Kali, the wish-fulfilling tree,
And there beneath It gather the four fruits of life.

"You must go to the Kalpataru and pray. Only then will you obtain the fruits. Only then will the fruits fall from the tree. Only then will you be able to gather them. These are the four fruits: dharma, artha, kama, and moksha."*[7]

Many years have passed since that New Year's Day so long ago, yet Ramakrishna, the wish-fulfilling tree, still waits to distribute to his devotees the immortal fruit of liberation.

---

*Dharma – righteous conduct; artha – wealth; kama – legitimate desires; moksha – liberation.

13

The Gospel of Sri Ramakrishna

Tava kathāmritam tapta jivanam kavibhir-iditam kalmasāpaham;
Shravana-mangalam shrimad-ātatam bhuvi grnanti ye bhuridā janāh.
— Bhagavata 10:31:9

O Lord, your nectar-like words stop the burning misery of afflicted souls; your words, which the poets have sung in verse, vanquish the sins of worldly people forever. Blessed are they who hear about your vast glory. Blessed indeed are they who speak of you, and how unparalleled is their bounty!"

The above-quoted invocation is taken from the *Gopi-Gita* of the *Bhagavata*. Krishna promised to meet the gopis, the milkmaids of Vrindaban, on a full-moon night in autumn. The gopis came to meet Krishna on the bank of the Yamuna River, and he played affectionately with them. But he sensed that they had become proud and egotistic due to this rare privilege. So he disappeared from them. Grief-stricken, the gopis wept and prayed to him to return. The above verse is from that prayer. M., the recorder of *The Gospel of Sri Ramakrishna*, used this verse on the title page of each of the five volumes of his original Bengali *Gospel.*

Tava kathāmritam: "Your words, O Lord, are like nectar." We speak sweet words. We sometimes say, "Oh, your words are so sweet!" But having no nectar ourselves, we do not know how to speak nectar-like words. The Divine Incarnations have this nectar within and so their words are full of sweetness.

Amrita means "nectar" or "immortality." According to Hindu mythology, the gods and the demons churned the ocean in order to obtain nectar. After a hard struggle, they extracted a jar of it. But the gods deceived the demons and drank it all, becoming immortal. This immortality, however, was relative: Absolute immortality comes only from the knowledge of Brahman. That nectar is within all beings. Jesus said, "The Kingdom of Heaven is within you." Dive deep inside. Then you will find that nectar and attain immortality.

God is the ocean of *amrita*, nectar. Once Ramakrishna asked Swami Vivekananda: "Suppose there were a cup of syrup and you were a fly. Where would you sit to drink the syrup?"

Vivekananda replied: "I would sit on the edge of the cup and stretch out my neck to drink it."

"Why?" Ramakrishna asked. "What's the harm in plunging into the middle of the cup and drinking the syrup?"

Vivekananda answered: "Then I should stick in the syrup and die."

"My child," Ramakrishna said to him, "that isn't the nature of the Nectar of Satchidananda. It is the Nectar of Immortality. Man does not die from diving into it. On the contrary, he becomes immortal."[1]

We say that human beings are mortal, but this is not true. The body is mortal. The Atman, our real nature, is immortal. It is this immortality that mankind is always searching for. The Brihadaranyaka Upanishad says that when Yajnavalkya offered wealth to his beloved wife, Maitreyi, she replied: "*Yenāham nāmritasyām, kimaham tena kuryām* — What should I do with that wealth which would not make me immortal?"[2] This is the bold message of Vedanta to modern people. If you want immortality, give up whatever you have. Christ also said the same thing: "Sell what you have and then follow me. Ye cannot serve God and mammon."

The Bengali title of *The Gospel of Sri Ramakrishna* is *Sri Sri Ramakrishna Kathamrita*, which means "Sri Ramakrishna's immortal (or nectar-like) talks." We hear the *Gospel*; we read the *Gospel*; we speak about the *Gospel*; but we do not "drink" the *Gospel*. It does not matter if we drink a drop, a glass, a jar, or a barrel of amrita. We will be immortal. It is not a matter of quantity, but of the substance itself. If we could actually absorb the *Gospel*, all our worldly desires would quickly dissipate. But it is not easy. We like to hold onto our desires: That is our problem.

Sri Ramakrishna tells this beautiful parable:

Once a fishwife was a guest in the house of a gardener who raised flowers. She came there with her empty fish-basket after selling fish in the market, and was given a place to sleep in a room where flowers were kept. But, because of the fragrance of the flowers, she couldn't get to sleep for a long time. Her hostess saw her condition and said, "Hello! Why are you tossing from side to side so restlessly?" The fish-wife said: "I don't know, friend. Perhaps the smell of the flowers is disturbing my sleep. Can you give me my fish-basket? Perhaps that will put me to sleep." The basket was brought to her. She sprinkled water on it and set it near her nose. Then she fell sound asleep and snored all night.[3]

Worldly people like the smell of fish. They cannot stand a beautiful divine fragrance. Mere speaking, mere talking, mere hearing won't help us. We may repeat the word "wine" a thousand times but that will not make us intoxicated. We must drink the wine. Christ said, "Whosoever heareth these sayings of mine and doeth them, I will liken him unto a wise man, who built his house upon a rock."

Tapta-jivanam: "Your words stop the burning sensation of worldly life." The world is burning with misery. When we talk about life we heave a deep sigh. I remember that when I was a young student of Vedanta I heard a vivid description of this world. Our teacher was expounding the concept of maya. He said: "Do you know what this world is? A traveller was passing through a desert. The sun was scorching hot. He was dead tired, thirsty, hungry, and exhausted. He was trying to find shelter, a shady place where he could take a little rest. At last he found a place where he laid down his head and slept, not knowing that the spot was made shady by the shadow of a poisonous cobra's hood! A single hiss and one drop of poison from that cobra would finish his life. So is this world." We do not know how the mysterious maya traps, binds, and enslaves us.

Human life is tormented by desire, doubt, disease, death, passion, jealousy, hatred, and so many other things. This is the real hellfire. The word of the Lord alone rescues us from that awful situation. The gospel of the Lord carries solace and succour for suffering humanity. It soothes our nerves and brings peace and joy to our minds. Just as water extinguishes fire, the words of the Lord extinguish the burning misery caused by worldly desires and our enjoyment of them.

Kavibhir-iditam: "Poets eulogize the words of the Lord in many ways." A renaissance begins at the advent of each avatar. Many books and dramas are written, songs and music are composed, and art and sculpture are developed. Ramakrishna spoke but a few words. Swami Vivekananda expounded his message of the harmony of religions and the divinity of human beings, spreading it throughout the world. M. recorded the Master's immortal gospel. Girish Chandra Ghosh, the actor-dramatist, wrote several dramas that incorporated the ideas of Ramakrishna. Many poets composed songs based on the teachings of the Master. But Ramakrishna himself had no formal education: His knowledge came straight from God. He said one day, "If you want to understand in one sentence, come to me. If you want to understand the same thing with a thousand words, go to Keshab."[4] Keshab Chandra Sen, the Brahmo Samaj leader, was a famous orator. It was he who first wrote about Ramakrishna in his Brahmo papers and magazines. When the Master came to know about it, he said, "Keshab, by writing about me, you want to make me famous? Don't try. Whom Mother makes famous, becomes famous."

Kalmasāpaham: The words of God "destroy all kinds of sins and their results." God's name purifies bodies and minds. Try to visualize the world as a room freshly painted black. You are there, dressed in white clothes. You may be extremely cautious but you cannot be alert all the time. In one moment of forgetfulness, you will stain your clothes with black spots. So it happens in this world: Desire, doubt, pride, anger, jealousy, greed, and lust are continually polluting our minds. Human beings stumble and fall, overcome by temptation. But they should not yield. They must fight. The Atman manifests in a human being through three powers: The power of wisdom, the power of will, and the power of action. Life is a struggle. Only two groups of people do not struggle: The illumined and the dead. *The Gospel of Sri Ramakrishna* has the power to develop a strong discriminative faculty and protect the mind from weakness and temptation.

Shravana-mangalam: Anybody who hears the words of God will undoubtedly be benefited. If one eats a chili, knowingly or unknowingly, one's tongue will burn. One can't help it. Similarly, these words of the Lord positively, definitely do good to people. One may think that just hearing the *Gospel* will not give one the flavour of it, but it will.

Shrimad: Beautiful. The words of the Lord are beautiful; they are truly fascinating and overwhelming. *The Gospel of Sri Ramakrishna* irresistibly draws us to God.

Ātatam: "Vast and easily available." As we do not need to search for space and air because they engulf us, so the words of God are easily accessible. Those who are spiritual aspirants get divine inebriation from the *Gospel*. It comes gradually and slowly, as the *Gospel* reveals its truths according to the aspirant's spiritual development and understanding.

The Gospel has an intoxicating effect on the mind. We may read it a thousand times, yet it remains an endless source of inspiration. There is no end to spiritual experience, and *The Gospel of Sri Ramakrishna* is a unique record of the highest immeasurable realizations. Once a disciple of the Holy Mother said that he had read *The Gospel of Sri Ramakrishna* fifty times and still he was finding new light in it. The message of God is endless. An American student read the *Gospel* and remarked: "There is one defect in this book: it has an end."

Bhuvi Grnanti Ye Bhuridā Janāh: You may perform charity in various forms but the best of them is to distribute the word of God to humanity. This final Sanskrit phrase has another meaning: Those who are spiritual seekers, those who have done spiritual practices in previous lives and also in this very life, get bliss, which is the taste of that spirituality.

Christopher Isherwood wrote about *The Gospel of Sri Ramakrishna*: "It is a fascinating piece of biography, quite extraordinarily honest. And as for its being long, the truth about anyone is never dull. Try it. I don't think you will be disappointed."[5]

Hundreds of people came to Ramakrishna with their questions and problems. Some came out of curiosity. Scholars came, and so did scientists, doctors, lawyers, teachers, professors, and students. Some spiritual leaders and social reformers visited him, and so did actors, actresses, dramatists, singers, and dancers. Some hypocrites, drunkards, ruffians, and villains came to him. *The Gospel of Sri Ramakrishna* is the first-hand account of the conversations of these various characters with Ramakrishna. Each person can find his or her own personality reflected in a character in the *Gospel*.

Sitting on a wooden cot at Dakshineswar, Ramakrishna would solve the problems of those who came to him because his own life was free from problems. Only he whose life is free from problems can solve other's problems. Ramakrishna would also boost the spirits of his visitors. As he himself said: "One man makes fire and others enjoy the heat. I have cooked food for you; you need only come and eat it."

On another occasion he said: "I am the destroyer of karma. I am the French colony."[6] At that time India was divided among three colonial powers: British, French and Portuguese. If a man did something wrong in British India, he could take shelter in the French colony where the British had no jurisdiction. "I am the French colony" means that whatever sinful actions one does, one need only take shelter in Ramakrishna to be free from fear and punishment. No worldly rules can bind such a person. Only a saviour has the power to save and eradicate people's past karma.

The subject of *The Gospel of Sri Ramakrishna* is God and *God alone*. It is concerned with how to realize Him and nothing else. Ramakrishna's simple and unostentatious utterance was, "I know only God and nothing else." In the beginning, in the middle, and in the end of the *Gospel*, you will find only one thing: God.

Ordinary people preach religion, but Divine Incarnations like Buddha, Christ, Krishna, and Ramakrishna can *give* religion. Religion means realization. A single touch, a single glance or a word from one of the Incarnations can bring a revolution in human life and transform human character. Ramakrishna was a tremendous spiritual force who could awaken others' God-consciousness in an instant. He was a spiritual phenomenon! In the *Gospel* we find him in samadhi at one moment; the next moment he is making fun and cutting jokes. He was that prince who could travel through all seven stories of the royal palace (the seven levels of consciousness) without obstruction. Ordinary people live on the first floor and do not even know what is on the other six floors. Even Ramakrishna's jokes and frivolities and fun were connected with God. Christopher Wood wrote: "Another side of Ramakrishna which seems to me important is that he had a sense of fun and that he was joyous. It is a tragic mistake that the popular idea of a good person is so often that of someone rather dull and somber, someone who rarely laughs. Whereas in actual fact it seems that the joy, the sheer pleasure even, of approaching God surpasses anything we know."[7] In the *Gospel*, M. indicated in many places: "All laugh," or "Laughter."

Ramakrishna never turned anyone away. He said, "Let me be condemned to be born over and over again, even in the form of a dog, if by doing so I can be of help to a single soul. I will give up twenty thousand such bodies to help one man."[8]

Mahendra Nath Gupta, or M.

M., the recorder of *The Gospel of Sri Ramakrishna*, was the headmaster of a school in Calcutta. Christopher Isherwood writes: "M. would have been overwhelmed, no doubt, if he could have known that Aldous Huxley would one day compare him to Boswell and call his *Gospel* 'unique in the literature of hagiography.'"[9] M. had a terrible family problem. He at one time planned to commit suicide. He came to his sister's home near Dakshineswar and his nephew brought him to the Dakshineswar temple garden where Ramakrishna lived. The man who intended to commit suicide was brought by Providence to Dakshineswar, where he met the Divine Incarnation for this age. As far as we know the man who accompanied M. to Dakshineswar never visited Ramakrishna again.

M. had kept a diary since he was in his early teens. He had an amazing photographic memory, artistic skill, and, above all, poetic imagination. He boldly proclaimed: "My record [*The Gospel of Sri Ramakrishna*] is not a collection from other sources. I recorded whatever I heard with my own ears from the lips of the Master and whatever I saw of his life with my own eyes."[10] In the beginning of each volume of the Bengali edition, he wrote that there were three ways one could collect materials about Ramakrishna: the first being direct observation recorded on the same day; the second, direct observation but unrecorded during the lifetime of the Master; and the third, hearsay and unrecorded at the time of the Master. Since M. recorded what he heard the very same day that he heard it, the *Gospel* belongs to the first category.

You can challenge the historicity of Christ, Buddha, or Krishna, but you cannot challenge the historicity of Ramakrishna. M. meticulously documented his conversations with Ramakrishna, the date and time, the place, and the people who were present.

Did Ramakrishna say anything new? Not really. He reinterpreted the same ancient Truth. He said, "The money which was in vogue at the time of a Nawab [a Muslim king] was outdated with the rule of a Badshah [Muslim emperor]." The coin changes according to the rule of different dynasties. The ancient avatars preached the message that was needed for the particular age and situation in which they appeared. Now the new avatar has come and preached according to the need of our age. One hundred years ago people did not know much about modern medicine; they treated their diseases with herbs and natural medicines. Now we use antibiotics. Herbs and antibiotics are both medicines but their use changes with the times. Krishna said in the Gita, "Arjuna, I am speaking to you the same Truth again."[11] Tautology is a weakness in logic, but it is not a weak point in scripture. The scriptures never tire of declaring the same truth again and again in different languages in different ages.

M. was asked to remove the repetitions from the *Gospel*, but he could not do that. To M. each word of Ramakrishna was just like a precious diamond.

The Gospel of Sri Ramakrishna came directly from M.'s diary. He said: "Sometimes I meditated on one scene over a thousand times. Sometimes I had to wait for a word of the Master like a Chataka bird." The Chataka bird drinks only rainwater. It waits for that alone, no matter how thirsty it is. In the *Gospel* we find that M. not only recorded the teachings and conversations of Ramakrishna, but also graphically described beautiful scenes in order to make a deep impression on the reader's mind. I shall include an example of a description from the *Gospel*, 22 July 1883: "Sri Ramakrishna had enjoyed a little rest after his midday meal. The room had an atmosphere of purity and holiness. On the walls hung pictures of gods and goddesses, among them one of Christ rescuing the drowning Peter. Outside the room were plants laden with fragrant flowers and the Ganges could be seen flowing towards the south. It was the rainy season; the exuberant Ganges was hurrying to meet the ocean and was happy to touch and to see the holy ground of the great saint of Dakshineswar."[12]

M. was attempting to depict the attitude of the spiritual seekers who were coming to meet Ramakrishna, as being that of rivers merging into the infinite ocean of Satchidananda.

Ramakrishna's Teachings in the Gospel

It is hard to acquire the qualifications for the study of Vedanta. A Vedanta student should practise discrimination, renunciation, and control of the senses, and he or she should have a burning desire for liberation. But if you want to read *The Gospel of Sri Ramakrishna*, no qualification is necessary; no commentator is necessary; no teacher is necessary; because it is simple. Simplicity was Ramakrishna's style and his sentences are seldom compound or complex. And simplicity is holy. Aldous Huxley wrote in the Foreword to Swami Nikhilananda's translation of the *Gospel*: "What a scholastic philosopher would call the 'accidents' of Ramakrishna's life were intensely Hindu and therefore, so far as we in the West are concerned, unfamiliar and hard to understand: its 'essence,' however, was intensely mystical and therefore universal."[13]

Though the background and plots of Ramakrishna's stories and parables are Indian in origin, they are so vivid and simple, so enchanting, that even a child can understand them. A man once came to him and asked, "Sir, how can I realize God?" Ramakrishna answered: "You may see God if your love for Him is as strong as these three attachments put together, namely, the attachment of a worldly man to the things of the world, the attachment of a mother to her child, and the attachment of a chaste and devoted wife to her husband."[14]

Gospel means "godspell" or "good story." Ramakrishna's stories and parables are very positive, instructive, and constructive. He always inspired people. His parable of the woodcutter is typical of this. A holy man told a poor woodcutter, "Go forward." The woodcutter took his advice, advanced further into the forest, and found a sandalwood forest!

He sold the sandalwood and became very rich. Then one day he thought to himself: That holy man told me to go forward. He did not ask me to be satisfied. So he went further into the forest again and found a copper mine. Going further still, he found a silver mine and then a gold mine. Finally, he found a diamond mine with which he became exceedingly wealthy. Ramakrishna said that there was no end to spiritual bliss, spiritual illumination.

Ramakrisha's teachings are very simple: "To meditate, you should withdraw within yourself or retire to a secluded corner or to the forest."

"Sir, I cannot go to the forest."

"All right. Meditate in the corner of a room." "Sir, my house is full of people. I cannot get a corner of a room."

"Meditate in the inner chamber of your heart."

There are many alternatives. If you cannot do anything, surrender to the Lord and He will do everything for you. "Give me the power of attorney," said Ramakrishna. Only an avatar like Ramakrishna can speak that way. Ramakrishna gave the example of a mother cat carrying her kitten wherever she wants. The kitten completely surrenders to its mother.

A very simple and beautiful example that Ramakrishna used concerns three men who were curious to know what was on the other side of a high wall. The first man climbed up a ladder and found Infinite Bliss on the other side. He jumped into it. The second man did the same thing. The third man also climbed up and saw it, but he came back down to tell others of that Infinite Bliss behind the wall, behind maya. The third man is Ramakrishna. In the evening when the sound of the vesper bells reverberated through the Dakshineswar temple compound, Ramakrishna would climb up onto the roof of the kuthi [mansion] and call out for his future devotees: "Come to me, my boys!" Where are you? I can't bear to live without you!"

On his second visit to Ramakrishna, M. asked four vital questions on behalf of humanity. The first question was: "Sir, how may we fix our minds on God?"

Ramakrishna answered: "Repeat God's name and sing His glories, and keep holy company. When a tree is young it should be fenced all around; otherwise it may be destroyed by cattle."

The second question was: "How ought we to live in the world?"

Ramakrishna said: "Do all your duties, but keep your mind on God. Live with all — wife and children, father and mother — and serve them. Treat them as if they were very dear to you, but know in your heart of hearts that they do not belong to you."

In this connection, Ramakrishna gave several examples:

"A maidservant in the house of a rich man performs all the household duties, but her thoughts are fixed on her own home in her native village.

"The tortoise moves about in the water. But can you guess where her thoughts are? They are on the bank, where her eggs are lying.

"First rub your hands with oil and then break open the jackfruit; otherwise they will be smeared with its sticky milk. First secure the oil of divine love, and then set your hands to the duties of the world."

The third question was: "Is it possible to see God?"

The answer came: "Yes, certainly. Living in solitude now and then, repeating God's name and singing His glories, and discriminating between the Real and the unreal — these are the means to employ to see Him."

The fourth question was, "Under what conditions does one see God?"

Ramakrishna answered: "Cry to the Lord with an intensely yearning heart and you will certainly see Him. People shed a whole jug of tears for wife and children. They swim in tears for money. But who weeps for God? Cry to Him with a real cry. Longing is like the rosy dawn. After the dawn, out comes the sun. Longing is followed by the vision of God."[15]

The Gospel of Sri Ramakrishna is a big volume. But whatever the price may be, no price can be put on the value of those words. Ramakrishna had a householder disciple, an *ishwarakoti* (godlike soul) whose name was Purna Chandra Ghosh. Long after Ramakrishna passed away, there was trouble in Purna's family and he wanted to commit suicide. He decided first to take his bath, and then go to the shrine to salute his guru before killing himself. He took his bath, then went to the shrine and saluted the Master. But he then thought: "Let me read a little bit of *The Gospel of Sri Ramakrishna*. Taking the beautiful message of the Master, I shall depart from this world." At random he opened the book and his eyes fell on this sentence: "*Purna balak bhakta. Thakur Purner mangal chinta karitechen.*" (Purna is a young devotee. The Master was thinking of his welfare.) "What?" cried Purna to himself: "The Master is thinking of me and I shall commit suicide? Impossible! He is thinking of my welfare and I am contemplating killing myself. It cannot be."[16] He gave up the idea and thus his life was saved. Such is the power of the words of *The Gospel of Sri Ramakrishna*!

14

The Centenary of
The Gospel of Sri Ramakrishna

The *Gospel of Sri Ramakrishna* was born on 26 February 1882 in the pages of Mahendra Nath Gupta's diary. During the centenary celebration of this immortal literature, innumerable people worldwide expressed their love and gratitude to Mahendra, who used the penname "M."

M. never realized that his personal diary would occupy such an exalted position in the religious literature of the world. When he was a college professor, he would hide himself on the roof and read his diary, so that no one would learn about it. When the Master's devotees wanted to hear what he had recorded, he gave them an evasive answer: "It is nothing. I just wrote something for myself." There is a saying: "The more it is hidden, the more it becomes firm; and the more it is expressed, the more it becomes despicable."

This universe is beautiful because its Creator has hidden Himself within it. God never comes forward to tell people, "Look, I am the Creator of this universe." M. tried to hide himself in the pages of the *Gospel* by assuming different names, such as Master (schoolteacher), Mani, Mohinimohan, a devotee, a servant, an Englishman (an English-educated man), and other pseudonyms. Later, many people became curious about the various characters who appeared in the *Gospel*, and they went to M. Someone asked M. about Hazra. M. replied: "One day Hazra was on the southeast veranda repeating japa on his rosary. The

Master returned from the Kali temple, snatched the rosary from Hazra's hand, and threw it away. He said to Hazra: "Why do you tell your beads here [*meaning while living with him*]? Many people in Calcutta are repeating the mantra with a rosary — some for twenty years and some twenty-five — but what are they achieving? Without longing one cannot achieve anything. Seeing this place [*meaning himself*] one can have awakening of consciousness."

A devotee: "What happened to Hazra at last?"

M.: "Hazra died while repeating the name of the Master."

A devotee: "In the *Gospel* there was a gentleman named 'Mani.' What happened to him?"

M.: "I don't know what will happen to him."[1]

All laughed, because the inquirer did not know that M. and Mani were the same person.

M. used to sit on the doormat in Ramakrishna's room. What humility, faith, and love he had for the Master! One day the Master said to M.: "You don't want anything from me, but you love to see me and hear my words. My mind also dwells on you. I wonder how you are and why you don't come."[2] On another occasion the Master asked for M.'s address. It makes us feel good to learn how much an avatar thinks of his devotees. We find in the Bhagavata that Krishna sent Uddhava to get news of his devotees in Vrindaban and to console them. In the *Gospel* we find many examples of how Ramakrishna expressed concern for his devotees. This proves that God also thinks of us.

M. was humble, serious and a hidden yogi. He played many roles in the divine drama of Ramakrishna: recorder of the *Gospel*, messenger, close companion, attendant, "kidnapping master,"* and so on.

There are two things that make Ramakrishna unique as an incarnation: his photographs and his gospel. We have to imagine how other incarnations of God looked, but for Ramakrishna we have three photographs that were taken during his lifetime. Moreover, they were taken when he was in samadhi. These pictures help his devotees in their meditation. Not only do we have these pictures, but we can also learn more about Ramakrishna by reading the *Gospel*, which vividly describes the Master's daily life, the people he encountered, and what he said. This type of day-to-day record is not available for any other avatar. M. wrote in the introduction to the first volume (sixth edition) of his Bengali *Gospel*: "Srima or Master or M. (a son of the Lord and a servant) are the

---

*Devotees humorously gave that name to M. because he brought several of his school students to Ramakrishna.

same person. While living with Sri Ramakrishna, whatever he heard and saw he tried to record in this book. He did not write anything that he heard from other devotees. The subject matter of this book is the daily events of the Master that were recorded in his diary. Whatever he heard and saw on a particular day, he recalled on the same day and recorded in his diary. — Author."

An artist creates pictures on a canvas with brush and paint. In the *Gospel*, M. used his pen to draw unique pictures of Ramakrishna's life, conversations, movements, singing, dancing, and travelling.

The main theme of *The Gospel of Sri Ramakrishna* is: "First God and then the world: the goal of life is to realize God." One needs the company of holy people to understand this message. Holy company is rare, but *The Gospel of Sri Ramakrishna* is easily available. This *Gospel* provides holy company. Chaitanya said that one can attain devotion by five means: holy company, service to God, study of the Bhagavata, chanting God's name, and living in Vrindaban or another holy place. M. reminded his visitors repeatedly: "We have no alternative than to have the company of the holy. 'Have the company of the holy' — that was the beginning, middle, and end of the Master's advice to us." Holy company cures householders of worldliness and frees monks from the net of maya. Everyone needs holy company: Even monks need the company of other monks.

There is a saying: Criticism is the ornament of a pioneer. Buddha said in the *Dhammapada* (Verse 228): "There never was, there never will be, nor is there now, a man who is always blamed, or a man who is always praised." M. was not only praised for writing the *Gospel*; some people also cursed him. In this connection, M. once said:

> Swami Vivekananda wrote to me that after reading the *Gospel*, some would curse me and some would reward me. If these teachings go against someone's self-interest, that person would curse me. Renunciation is the predominant message of this book. Those who have a desire for worldly enjoyment will be mad at me. Perhaps a young man had read the *Gospel* and became a monk. His mother will say that the man who wrote that book has ruined my son's life by his brainwashing. If the husband becomes spiritual by reading the *Gospel*, the wife will blame me, and if the wife becomes spiritual, the husband will curse me. Only they will appreciate me who have finished their desires for enjoyment. They will say: The words of the *Gospel* are like nectar. We were burning with misery, but the words of the Master brought peace and joy to our lives.[3]

Many books have been written on *The Gospel of Sri Ramakrishna*, and many more commentaries will be written on it in the future. For many years, I have been watching how the message of *The Gospel of Sri Ramakrishna* is spreading in the West. This amazes me, and it reminds me of the words of Swami Premananda: "Look, who will preach? No one is needed to preach the Master. He preaches himself. I visit various places and see the glory of the Master. With a view to showing me how he is spreading his ideas among others, he takes me to those places out of grace."[4]

In 1981 I went to the Vedanta Society of Kansas City to give a lecture. A young American woman had read *The Gospel of Sri Ramakrishna* and she wrote a letter to me in St. Louis. I asked her to visit me in Kansas City, Missouri. She is a daughter of a farmer and has a Master's degree. She works on the family's farm. The Midwest is called the breadbasket of America. She drove a few hundred miles to see me. When she was telling me her story, tears began to trickle from her eyes. She said: "I bought a copy of *The Gospel of Sri Ramakrishna* from the Vedanta Press in Hollywood and read it. One night I was sleeping in the cottage near our farm; Ramakrishna appeared before me and gave me a mantra." She told me the mantra that she had been given. I was dumbfounded and happy knowing the Master had bestowed his grace on her. I marvelled at how the Master was roaming around the vast farmlands of the Midwest in America and spotting those who feel sincere longing for God. Yearning for God is the only thing needful in spiritual life.

"Woman and Gold"

Another young woman in Kansas City bought a copy of the *Gospel* and read it. I asked her: "Does it bother you when you read in the *Gospel*, 'Woman and gold are maya'?" She replied: "No, it does not. I mentally change it to 'man and gold are maya.'" I was pleased to hear that. When I was in Hollywood, I presented a copy of the *Gospel* to a Catholic woman. When she read "Woman and gold are maya," she stopped reading the book. She wrote in her will that when she died the book should be returned to me. A few years later, that woman died, and her sister sent the book to me.

Swami Nikhilananda wrote an exhaustive note on page 82 in his translation of the *Gospel*:

> The term "woman and gold," which has been used throughout in a collective sense, occurs again and again in the teachings of Sri Rama-krishna to designate the chief impediments to spiritual progress. This

favourite expression of the Master "kamini-kanchan," has often been misconstrued. By it he meant only "lust and greed," the baneful influence of which retards the aspirant's spiritual growth. He used the word "kamini," or "woman," as a concrete term for the sex instinct when addressing his men devotees. He advised women, on the other hand, to shun "man." "Kanchan," or "gold," symbolizes greed, which is the other obstacle to spiritual life.

Sri Ramakrishna never taught his disciples to hate any woman, [or] womankind in general. This can be seen clearly by going through all his teachings under this head and judging them collectively. The Master looked on all women as so many images of the Divine Mother of the Universe.

To avoid any misunderstanding, I generally translate the term *kamini-kanchan* as "lust and gold." The root word of *kamini* is *kama*, which means desire; one needs gold or money to fulfill that desire. Desires for lust and gold or sex and money take away the mind from God — that is why Ramakrishna said that lust and gold are maya.

In 1942, when the English translation of the *Gospel* was published, American society was different from what it is now. When I find a Western woman buying the *Gospel*, I caution her not to get upset when she reads the phrase "woman and gold are maya." I explain that Sri Ramakrishna's Chosen Deity was Mother Kali; one of his gurus was the Bhairavi Brahmani; and his first disciple was his wife, whom he worshipped as the Divine Mother. He was extremely devoted to his own mother: Even though he was a monk, he did not wear ochre robes because he thought this would hurt her. He preached the motherhood of God. He taught his disciples to love and respect all women, as they are manifestations of the Divine Mother. He would feel pained if he found out a woman was fasting. Such a person cannot possibly hate women.

One of our swamis in the United States lent a copy of the *Gospel* to a professor, but he returned the book when he came across the saying "Woman and gold are maya." The professor told the swami why he had not read the whole book. The swami suggested: "Please read that portion of the book which appeals to you. You will not have to accept everything that Ramakrishna said." Later the professor read the whole book and told the swami: "I think Ramakrishna is the answer to our society. I love this book very much. Our society is guided by two things: Dollar-king and Sex-queen. The teachings of Ramakrishna are a nice solution to those crucial problems."

I have an English friend who is a professor of mathematics. He read the *Gospel* and commented: "I love Ramakrishna for two reasons: First, he never says anything that is irrational. Second, he is an expert at solving problems. He tells his visitors, 'Listen to a story,' and solves their problems. As a professor of mathematics, I cannot accept anything that is irrational and my job is to solve mathematical problems."

I met a woman who was a theology student at Eden Seminary in St. Louis. She was a devout Christian but would sometimes come to our lectures at the Vedanta Society. After reading the *Gospel*, she told me: "Swami, one defect of this book is that it has an end."

Truth and Longing in Vedanta

Ramakrishna was compelled to speak the truth: It was not possible for him to please people with sweet lies or flattery. He told people what was good for them. Swami Vivekananda said: "The duty of the common man is to obey the commands of his 'God' — society. The children of light never do it. This is an eternal law. The one accommodates himself to his surroundings and to social opinion and gets all good things from his *giver of all good things* — society. The other stands alone and drags society up towards him. The accommodating man finds a path of roses — the non-accommodating, one of thorns. But the worshipper of 'vox populi' goes to annihilation in a moment — the children of Truth live forever."[5]

In 1976 the Catholic church convened the Eucharistic Congress in Philadelphia. Mother Teresa of Calcutta coined a slogan, "Hunger for God," which created a tremendous commotion in America. In one of my lectures at the Vedanta Society in Hollywood, I told the audience: "This slogan of Mother Teresa may be new to you, but to us it is an old saying. The avatar comes to create hunger for God in the minds of people. Please open *The Gospel of Sri Ramakrishna*, which consists of 1063 pages. You will see that on almost every page the Master talks about longing for God. He said repeatedly: 'Yearning is like the red sky in the east at dawn. After such a sky the sun must rise. Immediately after that yearning one sees God.'"[6] In *Sri Ramakrishna and His Divine Play*, Swami Saradananda wrote that when the Master accepted the position of priest in the Kali temple, his longing was so intense that soon after he had a vision of the Mother. This first vision resulted from his longing, not through sadhana. Without longing, spiritual life lacks intensity and becomes monotonous.

In the Puranas, we find descriptions of devotees' love and longing for God; but God's love for the devotees is not mentioned. This is because human beings are incapable of expressing God's infinite love, and those scriptures were written by human beings. M. once said: "If the Master heard that someone had developed longing for God, he would rush to that person on his own initiative. One dark night the Master hired a carriage and went to a devotee's house in Calcutta. I was with him. As soon as the devotee learned that the Master had come, he said: 'Sir, why did you take so much trouble to come to see me in the dark of the night? If you had called for me, I would have come to you.' The Master told him: 'Look, in the beginning God becomes the magnet, and the devotee, the needle. But in the end the devotee becomes the magnet, and God the needle. One attains God who has longing.'"

Ramakrishna's Influence on the West

For most of the Church's history, Catholics kept themselves separate from adherents of other religious paths and maintained their exclusive identity. They did not even have much communication with other Christian denominations. On 7 December 1965, Pope Paul VI began to change this when he declared: "Let them reflect attentively on how Christian religious life may be able to assimilate the ascetic and contemplative traditions whose seeds were sometimes already planted by God in ancient cultures prior to the preaching of the Gospel." — Vatican Council II (Ad Gentes, 7 December 1965)

In August 1981 I had a talk with Swami Bhavyananda of the London Centre. He told me that in 1977 he had been invited to Italy by some Benedictine monks who were hosting a seminar on worship, prayer, and meditation as practised by Buddhists, Hindus, and Christians. On the dais of the monastery's altar, Bhavyananda set a picture of Ramakrishna and then worshipped him with flowers, incense, and candles. He then sang "Hari Om Ramakrishna" with instruments; the Christian monks joined with him. An Italian television station broadcast this event.

Pope Paul VI was in Rome at the time. This great soul met privately with Swami Bhavyananda. When the group photo of the seminar participants was taken, he took the swami's hand and made him sit next to him. At that time Swami Bhavyananda presented a copy of *The Gospel of Sri Ramakrishna* to him. He accepted the gift, and he told the swami that he had read about Ramakrishna.*

---

*When I visited Rome in 1990, I met the pope's ecumenical secretary and a monk who was the ecumenical representative for Asia. This monk was from Kerala, South India. He took me to his office and showed me *The Complete Works of Swami Vivekananda* on his desk. He was writing a thesis on Vivekananda's Bhakti Yoga, and asked me for some books on bhakti by other writers. I sent him a copy of *Bhakti Yoga* by Aswini Kumar Datta.

In 1981 I went to Mexico City to visit an unaffiliated Vedanta centre there. Every Monday the devotees met to meditate in front of a picture of Ramakrishna and discuss his life and message. I gave a talk on Vedanta, and the president of the Society translated it into Spanish.

There are many yogis, gurus, babas, and other religious leaders in America who are tremendously active in teaching Eastern religions and hatha yoga. Many of them use Ramakrishna's teachings in their sermons, directly or indirectly. In addition, I often find Ramakrishna's name in the index of many American books on religion, philosophy, and psychology. A student attending Los Angeles City College gave me a copy of *The Portable World Bible* (edited by Robert O. Ballou, Penguin Books), which is in their curriculum. When I examined that book, I found twelve pages of material taken from *The Gospel of Sri Ramakrishna*. In 1975 Christopher Isherwood presented me with a copy of *A Treasury of Traditional Wisdom* (published by Simon and Schuster, New York). I counted 167 quotations from *The Gospel of Sri Ramakrishna* in this huge volume.

In the *Gospel*, apart from spiritual wisdom, one finds sweetness and humour — that is the reason it is spreading. One of our friends from the Hollywood centre was a Major in the United States Air Force. He is a disciple of Swami Prabhavananda and a very jovial person. He said: "Perhaps in my previous life I was that troublemaker Hazra in Dakshineswar." So we call him "Hazra." He is now retired and the editor of *Judo* magazine. He said that he mentally connects himself with the devotees of Ramakrishna in Dakshineswar, and thus enjoys the company of the Master.

When I was at the Hollywood Centre in 1971, I would shake hands with the audience after the lecture. Once a man came forward and introduced himself saying, "Swami, I am Girish." When I shook hands with him, I smelled the odour of alcohol on his breath. I was delighted to see how the Master's devotees with all their different propensities live in different parts of the world. Let people connect themselves with the Master in whatever way they like. Krishna promised in the Gita: "*Na me bhakta pranashati* — My devotee never perishes."

Another friend from Santa Barbara is a staunch devotee of the Master. He is extremely intelligent and very outspoken. His friend gave him a book written by a yogi and asked him to read it. Our friend opened the book and counted eighteen "I-s" in two pages. He then handed Ramakrishna's *Gospel* to his friend and said: "I see your yogi's book is full of 'I-s'; now see this huge volume and see how many times

Ramakrishna used the word 'I.'" Ramakrishna could not utter the word "I"; he would use the term "here" or "in this place" instead.

In *The Gospel of Sri Ramakrishna*, there are many places in which one finds, "All laugh," or "Laughter." Sometimes American devotees say, "Swami, you laugh but we don't find anything there to laugh about." I reply: "Humour lurks in language, in gestures, in social customs, and in the prevailing practices of the people and place. If you want to understand Ramakrishna's humour, you will have to know his language, mood, behaviour, social customs, interpersonal relationships, and so on. I have a book, *10,000 Jokes, Toasts and Stories*, which I read sometimes to understand American humour. I don't understand most of the jokes because I don't get the point or the punch line. You see, if you are not born and brought up in a particular language, you can't get its subtle meaning, and you cannot understand the slang and colloquial expressions." There is a saying: A foolish man laughs thrice: At first he laughs without understanding; second, he laughs when he does understand; and third, he laughs when he wonders why it took so long to understand.

Once I was listening to a comedian on the radio. He told a story about a pastor who was giving a sermon in a village church. The pastor said: "Only Christ is perfect. You are all imperfect and sinners. Have you seen or heard of anyone who is perfect? If so, please raise your hand." There was deep silence in the church. At last a middle-aged man from the back raised his hand. The pastor challenged him: "Are you perfect?"

"No, sir."

"Have you seen anyone who is perfect?"

"No, sir."

"Have you heard of anyone who is perfect?"

"Yes, sir."

"Who is that person?"

"My wife's first husband," replied the man. Everyone laughed except myself. I then asked a friend, "Where is the humour?" He replied: "Whatever this man does, his wife says that her first husband was perfect in that respect." I don't understand many Western customs, especially courtship; so I can't find any humour in jokes about courtship. Similarly, Western people do not understand much of Ramakrishna's humour. Two things are in the blood of the American people: Love of freedom and a sense of humour. Ramakrishna appeals to both.

We know very little about how Ramakrishna's gospel is spreading throughout the world. Once I went to Washington University to attend a lecture by Joseph Campbell, a famous American writer and Orientalist.

He finished his lecture by telling the Master's parable about a tiger that was brought up by sheep.

Once there was a religious conference at a Baptist Church in Illinois. In his presidential speech one minister referred to the Master's story about the blind men trying to describe an elephant. Of course, neither Joseph Campbell nor the Baptist Minister mentioned Ramakrishna's name. That does not matter: the Master never craved name and fame; he spat on them.

It is hard to say how the *Gospel* works on the human mind. In the 1970s I gave a lecture in the Hollywood temple, entitled "Yearning for Illumination." I quoted a saying of Ramakrishna: "It is said, in the Kaliyuga, if a man can weep for God one day and one night, he sees Him." After hearing this, an actress went to her apartment and began to cry. She cried till midnight and then fell asleep. She said to me later, "I cried for the Master but he did not come." I replied: "You have wept for only seven or eight hours. The Master said that one would have to cry for twenty-four hours. So you will have to cry more." Truly, tears wash away all impurities of the mind that have accumulated birth after birth.

In 1973 I went to Portland to give a lecture. I mentioned the Master's saying: "Cry to the Lord with an intensely yearning heart and you will certainly see Him. People shed a whole jugful of tears for wife and children. They swim in tears for money. But who weeps for God? Cry to Him with a real cry." A middle-aged man said: "In America it is disgraceful for a man to cry. It is a sign of cowardice." I replied: "The Master asked his devotees to cry to God secretly and in solitude. You do not have to show everyone that you are crying for God."

A young man once asked for some advice from a disciple of Swami Brahmananda. He replied: "Read *The Gospel of Sri Ramakrishna* every day. It contains the answers to whatever spiritual questions arise in the human mind. If Ramakrishna's words cannot remove doubt from your mind, then do you think my words will?" A disciple of the Holy Mother joyfully said to a young monk: "Today is a memorable day in my life. I have read the five volumes of *The Gospel of Sri Ramakrishna* in Bengali fifty times." Another time a young man went to another disciple of the Holy Mother and said that he was studying the *Gospel* so that he could be a monk. The monk remarked: "Look, one cannot become a monk by reading the *Gospel*. Read the books of Swami Vivekananda. They will inspire you and then only will you need to join the monastery. One sees God when reading the *Gospel*. Why should such a person need to become a monk?"

I know quite a few Westerners who read *The Gospel of Sri Ramakrishna* every day and try to follow the Master's teachings. The *Gospel* is an antidote for depression and spiritual dryness. This reminds me of a wonderful incident that took place in 1932. A young monk moaned and complained to Swami Shivananda, saying: "I have not seen God, nor have I any peace of mind. Sometimes doubt prevails in my mind, and I even doubt the instructions that you gave me." At this, the swami's face turned red. He said excitedly: "Look, my son, if the Master is true, we too are true. Whatever I say is nothing but the truth; we have not come to cheat people. If we sink, you too will sink with us; but by his grace we have realized that we shall never sink, nor will you."[7]

Like an opium-addicted peacock, M. was always intoxicated with the nectar of Ramakrishna's words. He distributed the Master's message to everyone who went to him, and he left his magnum opus for future generations.

Finally, I shall quote a few lines from Aswini Kumar Datta's memorable letter to M.:

> You are blessed indeed. What heavenly nectar you have sprinkled all over the country! I was not born under the lucky star of an M., that I might jot down the days, the dates, and the hours of my visits with the Master and note down correctly all the words uttered by his holy lips.
>
> I saw the Master not more than four or five times. What I saw and received in those few days has sweetened my whole life. That Elysian smile of his, laden with nectar, I have locked up in the secret closet of my memory. That is the unending treasure of a hapless person like myself. A thrill of joy passes through my heart when I think how a grain of the bliss shed from that laughter has been sweetening the lives of millions, even in distant America. If that be my case, you may very well understand how lucky you are.[8]

15

The Gospel of Ramakrishna According to Girish Chandra Sen

The Brahmo Movement

In 1828 Raja Ram Mohan Roy (1777-1833) founded the Brahmo Samaj in Calcutta. At the centre of this socio-religious movement is the belief that there is one God, who is omnipresent and omniscient. The Brahmo Samaj played a significant role in the renaissance of India, and the roots of some significant modern thinking in India can be traced back to the Brahmo movement. The organization promoted a monotheistic, reformed Hinduism with strong Islamic and Christian overtones, support for the rights of women, and opposition to such aspects of Hinduism as idolatry, the caste system, and animal sacrifice. When Ram Mohan Roy died in 1833, the Brahmo movement declined. It was revived in 1843 by Devendra Nath Tagore, who founded the Adi Brahmo Samaj and became its leader. Devendra was a classmate of Mathur Mohan Biswas, a great devotee of Ramakrishna and son-in-law of Rani Rasmani, founder of the Dakshineswar Kali temple. Ramakrishna went with Mathur to see Devendra in Calcutta and also visited the Adi Brahmo Samaj.

Keshab Chandra Sen (1838-1884), a charismatic leader in Calcutta, joined the Brahmo Samaj in 1859. In 1863 he became a Brahmo minister and became the leader of the youth wing. In 1868 he had a personal conflict with Devendra, and the organization split. Keshab started the

Brahmo Samaj of India along with Shivanath Shastri and Vijay Krishna Goswami. He went to England in 1870, where he preached monotheism. He wanted to abolish the caste system, and he introduced inter-caste marriage. Queen Victoria praised his oratory and leadership.

The Brahmo leaders decided that the minimum marriage age for girls should be fourteen, and for boys, eighteen. In 1878 Keshab broke that rule when he married his own daughter, who was not yet fourteen, to the Maharaja of Coochbehar. This created a tremendous controversy and another schism formed. Keshab's followers formed a new group, the Navavidhan (the New Dispensation), while the dissidents founded the Sadharan Brahmo Samaj, which became more popular.

Ramakrishna and Keshab Chandra Sen

On 15 March 1875, Ramakrishna met Keshab at the Belgharia retreat of Jaygopal Sen, where Keshab was training his ministers. As soon as the Master arrived with his nephew Hriday, he went into samadhi. When he had regained partial consciousness, he began explaining profound spiritual topics in simple language illustrated with such commonplace examples that all present gazed at him, enthralled. They did not notice when the times for bathing and eating came and went. The time for the next prayer was nearly upon them when Ramakrishna remarked: "If any other kind of animal comes to a herd of cattle, they'll turn on it and gore it with their horns. But if a cow joins the herd, they'll lick its body and welcome it as one of themselves. That's what has happened to us here today." Then addressing Keshab, the Master added, "Your tail has dropped off." That odd remark seemed to startle and displease Keshab's disciples. Realizing that they had not understood him, the Master went on to explain: "As long as a tadpole has its tail, it can live only in the water; it can't come on land. But when its tail drops off, it can live on land or in the water. Similarly, as long as a man wears the tail of ignorance, he can only live in the world; but when the tail drops off, he can live either in Satchidananda or in the world, whichever he pleases. Your mind, Keshab, has reached that state now. You can live in the world and still be aware of God." All were overwhelmed. That day the Master discussed various topics, spent some delightful hours with them, and then returned to Dakshineswar.

After this first meeting, Keshab's newspaper, *The Indian Mirror,* published this news on 28 March 1875: "A Hindu Saint: We met one (a sincere Hindu devotee) not long ago and were charmed by the depth, penetration, and simplicity of his spirit. The never-ceasing metaphors and analogies, in which he indulged, are most of them as apt as they are beautiful. Hinduism must have in it a deep sense of beauty, truth, and goodness to inspire such men as these."[1]

It is Keshab Chandra Sen who first introduced Ramakrishna to the public. Most of the Master's disciples came to know about him through this religious leader. In Dakshineswar one day, Keshab said to the Master: "Sir, if you permit, I want to make your message known to the public. It will definitely do people good and bring peace to the world." Ramakrishna replied in an ecstatic mood: "It is not the time to spread the message of this place [i.e., his message] through lectures and newspapers. The power and ideas that are within this body will automatically spread all around in the course of time. Hundreds of Himalayas will not be able to suppress that power." As the Master said this his eyes were wide open and his face radiated a wonderful glow. All were quiet. Then the Master went into samadhi.[2]

Despite the Master's discouragement, Keshab continued to spread news of the Master in his papers. *The Indian Mirror* printed on 20 February 1876: "Ramakrishna, a Hindu devotee known as a Parama-hamsa, now living at Dakshineswar, is a remarkable man and appears to have attained an extraordinary elevation of moral character and spirituality. Several Brahmo missionaries who have visited him from time to time speak highly of his devotion and purity and his deep insight into the realities of the inner world. Though a true Hindu he is said to sympathize heartily with the Brahmos of the advanced schools."[3]

Keshab Introduces Ramakrishna's Message

On 24 January 1878 Keshab collected the sayings of Ramakrishna and published a ten-page pamphlet in Bengali entitled *Paramahamser Ukti*. The Indian Brahmo Samaj published it, and it sold for two pice.[4] Whenever Keshab met with Ramakrishna, his teachings were recorded and published in the *Dharmatattwa* magazine of the Brahmo Samaj. Keshab was a charismatic orator and a powerful writer. He was behind several newspapers and journals that propagated his ideas, including *The Indian Mirror*, *The Sunday Mirror*, *Liberal*, *Theistic Annual*, and *New Dispensation* in English, and *Dharmatattwa*, *Sulabh Samachar*, *Mahima*, *Paricharika*, *Balak Bandhu*, *Dharmaprakash*, *Bangabandhu*, *Deshahitaishini*, *Bishavairi*, and *Bamabodhini Patrika* in Bengali. These Brahmo publications continued to spread the teachings of Ramakrishna. Thus the Brahmo version of *The Gospel of Sri Ramakrishna* began to take shape during his lifetime.

The Theistic Quarterly Review published the following report in October 1879:

If all his [Ramakrishna's] utterances could be recorded, they would form a volume of strange and wonderful wisdom. If all his observations on men and things could be reproduced, people might think that the days of prophecy, of primeval unlearned wisdom had returned. But it is most difficult to render his sayings into English. We here try to give some stray bits:

1. So long as the bee is outside the petals of the lily, it buzzes and emits sounds. But when it is inside the flower, the sweetness hath silenced the bee. It drinks the nectar, forgets the sounds, and forgets itself. So the man of devotion.

2. Put the *gharā* (earthen pot) inside the brook of clear water. There is bubbling, there is noise, as long as the vessel is empty. When it is full, the bubbling ceases, the disturbance ceases. In silence and fullness the vessel lies in the depth of the element. So the heart of devotion.

3. Boil your sugar well in a living and active fire. As long as there is earth and impurity in it, the sweet infusion will smoke and simmer. But when all impurity is cast out, there is neither smoke nor sound, but the delicious crystalline fluid heaves itself in its unmixed worth, and, whether liquid or solid, is the delight of men and gods. Such is the character of the man of faith.

4. Through the stream of the troublous world I float a frail half-sunk log of wood. If men come to hold onto me to save their lives, the result will be this: they will drown me without being able to save themselves. Beware of [false] gurus.

5. Unshod and with bare feet who will venture to walk upon thorns and sharp stones? Shod with faith in Hari, what thorn or sharp stone can harm you?

6. Hold the post well-driven into the ground with your hand, and then you can quickly revolve round and round without falling. Have faith in a fixed and strong principle, and then, though your movements may be many and rapid, no harm will ever befall you. Without principle, every movement is a step towards a fall.

7. Churn your pure milk before the sun rises, and the butter that is thrown up, gather, and put in clear water. There is another kind of butter that is obtained by churning whey after sunrise, and that is allowed to float in the whey out of which it is churned. The latter kind of butter represents the religion of the Brahmo Samaj, while the former is pure Hinduism.

8. Woman and wealth have drowned the whole world in sin. Woman is disarmed when you view her as the manifestation of the

divine Vidya Shakti, the power of pure wisdom, as the mother of the human race.

9. O Mother Divine, I want no honour from men, I want no pleasure of the flesh, only let my soul flow into Thee as the permanent confluence of the Ganges and Yamuna. Mother, I am without bhakti, without yoga, I am poor and friendless. I want no one's praise, only let my mind always dwell in the lotus of Thy feet.

10. God alone is true, all else is false.[5]

Keshab and Ramakrishna had a wonderful relationship. The Master was very fond of Keshab. When Keshab was sick, the Master went to see him and made a special offering to the Divine Mother for his well-being. Keshab had tremendous love and respect for the Master as well. Sometimes the Master teased Keshab and his followers. Once he said: "I went to Keshab's place and watched their prayer service. After speaking at length about the glories of God, Keshab announced, 'Let us now meditate on God.' I wondered how long they would meditate. But, oh dear, they'd scarcely shut their eyes for two minutes before it was all over! How can one know God by meditating like that? While they were meditating, I was watching their faces. Afterwards I said to Keshab: 'I've seen a lot of you meditate, and do you know what it reminded me of? Troops of monkeys sometimes sit quietly under the pine trees at Dakshineswar, just as if they were perfect gentlemen, quite innocent. But they aren't. As they sit there, they're thinking about all the gourds and pumpkins that householders train to grow over their roofs, and about all the gardens full of plantains and eggplants. After a little while, they'll jump up with a yell and rush away to the gardens to stuff their stomachs. I saw many of you meditating like that.'" When the Brahmos heard that, they laughed.[6]

Before he died in 1884, Keshab trained his Navavidhan followers to respect others' faiths. Each minister became adept in a particular faith; for example, Pratap Chandra Majumdar specialized in Christianity, Aghorenath Gupta in Buddhism, Trailokya Nath Sanyal in Vaishnavism, and Girish Chandra Sen in Islam.

Girish Chandra Sen and the Adi Kathamrita

Girish Chandra Sen (1835-1910) was born in Dhaka, East Bengal (now Bangladesh). He was a linguist and knew Bengali, Sanskrit, Persian, Arabic, Urdu, and English. When he joined the Brahmo Samaj in 1872, Keshab entrusted him with teaching the Koran. He spent thirty years translating the Koran from Arabic into Bengali, earning the title "Maulavi." He translated the lives of the Sufi saints from Persian into

Bengali and edited them in six volumes under the title *Tapasamala*. A wonderful journalist, he regularly contributed to Brahmo newspapers and magazines. In 1875 he came in contact with Ramakrishna, and he associated with him for the next eleven years. When Ramakrishna passed away on 16 August 1886, Girish took part in the funeral procession.

After Ramakrishna's passing away Girish Sen wrote a short biography in Bengali that was published in *Dharmatattwa* in 1886. It has been translated into English and published in *Ramakrishna as We Saw Him* (Vedanta Society of Saint Louis, 1990).

While Ramakrishna was still alive, Girish began recording the Master's wisdom. He collected sayings from 1875 to 1878, then published them in Bengali as *Srimat Ramakrishna Paramahamser Ukti* (Sayings of Ramakrishna Paramahamsa).

In 1983 Shyamal Basu edited this collection and published it in Bengali under the title of *Adi Kathamrita* (Original Gospel). This book, which contains 184 teachings of Ramakrishna, has not been translated into any other language. Ramakrishna's colloquial Bengali language was a blend of formal language and rural dialect. In the *Adi Kathamrita*, Girish set Ramakrishna's dialogues in a question and answer form, and changed his village patois into the more formal, elegant Bengali that was commonly spoken in the 1870s.

The language of the *Adi Kathamrita* is different from *The Gospel of Sri Ramakrishna* recorded by M. The latter tried to preserve Ramakrishna's words intact, whereas Girish Sen took Ramakrishna's ideas and put them into his own language. We don't find the simplicity, originality, freshness, beauty, and sweetness of Ramakrishna's words and expressions in his book that we find in M.'s *Gospel*. Moreover, Ramakrishna's teachings are packed with similes, metaphors, and day-to-day examples that are understandable even to common folk. Girish heard the conversations, stories, and parables of Ramakrishna and then recast them in his own language. But in this book one finds some teachings that do not appear in the *Gospel* or in any other collection of Ramakrishna's sayings.

It should be mentioned that not all Brahmos were devoted to Ramakrishna. Some were his friends and admirers, but others were very critical of his teachings, and sceptical about his life. Some even considered Ramakrishna's episodes of samadhi to be epileptic fits. Keshab and his followers, however, were greatly influenced by Ramakrishna. For example, they learned to sing and dance in the name of God. Before they met Ramakrishna, they would not show any emotion in their sadhana;

they followed the Vedas and repeated their prayers, quoting texts from the scriptures. After coming in contact with Ramakrishna, the Brahmos introduced the concept of the Motherhood of God into their tradition. Ramakrishna visited both Keshab's Navavidhan and the Sadharan Brahmo Samaj guided by Shivanath Shastri and Vijay Krishna Goswami.

Ramakrishna's audience was composed of Indians who had been influenced by Western education and culture, religion and philosophy. Ramakrishna presented ancient India's spiritual tradition to his Westernized audience. Some of the monastic disciples of Ramakrishna, including Swami Vivekananda, were members of the Brahmo Samaj. These English-educated disciples used logic and reason to challenge the Master's views, and Ramakrishna easily and joyfully faced their challenges and used his own experience to convince them of the truth of what he said. One can counteract a particular scriptural text with another and a lower reasoning by a higher reasoning; but one cannot nullify experience. For example, one who has tasted sugar and knows it to be sweet will laugh if scientists and philosophers say that sugar tastes sour or bitter. Similarly, Ramakrishna's experience of God and his samadhi overwhelmed the atheists, agnostics, and sceptics that he encountered, and all their arguments were refuted.

Excerpts from the Adi Kathamrita

Some of the following teachings are not found in any English translations of Ramakrishna's sayings:

Question: "Do the great spiritual souls sometimes face depression and doubt?"

Ramakrishna: "The tremendous current of the Padma River sometimes turns into whirlpools on its course, but shortly it again begins to flow in a straight way. Similarly, depression and doubt arise momentarily in the minds of the great souls; but they do not last. They disappear quickly."[7]

Question: "The Muslims loudly pray 'Allahu Akbar.' Does it mean that they have seen God?"

Ramakrishna: "He who has realized Allah becomes overwhelmed and is silent. He who has not seen Allah shouts, saying 'Allah, Allah.'"[8]

Question: "If the body is impermanent, why then is a devotee careful about it?"

Ramakrishna: "Nobody cares for an empty iron safe. But people take special care of it if it is full of gold coins and precious gems. Similarly, if

God manifests in the heart of a holy person, people cannot help but serve and care for that person's body."[9]

Question: "Why do tears trickle from the eyes during upasana or prayer?"

Ramakrishna: "When one side of a log starts to burn, its moisture comes out as drops of water from the other side of the log. Similarly during meditation, the spiritual fire enters the heart and causes tears."[10]

Question: "We are mentally and physically weak. Is it possible for us to do any great things?"

Ramakrishna: "As the strong wind carries a fallen dry leaf a long distance, so weak and incapable people receive tremendous power by the grace of Brahman and accomplish great works."[11]

Question: "How can one make one's devotion steady and permanent?"

Ramakrishna: "If you hang a jar of water with a sling in your room, the water will dry up after a few days. But if you keep your jar under the surface of the Ganges, it will never dry up. Similarly, if one's mind is immersed in the all-loving God, one's love and devotion never dries up. One should not feel secure after having love and devotion only for a day; it will soon dry up like the water in the hanging jar."[12]

Question: "What is your opinion about modern preachers?"

Ramakrishna: "They have food for two hundred people, but they invite thousands. They practise very little sadhana, but they declare themselves to be gurus and start preaching religion."[13]

Question: "Why can we not see the Divine Mother?"

Ramakrishna: "She is the aristocratic daughter of a very rich person and lives behind a screen. Those who are devotees of the Mother go behind the screen and see Her."[14]

Question: "Jesus' enemies crucified him, but he prayed for their welfare. How could this be?"

Ramakrishna: "If one drives a nail into an ordinary unripe coconut, it penetrates through the fibre, shell, and kernel; but when the coconut becomes ripe and water evaporates from the inside, the kernel is separated from the shell. At that time the nail cannot pierce the dry kernel. Jesus Christ was like that dry coconut. His Atman or Soul was separated from the body. His enemies nailed his body but not his Soul. That is why his body endured the pain of that piercing nail, but his Soul prayed for the good of his enemies."[15]

Question: "What is the strength of the spiritual aspirant?"

Ramakrishna: "As a child cries for the mother, so crying for God is the strength of an aspirant."[16]

Question: "How does God dwell in the human body?"
Ramakrishna: "He lives in the body like the plunger in a syringe."[17]
Question: "Will all people see God?"
Ramakrishna: "Nobody can live in this world without food; some eat at 2:00 p.m., some in the evening. Similarly, all will see God sometime or other."[18]

Ramakrishna's similes and metaphors glitter like gems. They create wonderful images in readers' minds, helping them to visualize the truths of which he spoke. Ramakrishna explained lofty spiritual concepts using such simple language and homespun examples that left hardly any room for one to doubt him.

The *Adi Kathamrita* of Girish Chandra Sen has a historical value. It was published 25 years before M.'s popular *Gospel of Sri Ramakrishna*, while Ramakrishna was still alive. Some devotees might have read it to him.

Ramakrishna did not care for publicity; he was happy to lead his own life. His attitude was: When flowers bloom, bees come of their own accord. He also felt that one should not quarrel or fight about religion. He simply declared: First be spiritual, and then love and serve human beings as God. The goal of human life is to realize God.

16

The Gospel of Ramakrishna According to Suresh Chandra Datta

The Life of Suresh Chandra Datta

Suresh Chandra Datta, one of the recorders of Ramakrishna's gospel, was born in West Calcutta in 1850. From his boyhood onward Suresh was honest, humble, simple, and self-reliant. He was a highly educated and talented man. From time to time Suresh would attend Keshab Chandra Sen's lectures with Durga Charan Nag, a neighbour. At night they would meditate with Keshab's devotees on the bank of the Ganges. Durga Charan longed for God and sought a guru to guide him.

Every evening Suresh went to Durga Charan's house to discuss religion. Suresh was a staunch follower of Keshab's Brahmo Samaj, which advocated the belief in God without form. Like Christians, Brahmos considered God as formless but full of divine qualities: God is omnipotent and omniscient, merciful and forgiving, kind and loving, and so on. Durga Charan, however, was an orthodox Hindu who obeyed every scriptural injunction. The two men had heated religious discussions every evening, but their different views were never reconciled. During one of their friendly squabbles, Durga Charan said to Suresh: "The gods and goddesses of the Hindus as well as the formless Brahman are all true. But attaining Brahman is so difficult, I doubt whether one or two in a million can ever reach this stage. Hence arises the necessity of believing in the various gods and goddesses of Hinduism. Do you think that the

Vedas, Puranas, Tantras, and mantras are all false?" Suresh retorted: "Uncle, set aside your scriptures. I have no faith in them."

Fortunately, during one of his visits to the Brahmo Samaj, Suresh happened to hear about Ramakrishna, the saint of Dakshineswar. He waited for two months before he suggested to Durga Charan that they visit the Master. After lunch that very day, they left for Dakshineswar.

It was a hot summer day in April or May, probably in 1883. They arrived at Dakshineswar at 2:00 p.m. Both men were delighted by the beauty of the temple garden, and they enjoyed its peaceful atmosphere. Ramakrishna received them graciously and asked them to sit down. He talked to them for some time. In the course of conversation, Ramakrishna said: "Live in this world like a mudfish. There is nothing wrong in staying at home. The mudfish lives in the mud but is not soiled by it. Similarly, live in this world but never be contaminated by its evils."[1] Then Ramakrishna sent them to the Panchavati grove to meditate. After half an hour they returned to the Master's room, and Ramakrishna took them around to the various temples in the Dakshineswar compound. He first walked to the twelve Shiva temples and prostrated before each deity, circumambulating their respective shrines. Durga Charan followed the Master's example, but Suresh merely looked on, for he had no faith in Hindu gods and goddesses.

Ramakrishna next took them to the Krishna and the Kali temples. Both Suresh and Durga Charan were astonished by the ecstatic mood that came over the Master when he entered the Kali temple. As a restless child holds onto the hem of its mother's garment and moves around her, so the Master went around the image of Kali and prostrated before Her. About 5:00 p.m., after returning to the Master's room, Suresh and Durga Charan took their leave. Ramakrishna gave them this parting advice: "Come again. Our acquaintance will grow deeper if you keep coming regularly for some time."

The experience of that first meeting left an indelible impression on their minds, and they could not help but talk about Ramakrishna. The next week they both visited the Master again. On seeing these two sincere seekers, Ramakrishna exclaimed in an ecstatic mood: "You have done well in coming again. I have been waiting here for you for a long time." The Master once again asked them to meditate in the Panchavati grove.

Suresh visited the Master eight or nine times in the company of Durga Charan. Undoubtedly he must have visited Ramakrishna many more times alone or with others; otherwise he could not have collected so many of the Master's teachings. He published these teachings in a book during Ramakrishna's lifetime. Suresh was not the first to record and publish Ramakrishna's teachings, but the second. (Ram Chandra Datta published *Tattawasara* in 1885.)

In 1885, during the Afghan War, Suresh was given a job in a military department that paid a monthly salary of two hundred rupees. He was assigned to Quetta, in the northwestern part of India. Before his departure from Calcutta, Durga Charan urged Suresh to receive initiation from the Master. But Suresh had no faith in mantras or in God with form. After a prolonged discussion with Durga Charan on this point, they agreed that Suresh should abide by the Master's wishes.

The next day both men went to Dakshineswar, and Durga Charan raised the question of initiation. "Yes, Durga Charan is right," Ramakrishna said to Suresh. "A person should practise spiritual disciplines under the direction of a guru. What prevents you from admitting this?"

"Sir, I have no faith in mantras," replied Suresh humbly.

"All right," said the Master. "Do not worry about it now. Everything will come in time."[2]

In Quetta it was not long before Suresh began to feel the need for initiation very keenly. He continued his spiritual disciplines as usual. During this time an ugly incident tested his strength of character. Suresh was extremely honest. His manager tried to embezzle some money, and he asked Suresh to sign false bills. Suresh refused to do this, and as a result he was forced to resign and return to Calcutta.

One day in 1886 Suresh went to see Ramakrishna at the Cossipore garden house. The Master was then bedridden because of his illness. He asked Suresh: "Where is your doctor friend [Durga Charan]? He is said to be a good physician. Tell him to come here sometime soon."[3] Seeing the Master's fragile condition, Suresh could not bring himself to ask for initiation. Instead, he went home and informed Durga Charan that the Master wanted to see him.

After the Master's passing on 16 August 1886, Suresh regretted not having followed his friend's advice about asking for initiation. He lamented his poor decision and passed his nights in prayer and meditation on the bank of the Ganges. One night he fell asleep while crying to God on the riverbank. Some time before daybreak the next morning he dreamt that Ramakrishna had come out of the water and approached him, and then uttered a mantra in his ear. As Suresh was about to take the dust of Ramakrishna's feet, he disappeared. At this point, Suresh's life changed and he became an ardent devotee of the Master.

A Brief Biography of Ramakrishna

Suresh Chandra Datta wrote a small biography[4] as an introduction to his collection of the Master's teachings, *Sri Sri Ramakrishnadever Upadesh*. In this biography Suresh published some wonderful stories about the Master. I present some of these stories here.

Kshudiram's vision: Before Ramakrishna was born, his father, Kshudiram, had a vision of Vishnu in which the god said He would be born as his son.

Ramakrishna's early days in Dakshineswar: The Master had wonderful relationships with Rani Rasmani, the founder of the Kali temple, and her son-in-law Mathur. Ramakrishna practised Tantra, Vedanta, and various other spiritual disciplines. He eventually realized God by practising different spiritual disciplines and religions. Due to his intense longing, he had his first vision of the Divine Mother.

Ramakrishna's renunciation: To test his purity, Mathur once took the Master to visit some alluring young women. But the Master had renounced lust. As soon as the Master saw the women, he addressed them as "Oh my blissful mothers," and then went into samadhi. They were embarrassed and begged forgiveness from the Master, asking him to bless them. Ramakrishna had also given up money; he could not even touch it. Saying, "Money is clay and clay is money," he threw a rupee and a clod of dirt into the Ganges. When Mathur offered money and property to him, the Master was so angry that he almost hit Mathur.

Ramakrishna's childlike nature: The Master was a true paramahamsa, so his nature was childlike. Once in ecstasy, while trying to embrace Lord Krishna, he fell and broke his right arm. He cried like a boy and was deeply distressed. But he had the faith of a child. During that time a man came from Calcutta and said: "Sir, your hand will be all right. It will heal." The Master was immediately relieved. He told his visitors: "Look, this man has come from Calcutta and says that my hand will be all right, so I will be all right."

Once he saw steamers passing on the Ganges, and a desire arose to see a steamer up close and find out how its engine makes that *jhak jhak* sound. He was a real paramahamsa so his nature was childlike.

The Master's Vaishnava sadhana: When Ramakrishna was practising spiritual disciplines in the mood of Radha, he dressed and acted like a woman. When he practised the servant attitude towards Ramachandra, he behaved like Hanuman. While practising humility, he cleaned the privy of the Dakshineswar temple garden. Although he was a brahmin priest, he did not consider himself to be higher than the untouchable sweeper whose job it was to clean the privy.

One day a wealthy doctor came to the Dakshineswar temple garden. When he saw Ramakrishna, he thought he was a gardener and asked him to pick some flowers for him. The Master immediately obeyed him. Later on, the doctor was embarrassed when he learned that Ramakrishna was that man.

The Master as an Avatar: In the course of time, Ramakrishna became known among Calcutta people through Keshab Chandra Sen, Vijay Krishna Goswami, and other Brahmo leaders. The famous scholars Pandit Vaishnavcharan, Pandit Gauri, and Pandit Padmalochan all recognized him as an avatar.

Once a great scholar visited Dakshineswar to evaluate Ramakrishna's spirituality. The Master was in his room, surrounded by his devotees. The scholar entered the room and asked: "Are you a paramahamsa?" He found the Master seated on a soft bed, with a bolster at his back. He saw the Master's shoes and other articles in his room. He then sat on the Master's bed and told the devotees: "You have come from Calcutta to see a paramahamsa! You are all deceived by this man. I have read the scriptures and I know the signs of a paramahamsa." He then quoted the scripture where the signs of a paramahamsa are mentioned. Disgusted, the scholar left the room; he had expected Ramakrishna to be an austere hermit. The scholar went to the bank of the Ganges to practise his evening meditation. While he was concentrating on his Chosen Ideal, he had a vision. He immediately rushed to the Master and found him in samadhi. The scholar stood in front of Ramakrishna and exclaimed with folded hands: "You are God."[5]

When he talked about God, the Master would merge into samadhi. He lost consciousness of the outside world, his face would beam with a sweet smile, and tears would trickle from his eyes. Only after hearing the Lord's name would he become normal again. Ramakrishna passed away on 16 August 1886. Pointing to his picture, Ramakrishna said: "In the future, I will be worshipped in many homes."

Sri Sri Ramakrishnadever Upadesh

As was mentioned earlier, Suresh met Ramakrishna in 1883. After associating with him for a couple of years, he discovered that the Master's teachings are more precious than gems and jewels. He felt that the words of the Master must be recorded. He had heard many sermons at the Brahmo Samaj and had read its literature. Ramakrishna's simple convincing words and examples, stories and parables made a deep impression on his mind. He asked some of the Master's close disciples who lived with him to record his teachings. But the disciples were too absorbed in the bliss of the Master's holy presence and overwhelmed by his personality to do such a thing at that time.

So, driven by evangelical inspiration, Suresh began recording the teachings of the Master that he heard directly from him. Haramohan Mitra, another householder disciple of the Master, had some experience in publishing. He came forward to help Suresh, and in December 1884 he published 100 of the Master's teachings while Ramakrishna was still alive. The second part, which comprised another 100 teachings, came out in 1886. Inspired, Suresh started collecting even more of the Master's teachings from other disciples who had heard them directly from the Master. Thus Suresh collected 600 teachings. In 1894 he combined all of the teachings he had collected and added a biography of the Master. Thus *Sri Sri Ramakrishnadever Upadesh* came into existence. The rapid sale of the book inspired both Haramohan and Suresh. Over time, Suresh added to his collection; the book now contains 950 teachings.[6] These wonderful teachings of Ramakrishna have not yet been translated into English in their entirety. Some stories and teachings appear in different forms in *Teachings of Sri Ramakrishna* (published by Advaita Ashrama, Calcutta) and *Sayings of Sri Ramakrishna* (published by Ramakrishna Math, Chennai).

Suresh wrote in the introduction that if anybody could prove that any of the teachings or stories in his collection were not true, or distorted or exaggerated, he would make corrections in the next edition. He did not accept any secondhand information. Moreover, he verified the information that he collected by checking with at least one other source. Suresh did not interpret the Master's teachings because he wanted to let the readers understand Ramakrishna in their own way. Suresh died in 1912.

Some Teachings from Sri Sri Ramakrishnadever Upadesh

1. You see many stars in the sky at night, but not when the sun rises. Can you therefore say that there are no stars in the heavens during the day? O human beings, because you do not find God in your ignorance, say not that there is no God.

581. God dwells in all beings, but all beings do not identify themselves with God, so they suffer.

567. Some people shed a jugful of tears to have children; some cry for money and property; but who longs to see God? Those who want God, find Him.

569. In this Kaliyuga a human being can attain perfection in three days. Those who cry with a longing heart for God day and night see Him.

11. Question: "How can one ascertain the state of perfection?"

Answer: "As potatoes and eggplants become soft when they are boiled, so people become very soft or humble when they attain perfection. Their egos dissolve completely."

30. A room may be dark for a thousand years, but it is lighted instantly as soon as a lamp is lit. Similarly, one glance of God's grace can wipe away sins accumulated in thousands of births.

160. If one drops a salt doll, a cloth doll, and a stone doll in the ocean, the salt doll melts instantly and loses its individual existence. The cloth doll becomes soaked with water: It does not become one with it, and it maintains its own separate existence. Water does not enter into the stone doll at all. A free soul is like the salt doll, a worldly soul is like the cloth doll, and a bound soul is like the stone doll.

157. The sun may shine equally everywhere, but it reflects more clearly in clean water, mirrors, and other transparent objects. Similarly, God may dwell in every heart, but He manifests more completely in the hearts of holy people.

234. Tears of repentance and tears of joy come out from opposite corners of the eyes: the former from the inner corner and the latter from the outer corner.

235. Question: "Nowadays many preachers are preaching religion. What do you think of them?"

Answer: "It is like a man who has food for one person, but he has invited one hundred. After practising a little sadhana, he has started to make money by initiating disciples like a professional guru."

236. Question: "What is real preaching?"

Answer: "Real preaching requires that one be absorbed in God before preaching spirituality to others. He who tries to make himself free, preaches well. Hundreds of people from all directions come to one who is free and they ask for instruction. When the flowers bloom, bees come of their own accord."

303. Let the boat be in the water, but let not water be in the boat. Let a spiritual aspirant live in the world, but not let worldliness enter inside him.

364. The same God manifested here as Krishna and manifested there as Jesus.

383. God laughs twice. When two brothers divide the land, saying, "This part is mine and that part is yours," God laughs. He says to Himself, "The whole universe belongs to Me, but they say they own this portion or that portion." When the physician says to a patient's mother, "Don't be afraid, mother; I shall certainly cure your boy," God laughs. He says to Himself, "I am going to take his life, and this man says he will save it!"

376. When shall I be free? When "I" ceases to be. If "I" wants to remain, let it stay as a servant-I of God.

405. Neither sin nor mercury can be hidden.

406. One who eats radish belches radish; one who eats cucumber belches cucumber. What is inside of a person comes out through his or her speech.

471. One cannot see God without renouncing lust and gold.

570. Question: "What should I do with bad thoughts?"

Answer: "Let bad thoughts arise in the mind; they cannot do any harm until you do something wrong."

593. Once the Master said, "If you want to understand after hearing one sentence, come to me. And if you want to understand after hearing a million sentences, go to Keshab Chandra Sen." A man asked him, "Please give me knowledge in one sentence." He said, "*Jagat mithya Brahma satya* — This world is impermanent and Brahman is real."

621. One cannot achieve anything if there is any theft in the chamber of the heart [meaning hypocrisy].

688. Friend, as long as I live so long do I learn.

720. As many faiths, so many paths. Have steadfast devotion to your path, but never hate or criticize the paths of others.

744. God loves simplicity. Call on Him with a simple and pure mind. You will then surely find Him.[7]

17

The Gospel of Ramakrishna According to Ram Chandra Datta

The Life of Ram Chandra Datta

Ram Chandra Datta, a householder disciple of the Master, was one of the recorders of Ramakrishna's gospel. Ram was born in Calcutta on 30 October 1851. From his boyhood onward Ram was very bold and straightforward in his convictions, and no one could persuade him to act contrary to them. He studied at the General Assembly's Institution and later was admitted to the Campbell Medical School in Calcutta. Sometime after his graduation he was appointed as an assistant to the Government Quinine Examiner. He also married around this time. Later, when he became financially solvent, he bought a house for his family at Simla, in the central part of Calcutta.

Ram was deeply interested in science and studied chemistry under his English supervisor with great diligence. Having learned this subject thoroughly, Ram extracted from an indigenous medicinal plant an antidote for blood dysentery. This drug was approved by the government and was recommended by leading doctors. As a result, Ram's fame spread and he was appointed a member of the Chemist Association of England. He was also promoted to the post of Government Chemical Examiner and was asked to teach the military students at the Calcutta Medical College.

Ram's great enthusiasm for science and modern knowledge made him an inspiring lecturer, but it also made him an atheist. In his own words: "In those days we did not believe in God. We considered that everything happens, changes, or dissolves by the force of nature. We were rank materialists, and we held the view that eating, sleeping, and creature comforts were the *summum bonum* of life."[1] Ram was fond of debating with others about God and religion and found great satisfaction in defeating his opponents. This ardour for atheism lasted five years.

Grief is an eye-opener that forces a person to face the harsh realities of life. The death of his young daughter was a terrible shock to Ram, and a great change came over his life. On the evening of Kali Puja, sometime after his daughter's death, he went up to the roof of his house and observed the houses of Calcutta glittering with lights. Above, the dark, clear sky was studded with twinkling stars. His grief-stricken heart seemed to be searching for something meaningful in that panorama of nature. All of a sudden he noticed some clouds passing overhead, driven by the wind. They quickly disappeared. Ram asked himself: "Where do they come from and where do they go? Does God exist? If so, can He be seen?"[2]

He started to visit different religious leaders of the Brahmo, Christian, and Hindu faiths, but no one could answer his questions about God and religion. During this time Ram's family guru came to his house and wanted to initiate him. Ram was forthright. He said: "Sir, I don't believe in God. I have terrible doubts about His existence. Can you tell me the way to realize God?" The guru kept quiet. He did not know what to say.

"The great inquiry" began to possess Ram. He became more and more determined to have his doubts removed and to satisfy his hunger for God. He studied many religious books but could find no satisfactory answers to his questions. At last he came to know about Ramakrishna from the writings of Keshab Chandra Sen, a Brahmo leader of Calcutta.

On 13 November 1879, Ram went to Dakshineswar by boat with Gopal Chandra Mitra and a cousin, Manomohan Mitra. As soon as they reached the Dakshineswar temple garden, they inquired about Ramakrishna and were directed to his room. But when they reached it they found the door shut, and their Western education made them hesitate to call out or knock. Just then Ramakrishna opened the door himself and asked them to come in. Ram noticed that Ramakrishna did not look like the traditional ochre-clad monk with matted hair and ash-smeared body. On the contrary, the Master was the embodiment of simplicity.

Ramakrishna saluted them, addressing them as Narayana, and asked them to sit down. Then he smiled at Ram and said: "Hello, are you not a doctor? [*Pointing to Hriday*] He is suffering from fever. Could you check his pulse?" Ram was astonished that Ramakrishna knew he was a doctor. After examining Hriday, Ram reported that his body temperature was normal.

From the very beginning Ramakrishna made Ram his own and would often inquire about his personal life and mental conflicts. Ram was greatly attracted to the Master and started visiting him every Sunday, returning home in the evening. Soon Ram felt bold enough to ask the questions that had been haunting him.

Ram: "Does God exist? How can one see God?"

Ramakrishna: "God really exists. You do not see any stars during the day, but that does not mean that the stars do not exist. There is butter in milk, but can anyone know it merely by sight? In order to get the butter you must churn the milk in a cool place before sunrise. If you want to catch fish in a pond, you have to learn the art of fishing from those who know it, and then you must sit patiently with a fishing rod, throwing the line into the water. Gradually the fish will grab your bait. Then, as soon as the float sinks, you can pull the fish to the shore. Similarly, you cannot realize God by a mere wish. Have faith in the instructions of a holy man. Make your mind like a fishing rod and your prana, or life-force, like a hook. Your devotion and japa are like the bait. Eventually you will be blessed by the vision of God."

Ram had recently been connected with the Brahmo Samaj, whose members did not believe in a God with form, so he was wondering how one could see a formless God. The Master read his mind and said: "Yes, God can be seen. Can God, whose creation is so beautiful and enchanting, be imperceptible?"

Ram: "Is it possible to realize God in this life?"

Ramakrishna: "You get what you desire. Faith alone is the key to success." Then he sang a song:

As is a man's meditation, so is his feeling of love;
As is a man's feeling of love, so is his gain;
And faith is the root of all.
If in the Nectar Lake of Mother Kali's feet
My mind remains immersed,
Of little use are worship, oblations, or sacrifice.

The Master continued: "The more you advance in one direction, the more you leave behind the opposite direction. If you move ten steps towards the east, you move ten steps away from the west."

Ram: "But one must have tangible proof. Unless we have direct experience of God, how can our weak and doubting minds have faith in His existence?"

Ramakrishna: "A typhoid patient in a delirious state clamours to take gallons of water and heaps of rice. But the physician pays no heed to these entreaties, nor does he prescribe medicine at the patient's dictation. He knows what he is doing."[3]

Ram was very moved; he was impressed by Ramakrishna's simple, convincing answers. He became so intoxicated listening to these divine discourses that he was reluctant to return home. Whenever he visited the Master, he would forget all about the world, his family, and his duties.

Once, at the Master's request, Ram spent a night at Dakshineswar. When he was alone with the Master, he started looking at him in wonder.

Ramakrishna: "What are you looking at?"

Ram: "I am looking at you."

Ramakrishna: "What do you think of me?"

Ram: "I consider you to be Chaitanya."

Ramakrishna was silent for a moment, and then he said, "Well, the Bhairavi Brahmani used to say the same thing."[4]

As days went by, Ram saw more and more of Ramakrishna's extraordinary spiritual powers, and his scepticism was replaced by faith.

Quite often the devotees of Ramakrishna would arrange festivals in their homes and would invite the Master and other devotees to attend. At these gatherings the Master would talk about God and sing and dance in ecstasy, filling the whole house with an intense atmosphere of spirituality. The host generally bore all the expenses of the feast, including paying the Master's carriage fare and sometimes hiring a musician. Now Ram was known for his miserliness, and when he started to calculate the expenses involved in hosting such a festival, he hesitated. But when Ramakrishna set a date to visit his home, Ram had a change of heart and gladly began to make the necessary preparations.

In the early 1880s, on a full moon day of the Bengali month of Vaishakh, Ramakrishna went to Ram's house. Ram felt so blessed on this occasion that afterwards he would arrange a festival every year to celebrate that auspicious day. After this, Ram invited the Master to his house many times and became so expert in festival management that other devotees would consult him before inviting the Master to their homes. Slowly the Master uprooted Ram's miserliness and made him a generous devotee.

A true disciple carries out his teacher's instructions to the letter, proving thereby his love for the teacher. The Master had said, "Those who serve the devotees, serve me." Ram strictly observed this commandment of the Master, serving the followers of Ramakrishna with great devotion until the end of his life. He used to say, "He who calls on Ramakrishna is my nearest relative." His wife, Krishnapreyasi, was also very devout, and she cheerfully helped her husband in his spiritual path. Ram, furthermore, had heard the Master cautioning the devotees about money: "Just as water under a bridge is constantly flowing and as a result it never becomes stagnant and foul, so also the money earned by a real devotee should be spent for a noble cause rather than be accumulated. The desire for accumulation breeds the poison of attachment."[5] Ram, therefore, did not save his earnings, but spent money freely for the good of others — especially for the poor, the needy, and the afflicted. He helped many students financially, even to the extent of providing free board and lodging in his own home. But Ram's main interest was in arranging kirtan every evening in his home and feeding the thirty or so participants.

Spiritual life is not always smooth. Ram and the other devotees would be absorbed in their singing until the late hours of the night, and this naturally caused much disturbance. Soon Ram's neighbours began to complain. He then decided to buy a secluded garden house where he could hold kirtans and practise spiritual disciplines. When he informed the Master of his intention, Ramakrishna advised him, "Buy such a solitary garden house that if a hundred murders were committed there no one would know it."[6] Accordingly, in the middle of 1883 Ram purchased a garden house at Kankurgachi, a suburb just east of Calcutta.

After a few months the Master said to Ram: "How is it that you have not yet taken me to the new garden you have purchased for holding kirtan? Let us go one day to your garden to see what it is like."[7] Ram was exuberant. Immediately he arranged everything for the Master's visit. On 26 December 1883 the Master visited Ram's garden house. That visit is recorded in M.'s *Gospel of Sri Ramakrishna*.

In September 1885 Ramakrishna moved to Shyampukur, in the northern section of Calcutta for his cancer treatment. Ram took an active part in the arrangements that were made for the Master's care. The stuffy and polluted atmosphere of Calcutta aggravated Ramakrishna's illness. In accordance with his doctor's advice, the devotees moved him to a garden house in Cossipore, a suburb north of Calcutta. Ram, as usual, took the managerial role there, and he also contributed money towards the Master's living expenses according to his means.

On 1 January 1886, Ramakrishna went into an extraordinary spiritual mood and blessed many devotees, saying, "Be illumined." Ram was one of those present on that occasion. Later he celebrated that day every year as "Kalpataru Day" (Wish-Fulfilling Day) at his garden house.

On 17 January 1899, at 10:45 p.m., Ram breathed his last. His body was cremated on the bank of the Ganges and the relics were placed next to Ramakrishna's temple at Yogodyana. Before he passed away he told his disciples: "When I die please bury a little of the ashes of my body at the entrance to Yogodyana. Whoever enters this place will walk over my head, and thus I shall get the touch of the Master's devotees' feet forever."

Ramakrishna's First Biography

Ram Chandra Datta was an ardent devotee of Ramakrishna. In 1885 when the Master heard that Ram was writing something about him, he cautioned Ram, saying: "Do not publish my biography now. If you do, my body will not last long." Ram honoured this request. But in July 1890, four years after the Master's passing away, he wrote the first biography of Ramakrishna, *Sri Sri Ramakrishna Paramahamsadever Jivanvrittanta*.

In the introduction to the biography Ram wrote: "Whatever I have written in this book about Paramahamsadeva is based on some incidents I have witnessed myself, some I have heard directly from the Master, and some on information sent by Hridayram Mukhopadhyay, the Master's nephew. I verified some incidents of the Master's early life supplied by Hriday through Manomohan Mitra who went to Kamarpukur and compared them with the statements of the local people."

Ram further wrote: "I had a keen desire to write a chronological biography of Paramahamsadeva, but failed because only the Master knew what he had done and none else. Even Hriday did not know everything about him although he constantly lived with him. I asked questions of the elderly people of Dakshineswar, but they also could not give any information about the Master. When the Master talked, he did not say anything about the date, month, or year. He only told us the chronology of his practising sadhana that we have recorded accordingly."[8]

Ram's biography of Ramakrishna is 240 pages long, with 22 chapters and an appendix. He describes the Master's birth and early life, his coming to Calcutta and accepting the post of priest in the Kali temple of

Dakshineswar, his vision of Kali, his various sadhanas, his marriage, his practice of Christianity and Islam, his pilgrimage, his meeting with great people of India, the coming of his devotees, the training of his disciples, and his passing away. Although this biography has tremendous historical value, it seems that Ram wrote and interpreted it according to his understanding.

Tattwasara

Ram was so moved by the teachings of Ramakrishna that he would go to Dakshineswar with paper and pencil to write down the Master's immortal words. Seeing him taking notes, the Master said to Ram: "Why are you writing all these things? You will see, later your mind will be your guru." However, in May 1885 Ram compiled some of Ramakrishna's important teachings that he had noted down and brought them out in a Bengali book entitled *Tattwasara*. A few of the devotees objected to this and they reported it to the Master. Ramakrishna called Ram aside one day and said: "Look here, some devotees informed me that you were publishing a book. What have you written?" Ram replied that he had collected some of his teachings and put them together in a book. Ram then read some of it to the Master, who said: "Oh, you have written those teachings? Very good. Listen, if you think that you have written them you will get very little response from others; but if you think that the Lord is working through you then it will be in great demand."[9]

Ram wrote in the introduction to his version of the Master's gospel:

The goal of *Tattwasara* is to spread the teachings of a holy man. It would be nice if a wise pandit would take over this task, but I am sorry to say that no one came forward. However, I have given a start and I believe that henceforth some competent people will write many books based on the teachings of Paramahamsadeva like *Tattwasara* and spread many profound truths of the spiritual realm.

Finally I should say that it is extremely difficult to express fully the words and ideas of the Master. For that reason, I suggest that those who want to attain true knowledge, should go to Paramahamsadeva at the Kali temple of Dakshineswar. Once in an ecstatic mood the Master said: "Those who come here with simple faith for pure knowledge and God-realization, their desires will certainly be fulfilled."[10]

There are six chapters in *Tattwasara*: God; The Nature of God, with Form and without Form; Brahman and Shakti; Methods of Sadhana; How to Attain God; and The Necessity of Practising Sadhana. Ram included his own commentaries on Ramakrishna's teachings in this book.

Tattwa-prakashika, or Teachings of Ramakrishna Paramahamsa

In 1886 Ram collected more of the Master's teachings, which he published in three volumes in 1886 and 1887 under the title *Tattwa-prakashika, or Teachings of Ramakrishna Paramahamsa*. This 460-page book includes 300 teachings. It should be noted that the gospel Ram recorded is different from other gospels. He wrote commentaries on the Master's teachings according to his own understanding. They were based on science, philosophy, folklore, and scripture.

Ram wrote in the preface to this book:

> The gems of my heart are now published in the form of *Tattwa-prakashika* for bringing happiness to humanity. The gems I received from the Master are undecaying and infinite. No thieves or robbers can steal them. None can have them until I offer them willingly. Previously I published some of these gems [in *Tattwasara*], and many people were eager to have more, so I have published this book in an enlarged form.
>
> As rainwater falls from above and takes form according to the container, so the Master's teachings have been understood by people according to their capacity. I interpreted his teachings according to my knowledge. Some people think that material science, mental science, and spiritual science are contradictory; but the Master's teachings harmonize all three sciences.[11]

Like the gospel according to Girish Chandra Sen, the teachings of Ramakrishna in these books are recorded in Ram's own language. In *The Gospel of Sri Ramakrishna*, however, M. tried to preserve the Master's language in his record. In *Tattwa-prakashika* Ram included 300 of the Master's teachings, with his own interpretations, in ten chapters: God; Difference between Brahman and Shakti; The Nature of God, with Form and Without Form; Maya; The Place for Sadhana; Methods of Sadhana; The Guru; God-realization; Who is a True Spiritual Aspirant?; and General Teachings: to the Monks and the Householders.

It is noteworthy that Ram was the first person to publish a biography of Ramakrishna, the first to build a temple for the worship of the Master's relics, and the first to preach publicly that Ramakrishna was an avatar. His burning faith, devotion, renunciation, erudition, and his power to convince people made him an ideal evangelist. And more important, he had the blessings of his guru, Ramakrishna.

From 1893 to 1897, Ram gave eighteen lectures on Ramakrishna's life and teachings at the Star, City, and Minerva theatres. These lectures created a sensation in Calcutta. At first some of Ramakrishna's devotees objected to these lectures, but Ram would not listen to them. He gave his first lecture on Good Friday in 1893, entitled "Is Ramakrishna Paramahamsa an Avatar?" Ram substantiated his belief that Ramakrishna was an avatar through scriptural quotations, reasoning, empirical evidence, and incidents from his own personal experience. Ram's writings and lectures about Ramakrishna are written in Bengali and have not been translated.

18

The Gospel of Ramakrishna According to Mahendra Nath Gupta

The Life of Mahendra Nath Gupta, or M.

M. was the pen name of Mahendra Nath Gupta. He was born in Calcutta on 14 July 1854. His parents were spiritually-minded people, and he was very devoted to his mother. When he was four years old, he went with his mother to attend the Chariot Festival of Jagannath at Mahesh, and on their way back they stopped at the Dakshineswar temple garden. He later recounted his memory of that day: "The temple was all white then, new and glistening. While going around the temple, I lost sight of my mother and was crying for her on the temple porch. Immediately a handsome brahmin came out of the temple and, touching my head, consoled me. Then he called out: 'Whose child is this? Where has his mother gone?'" M. told the devotees, "Most probably he was Sri Ramakrishna because at that time he was the priest in the Kali temple."[1]

From his childhood, M. had religious and mystical inclinations. When he was five years old, he used to climb to the roof of his house to gaze at the vastness of the sky or to stand there during the monsoon and experience the torrential rains. He had read in the Mahabharata that one should love and worship one's teacher, so when the family priest visited their home, M. saluted him and served him personally. On his way to school he would bow down at the temple of the Divine Mother, which was on the other side of the College Street Market. When he was in the eighth grade he started to keep a diary, and the following entries show his religious nature: "I got up in the morning and prostrated before my parents." "As usual, on my way to school I saluted Mother Kali and Mother Shitala." *The Gospel of Sri Ramakrishna* was the ultimate result of this habit of keeping a diary, and M. himself commented about his great work, "I was an apprentice for fifteen years."[2]

M. was a brilliant student. He received his school education at the Hare School in Calcutta, where he was second in his class, and in 1875 he graduated third in his class from the Presidency College. He was a favourite student of C.H. Tawney, a well-known professor of English, who later wrote a brochure on Ramakrishna. While M. was in college he married Nikunja Devi, a cousin of the Brahmo leader Keshab Chandra Sen. At that time Keshab was the hero of modern Bengal, and M. was very much influenced by him.

After graduating from college, M. became a teacher. He served as headmaster in several schools in Calcutta. In February 1882, when he met Ramakrishna, M. was the headmaster of the Shyambazar Branch of the Vidyasagar School. He was an excellent teacher, well versed in both Eastern and Western philosophy as well as in history, literature, astronomy, and science. Moreover, he had studied the New Testament so thoroughly that he could quote many passages from memory. Long after M. had met Ramakrishna, a Christian minister once expressed his amazement at the depth of M.'s knowledge of the Bible. M. told him politely, "Sir, we lived with Christ [to M., Ramakrishna and Christ were the same], so we understand his teachings a little."[3]

God's divine play in this world is such that we sometimes find suffering leading to happiness, and again, success leading to a downfall. M.'s mother died when he was young, and without her, squabbles gradually disrupted the harmony in their joint family. M. was a peace-loving soul, and he finally could no longer bear the pettiness and selfishness of his relatives. He decided to leave home. One night at 10:00 p.m. he left for his sister's house at Baranagore, accompanied by his wife. He hired a horse carriage, but one of the carriage wheels broke near Shyambazar. He approached a friend's house nearby to ask for lodging for the night, but got a cold reception. Luckily, at midnight he found another carriage and was able to reach his sister's house. M.'s brother-in-law, Ishan Kaviraj, happened to be Ramakrishna's physician.

The next afternoon M. went for a walk with his nephew Sidhu, who took him to the temple garden of Dakshineswar, and there M. met Ramakrishna for the first time. M. put it beautifully: "I was thinking of killing myself, but instead I found my real Self. My family troubles led me to God."[4] It is interesting that Sidhu, who took M. to Ramakrishna, never visited Ramakrishna again. M. writes of that first visit:

They [M. and Sidhu] arrived at the main gate at dusk and went straight to Ramakrishna's room. And there they found him seated on a wooden couch, facing the east. With a smile on his face, he was talking of God. The room was full of people, all seated on the floor, drinking in his words in deep silence. M. stood there speechless and looked on. It was as if he were standing where all the holy places met and as if Sukadeva himself were speaking the word of God, or as if Sri Chaitanya were singing the name and glories of the Lord in Puri. M. looked around him with wonder and said to himself: "What a beautiful place! What a charming man! How beautiful his words are!"

As he left the room with Sidhu, he heard the sweet music of the evening service arising in the temple from gong, bell, drum, and cymbal. He could hear music from the nahabat, too, at the south end of the garden. The sounds travelled over the Ganges, floating away and losing themselves in the distance. A soft spring wind was blowing, laden with the fragrance of flowers; the moon had just appeared. It was as if nature and man together were preparing for the evening worship.[5]

On that first day, M. spoke very little with Ramakrishna. He later said to the devotees: "After meeting Sri Ramakrishna, I completely forgot my past. His towering personality and spiritual magnetism erased my sad memories."[6]

On his second visit, M. was scolded by Ramakrishna and, as he described it, his ego was crushed. With humility born of greatness, he immediately perceived the truth of Ramakrishna's words and accepted it. It seems that M.'s belief in intellectual knowledge was overpowered by Ramakrishna's spiritual wisdom once and for all. Generally people prefer to hide their weaknesses, but M. was so sincere that he meticulously recorded all the scoldings he received from the Master, as well as his reactions to them. M.'s record runs: "Thus rebuked, M. sat speechless. His pride had received a blow. After a few minutes Sri Ramakrishna looked at him kindly and said affectionately: 'You see, you have certain good signs. I know them by looking at a person's forehead, his eyes, and so on.'"[7]

On this occasion M. asked Ramakrishna four vital questions about life. For readers of *The Gospel of Sri Ramakrishna*, it is as though M. had asked them on behalf of humanity: (1) "How may we fix our minds on God?" (2) "How ought we to live in the world?" (3) "Is it possible to see

God?" (4) "Under what conditions does one see God?" Reading Rama-krishna's responses to these questions in the first few pages of the *Gospel*, one can already see how the Master incorporated in his teachings para-bles, symbols, songs, stories, folklore, myths, scientific reasoning, day-to-day household examples, and examples from nature and the behaviour of animals and humans. He seldom used scriptural testi-mony. He taught from his personal experience and explained the deep truths of spiritual life in an utterly simple way, and this captivated M. Never before had he met such a man.

On his fourth visit, M. found Ramakrishna in his room surrounded by a group of young men. As soon as M. came into the room, the Master laughed and said to them: "There! He has come again." Then he explained the reason for his laughter: "A man once fed a peacock with a pill of opium at 4:00 p.m. The next day, exactly at that time, the peacock came back. It had felt the intoxication of the drug and returned just in time to have another dose."[8]

For the remaining four and a half years of the Master's life, M. returned for dose after dose of this divine intoxicant — direct association with God Incarnate — and then shared it freely with other seekers of God. At the beginning of each volume of the Bengali *Gospel*, he quotes a verse from the Bhagavata: "O Lord, your words, like sweet nectar, refresh the afflicted. Your words, which poets have sung in verses, vanquish the sins of the worldly. Blessed are they who hear of you, and blessed indeed are they who speak of you. How great is their reward!"[9]

As other Incarnations of God have had someone to witness or collect their teachings, perhaps M. was this same great soul born again for that purpose. At first sight, Ramakrishna recognized M.'s worth, and the following comments he made about M. indicate that M. was not an ordi-nary person: "I recognized you on hearing you read the *Chaitanya Bhagavata*. You are my own. The same substance, like father and son. Before you came here, you didn't know who you were. Now you will know." "Once [in a vision] I saw Gauranga and his devotees singing kirtan in the Panchavati. I think I saw Balaram there and you too." "Yes, I know everything: what your Ideal is, who you are, your inside and outside, the events of your past lives, and your future."[10] "I can see from the signs of your eyes, brows, and face that you are a yogi. You look like a yogi who has just left his seat of meditation."[11]

At one of their first meetings Ramakrishna wanted to evaluate M.'s understanding of his spiritual state. He asked M.: "What do you think of me? How many annas of knowledge of God have I?" "I don't understand what you mean by 'annas,'" replied M. "But of this I am sure: I have never before seen such knowledge, ecstatic love, faith in God, renunciation, and catholicity anywhere."[12]

On another occasion Ramakrishna asked, "Have you found anyone else resembling me — any pandit or holy man?" M. replied, "God has created you with His own hands, whereas He has made others by machine."[13] This remark made the Master laugh.

After he had been visiting the Master for some time, M. felt the urge to renounce family life and become a monk. But Ramakrishna had set out a different path for him and discouraged him from this idea, saying: "You are well established in God already. Is it good to give up all? God binds the Bhagavata pandit to the world with one tie; otherwise who would remain to explain the sacred book? He keeps the pandit bound for the good of men."[14] When M. insisted, the Master said: "Let nobody think that if he does not do Mother's work, it would remain undone. The Mother can turn even a straw into a teacher."[15]

Ramakrishna knew the mission of M.'s life: M. would be the recorder of his gospel. Ramakrishna trained him accordingly, making him a perfect instrument to propagate his message to the world.

Ramakrishna remarked about M.: "This man has no ego." This was true because he had crushed M.'s ego. On his second visit, M. tried to argue with the Master on the question of whether God has form or is formless. About the incident M. recorded in the *Gospel*: "This was M.'s first argument with the Master, and happily his last." An egotistic person cannot carry God's message. There is a saying: "Where there is I, there is no God; and where there is God, there is no I. As darkness and light never stay together, so ego and God." Anyone who wants to be a perfect instrument of God, will have to efface his or her ego. M. wanted to be in the background in the divine drama of Ramakrishna. In the *Gospel*, he hid himself behind many names: M., Mani, Master, Mohinimohan, an Englishman, a devotee, a servant, and so on.

Introduction and the Kali Temple of Dakshineswar

M. wrote a short biographical introduction about Ramakrishna for the first part of the original Bengali *Gospel*. Swami Nikhilananda's translation does not include this introduction; the translator includes his own more elaborate biography instead. In the original *Gospel*, M. wrote about Ramakrishna's birth, his parents, his boyhood days in Kamarpukur, his education, his association with holy men, and his first samadhi. He described Ramakrishna's move to Calcutta, his acceptance of the position of priest in the Kali temple of Dakshineswar, and his vision of the Divine Mother. M. discussed Ramakrishna's marriage to Saradadevi. M. also wrote that Ramakrishna became so god-intoxicated that he could not continue to do the worship service, but instead practised Tantra, Vedanta, Christianity, and Islam, and thereby realized God through many religious paths. The Master cried: "Mother, I shall listen only to you. I don't know any scriptures, nor have I anything to do with the scholars who are well versed in them. You teach me, Mother."[16]

Ramakrishna realized that the Supreme Brahman and the Divine Mother are the same. According to M., the Divine Mother told Ramakrishna: "You and Myself are identical. Endowed with devotion, you stay in this world for the good of humankind. When pure devotees come, talk to them about God."[17]

During the vesper service, the Master would cry from the roof of the Kuthi: "O devotees, where are you? Please come quickly." Gradually, the devotees began to come. M. gave a list of the Master's men and women devotees and the year in which they came. M. also mentioned Ramakrishna's pilgrimages and meetings with distinguished people of the East and West.

In his original introduction to the Bengali *Gospel*, M. left a beautiful description of the temple garden of Dakshineswar. This introduction is discussed in detail in this book in the chapter entitled "The Stage for Ramakrishna's Divine Play."

Sri Sri Ramakrishna Kathamrita

In 1897 M. published two pamphlets in English under the title *The Gospel of Sri Ramakrishna*. A few years later, the *Gospel* started being published in Bengali in five volumes as *Sri Sri Ramakrishna Kathamrita*. Volume one was published in 1902, volume two in 1904, volume three in 1908, volume four in 1910, and volume five in 1932. The *Gospel* contains nearly 176 entries that M. recorded during Ramakrishna's lifetime and eight entries that he added after the Master passed away. In addition, M. collected a few more entries from other sources and included them in the appendix.

M. also discussed the history of *The Gospel of Sri Ramakrishna*:

To what extent can we foresee God's plan? The Master made me start keeping a diary in 1867 when I was a student in class eight at Hare School. Since then I recorded in my journal my daily activities, the places I visited, and so on. I met the Master in the later part of February 1882. That is when my habit of maintaining a diary really became fruitful. When we look back on our past we realize that God is making us do everything. God determines beforehand what he will do through a particular person and then gets it done through him. There were many people around the Master, but he made me write the chronicle. As a result, *The Gospel of Sri Ramakrishna* came into existence. I was an apprentice for fifteen years. The hard discipline greatly helped me. It sharpened my memory and increased my skill in writing. I could recall the sequence of all of the incidents that had occurred during the day after I returned home at night. I would try to remember the first lines of the songs I had heard. This is the way the Master worked through me.

I was involved in worldly activities, bound to my work, and could not visit the Master whenever I wished. Therefore I used to note down his words so that I could think over what he had said between my visits to him. In this way the impressions made on my mind might not be counteracted by the stress of worldly work and responsibilities. It was thus for my own benefit that I first took notes, so that I might realize his teachings more perfectly.

I used to memorize the Master's words, and then after returning home I would write brief notes in my diary. Sometimes I would spend the whole night in completing my record. Later I would fill in all the details from memory. Sometimes I would spend seven days completing the record of one day's happenings. Thus *The Gospel of Sri Ramakrishna* appeared in book form from the notes of my diary. Sometimes I had to wait for a word of the Master's to come to my mind as a chataka bird waits for a drop of rainwater to fall. Sometimes I meditated on one scene over a thousand times. As a result I could vividly visualize the Master's divine play, though it had happened long before. By the grace of the Master I used to feel that his play had just happened. Therefore one can say that it was written in the Master's presence. At times I would not be satisfied with a particular description of an episode, so I would get absorbed in meditation on the Master. Then the correct picture would vividly appear in my mind. Therefore, from a human standpoint there was a great distance of time, but in my thought world I felt that it had happened just before I recorded it. My account is not culled from other sources. I recorded whatever I heard from the Master's lips with my own ears and whatever I saw of his life with my own eyes.

The Gospel of Sri Ramakrishna is the world's only firsthand record of the life and teachings of an avatar. One can collect materials about Sri Ramakrishna in three ways: First, direct observation recorded on the same day; second, direct observation but unrecorded during the lifetime of the Master; and third, hearsay, also unrecorded during the lifetime of the Master. *The Gospel of Sri Ramakrishna* belongs to the first category. I was present during each scene of the *Gospel*.

I have published my diary very carefully. If there is any mistake in it, then its value will diminish. People do not realize that at one time I had to study the rules of evidence. If a witness makes a single mistake, the entire case becomes nullified. Addressing the judge, the lawyer says, "My Lord, this witness is not reliable." I used to visit the court and observe all these details. The evidence of an eyewitness is very valuable. For that reason the judge asks, "Did you see this yourself?" If a person has seen and heard something himself, his words carry weight. I checked all the facts and details before I published *The Gospel of Sri Ramakrishna*.[18]

When somebody asked M. to remove some of the repetitions from the *Gospel*, he replied:

I cannot do that. The Master told the same parable to different people. If I remove a particular section, the train of the conversation will be broken. Moreover, you won't be able to see the effect of the *Gospel* on a particular person's life. The Master gave the same teaching to five different people in five different places. What he said to Bankim, he said to others also; and whatever conversation he had with Vivekananda, he had with others too.

You see, sometimes the brilliance of a diamond is enhanced by changing its setting. Putting it on the dusty ground produces one effect, and putting it on a green lawn produces another. But putting it in a casket lined with blue velvet produces the most brilliant effect of all. The same is true of the words in the *Gospel*. The rays of the sun look different when they fall on water, on the earth, and on glass, but the maximum brilliance is produced when the sun is reflected on glass. So I cannot avoid the repetitions in the *Gospel*, because removing them would disturb the Master's dialogue.

Once Hriday said to the Master: "Uncle, please reserve some of your best teachings. Otherwise, if you say everything all at once, and then repeat the same thing again and again, people will not come to you anymore." The Master replied: "You rascal! I shall repeat my words fifty times. What does it matter to you?"[19]

The Gospel of Sri Ramakrishna was in the curriculum of M.'s school. When M. was accused by some people of trying to sell his books to the students, he calmly replied:

The students will understand the effect of reading the *Gospel* when they enter family life. The Master used to say, "The world is a burning fire." And I fully realized it. After the boys enter the world and are tormented by sorrows and sufferings, the Master's immortal words will save them, like a loving mother. If they remember at least one of the Master's teachings, that will be like a boat to ferry them across the turbulent ocean of maya and it will bring peace to their lives.[20]

In spite of his illness, M. read the proofs of the last part of the Bengali *Gospel* at one o'clock in the morning by the light of a kerosene lantern. Being lovingly chastised by a colleague, he said:

People are finding peace by reading this book, the Master's immortal message. It is inevitable that the body will meet its end, so it is better that it be used for spreading peace to others. We are in the world and have fully experienced how much pain there is in it, yet I have forgotten that pain through *The Gospel of Sri Ramakrishna*. I am hurrying so that the book may come out soon.[21]

The Gospel of Sri Ramakrishna is an authentic record of Ramakrishna's life and teachings, deep and yet very simple and appealing. Ramakrishna's language and the expressions he used are fascinating. Many people learn Bengali just so that they may read this wonderful piece of literature in the original language and get a taste of how Ramakrishna talked.

When we read the *Gospel*, its vivid descriptions help us to visualize Ramakrishna as he moved about in his environment. We see the places he knew and the people he came in contact with. This vivid and artistic depiction of an avatar's life is unique. Swami Vivekananda wrote: "The move is quite original, and never was the life of a great Teacher brought before the public untarnished by the writer's mind as you are doing. The language also is beyond all praise — so fresh, so pointed, and withal so plain and easy. Moreover, the dramatic part is infinitely beautiful."[22]

As we read the *Gospel*, we enjoy the holy company of the Master. In the *Gospel*, festivities are always going on, with Ramakrishna at the centre. We enjoy the theatre, music, singing, dancing, humour, worship, meditation, and samadhi. Reading the *Gospel* chases away loneliness and boredom. The *Gospel* presents to us the divine drama of Ramakrishna with various characters representing all types of people: jnanis, devotees, hypocrites, drunkards, householders, monks, actors, actresses, musicians, and so on.

Swami Bhajanananda wrote: "Every great religion has its own scripture. There are several scriptures already existing in the world, including the Vedas, Avesta, Tripitaka, the Bible, and the Koran. Do we need one more? Yes, precisely because there are several scriptures: We need just one more to show the validity of every one of them and to establish their overall harmony. *The Gospel of Sri Ramakrishna* compiled by M. serves this purpose admirably well."[23]

M.'s record of Ramakrishna's life is extremely interesting, in part because he himself played a vital role. Sometimes he was a silent witness of the divine drama of Ramakrishna; other times, an active participant in the play. In addition, M.'s love for the Master was phenomenal; his I-consciousness was saturated with Ramakrishna-consciousness. If this were not so, he never could have produced *The Gospel of Sri Ramakrishna*, which is unique among the world's religious literature. Faithfully and vividly, M. recorded the Master's samadhi and meditation, his prayer and worship, his dreams and visions, actions and devotion, purity and renunciation, singing and dancing, humour and mimicry, sadhana and pilgrimage, behaviour and psychology, religion and philosophy, and his social and scientific outlook. But most important, M. recorded Ramakrishna's conversations with God, as well as his talks with the people who came to him, his love and empathy for others, and his fervent concern for his devotees.

M. writes in the *Gospel*: "The Master was weeping and praying to the Mother. In a voice choked with emotion, he prayed to Her with tearful eyes for the welfare of the devotees: 'Mother may those who come to You have all their desires fulfilled. But please don't make them give up everything at once, Mother. Well, You may do whatever You like in the end. If You keep them in the world, Mother, then please reveal Yourself to them now and then. Otherwise, how will they live? How will they be encouraged if they don't see You once in a while?'"[24]

19

The Gospel of Ramakrishna According to Swami Brahmananda

A Bird's-Eye View of Ramakrishna's Gospels

The word *gospel* comes from *godspell* or *goodspell*, which means glad tidings, good news. This good news uplifts human minds. We may notice that some of Ramakrishna's teachings have been recorded differently by different writers. Although each of his teachings is the same, the wording and language he used were different. Stories have been recorded in more or less detail, depending on the writer. When we read the Bible, we find the same phenomenon: The same teachings or stories of Jesus were recorded differently by Matthew, Mark, Luke, and John. The wording of each gospel is different; some stories have more details than others. It is quite natural for two persons to see and hear the same thing at the same time and yet record different descriptions of the event.

The first gospel of Ramakrishna was recorded in 1878 by Girish Chandra Sen, a disciple of the Brahmo leader Keshab Chandra Sen; it consists of 184 of the Master's teachings. The second gospel was recorded in 1884 by Suresh Chandra Datta, a householder devotee of Rama-krishna, and comprises 950 teachings of the Master. The third gospel was recorded in 1885 by Ram Chandra Datta, a householder devotee of Ramakrishna. It consists of 300 teachings of the Master. The fourth gospel was recorded in diary form by M. (Mahendra Nath Gupta) from 1882 to 1886. Published in five volumes between 1902 and 1932, it has 176 entries. The fifth and last gospel was recorded by Swami

Brahmananda, a monastic disciple of Ramakrishna. It was published serially from 1898 to 1900 in *Udbodhan* magazine. In 1905 the teachings were collected in a book, *Sri Sri Ramakrishna Upadesh,* containing 248 teachings of the Master.

All of these gospels were recorded in Bengali, Ramakrishna's mother tongue. The first three of these gospels have not yet been translated into English in their entirety. M.'s record was published in five volumes, which in 1942 was published in English as *The Gospel of Sri Ramakrishna.* Swami Nikhilananda of the Ramakrishna-Vivekananda Centre in New York translated this huge work, and Aldous Huxley wrote the foreword. The gospel according to Swami Brahmananda was translated into English and edited by Jnanendra Nath Mukhopadhyay and F.J. Alexander as *Words of the Master* and published by Udbodhan Publication Office, Calcutta, in 1924.

The Master's words were so impressive and instructive that Swami Shivananda, as a young disciple, had felt tempted to take notes. He recalled: "One day at Dakshineswar I was listening to the Master and looking intently at his face. He was explaining many beautiful things. Noticing my keen interest, the Master suddenly said: 'Look here! Why are you listening so attentively?' I was taken by surprise. He then added: 'You don't have to do that. Your life is different.' I felt as if the Master had divined my intention to keep notes and did not approve of it, and that was why he had spoken in that way. From that time on I gave up the idea of taking notes of his conversations, and whatever notes I already had I threw into the Ganges."[1]

Ramakrishna advised his young monastic disciples to renounce both externally and internally; he advised his householder disciples to renounce internally. Many years later Swami Premananda related how the Master taught the monastic disciples: "Very little of the Master's teachings are recorded in the *Gospel,*" he said. "M. used to visit the Master occasionally and would note down his teachings as he heard them. . . . His teachings to the monastic disciples were given in private. As soon as the householder devotees would leave the room, he would get up and lock the door and then speak to us living words of renunciation. He would try to impress upon our young minds the emptiness and vanity of worldly enjoyments."[2]

The Life of Swami Brahmananda

Swami Brahmananda, a monastic disciple of Ramakrishna, was born in 1863 as Rakhal Chandra Ghosh. His father was a rich landlord of their village, Sikrakulingram, located some thirty miles from Calcutta. His mother died when he was very young and his father remarried. When Rakhal was twelve years old, he moved to Calcutta to attend school, but he was not interested in his studies. He was mainly interested in spiritual life and practising meditation. He met Narendra (later Swami Vivekananda) in a gymnasium. The two boys became close friends and remained so throughout their lives. He and Vivekananda joined the Brahmo Samaj, a socio-religious movement, in Calcutta. When Rakhal was eighteen, his father became concerned by his indifference to his studies and family life, so he arranged his marriage to a sister of Manomohan Mitra, an ardent devotee of Ramakrishna.

Ironically, it was Rakhal's brother-in-law who took him to Ramakrishna in June 1881, and later made it possible for him to renounce the world. As soon as the Master saw Rakhal, he told Manomohan with a smile, "A wonderful receptacle!" Then the Master asked him, "What is your name?" "Rakhal Chandra Ghosh." Hearing the word "Rakhal," the Master went into ecstasy and softly uttered: "That name! Rakhal — the cowherd boy of Vrindaban!" After regaining normal consciousness, the Master treated him as his own and at last said, "Come again." Earlier in a vision Ramakrishna had seen Rakhal dancing with Krishna and realized that he had been a companion of Krishna in his previous life.

In the beginning Rakhal visited the Master now and then; later he began staying at Dakshineswar. His father objected to this, telling him to concentrate on his studies. When he found that Rakhal was not listening to him, he became angry and locked him in a room. But there is a saying: "The more love is obstructed, the more intense it becomes." The lonely, homebound Rakhal longed for the Master. On his part Ramakrishna worried about Rakhal. He went to the temple and prayed: "Mother, my heart is breaking for Rakhal. Please bring him back to Dakshineswar." The Divine Mother answered Ramakrishna's prayer, and Rakhal resumed his visits to Dakshineswar after his father relented. His wife and her family were also sincere devotees and did not object to his remaining with the Master.

Under Ramakrishna's guidance Rakhal began to practise intense spiritual disciplines. He forgot day and night as well as food and family. The Master taught him various kinds of spiritual disciplines, such as *asanas* (postures), *mudras* (gestures), japa, meditation, yoga, and other practices. One day the Master initiated Rakhal into the path of Shakti before the Divine Mother and taught him how to practise meditation on the different centres of the kundalini. Rakhal used to practise these disciplines in private. Rakhal recalled: "Once I was meditating in the Panchavati at noon while the Master was talking about the manifestation of Brahman as sound [Shabda-Brahman]. Listening to that discussion, even the birds in the Panchavati began to sing the Vedic songs and I heard them."

Rakhal served his guru in Dakshineswar, and also in Cossipore during his last days. Ramakrishna passed away on 16 August 1886. The Master's disciples established the Baranagore Monastery and took their final monastic vows. Rakhal became Swami Brahmananda. He then went on pilgrimage and travelled throughout India. In 1893 Swami Vivekananda went to the United States of America and represented Hinduism at the Parliament of Religions in Chicago. He became very famous. In 1897 he returned to India, where he established the Ramakrishna Math and Mission and appointed Brahmananda its president. After Vivekananda passed away in July 1902, Brahmananda guided the Ramakrishna Order until his own passing away in 1922.

Brahmananda's Reminiscences of Sri Ramakrishna*

Sometimes devotees would tell Sri Ramakrishna about their spiritual experiences. Hearing them, one young disciple [Brahmananda himself] asked the Master to grant him some spiritual experiences. The Master told him: "Look. That kind of experience comes when one practises meditation and prayer regularly and systematically. Wait. You will get it eventually."

A couple of days later, in the evening, the young disciple saw the Master walking towards the Divine Mother's temple, and he followed him. Sri Ramakrishna entered the temple, but the disciple did not dare go inside, so he sat in the natmandir [the hall in front of the Mother's temple] and began to meditate. After a while he suddenly saw a brilliant light, like that of a million suns, rushing towards him from the shrine of the Divine Mother. He was frightened and ran to the Master's room.

A little later Sri Ramakrishna returned from the shrine. Seeing the young disciple in his room, he said: "Hello! Did you sit for meditation this evening?" "Yes, I did," answered the young disciple, and he related to the Master what had happened. Then the Master told him: "You complain that you don't experience anything. You ask, 'What is the use

*The material in this section was previously published in *Ramakrishna as We Saw Him* (Vedanta Society of Saint Louis, 1988).

of practising meditation?' So why did you run away when you had an experience?"

It is natural to experience depression now and then. I [Swami Brahmananda] also felt like that once while I was in Dakshineswar. I was then quite young and the Master was about fifty years old, so I was shy about speaking openly with him. One day I was meditating in the Kali temple. I could not concentrate my mind. This made me very sad. I said to myself: "I have been living here so long, yet I have not achieved anything. What is the use of staying here then? Forget it! I am not going to say anything about it to the Master. If this depressed condition continues another two or three days, I shall return home. There my mind will be occupied with different things." Having decided this in the shrine, I returned to the Master's room. The Master was then walking on the veranda. Seeing me, he also entered the room. It was customary after returning from the shrine to salute the Master and then eat a light breakfast. As soon as I saluted the Master, he said: "Look. When you returned from the shrine, I saw that your mind seemed to be covered with a thick net." I realized that he knew everything, so I said, "Sir, you know the bad condition of my mind." He then wrote something on my tongue. Immediately I forgot all my painful depression and was overwhelmed with an inexpressible joy.

As long as I lived with him I had spontaneous recollection and contemplation of God. An ecstatic joy filled me all the time. That is why one requires a powerful guru — one who has realized God. Before initiation the guru and the disciple should test each other for a long time. Otherwise there may be regrets afterwards. This is no passing relationship.

Ah, how joyfully we lived with the Master at Dakshineswar! Sometimes we would be convulsed with sidesplitting laughter by his humour and wit. What we now cannot experience by meditation, we then attained automatically. If my mind went astray even a little, he would understand it from my appearance and would pass his hand over my chest, setting my mind right. And how free I was with him! One day, on the semicircular west porch, I was rubbing oil on his body. For some reason I got angry with him. I threw away the bottle of oil and strode off with the intention of never returning. I got as far as Jadu Mallick's garden house but could not move further. I sat down. In the meantime he had sent Ramlal to call me back. When I returned he said: "Look. Could you go? I drew a boundary line there."

On another occasion I did something wrong and became extremely penitent. I went to confess it to him. As soon as I arrived he asked me to follow him with his water jug. While returning he said: "You did this certain thing yesterday. Never do it again." I was surprised. I wondered how he had known.

Another day when I returned from Calcutta he said: "Why can't I look at you? Have you done anything wrong?" "No," I replied, because I understood "wrong action" to mean stealing, robbery, adultery, and so on. The Master again asked me, "Did you tell any lie?" Then I remembered that the day before, while chatting and joking, I had told an untruth.

There is nothing outside. Everything is inside. People are fond of music, but they do not realize that the music we hear with our ears is trivial compared to the music within. How sweet and soothing it is! During his meditation in the Panchavati, Sri Ramakrishna used to listen to the melody of the vina [a stringed instrument] within.

Sri Ramakrishna rarely slept for more than an hour or so at night. He would pass the night sometimes in samadhi, sometimes singing devotional songs, and sometimes chanting the Lord's name. I often saw him in samadhi for an hour or more. In that state he could not talk in spite of repeated efforts. Regaining outer consciousness, he would say: "Look. When I am in samadhi I want to tell you my experiences, but at that time I lose my power of speech." After samadhi, he used to mutter something. It seemed to me that he was talking with somebody. I heard that in earlier years the Master stayed in samadhi most of the time.

The Master would go into different kinds of samadhi at different times. Sometimes his whole body would become stiff like a log. Coming down from this state, he could easily regain normal consciousness. At other times, however, when he was absorbed in deep samadhi, it would take a longer period for him to return to consciousness of the outer world. On such occasions he would take a deep breath after gasping for a while, like a drowning man coming up out of water. Even after he had composed himself, he would talk like a drunkard for some time, and not all of his speech was intelligible. At that time he would often express some small desire: "I shall eat *sukta* [a bitter squash curry]," "I shall smoke tobacco," and so on. And sometimes he would rub his face, moving his hands up and down.

Before the Master passed away at the Cossipore garden house, he would tell us about his visions of the Infinite. One day Girish and Swamis Vivekananda, Ramakrishnananda, Niranjanananda, and I were present in his room. We were then young boys, but Girish was elderly and extremely intelligent. Hearing a few words about the Infinite from the Master, Girish exclaimed: "Sir, don't talk anymore. I get dizzy." Oh, what a conversation! The Master used to say: "Sukadeva is like an ant that is satisfied with a small particle of sugar. Rama, Krishna, and other Incarnations are like bunches of grapes hanging on the tree of Satchidananda." These are mere thoughts about the Infinite. It is hard to comprehend.

On one occasion Sri Ramakrishna said: "One day as I was meditating in the Kali temple, I saw in a vision the veils of maya disappearing one after another. In another vision the Divine Mother showed me the light of Brahman, which surpassed the light of even millions of suns together. I then saw that a luminous form emerged from that infinite light and again merged back into its source. I experienced that the formless Brahman took a form and again became formless."

Oh, what superhuman power the Master had! At that time we thought it was merely a peculiar power with him, and we could not understand the nature of it. Now we realize what a wonderful power it was!

It would have been wonderful if the Master's sayings, especially those about his devotional practices, spiritual unfoldment, and experiences, could have been recorded exactly and correctly — that is to say, immediately after hearing them from him. When he talked about knowledge [jnana], he did not talk about anything else. Again, when he talked about devotion [bhakti], he spoke of nothing but devotion. He repeatedly imprinted in our minds that worldly knowledge is insignificant and futile, that one must exert oneself to attain spiritual knowledge, devotion, and love alone.

The Master could seldom sleep at night. He did not allow the boys who lived with him to sleep either. When others had gone to bed he would wake up his disciples, saying: "What is this? Have you come here to sleep?" Then he would instruct each disciple and send him for meditation to the Panchavati, Kali temple, or Shiva temple, according to his inclination. After practising japa and meditation as directed, each would return to the room and sleep. Thus the Master made his disciples work hard. Often he would say: "Three classes of people stay awake at night: the yogi, the enjoyer, and the sick person. You are all yogis, so sleeping at night is not meant for you."

Sri Ramakrishna used to say, "Eat as much as you like during the day but eat sparingly at night." The idea is that the full meal taken at noon will be easily digested, and if you eat lightly at night, your body will remain light and you can easily concentrate the mind. A heavy meal at night produces laziness and sleep.

Sri Ramakrishna used to encourage everybody to practise meditation. A person falls from spiritual life if he does not practise meditation regularly. The Master asked his guru Tota Puri, "You have attained perfection, so why do you still practise meditation?" Pointing to his shining brass pot, Tota Puri replied, "If you do not clean brass every day, it will be covered with stains." The Master used to say: "The sign of true meditation is that one forgets one's surroundings and body. One will not feel even a crow sitting on one's head." Sri Ramakrishna attained that state. Once while he was meditating in the natmandir, a crow sat on his head.

The temple garden of Dakshineswar, which Rani Rasmani had built, provided everything Sri Ramakrishna needed for practising sadhana. If you have true faith, love, and devotion, God will provide everything you need.

A monk saved ten thousand rupees in a bank. Hearing this, the Master said, "He who calculates pros and cons and plans for the future will ruin his spiritual life."

Usually the Master would not allow anyone to stay with him for more than two or three days, but once a young man stayed with him for several days. This annoyed some devotees, and they complained to the Master that he was teaching the young man the path of renunciation. The Master answered: "Let him take up a worldly life. Am I dissuading him from it? Let him first attain knowledge and then enter the world. Do I teach everybody to renounce lust and gold? I talk about renunciation to the ones who need only a little encouragement." He used to say to the rest, "Go and enjoy hog-plum pickle, and come here for medicine when you have colic."

Sometimes the Master would ask people: "Can you tell me what kind of state I am passing through? What makes me go so often to those who cannot buy me a penny's worth of puffed sugar cakes and who have not even the means to offer me a torn mat to sit on?" He used to explain afterwards: "I find that certain people will easily attain success. It will be very difficult for the rest, for they are, as it were, pots for curd. One cannot keep milk in them." He would tell them, "I pray for you so that you may realize God quickly."

The Master used to say, "Wherever there is extreme longing, God reveals Himself more." He also said to some people, while pointing to himself: "Have love for this. That will do." Oh! Such a wonderful play is over!

Again, he used to say, "One needs intense longing to realize God." In this connection the Master often told a story: Once an aspirant asked his teacher how to realize God. The teacher, without answering, took the disciple to the nearest pond and held him under the water. After a while, when the student was extremely restless and about to collapse, the teacher pulled him out of the water and asked, "How did you feel under the water?" "I was dying for a breath of air," he answered. "When you feel like that for God," said the teacher, "you will realize Him."

Another time he said: "Do you know what type of love is necessary for God-realization? As a dog with a wound in its head becomes frantic and jumps around, so one should desperately seek God."

The Master used to say that there should not be any theft [i.e., hypocrisy] in the inner chamber of the heart. He had great affection for the simple-hearted. He used to say: "I don't care for flattery. I love the person who calls on God sincerely." The Master also said that all impurities of the mind disappear by calling on God with a sincere heart.

Oh, how deep was the Master's devotion to truth! If he happened to say that he would not eat any more food, he could not eat more, even if he was hungry. Once he said that he would go to visit Jadu Mallick [whose garden house was adjacent to the Dakshineswar temple garden] but later forgot all about it. I also did not remind him. After supper he suddenly remembered the appointment. It was quite late at night, but he had to go. I accompanied him with a lantern in my hand. When we reached the house we found it closed and all apparently asleep. The Master pushed back the doors of the living room a little, placed his foot inside the room, and then left.

He could see the inside of a man by merely looking at his face, as though he were looking through a glass pane. Whenever a visitor came he would look him over from head to foot, and he would understand everything. Then he would answer that person's questions.

One day the son of a public woman came to Dakshineswar. The Master was sleeping in his room. The man entered and touched his feet. The Master at once jumped up, as if someone had thrown fire on him. He said: "Tell me frankly all the sins you have committed. If you cannot, then go to the Ganges and say them out loud. You will be freed from them." But the man was ill-fated and could not do so.

Sri Sri Ramakrishna Upadesh (Words of the Master)

Swami Saradananda wrote in his introduction to Swami Brahmananda's *Words of the Master*:

The present brochure is from the pen of one who was regarded by the

Master as next to the Swami Vivekananda in his capacity for realizing religious ideals. And everyone who had the great fortune to come directly under the hallowed touch of the Mahapurusha [saint] of Dakshineswar could testify to the great love which Sri Ramakrishna always bore towards the author of the volume.

The little volume therefore assumes a great importance in consideration of the source from which it has come. For the only motive which has moved the author to compile these selected sayings of the Master is to present them to the public as nearly as possible in the form in which they were originally uttered. It is indeed the labour of grateful love of the beloved disciple, who, more than anyone else, used to live so constantly with the Master, to set him aright before the public, seeing how his invaluable words are becoming roughly handled, deformed, and distorted nowadays at the hands of many.[3]

Brahmananda completed his book, *Words of the Master*, when he was in Varanasi in 1914. Swami Prabhananda wrote in his *Brahmananda Charit*:

Maharaj [Brahmananda] used to write the Master's teachings sitting in his room at the Home of Service, and he would not allow anyone to be there when he wrote them. His attendants observed that sometimes at midnight, he would ask to have the manuscript brought to him. Once, after correcting it, he said: "The Master came and told me: 'I didn't say that. I said this.'" This incident occurred towards the end of his compilation. Another day the Master appeared before Maharaj and said that one of the teachings that had been recorded was not his. Then Maharaj remembered that he had heard that teaching* from a Gujarati monk. Referring to this incident, Maharaj remarked: "The Master protected me from a falsehood." He immediately removed that teaching from his manuscript and completed his compilation project.[4]

---

*There was a holy man who used to practise meditation sitting on the bank of a river. One day he saw a scorpion being carried away by the current of the river. Out of compassion he grabbed hold of it and released it on the ground. As soon as he touched the scorpion it stung his hand, causing him terrible pain. After a while the scorpion fell back into the water and was again about to be carried away by the current. Again the monk rescued it and was stung by the ungrateful creature. A third time the scorpion fell into the river, and seeing its pitiable condition the compassionate monk started to rescue it. At that moment a bystander said to the monk: "Sir, I have been watching you. I saw how that scorpion stung you several times. Still you are trying to save its life?" The monk replied: "The nature of a scorpion is to sting, and the nature of a holy person is to do good to others, so I am following my nature." Saying so, the monk picked up the scorpion once more and carried it to a distant place so that it could not again fall into the water. The nature of a holy man is to do good to the world, and he never gives up his divine nature. [Swami Chetanananda, *A Guide to Spiritual Life* (Vedanta Society: St. Louis, 1988),104.]

Truth is deathless. The life and teachings of avatars are based on truth, so they are immortal. As the gospels of Buddha and Christ are passing from generation to generation without any interruption, so the gospel of Ramakrishna will continue to flow throughout the ages.

20

After Ramakrishna's Passing Away

By M. (Mahendra Nath Gupta)

The five volumes of Sri Sri Ramakrishna Kathamrita, recorded by M. (Mahendra Nath Gupta) in Bengali, were not written in chronological order. At the end of the first four volumes, M. added some information about the disciples of the Master and the Ramakrishna monastery at Baranagore that was established after Sri Ramakrishna's passing away. A few years ago, some researchers discovered that four of M.'s diary entries (25 August 1886, 2 September 1886, 12 October 1886, and 17 February 1887) had been published in 1904 in the Navya Bharat (Jaishtha-Ashar 1311 B.E.), a monthly magazine. Perhaps M. intended to add these entries at the end of the fifth volume of the Kathamrita, but unfortunately that volume was only published posthumously. I have translated this newly-found material from Bengali into English. I must acknowledge that I have used some songs from Swami Nikhilananda's translation, The Gospel of Sri Ramakrishna, which I have referred to in the footnotes. In this precious historical record we learn that the Ramakrishna Math at Baranagore was inaugurated sometime before 12 October 1886. — Translator

*Translated by Swami Chetanananda from Udbodhan, vol. 102, issue 10 and vol. 103, issues 2 and 3.

Chapter 1
Wednesday, 25 August 1886

It has been ten days since Sri Ramakrishna went to his own abode, leaving his devotees behind. Imbued with renunciation, Narendra and his brother disciples have been practising sadhana.

Narendra and the Master's devotees have assembled in the parlour of Balaram Basu's house in Calcutta. They are like motherless orphans. By merely looking at them, one can feel their intense grief, the result of the Master's passing away. One thought fills their minds: The Master has gone to his own abode; what should we do now? The devotees have no place where these young disciples can stay together. They are forced to return home for food and shelter every day. The thread holding the pearls together as a necklace has broken, and the group is about to fall apart. The disciples continually think: Where shall we go? What shall we do? Sitting in seclusion, they think of the Master and cry for him.

Narendra, Rakhal, Kali, Sharat, Shashi, Tarak, Gopal, Bhavanath, and M. arrived first, and later Niranjan came.

Every one looks to Narendra. He is planning to send some of his brother disciples to Vrindaban, so he has been collecting some money from the devotees.

Sri Ramakrishna's Advice: Renounce Lust and Gold

Narendra leaves for Girish's house nearby, accompanied by some of his brother disciples. He and M. talk on the way.

Narendra (*to M.*): "Sir, please pay for a one-way fare for Baburam."

M.: "Certainly. I will pay."

Narendra: "Right now, if you would, please."

M.: "Right now?"

Baburam is one of those who has been chosen to go to Vrindaban. The group of devotees arrives at Girish's parlour. Narendra asks Girish for money.

Girish: "I don't have much money with me at present, but if you want I can contribute 10 or 11 rupees right now. Why are they going to Vrindaban?"

Narendra (*gravely*): "The Master told us to renounce lust and gold."

A Devotee: "Are you also going away?"

Narendra: "Let us all renounce home first. I have some business at home. The litigation has not yet been settled. (*After some thought*): Let the litigation take its own course. I haven't understood the truth. Getting involved in this family affair is useless."

Rakhal: "If I stay here, I shall feel pulled by my family."

Narendra's father had passed away, and he has two younger brothers and some sisters. They have no guardian and no money to purchase food and clothing. Narendra has passed his B.A. examination, and if he so wishes, he can get a job to maintain his family. Rakhal has his father, wife, and child at home.

The topic of the Kankurgachi garden house [where Ramakrishna's relics were installed] arises and they discuss how the trustees should be appointed.

Rakhal: "We will be pleased if they make Narendra a trustee."

Narendra: "No, no. What good is there in being a trustee?"

When everyone asks Narendra to be a trustee, he tells Girish: "All right. Let it be so." But Narendra is not appointed.

The Devotees are Grief-stricken Because of the Master's Passing Away

In Girish's room Mani* and a devotee begin to talk. The devotee heaves a sigh and says: "I shall not pray to the Master for anything."

Mani: "Not for anything?"

Devotee: "No, I will not pray for anything — neither for devotion nor for my family."

Having thus spoken, the devotee again sighs deeply.

Devotee: "The Master said: 'Why so much milk? Devotees have their families; how can they afford to pay for it?' How painful! I will never forget it."

While the Master was suffering from cancer at the Cossipore garden house, the householder devotees had borne all the expenses for the Master's service. The Master was always watchful so that they might not spend too much money.

Devotee: "I wanted to engage a full-time doctor to treat the Master, but I couldn't do it."

The devotee remains silent for a while and then says: "Well, do you think that I would try to improve the condition of my family by chanting the Master's name? What do I care whether people call me good or virtuous?"

---

*"M." and "Mani" are pseudonyms for Mahendra Nath Gupta, the recorder of *The Gospel of Sri Ramakrishna*.

Chapter 2
Thursday, 2 September 1886

Shashi has come to M.'s house on Guruprasad Chaudhury Lane in Calcutta. He and M. are seated on a wooden cot in the study. Shashi and Sharat live in their family home at Pataldanga. Today Shashi wears clean clothes and carries a new umbrella. Shashi and M. begin to talk about the Master.

M.: "The Master told me that Narendra was the main disciple among the group."

Shashi: "I vividly remember that the Master said that Narendra would be our leader."

M.: "Do you remember what the Master said about further study?"

Shashi (*with a smile*): "Yes, I distinctly remember that the Master told Narendra one day, 'Don't allow them [the young disciples] to study in school anymore.'"

M.: "What about Kali?"

Shashi: "Yes, the Master scolded Kali and said to him, 'You have introduced studies here.' I had begun to study the Persian language, and as a result I got a scolding from him."

Then Sharat and Narendra arrived, and they all began discussing when Sri Ramakrishna's message would be preached. Who would preach it first?

M.: "Who has understood the Master? Do you remember what the Master said about Vaishnavcharan's writing?"

Sharat: "Yes, I remember. The Master said: 'Vaishnavcharan understood every one of my spiritual experiences. I thought that he would be the first to make them public.'"

Narendra: "The Master told me, 'The knowledge of Brahman is the goal. Vaishnavcharan was supposed to spread the message first, but it didn't work out. Keshab Sen was the first to make the message public.'"

Chapter 3
Sri Ramakrishna's First Monastery at Baranagore
Tuesday, 12 October 1886

Nearly two months had passed since the Master left this world, after binding his devotees with a cord of love. Where would they go now? They could no longer enjoy staying at their homes. They wanted to be together always and to spend their days and nights thinking of him and talking about him. Two or three of the disciples had no home. At this juncture Surendra came forward and told them: "Brothers, you have no place to live, and we have no place to give rest to our hearts. Let us rent a house in Baranagore, where you will live, and we shall visit from time to time."

Surendra used to pay fifty [actually eighty] rupees every month for the Master's service at the Cossipore garden house. He now said: "Brothers, I used to contribute a little money for the Master's service. I shall provide that amount to pay the expenses of this house in Baranagore."

Gradually, Narendra and the Master's other unmarried disciples moved to the Baranagore monastery and they did not return to their homes. The number of monastic brothers increased over time, and eventually Surendra was donating one hundred rupees per month.

Blessed Surendra! It is you who have laid the foundation of this first monastery. This Ashrama owes its existence to your good wishes! Through you the Master has made it possible for his disciples to live in the world as the embodiment of his central teaching — the renunciation of "woman and gold." Through Narendra and other young renunciants he has demonstrated the Eternal Hindu Dharma among people. Who can forget the debt owed to you? The brothers lived at the monastery like orphan boys. Sometimes they would not have the money to pay their rent; sometimes they would have no food. They would wait for you to come and settle all these difficulties. Who would not shed tears on remembering your selfless love!

Narendra and Jnana Yoga

Baranagore Math. On this moonlit night Narendra and Mani are walking on the eastern veranda of the Master's shrine. It is the night of the full moon, when the goddess Lakshmi is worshipped.* Narendra and Mani converse about the Master and also about jnana yoga and bhakti yoga.

Mani: "The Master described two paths — knowledge and devotion — and said that both lead to the same goal. The followers of jnana and the followers of bhakti reach the same place."

Narendra: "But the Master told me: 'The Knowledge of Brahman is the goal. Devotion is meant to maintain the external aspect of life. The elephant has outer tusks and inner grinders as well. The tusks are mere ornaments; but the elephant chews its food with the grinders.'"

Mani: "The Master also said that one can attain the Knowledge of

*In that year it was on 12 October 1886.

Ramakrishna Math,
Baranagore

Baranagore Math, 1887

Standing, left to right: *Swamis Shivananda, Ramakrishnananda, and Vivekananda, the monastery cook, Devendra Mazumdar, Mahendra Nath Gupta (M.), Swami Trigunatitananda, Harish Mustaphi (maternal uncle of Devendra Mazumdar).* Sitting, left to right: *Swamis Niranjanananda and Saradananda, Hutko Gopal, Swami Abhedananda*

Brahman through the path of devotion. The Knowledge of Brahman can be attained from the path of knowledge as well as from the path of devotion. Perhaps you remember that the Master also said: 'After attaining the Knowledge of Brahman, some embrace devotion and live in this world. One can then ascend from the *lila* (Relative plane) to the *nitya* (Absolute plane) and descend from the nitya to the lila.'"

Narendra: "Were you present that day when the Master talked about the Knowledge of Brahman at the Cossipore garden house?"

Mani: "I was not present at that time; but I heard that he talked about it for a long time. Do you remember what he said about Sukadeva?"

Narendra: "No, I don't remember."

Mani: "I have heard that the Master said on that day: 'Sukadeva and sages like him may have been big ants; but even they could carry at the utmost a few grains of sugar. Shiva touched the water of the Ocean of Brahman-Consciousness, or at the most drank a handful of that water.' Did you hear such things?"

Narendra: "Yes, the Master said many such things on that day."

Narendra's Vision and Abnegation of Ego

Mani and Narendra begin a discussion about the brothers of the monastery.

Mani: "Now everything depends on you. You will have to look after them."

Narendra: "The ego is very troublesome. The other day I scornfully scolded H. a little. Immediately I had a vision of the Master. Do you know what he told me? He said: 'What are you thinking? Know for certain that I can make any one amongst you who is the smallest, the greatest, and again I can make any one amongst you who is the greatest, the smallest.'* I have been extremely careful since I had that vision. 'The least shall be greatest and the greatest, the least.'"

Mani: "You are right. One attains God by His grace only. He can make a person great, and also small. Can anyone attain Him by one's own efforts? One needs His grace."

Narendra's Longing for God-vision

Narendra enters the room. It seems that his hope for God-realization has weakened a little. He begins to sing:

*Compare: "I teach the Knowledge of Brahman to the gods and human beings. I am endowed with the Knowledge of Brahman. I make a person great if I want to. I can make a person Brahma, a rishi, or a knower of Brahman." — Devi-sukta, 5.

Can everyone have the vision of Shyama? Is Kali's treasure for
  everyone?
Oh, what a pity my foolish mind will not see what is true!
Even with all His penances, rarely does Shiva Himself behold
The mind-bewitching sight of Mother Shyama's crimson feet.
To him who meditates on Her the riches of heaven are poor indeed;
If Shyama casts Her glance on him, he swims in Eternal Bliss.
The Prince of yogis, the King of the gods, meditate on Her feet in vain;
Yet worthless Kamalakanta yearns for the Mother's blessed feet![1]

Narendra goes to another room in the monastery. What is he
thinking? Has Sri Ramakrishna's loving form suddenly come alive in his
heart? He again begins to sing:

Dear friend, my religion and piety have come to an end:
No more can I worship Mother Shyama; my mind defies control.
Oh, shame upon me! Bitter shame!
I try to meditate on the Mother with sword in hand,
Wearing Her garland of human heads;
But it is always the Dark One,* wearing His garland of wild
  wood-flowers
And holding the flute to His tempting lips,
That shines before my eyes.
I think of the Mother with Her three eyes, but alas! I see
Him alone with the arching eyes, and I forget all else!
Oh, shame upon me! Bitter shame!
I try to offer fragrant flowers at the Mother's feet,
But the ravishing thought of His graceful form unsettles my helpless
  mind,
And all my meditations meant for the Naked One** are drawn away
By the sight of His yellow scarf.[2]

After singing this song, Narendra remains silent for a while and then
suddenly announces, "Let us go to the cremation ground." He then
remarks: "My goodness! It seems to be a parlour and not a cremation
ground." (All laugh.)
Paramanik Ghat is near the monastery, and the cremation ground is
near that ghat. The cremation ground is surrounded by walls, and there
is one brick building with three rooms at the east end. Sometimes at
night Narendra and others go there alone to practise sadhana.

*Krishna.
**Shyama.

*　　　　　*　　　　　*

The Holy Mother now lives in Vrindaban. Narendra and M. are talking about her. One day at the Cossipore garden house, the young devotees told Sri Ramakrishna about the Holy Mother's affection for them. At that time she was living at the garden house to serve the Master. The disciples told the Master that they had never met another woman as large-hearted as she was.

M.: "What did the Master say?"

Narendra: "The Master began to laugh and then said: 'She is my Shakti [Power]. So she loves all.'"

Chapter 4
Friday, 17 February 1887

It is 12:30 p.m. at the Baranagore monastery. Narendra and the other monastic brothers are living at the monastery. Haramohan and M. have arrived. Shashi is busy with the Master's worship service. Narendra is about to go to the Ganges for his bath.

Narendra: "Krishna mainly discussed japa and austerity in the Gita."

M.: "How is that? Then why did he give so much advice to Arjuna?"

Narendra: "Krishna did not ask Arjuna to perform family duties."

M.: "When Krishna asked Arjuna to fight, Arjuna was a householder. He, therefore, was advising Arjuna to perform his family duties in a detached way."

(Narendra later changed his opinion about this. While in America he lectured on karma yoga, and there he advised his students to perform action without attachment. When Narendra first took the vows of sannyasa, he was extremely disgusted with the duties of the world, so he said that japa and austerity were the main focus of the Gita.)

A householder devotee is talking with a monastic brother; his intention is to stay at the monastery. The devotee is impressed with the spiritual atmosphere of the monastery, and family life has become distasteful to him. They are talking on the southern veranda of the kitchen, where Niranjan is working.

The Devotee: "If I stay in the monastery, will I be blamed for neglecting my family?"

The Monk: "No one will blame you for living here, but you have a responsibility to look after your family."

Niranjan (*from the kitchen*): "Hello brother, what are you doing? What kind of advice are you giving to him?" (*All laugh.*)

Narendra and Kali have returned from their bath in the Ganges. Kali is always engaged in studying Vedanta. He does not care for the attitude: "You are my Lord and I am Your devotee." He reflects continually: "I am that Brahman. I have no name and form." So after returning from his bath, he goes to his room and starts repeating: "I am beyond name and form. I am that Absolute Being. I salute You, I salute You, I salute You and Myself."

The devotees sit down to have lunch. There is only one cook at the monastery. After lunch everyone clears away their own leaf-plates; but Narendra removes M.'s leaf-plate. When M. objects, Narendra replies, "Here all are equal."

After lunch everyone assembles in the parlour. Some are chewing betel-rolls; some are smoking hubble-bubbles.

Rakhal (to M.): "I want to visit you someday. I am eager to hear what you are writing about the Master."

M.: "I have decided that until my life is transformed I will not share those teachings with anybody. Each of the Master's words is like a mantra. Is it not good to translate those teachings into one's life?"

Rakhal: "Yes, indeed. Well, how do you like your family life?"

Shashi: "Look, brothers, Rakhal is lecturing."

Rakhal (smiling, to M.): "Previously I was not inclined to come here. Now I see that the company of the brothers is beneficial."

Narendra: "Where is the real substance in human beings? I care for no one, except one. [Perhaps he meant Sri Ramakrishna.] Who has his own power? Everyone is subject to circumstance — a slave to maya. Everyone is a slave like me — a sport of circumstances."

Rakhal smiles and whispers to Haramohan. Prompted by Rakhal, Haramohan asks: "What about Brother X?"

Narendra: "Brother X is a wretched fellow. If he wants to be a monk, why is he saving money? A sadhu should be penniless."

A Monk: "Everyone is wretched and you consider yourself great."

Narendra: "I am also wretched because I am a slave of circumstances. Do I have any power?"

M. (to himself): "Is it circumstance or God? The Master used to say, 'Everything happens by the will of Rama.'"

Narendra: "How can a man who has money be a monk? Moreover, he gives lectures to people. Is he not ashamed to preach?"

Narendra and Buddha

Haramohan: "Well, if a man experiences ecstasy or samadhi, he must be great."

Narendra: "Go and study Buddha. According to Shankara the ultimate spiritual experience is nirvikalpa samadhi, which is the first stage that Buddha attained."

A Devotee: "If nirvikalpa samadhi is the first stage, then there must be higher stages than that. Why don't you describe a few to us? Buddha must have said something about it."

Narendra: "I don't know."

A Devotee: "If nirvikalpa samadhi is the first stage of Buddha's experience, then why did he later preach this doctrine: 'Nonviolence is the supreme dharma?'"

Narendra: "It is hard to understand this view, but the Vaishnavas learned their nonviolence from Buddha."

A Devotee: "Is it necessary for one to learn nonviolence from Buddha? It often happens that one gives up eating fish without having any instruction from anybody. It may not be true that the Vaishnavas learned nonviolence from Buddha."

Narendra: "If someone renounces the killing of animals without being asked to, then it is to be understood as hereditary transmission."

A Devotee: "Then what about the people in Europe who have given up killing animals? They were beef-eaters. They have not learned from Buddha."

Narendra: "However, Buddha discovered this path."

M. (to himself): "Wonderful! Each disciple of the Master is a hero. Everyone is an independent thinker, not just Narendra. And why not? They are disciples of the Master and he trained them himself."

*　　　　*　　　　*

Narendra is reading the Gita and explaining it to the brother disciples. He has been elucidating the following verses from the Gita (5:7-9): "He who is devoted to yoga and is pure in mind, who has conquered his body and subdued his senses, who has realized his Self as the Self of all beings — he is undefiled though he acts. 'I do nothing at all,' thinks the yogi, the knower of Truth; for in seeing, hearing, touching, smelling, and tasting; in walking, breathing, and sleeping; in speaking, emitting, and seizing; in opening and closing the eyes, he is assured that it is only the senses busied with their objects."

After reading the Gita for a while, Narendra says: "I am leaving; now you have the joyful company of M." But Narendra cannot go.

Baburam: "I don't understand the Gita and other scriptures. The Master said the right thing, 'Renounce, renounce.'"

Shashi: "Do you know what the real import of the word 'renounce' is? It means to remain in this world as an instrument in the hands of God."

Prasanna begins to study the Gita in Kali's retreat room; Sharat is also there reading Lewis' *History of Philosophy*. Another monk is meditating in the Master's shrine.

Narendra and the Vision of God

The discussion turns to the vision of God.

Narendra: "The vision of God is a kind of false perception."

Rakhal: "What do you mean? You have experienced it."

Narendra (*with a smile*): "One gets such a vision because of a derangement of the brain, like a hallucination."

Mani: "Brother, whatever you may say, the Master had visions of divine forms; so how can you say that it is a derangement of the brain? Do you remember when Shivanath remarked that the Master's samadhi was a kind of nervous disorder or mental illness, and the Master replied, 'Does anyone become unconscious thinking of Consciousness?'"

Narendra and the other brothers have assembled in the parlour. Some are chewing betel-rolls, some are smoking hubble-bubbles. It is spring, and nature is as if pulsating with joy. The monastic brothers are also joyful. They practise celibacy and renunciation and think of God day and night. Always before them is their great ideal, their guru, Sri Ramakrishna. Sometimes out of exuberant joy, they shout the great saying of the Sikhs: "*Wah guruji ki fate!*" — Victory to the guru! Narendra taught them this mantra, prefacing it with "Om."

M. asks Sharat to join him in repeating "Victory to the guru," one hundred times, which makes him happy.

Narendra: "It does not work to just give an order. One should first start repeating the mantra. Then others will join in."

Balaram has sent some sweets and other things from his Calcutta residence. The kachuris (fried bread with a spicy filling) are delicious. All of the brothers enjoy the refreshment. One brother tries to eat more than his share.

Narendra (*to the brother*): "You greedy rascal! It is not good to eat too much."

The Vesper Service in the Monastery

It is evening. Shashi burns incense in the shrine and bows down to the Master, glorifying his sweet name. Then he goes to the pictures of the gods and goddesses in each of the rooms, addressing them one after another and waving incense in front of each of them. He chants in his melodious voice: "Salutations to the guru"; "Salutations to Mother Kali"; "Salutations to Chaitanya taking the form of Rama and Krishna"; "Salutations to Radha and Krishna"; "Salutations to the beloved of Radha"; "Salutations to Advaita Acharya and other devotees"; "Salutations to Gopala and Mother Yashoda"; "Salutations to Rama and Lakshmana"; "Salutations to Vishwamitra."

The senior Gopal performs the vespers by waving the light, and the devotees watch him. Narendra and M. are in the main hall. M. had asked Narendra to join the vesper service, but due to some work he could not do so.

After the vespers, the devotees sing a hymn to Shiva in chorus: "Jaya Shiva Omkara, Bhaja Shiva Omkara; Brahma Vishnu Sadashiva, Hara Hara Hara Mahadeva."

As night falls, everyone sits for a light supper, which Baburam serves. Each person is served a few chapatis, some vegetable curry, and a little bit of molasses. M. is eating with them, sitting next to Narendra. When Narendra sees a couple of burnt chapatis on M.'s plate, he immediately replaces them with good ones. Narendra keeps a vigilant eye on everything.

After supper everyone sits together in the parlour. A monastic brother tells M.: "Nowadays we hardly get to hear any songs on the Divine Mother. Why don't you sing that favourite song of the Master?"

M. sings:

O Mother Shyama, full of the waves of drunkenness divine!
Who knows how Thou dost sport in the world?
Thy fun and frolic and Thy glances put to shame the god of love.
O Wielder of the sword! O Thou of terrifying face!
The earth itself is shaken under Thy leaps and strides!
O Thou Abode of the three gunas! O Redeemer! Fearsome One!
Thou who art the Consort of Shiva!
Many the forms Thou dost assume, fulfilling Thy bhaktas' prayers.
Thou dancest in the Lotus of the Heart,
O Mother, Eternal Consort of Brahman![3]

While talking with M., Rakhal says: "I want to visit Varanasi. I feel I should go there alone."

Rakhal has his father, wife, and son at home, but he has renounced everyone and everything for God-realization. He is endowed with intense renunciation. His mind is longing for God all the time, so he wants to wander alone.

21

Ramakrishna and His Divine Play According to Swami Saradananda

The Life of Swami Saradananda

Swami Saradananda was a monastic disciple of Ramakrishna. He was born Sharat Chandra Chakrabarty in an affluent family in Calcutta in 1865. While attending college in 1883, he met Ramakrishna in Dakshineswar and began to visit him regularly. Speaking of him and his cousin, Ramakrishna recalled, "In a vision I saw that Shashi and Sharat were among the followers of Christ."[1]

One day at Dakshineswar, Ramakrishna fulfilled the wishes of his disciples like a Kalpataru (wish-fulfilling tree). Some asked for devotion, some knowledge, and some liberation. Seeing Sharat silent, the Master asked him: "How would you like to realize God? What divine vision do you prefer to see in meditation?"

Sharat replied: "I do not want to see any particular form of God in meditation. I want to see Him in all beings. I do not like visions." The Master said with a smile: "That is the last word in spiritual attainment. You cannot have it all at once."

"But I won't be satisfied with anything short of that," replied Sharat. "I shall strive my best until I am able to attain it." At last the Master blessed him, saying, "Yes, you will attain it."[2]

Ramakrishna continued to train his disciples until he passed away in 1886. Sharat served his guru during his last days and witnessed the final divine play of the Master. In January 1887, he took final monastic vows under the leadership of Swami Vivekananda at Baranagore Math and then left to practise austerities in the holy places of India.

In 1893 Swami Vivekananda went to America and represented Hinduism, or Vedanta, at the Parliament of Religions in Chicago. After teaching Vedanta in the United States and Europe for a few years, he asked Saradananda to help him. In March 1896 Saradananda left for England and met Vivekananda there in April. Swamiji then sent him to America with Mr. Goodwin towards the end of June.

Saradananda was very successful in preaching Vedanta. He lectured at the Cambridge Conferences also. It is a great loss that only one of the swami's lectures was recorded, "The Vedanta: Its Theory and Practice."

After successfully preaching Vedanta in the West for a couple of years, Saradananda was called back to India by Swamiji, who then made him the secretary of the Ramakrishna Math and Mission, which he had founded in May 1897. Saradananda carried the responsibility of this important position until he passed away in 1927.

The Origin of Sri Sri Ramakrishna Lilaprasanga

In 1909 Saradananda began to write his monumental work *Sri Sri Ramakrishna Lilaprasanga* in Bengali. This biography was translated as *Sri Ramakrishna, The Great Master* by Swami Jagadananda in 1952. My translation as *Sri Ramakrishna and His Divine Play* was published in December 2003 by the Vedanta Society of St. Louis. It is not only an authoritative biography of the Master, but also a classic of Bengali literature. Saradananda wrote his magnum opus in five volumes, beginning with volumes three and four, then completing two, one, and five. He explained why he did not follow a chronological sequence as he worked: "Unless people understand how the Master remained in bhavamukha [an exalted state between the Absolute and the Relative] and how the mood of a guru was natural to him, they will not be able to comprehend the Master's wonderful character, unprecedented mental state, and extraordinary activities. That is why we tried to make the reader understand this subject at the outset [by first writing the third volume]." He published serially some parts of *Lilaprasanga* in the magazine *Udbodhan*, beginning in 1909 and continuing until 1919.

Saradananda described several reasons for this great undertaking: First, he wrote it to repay the money that he had borrowed to build a house in Calcutta for Sri Sarada Devi, the Holy Mother, and to publish *Udbodhan* (a Bengali magazine started by Vivekananda).

Second, he wished to publish an accurate and complete account of the Master's life. As an editor of *Udbodhan*, he had to correct and rewrite many articles about Sri Ramakrishna that were full of misinformation. As an eyewitness to the Master's life, he could not bear that any untruth about the Master be published.

Third, by 1909 several books had been published about Ramakrishna, including *Sri Sri Ramakrishna Paramahamsadever Jivanvrittanta* by Ram Chandra Datta, *Sri Ramakrishna Punthi* and *Sri Ramakrishna Mahima* by Akshay Kumar Sen, *Sri Ramakrishna Charit* by Gurudas Barman (the pen name of Priyanath Sinha, a classmate of Vivekananda), and *Sri Sri Ramakrishna Kathamrita* by M. Some of these writers' records were not accurate, and some focussed on the miracles that the Master had performed — which he himself had despised. With the goal of presenting a flawless biography of Ramakrishna, Saradananda began to write the *Lilaprasanga*. He appealed to the Master's devotees to send him or the president of the Order their authentic stories or other incidents concerning the Master.[3]

Fourth, Saradananda wrote in the preface to volume three of his work: "When Swami Vivekananda, the foremost disciple of Sri Rama- krishna, came to the West to preach religion, people became eager to know more about the Master's life. As a result, many people have written many things about the Master, but until now no one has clearly indicated that his extraordinary life was deeply connected to the eternal Hindu, or Vedic, religion. While reading those other books one might come to the opposite conclusion, that Sri Ramakrishna was an indi- vidual, separated from the eternal Hindu religion, who had created a particular religious sect."[4] He also reproduced Swamiji's article on "Hinduism and Sri Ramakrishna" at the beginning of the third volume as testimony that the Master's life was the meeting point of all sects and that his message harmonized all religions.

Fifth, Saradananda tried to justify the philanthropic activities of the Ramakrishna Mission and also to remove misunderstandings about Ramakrishna's teaching, "Serve human beings as God." M., the recorder of *The Gospel of Sri Ramakrishna*, had commented that the monastic disci- ples had changed the focus of the Master's teaching, which according to M. was God-realization and not social service. Of course, M. revised his opinion in 1912, when the Holy Mother visited the Ramakrishna Mission Home of Service in Varanasi and said, "The Master is ever-present in this place, and Mother Lakshmi always casts Her benign glance upon it."[5]

Once Girish Chandra Ghosh had asked Vivekananda to write a biography of Sri Ramakrishna. Swamiji declined, expressing his inability, saying, "Shall I make the image of a monkey while trying to make that of Shiva?" On another occasion Swamiji said, "Sharat will write." Later Girish asked Saradananda to write about Sri Ramakrishna's divine life, his sadhana, and his message. He feared that otherwise, in the future some less adept people might present the Master in a narrow, incorrect way, which might eventually form a cult and defeat the purpose of his incarnation. There was cause for such apprehension: It was well known that Girish had given his "power of attorney" to the Master, who took complete responsibility for him. Some people began trying to imitate this and deceive themselves, not understanding the importance of self-surrender.

Saradananda first wrote "Sri Ramakrishna as a Guru," the third and fourth volumes of *Lilaprasanga*, and then wrote the remaining volumes. In the beginning of the third volume, Saradananda explained the mystery of the "power of attorney" that the Master had accepted from Girish. Before publication, Saradananda read the chapter to Girish, who wholeheartedly approved it.[6]

Once a monk asked Saradananda to write about the life of Ramakrishna and to include all the stories about him. The swami replied: "Is it so easy to write about the Master? One should not undertake such work without having his command. If I get his command, I shall try." Some years later when the *Lilaprasanga* was published, the same monk asked Saradananda whether he had received the command before writing the book. He avoided the question, saying, "That is none of your business."

One day, Asitananda, an attendant of Saradananda, worked up the courage to ask the swami if he had experienced nirvikalpa samadhi. "Did I waste my time cutting grass [i.e., living meaninglessly] when I lived in the company of Sri Ramakrishna?" Saradananda replied. When the attendant pressed him for details, the swami said: "Read the chapter on samadhi in the *Lilaprasanga*. I have not written anything about samadhi without experiencing it myself."[7]

Christopher Isherwood, the author of *Ramakrishna and His Disciples*, wrote:

Although Saradananda did not begin his work until more than twenty years after Ramakrishna's death, there is no doubt of its authenticity.

Many of those who had known Ramakrishna were then still alive, and Saradananda carefully compared his memories with theirs. *The Great Master* has also the value of having been written by a monastic disciple, who has actually shared the extraordinary experiences he describes. "Nothing beyond my spiritual experience has been recorded in the book," Saradananda once told a questioner. This seemingly cautious answer is in fact a claim so tremendous that it silences all suspicion of boastfulness; a man like Saradananda could not have made it unless it was literally true.[8]

With permission from the Holy Mother as well as her blessings, Saradananda began to write *Sri Sri Ramakrishna Lilaprasanga*. All of the information about Holy Mother in the book came directly from her. When the Mother was in Calcutta, Saradananda used to read the manuscript to her, as it was then being published serially in *Udbodhan* magazine. When she was in Jayrambati, someone else would read it to her. She commented: "Everything has been written correctly in Sharat's book." Once a learned disciple of the Mother said, "Mother, what a wonderful book Sharat Maharaj has written!" The Mother replied, "Yes, one needs learning and intellect to understand Sharat's book."[9]

Swami Saradananda painstakingly gathered stories of the Master's early life from the villagers of Kamarpukur. For information on the Master's sadhana, he relied on accounts supplied by Hriday, the Master's nephew and attendant, as well as stories told by the Master himself. The Master's wife (Sarada Devi) and other relatives, his men and women devotees, and his disciples contributed many stories and eyewitness accounts. Swami Saradananda wrote in the preface to his fifth volume: "When we first started writing about the Master's divine play, we never imagined that we would proceed so far. It was possible only by his inconceivable grace." This detailed biography of Sri Ramakrishna is unique in spiritual literature; we can find no similar detailed accounts for Krishna, Buddha, or Christ.

The swami wrote in the preface to the third volume: "The Master told us explicitly again and again: 'He who was born as Rama and as Krishna in previous ages is now in this sheath,' as he pointed to his own body. 'The spiritual experiences of this place (*meaning himself*) have surpassed even the Vedas and Vedanta.' While recounting as impartially as possible the biography of Sri Ramakrishna, who was established in bhavamukha, we were forced to admit that such an extraordinary life had never before been seen in the spiritual world."[10]

In 1925, during the Chariot Festival in Puri, Saradananda talked about the adverse conditions in which he wrote the *Lilaprasanga* in the Udbodhan house:

> Holy Mother was living upstairs along with Radhu; I was surrounded by devotees and I had to keep the accounts also; the burden of the loan for the house was on me. I used to write the *Lilaprasanga* sitting in the small room downstairs. Then nobody dared to talk to me, as I had no time to chat for a long time. If anybody would ask anything, I would say, "Be quick," and finish the talk briefly. People would think that I was egotistic. I could not write much about the devotees [except Gopal-ma and Vivekananda], because there was so much material to write about the Master. When the mind was ready, only then could I write.[11]

The Bhagavad Gita (4:18) says, "He who finds action in inaction, and inaction in action, he is a perfect yogi." Amidst the hectic surroundings and crowds of devotees and monks, Saradananda continued working on his important project. One day some young monks were talking loudly and laughing in the Udbodhan office, adjacent to the swami's room. Golap-ma, an attendant of the Holy Mother, scolded them: "Shame on you! Mother is upstairs and Sharat is doing serious work, and you boys are making such great noise!" Overhearing Golap-ma's loud voice, the swami said to her: "Well, Golap-ma, please don't give your ears to them. It is the nature of the boys to behave like that. I am so close to them, but I don't listen to what they are talking about. I have told my ears, 'Don't listen to anything that is unnecessary.' So my ears are not listening to them."[12] Saradananda had total control over his senses.

Saradananda's life was extremely disciplined and he followed his routine strictly. After having his morning bath in the Ganges, Saradananda would go to the shrine and bow down to the Master and then to the Holy Mother. At 7:00 a.m., he would come downstairs and sit in a small room to the left of the entrance to the Udbodhan house. This was his office and reception room. There was a cotton mattress on the floor and no furniture except for a small wooden desk. On his desk was a blotting pad; at the right, on the mattress were several bundles of letters. There were also a tin of cigarettes and a match-box; two inkpots — one with ink and the other with clean water for washing the nib of the pen; a small rag for cleaning the nib; a towel for wiping his perspiration; and another cloth for dusting the desk and papers.[13]

Saradananda would write for hours daily sitting in the same place. Sometimes he would rub his chin with the back of his left hand; this was what he did when he was thinking. Sometimes he would stretch his legs, but without leaving his seat. As a result, in later years the circulation in his legs was greatly impaired, and they would sometimes tremble. Between writing sessions he would drink tea and smoke his hubble-bubble, which was kept at his left side. He would have lunch at 1:30 p.m., and after that he would rest for an hour and a half on his mattress. He would write again until evening, then finally close his office, putting everything in its place. He would then meet with devotees and answer their questions. Sometimes he would go to Belur Math and stay for a couple of days.

In his memoirs, Swami Nikhilananda wrote about an important incident:

> Before we left for Varanasi [in 1925], Swami Shuddhananda asked Swami Saradananda in front of me to finish the Cossipore chapter of the *Lilaprasanga* [which would describe Sri Ramakrishna's last days]. Swami Saradananda said that he had some notes but he was not well enough to write the article. Swami Shuddhananda then said: "You can dictate it and Nikhilananda will write it." He said he would see what could be done. I believe he took his notebook with him. He did not feel well in Varanasi, so nothing was done. When we were leaving for Puri, Swami Shuddhananda reminded him about the article and again asked him to dictate the whole thing to me. Then the swami made the following significant remark: "When the Holy Mother was alive I felt a great deal of inner strength and began to write the *Lilaprasanga*. She died and I felt as if all my powers were gone. Then I saw Swami Brahmananda and began to feel strong again. When he died I felt as if my brain was completely paralyzed. I simply cannot finish the book." Then he added: "When I began to write the *Lilaprasanga* I thought I understood the Master. But now I clearly see that the life of the Master is very deep. I was merely hovering over the top branches; the root is far beneath the ground."[14]

Neither M. nor Saradananda recorded the last days of Sri Ramakrishna. Perhaps it was the will of the Master that it not be written. In 1925 when a disciple asked him to complete the Master's life, Saradananda said humbly: "Perhaps it will never be completed. I am not getting any inspiration from within. The Master made me write whatever he wanted. Now when I read the *Lilaprasanga*, I wonder, have I written all these things? I have no more inclination to do anything. It seems that the Master is doing everything."[15]

Swami Saradananda had planned to write a sixth part of the

Lilaprasanga. With that in mind, he kept two small notebooks in which he jotted down information gathered from various people as they reminisced about the Master, as well as ideas that came to him from time to time. It was in one of these notebooks that he made a note of his plan for a sixth part of the *Lilaprasanga,* to be called "Sri Ramakrishna in Cossipore."

Swami Saradananda's plan never materialized, but he did write three further articles, based on his notes, which were incorporated in the fifth part of the *Lilaprasanga.* The unused portions of Swami Saradananda's notebooks have been published by Swami Nirlepananda (a grandson of Yogin-ma) in a small book, *Bhagavan Sri Sri Ramakrishnadeva.* It has been translated and printed in the appendix of *Ramakrishna as We Saw Him* (published by the Vedanta Society of Saint Louis) as 'Sri Ramakrishna: Some New Findings' by Swami Saradananda. He said that he had covered only the Master's relationship with Gopal-ma and Swami Vivekananda in the *Lilaprasanga.* He wanted to write details of the Master's connection with other disciples and devotees, and for that reason he began to write notes in his diary.

A Note on Sri Ramakrishna and His Divine Play

In the translator's note of *Sri Ramakrishna and His Divine Play,* I wrote in detail the history, importance, and magnitude of Swami Saradananda's magnum opus, *Sri Sri Ramakrishna Lilaprasanga.* Here is part of that note:

In addition to an account of the god-intoxicated life of Sri Rama-krishna, the reader will find in this book glimpses of mysticism, discussions of various religious and philosophical traditions of India, accounts of different religious leaders, and descriptions of the social customs, the educational system, and the socio-religious movements of nineteenth-century India. It is really astounding how Sri Rama-krishna, who had no formal education, overwhelmed the great savants and religious leaders of India with his spiritual power. In this book the reader will see how Sri Ramakrishna, the avatar of our modern age, lived and behaved, how he practised sadhana and taught spirituality, how he evaluated and trained his disciples by observing their physical characteristics and reading their minds as one would a book, how he used parables and folktales in his teachings, how he laughed and cried, sang and danced, made jokes like an ordinary human being, and at the same time frequently experienced spiritual visions and samadhi. It is important to see how Sri Ramakrishna's divine life reflected his phenomenal renunciation, passion for truth, childlike simplicity, complete lack of egotism, longing for God, and love for humanity.

This book bears witness to Sri Ramakrishna's testimony that all religions are equally valid. He found a place for each one in his own life. He first realized God by following Hindu practices, and then by following the Christian and Muslim paths. Such a journey is unique in the religious history of the world. He afterwards proclaimed, "As many faiths, so many paths," thus establishing an ideal harmony of religions for our present age, in which religions are in conflict and hatred and violence are rampant. He taught a religion so badly needed today — a religion that is constructive and not destructive, scientific and not fanatical, practical and not theoretical, rational and not superstitious, universal and not parochial. Truly, Sri Ramakrishna worked to create unity in our time and he repeatedly stated that the goal of human life is to realize God.[16]

22

My Master According to Swami Vivekananda

The Life of Swami Vivekananda

Swami Vivekananda was born in Calcutta on 12 January 1863, and was given the name Narendranath Datta. He was a precocious boy, truthful and very idealistic. Brought up and educated in nineteenth-century Calcutta, Narendra was introduced at an early age to the principles of Western thinking, one of these being that one should not accept anything without evidence. He was a bold and free thinker as well as a doubter. In his intense desire to realize the truth, Narendra practised meditation, studied different religious and philosophical systems of the East and the West, and met a number of religious leaders, but to no avail. At last he met Ramakrishna at Dakshineswar and asked a straightforward question: "Sir, have you seen God?"

Ramakrishna replied immediately: "Yes, I have seen God. I see Him as I see you here, only more clearly. God can be seen. One can talk to Him. But who cares for God? People shed torrents of tears for their wives, children, wealth, and property, but who weeps for the vision of God? If one cries sincerely for God, one can surely see Him."[1]

"That impressed me at once," said Narendra. "For the first time I found a man who dared to say that he saw God, that religion was a reality, to be felt, to be sensed in an infinitely more intense way than we can sense the world. I began to go to that man, day after day, and I actually saw that religion could be given. One touch, one glance, can change a whole life."[2]

From 1881 to 1886, a close relationship developed between Ramakrishna and Narendra. Narendra's doubts and scepticism were gradually dispelled by Ramakrishna's spiritual power and the realizations that Ramakrishna shared with him. Ramakrishna's love and concern made Narendra his own forever. He trained Narendra in a number of spiritual disciplines and initiated him into the teachings of nondualistic Vedanta. From the Master Narendra also learned practical Vedanta and how to serve human beings as God.

Before his passing away on 16 August 1886, Ramakrishna transmitted his spiritual power to Narendra and said: "Today, after giving you everything, I have become a beggar. With this power you are to do much work for the good of the world before you return."[3] In October 1886, the young disciples of Ramakrishna established Baranagore Math (monastery) under Narendra's leadership. In January 1887 they took monastic vows and dedicated their lives to benefiting humanity.

From 1887 to 1893 Vivekananda travelled throughout India, and then left for the United States to represent Vedanta, the basis of the Hindu religion, at the Parliament of Religions in Chicago. He preached the universal message of Vedanta in America and then Europe and returned to India. In 1897 he established the Ramakrishna Math and Mission in Calcutta and made Belur Math the headquarters of the Order. In 1899 he again travelled to the West and stayed there for a year and a half before finally settling in Belur Math. He passed away on 4 July 1902 at the age of thirty-nine.

Ramakrishna and His Message*

Once Girish Chandra Ghosh, a great devotee of Ramakrishna, asked Swami Vivekananda to write a biography of Ramakrishna. Swamiji replied: "Please don't request that. I shall very gladly do whatever you ask of me other than this. I would not even hesitate to revolutionize the world at your request, but I shall not be able to do the work you have suggested. He [Ramakrishna] was so profound, so great, that I have not

*In 1970 Swami Abhayananda, a trustee and the manager of Belur Math, told me: "Many foreigners come to Belur Math and want to know about Ramakrishna and Vivekananda. Can you make two booklets on the Master and Swamiji that I can present to them?" I was then working in the Advaita Ashrama publication department, Calcutta. I compiled *Ramakrishna and His Message* by Swami Vivekananda and *Swamiji and His Message* by Sister Nivedita and they were published anonymously. The information in this section is taken from the former. — *Author.*

understood him at all. I have not been able to know even a fraction of his life. Do you advise me to fashion a monkey while trying to mould an image of Shiva? I can't do it."[4]

On another occasion, a disciple of Vivekananda asked him: "Do you believe Ramakrishna to be an avatar [an incarnation of God]?"

Swamiji: "Tell me first — what do you mean by an avatar?"

Disciple: "I mean one like Ramachandra, Krishna, Buddha, Jesus, and others."

Swamiji: "I know Bhagavan Sri Ramakrishna to be even greater than those you have just named. What to speak of believing, which is a petty thing — I *know*!"

Disciple: "Why do you not preach Ramakrishna as an avatar? You have indeed power, eloquence, and everything else needed to do it."

Swamiji: "Truly, I tell you, I have understood him very little. He appears to me to have been so great that whenever I have to speak anything of him, I am afraid lest I ignore or explain away the truth, lest my little power does not suffice, lest in trying to extol him I present his picture by painting him according to my lights and belittle him thereby!"[5]

Although he expressed his inadequacy many times, Swamiji did speak and write about Ramakrishna. His reminiscences of and reflections on his beloved Master are scattered throughout the nine volumes of *The Complete Works of Swami Vivekananda* and in other literature. It is worth adding that Vivekananda's own life appeared to be Ramakrishna himself in action. Not only in Swamiji's explicit utterances, but also implicitly all through his *Complete Works*, Ramakrishna is present, for the mind of the disciple was not other than that of the Master. In fact, Vivekananda's writings and lectures are all commentaries on Ramakrishna's message. Swamiji himself said: "All the ideas that I preach are only an attempt to echo his [Ramakrishna's] ideas."[6]

Once in London Vivekananda said to his audience: "I am what I am and what I am is always due to him [Ramakrishna]; whatever in me or in my words is good and true and eternal came to me from his mouth, his heart, his soul. Sri Ramakrishna is the spring of this phase of earth's religious life, of its impulses and its activities. If I can show the world one glimpse of my Master, I shall not live in vain."[7]

My Master

In the West, Vivekananda seldom talked about Ramakrishna, his beloved Master. Why? Swamiji was strongly opposed to religious dogmatism, fanaticism, and personality cults; he knew that a personality cult grows speedily and dies quickly. He preached the eternal and universal principles of Vedanta. In 1897 at Lahore when Lala Hansaraj, the leader of the Arya Samaj, was defending his orthodox view concerning the Vedas, Swamiji told him: "Sir, you emphasize that there can be only one interpretation of the Vedas, which I consider a kind of fanaticism. I know it helps to spread a sect rapidly. Again a personality cult spreads faster than scriptural dogma. I have the power to bring one-third of the population of the world under the banner of Sri Ramakrishna, but I have no intention of doing that, because that would counteract my guru's great message of harmony, 'As many faiths so many paths.' And a new sect would originate in India."[8]

When Swamiji returned to Calcutta after teaching Vedanta in the West, Ram Chandra Datta, a staunch follower of Ramakrishna, said to him: "Well, you went to the West and all the time you harped on Vedanta. Why did you not preach Ramakrishna, whose very name is conducive to man's liberation?" Swamiji replied: "If I had talked to them about Ramakrishna, they would have at once replied, 'We have our Jesus Christ. What more have you to say?' Now I have preached to them the religion and philosophy of Vedanta and the Vedantic ideal of God-realization. Naturally they would inquire, 'Who is the man who has realized the ideal in this age?'"[9]

Swamiji used logic and science when explaining the eternal principles of Vedanta. Only to close students did he speak about his Master who was the embodiment of the Vedas and Vedanta.

On 1 July 1895 Swamiji talked about Ramakrishna to a group of his students at Thousand Island Park in New York state. He said:

Sri Ramakrishna was the son of very orthodox brahmins, who would even refuse a gift from any but a special caste of brahmins. Owing to the extreme poverty of his family, Sri Ramakrishna was obliged to become in his boyhood a priest in a temple dedicated to the Divine Mother Kali. The daily service of Mother Kali gradually awakened such intense devotion in the heart of the young priest that he could no longer carry on the regular temple worship; so he abandoned his duties and retired to a small woodland in the temple compound, where he gave himself up entirely to meditation. A relative fed him once a day and watched over him. Whatever teachers he needed came to him unsought; from every sect some holy saint came and offered to teach him, and to each he listened eagerly. But he worshipped only Mother; all to him was Mother.

Sri Ramakrishna never spoke a harsh word against anyone. So beautifully tolerant was he that every sect thought that he belonged to them. He loved everyone. To him all religions were true. He found a place for each one. The waves of religious thought rise and fall, and on the topmost wave stands the Prophet of the period. Ramakrishna came to teach the religion of today — constructive, not destructive. He had to go afresh to nature to ask for facts, and he got scientific religion, which never says "Believe," but "See" — "I see, and you too can see." Use the same means and you will reach the same vision. God will come to everyone; harmony is within the reach of all. Sri Ramakrishna's teachings are the gist of Hinduism; they were not peculiar to him. Nor did he claim that they were; he cared naught for name and fame.

He began to preach when he was about forty; but he never went out to do so. He waited for those who wanted his teachings to come to him.

Sri Ramakrishna is worshipped in India as one of the great Incarnations, and his birthday is celebrated there as a religious festival.[10]

Vivekananda gave two public lectures titled "My Master": one on 23 February 1896 at Madison Square Concert Hall in New York City and the other in autumn 1896 in Wimbledon, near London. The Wimbledon lecture was later published in two issues of *Brahmavadin* (15 September and 1 October 1897). J.J. Goodwin recorded both of the lectures and Miss S.E. Waldo compiled and edited them, then published them as *My Master* (The Baker & Taylor Company, New York, 1901). This version of *My Master* has been incorporated into the fourth volume of *The Complete Works of Swami Vivekananda*. Swami Saradananda published another version of *My Master* from Udbodhan Office. It would be wonderful if the original lectures given in New York and Wimbledon* were to be published separately: it would be helpful to read these two vivid and inspired accounts of the Master told by his main disciple who was reticent to talk about his guru. Moreover, Swamiji once said: "I can talk on the same subject, but it will not be the same lecture."[11]

In the Udbodhan version, Saradananda wrote in the editor's note:

One who was present [probably Sister Nivedita] at the second of the two lectures has told us how strange, to an English audience, seemed the story of a saint whose absorbing struggle was against the thought of woman and gold. The tale of the coin offered in sleep was, to those who heard it, simply incomprehensible. But there was one passage in

---

*This Wimbledon lecture on My Master has been reprinted in *Vedanta* Magazine (Ramakrishna Vedanta Centre: England, 1995), pp.200-222.

the lecture that, even in the West, carried all before it: it was that in which the speaker talked of the soul's search for God. Possibly many of the guests of that evening still remember the passionate declaration on which he ended: "And even now, after four years spent in all the luxury and splendour of the West, I hold still that there is nothing in the whole universe worth possessing, save God!"

With that unconsciousness of self, and finality of touch, which are the signs of "the competent witness," the Swami tells us now of his Master's inner history — and again of those dramatic incidents in which every *epos* must be written, even though of an avatar. How Ramakrishna Paramahamsa overcame the temptations of pride, of wealth, and of sex; and how he added realization to realization, till his thought had become as vast as his love, and neither fell short of all humanity; these things form the good tidings, the wondrous tale, that is borne out amongst the nations, to bring men back, to learn of him. And yet even these seemed to the teller himself inadequate, as revelation of the Master he had seen and loved. Of all such attempts he exclaimed impatiently, one day: "But after all, it was not even what he taught us! It was that great life that we lived with him! And that can never be told!"[12]

In New York on 16 February 1896 Swamiji gave a lecture titled "The Real and the Apparent Man" and concluded: "My whole life has been changed by the touch of one of these divine men, about whom I am going to speak to you next Sunday."[13]

Swami Nirvanananda, an attendant of Swami Brahmananda, told us the following story: "In New York Swamiji went to the podium to speak on 'My Master.' Seeing the audience he changed his mind. He thought that these worldly people would not understand the Master whose life was completely free from lust and gold. So it would be better not to speak on him. Meanwhile, the Master appeared before him and asked him to speak as it would do good to them."

Sister Devamata (Laura Glenn) left this eyewitness account:

[Madison Square Concert Hall] was full to the uttermost at that closing lecture — every seat, every foot of standing room was occupied. As he entered the hall from a door at the side of the platform, one sensed a different mood in him. He seemed less confident, as if he approached his task reluctantly. He began his lecture with a long preamble [a not unimportant historical background]; but once in his subject, it swept him. The force of it drove him from one end of the platform to the other. It overflowed in a swift-running stream of eloquence and feeling. The large audience listened in awed stillness and at the close many left the hall without speaking. As for myself, I was transfixed. The transcendental picture drawn overwhelmed me. The call had come and I answered.[14]

"My Master" is a long lecture, so I will offer some highlights.

Swamiji opened the lecture by quoting the well-known verse from the Gita: "When virtue subsides and vice prevails, I come down to help mankind." Then Swamiji compared the ideals of the Orient and the Occident and indicated the necessity of harmonizing both. Then he stated that if anyone wishes to be a true reformer, three things are necessary:

1. Do you really feel for your brothers?
2. Have you found any remedy to mitigate their sufferings?
3. Are you really sure that you can stand up for your ideals and work on, even when the whole world wants to crush you down?

Swamiji talked about the character of Ramakrishna's parents and their poverty; his schooling, relocation to Calcutta, and acceptance of the job of a priest; his spiritual adventures; his longing and vision of God; his sadhana and conquest of the desires of lust and gold, name and fame.

Swamiji said: "First, form character. That is your highest duty. Know truth for yourself, and there will be many to whom you can teach it afterwards. They will all come. That was the attitude of my Master. He criticized no one. For years I lived with that man, but never did I hear those lips utter one word of condemnation for any sect."[15]

Swamiji continued:

For the first time I found a man who dared to say that he saw God, that religion was a reality. Religion is not talk or doctrines or theories, nor is it sectarianism. It is the relation between the soul and God. Religion does not consist in erecting temples or building churches or attending public worship. It is not to be found in books or in words or in lectures or in organizations. Religion consists in realization. The first idea in this attempt to realize religion is that of renunciation. As far as we can, we must give up. Darkness and light, enjoyment of the world and enjoyment of God, will never go together. "Ye cannot serve God and Mammon."

The second idea that I learnt from my Master, which is perhaps the most vital, is the wonderful truth that the religions of the world are not contradictory or antagonistic; they are but various phases of one Eternal Religion.[16]

Towards the end of his lecture, Swamiji said: "Today the name of Ramakrishna Paramahamsa is known throughout India with its millions of people. Nay, the power of that man has spread beyond India, and if there has ever been a word of truth, a word of spirituality, that I have spoken anywhere in the world, I owe it to my Master. Only the mistakes are mine."[17]

Swamiji concluded the lecture by saying, "My Master's message to mankind is: 'Be spiritual and realize truth for yourself.'"[18]

The following criticism of the materialistic West is found only in the Udbodhan edition that was edited by Swami Saradananda:

Men and women of today! If there be among you any pure, fresh flower, let it be laid on the altar of God. If there are among you any who, being young, do not desire to return to the world, let them give up. Let them renounce! This is the one secret of spirituality — renunciation. Think of every woman as your mother. Give up this wealth. What does it matter? Wherever you are, the Lord will protect you. The Lord takes care of His children. Dare to do this. Be brave enough to do it. Such great sacrifices are necessary. Can you not see the tide of death and materialism that is rolling over these Western lands? How long will you keep the bandage over your eyes? Can you not see the power of lust and unholiness that is eating into the very vitals of society? Believe me, you will not arrest these things by talk or by movements of agitation for reform, but by renunciation, by standing up, in the midst of decay and death, as mountains of righteousness. Talk not, but let the power of purity, the power of chastity, the power of renunciation, emanate from every pore of your body. Let it strike those who are struggling day and night for gold, that even in the midst of such a state of things, there can be one to whom wealth counts for nothing. Nor let there be lust! Put away lust and wealth. Sacrifice yourselves.

But who is it that will do this? Not the worn-out or the old, bruised and battered by society, but the Earth's freshest and best, the strong, the young, the beautiful. Such are they who must be laid upon the altar, and by their sacrifice save the world. Lay down your lives. Make yourselves servants of humanity. Be living sermons. This, and not talk, is renunciation. Stand up and strike! The very sight of you will fill the worldly mind, the wealth-seeking mind, with terror. Words never do anything. Preaching has been all in vain. Every moment, prompted by the thirst for wealth, books are brought out. But they do no good because the power behind their words is zero.

Stand up, and realize God! If you can renounce all wealth and all sex, it will not be necessary for you to speak. Your lotus will have blossomed, and the spirit will spread. Whoever approaches you will be warmed as it were by the fire of your spirituality.[19]

Marie Louise Burke wrote about the reason why the above passage was kept out of *The Complete Works of Swami Vivekananda*. She wrote: "It would appear that because of his forthright denunciation of Western materialism during the course of the New York lecture, Swamiji had banned its publication. 'I did not allow it to be published,' he is quoted as having said a year or so later, 'as I had done injustice to my Master. My Master never condemned anything or anybody. But while I was speaking of him I criticized the people of America for their dollar-worshipping spirit. That day I learnt the lesson that I am not yet fit to talk of him.'"[20]

The Life of Swami Vivekananda, by His Eastern and Western Disciples described the reactions to this lecture:

It so happened that he once spoke before a large audience gathered to hear him on "My Master." Full of the fire of renunciation that he was, when he saw before him the audience composed, for the most part, of worldly-minded men and women lacking in spiritual sympathy and earnestness, he felt that it would be a desecration to speak to them of his understanding of and his real feelings of devotion for Sri Rama-krishna. So, instead, he launched out on a terrible denunciation of the vulgar, physical, and materialistic ideas which underlay the whole of Western civilization. Hundreds of people left the hall abruptly, but in no way affected, he went on to the end. The next morning the papers were filled with varying criticisms, some highly favourable, others severely critical in their analysis of what he had said, but all comment-ing on his fearlessness, sincerity, and frankness. When he himself read the report of his speech, he was stung with remorse. He wept bitterly for thus denouncing others and said: "My Master could not see the evil side of a man. He had nothing but love even for his worst vilifiers. It is nothing short of sacrilege on my part to abuse others and wound their feelings while speaking about my Master. Really I have not under-stood Sri Ramakrishna and am totally unfit to speak about him!"[21]

Swamiji wept and confessed his mistake of intolerance towards the Western materialistic outlook; he also expressed his humility and inability to talk about his Master, who never criticized others. Swamiji's behaviour proved that he was a great soul! He did not try to hide or justify his mistakes.

The scriptures say: "Speak the truth, speak in a pleasant way, but do not speak the unpleasant truth. If you love someone, speak the unpleasant truth for that person's welfare." Swamiji said, "I love the Yankees." "The people I love most, I scold most."[22] He was a universal man and truly loved humanity, but he had a soft spot for the American people who had helped him immensely. When some of his American friends cautioned him not to be too outspoken, he replied: "I do everything to be sweet, but when it comes to a horrible compromise with the truth within, there I stop. I have a message to give; I have no time to be sweet to the world — and every attempt at sweetness makes me a *hypocrite*. I will die a thousand deaths rather than lead the jelly-fish existence of yielding to every requirement of this foolish world."[23] In San Francisco, while speaking on the monistic concept of God and man, he said: "You may not like what I am saying. You may curse me today, but tomorrow you will bless me."[24]

23

Disciples of Ramakrishna in the West

hen God incarnates on this earth as a human being, He is called an *avatar*, which literally means "one who descends." The avatar comes to restore religion when it has been degraded. Ramakrishna said that just as the same moon rises again and again, the same God appears in different places at different times, according to the need of the age. The avatar does not come alone; he is accompanied by companions who help to fulfill his mission. These companions are not ordinary mortals: some of them are *ishwarakotis* (godlike souls) and some are *nitya-siddhas* (ever-free souls). They are born to serve humanity and not for any personal motive.

There are three missionary religions: Buddhism, Christianity, and Islam. Buddhism spread through love and friendship; Christianity and Islam used force.

When Buddha had fulfilled his mission and decided to leave the body, his disciples began to lament. Aniruddha rushed to Ananda, Buddha's attendant, and requested him to ask four vital questions of Buddha before he passed away. Ananda took those questions to the dying Buddha and begged him to clear their doubts. "All right, speak," said Buddha.

Ananda: "The first question: After Buddha enters nirvana we want to compile the Sutras. What words should we begin them with to show that they are the Buddha's?"

Buddha: "Use the four words 'Thus I have heard.'"

Ananda: "The second question: Where should we live? There are so many of us. How will we get along? Where will we dwell?"

Buddha: "That's a small problem. You should dwell in the 'Four Dwellings of Mindfulness.' These are: 1. Contemplation of the body as impure. 2. Contemplation of feelings as suffering. 3. Contemplation of thoughts as impermanent. 4. Contemplation of dharmas as devoid of Self."

Ananda: "The third question: Buddha has been our teacher. When he enters nirvana who will be our Master?"

Buddha: "Take the Pratimoksha as your Master. The Pratimoksha is the Vinaya — the precepts and rules. Take the precepts as Master."

Ananda: "The fourth question: What should we do about bad-natured *bhiksus* [monks]? While Buddha was in the world he could control them easily. What should we do about them?"

Buddha: "Oh, that is very easy. You should be silent and they will go away. Don't talk to them. After all, aren't they bad? Aren't they boisterous and disobedient? Ignore them. Don't speak to them. They'll get bored and leave on their own."[1]

Buddha's messages of nonviolence, love, compassion, and friendship still inspire millions of people all over the world.

Jesus lived for only thirty-three years. His disciples saw how Jesus cured the sick, brought the dead to life, transformed water into wine, walked on water, and stopped a storm with a mere word. After three years of intense ministry, Jesus was crucified.

Within two months after Jesus' crucifixion and resurrection, the Holy Spirit descended on his disciples and inspired them to preach. They began to spread the message of Christ: love, forgiveness, renunciation, purity, and service to humanity. Peter, whose fear had compelled him to deny Christ three times, fearlessly went to Jerusalem and said: "O children of Israel, Jesus of Nazareth was the messiah. You have witnessed how his divine power manifested during his lifetime. And you people mercilessly crucified him." Peter created tremendous guilt and fear in the minds of the people, and then told them: "Now you must be repentant and take refuge in Christ. Thus you will be free from sin and receive God's grace." With this first lecture, Peter converted 3,000 people to Christianity. Thus Christ's mission continued.

Christ's disciples also performed many miraculous deeds. One day while Peter and John were entering a temple, a lame man asked Peter for alms. Peter said to him: "Silver and gold have I none; but such as I have give I thee. In the name of Jesus Christ of Nazareth rise up and walk."[2] Immediately that man's lameness was healed and he walked with Peter to the temple. People were amazed seeing the power within Peter. Nonetheless, the disciples of Christ were persecuted as they continued to carry out their Master's mission. Some of them became martyrs.

It is extremely difficult to carry the message of an avatar. His disciples fight constantly against unrighteousness and evil. They move through adverse circumstances; they struggle with hypocrites and selfish, fanatical, and evil-minded people; and at the same time they declare the glory of God and the message of Truth.

An enthusiastic young disciple of Buddha asked permission to carry his message to Suraparanta. Buddha said to him: "I heard that the people of Suraparanta are very rough, cruel, and tyrannical. What will you do if they criticize and ill-treat you?"

"I shall keep quiet," answered the disciple.

"If they beat you?"

"I shall forbear."

"If they try to kill you?"

The disciple replied: "There is no way one can escape death. Some people pray for death in order to get rid of suffering in the world, but I shall not do that. Neither shall I invite death nor stop death if it comes to me."

Buddha was pleased and gave him permission to carry his message.[3]

Jesus also sent out his disciples, saying: "Go and preach 'The Kingdom of heaven is near.' Do not carry any gold, silver, or copper money in your pockets. Do not carry a beggar's bag for the trip or an extra shirt or shoes or a walking stick. A worker should be given what he needs.

"Listen, I am sending you out like sheep to a pack of wolves. You must be as cautious as snakes and as gentle as doves. Watch out, for there will be men who will arrest you and take you to court, and they will whip you. Do not worry. Do not be afraid of those who kill the body but cannot kill the soul."[4]

God's power works through the avatar. He transmits that power to his disciples so they can carry out his mission. Ramakrishna empowered each of his disciples according to each one's capacity. Ramakrishna's mission is as deep as the ocean and as vast as the sky. His main teachings were: The goal of human life is to realize God; serve human beings as God; be unattached and do your duty; be pure and love all; practise the four yogas (jnana, karma, bhakti, and raja yoga); respect others' faiths. Ramakrishna said: "When flowers bloom, bees come of their own accord. They do not need to be invited. It is an inexplicable spiritual law that if love and devotion for God are truly manifest within you, those who have dedicated their lives to searching for God and experiencing the Truth, or have resolved to do so, will definitely come to you."[5]

Ramakrishna further said that if anyone wanted to preach, that person needed to receive a command from God or people would not listen. At the Cossipore garden house, Ramakrishna wrote on a piece of paper, "Narendra will teach people." He later transmitted his power to Narendra and said, "Today I have become a beggar after giving you my all. With this power you are to do much work for the good of the world before you return." Ramakrishna also empowered M., the recorder of *The Gospel of Sri Ramakrishna*, saying, "You will have to talk about the Bhagavata [the scriptures] to people."

The Ramakrishna Mission was officially inaugurated on 1 May 1897 at Balaram Bose's house in Calcutta, but it was actually started at Dakshineswar by the Master himself. Ramakrishna's life and his message imperceptibly formed the shape of his mission, and finally at Cossipore he launched his Order by giving ochre cloths to some of his young disciples. He knew that those monastic disciples would carry his message all over the world.

Swami Vivekananda
(Five years: July 1893 to December 1896 and July 1899 to December 1900)

It was actually at the behest of Ramakrishna that Vivekananda went to the West to represent Vedanta or Hinduism. One day in the spring of 1893 while in Madras, Swamiji had a dream in which he saw Ramakrishna walking into the ocean and beckoning him to follow. He also heard the command: "Go!" Although Swamiji was certain of his journey, he still felt it necessary to ask for Holy Mother's permission and her blessing. He wrote to Swami Saradananda: "I have had a vision in which the Master told me to go to the West. My mind is quite disturbed. Please tell Holy Mother everything and let me know her opinion." Saradananda went to Holy Mother and read Swamiji's letter to her. She did not give her opinion immediately, but asked Saradananda to wait. After a couple of days, Holy Mother had a dream. She saw Ramakrishna walking over the ocean waves and asking Narendra to follow him. Then Holy Mother told Saradananda: "Please write to Naren that he should go to the West."[6] Swamiji was overjoyed when he received Holy Mother's approval and blessing.

Vivekananda was the first Indian monk to bring to the West Ramakrishna's message on the harmony of religions and the universal teachings of Vedanta. The ancient message of Vedanta and Ramakrishna's teachings are the same. Swamiji described Ramakrishna as an embodiment of the Vedas. On 30 December 1894 Swamiji declared at the Brooklyn Ethical Society in New York: "I have a message to the West as Buddha had a message to the East."[7] Marie Louise Burke wrote a biography of Swamiji in six volumes under the title *Swami Vivekananda in the West: New Discoveries*. Burke describes how Swamiji endured tremendous difficulties during his mission to the West: he was ill-treated, humiliated, and slandered in Detroit; he was stoned in Boston and elbowed down in Chicago because of his Indian clothing; he was refused entrance to a restaurant because of his dark complexion. Someone even poisoned his coffee, but fortunately Ramakrishna stopped him from drinking it.

Nowadays many teachers from the East teach religion and yoga in the West without obstruction. Vivekananda was the pioneer. He gave his life to spread India's religion and culture in Western countries. He also laid the groundwork that opened the doors for future Ramakrishna monks to come to the West. Robert Ingersol, a famous American agnostic, said to Swamiji: "Fifty years ago you would have been hanged if you had come to preach in this country, or you would have been burned alive. You would have been stoned out of the villages if you had come even much later."[8]

At the Parliament of Religions in Chicago, the various representatives glorified their respective faiths; but Vivekananda glorified all religions. He tried to rejuvenate the universal, eternal religion of the world by warning about the dangers of narrowness, superstition, and bigotry. He presented Ramakrishna's wonderful message of the harmony of religions. Years later a Jewish scholar told Swami Nikhilananda: "After hearing Swami Vivekananda [at the Parliament] I realized that my religion was also true."[9]

To those who believed in the doctrine of original sin, Vivekananda said: "Ye are the children of God, the sharers of immortal bliss, holy and perfect beings. Ye divinities on earth — sinners! It is a sin to call a man so; it is a standing libel on human nature."[10] It is easy to kill a man, but it is not so easy to destroy doubt and guilt entrenched in the human mind. Swamiji did not seek praise and applause like other religious leaders. He told the American people clearly: "I am a plain-spoken man, but I mean well. I want to tell you the truth. You are my children. I want to show you the way to God by pointing out your errors. Therefore, I do not flatter you, or always say fine things about your civilization."[11]

Vivekananda's contribution to the West is now in the pages of history. In 1976, there was an exhibition in the Smithsonian Institution in Washington D.C, as part of the bicentennial celebration of American independence. There were 31 pavilions in that exhibition, each depicting the story of a foreigner who came to America and contributed new thoughts and ideas to the American heritage. Swami Vivekananda was the only Indian represented there. The National Portrait Gallery of the Smithsonian Institution produced a commemorative volume, *Abroad in America* (*Visitors to the New Nation: 1776-1914*), in which Swami Vivekananda was included.

Even now researchers are uncovering new incidents and stories about Swamiji. For example, during an interview with a reporter from the *Detroit Evening News* on 16 February 1894 Swamiji told the following story:

> I was travelling on the train from Minneapolis a few months since, when an American gentleman came and sat down beside me. He began to ask me: "Are you a Spaniard?"
> "No, I come from India."
> "India? Where's that? I never studied jography [sic]."
> I told him, "On the other side of the globe, in Asia."
> "Oh, you are a heathen."
> "Yes, that's what they call me in this country."
> "Then you'll go to hell."
> "I hope not," I said, "for though you people with the thermometer below zero may not care so much, we who live in a hot country where it is 120 in the shade, do not want to go where it is any hotter."
> "Well, you will go, all the same," he said.
> Then I asked him who he was.
> "I'm a cowboy," he answered.
> "Oh, yes, I've heard of you. What religion are you?" I asked.
> "I am a Presbyterian," he answered.
> "Then he asked me other things, and I told him about our theory that every soul lived in the past as well as in the present and that because we did not remember was no more sign than that we did not live before we were 3 or 4 years old, because we did not remember it. Then my friend, the cowboy, held out his hand and said, 'Shake! I believe that, too. My sister, now dead, one day dressed in boy's clothes

and always wore them afterward because she said she had been a man once and she remembered liking it so much better than being a girl. But you're a heathen and you will go to hell. Don't you forget that.'"[12]

Swamiji must have chuckled to himself after this wonderful encounter with the rustic cowboy. Although it was a trifling incident, it showed how ordinary Americans viewed non-Christians, especially foreigners. However, Vivekananda touched the hearts and minds of many Westerners. His ideas are at work in the West even now.

Swami Saradananda
(Two years: March 1896 to January 1898)

Vivekananda was extremely busy preaching Vedanta in America and England. He called for Swami Saradananda to take over responsibility for his work in England. After receiving permission from the Holy Mother, Saradananda left for London. His boat encountered a hurricane during the trip, but he was unperturbed. When the boat docked in Rome, Saradananda went to visit St. Peter's Basilica. Upon seeing the statue of St. Peter, he went into ecstasy and lost outer consciousness. Ramakrishna had once said: "In a vision I saw that Shashi and Sharat [Saradananda] had been among the followers of Christ."[13]

Saradananda arrived in London on 1 April 1896. When Vivekananda returned to London from America at the end of April, he asked Saradananda to speak to the English audience about Vedanta. On 28 May 1896 Swamiji met Professor Max Müller at Oxford, who wrote an article in *Nineteenth Century* on Ramakrishna entitled "A Real Mahatman." Professor Müller later wrote the book *Ramakrishna: His Life and Sayings*. Saradananda recalled: "He asked Swamiji to furnish him with enough material for a book so he could write about Sri Ramakrishna in greater detail. Swamiji agreed to help. When he returned, he asked me to undertake the job forthwith. I worked hard and gathered all the incidents in the life of the Master and the teachings of the Master and showed the manuscript to Swamiji. I thought Swamiji would edit it and make extensive corrections. He didn't do that. He simply changed a few words for fear of exaggeration and sent the whole manuscript to Professor Müller. As I remember, Professor Müller incorporated the complete manuscript in his book and published it without making any alterations."[14]

At the end of June 1896 Swamiji sent Saradananda to America, along with J.J. Goodwin, his stenographer and disciple. Saradananda's sweet and gentle personality and his masterly exposition of Vedanta philosophy immediately proved attractive. He was invited to speak at the Green Acre Conference of Comparative Religions in Maine, where he lectured on Vedanta and held classes on yoga. After the sessions closed, Saradananda lectured in Brooklyn, New York, and Boston. At the Brooklyn Ethical Association he presented a lecture entitled "The Ethical Ideas of the Hindus." Wherever Saradananda went he made friends and won staunch followers to Vedanta. Finally he settled down in New York City to carry on the Vedanta work in an organized way.

Saradananda also held classes regularly in Montclair, New Jersey, where he stayed at the home of Mr. and Mrs. Wheeler. Swami Atulananda, a Western monk, wrote in his book *With the Swamis in America*:

> An interesting incident took place when Swami Saradananda was living at this happy home. The swami had often spoken about Sri Ramakrishna and one day he produced his Master's photograph and showed it to the lady of the house. "Oh, swami," she exclaimed, "it is the same face!" "What do you mean?" said the swami. And then she told him that long ago, in her youth, before she was married, she had had a vision of a Hindu and that it was the same face that now she saw in the photograph. "It was Sri Ramakrishna," she said, "but I did not know it until now. I was so much impressed and charmed at the vision at the time, that I remember the face very distinctly, and I have been going about here and there ever since I had the vision, wherever I heard that a Hindu had come to America, but I was always disappointed, not finding the same face. And now at last I see that it was Sri Ramakrishna."[15]

Referring to this incident, Saradananda later recalled: "The Master chooses his own men and women. We are mere instruments in his hands. It is a privilege to work under his banner. In America he had already prepared the ground for me; I was not alone. He brought to me men and women of exalted character who helped me in our work and bore great love for our Master."[16] Mrs. Ole Bull of Boston, who greatly supported Vivekananda's Vedanta work in the West, invited Saradananda to her home. She introduced the swami to her influential friends, including Professor William James and other academics at Harvard University. Mrs. Bull often said that Swamiji was like the brilliant scorching sun and Saradananda, the cool, refreshing moon.

Just at the time when Saradananda was at the height of his usefulness in America, Vivekananda recalled him to India to help him organize the Ramakrishna Mission at Belur. After having spent two years in America, he sailed with Mrs. Ole Bull and Miss Josephine MacLeod for India on 12 January 1898, handing over responsibility for the Vedanta Society to Swami Abhedananda. Saradananda reached London on 20 January and Paris on 21 January. He admired the creative talents of the French people, including their art and music. The party went to Rome and then continued on to India via Naples and Brindisi, Italy. They arrived in Calcutta on 8 February 1898; Swamiji and other monks went to Howrah Station to receive them. Swamiji appointed Saradananda General Secretary of the Ramakrishna Math and Mission. His Western experience proved to be an immense help to him in managing the Order.

Swami Abhedananda
(Twenty-five years: August 1896 to November 1921)

After Vivekananda sent Saradananda to America in June 1896, he asked Swami Abhedananda to take responsibility for the Vedanta work in London. Abhedananda arrived in London in September 1896. After three months of teaching him how to work in the West and introducing him to the famous orientalists Max Müller and Paul Deussen, Swamiji returned to India. Abhedananda preached Vedanta in London for a year and then sailed to America when Saradananda was called back to India. Abhedananda arrived in New York on 9 August 1897 to take charge of the Vedanta Society.

Abhedananda did not confine himself to New York; he travelled to various American cities and preached Vedanta. He met Thomas Edison and talked to him about Vedanta and India. Mr. Edison showed the swami his laboratory. Abhedananda also met President William McKinley and Elmer Gates, a famous scientist and psychologist. John G. Brady, the governor of Alaska, was impressed with the swami and invited him to visit Alaska one summer. Abhedananda was acquainted with many intellectuals of Boston and Cambridge, Massachusetts, such as Charles Rockwell Lanman, Josiah Royce, Nathaniel Southgate Shaler, and William James, the author of *The Varieties of Religious Experience* and *Pragmatism*. Abhedananda also attended conferences held at Green Acre and Cambridge, where he talked about Vedanta.

It is said that libel and slander, censure and criticism are the ornaments of those who pave the way for truth. Attacks from backbiters and faultfinders make a pioneering soul more strong and determined. When Abhedananda became popular in New York, some Christian missionaries could not bear it. Some of them fabricated scandalous stories to defame the swami's character. Undaunted, Abhedananda paid them no heed; he continued to work with his usual vigour and equanimity.

Abhedananda later told his disciples how he faced his trials and tribulations: "When I was in America, I would try to forget my sorrows and sufferings by singing or praying to the Master. I would spend my time practising japa and meditation, or studying books. There was none with whom I could open my heart, so I lived in my own world. . . . If a person upholds the truth, he encounters more obstacles; but one should never give up the truth. One should hold the post [i.e., God] with might and main. Don't you see how I have confronted the storms of obstacles? I don't care even if the whole world stands against me. I am holding onto the Master."[17]

When Vivekananda came to America for the second time on 28 August 1899, accompanied by Turiyananda, Abhedananda was then busy with the Green Acre Conference. Vivekananda and Turiyananda went to Mr. Francis Leggett's country home, Ridgely, in Stone Ridge, New York. On 7 September Abhedananda received a cable from Vivekananda asking him to come to Ridgely, and the next day he travelled there from Boston. Abhedananda was delighted to see Swamiji and Turiyananda and told them all about what he had been doing. He stayed with them for ten days and then went to New York. On 7 November Vivekananda attended a reception given by Swami Abhedananda and members of the Vedanta Society.

Starting in 1901, Abhedananda's audience began to increase dramatically, eventually reaching 600. The number of students in his yoga class increased so much that he had to give the class twice a day. To accommodate the overflowing audience, the Vedanta Society rented Carnegie Lyceum for Abhedananda's lectures. *The New York Sun* described the lecture that Abhedananda gave on the first Sunday of 1901:

> Swami Abhedananda lectured in the Carnegie Lyceum yesterday afternoon on the "Religious Need of the Twentieth Century." He spoke of tuning the molecules of the brain cells to harmonize with the vibrations of the Cosmic Mind, and so gaining power, and he said that the mind and matter were not dual entities, but the subjective and objective manifestations of the unknown.
>
> "The twentieth century needs a religion," he said, "with no scheme for salvation, no need for heaven or hell, no fear of eternal punishment. The twentieth century needs a religion free from sacerdotal institutions and free from all books, scriptures, and personalities. The twentieth century needs a religion with a concept of God, not personal, not impersonal but beyond both, a God whose supreme aspect will

harmonize with the ultimate Reality of the universe. The twenti-eth-century religion must accept the ultimate conclusions of all the philosophies of the world."[18]

Abhedananda travelled extensively in the United States and in Canada, preaching the message of Vedanta. In August 1901 he visited San Francisco and went to Shanti Ashrama in the San Antonio Valley of Northern California, where he lived with Swami Turiyananda for some time. During his twenty-five year stay in the West, Abhedananda crossed the Atlantic seventeen times. He also travelled and taught Vedanta in many European countries, including England, France, Germany, Italy, Switzerland, Austria, Bavaria, Holland, Belgium, and Czechoslovakia.

In 1906 Abhedananda visited India for six months and when he returned to America, he brought Swami Paramananda with him as his assistant. In 1907 he decided to establish a retreat site for students of Vedanta. Accordingly, a plot of 370 acres was purchased in the Berkshire Hills, not far from the picturesque little village of West Cornwall, Connecticut. It was 107 miles from New York and the train trip there took about four hours. Abhedananda duly inaugurated the Berkshire retreat in March 1907, and he remarked, "The Ashrama looks like a fairy-land." In the meantime, Paramananda moved to Boston and opened a Vedanta centre there. Abhedananda handed over responsibility for the Vedanta Society of New York to Swami Bodhananda, a disciple of Vivekananda, and began to stay in the Berkshire retreat.

It is amazing how Ramakrishna protected his disciples in the West. Abhedananda recalled:

> In 1915 I was in London. On 6 May I went to the booking office to pur-chase a ticket from London to New York by the *S.S. Lusitania*. While I was in that office, a mysterious thing happened. I was about to buy the ticket, but immediately I heard a clear voice forbidding me to buy it. I was dumbfounded. I thought it might be a freak of my mind. I looked around but couldn't find anybody. So again I went to the counter and the same thing happened. Then I decided to return to the apartment without buying any ticket.
>
> However, I planned to buy the ticket the following day. The next morning I saw in the newspaper in big letters 'S.S. Lusitania Is No More.' I was overwhelmed. Tears rolled down my cheeks. I realized that the Master had saved my life.[19] [*See footnote p. 77.*]

Abhedananda gathered valuable experience from travelling and lecturing extensively in the West for twenty-five years. His writings made a tremendous impact on the Western mind. His books are still popular in the West: *Doctrine of Karma, Reincarnation, Life Beyond Death, Mystery of Death, How to be a Yogi, Self-knowledge,* and *Spiritual Unfoldment.* On the eve of his return to India from San Francisco, the swami said: "The East and the West will unite — such is God's will. The signs of the times greatly encourage me, and my visit and prolonged stay in this country has clearly convinced me that it is possible to make the world our home, and to love all as brothers and sisters. God's spirit is working everywhere. Blessed is he who sees the work, and realizes the Divine Spirit."[20]

Swami Turiyananda
(Three years: July 1899 to July 1902)

The great monk Swami Turiyananda was austere by nature. He wanted nothing more than to pass his days practising spiritual disciplines. In 1897-98 Vivekananda was suffering from various physical problems, so his physicians advised him to return to the West to recuperate. He wanted Turiyananda to accompany him, but the latter was reluctant. Swamiji insisted: "Brother, can't you see I have been laying down my life, inch by inch, in fulfilling the mission of the Master, till I am on the verge of death? Can you merely stand looking on and not come to my help by relieving me of a part of my great burden?"[21] Turiyananda could not refuse his leader's entreaties.

In June 1899 Turiyananda left for England and America with Vivekananda and his Irish disciple, Sister Nivedita. On the boat to England, Turiyananda asked Nivedita to teach him Western customs. She explained with an illustration. Picking up a knife, she held the sharp edge in her hand and gave the handle to Turiyananda, saying, "Swami, whenever you give something to someone, always take the inconvenient and unpleasant side yourself, and give the convenient and pleasant side to the other."[22]

After spending a short time in England, Vivekananda and Turiyananda left for America on 16 August 1899. Soon after their arrival in New York, they went to Ridgely Manor, the Leggett family's country home, where they rested for a few weeks. One day Mrs. Leggett visited Swamiji's cottage and found Turiyananda's mattress and bedding on the floor. "What is the matter, swami?" she exclaimed. "Is something wrong with the bed?"

"No, no," he assured her; "the bed is fine. But, you see, I cannot bring myself to sleep on the same level with Swamiji — so I have put the mattress on the floor."[23] This shows how much love and reverence Turiyananda had for Swamiji.

Seeing that Turiyananda was hesitant to give lectures and classes, Swamiji said to him: "Don't be frightened when I say you have to conduct classes and lectures. Whatever you say will do good to the people. Show them what spirituality is."[24] Turiyananda moved to Mrs. Wheeler's residence at Montclair in New Jersey, forty miles from New York City, where the Vedanta Society was led by Abhedananda. Turiyananda carried on the Vedanta work in the New York area for a year; during that time Vivekananda preached in California. Turiyananda startled the sophisticated Western audience with the bold, uncompromising message of Vedanta: "Brahman alone is real; everything else is unreal. The human soul is that Brahman. We are bound by the delusion of ignorance. Tear away the delusion and be free. All power is within you, for you are the Atman. Assert your divine nature."

Students of the New York Vedanta Society found Turiyananda to be an inexhaustible mine of spiritual wisdom. While walking, eating, or sitting, his spiritual conversation flowed like a perennial spring. Once he was asked: "Swami, how is it possible for you to always speak of holy subjects? Don't you ever get exhausted?"

Turiyananda replied: "You see, I have lived this life from my youth; it has become part and parcel of me. And the Divine Mother keeps the supply filled up. Her store can never be exhausted. Whatever goes out, She at once fills up again."[25]

Some of the Vedanta students considered the big city with all its comforts to be unsuitable for spiritual practice, and they wanted a quiet spot where they might devote themselves to a life of renunciation. One of the students, Minnie C. Boock, offered 160 acres in Northern California for a retreat. When Vivekananda arrived in New York in June 1900, he accepted her offer and asked Turiyananda to take up the project, but he did not want to assume this responsibility. Swamiji said, "It is the will of the Mother that you should take charge of the work there."[26] When Turiyananda agreed to the proposal, Swamiji said: "Don't trouble yourself about lecturing. You just live the life. Be an example to them. Let them see how men of renunciation live."[27]

On 4 July 1900 Turiyananda left New York by train, accompanied by Swamiji and Miss Boock. This was the last time the two brother disciples would be together. Just before Swamiji disembarked at Detroit, Turiyananda asked for advice regarding his future work. Swamiji told him: "Go and establish the Ashrama in California. Hoist the flag of Vedanta there. From this moment destroy even the memory of India. Above all, live the life, and Mother will do the rest."[28] Turiyananda arrived in Los Angeles on 8 July 1900. He became the guest of Miss Boock's sister in Alhambra, and later went to the Mead sisters' house in Pasadena. After a couple of weeks, he went to San Francisco, where he was cordially received by members of the Vedanta Society. They told him that Vivekananda had said, "I will send you a real Hindu monk, who lives what I talk about." Turiyananda responded: "I am a rowboat: I can take two or three to the other side of this ocean of the world. But Swamiji is an Atlantic liner: he can take thousands."[29] While he was in San Francisco, he gave lectures and conducted morning meditation at the Society.

On 2 August he left for the new retreat with a dozen enthusiastic men and women. They travelled by train to San Jose, by four-horse stage coach to Mount Hamilton, and then by private horse carriage some twenty-two miles over narrow mountain roads to the San Antonio Valley.

Ashrama life began under primitive conditions: There was no running water, no electricity, and no bathroom facilities. There were snakes, scorpions, and tarantulas all around. They had to bring water from a distance of six miles; they lived on vegetarian food. There was no market nearby. Turiyananda found himself in a wilderness, with all these people depending on him. He was disheartened. He complained to the Divine Mother: "Mother, what have You done? What do You mean by this? These people will die. No shelter, no water — what shall they do?" Agnes Stanley immediately said to him: "Swami, why are you dejected? Have you lost faith in Her? You have less faith than even Baby [Ida Ansell]." Having said this, she emptied her purse in his lap.

Turiyananda now caught a glimpse of the enterprising American mind. These students came from the old pioneer stock and were not about to be cowed by hardships. Turiyananda was delighted to hear Mrs. Stanley's bold words. He said to her: "You are right. Mother will protect us. How great is your faith! Your name henceforth will be Shraddhā [one who has firm faith in God]."[30]

The ordeals and hardships continued in that remote, rugged mountain area. The students, however, had a wonderful teacher of Vedanta, who had the power to raise their minds to a higher realm of spirituality where they could lose body-consciousness. In the beginning they had only one small cabin and a shed, and their first meal was boiled rice and brown sugar. After supper they gathered around a campfire, and the swami chanted: "We meditate on the adorable and effulgent light of Brahman who has produced this universe. May He enlighten our understanding."

Turiyananda named the retreat "Shanti Ashrama," the abode of peace. Everyone worked hard to create a spiritual atmosphere there. First, they built the meditation cabin; then they gradually added more cabins for the Ashrama members. Although there was an informal daily routine in the Ashrama, one day someone suggested that formal rules be set. Turiyananda replied: "Why do you want rules? Is not everything going on nicely and orderly without formal rules? Don't you see how punctual everyone is — how regular we all are? No one is ever absent from the classes or meditations. Mother has made Her own rules. Let us be satisfied with that. Why should we make rules of our own? Let there be freedom, but no license. That is Mother's way of ruling. We have no organization, but see how organized we are. This kind of organization is lasting, but all other kinds of organization break up in time. This kind of organization makes one free; all other kinds are binding. This is the highest organization; it is based on spiritual laws."[31]

In Shanti Ashrama, Turiyananda's main focus was to build his students' character according to the Vedantic way. He told them: "Be yourself and be strong. Realization is only for the strong, the pure, and the upright. Remember that you are the Atman. Swamiji has taught you that every soul is potentially divine. Realize your divinity, then you will realize that all souls are divine. Remove the cloud of ignorance, and the Atman will reveal itself in your heart."

When asked how this can be realized, he answered: "Through meditation. Meditation is the key that opens the door to Truth. Meditate till light flashes into your mind and the Atman stands self-revealed."[32]

After teaching Vedanta for three years in the West, Turiyananda's health broke down due to excessive austerity. He decided to return to India. In addition, Swamiji wanted to see him. Turiyananda handed over responsibility for Shanti Ashrama to Brahmachari Gurudas (later Swami Atulananda) and instructed him: "Control your passions, anger, jealousy, pride. And never speak ill of others behind their backs. Let everything be open and free. When anything has to be done, always be the first to do it. Others will follow. But unless you do it first, no one will. You know how I have done all kinds of physical work here, only for that reason."

Gurudas asked, "But what about the classes, swami? What shall I teach? I am a student myself."

Turiyananda replied, "Don't you know yet, my boy, that it is life that counts? Life creates life. Serve! Serve! Serve! That is the great teaching. Be humble. Be the servant of all. Only he who knows how to serve is fit to rule. But you have studied many years; teach what you know. As you give out, so you will receive."

"Swami," Gurudas ventured, "when you are gone we will be like sheep without a shepherd." "But I will be with you in spirit," Turiyananda said solemnly.[33]

On 6 June 1902 Turiyananda left San Francisco by boat. When he arrived in Rangoon, he read in the newspaper that Swamiji had passed away on 4 July. Broken-hearted, he arrived at Belur Math on 14 July 1902.

Swami Trigunatitananda

(Twelve years: January 1903 to January 1915)

When Swami Turiyananda's health broke down, Dr. M.H. Logan, the president of the Vedanta Society of San Francisco, asked Swami Vivekananda to send another swami for the Society. Swamiji selected Swami Trigunatitananda, and soon afterwards passed away on 4 July 1902. Trigunatitananda handed over the editorial responsibility for *Udbodhan* magazine to Swami Shuddhananda and prepared to leave for America. The swami left Calcutta on 27 September 1902 and travelled to California via Puri, Waltair, Madras, Pamban, Colombo, Shanghai, and Yokohama in Japan, finally reaching San Francisco on 2 January 1903.

Trigunatita was received by Dr. Logan, Mr. and Mrs. C.F. Peterson, and other members of the Society. He began lecturing at the Petersons' house, but it could not accommodate the large crowds. In March 1903, the Society rented a large house at 40 Steiner Street where Trigunatita and the Peterson family could live and he could conduct the services. Trigunatita gave classes on the Gita on Monday evenings and on the Upanishads on Thursday evenings; he lectured in the morning and evening on Sundays. Music, of course, was part of every service.

In 1904 some students invited Trigunatita to establish a Vedanta centre in Los Angeles, nearly 500 miles south of San Francisco. The swami began the work there, but later found it difficult to manage both places; so he asked for an assistant from India. The authorities of Belur Math sent Swami Satchidananda, who received a hearty welcome in San Francisco and then, under Trigunatita's guidance, started working in Los Angeles. But after only a year, Satchidananda was compelled to return to India because of poor health.

In the same year, the work in San Francisco had grown to such proportions that Trigunatita felt the Society should have a suitable building of its own. With Trigunatita, to think was to act, and a committee was at once appointed to look for a suitable site. Soon a meeting of all the members was called, funds were quickly raised, and a plot of land was purchased on the corner of Webster and Filbert streets. On 25 August 1905 the cornerstone was laid. The swami placed in it pictures of Ramakrishna, Holy Mother, and others within a metal box. Regarding the future of the temple, Trigunatita said, "I shall not live to enjoy; others will come later who will enjoy"; and, referring to his own participation, he boldly proclaimed: "Believe me, if there is the least tinge of selfishness in building this temple, it will fall; but if it is the Master's work, it will stand."[34] And amazingly enough, the temple emerged unscathed from the terrible earthquake of 1906 and the fires that followed, which destroyed much of San Francisco. This was the first Hindu temple in the Western world. It was dedicated on 7 January 1906 and the first services were held there on Sunday, 15 January 1906.

Trigunatita planned the temple himself, incorporating elements from a Hindu temple, a Christian church, a Muslim mosque, and an American residence. It was designed by the architect Joseph A. Leonard, in a style generally called Pointed Architecture of Grecian and Roman origin. All the mouldings, ornaments, and the arches of the veranda are of Moorish style. The points of the domes, towers, and pinnacles, directed upwards to the sky, have a religious meaning: Let us move towards God, rising higher and higher until we reach the very highest.

Shortly after the temple dedication, Trigunatita was inspired to start a monastery for the young American students. He recruited ten young men and housed them on the third floor and in the tower rooms. These men were subjected to strict discipline. They had to rise early in the morning, meditate regularly, and do household duties such as cleaning, sweeping, and gardening. Trigunatita was fond of teaching by means of forceful maxims. When someone at the dining table recited the great watchword of the American Republic, "Eternal vigilance is the price of liberty," he asked him to repeat it. Some of the mottoes hanging in rooms of the monastery were: "Live like a hermit, but work like a horse"; "Do it now"; "Watch and pray"; "Do or die — but you will not die."[35]

Trigunatita was an uncompromising ascetic. He taught his students through personal example more than through words. He set a consistent example of regularity and punctuality. He would go to bed last and rise before any of the other members of the monastery. His office was his bedroom, but he had no bed: He would spread one blanket on the carpet, put another blanket over himself, and use the upper part of his right arm as his pillow. The swami strongly believed that through discipline a strong character is formed, which is absolutely essential as a foundation for spiritual life. To the earnest disciple he would say: "I don't mind if I break every bone in your body if I can drag you up to the shores of the ocean of Immortality and throw you in. Then my work will be finished."[36]

Trigunatita also started a convent at the earnest entreaties of some women disciples who wanted to live a life of discipline under his guidance.

The life of Trigunatita was one long sacrifice. He veritably radiated holiness, for he always lived in the consciousness of the Divine Mother. However, he was overworked and his health was failing, so in April 1906 Swami Prakashananda was sent to assist him.

One of the members of the monastery, a Hungarian named Joseph Horvath, was a printer. This gave Trigunatita the idea of starting a printing press in the temple basement. A complete printing outfit was secured, and Mr. Horvath devoted all his time to the swami's publication projects. In April 1909 Trigunatita started a monthly magazine called *Voice of Freedom*. This magazine served as a channel through which the message of Vedanta reached many souls who could not attend the swami's lectures.

When Trigunatita came to San Francisco, he took charge of Shanti Ashrama, but Gurudas (later Swami Atulananda) continued to manage it. Trigunatita planned a rigorous schedule for the retreat. From 3:45 a.m. to 10:00 p.m. the students were busy with chanting, meditation, and scripture classes, along with chopping wood, carrying water, cooking, cleaning, and maintenance. They were also placed on a strict vegetarian diet. The swami provided plenty of relaxation in between periods of work. Those who had the privilege of attending the classes at Shanti Ashrama could hardly forget their unique experiences. They were charged with the spirituality of Trigunatita.

For the last five years of his life, Trigunatita suffered from rheumatism and Bright's disease. However, he continued to follow his routine faithfully; he did not deviate from his strict diet; and he did not reduce his workload. As a result, his health became even worse. Once he told a disciple: "A number of times during moments of excruciating pain, I would think, 'Let the body go, and end it all.' But I could not do it — the thought would come that the Mother's work must go on, and I set my will to force the body to carry on. This body has become a mere shell and may go to pieces at any time. For three years now I have held the body together by sheer force of will."[37]

On Friday, 25 December 1914 Trigunatita conducted the all-day Christmas service from 6:00 a.m. to 9:00 p.m. Two days later, on Sunday afternoon, 27 December 1914, Trigunatita was lecturing from the podium of the Hindu Temple of San Francisco. Suddenly a mentally unbalanced young man threw a bomb onto the pulpit; there was an explosion and a cloud of dense blue smoke obscured the platform. When the smoke cleared it was found that the young man, one of Trigunatitananda's former students, had been killed and that the swami had received severe injuries. He was taken at once to the Affiliated Colleges Hospital. On the afternoon of 9 January the swami told one of his young disciples that he would leave his body the next day, which was the birthday of Vivekananda according to the Indian lunar calendar. And as he foretold, Swami Trigunatitananda, the great yogi and disciple of Ramakrishna, passed away at 7:30 p.m. on 10 January 1915.

On 13 April 1916 Swami Prakashananda carried Swami Trigunatita's relics to Shanti Ashrama and installed them on the top of the highest hill, Siddha Giri, the "Hill of Realization." Swami Trigunatitananda's ashes remain as a symbol of his vanished form, but his immortal message lives on after him: Work hard. Discipline yourself. Build your character. Endure to the end. Realize your Self. And be free.[38]

*   *   *

Like Ramakrishna's direct disciples, the generations that followed them have sacrificed their lives to carry his mission all over the world. The spiritual current of Ramakrishna has not yet become fully manifest. The Master himself said: "I have seen big steamers going by on the Ganges, at the time hardly noticing their passing. But oh, my! What a terrific noise is heard after a while, when the waves splash against the banks!" Similarly, people cannot recognize the avatar when he comes; his life and mission become more apparent after some time has passed.

Swamiji forecast the spiritual tidal wave that Ramakrishna would initiate. He wrote to Alasinga Perumal on 28 May 1894 from Chicago: "Up, up, the long night is passing, the day is approaching, the wave has risen, nothing will be able to resist its tidal fury. . . . Rejoice that you are the chosen instruments in His hands. The flood of spirituality has risen. I see it is rolling over the land resistless, boundless, all-absorbing. Every man to the fore, every good will be added to its forces, every hand will smooth its way, and glory be unto the Lord!"[39]

Sister Nivedita wrote to Josephine MacLeod on 11 April 1906: "You see, when we who understood Swamiji and remember Him are dead, there will come a long period of obscurity and silence, for the work that He did. It will *seem* to be forgotten, until, suddenly, in 150 or 200 years, it will be found to have transformed the West."[40]

Once in Belur Math Swamiji said to Swami Premananda: "Here, here [pointing to the Belur Math] — whatever gems and jewels [precious spiritual treasures] I have kept, please preserve them with great care. You only guard them, take care of them. Those who will work with these treasures, they are coming — coming from far away. They will come after five or six generations. They will enjoy and reap the results. I only sang the song of the advent. You protect and preserve this spiritual tradition."[41]

24

Ramakrishna and the Renaissance of Art

uman beings perceive this world through the senses. Since no two persons are alike, taste and sense of beauty tend to differ from person to person. For example, the philosopher and the poet do not see the world in the same way. The philosopher says: "If you want to realize Reality, withdraw your senses and your mind from worldly objects." But the poet says: "No, you do not have to do that. Use your senses and your mind. Open your eyes and see God in every thing and every being. God is immanent." The philosopher says: "Brahman is 'not this, not this.' It cannot be an object of perception." But the poet says: "Everything is verily Brahman."

Again the philosopher says: "Reality is Truth, Consciousness, and Infinity." The poet says: "Reality is Truth, Bliss, and Beauty." Both are talking about the same Reality from different perspectives; only their expressions are different. Ramakrishna, however, harmonized both approaches. He said: "Does God exist only when the eyes are closed, and cease to exist when the eyes are opened? The Lila [manifestation] belongs to Him to whom the Nitya [absolute] belongs, and the Nitya belongs to Him to whom the Lila belongs."[1] Ramakrishna thus reconciled these two approaches to Vedanta: When you close your eyes, say: "I am Brahman." And when you open your eyes, say: "Thou art That. You are Brahman too."

If five artists are commissioned to produce a painting of a tree, all five paintings will be different. The first artist might be impressed by the green colour of the leaves; the second, by the effect of light and shadow; the third, by the colour of the flowers; and the fourth, by the structure of the branches. The fifth artist's impression may be completely different. He may think of that tree as an ascetic, absorbed in deep meditation. Or, he may visualize the tree meditating like a nun in breathless adoration. The same tree is painted by five artists, but each painting is different.

It is as difficult to define art as it is to define God. The ancient sages tried their utmost to convey a glimpse of the Infinite in the Upanishads. The Infinite Brahman is described as soundless, intangible, formless, tasteless, odourless, birthless, deathless, changeless, and so on. "Without hands He grasps everything; without feet He walks everywhere; without eyes He sees everything; without ears He hears everything. Brahman knows everything, but no one knows Brahman. He is the Full, the Great, the Eternal Being."[2] Those who know how to unveil this mystery of the Reality are saints as well as true artists.

The old meaning of art implied skill and ability acquired through patient practice and directed towards a definite end, whether this end be aesthetical, ethical, or useful. Art in this sense includes the fine arts, arts of conduct, and liberal arts: the fine arts being concerned with the attainment of the beautiful, the arts of conduct with the good, and the liberal arts with the useful.

In modern times the term *art* applies only to the fine arts, which mainly consist of painting, drawing, sculpture, architecture, music, dancing, literature, and drama.

According to the Encyclopaedia Britannica:

The function of art is the creation of beauty. Indeed, it may be said that there is no beauty outside art, or to be more exact, no beauty that has not been revealed by art. Nothing in nature is either beautiful or ugly, for beauty and ugliness are not positive attributes of matter, but matter is invested with these attributes by the artist's emotional reaction to some outside stimulus. It is doubtful if anybody found anything other than dinginess and "ugliness" in the mist and fog of the Thames-side in London before Whistler, by the work of his brush and the poetic imagery of his "Ten O'clock Lecture," invested the murky London atmosphere with permanent beauty. Until the dawn of the Renaissance in Italy, the beauty of mountain scenery was a closed book to the mediaeval mind. A mountain was a thing to be shunned, an impediment to traffic, a source of danger and fatigue. Mountains only became beautiful in the eyes of mankind after Giotto and his followers had introduced them into their pictures to replace the traditional old backgrounds of early mediaeval art.[3]

Actually, it is the soul of beauty itself that artists try to express in their work; but the "degree of expressional power" is what separates the master from the ordinary artist. This idea is especially emphasized in Eastern traditions. We find in both oriental and occidental art various schools or styles, such as idealistic, impressionistic, romantic, realistic, and so on. "Yet, taken as a whole," according to the Encyclopaedia Britannica, "one may note that oriental paintings are distinct, not only in aesthetic expression, but also in technical achievement. In creating a picture, the Far Eastern artist, before all else, grasps the spirit of his subject, then conveys this mood to the brush. He paints, not what he sees, but what he feels."[4] Moreover, "An artist is urged to examine every significant feature of his subject and imagine himself to be it before delineating it. By this means and this alone may he be able to express its spirit."[5] This describes the same unity of life that the artist tries to approach in his work and the seeker of God tries to approach in his prayer and meditation. Nandalal Bose, a famous artist of modern India, once described art in this way:

> Art is imagination. It is feeling expressed in line, form, and colour. Art must evoke feeling. There is, however, a grammar, a science of art. But feeling is of the highest importance. It precedes science. It leads first to form particular life movements to merge ultimately into cosmic movement. It is that sympathy in virtue of which the artist becomes one with the object he contemplates. He lives in his art. The aim of art is creation and not imitation of nature. The same creative impulse that moves in nature impels and inspires the artist. Art is rhythm. Ideas, feelings, forms, colours, and movement appeal to our aesthetic nature only when they are rhythmically composed.[6]

The word *renaissance* means "rebirth, or revival." At the advent of an avatar, or divine incarnation, a renaissance occurs, a new civilization begins, and a cultural revival takes place. Although Christ's public life lasted only three years, his contribution to the world of thought and culture was immense. His life and teachings have been sources of inspiration to countless artists in every field — painters, sculptors, architects, poets, writers, musicians, actors, and dramatists. Two thousand years have passed, and still people are writing books and composing songs about him. Painters and sculptors still strive to depict his form. And the avatars who lived before Christ — Rama, Krishna, and Buddha — also continue to inspire artists all over the world.

The history of Indian art covers a span of about 5000 years and presents a rich heritage. The Aryans of India were acquainted with the arts of dancing, singing, weaving, building, and making ornaments of gold and silver. Indian art flourished in the Maurya period (325-185 B.C.) and in the Gupta period (320-600 A.D.).

Indian art has always been based on Indian religious traditions. Nowhere else in the world will one find so many paintings and images of gods and goddesses. This is because the ideals and heroes of Indian society are spiritual in nature. The influence of social and political leaders is not nearly as great as that of religious leaders.

Ananda Coomaraswamy of the Boston Museum of Art gives an interesting description of the mystical aspect of the Indian artist's creative process:

> The artist sits in meditation and purges his mind of all disturbing elements and concentrates like a Yogin on the subject of his creation. The result of such a concentration is that his mind leaves the world of forms and soars high in the world of the formless. When the mind is thus merged in the formless, the impregnated desire of creating forms draws spontaneously from out of the formless the desired form, the deity associated with its particular posture, gesture, colour, and his whole mind becomes suffused as it were, with the radiant form of the deity which emerges from the depth of this consciousness and fills the canvas of his mind. The next duty of the artist is to transfer the picture of the mental canvas to the external canvas of matter.[7]

Ramakrishna was born at a critical period in Indian history. Western culture and civilization were spreading rapidly throughout Indian society, and Christian missionaries were converting the population. But Ramakrishna's divine life and his spiritual teachings touched people's hearts and restored their culture and religious heritage. He had a great influence on many social and religious leaders.

Ramakrishna is a living force even now: His ideas are growing and spreading day by day. His life is like a dazzling diamond with many facets, with each facet revealing one of his talents. Once Swami Vivekananda remarked: "The artistic faculty was highly developed in Sri Ramakrishna, and he used to say that without this faculty none could be truly spiritual."[8] Although Ramakrishna was mostly in a god-intoxicated mood, his artistic abilities permeated his life.

Ramakrishna as a Painter

When Ramakrishna was a young boy, he visited his married sister. Observing how cheerfully she served her husband and how contented her husband was, he painted a picture depicting the couple in that happy mood and presented it to them. People were amazed to see how life-like it was.

Ramakrishna had an artist's eye for perfection. In addition, he was familiar with the physical characteristics of different types of people. In Kamarpukur Ramakrishna once visited the studio of a professional sculptor who made clay images of gods and goddesses. He pointed out that the sculptor was not painting the eyes of the deity correctly. "Divine eyes," he said, "should be lotus-shaped. They should be long and pointing towards the ears." He then demonstrated with a brush and paint, astonishing the sculptor. In later years Ramakrishna used charcoal to draw pictures on the wall of the veranda of his room in Dakshineswar.

Ramakrishna as a Sculptor

As a boy in Kamarpukur, Ramakrishna would make clay images of gods and goddesses. Swami Saradananda described how he continued to do this in Dakshineswar:

He gathered some clay from the bed of the Ganges and made an image of Shiva with His bull, His drum, and His trident. While he was worshipping that image, Mathur happened near in the course of his walk. Curious about what the Master was worshipping so intently, he drew closer and found an image that was small but beautiful. Mathur was amazed, and realized that such a divine image was not available in the market. Curious, he asked Hriday where he got the image and who made it. Mathur was astonished to hear that the Master knew how to make the images of gods and goddesses and also how to repair broken images. He asked Hriday to give him the image after the worship. Hriday agreed, and with the Master's permission brought it to Mathur when the worship was over. Mathur scrutinized the image closely and was extremely impressed by what he saw. He then sent the image to the Rani for her to see it. She praised the maker of the image and, like Mathur, was amazed when she was told the Master had made it.[9]

In August 1855 the priest of the Radha-Krishna temple slipped while he was carrying the deity, accidentally breaking one of the feet of the Krishna image. According to Hindu tradition, a broken image cannot be worshipped; it should be immersed in the Ganges. Rani Rasmani ordered that a new image of Krishna be made, but she was fond of the old one and wanted to keep it. She asked scholars for their opinions, and all advised that the image should be replaced. But Ramakrishna said: "If any one of the Rani's sons-in-law were to break a leg, would she forsake him and put someone else in his place? Wouldn't she rather have him treated by a doctor? Let it be the same in this case. Mend the image and worship it as before. Why should the image be discarded?"[10] Ramakrishna himself then skillfully mended the image and the worship continued. Unfortunately in 1929 this old image again broke and in 1930 the temple trustees installed the new one on the main altar and the old broken one was kept in the left-side room of the Krishna temple.

Ramakrishna as a Dancer

When children or youths dance, their movements tend to be uninhibited and graceful; but when older people dance, their movements are often self-conscious and awkward. Swami Saradananda wrote:

> When we first met the Master, he was about forty-nine years old — or perhaps five or six months short of that. Before we became acquainted with the Master, we thought that although people love to see children dance and make gestures, it disgusts them or becomes ludicrous if a robust man acts that way. Swami Vivekananda used to say, "Does anyone enjoy watching a rhinoceros dance like a dancing girl?" When we came to the Master, we had to change our views. Although the Master was advanced in age, when he danced, sang, and made gestures — they were so sweet and beautiful! Girish once remarked: "I never dreamt that an old fellow could look so beautiful when he danced!"[11]

Once Swami Saradananda saw the Master dance in Mani Mallick's house. He recalled:

> The Master was dancing in the centre of that god-intoxicated group, rapidly moving forward and backward with rhythmic steps. In whatever direction he moved the crowd made room for him, as if enchanted.
>
> An extraordinary combination of tenderness, sweetness, and leonine strength was visible in every one of the Master's limbs. His face shone with a divine smile. What a superb dance! There was no artificiality or affectation in it — no jumping, no unnatural gestures or acrobatics. Nor was any absence of control apparent. Rather, one saw in the Master's dancing a rhythm of natural gestures and movements that sprang from his overwhelming bliss, sweetness, and zeal. His

phenomenal dance was like that of a big fish that swims freely and joyfully throughout a vast clear lake, sometimes slowly and sometimes
quickly. Absorbed in the ocean of blissful Brahman, the Master used
his body to express his inner feelings.[12]

Ramakrishna as a Singer

"Music is the art of the prophets," said Martin Luther. Ramakrishna
knew at least 181 songs, all of which he had learned after having heard
them only once. His voice was sweet and melodious; people loved to
hear him sing. Whenever Rani Rasmani came to the Kali temple, she
would ask Ramakrishna to sing some songs about the Divine Mother.

Ramlal recalled: "If someone broke the rhythm while singing, the
Master would cry out 'Oohu, oohu.' But if the person sang with
devotion and deep absorption, such irregularity would not disturb
him. He was not interested in ragas, raginis [metres], or the science
of music. The Master sang in ecstasy, and his voice was soft, sweet,
and melodious. Sometimes when he was singing, he would impro-
vise some joyous phrase. I saw the Master enter into samadhi many
times while singing. Sometimes he would ask me or Swamiji to
sing, and while listening he would again enter into samadhi."[13]

Ramakrishna as an Actor

Swami Saradananda wrote:

In Kamarpukur at that time there were three *yatra* [theatrical] groups,
one *baul* [minstrel] party, and a couple of *kavis* [versifiers who compete
in tournaments]. Furthermore, many Vaishnavas lived there, and they
would read the Bhagavata and sing *kirtan* in their homes every evening. From his childhood Gadadhar had heard the operas, songs, and
kirtans of these groups and had committed everything to memory. To
entertain the women, one day he would recite dialogues from a drama,
another day he would sing baul songs, and other days he would recite
the compositions of the kavis or sing kirtan. While enacting a play, he
alone would act out all the roles, changing his voice to suit each character. If he noticed that his mother, or any other woman, was
depressed, he would portray the role of a clown from a play or mimic
the particular manner and gestures of someone well known in the village, making them burst into laughter.

Observing Gadadhar's acting talent, one day some of his friends
proposed that they form a *yatra* [theatrical] party and asked him to
train them. Gadadhar agreed. However, the boys knew that their
guardians would object, so they were worried about finding a

secluded place in which to rehearse. The quick-witted Gadadhar suggested the secluded mango orchard of Manikraja, and they decided that every day at a particular time they would slip away from school and meet there.

The plan was soon carried out. Under Gadadhar's direction the boys quickly learned their roles and memorized the songs of the dramas based on the lives of Ramachandra and Krishna, and their performance resounded throughout the mango orchard. Of course Gadadhar had to draw upon his creativity to direct every aspect of those performances, as well as to perform the main roles. The boys were very happy when they found their little group was working well together. It is said that while performing in the mango orchard, Gadadhar would experience bhava samadhi.[14]

One night during the Shivaratri festival in Kamarpukur, a theatrical group came to perform a drama. But the main actor who was supposed to act in the role of Shiva fell sick. The villagers asked Ramakrishna to act in that role, and he was dressed accordingly. As soon as he went on the stage, he went into samadhi. Like a true actor, he became one with the character.

Ramakrishna as a Humorist

Humour is a mixture of love and wit. It is an art that makes people laugh. And people laugh when they are happy. It is truly joyful to live with a person who is inspiring and full of fun. Ramakrishna realized the blissful Brahman and shared that bliss with everyone who went to him. When depressed, one should read *The Gospel of Sri Ramakrishna*. His life and teachings are so simple and powerful that they can awaken and elevate the most despondent soul.

Story-telling is a wonderful medium in all religious traditions. We never get tired of telling and listening to the same story again and again. It reminds me of an anecdote:

Nicholas Murray Butler and Brander Matthews were discussing stories. Said Matthews, "When the first man tells an anecdote, it is originality; when the second tells it, it is plagiarism; with the third it is lack of originality; and with the fourth it is drawing from a common stock."

"Yes," broke in Butler, "and in the case of the fifth it is research."[15]

However, Ramakrishna knew a special technique for telling humorous stories. One may tell a story and get no response, while another person telling the same story may put his audience in stitches.

Of course Ramakrishna amused his listeners with his stories but at the same time these stories helped them solve their problems.

M. recorded various stories of the Master in the *Gospel*:

A job-seeker got tired of visiting the manager in an office. He couldn't get the job. One day he told his tale of woe to a friend. The friend said: "How stupid you are! Why are you wearing away the soles of your feet going to that fellow? You had better go to Golap. You will get the job tomorrow." Golap was the manager's mistress. The candidate called on her and said: "Mother, I am in great distress. You must help me out of it. My children are about to starve to death. I can get a job if you but say the word." Golap said to him, "Child, whom should I speak to?" The candidate said, "I am sure to get the job if you just put in a word about it to the manager." Golap said, "I shall speak to him today and settle the matter." The very next morning a man called on the candidate and said, "You are to work in the manager's office, beginning today." The manager said to his English boss: "This man is very competent. I have appointed him. He will do credit to the firm."[16]

*　　　*　　　*

Once a barber was shaving a gentleman. The latter was cut slightly by the razor. At once he cried out, "Damn!" But the barber didn't know the meaning of the word. He put his razor and other shaving articles aside, tucked up his shirt-sleeves — it was winter —, and said: "You said 'damn' to me. Now you must tell me its meaning." The gentleman said: "Don't be silly. Go on with your shaving. The word doesn't mean anything in particular; but shave a little more carefully." But the barber wouldn't let him off so easily. He said, "If 'damn' means something good, then I am a 'damn,' my father is a 'damn,' and all my ancestors are 'damns.'" (*All laugh.*) "But if it means something bad, then you are a 'damn,' your father is a 'damn,' and all your ancestors are 'damns.'" (*All laugh.*) "They are not only 'damns,' but 'damn — damn — damn — da-damn — damn.'" (*Loud laughter.*)[17]

Ramakrishna's Art of Teaching

Artists express their feelings through symbolism and imagery. Similarly, Ramakrishna taught spirituality through similes and metaphors, illustrations and comparisons, stories and parables. Buddha and Christ used the same method, which was simple and effective because it helped their audiences to visualize the teachings. Using ordinary scenes from day-to-day life, Ramakrishna answered the most intricate questions of philosophy.

The Upanishads say that knowers of Brahman are omniscient. If this is true, one may ask how the ancient knowers of Brahman could be omniscient without having knowledge of physical sciences.

The Master explained this by using examples from village life:

When rice is boiling in a pot, if you take one grain and press it between your fingers, you instantly know whether all the grains in the pot are soft or not. Why is this? You have not pressed all the grains one by one. How then do you come to this conclusion? Similarly, by examining two or three things in the world, one can know whether the world is eternal or transient, real or unreal. A man is born, lives for some time, and then dies. The same is true of a cow and a tree. After thus observing one thing after another, you come to the conclusion that whatever has name and form follows the same law. The earth, the sun, the moon, and so on have names and forms: they are therefore under the same law. Thus, you become aware that everything in this universe is of a similar nature. Do you not then know the nature of everything in this world? When you thus realize that this world is transient and unreal, you cannot love it anymore; you will remove it from your mind and will be without desire. As soon as you give up desire for the world, you will see God, the source of the world. So when a man has the vision of God, tell me: Is he omniscient or not?[18]

Someone asked the Master: "Maya is God's power and dwells in God. Is God then bound by maya as we are?" He replied: "No, not at all. Although maya belongs to God and dwells always with God, He is never bound by maya. Look, whoever is bitten by a snake dies. But there is always poison in the fangs of the snake, and the snake eats and gulps saliva through its mouth, but the snake does not die. It is just like that."[19]

Ramakrishna's Influence on the Arts

Ramakrishna encouraged and supported many artists, writers, actors, singers, dancers, and musicians who came to visit him. When Girish Chandra Ghosh, the famous playwright and actor, wanted to give up his career and become a monk, Ramakrishna discouraged him and told him that many people benefited by watching his dramas. Girish once said, "I learned how to write drama and how to act from Sri Ramakrishna." M., who was a schoolteacher, said, "I learned how to teach in school from Sri Ramakrishna." And Swami Vivekananda said, "I learned how to reason scientifically from Sri Ramakrishna."[20]

Not only did Ramakrishna keep several religious pictures in his room, but he also advised his devotees to do the same. "Divine feeling is awakened through such pictures," he said. Once he went to see the home of a devotee, hearing that he had a large collection of religious pictures.

Professor Nalini Ranjan Chattopadhyay has written a book about Ramakrishna and the Bengali stage. This book, written in Bengali, describes the tremendous influence that Ramakrishna had on Bengali actors, actresses, and musicians. He is worshipped as the patron deity of the stage. Even today many Bengali actors and actresses salute the picture of Ramakrishna before going onstage, following a tradition started by Girish Ghosh. At one time, men would act in the roles of women because women of good families were reluctant to act on the stage. Girish introduced some courtesans to act in his dramas. During Ramakrishna's time, actresses were considered immoral, and puritanical people would not attend their performances. But Ramakrishna gave these women his blessings and approval, thereby gaining for them society's approval as well. He acknowledged the gift of the artist and elevated actresses to a higher status. He actually brought about a revival of the Bengali stage.

Ramakrishna went to see several plays in the theatre. After he attended a performance based on the life of Chaitanya, someone asked him how he had enjoyed the play. Ramakrishna answered, "I found the representation the same as the real." To him, the woman who had acted in the role of Chaitanya and the real Chaitanya were the same. He was so pleased with this actress's talent and sincerity that he blessed her, saying, "Be illumined." As a result, she was transformed and henceforth lived like a nun.

Once, explaining to someone his wide-ranging interests, Ramakrishna said: "I do not like a monotonous life. I want variety. I want to make a bouquet with five kinds of flowers. I want to play music with a flute that has seven holes. I like to taste a variety of foods. I don't want to be a dry monk."

Behind Ramakrishna's words, behind his expressions, behind whatever he did there was his intense spiritual feeling and his experience of Oneness. This is exactly what artists struggle to achieve. The nineteenth-century British painter, Joseph Mallord William Turner, wanted to paint a picture of a storm at sea. During a storm he approached a boatman and asked him to take him out in his ship and tie him to the mast while the ship sailed through the worst of the storm. He experienced the dance of destruction. He was shivering; he thought he would die. When he finally returned to shore, he went to his studio and painted the picture. It was so vivid that a friend asked him in amazement, "How did you do it?" "I experienced it," Turner replied. "Not only did I see the storm and feel it, but it blew itself into me till I became part of the storm."[21]

We have read many times how the scriptures describe samadhi, but we had never seen a person in that state until we saw the photographs of Ramakrishna. This is the first time in the religious history of the world that the joy of samadhi has been photographed. It is amazing that all three pictures of Ramakrishna were taken when he was in samadhi. One of them was taken in 1879 at the home of the Brahmo leader, Keshab Chandra Sen. A religious discussion was going on when, all of sudden, Ramakrishna stood up, raised his arms, and merged into samadhi. His nephew Hriday supported him so that he would not fall. When the photograph was taken, his face was beaming with joy. A Bharat Natyam* dancer came one day to visit one of our monasteries in India. He did not know anything about Ramakrishna, but he happened to see that picture. He asked: "Who is this great dancer? His mudra [posture] is perfect." One of the monks asked him to explain what he meant, and the dancer replied: "According to our dancing tradition, this mudra signifies the Infinite."

Ramakrishna's smiling face in this picture is truly a masterpiece. It shows the kind of experience that comes when a person is in nirvikalpa samadhi, completely united with Cosmic Consciousness. Swami Vijnanananda, a monastic disciple of Ramakrishna, once commented: "When I first saw the Master in samadhi, his face was beaming with joy. It seemed as if he would not be able to hold that joy within and his face would crack. There is a certain kind of melon that cracks when it is ripe. I saw that the Master's face was like that melon. There was so much joy inside, it was about to crack open." This is real art: The expression of energy, rhythm, bliss, beauty, and truth; the expression of the Infinite.

It is clear, then, that Ramakrishna was born in this age to revitalize religion and philosophy, science and literature, art and culture. Only future generations will be able to accurately assess his total contribution to the renaissance of art. His life and universal message awakened a cosmic spiritual power, and the vibration of that power is still encircling the globe, touching and inspiring innumerable hearts. In *The Life of Ramakrishna*, Romain Rolland pointed out to his Western readers:

> I am bringing to Europe, as yet unaware of it, the fruit of a new autumn, a new message of the Soul, the symphony of India, bearing

*A type of classical Indian dance.

the name of Ramakrishna. It can be shown (and we shall not fail to point out) that this symphony, like those of our classical masters, is built up of a hundred different musical elements emanating from the past. But the sovereign personality concentrating in himself the diversity of these elements and fashioning them into a royal harmony is always the one who gives his name to the work, though it contains within itself the labour of generations. And with his victorious sign he marks a new era.[22]

25

Ramakrishna and Monasticism

The traditional concept of Indian monasticism is one of austerity, withdrawal from society, and striving only for one's own liberation. Shankara described the traditional monk in his famous hymn, *Kaupinapanchakam* (verse 1):

Roaming ever in the grove of Vedanta,
Ever pleased with his beggar's morsel,
Ever walking with heart free from sorrow,
Blest indeed is the wearer of the loincloth.[1]

In contrast, Ramakrishna would pray, "Oh, Mother, don't make me a dry monk." But he did not come to oppose the traditional values of monasticism. Instead he built a new, beautiful, and harmonious edifice upon the old structure of monastic life, preserving all the ancient values and blending them with the lifestyle and temperament of modern times, thus providing a much-needed restatement, in contemporary terms, of the ideals of the past.

Shankara wrote in the introduction to his commentary on the Bhagavad Gita: "Of two kinds is the dharma dealt with in the Vedas: the one characterized by activity and the other by renunciation. This twofold dharma, the cause of the stability of the world order and also the direct means by which human beings attain prosperity and the Highest Good, was followed by members of the different ashramas, desirous of securing their welfare. People practised Vedic dharma for a long time. Then lust arose among them; discrimination and wisdom declined.

Unrighteousness began to outweigh righteousness. Thus, when unrighteousness prevailed in the world, Vishnu, the first creator, wishing to ensure the continuance of the universe, incarnated Himself as Krishna."[2]

When God incarnates as a man, he behaves like a human being, but at the same time every one of his actions is extraordinary and has meaning. In the case of Ramakrishna, we see that he married, he became a sannyasin, and he also preached religion. But throughout his life, his main focus was on the experience of unity in diversity. He said: "One player is producing only a monotone on his flute, while another is creating waves of melodies in different ragas and raginis. That is my attitude. Why should I produce only a monotone when I have an instrument with seven holes? Why should I say nothing but, 'I am He, I am He?' I want to call on God through all the moods — through *shanta*, *dasya*, *sakhya*, *vatsalya*, and *madhura*. I want to make merry with God. I want to sport with God."[3] Thus, Ramakrishna was the prophet of the harmony so badly needed in this age, who could serve all, irrespective of caste or creed. His life became the meeting point of all sects and paths.

One day the Master asked one of his disciples, "What do you think of me?" The disciple replied, "Sir, you are neither a householder nor a monk." Apparently pleased, Ramakrishna said, "How do you know such a truth?" Ramakrishna was an incarnation of God. God is neither a monk nor a householder; He is beyond both.

The goal of human life is to realize God. This realization does not depend on whether one leads a monastic life or the life of a householder. Some people think that Ramakrishna came for householders and some think that he came for monks. Actually, he came for anyone who sincerely wants to realize God, and to demonstrate to modern people how to lead a God-centred life.

Once one of his householder disciples expressed his desire to renounce the world, but Ramakrishna did not give him permission. "What harm is there in remaining a householder?" he asked the disciple. "Only keep the mind fixed upon God. The life of a householder is fighting from within the fortress."[4] Ramakrishna taught that it was better to grow in one's own way naturally, and that it was not good to force oneself into renunciation. He once said: "There are two kinds of yogis, the 'revealed' and the 'hidden.' The householder may be a 'hidden' yogi. None recognizes him. The householder must renounce mentally, not outwardly."[5]

Kamini-kanchan maya (lust and gold are maya) was an oft-repeated utterance of Ramakrishna. And regarding monastic rules he was uncompromising. For the good of the many, for the happiness of human beings, is the sannyasin born. One who forgets his or her ideal after embracing sannyasa has lived in vain. Ramakrishna's attitude regarding this was unequivocal, as these remarks show: "A sannyasin associated with 'woman and gold' is like a beautiful damsel with a bad odour. The odour makes her beauty useless."[6]

"Do you know how it looks for a sannyasin to accept money or to be attached to an object of temptation? It is as if a brahmin widow who had practised continence and lived on simple boiled rice and vegetables and milk for many years, were suddenly to accept an untouchable as her paramour."[7]

"Sadhus [monks] should depend one hundred percent on God. Birds and monks do not hoard. Don't trust a sadhu if he keeps bag and baggage with him and a bundle of clothes with many knots."[8]

According to Hindu tradition, a person must pass through four successive stages during his or her lifetime: Brahmacharya (student), Garhasthya (householder), Vanaprastha (forest-dweller), and Sannyasa (monk). So at the end one is supposed to embrace the monastic life, severing all worldly ties and attachments. However, this Hindu view — that renunciation is the culmination of human life — is very flexible; it does not bind one with strict rules. For example, the Jabala Upanishad says: "Let one renounce even from the state of a student or from the state of a householder or from that of a forest-dweller. On whatever day a man has the spirit of renunciation, that very day let him renounce."[9]

Once Sarada Devi, the spiritual consort of Ramakrishna, was asked about Ramakrishna's specialty and she replied: "Renunciation is his specialty in this age. Did anyone see such natural (and total) renunciation ever before?"[10]

The Brihadaranyaka Upanishad (4:4:22) says: "Desiring the Atman alone, monks renounce their homes. The ancient sages, having risen above the desire for offspring, the desire for wealth, the desire for name and fame, led the life of mendicants." These three desires were so completely absent from Ramakrishna's mind that he had to *create* trivial desires in order to bring his mind down to the level of ordinary consciousness.

Mathur Nath Biswas, a son-in-law of Rani Rasmani and owner of the Dakshineswar temple, tested Ramakrishna in many ways. He offered him vast property worth millions of rupees, which Ramakrishna refused to accept. Then he took him to a famous courtesan in Calcutta, but the very sight of her plunged Ramakrishna into deep samadhi. The highest respect one can offer another person is to worship him as God. Mathur honoured Ramakrishna in this way, but not even a trace of ego cropped up in the Master's mind.

The Hindu scriptures describe four types of sannyasins: Kutichaka, a man of renunciation who does not move from place to place; Bahudaka, an itinerant monk; Hamsa, a monk of superb renunciation and discrimination; and Paramahamsa, an illumined soul who has transcended all duality and so is beyond injunctions and prohibitions.

There are two stages of sannyasa: *Vividisha-sannyasa*, when a person takes monastic vows with a view to attaining the knowledge of Brahman; and *Vidvat-sannyasa*, when, after illumination, a person takes formal vows in order to enjoy the bliss of living free of all bondage.

Ramakrishna was a Paramahamsa and he took sannyasa after he had realized God. In his own words: "My experiences are for others to refer to."[11]

Ramakrishna took monastic vows from Tota Puri, an illumined monk of the Puri sect, which is one of the ten sects founded by Shankara. It is interesting to note that whenever Ramakrishna needed a teacher, that teacher appeared of his or her own accord. Ramakrishna followed each guru's bidding to the letter with complete faith.

Swami Saradananda provided a detailed description of Ramakrishna's initiation into sannyasa in *Sri Ramakrishna and His Divine Play*:

At the end of the night the auspicious *brahma muhurta* [48 minutes before sunrise] arrived. Guru and disciple entered the hut. After they completed the preliminary rituals, they ignited the *homa fire*. The Panchavati and the surrounding groves reverberated with the holy and profound sound of the mantras chanted prior to the monastic vows. From ancient times these vows to renounce everything for God have been passed along in succession from guru to disciple, making India a land of knowers of Brahman. When that sweet sound touched the gentle undulating surface of the holy river Ganges, it seemed that She came to life. She flowed joyfully with a sweet murmuring sound as if carrying this message in all directions: After a long time, here in this age an extraordinary aspirant was taking the all-renouncing monastic vows for the good of all people in the world.

The guru was prepared to recite the mantras; he instructed the disciple to follow them attentively and repeat them while pouring oblations into the homa fire. The prayer mantras were uttered first.

"May the truth of Supreme Brahman be revealed unto me. May the blissful Reality be realized by me. May the indivisible blissful Brahman become manifest in me. O Supreme Self, You eternally coexist with Your Power to reveal the knowledge of Brahman! Among Your children — gods, humans, and other beings — I am Your child and servant, a special object of compassion. O Supreme Lord, destroyer of the dreary dreams of the world, please destroy all my painful dreams, the perception of duality. O Supreme Self, I offer my vital forces as oblations to You, and controlling my senses I focus my mind on You alone. O Shining One, creator and director of all beings, do remove from me all the impurities that obstruct true knowledge, and bestow upon me Self-knowledge free from doubt and error. At Your command may the sun, the wind, the pure water of the rivers, plants and trees, grains such as rice, wheat, barley, and everything in this world be favourable to me and help me to attain the knowledge of Reality. O Brahman, You become manifest in various forms in this world through Your special power. I offer my oblations to You in this fire so that I may become fit to retain knowledge of the Self by purifying the body and the mind. Be gracious unto me."[12]

Then the *viraja homa* began: "May this oblation purify the five elements I am made of: earth, water, fire, air, and ether. Freed from impurities and ignorance, may I become the self-luminous Brahman. Swaha!

"May this oblation purify my five vital forces: *prana, apana, vyana, udana,* and *samana.* Freed from impurities and ignorance, may I become the self-luminous Brahman. Swaha!

"May this oblation purify the five sheaths: *annamaya, pranamaya, manomaya, vijnanamaya,* and *anandamaya.* Freed from impurities and ignorance, may I become the self-luminous Brahman. Swaha!

"May this oblation purify the five objects of my senses: sound, touch, form, taste, and smell. Freed from impurities and ignorance, may I become the self-luminous Brahman. Swaha!

"May this oblation purify my mind, speech, body, and actions. Freed from impurities and ignorance, may I become the self-luminous Brahman. Swaha!

"Awake, O red-eyed Divine Being dwelling in the fire. You are expert in removing the obstacles to knowledge. O fulfiller of desires, please destroy whatever impediments lie in the path of Self-knowledge and purify completely all the impressions of my mind, so that the knowledge imparted by my guru may be manifest in my heart. May this oblation make me free from impurities and ignorance, so that I become the self-luminous Brahman. Swaha!

"I am identified with the consciousness of Brahman. I offer all my desires for sex, progeny, wealth, honour, physical beauty, and so on in the fire as oblations. I renounce everything completely. Swaha!"[13]

Ramakrishna said emphatically that "the spiritual experiences of this place (*meaning himself*) have surpassed even the Vedas and Vedanta";[14] yet when he took the vows of sannyasa he followed all the injunctions of the scriptures. He then offered his tuft of hair and sacred thread into the fire as oblations, according to scriptural injunctions. The Master received a loincloth, an ochre robe, and a name* from his guru, in accordance with the tradition followed by generations of aspirants since ancient times. He then asked Tota Puri for instructions.

"Nangta instructed me in Vedanta," Ramakrishna said. "In three days I went into samadhi. At the sight of my samadhi, he was quite taken aback and exclaimed, 'Ah! What is this?' We talked only of Vedanta. The Brahmani used to say to me: 'Don't listen to Vedanta. It will injure your devotion to God.'"[15]

It is a widespread misconception that monistic Vedanta is antagonistic to the path of devotion. This is not true, as was pointed out by Narahari in his *Bodhasara* (32:42): "Before the dawn of knowledge, duality is the cause of delusion; but when true knowledge is awakened through intuition, duality is imagined for the sake of devotion to God. This blissful state is even more beautiful than nondualism."

Ramakrishna never cared for dry philosophical discussion or crude forms of asceticism. After reaching the nitya (the absolute) he would return to dwell in the lila (the relative), and again climb from the lila to the nitya. His description of this is unique: "Mere dry knowledge is like an ordinary rocket: it bursts into a few sparks and then dies out. But the Knowledge of sages like Narada and Sukadeva is like a good rocket: for a while it showers balls of different colours, and then it stops; again it throws out new balls and again it stops; and thus it goes on. Those sages had prema [divine love] for God. Prema is the rope by which one can reach Satchidananda."[16]

Traditional Vedanta monks hold that action originates from desire, and desire from ignorance. Therefore, monks should give up action and

*Some say that during the sannyasa ceremony Tota Puri gave the name "Ramakrishna" to the Master. Others say that the great devotee Mathur gave that name to the Master. The first opinion seems to be reasonable.

Later, some researchers found that the name "Ramakrishna" was given by his father, as he was a devotee of Ramachandra. He gave similar names to his two other sons, Ramkumar and Rameswar. A deed of document executed by Rani Rasmani on 18 February 1861 shows that in 1858: "Sri Sri Radhakantaji — Sri Ramakrishna Bhattacharya: Rupees 5/-, 3 pairs of cloths, plus Rs. 4.50." – vide *Sri Sri Ramakrishna Kathamrita* — Part 2, by M. This proves that in 1858 the Master was the priest of the Krishna temple and his monthly salary was five rupees, whereas Tota Puri arrived at Dakshineswar in 1864. It seems Tota Puri gave the same name to the Master.

452 ▪ How to Live With God

desire so that they can get rid of the ignorance that covers the Atman. There is no action in the Atman, or in Brahman. The Mahanarayana Upanishad says, *na karmanā*; that is, liberation is not possible through action. Moreover, Shankara wrote in his commentary on the Gita (18:30): "The path of action as taught in the scriptures is the path of bondage." But he also admitted (Gita 18:10): "For him whose mind has thus been purified by performance of regular acts and who thus becomes inclined to knowledge of the Self, *jñānanishthā* [steadfast meditation on the Self] is the next step."

The monks of the Ramakrishna Order, however, are involved in various activities. This is misunderstood by traditional Vedanta monks. The question of whether activity or contemplation is the appropriate path for monastics has been an eternal dilemma for traditional monks. But Ramakrishna's succinct saying, "Tie the nondual knowledge in the corner of your cloth and then do as you please," resolves that quandary. If God can be seen with closed eyes, why not with open eyes? If the all-pervading God appears in the temple, then why not in the forest or even the factory? This, of course, means that every one of a spiritual aspirant's actions must be transformed into worship.

Swami Vivekananda put this quite clearly in his lecture "Sannyasa: Its Ideal and Practice": "You must try to combine in your life immense idealism with immense practicality. You must be prepared to go into deep meditation now and the next moment you must be ready to go and cultivate these fields [the meadows of the Belur monastery]. You must be prepared to explain the difficult intricacies of the scriptures now, and the next moment to go and sell the produce of the fields in the market."[17]

This new approach to the Indian monastic ideal is based on the concept that there is no contradiction between *Aham Brahmāsmi* (I am Brahman) and *Tattwamasi* (Thou art That). By closing the eyes, a spiritual aspirant can say, "I am Brahman." Opening the eyes, one can say "Thou art That" and, with that attitude, worship all beings.

Ramakrishna never advised his disciples to work only for their own liberation. He regarded such aspirants as inferior. One day in the Cossipore garden house, Narendra (later Swami Vivekananda) expressed a desire to be immersed in samadhi for three or four days at a stretch, interrupting his meditation now and then for a bite of food. Ramakrishna reprimanded him for his selfish attitude. "Shame on you!" he said. "You are asking for such an insignificant thing. I thought that you would be like a big banyan tree, and that thousands of people would rest in your shade. But now I see that you are seeking your own liberation."[18]

Later, Swami Vivekananda formulated the motto of the Ramakrishna Order: "*Ātmano mokshārtham jagat hitāya cha.*" "[A monk should live] for the emancipation of the Self and for the well-being of the world." Thus, Swamiji tried to express the ancient monastic ideals not only through the old methods of spiritual discipline and teaching by example, but also by utilizing the spiritual energy generated by spiritual practices for the good of humanity. Swamiji said: "The sannyasin, verily, is born into this world to lay down his life for others, to stop the bitter cries of men, to wipe away the tears of the widow, to bring peace to the soul of the bereaved mother, to equip the ignorant masses for the struggle for existence, to accomplish the secular and spiritual well-being of all through the diffusion of spiritual teaching, and to arouse the sleeping lion of Brahman in all by throwing in the light of knowledge."[19]

But it should be understood that the Ramakrishna Order is not like other philanthropic organizations, which are maintained only for social services, relief work, and so on. Service to human beings is akin to worshipping God because God dwells in the hearts of all beings. The Ramakrishna Order is preeminently a religious body, its service to others forming part of its spiritual practice.

Religiosity was unbearable for Ramakrishna. Though he took monastic vows, he continued to wear an ordinary white cloth instead of ochre robes throughout his life. As the scripture says: "Where is there any injunction or prohibition for him whose mind is always above the play of the three gunas?"

Once a stranger dressed in the ochre cloth of a monk came to visit Ramakrishna in Dakshineswar. On seeing such ostentatious dress the Master commented: "Why this gerua [ochre cloth]? Should one put on such a thing for a mere fancy? If the outer garb does not correspond to the inner thought, it gradually brings ruin. Uttering false words or doing false deeds, one gradually loses all fear. Far better is the white cloth of a householder. Attachment to worldliness, occasional lapses from the ideal, and an outer garb of gerua — how dreadful!"[20]

Long before his disciples came to him, Ramakrishna initiated the great scholar and logician Narayana Shastri into sannyasa. After coming in contact with Ramakrishna in Dakshineswar and observing his nirvikalpa samadhi, Shastri thought: "Ah! How wonderful! Where shall I find another person like him who can teach me and explain the hidden meaning of the scriptures? I must not miss this opportunity. I must learn from him the means of immediate knowledge of Brahman at any cost."[21]

He prayed for monastic vows with such eagerness that Ramakrishna agreed to initiate him on an auspicious day. As far as we know, this was the first time Ramakrishna conferred sannyasa.

Ramakrishna founded his Order towards the end of his life, while he was at the Cossipore garden house. One of his biographers wrote:

> One day Gopal Senior [later Swami Advaitananda] expressed his desire to the Master to distribute ochre cloths and rudraksha rosaries among sannyasins. Pointing to his young disciples, Sri Ramakrishna answered: "You won't find better monks than these anywhere. Give your cloths and rosaries to them." Gopal placed a bundle of ochre cloths before the Master, who distributed them among his young disciples. One cloth was left, and the Master ordered it to be preserved for Girish, who was second to none in his spirit of renunciation. One evening the Master made the young boys go through a ceremony and permitted them to receive food from the houses of all, irrespective of caste. Thus it was that the disciples were initiated into the monastic order by the Master himself, and the foundation of the future Ramakrishna Order was laid.[22]

Chaitanya said to his disciple Sanatan: "Listen, there is no greater dharma than practising compassion for all living beings, love of God's name, and service of devotees."[23] This traditional attitude was given a new direction by Ramakrishna. He said: "Compassion for all beings? How foolish to speak of compassion! Human beings are as insignificant as worms crawling on the earth — and they are to show compassion to others? That is absurd. It must not be compassion, but service to all. Recognize all as manifestations of God and serve them as such."[24] Swami Vivekananda later formulated his Practical Vedanta based on these teachings of his Master. Proclaiming the monasticism of the new era, he heralded in a trumpet voice: "Embodied beings cannot remain without activity for even a moment, so their duty is to perform every action as service to God within human beings; thus they will soon reach the goal."[25]

Manu, the Hindu lawgiver, described the life of a monk in his *Samhita* (6:40-43,45):

> For that monk, by whom not the slightest danger even, is caused to created beings, there will be no danger from any quarter, after he is freed from his body.
>
> Departing from his house fully provided with the means of purification, let him wander about absolutely silent, and caring nothing for enjoyments that may be offered to him.
>
> Let him always wander alone without any companion, in order to

attain final liberation, fully understanding that the solitary man, who neither forsakes nor is forsaken, gains his end.

He shall neither possess a fire, nor a dwelling. He may go to a village for his food. He shall be indifferent to everything, firm of purpose, meditating and concentrating his mind on Brahman.

Let him not desire to die, let him not desire to live; let him wait for his appointed time of final departure, as a servant waits for the payment of his wages.

Similar injunctions for the monastic may be found in the *Shanti Parvan* (Chapter 192) of the Mahabharata. So it can be seen that there is a definite contrast between the old and the modern approaches to monastic life. For monasticism as propounded by Ramakrishna and Vivekananda is more a renovation than a revival of the ancient system. It is undoubtedly a new turn with a new purpose: to work for one's own liberation by doing good to humanity and to the world at large. According to nondualistic Vedanta, while doing good to others, we do good to ourselves because the Atman is one and It pervades all beings. Selfishness and body-consciousness are the two main obstacles to Self-knowledge. That is why Vivekananda told his followers: "Go to hell yourself to buy salvation for others."[26]

26

If Ramakrishna
Were Alive Today

The word *if* comes from doubt, which generates a lot of problems in human life. There is a fascinating story about Kumarila Bhatta, a teacher of the Vedic ritualistic school (Mimamsa), who used the word *if* at a very critical moment and saved his life. Kumarila was a South Indian brahmin and a famous Vedic philosopher. He was defeated in a debate with Dharmakirti, a Buddhist logician. According to their agreement, he had to become a Buddhist, so he went to Nalanda to learn Buddhism from Dharmapala. One day his guru, Dharmapala, was criticizing the Vedas. This saddened Kumarila, and he wept in secret. A Buddhist student saw him and informed Dharmapala. Enraged, the guru told Kumarila: "You still have respect for the Vedas! You are pretending that you are a Buddhist and taking lessons from me. I challenge you to disprove my view, if you are capable enough." A fierce debate ensued between the guru and the disciple. Dharmapala was tormented and defeated by Kumarila's sharp arguments. Then Kumarila said: "Without instruction from one who is omniscient, a jiva cannot become omniscient. Buddha was illumined by the knowledge of the Vedas, yet he discarded the Vedas. Is that not theft?"

The angry Buddhists attacked Kumarila, and Dharmapala ordered them to throw him from the top of the palace and kill him. The mob took Kumarila to the top of a tower and pushed him off. As he fell, Kumarila shouted: "If the Vedas are true, may I remain alive without injury." Kumarila fell to the ground but did not die. The onlookers were dumbfounded. Kumarila told them: "O nonviolent Buddhists, I see that one of my eyes has been slightly injured. That would not have happened if I had not said '*if* the Vedas are true.'" The Buddhists recognized the divine power in Kumarila and released him.

Kumarila escaped death by the power of his faith, but what about us? Our minds are constantly oscillating between doubt and faith: What if Ramakrishna were alive today? Does he really exist or has he merged into nirvana? *But, as if, seems to be* — these words are constantly popping up in our minds. To remove this horrible doubt, we read the scriptures, practise japa and meditation, seek out holy company, and perform unselfish actions. Still doubt persists. How can we be rid of it? The human intellect cannot comprehend how a huge banyan tree can exist in a seed. Similarly, one cannot understand how the Cosmic God can inhabit an ordinary human body.

Ramakrishna's nephew Ramlal described his doubt to a devotee:

I used to address the Master as *apani* [a term of respect used for seniors or revered persons] because I did not feel that he was my own uncle. As I could not understand his behaviour, moods, or samadhi, a doubt arose in my mind. I thought: "The Master is an unlettered person, but still all great scholars are defeated by him. Is he truly an Incarnation of God?" One day I said to the Master: "A doubt has arisen in my mind about you. I am confused." The Master replied: "Look, Ramlal. One cannot understand this mystery through the intellect. You have seen jilipis [a type of sweet]. From the outside they look dry. How would one know that they are full of sweet syrup inside? If you think of me as an avatar, then you are blessed that you have the opportunity to serve me. In addition, you are my blood relative. What else do you want?"

In those days I did not recognize the Master's greatness. Although we were his blood relatives, we did not realize who he was. But through his grace, I have this much faith: since we were born into his family, we have found refuge at his lotus feet. From his own lips I heard that when a man attains illumination, seven generations of his family before and after him become liberated. And to think that the Lord himself was born in our family as a human being! Through his grace and his holy company we too have had many visions and spiritual experiences. Thus he gave us faith and devotion for him.[1]

When we are separated from our dearest ones, we feel empty. This is a natural law. When the Master was about to leave Dakshineswar for his cancer treatment, Ramlal told him: "Uncle, you are going to Calcutta for treatment. I shall miss you terribly." The Master consoled him, saying: "Think that I have gone to the pine grove or to Calcutta for a visit, and I shall be back soon. This way you won't feel sad."

Ramlal later said to the devotees:

From then on I have never felt that the Master is absent. I experience his presence here and sometimes see him.

The Master told me: "Whoever comes to Dakshineswar — whether known to you or not — please give that person a little bit of prasad and a glass of Ganges water. You will not have to do anything else. This service will give you the result of japa, austerity, or sacrifice." So I do as he told me, and I get immense joy. Truly, I don't have good concentration in japa and meditation, but I practise according to my routine.

Now the number of the Master's devotees has increased. His message has spread within a few years. I see some people who have come from different countries. I don't even know their languages. They roll on the ground of the Panchavati and take dust from that place; and they also take leaves from the banyan tree and bel tree.[2]

These are the signs of love according to the devotional scriptures: In the eyes of the lover, the beloved's face is beautiful; and sweet are the beloved's lips, face, smile, speech, song, and dance. Even the beloved's home and belongings are sweet.

People experience both pain and joy when they are separated from the one they love. When the full moon reflects on shallow water, the fish play with it and believe that the moon is their companion. When the moon sets, they feel pain; but they wait patiently, thinking of their beloved's return. The lotuses unfold their petals when the sun rises and close them at sunset. They pass their nights meditating on their beloved, the sun. There is joy in that meditation. We are gross-minded people, so we understand only the joy of physical union. We are unaware of the everlasting joy that comes from union with the Atman. Rabindranath Tagore wrote in his *Gitanjali*:

O Lord, my eyes always remain open for you;
I may not see you,
But I am always eager to see you.
This makes me happy.

Sometimes we think about the joy we would have experienced if we had lived with the Master in Dakshineswar. Swami Brahmananda said: "As long as I lived with the Master I had spontaneous recollection and contemplation of God. An ecstatic joy filled me all the time. Ah, how joyfully we lived with the Master at Dakshineswar! Sometimes we would be convulsed with side-splitting laughter by his humour and wit. What we now cannot experience by meditation, we then attained automatically."[3]

Swami Turiyananda wrote:

Ah, those days at Dakshineswar were like heaven itself! From morning till one o'clock in the afternoon everyone would be busy picking flowers and making other preparations for worship until the poor were fed. In the meantime Sri Ramakrishna would discuss spiritual subjects, and the devotees would listen to him with rapt attention. Even his fun and jokes were related to God. There was no other topic. Everything culminated in his samadhi.

An hour of congregational singing in the company of the Master filled us with such exuberant joy that we would feel transported, as it were, into an ethereal region. But now even meditation fails to evoke that celestial bliss, or even a semblance of it. That bliss would stay with us continuously for a week. We used to feel intoxicated, though we did not know why or how. Who would believe it? It is difficult to convince anyone.[4]

M. wrote: "One may live with an avatar, but one cannot necessarily know him if he does not want to be known. Hriday was asked to leave the Dakshineswar temple. One day he came to see the Master, and standing outside the gate he cried: 'Uncle, take me back. I am deprived of your company and so I suffer.' The Master replied: 'Why, was it not you who said to me, "You follow your ideal and let me follow mine?"' Hriday: 'Yes, I did say that. But what did I know?' Tears also appeared in the Master's eyes. No one can recognize him if he does not want to be recognized. When Hriday lived with the Master, he did not know who the Master was. When he was separated from him, he realized the Master's greatness."[5]

Seeing Through the Physical Eyes and the Spiritual Eye

With our physical eyes we see the world and all its beings, which are created by God's maya. There is no end to this visualization. It is because maya makes the One into many that this world is full of variety and diversity. When through sadhana we develop a spiritual or mental eye, we see unity in the multiplicity. This is called same-sightedness or knowledge of Oneness. At that time one realizes: "As the same nondual fire, after it has entered the world, becomes different according to whatever it burns, so also the same nondual Atman, dwelling in all beings, becomes different according to whatever It enters. And It also exists without."[6]

M. wrote:

> Once somebody asked the Master, "Is God with form or without form?" The Master answered: "I have seen the Mother both ways. She is the indivisible Satchidananda, and again She assumes various forms for the devotees. At Kalighat [in South Calcutta] I saw the Divine Mother playing with some children and chasing a butterfly. Another time I saw Her walking on the Adi Ganga." On one occasion the Master told us: "Mother has come. She is wearing a red-bordered sari and has tied a bunch of keys in the corner of Her cloth." He said this in the presence of Keshab Sen and others in his room at Dakshineswar. People heard the Master's words, but the Master alone heard the Mother's words. Another day he said: "The Mother is going up and down the stairs in the temple. Her hair is dishevelled, and Her anklets are making a *jhun-jhun* sound." Once in Cossipore he said, "Today I saw the Mother playing a vina [a stringed instrument]." The Master was absorbed in the formless aspect of the Mother for six months during his sadhana.
>
> Not only did he see God, but he also used to talk to the Divine Mother, as we talk among ourselves, in front of people. One day he said, "The Mother has come." Then he began to talk to Her, saying: "Well, Mother, to whom should I listen? This person is saying this and the other person something else." Then the Divine Mother said something to him. Again the Master said: "I understand, Mother. I shall listen to You and no one else."[7]

Our eyes and ears are not as subtle as Sri Ramakrishna's, so we do not see the Divine Mother as he did. We read about the Master; we listen to his message; we think of his divine play; but still he is not living to us. Sadhana is sweet and joyful when the aspirant uses his or her feeling and thinking capabilities together. Some people try to understand God only through the intellect; but they do not realize that intellectual understanding and true realization are not the same. For example, a man understands that smoking causes cancer, but he still smokes.

M. sometimes advised the devotees to meditate on various scenes in the Master's life, such as the following three scenarios:

1. In the evening the Master is seated on his bed, absorbed in deep meditation. After meditation he says, "Those who think of God day

and night don't need to practise spiritual disciplines at the stipulated times."

2. There is a dark cloud over the north side of the temple garden; its reflection falls on the Ganges. This cloud is behind the Master as he is returning to his room from the Panchavati.

3. At Balaram Mandir the Master says to Balaram's father: "All religions and all paths call upon their followers to pray to one and the same God. Therefore one should not show disrespect to any religion or religious opinion."[8]

The famous writer Ishan Chandra Roy wrote an article titled "How to See Sri Ramakrishna," from which the following is taken:

One of my Christian friends lamented to me: "If I had been born 1900 years ago, I could have seen Jesus Christ." A devotee of Ramakrishna also said, "If only I could have lived with the Master!" Their attitude is that their lives would be blessed if they could see their Chosen Ideals. Once the present writer also had a desire to see Ramakrishna. God always fulfills a sincere wish. Someone may say that when a person dies one can no longer see that person with his physical eyes, so how can a person see Ramakrishna when he is no longer in a physical form?

Undoubtedly it is a great fortune to see a great soul or an avatar. But would every human being truly see and recognize them? Thousands of people saw Lord Jesus. But the Pharisees and Roman soldiers did not see Jesus the way Mary Magdalene and Joseph of Arimathea saw him. They would not have persecuted and crucified him if they had seen the real nature of Jesus Christ. So, true seeing is not seeing through these mortal eyes only.

In the eyes of a mother, a dark ugly boy is *Nilmani* [the blue jewel]; and a blind boy is *Padmalochan* [the lotus-eyed one]. A lover sees Helen's beauty in Ethiope's brow. A man neglects a woman, and another man accepts the same woman, offering her everything he owns. Why do such things happen? Because it is better to see through the mental eye than through the physical eyes. What one cannot see through the physical eyes, one can see or catch through the mental eye.

Some may think that seeing through the mental eye is actually imagination, so it is unreal. This is not true. The beauty of the child is reflected in the mother's eyes. That beauty really exists, so it is real. Therefore, just as the result of seeing through the physical eyes is true, so also is the result of seeing through the mental eye true.[9]

The scriptures say that one can achieve everything through love — even the vision of God. When we see Ramakrishna's pictures and the places where he enacted his lila, when we read his conversations and listen to the songs he sang, we feel the Master awaken in our hearts.

The Fortunate Ones Can See

According to the *Chaitanya Charitamrita*: "Gaur [Chaitanya] is still enacting his divine play; only a fortunate few can see it."

We sometimes lament our bad luck that we never had the opportunity to see Ramakrishna. While reading *The Gospel of Sri Ramakrishna* and *Sri Ramakrishna and His Divine Play*, we are inspired for the moment, but afterwards we are again depressed. We lament that our lives have been lived in vain.

In this respect, M. gives us a little hope. He told some devotees: "One can see the Master even now in Dakshineswar. First one should know by reading the books when and where the Master sat and what he did; then one should connect oneself with that place and imagine the presence of the Master at that time. Thus one can have the association of the Master and one can even see him. What is imagination today is realization tomorrow. One can have this vision when one's imagination is deeply intensified. According to the Yoga scriptures, everything is present; there is no past or future."[10]

One day Latu came to Dakshineswar to visit the Master, but he was told the Master had left for Kamarpukur. This news did not lessen his tremendous longing to see the Master. He sat on the bank of the Ganges and started to weep. Someone had told him that Sri Ramakrishna was ever-present at Dakshineswar and that anyone who called on him would see him. Holding steadfastly to this idea, the boy sat there from midday until evening. Ramlal, the Master's nephew, was employed as a priest in the Kali temple at that time. He noticed Latu in the temple garden. He describes the scene in his own words: "As many times as I said to Latu, 'The Master has gone home,' so many times did he repeat, 'No, you do not understand; the Master is definitely here.' I found I could not convince the boy, so I went to the temple to conduct the vesper service. When it was over, I returned to the spot where I had left Latu, taking with me some prasad for him to eat. There I discovered him bowing down and touching his forehead to the ground. Mystified, I kept quiet. After a moment or two, when the boy rose and saw me standing before him, he seemed surprised and asked me: 'Ah! Where has the Master gone?' Dumbfounded, I gave him the prasad and went back to the temple."[11]

Ramlal described a similar incident, in which the Master appeared before a monk:

A young Ramait monk [a worshiper of Ramachandra] in Ayodhya had a vision that God had again incarnated on earth, somewhere in the East. In order to see him, the monk started on foot eastward from Ayodhya. When he reached Bengal he heard that there was a great saint named Sri Ramakrishna near Calcutta. He finally found Dakshineswar after a long search and asked someone, "Where is Ramakrishna Paramahamsa?" The people of the Kali temple told him that the Master had just passed away a few days before. Hearing this heartbreaking news, the monk exclaimed: "What! He passed away? I have come from Ayodhya on foot [nearly a thousand miles] just to see him. I went through so much hardship to get here and he has left the body!" The young monk began to sob.

The manager of the Kali temple offered him some food from the temple store but he refused it. He went to the Panchavati and stayed there for two or three days without eating. One night Sri Ramakrishna appeared before him and said: "You have not eaten anything for several days. I have brought this pudding for you. Please eat it." He fed the monk and disappeared.

The next morning I went to the Panchavati and found the monk full of joy. I asked: "What happened? You were so unhappy yesterday. Why are you so cheerful today?" Then he told me everything. He even showed me the earthen bowl in which the Master had brought the pudding.*[12]

To Live in the Abode of Ramakrishna

Is Ramakrishna only in Kamarpukur, Dakshineswar, Cossipore, or Belur Math? He is God; he is everywhere, beyond space and time. He dwells in every creature, but he manifests especially in human beings. M. said: "The Master graciously put special glasses on my eyes, so I see everything red [the colour of love]. I feel that everyone is my relative, my very own."[13] This is called the eye of love. When this eye opens, one feels that all are children of God and everyone belongs to the Master.

Sometimes devotees imagine that after death they will go to *Ramakrishna-loka*, the abode of Ramakrishna. Once Swami Vijnanananda said: "Sometimes this question arises in my mind, 'Where shall I go after death?' In this respect Swami Shivananda says: 'We shall go to *Ramakrishna-loka*. We will live there with the Master.' I say that I will not go to any place like that. I will not go to any external world. If one can keep the Master always in the mind, if one does not forget him even for a moment, then one is living with the Master. If one's mind is constantly

*Ramlal preserved that bowl for a long time, but later it was somehow destroyed.

absorbed in the thought of the Master, wherever that person lives, he or she dwells in the abode of Ramakrishna."[14] Krishna says in the Gita (12:8): "Fix your mind on Me alone, rest your thought on Me alone, and in Me alone you will live hereafter. Of this there is no doubt."

M.'s Diary Is the Honeycomb

Bees fly from flower to flower for honey; they gather it and fill the honeycomb. People extract the honey and enjoy it. M. used to run to the temple garden of Dakshineswar and to places in Calcutta to gather Ramakrishna-honey, the Master's immortal words. He gathered Ramakrishna-honey over a period of five years, recorded it in the *Gospel*, and dispensed it himself for nearly fifty years. He strongly believed that anyone who imbibes these immortal words of the Master will be immortal.

Once M. told some devotees: "I don't claim any credit for it. The Master's life was a glowing example of *jivanmukti* [liberated while living] and *videhamukti* [liberated at the time of death]; we lived with him and witnessed those states. One cannot understand Vedanta only through reasoning; one needs experience. That depends on sadhana. Our doubts disappear when we see a person who is illumined and free. God descends as an avatar to manifest the true meaning of the scriptures and to correct their distorted interpretations. I am lucky because I associated with the Master over a period of five years, and I now understand a little. 'Just as by one clod of clay all that is made of clay is known, the modification being only a name arising from speech, while the truth is that all is clay.' — This statement of Chandogya Upanishad (6:1:4) is an example of videhamukti."[15]

It is said that relationships develop through frequent contact. Related to this is the saying, "Out of sight, out of mind." If we can establish a strong relationship with God, our lives will be free from anxiety, uncertainty, and fear. The Master used to say, "I am and my Divine Mother is." He depended on the Divine Mother alone, and none else. As a result, the Mother took care of him.

The Master taught his devotees various ways to establish a relationship with God. The Vaishnava scriptures describe five kinds of sadhana: shanta, dasya, vatsalya, sakhya, and madhura. One can create a relationship with God by cultivating any one of those attitudes. Standing on the southern ghat of the goose pond, the Master told Narendra: "Look here. Come a little more often. You are a newcomer. On first acquaintance people visit each other quite often, as is the case with a lover and his sweetheart. (*Narendra and M. laugh.*) So please come, won't you?" Narendra, a member of the Brahmo Samaj, was very particular about his promises. He said with a smile, "Yes sir, I shall try."[16]

The Master said to some people: "It will be enough if you visit this place occasionally." By "this place" he meant himself in particular; but more generally he was referring to God. The Master was God in human form. M. wrote: "The Master said, 'Seeing an avatar is the same as seeing God.' Jesus also said: 'He that hath seen me hath seen the Father. I and my Father are one.' Why did the Master say that it would be enough to visit him? Because people would be awakened by seeing him. Why do people practise japa and meditation? So that they can feel the presence of God. We saw with our own eyes that God was seated in front of us in human form. So the Master would say, 'It will be enough if you visit this place occasionally.' He meant himself."[17]

I Do Not Know Thy True Nature

To understand Ramakrishna, we go to different teachers and monks, pray in temples, practise spiritual disciplines, and read many books and scriptures. Sometimes we cry and lament, blaming our karma and our previous lives, and some of us think that we have been cursed. But we do not realize that time is a factor. Krishna said in the Gita: "*Kalena atmani vindati* — One knows in the course of time." Ramakrishna said: "The mother bird does not break the shell of the egg until the right moment arrives." One cannot get fruit as soon as one plants a seed in the ground. One may have to wait several years before one reaps a harvest. Similarly, in spiritual life one should be like a farmer who tills the ground whether there is rain or drought. If one continues practising spiritual disciplines, one day divine grace will dawn.

Once a brahmachari told Swami Saradananda: "Swami, we have so many defects, I doubt whether the Master will ever reveal himself to unfortunate ones like us." Consoling the brahmachari, the swami said: "Go on calling the Master. As a goldsmith heats an alloy to remove the impurities, so the Master will remove all impurities from your mind and give shape to it. He will definitely reveal himself to you. Don't fear. Have faith."[18]

Some householder devotees believed that because they had met the Master, they would definitely attain liberation. They therefore had no anxiety on that account. Some even believed that they no longer had to practise spiritual disciplines because they had seen the Master. But Swami Vivekananda had a different opinion on this subject. He said: "It

is not true that those who have not met the Master will not attain liberation and those who have seen him three times will be liberated."[19]

Even the great soul Swami Vivekananda said that he understood the
Master very little. Sometimes we try to understand Ramakrishna's true
nature by studying the conversations of the Master's direct disciples and
close devotees. We are frustrated in our efforts at times, but sometimes
we see some rays of hope. According to the devotional scriptures,
āshābaddha (holding on to hope) is a good sign; it indicates love for God.
Swami Shivananda told this story:

> You will be surprised to hear that many Muslim men and women these
> days worship Sri Ramakrishna as Muhammad, the messenger of God.
> One year I visited the Nilgiri Hills [in South India]. The devotees there
> arranged for my residence in a bungalow at Koonoor. Learning that I
> was there, a Muslim doctor and his family came all the way from Bom-
> bay to see me. Upon inquiry I found that he was a famous physician in
> Bombay who had been educated in England and had a very good prac-
> tice. He was accompanied by his wife and two handsome sons.
>
> In the course of conversation the doctor said to me, "We have come
> to see you, but my wife is especially eager to speak to you." Saying
> this, he moved to the adjoining room. His wife saluted me with great
> devotion and disclosed many intimate things related to her spiritual
> life. Since childhood she had been a devotee of Krishna. She wor-
> shipped Krishna as a child and occasionally had visions of him. After
> reading the Master's life and teachings, she had become very devoted
> to him. It was her conviction that her Chosen Deity Krishna had been
> born again as Sri Ramakrishna.
>
> I noticed that she had profound love and devotion for the Master.
> She was quite intense in her spiritual practices and the Master had
> blessed her in many ways. When taking leave of me, she knelt down
> and bowed to me, saying, "Please bless me by touching my head with
> your hand. You had the blessed privilege of associating with Sri Rama-
> krishna and you were blessed by him. Please touch my head with the
> hand that once touched Sri Ramakrishna!" And how she wept! I felt in
> my heart again and again: "Glory be unto the Lord! Blessed is Thy
> power! Who will understand Thee?" The hymn describing the great-
> ness of Shiva came to my mind.
>
> > O Lord, I do not know Thy nature nor what Thou art.
> > Whatever Thou art, O Great God, my salutations to Thee again and
> > again.
>
> Actually the same thing can be said about the Master.[20]

Shall We Be Satisfied With the Picture Only?

There were no cameras during the times of Rama, Krishna, Buddha, and Christ, so we really do not know what they looked like. Different painters and sculptors have used their imagination when making images of those avatars; we satisfy our souls by visualizing those images. Six photographs of Sri Ramakrishna were taken: four while he was alive and two after he had passed away. We know from these pictures exactly how the Master looked. We do not need to try to imagine what he looked like. This helps our meditation.

The three well-known pictures of the Master were taken while he was in samadhi: the first one was taken during kirtan at Keshab Sen's house in Calcutta; the second one, a standing pose, at the Bengal Studio at Radhabazar, Calcutta; and the third one at Dakshineswar, while he was seated in front of the Krishna temple. A fourth picture was taken by the arrangement of Ram Chandra Datta. When he saw this picture, the Master remarked: "I don't look like that."[21] According to Swami Akhandananda, a direct disciple of Sri Ramakrishna, when the Master saw the print, he remarked: "Who is this? Am I such an angry man?" Ram gave no reply. He understood that the Master did not approve of the photo, so he threw both the print and the negative into the Ganges.[22]

The Master's devotees would love to see him with their own eyes. Once a monk asked Swami Shivananda: "Swami, will my life end after only having seen the picture of the Master? Shall I have no realization?" "No, no," replied Swami Shivananda encouragingly, "why should it be in the picture alone? You will have your living vision here (*pointing to his own heart*)."[23]

The Holy Mother told a thrilling story about the shrine picture of the Master (the seated pose). When she was in Puri, she had no altar, so she put the picture on a large can that contained ghee. One day she performed her ritual, then went to visit Lord Jagannath in the temple. Upon her return, she saw that the picture was on the floor. The Holy Mother said later: "I saw that many red ants were crawling over the can, which contained ghee. Because those ants crawled over the picture of the Master, he moved to the floor."

Another time a devotee asked: "Does the Master exist in the picture?" Holy Mother: "Of course he does. The body and the shadow are the same. And what is his picture but a shadow? If you pray to him constantly before the picture, then he manifests himself through the picture."[24]

Sri Ramakrishna said: "An imitation custard-apple reminds one of the real fruit." Similarly, Ramakrishna's picture reminds us of Ramakrishna. One of our well-known Hindu families went to Saudi Arabia on business. According to government policy, religious pictures are not allowed there. At the airport, the customs officer found a framed picture of Ramakrishna in one of the suitcases and asked, "Who is this?" The wife replied, "He is my father." The officer raised no objection. The lady did not lie; truly, the Master is our real father.

After the Master's passing away, people flocked to see the Holy Mother and the disciples and devotees of the Master. They wanted to touch those people who had touched Ramakrishna. On 1 September 1986 I went to Rameswaram with Swami Sarvajnananda, a disciple of Swami Shivananda. I tape-recorded his reminiscences, and I include one of them here:

I knew a devotee named Narayanaswamy Iyer, who lived about 75 miles from Madras. He subscribed to the *Brahmavadin* and knew much about Sri Ramakrishna, Swami Vivekananda, and the direct disciples of the Master. He was a bachelor and looked after his mother. He worked in a garden for eight rupees a month. He had a great desire to touch someone who had touched Sri Ramakrishna. When he heard that the Holy Mother was coming to Madras [in 1910], he made arrangements to visit her. Unfortunately someone in his family died, and he was unable to make the trip.

In 1921, when Swami Brahmananda was in Madras, Narayana-swamy was again hopeful of fulfilling his desire. He went to see Maharaj at the Madras Math. Finding that Maharaj was at the Students' Home, Narayanaswamy went there. Narayanaswamy, who was the embodiment of humility, arrived at 1:30 in the afternoon. Maharaj usually rested after lunch, and his attendant scolded Narayanaswamy for coming to visit at that hour. But Maharaj over-heard the conversation and told the attendant to send the devotee to his room. I later asked Narayanaswamy about his meeting with Maharaj. He said: "I went inside the room and put flowers and fruit near his feet. Then I held his feet and touched them with my head. Tears were flowing from my eyes. I don't know how long I was there. I was overwhelmed with joy. I felt that my desire had been fulfilled; I had touched Maharaj, who had been touched by Sri Ramakrishna. Maharaj put his hand on my head and blessed me and then asked me to stand up. I saw his serene face. Then, facing him, I walked backward out of the room, as a sign of respect. Meeting the spiritual son of Sri Ramakrishna was the greatest moment of my life."[25]

Nowadays some devotees lament that we have not seen the Master, the Holy Mother, and the direct disciples. Is it possible to establish a relationship with the Master by merely seeing his picture and reading books?

Once a devotee said to M.: "You are very fortunate. You have seen and heard Sri Ramakrishna. You have even touched him and served him." M. replied: "Don't think in that way. The Master said that all his wealth and power will go to his children. Discrimination, renunciation, knowledge, devotion, and love are his wealth. These good qualities will come to the soul who thinks of him. It is God's grace that a devotee calls on God. It is God who attracts the devotees. It is not to the devotees' credit. He has become everything. Even now if people meditate on the form and qualities of the Master, they will feel his living presence in their hearts and will get the same result as we did while living with the Master."[26]

On another occasion, M. told a devotee: "Do you know what we received from the Master? Burning faith."[27]

Inquiry on Ramakrishna

The first aphorism of the *Brahma-sutra* is: *Athāto Brahma jijñāsā* (Hence, thereafter, an inquiry on Brahman). One should inquire about Brahman after becoming a qualified student of Vedanta. Now one asks: Is Brahman known or unknown? If It is a known entity, we all know It; and if not, then it is useless to try to know It. The unknown cannot be known. There are long discussions on this subject.

Who is Ramakrishna? Many people have raised this question in the past, many are questioning at present, and many will do so in the future. Ramakrishna's personality is subtle, inscrutable, and full of mystery. In the future, the Ramakrishna-sutra will be written as was the *Brahma-sutra*. Scholars and philosophers will write books, philosophies, commentaries, and so on based on the Master's teachings. Here are some Ramakrishna-sutras:

"As many faiths, so many paths."

"Lust and gold are maya."

"Tie the nondual knowledge in the corner of your cloth, and then do as you please."

"When the 'I' dies, all problems are cleared."

"Where there is jiva there is Shiva."

The Master said that some people have seen Varanasi and some have heard about Varanasi. People believe those who have seen Varanasi:

There is a power in the words of eyewitnesses. So if we want to learn about Ramakrishna, we must proceed by following the words and writings of those who saw him with their own eyes. These people were not ordinary human beings; they were companions of the avatar Ramakrishna. Later, others went to the Master's companions and asked questions about him.

Ram Chandra Datta, an ardent devotee of the Master, believed that whoever saw Ramakrishna only once became pure and blessed. He even believed that with a mere touch, the Master had purified carriages, coachmen, and even their horses. Upon hearing this, a man remarked: "Well, then there is nothing to worry about. Many people have seen Ramakrishna on the street, and so have the carriage drivers and temple employees. Will all of them be liberated?" Enraged, Ram retorted: "You go and take the dust of the feet of those drivers who drove the Master. Go — go! You take the dust of that sweeper's feet who has seen the Master. That will make your life pure."[28] On another occasion, a young man inquired, "What happened to those boatmen who saw Ramakrishna?" Ram angrily replied: "You rascal, you are asking what happened to those boatmen who saw the Master? Know for certain that they saw the Master through their good karma and that they were more fortunate than you." The young man apologized to Ram and later wrote: "I understood afterwards that a person who saw the Master even once, unknowingly, is blessed and fortunate. I am not fit to touch his feet."[29]

Vijaynath Majumdar wrote in his diary: "Kankurgachi Yogodyana, 1898. The Master's devotees — Ram Datta, Girish Ghosh, Akshay Sen, Haramohan Mitra, Kalipada Ghosh, and Manomohan Mitra — were present. We three or four devotees were also present on that occasion. Someone said, 'Those who had an opportunity to come to the Master were all spiritual aspirants and very pure.' Manomohan commented: 'I don't agree with what you have said. If that were true, what would happen to us? When we went to the Master, we were like these young people [pointing to us]. At that time we had neither any faith, nor devotion, nor goal, nor any enthusiasm to reach the goal. We didn't have any self-control. I tell you from my experience that those qualities did not come to me beforehand. They came to me later by the Master's grace. It is his grace that he accepted us and then faith, devotion, longing, and so on came to us. We did not achieve those by our own effort. We got them by his grace.'"[30]

On 15 August 1897, during the weekly meeting of the Ramakrishna

Mission, this question was put to Girish Chandra Ghosh: "What is your opinion about Ramakrishna as an avatar?"

Girish replied: "It annoys me even to consider any other man as possessing his divinity! When I went to see him once, I had just left a house of ill-repute — and yet he offered me a seat. Once he came to see me at that profane theatre of mine, bearing sweets! And just for me!

"I have never received such love from anyone. To me, Sri Ramakrishna is the Lord; he is God incarnate. A single utterance of his removed the doubts of a lifetime from my mind. Even now, if I find doubts begin to stir, I think of him. Immediately they vanish and do not rise again. I find that it is not difficult to obey him, love him, and worship him. But, indeed, it is difficult to forget him."[31]

In later days, Ramakrishna's disciples faced many questions from the new monks and devotees about the Master. A young monk asked Swami Brahmananda: "Maharaj, does Sri Ramakrishna exist even now?"

Maharaj: "I see you have lost your mind. Why would we have renounced hearth and home to lead such a life? He exists always. Pray to him day and night for a vision of him. He will dispel all your doubts and will make you understand his true nature."

Monk: "Do you see the Master nowadays?"

Maharaj: "Yes, I see him whenever he shows himself out of his mercy. Anybody who has his grace can see him. But how many people have the love and longing to see him?"[32]

Once a devotee asked Swami Saradananda: "Does Ramakrishna have any real existence other than his ideal existence?"

Saradananda: "Yes, he does. Many people have seen him and even talked to him."

Devotee: "Do you have any proof of your own?"

Saradananda: "Yes, I have had some experiences. Why else would I stay here?"

Devotee: "If the Master did exist, why was it that Swami Vivekananda could not talk to him at will?"

Saradananda: "Of course Swamiji talked to the Master. We know that Swamiji talked to the Master as I am talking to you. But it did not happen all the time at Swamiji's wish. For example, you live in Sankharitola; if you want to talk to me you have to come here. Swamiji was not always on the same plane as the Master. Moreover, when you are engaged in action, your mind remains on a lower plane. So if you want to talk to the Master, you will have to control your mind and lift it up to a higher plane."[33]

On one occasion a student asked Swami Premananda: "We hear many stories concerning Ramakrishna, but they are hard to believe since we have not seen him with our own eyes. And without that belief or conviction, everything becomes unreal."

Swami Premananda: "In a legal case the judge trusts the evidence of a good witness, a well-respected person. Suppose you are the judge and I am the witness. I am telling you that I have seen the Master's wonderful ecstasy, intense renunciation, incomparable knowledge, and unique activities. Can everyone see everything? Some believe by seeing, some by hearing, and some by reading. One needs faith — firm, unflinching faith. In spiritual life one needs simple, guileless faith."[34]

If I Had Been Born in Ramakrishna's Day

There is no limit to human imagination. But some people disregard imagination, considering it to be mere daydreaming. They do not know that imagination turns into realization. For example, seldom will one find a person in America who does not recognize Mickey Mouse and Disneyland, a famous amusement park. Walt Disney was the founder of this beautiful institution. Once he visited England and found that the government was demolishing old and dilapidated castles. He said to them: "Look, there are some ghosts living in those castles. Why are you making them refugees? If you don't build homes for them, I shall take them to America." With this idea in mind, Walt built the Haunted House in Disneyland. It is an interesting show. One can see those British ghosts singing, dancing, weeping, laughing, and reading the Bible. Thus Walt's imagination became manifest. Ordinary people cannot hold on to anything they imagine firmly enough for it to take form in reality.

In his poem *In the Days of Yore*, Rabindranath Tagore wrote:

If I had been born in the days of Kalidasa,*
I would have become the tenth jewel in the garland of nine jewels.
I would give up all tension and anxiety,
I would move at a slow pace, as if there were no disease or death.
My lifeboat would pass rhythmically over the gentle waves,
If I had been born in the days of Kalidasa.

If I had been born at the time of Ramakrishna, what would have happened? Once I put a question to some Americans: "Suppose you are sleeping in your bed alone in a dark room. If Jesus were to appear before you at that time, what would you do? Think about it deeply." Observing

*A famous medieval Sanskrit poet.

their silence, I said: "I know what you would do: You would dial 911.* We are timid. We are not yet ready to see Jesus. Some would say, 'O Lord, please stay in the picture on my wall. I am afraid to see you.'"

It was not easy to live with Ramakrishna. He would call for his niece Lakshmi and the Holy Mother to get up at 4:00 in the morning and practise meditation. If he got no response, he would pour water under the door of the nahabat to awaken them. Since the Holy Mother and Lakshmi slept on the floor, sometimes their beds would get wet. Sometimes I tease American women: "If you had Ramakrishna as your husband, what would you do? I am sure you would file for divorce."

Rani Rasmani once sat inside the Kali temple, thinking of a lawsuit. Ramakrishna slapped her. The Master also slapped Jay Mukhopadhyay of Baranagore, who had been repeating the mantra absent-mindedly as he sat on the bank of the Ganges. Those who were admonished by the Master in this way were truly blessed. From then on, whenever they became distracted during their spiritual practices, they would think of the Master. Thus he turned their minds towards God forever. Sometimes devotees think that their meditation would be deeper if they received a few slaps from the Master.

Mathur was very grateful to the Master, who protected him and his family from many calamities. For his part, Mathur took care of the Master's needs for fourteen years. They had a wonderful relationship. Mathur wanted to plan for the Master's welfare during his absence. He consulted with Hriday and planned to transfer a large property into Ramakrishna's name. When the Master heard about it, he became angry and tried to hit Mathur, saying, "You rascal, you want me to be a worldly person!" Mathur ran out of the room, closing the door behind him.

When the Master saw Latu sleeping one evening, he scolded the boy and told him his service was no longer needed. The evening was meant for meditation. Latu apologized and vowed that he would no longer sleep at night. He followed this vow until his death. The Master asked the Holy Mother to give Baburam four chapatis for his supper. When he heard that Baburam had eaten more than four chapatis, he told the Holy Mother not to give extra food to the disciples: If they ate too much, it would make them drowsy and they would not be able to meditate at night. The Holy Mother said: "Why are you so worried because he ate two more chapatis? I shall watch the boys in the future. Please don't scold them for eating their food."

*In America, 911 is the emergency number. It is used to summon help from police, or to call for an ambulance, or fire fighters.

The great writer Kshirod Prasad Vidyavinod decided to visit Rama-krishna in Dakshineswar. He got as far as Alambazar, which is very close to Dakshineswar, but then returned home. He heard that Ramakrishna could read others' minds; he would be terribly embarrassed if the Master should mention what was in his mind in front of others. It was for this reason that he did not visit Ramakrishna.

Ramakrishna was the embodiment of purity and renunciation. He came to the world to show people how to love God, teaching each person according to his or her aptitude and capability. Sometimes he was as strong as a thunderbolt, and sometimes as soft as a flower.

We often wish that we could have lived with the Master. This reminds us of the Holy Mother's situation. She recalled: "Sometimes it happened that I could not see the Master even once in two months. I would console my mind by saying: 'O mind, what good karma have you done to see him every day?' I would stand behind the split bamboo fence to listen to his kirtan. Thus I developed rheumatism in my feet." This brings tears to our eyes. She served her husband and sacrificed her personal happiness for the good of humanity.

We Are Blessed and You Are Blessed

In this world those who doubt are miserable. Doubt destroys happi-ness and peace of mind. In the Bible, we read the story of Doubting Thomas, a direct disciple of Jesus. When Jesus appeared before his disci-ples after his resurrection, Thomas was not there. When they told him of the resurrection, he replied that he would believe it only if he could touch the marks that the nails had made on Jesus' body. After eight days, Jesus again appeared before the disciples. He said to Thomas: "Reach hither thy finger, and behold my hands; and reach hither thy hand, and thrust it into my side: and be not faithless, but believing." Over-whelmed, Thomas responded: "My Lord and my God." Jesus then said to him: "Thomas, because thou hast seen me, thou hast believed: blessed are they that have not seen, and yet have believed."[35]

Blessed they are who have taken refuge in the Master after only hearing his name. Swami Turiyananda said: "Never forget this adage of Swami Vivekananda: 'Make your own fair — whether you have a companion or not.' To whom else should you look for help? The Master used to say. 'I am and my Divine Mother is.' That is all. Whom else do you want? The main thing is to patiently adhere to the ideal. If you can do that, gradually everything will become favourable. Hold on to the Master; you will be surprised at what will follow. The Master used to say,

'An imitation custard apple reminds one of the real fruit.' Similarly, the Master's photograph will remind you of the Master. Feel his presence in his photograph and devote yourself to his service and worship. You will surely be imbued with his spirit."[36]

Some people lament: "Our samskaras are bad"; "We are unfortunate and hopeless"; "This life has gone in vain" and so on. The Master and his disciples did not like such negative attitudes. Once Swami Vijnanananda reminded the devotees of their greatness by saying: "We became inspired by seeing the Master, and you have become intoxicated by just hearing his name."[37]

Once a monk said to Swami Shivananda: "Maharaj, we did not see the Master. You are here and it brings us great joy. You are a direct disciple of the Master. Is it a small privilege that we can be with you? Because of your presence, all of us — the monks and devotees — are very happy. When I think about how many people from distant places spend so much money and travel all the way here to see you only once, I realize how fortunate we are to be able to stay with you all the time."

Shivananda: "The Master is especially merciful to you. That is why he is making you serve his devotee (*meaning himself*). You are blessed; I too am blessed because I am with you. Who knows where I would have been otherwise!"[38]

When talking to some devotees, M. described Brahma's prayer to Krishna from the Bhagavata (10.14). In it, Brahma said:

> I enjoy being born in the world, and particularly in Vrindaban. The people of Vrindaban think of Krishna day and night; as a result they are always united with Krishna. O Lord, the dust of Vrindaban is blessed by the touch of your feet and your devotees' feet. My life will be blessed if I can touch that dust with my head.
>
> O Krishna, as long as people are not absorbed in you physically, mentally, and verbally, their worldly thoughts rob them of everything and throw them into a vortex of suffering. Moreover, their home becomes like a prison and their feet are tied with a chain of delusion.
>
> O Lord, you descend to the world as an avatar only to bestow peace and joy upon your devotees. In fact, you are transcendental.

M.: "Ah, what a beautiful statement Brahma made! Being the creator of the universe, he wants to be born as a man in Vrindaban. Why? Because the people of Vrindaban constantly think of Krishna and have become one with him. Brahma would consider himself blessed if he could get the dust of that holy place on his head. Brahma further said that the avatar assumes a body to give joy to his devotees.

"We are truly blessed. We lived with the Master and loved him. We also received his love and affection. We touched his feet with these hands, ate his prasad, saw him with these eyes, heard his words with these ears. It was through his grace that we saw his divine form; truly he led us from death to immortality, from fear to fearlessness. We are truly blessed. You are also blessed because you have loved the Master without seeing him, only hearing about him. The monks have renounced everything for him. The Master said that his devotees who lived at home were not truly householders."[39]

A devotee said to the Holy Mother: "Mother, some of your children see the Master with eyes closed and some with eyes open. I am unfortunate that I have not seen the Master." The Holy Mother replied: "One can see the Master if one's body and mind become pure." Later, the Mother blessed that devotee by touching his head and saying: "I say that you will not pass away without seeing the Master. This is your last birth."[40]

Once Swami Premananda said to Girijananda, a disciple of the Holy Mother: "Are you an ordinary person? Are the children of the Mother inferior to the children of the Master? Do you think that because people take the dust of our feet, we have become great? We came after seeing the Master and you have come without seeing him. You are greater than we are." [Krishna said: "Those who are my devotees' devotees, they are the supreme devotees."]

Girijananda: "The Master made you great."

Premananda: "The Master did not make us great; he made us small and humble. Always try to be small and humble. Drive away all ego from the mind. The Master used to say: 'All trouble and botheration come to an end when the "I" dies. Not I, not I, but Thou, Thou.'"[41]

When people lamented their ill luck for not having the chance to meet Sri Ramakrishna, Girish would reply, "As Mother Ganges flowed in a hundred streams in order to redeem the Sagara* dynasty, so the exuberant love of Sri Ramakrishna is flowing through hundreds of devotees in order to eventually redeem the world."[42]

If Ramakrishna Were Alive Today

When we are tormented by worldly maya, and we see darkness all around and cannot find a way out, at that time we think that if Ramakrishna were alive today, we would go to him for peace and nourish our

---

*Bhagirath, a descendant of King Sagara, brought the Ganges from heaven to save the souls of his departed ancestors who were destroyed by the curse of a sage.

hearts with his advice. Poverty and misery, disease and grief are constantly burning human beings. The funeral pyre burns only once, but worries and anxieties burn constantly. For that reason people went to Ramakrishna for bliss, which is the most essential thing in life. Once Swami Akhandananda said: "Don't show your gloomy, grouchy face. Always be cheerful. The Master was always joyful and would make us laugh with his stories. He was very humorous."[43]

Kedar Nath Bandyopadhyay, a native of Dakshineswar, wrote in his reminiscences:

> One day I started for my office and crossed the Ganges by boat. Due to some family trouble, my mind was very disturbed. It occurred to me that it would be better to go to the Master than to the office, so I took another boat and landed at the temple ghat of Rani Rasmani.
>
> The Master was standing on the western veranda of his room, looking at the Ganges. As I walked up to him, he said: "What! You ran away from your office? That is not good. Live in this world like a crocodile. It lives under water, but sometimes it raises its snout above water, takes a deep breath, and again dives below the surface. People are submerged in their worldly life, and they come here only when they are suffocating at home. Does anybody tread the path of religion without first undergoing sorrows and sufferings? Misery has great value. It helps a person find the path to God."
>
> He continued: "I know you are married. Do you have a mother?"
>
> "Yes, my mother is still alive," I replied.
>
> He was silent for some time, and then said: "All right, now stay at home. A little misery is good. It helps one to make progress in spiritual life. If there were no misery, would anyone chant the Lord's name?"
>
> He went on talking in this way, but it seemed to me that he was tired. Indeed, the cancer in his throat was developing day by day. I said to him: "Sir, please take a little rest. You have just finished your lunch and I am disturbing you."
>
> "It is true," he said, "the pain is there. But if you wish to know anything, you may ask."
>
> Smiling, I replied, "We want to know so many things, but where is our capacity for understanding?"
>
> The Master said: "Know God. Make some effort and you will find Him. He is ever-present. Develop a deep longing for God."
>
> I then implored him, "Sir, please bless me."
>
> In reply, he said: "Longing does not come through blessings. It depends upon self-effort. Increase your love for God." He was ready to answer my questions, but I could not think of any. After accompanying him to his room, I left for home.

The Master came to awaken God-consciousness in us. We are fortunate to have had him in our midst. Now the more I think of him, the
more my heart yearns for him and tears flow from my eyes.[44]

After Ramakrishna passed away in 1886, Kedar went through a difficult time. A few years later he was going to Calcutta by boat. Seeing the
Kali temple of Dakshineswar, a thought arose in his mind: "If only the
Master were alive today." He disembarked at Baghbazar ghat in
Calcutta. He heard that the devotees had installed the Master's relics in
Ram Chandra Datta's Kankurgachi Yogodyana. Kedar did not know
where Kankurgachi was; he knew only that it was somewhere past the
rail line near Narkeldanga. He began to walk. He was possessed by the
thought, "If only the Master were alive today."

Kedar recalled:

I passed the rail line and the gardens on both sides of the road. The area
was sparsely populated. It was noon on a hot summer day. The road
was almost empty. I guessed that Ram Datta's garden would be somewhere nearby. I moved forward. I found a lane that turned to the right;
at the end of it there was a gate and a bamboo grove. The gate was not
locked. I entered the compound and closed the gate behind me.

But where was the temple — the Master's temple? Was this not the
right garden? I felt that it was. I proceeded a little and found a small
pond extending east to west, and a path around it. There was a small
painted brick building at the east side of the pond, facing west. I
looked at that building and noticed that the door was open. What was
this? It was the Master! My heart was overwhelmed with joy. Blessed
are these devotees who installed the living image of the Master. I saw
the same joyful face, and the same cloth, with part of it placed on his
shoulder. I also observed that parts of his beard were moving in the
breeze. It was amazing to see! The same living form of the Master that I
used to see in Dakshineswar."

After a few minutes, Kedar heard the priest call out from the northeast
corner of the garden: "Who are you? What are you looking for here?"

"I am looking at the Master. Is this the garden of Ram Datta?" Saying
so, Kedar moved towards the priest.

Priest: "What did you say?"

Kedar: "I was gazing at the image of Ramakrishna Paramahamsa."

Priest: "Where is the image? What are you saying?"

Kedar: "I saw the Master inside that room."

Priest: "The room is closed and here is my key. Do you want to see
inside? After I finished the worship an hour ago, I went for lunch. There

Kankurgachi Yogodyana, where Ramakrishna visited on 26 December 1883

Marble image of
Ramakrishna at
Kankurgachi

are some silver vessels for worship, so I locked the door. But you say that you saw the Master's image?"

Then both went in front of the shrine and saw that the western and southern doors of the room were open. There was no image of the Master inside. Controlling himself, Kedar said to the priest, "Sir, please check your silver vessels and other things in the shrine." The priest was dumbfounded and said: "I see that everything is intact. I have worshipped here for the last few years, and I have never forgotten to lock the shrine."

Kedar then wanted confirmation: "Is this the garden of Ram Datta?"

Priest: "Yes, it is Ram Datta's Yogodyana. And this is the memorial temple of Ramakrishna Paramahamsa. Well, may I know who you are? Where have you come from? Many people come here, but I have never seen you. Shall I inform Ram Babu?"

Kedar: "No, it is not necessary to inform him. I came as many people have, to bow down to the Master."

Then the priest served Kedar some of the Master's prasad: cucumber, banana, papaya, sweets, and a glass of water. Kedar enjoyed the prasad on that hot summer day and left for Dakshineswar.

As soon as he returned to the street, a coachman stopped his horse carriage in front of him and asked, "Sir, where do you want to go?"

Kedar replied: "Dakshineswar."

"Please come," replied the coachman. "This carriage belongs to Beni Saha of Baranagore. I am returning there."

Kedar got into the carriage and began to think about the wonderful lila of the Master and how the Master had fulfilled his wish: "If only the Master were alive today."[45]

27

The Second Coming of Ramakrishna

Introduction

"Ramakrishna's Second Coming" is a somewhat controversial topic. One of our American devotees read that after 100 years Ramakrishna would be born again as a baul (a minstrel). So in 1986 (Ramakrishna passed away in 1886), she went to attend the Jaydev Fair in the Birbhum District of West Bengal, an annual gathering of all bauls. She moved among the bauls, and then told me of her disappointment. I wrote this as an article in Bengali at that time.

In *The Gospel of Sri Ramakrishna*, Ramakrishna is quoted as saying: "I shall have to assume a human body again, in a northwesterly direction."[1] Northwest from Dakshineswar are located places such as Burdwan, Punjab, Afghanistan, Russia, Finland, Sweden, Norway, Greenland, and so on. Some disciples have said that the Master would return again after one or two hundred years; some have said that they did not know when he would return.

When Swami Vivekananda was visiting the West, someone asked him: "When will Christ come again?" Swamiji replied: "I never take much notice of these things. I have to deal with principles. I have only to preach that God comes again and again, and that He came in India as Krishna, Rama, and Buddha, and that He will come again. It can almost be demonstrated that after each 500 years the world sinks, and a tremendous spiritual wave comes, and on the top of the wave is a Christ."[2] Swamiji knew that the Master was the avatar of this age.

The Holy Mother said: "The Master will live in the hearts of the devotees for a hundred years."[3] When the Holy Mother said "a hundred," she must have meant "hundreds"; because one hundred years have already elapsed since the Master's passing away, and innumerable devotees all over the world are still carrying Ramakrishna in their hearts. If one takes every word in the Ramakrishna literature literally, it is possible to fall into confusion. It may be that the recorder of the Mother's reminiscences wrote "a hundred" instead of "hundreds."

Rama was born in the Treta age, Krishna in the Dwapara age, Buddha 2500 years ago, and Christ 2000 years ago. But they are still alive in the hearts of millions of people, and will remain so. The lives of avatars, as well as their messages, are beyond space and time. It does not matter if Ramakrishna appears at any time, at any place, in any form; his life and message will continue eternally like those of Rama, Krishna, Buddha, and Christ.

I kept this manuscript with me for many years. Some monks discouraged me from publishing it because they thought it might confuse devotees. However, some devotees in the East and the West were already confused by reading what the Master said about this subject in addition to many contradictory statements made by others. To solve this dilemma, in 1997 I read this manuscript to a learned, senior monk of the Ramakrishna Order at Belur Math. He listened attentively as I read the manuscript and at the end encouraged me to publish it.* Truly, I have not formed any opinion about the Master's second coming; I have tried only to reconcile the various statements published in the Ramakrishna literature.

Imagination and Expectation

Ramakrishna was a joyful, loving, and lovable person. He was a spiritual magnet; it was hard to resist his attraction. Everyone loves to think about a loved one, and to imagine that one is with the beloved. This is inherent in human nature. One is fulfilled when one can establish a strong and steady relationship with the beloved. Rupa Goswami wrote in his *Bhakti-rasāmrita-sindhu* about the characteristics of one who has a passionate love for the Beloved, God: "The minds of those who have developed this love never oscillate; they do not spend time on anything

*It has been printed in *Udbodhan,* vol. 100, issue 2 (February-March 1998).

other than in thinking of God; they are humble and unattached to sense objects; they cultivate hope and are always eager to reach God; they love to chant God's name and praise His glories; they are eager to live in a holy place, and so on." It is natural for a genuine devotee to live in the expectation of seeing God. "I shall surely see my beloved Lord in this life" — one should hold this hope firmly in one's heart. The devotional scriptures say: "For those who hold this hope, there is a strong possibility that they will attain God."

We would not expect Ramakrishna to return if he had not said he would. The places and persons connected with his divine play are still vivid; his conversations, stories, and songs still reverberate in our memories. Although he passed away nearly 120 years ago, the clothes he wore, his coat, his cot and bed, his cups and plates, his hubble-bubble, his caps and shoes, his photos and manuscripts, and so on still exist. When we see those things with our own eyes, we tell our nonbelieving minds, "Look, these things were used by an avatar himself." This enhances and strengthens our faith. When we read about Ramakrishna's life and his teachings, we feel that he is our very own. An American disciple of Swami Satprakashananda, who was a disciple of Swami Brahmananda, told me candidly: "Swami, Ramakrishna is my [spiritual] great-grandfather."

M. said: "I get joy when I see a person thinking of the Master, the highest ideal. His teachings are living and inspiring. He just recently came, so his ideas are very fresh; they are spreading all over the world. Those who cannot achieve the goal in this life will have to spend many more lifetimes to reach it."[4]

It is a great unfathomable mystery how the infinite God takes a human form made of flesh and blood. One day the Master said to M.: "God speaks through this mouth, so this [*meaning himself*] is an avatar. What comes out through this mouth are the Vedas. A person will achieve everything if he or she visits this place." Another day, while going to Calcutta by carriage, the Master said to M., "God is seated near, and still people are searching for God here and there."[5]

The avatar comes to fulfill the need of the age. When religion declines and irreligion prevails God incarnates — this is a historical fact. The advent of Rama, Krishna, Buddha, Christ, Chaitanya, and Ramakrishna substantiate this truth. When people feel emptiness, dryness, restlessness, and a lack of peace and joy, they long for someone who can give them peace and bliss. Just such a person is an avatar. M. remarked: "When the avatar comes, many great souls come with him to enjoy and share in his lila [divine play]. For example, if there are a few trees and a pond in the midst of a vast desert, people stop there and take rest during their journey. Similarly, people take rest and refresh themselves at that source of eternal freshness — the avatars. Some among the Jews waited with great longing and said, 'Our Messiah is coming.' Bharadwaja and other sages waited for Ramachandra. Advaita Goswami said, 'Chaitan-yadeva will come.'"[6]

The avatar does not come alone; he comes with his companions. The avatar is the very embodiment of spirituality like a mighty glacier; his disciples are like streams carrying the melted water to a parched continent. They are the avatar's messengers. Ramakrishna said: "The illumined rishis of previous cycles come to this world along with the avatar. They are intimate companions of God. God spreads spirituality in this world through them."[7]

Awakening of the Brahma-kundalini

It is truly astounding how radio, television, internet, telephone, and other communication systems can carry information around the globe within a few seconds. Human beings can travel from one part of the world to another in a very short time. The world is now very small. The lives and messages of the previous avatars were limited to small geographical areas during their lifetimes and for a couple of centuries afterwards. We find that Rama's influence extended only from Ayodhya to Sri Lanka, Krishna's from Mathura-Vrindaban to Dwaraka-Prabhas, Buddha's from Kapilavastu to Gaya-Varanasi, Christ's from Judea to Samaria-Galilee, and Chaitanya's from Navadwip to Puri-Vrindaban. It was not possible for Ramakrishna to go to distant places to spread his message because he was in samadhi most of the time. But as he sat in the village of Dakshineswar, he shook the Cosmic-kundalini so vigorously that his message encircled the globe within a short time of his passing. This Cosmic-kundalini is the Divine Mother Kali. Swami Shivananda said: "The Master was after all none other than Mother Kali, who in the form of the Master is saving the world even now."[8]

Swami Shivananda continued: "Swami Vivekananda once said: 'In this age the Brahma-kundalini — the Mother who is responsible for the creation, preservation, and destruction of the universe — has been awakened by the fervent prayers of Sri Ramakrishna. No wonder the individual kundalini will be awakened now!'"[9]

At Cossipore, the Master told Swamiji: "Wherever you take me on your shoulders, there I will go and stay, be it under a tree or in a hut."[10]

That is why Swamiji carried the relics of the Master on his own shoulder and installed them at Belur Math. Then he said to the Master's disciples: "Know for certain, the Master will dwell in this place for a long time and benefit humanity."[11] The power of the Brahma-kundalini that appeared in the form of Ramakrishna was transmitted to Vivekananda by Ramakrishna himself. Later, Swamiji wrote in the Belur Math rule book: "The Lord has not yet given up the Ramakrishna form. Some see him in that form even now and receive instructions from him, and all can see him if they so desire. This form will last until he comes again in another gross body. Though he is not visible to all, that he is in this Order and is guiding it is a fact of everybody's experience. Otherwise such a worldwide movement could never have been set on foot in so short a time by this handful of insignificant, helpless, and persecuted boys."[12]

The Ramakrishna Order firmly believes that the Master is working through this organization. Swami Shivananda once said: "It will take a long period of time to understand who Ramakrishna and Vivekananda were. It had been thousands of years since such a great power had appeared in the world for the benefit of humanity. People understood the greatness of Buddha hundreds of years after his advent. Gradually his all-inclusive message spread all over the world. It is amazing to consider the great event that took place for just one of his teeth! A huge temple was built over one tooth of Buddha. Here at Belur Math we have the relics of Ramakrishna, the Holy Mother, and Swami Vivekananda. I get goose bumps when I think about it. People from all over the world will come and roll on the ground of Belur Math. We see signs of this already. What great commotion is rising centred on the Master! We are blessed that we can see it. You will also see so many things in the future!"[13]

The Golden Age Has Begun

As the moon waxes and wanes, so the ocean has a flood tide and an ebb tide. These tides are part of an ocean's life. Similarly, the rise and the fall of religion are an integral part of human existence. Hypocrites and cheats bring religion down, but avatars raise it up. In every age each religion flows like a wave in an up-and-down motion. Ramakrishna's advent counteracted the evil tendencies of the Kaliyuga and started a new age. He demonstrated to the materialistic world how to move one's mind from a lower plane to a higher one. He said again and again: "The goal of human life is to realize God. God first, and then the world." Lust and gold cannot be goals of human life.

In 1895 Swamiji wrote a letter to Swami Ramakrishnananda from America: "The Satyayuga [Golden Age] started the day Ramakrishna was born as an Incarnation."[14] In another letter, to Alasinga Perumal in Madras, he wrote: "I believe that the Satyayuga will come when there will be one caste, one Veda, and peace and harmony. This idea of Satyayuga is what would revivify India. Believe it."[15]

The Holy Mother concurred: "The Satyayuga has begun with the birth of the Master. Many luminaries have accompanied him. . . . Countless ordinary people take birth and die; but the foremost ones come with the avatar for the sake of his mission."[16]

People expect peace and happiness in a golden age; but within sixty years of Ramakrishna's passing away, two world wars took place and millions of people were killed. When the Holy Mother was asked about this she answered that the storm comes before the rain. Storms obscure people's vision by blowing the dust, they break trees and plants, and destroy homes. After the rain comes and settles the dust, people can see clearly. Similarly, at the advent of an avatar terrible disasters happen in the world, clearing all unrighteousness, falsehood, hypocrisy, and evil from society. At that time the realm of dharma (righteousness) manifests. People's happiness and peace depend on that dharma.

As Swami Vivekananda stood in the courtyard of Belur Math a few days before his passing away, he said: "The spiritual current that has been released will run unimpeded for seven or eight centuries — nobody will be able to stop it. This spiritual current of the age will flow on out of its own inner strength; it will not depend on any person. This has been ordained by the divine power. What can ordinary human beings do? But the man who plays a role in fulfilling the need of the age will be blessed."[17]

While in San Francisco in 1900, Swami Vivekananda had a conversation with Mrs. Alice Hansbrough about Ramakrishna's return, which she recorded in her memoirs: "Swamiji longed to be free of the body. 'I have to come back once more,' he said. 'The Master said I am to come back once more with him.' 'You have to come back because Sri Ramakrishna says so?' I asked. 'Souls like that have great power, Madam,' he replied. It was probably during an after-lunch conversation [in Pasadena] when he was walking up and down the living room, that Swamiji told us, 'The Master said he would come again in about two hundred years — and I will come with him. When a Master comes, he brings his own people.'"[18]

Where Will Ramakrishna Appear?

When we study the history of world religions, we find that there is no particular place for the advent of an avatar. Sometimes he is born in a king's palace, sometimes in a poor family's hut, sometimes in a prison or in a manger. But it is certain that the avatar takes birth in the house of virtuous parents. The parents of avatars are very special people, endowed with love, compassion, purity, detachment, devotion, simplicity, sincerity, austerity, and truthfulness.

One of my friends used to tease me, saying: "Hinduism must be a weak religion because God incarnates there again and again. But in Christianity, Christ is the only Son of God." I jokingly replied: "God is afraid to be born in Christianity because He would be crucified again. So He goes to India and takes birth among the Hindus. The Hindus love God in many forms and they will not kill Him. Moreover, the Christians will not accept or recognize another incarnation or prophet. So God does not want to be born among them anymore."

However, many people are eager to see Ramakrishna. When we read *The Gospel of Sri Ramakrishna* and *Sri Ramakrishna and His Divine Play*, we wish we could live with the Master. The Master's life was based on truth, and every word of his was true. He himself said that he would come again. Now three questions are in front of us: Where will he come? When will he come? And in what manner will he come?

In the *Gospel*, in some places Ramakrishna gave distinct hints about his reappearance, and in other places he was more indirect. He said:

"What am I? It is all He. I am the machine and He is its Operator. It is God alone who exists in this [*meaning his body*]. That is why so many people are feeling more and more attracted to it. A mere touch is enough to awaken their spirituality. This attraction, this pull, is the attraction of God and none else. Tarak of Belgharia was going home from Dakshineswar. I clearly noticed that a flame-like thing came out of this [*meaning his body*] and followed him.

"Many troubles and worries follow in the wake of a birth in a physical body. One has to assume a human body if one cherishes the slightest desire."

A Devotee: "What are the desires of those who are Incarnations of God?"

Master (*smiling*): "I find that I have not got rid of all my desires. Once I saw a holy man with a shawl, and I too wanted to put on one like it. Even now I have that desire. I don't know whether I shall have to be born again for it."

Balaram (*smiling*): "Then will you be born again just for a shawl?"

Master (*smiling*): "One has to keep a good desire so that one may give up the body meditating on it."[19]

On 24 December 1883, the Master told M.: "I shall have to be born once more. Therefore I am not giving all knowledge to my companions. (*With a smile*) Suppose I give you all knowledge; will you then come to me again so willingly? I recognized you on hearing you read the *Chaitanya Bhagavata*. You are my own. The same substance, like father and son. All of you are coming here again. When you pull one part of the kalmi creeper,* all the branches come towards you."[20]

On 9 August 1885, the Master said to Mahimacharan: "It will be sufficient for the youngsters who come here if they know only two things. If they know these, they will not have to practise much discipline and austerity. First, who I am, and second, who they are. Many of the youngsters belong to the inner circle.

"Those belonging to the inner circle will not attain liberation. I shall have to assume a human body again, in a northwesterly direction.

"I feel peace of mind when I see the youngsters. How could I live without seeing pure-souled persons?"[21]

Ramakrishna himself said that he would be born again somewhere northwest of Dakshineswar. There has been much speculation about the exact place. A devotee once said to Swami Brahmananda: "I have heard that Sri Ramakrishna will soon reappear in the region of Burdwan [West Bengal]. Is this true?"

Brahmananda: "I have never heard that. I have only heard that he will come again in the region of the northwest."

Devotee: "Maharaj, some say the Master will come again after one hundred years, and some say after two hundred years."

Brahmananda: "I know nothing about the time of his coming, nor have I heard anything about it."[22]

Sharat Chandra Chakrabarty, a disciple of Vivekananda, wrote in his article on *Avatāravād* (the doctrine of the avatar): "I heard from Swami Subodhananda that once the Master went into samadhi in the Panchavati of Dakshineswar. He was seated facing the northwest. After regaining his normal state, he said: 'Look, the Mother is saying that the more a person thinks of this [*pointing to his body*] the more that person will understand the highest truth of religion.' Pointing to the northwest with his finger, the Master said: 'I will come again in that direction; at that time many people will attain knowledge.'"[23]

On 26 November 1935, Swami Vijnanananda said to the devotees in Barisal (which is now in Bangladesh): "This time the Master came secretly. He will come again after one hundred years in the northwest direction."

*A plant that grows on the surface of ponds.

A Devotee: "Did the Master say that he would be born in the Punjab?"
Vijnanananda: "No, the Master did not say that he would be born in the Punjab."[24]

Swami Abhedananda recalled: "One evening Sri Ramakrishna was attended by his faithful attendants Shashi [Ramakrishnananda] and Kali [Abhedananda], who were waiting upon him at Cossipore. The Master inspired them by saying: 'My Divine Mother has shown me that the photograph of this body will be kept upon altars and be worshipped in different houses as the pictures of other avatars are worshipped. My Divine Mother has also shown me that I shall have to come back again and that my next incarnation will be in the West.'"[25]

When Is Ramakrishna Coming?

Waves rise and fall. The deeper a wave goes down, the higher it comes up. When we study history, we find that it takes three to five hundred years for a religion to decline, and it takes the same length of time to rise again. Swamiji once told his disciple Sharat Chandra Chakrabarty: "Ah, it is quite enough if one all-renouncing great soul like Sri Ramakrishna comes in a thousand years! For a thousand years after his advent, people may well guide themselves by those ideas and ideals he leaves behind."[26]

Ramakrishna never directly stated when he would return, as far as the record shows. Some people say he will come one hundred years after his death, and some say two hundred years afterwards. It seems that he may return soon because at present the world is in deep turmoil and afflicted by violence, hatred, and war. People are hungry for peace and joy. Ramakrishna said: "Wherever there is any trouble in the Divine Mother's empire, I shall have to rush there to stop it, like a government officer."[27] So God must be born in every age to accomplish His mission — serving suffering humanity.

On different occasions the Holy Mother made various statements about the Master's return. Once she recalled: "The Master said he would come again after a hundred years. Meanwhile, for those hundred years he would live in the hearts of those who love him. Standing on the semicircular veranda of Dakshineswar, the Master said this, pointing towards the northwest. I told him I could not come again. Lakshmi also said she would not come again, even if she were chopped into shreds like tobacco leaves! The Master laughed and said: 'How can you avoid coming? Our roots are twined together like the kalmi plant. Pull one stem and the whole clump comes forward.'"[28]

The Holy Mother also stated: "The Master said that he would dwell in the hearts of his devotees for a hundred years in his subtle body. He further said that he would have many devotees among the white people."[29]

Swami Saradananda wrote on this subject in *Sri Ramakrishna and His Divine Play*: "The Master not only knew this about himself through his yogic insight, but he also told us many times, pointing to the northwest, that the next time he would reincarnate there. Some of us (Girish Chandra Ghosh and others) said that the Master even told them the time of his advent, stating: 'I shall have to be born in that direction after two hundred years. Then many will be liberated, and those who fail at that time will have to wait a long time for liberation.'"[30]

Once a devotee asked Swami Saradananda: "Does God really descend as an avatar?"

"Of course He does," replied Saradananda. "We have heard the Master say: 'He who was Rama and Krishna is now Ramakrishna.' In other words, the same power manifests according to the need of the age. He further said, 'I will be born again in the northwest after two hundred years.' You see, this universe and all beings are nothing but His manifestation. But at some times and in some places one can see His special manifestation according to need."[31]

Another time, a devotee said to Saradananda: "Swami, it was expected that the Master's advent would virtually change the country, but observing the activities of the Ramakrishna Mission it seems that it will not happen."

Saradananda answered: "Now the activities of the Mission are going on in a certain way; but they will spread vigorously when the Master comes after 200 years. Just as 250 years after Buddha, the Emperor Ashoka spread Buddhism all over the world, so the Master's religious ideals will spread when he comes back again."[32]

A devotee asked Swami Vijnanananda: "Swami, there is controversy about the Master's return. It is mentioned in one book that he will come back after 100 years and in another after 200 years." The swami said: "Whatever it may be, the Master will come back soon."[33]

Ramakrishna's niece Lakshmi said: "The Master said, 'I shall come back after 100 years.' I can't definitely say whether that year should be counted from his birth, or death, or on the day when he said it."[34]

Now there is a great dilemma in front of us: We have just started to build our lives and society according to the ideals of Ramakrishna and Vivekananda, and the Master's message has begun to spread all over the world. If Ramakrishna were to appear now in a new name and in a new form, there might be terrible confusion and friction. Will the new avatar change the activities and ideals of the previous avatar and establish his own mission? It is natural for devotees to feel such apprehension; but I think this anxiety is groundless, for three reasons.

First, because the avatar "comes to fulfill and not to destroy." He nullifies falsehood and not truth. Ramakrishna preached the truth. If he comes again, he will teach the same truth. The Rig Veda says: "Truth is one; sages call it by various names."

Once an old monk tested a young monk, saying: "If Ramakrishna appeared before you and said, 'The goal of human life is to enjoy lust and gold,' what would you do?" The young monk replied: "I would say, 'O hypocrite Ramakrishna, you can go. I don't need you.'" Jesus cannot say, "Blessed are the *impure* in heart for they shall see God."

Second, whether the owner of a house comes home in Western attire, or Indian attire, or any other type of clothing, the dog easily recognizes its master. Similarly, in whatever form the avatar comes, a true devotee will definitely recognize him.

Third, Patanjali defined God in the *Yoga Sutras* (1:24): "Ishwara [God, the Supreme Ruler] is a special Purusha, untouched by misery, actions and their results, and desires." The great sage Vyasa commented on this aphorism: "None can have power similar to God. Imagine that there are two gods with equal powers and they say they will change the same thing differently, such as, 'Let this one be new,' and 'Let this one be old.' If one's wish is thus fulfilled and the other's unfulfilled, one will lose his godhood. Both wishes cannot be fulfilled simultaneously. The same object cannot be new and old at the same time; that is contradictory. Therefore, the One whose power has no equal is God, and He is not separate from the Purusha." Swamiji said that the Master was *sarvam swatantram ishwaram* — the Lord Shiva, ever-free God.[35]

Again, we learn from Vyasa's commentary that He who possesses supreme power is God, and He is one and not many. God never becomes old or new — He is eternal. The same God comes again and again as an avatar to establish religion. As the Master used to say, "The same moon rises again and again." So if the new avatar comes, he will not nullify the mission of the old avatar.

In What Manner Will Ramakrishna Come?

Neither the *Gospel* nor the *Divine Play* includes any direct statement from Ramakrishna concerning how he will return. However, M. records that on 15 March 1886 Ramakrishna said: "A band of minstrels [bauls] suddenly appears, dances, and sings, and it departs in the same sudden manner. They come and they return, but none recognizes them."[36]

On 12 May 1913 Swami Arupananda told the Holy Mother that a devotee from Ranchi had had a vision of the Master. He had seen the Master wearing an ochre cloth, with wooden sandals on his feet, and tongs in his hand.

Arupananda: "Mother, why did the Master have wooden sandals and tongs?"

Holy Mother: "Those things are the signs of a monk. He said that he would come back as a baul. The bauls wear a long robe, grow a beard, and tie their long hair on their heads in a bun."[37]

On 9 February 1912 Gauri-ma said: "The Master will come back twice and once as a baul."

Holy Mother: "Yes, the Master said to me, 'You will carry my hubble-bubble.' I might have to cook in a broken pan and he will eat from a stone plate. He will travel continually without caring for his surroundings."[38]

Brahmachari Akshaychaitanya wrote in his book *Sri Sri Sarada Devi*: "The Holy Mother said to Nikunja Devi (M.'s wife): 'One day the Master said: "I know who you are and Lakshmi, but I shall not tell you. To repay my debt to you, I shall be born as a baul and make you my companion."'"[39]

Once an attendant of the Holy Mother said to her, "I heard that you and the Master would come back as bauls." The Mother replied: "Well, you will not escape either. Those who have come this time will have to come the next. Have you seen the moon in the sky? Does the moon rise alone? It rises along with the stars." The attendant said joyfully: "Mother, we are all ready to come back because we will be with you."[40]

We really do not know why Ramakrishna said he would come back as a baul. I think it will not be out of place to discuss the meaning of the word "baul," the baul way of life, their spiritual practices, and songs. The dictionary meaning of baul is a person who is god-intoxicated, mad, overwhelmed with divine love. Professor Upendranath Bhattacharya wrote in *Banglar Baul O Baulgan* (Bauls of Bengal and Baul Songs) that until the beginning of the 17th century, the word "baul" did not enter into the Bengali language as indicating a religious sect. The word *baul* originated from the Sanskrit word *batul*, or mad.[41] Later the bauls formed a religious sect centred on Chaitanya, the 14th century mystic of Bengal. They consider Chaitanya to be the founder of their sect. According to their philosophy, Radha and Krishna dwell in the human body, so it is meaningless to search for God anywhere other than within ourselves. The bauls say: "Whatever is in the human body is also in the universe." The sun, moon, Agni, Brahma, Vishnu, Shiva, heaven, Vaikuntha, Vrindaban, and so on exist within the body. That is why their doctrine is called *deha-tattwa*, the body as the seat of all truths.

Bauls are devotees of God, and they worship Him in human beings. They salute each other when they meet. They have no enemies and no caste. They are free from social norms and customs. They have no fixed homes: They travel from one place to another carrying their message in their songs. They inspire people through songs that appeal to the masses. The main themes of their songs are: worship of the Lord, grace of the guru, service to humanity, finding the truth in the body, knowing the six centres of the kundalini in the body, and so on. Their songs are full of humility, devotion, passion, longing, detachment, and self-surrender. Bauls practise various kinds of yoga and pranayama. Bauls are not monks, but great lovers of God.

In the *Chaitanya Charitamrita*, Chaitanya described to his disciples the pain of his separation from Krishna and declared himself to be *maha-baul*, the Great Baul. He said that as such he would first control the senses and make them his disciples. Then he would renounce the body-idea and objects of enjoyment and travel with his disciples to Vrindaban in a god-intoxicated mood.

From this statement of Chaitanya, the Great Baul, one can infer that when Ramakrishna returns as an avatar, he will travel with his disciples from place to place, from one country to another. During his last incarnation Ramakrishna was the embodiment of samadhi, so it was not possible for him to travel much. Once the Master lamented: "Gauranga and Nityananda carried the name of Hari from door to door, whereas I cannot go anyplace without a carriage."

One day the Master said to the Brahmo devotees: "Without desires the body cannot live. I had one or two desires. I prayed to the Mother, 'O Mother, give me the company of those who have renounced "lust and gold."' I said further: 'I should like to enjoy the society of Thy jnanis and bhaktas. So give me a little strength that I may walk hither and thither and visit those people.' But She did not give me the strength to walk."

Trailokya, "Have all the desires been fulfilled?"

Master, "No, there are still a few left."[42]

The desire of an illumined soul never remains unfulfilled. It seems that the Master will come back to fulfill some of his cherished wishes. He said: "I cherished a desire. I said to the Mother, 'O Mother, I shall be king of the devotees.'"[43]

Swami Vijnanananda said: "This time the Master came secretly. The next time he will come in the northwest as a king with tremendous physical strength." It seems that the Master will come as a king of devotees and not as a king of the material world.

Avatar: Real or False?

How can one recognize a real avatar or prophet? Nowadays so many people claim to be avatars; and sometimes disciples proclaim that their gurus are avatars. A monk jokingly said to me: "If anyone wants to be an avatar in the West, that person just needs to write an autobiography and collect three fanatic disciples who will declare their guru to be an avatar."

There is a saying: A jewel may be on the feet and a glass bead on the head, but their worth does not change. A jewel always remains a jewel and a bead, a bead. In the market both are sold according to their respective worth. Just as some unscrupulous traders try to sell glass beads as jewels, so some hypocrites try to achieve name and fame in the religious world. Later, when their true natures are exposed, they are humiliated.

A blazing fire cannot be suppressed. Ramakrishna tried to hide himself as a poor and illiterate temple priest, but he did not succeed. Swamiji said to Sharat Chandra Chakrabarty: "God appears as an avatar in this world every few hundred years. But when I was in Dhaka, I heard that five avatars had appeared in that area. Do you know why? When out of compassion for human beings, God takes a human form and then disappears after performing his wonderful divine play, some people then declare themselves to be avatars for self-glory and name and fame. Studying the religious history of the world, one can see that in every age such false prophets appear. This time God truly appeared as Ramakrishna. Its proof is that within a few years of his passing away, he has been worshipped in the East and the West as an avatar."[44]

Now the question is: If a new avatar comes, how shall we know that he is real, and not an imposter? Here are some general characteristics of an avatar:

1. Shows compassion for all beings;
2. Is the saviour of the fallen and downtrodden;
3. Treats everyone equally;
4. Is pure and all-loving;
5. Possesses supreme renunciation;

6. Is free from animal impulses;
7. Is endowed with divine knowledge and power;
8. Is omniscient and omnipotent;
9. Is the protector and preserver of religion;
10. Removes bad karma;
11. Is free from grief and delusion;
12. Is established in truth;
13. Has no body-consciousness.

Keep the Heart Open

If a new avatar comes, devotees of Ramakrishna should not be upset or sorrowful. Rather, they should rejoice upon seeing the Master's new lila. The Master never cared for narrowness or small-mindedness. Those who keep their hearts shut and form sects in the name of Ramakrishna are, in his own words, like a frog living in a well, who has never seen the outside world. He also said, "*Dal* [sedge] grows in a stagnant pool."[45] Ramakrishna was completely nonsectarian; he was the meeting place of all sects and religious paths. The Master used to say that blind people touch different parts of an elephant and form their own limited opinions, but a person with sight sees the whole elephant. Those who have the full experience of God cannot form any sect. For that reason, the Master imparted to Vivekananda various spiritual experiences, including nirvikalpa samadhi, the knowledge of Oneness, so that he could not form any sect.

Ramakrishna's return to the world is a serious subject. The Master's personality and ideas are spreading rapidly all over the globe. Numerous people are gathering day by day under the banner of the Ramakrishna Mission; and hundreds of centres based on his life and message are emerging. None can stop these developments. Ramakrishna's life and message were based on truth, which alone triumphs.

When the Master was living at the Cossipore garden house, there was a difference of opinion between the monastic and householder disciples regarding how to serve him. Sharat Chakrabarty asked his guru, Vivekananda, about this situation. Vivekananda replied:

Yes, but [it was] not exactly a split — it was only a misunderstanding, that's all. Rest assured that among those who are Sri Ramakrishna's devotees, and have *truly* obtained his grace, there is no sect or schism. There *cannot* be — be they householders or sannyasins. As to that kind of slight misunderstanding, do you know what it was due to? Well, each devotee colours Sri Ramakrishna in the light of his own understanding and each forms his own idea of him from his peculiar standpoint. He was, as it were, a great Sun, and each one of us is eyeing him, as it were, through a different kind of coloured glass, and coming to look upon that one Sun as parti-coloured. Of course, it is quite true that this leads to schism in the course of time. But then, such schisms rarely occur in the lifetime of those who are fortunate enough to have come in direct contact with an avatar. The effulgence of that Personality, who takes pleasure only in his Self, dazzles their eyes and sweeps away pride, egotism, and narrow-mindedness from their minds. Consequently they find no opportunity to create sects and party factions. They are content to offer him their heart's worship, each in his own fashion.[46]

Sharat then inquired whether there was a possibility that sects in the name of Ramakrishna would be formed in the future.

Swamiji replied: "Quite so. Hence, sects are bound to form in the course of time. Look, for instance, how the followers of Chaitanya have been divided into two or three hundred sects; and those of Jesus hold thousands of creeds. But all those sects without exception follow Chaitanya or Jesus and none else. But this Math [Belur monastery] that we are building will harmonize all creeds, all standpoints. Just as Sri Ramakrishna held highly liberal views, this Math too will be a centre for propagating similar ideas. The blazing lights of universal harmony that will emanate from here will flood the whole world."[47]

Swamiji was apprehensive about sects forming in the name of Ramakrishna, who was completely nonsectarian. At Lahore in 1897 Swamiji said to Lala Hansaraj, the leader of the Arya Samaj: "You see, I have such power that I can bring one-third of the world's population under the banner of Ramakrishna. Despite that power, I have no intention of doing that because that will refute my guru's message of harmony: 'As many faiths so many paths.' Furthermore, it would just create a new sect in India."[48]

Ramakrishna never said that he was the only avatar, or even the last avatar. His disciples also never tried to establish this view. It is natural that an organization develops around an avatar. A sect is not bad, but sectarianism is horrible. If Krishna, Buddha, Moses, Christ, Muhammad, and Ramakrishna were to travel in one car, they would laugh, joke, and even embrace each other. But if a Hindu, a Buddhist, a Jew, a Christian, and a Muslim were to travel together, they might well quarrel among themselves. This is the outcome of sectarianism and fanaticism. Observing this religious conflict and schism, narrowness and bigotry,

Ramakrishna told the Brahmo leaders Keshab Sen and Vijay Goswami: "Look here. Your quarrel seems like the fight between Shiva and Rama. Shiva was Rama's guru. Though they fought each other, yet they soon came to terms. But the grimaces of ghosts, the followers of Shiva, and the gibberish of the monkeys, the followers of Rama, would not come to an end!"[49]

Therefore, if we are true devotees of the Master, we shall not fight like ghosts and monkeys if Ramakrishna appears again. Swami Vivekananda, who was the voice of Ramakrishna, left clear directions for future generations:

Our watchword will be acceptance and not exclusion. Not only toleration; for so-called toleration is often blasphemy and I do not believe in it. I believe in acceptance. I accept all the religions that were in the past and worship with them all.

Not only shall I do all this, but I shall keep my heart open for all the religions that may come in the future. Is God's Book finished? Or is revelation still going on? It is a marvelous Book — these spiritual revelations of the world. The Bible, the Vedas, the Koran, and all other sacred books are but so many pages, and an infinite number of pages remain yet to be unfolded. I shall leave my heart open for all of them. We stand in the present, but open ourselves to the infinite future. We take in all that has been in the past, enjoy the light of the present, and open every window of the heart for all that will come in the future. Salutations to all the prophets of the past, to all the great ones of the present, and to all that are to come in the future![50]

The Spiritual Tidal Wave Is Coming

On 28 November 1883 Ramakrishna said to Keshab Sen: "I have seen big steamers going by on the Ganges, at the time hardly noticing their passing. But oh, my! What a terrific noise is heard after a while, when the waves splash against the banks! Perhaps a piece of the bank breaks loose and falls into the water."[51] Ramakrishna himself was a big steamer. He lived for only a little over fifty years but his spiritual legacy will continue to flow in the veins of humanity for thousands of years.

Swami Vivekananda was a rishi, a seer of truth and of the future. Observing the movement of the gigantic ship that was Ramakrishna, he wrote to Alasinga Perumal from America: "Up, up, the long night is passing, the day is approaching, the wave has risen, nothing will be able to resist its tidal fury. The flood of spirituality has risen. I see it is rolling over the land resistless, boundless, all-absorbing."[52]

At a later date Sharat Chakrabarty asked Swamiji: "Sir, what is the outcome of all your labours here and in foreign countries?"

Swamiji replied: "You will see only a little manifestation of what has been done. In time, the whole world must accept the universal and catholic ideas of Sri Ramakrishna. Of this, only the beginning has been made. Before this [spiritual] flood everybody will be swept off."[53]

Sometime before his passing away in 1902, Swamiji told Swami Adbhutananda: "Brother, what do you see now? You will see the results of what I have done. This is just the beginning. People of Europe and America have started to appreciate the greatness of our Master. After a few years they will accept his ideas. Now they are only a handful, but later hundreds will come. Then you will understand what this Vivekananda has done."[54]

A big ocean wave rolls up the sandy beach wetting the sand. Then the sand dries. After a while, another wave comes and wets the sand again. This is the way of nature. The spiritual tidal wave of Ramakrishna is spreading all over the world, but in the course of time this wave will recede and the sands will dry up. Again a new spiritual wave will come and Ramakrishna, perhaps as a baul, will be on its pinnacle. The new avatar will establish the great and all-inclusive view of Ramakrishna and spread his universal message throughout the world. The luminous sun does not introduce itself by saying, "I am the sun and the world is illumined by my light." Similarly, the "Great Baul" Ramakrishna will be endowed with knowledge, devotion, love, renunciation, purity, and power to the fullest extent. He will shine in his own glory, so we will have no difficulty recognizing him. If we can simply jump into his spiritual current, we will definitely reach our goal.

28

Some Glimpses of Ramakrishna

Biographers usually write about noteworthy events, marvellous achievements, and amazing stories that take place in the public life of great personalities, and neglect their daily routine, trifling events, and their relationships with their friends and family. As a result, readers do not get a full picture of those great people. Swami Vivekananda remarked: "As I grow older I find that I look more and more for greatness in little things. I want to know what a great man eats and wears, and how he speaks to his servants. I want to find a Sir Philip Sidney greatness! Few men would remember the thirst of others, even in the moment of death. But anyone will be great in a great position! Even the coward will grow brave in the glare of the footlights. The world looks on."[1]

We are human beings so we understand the human aspects of the avatars, who are actually God in human form. Otherwise who could understand the infinite God? It is impossible to comprehend God with our impure minds and puny intellects. The Mundaka Upanishad describes the Cosmic Being: "The heavens are His head; the sun and moon, His eyes; the quarters, His ears; the revealed Vedas, His speech; the wind is His breath; the universe, His heart. From His feet is produced the earth.

He is indeed the inner Self of all beings."[2] When we read this verse, we become afraid to love that Supreme Being, whose eyes are the sun and the moon. We cannot imagine approaching Him or establishing a relationship with Him. For that reason, we need Rama, Krishna, Buddha, Jesus, Ramakrishna, and other great teachers of the world, who can speak to our hearts and guide us along the path of blessedness.

The most important events, stories, and teachings of Ramakrishna are recorded in *Sri Ramakrishna and His Divine Play, The Gospel of Sri Ramakrishna, Ramakrishna as We Saw Him, They Lived with God, God Lived with Them*, and many other books. This chapter provides some further glimpses of Ramakrishna that reveal some facets of his private life, his daily routine, his interpersonal relationships, his love and concern for others, his surroundings, and so on. These brief and seemingly insignificant incidents draw us close to this Godman, and we get a chance to see his human side vividly. We see him become angry when he encounters hypocrisy; we see him cry when someone dies; we see his feeling for his mother, wife, relatives, and devotees. We see how he suffers from disease, how he sings and dances, laughs and makes jokes, scolds and loves his disciples. Observing all these things, we feel that he is not a god sitting in heaven but a human being like us moving on this earth. To a lover, every detail of his or her beloved's life is important, because it brings more familiarity, feeling, awareness, love, and joy.

Ramakrishna's Parents

An avatar's parents are extraordinary people. Ramakrishna's father, Kshudiram, was a man of truth and extremely devout; his mother, Chandramani, was pure and simple. When she was pregnant with Ramakrishna, she one day began to have labour pains. Kshudiram said to her: "How can you give birth to the child right now? Let me first finish the worship of Lord Ramachandra."[3] According to the Hindu custom, one cannot perform ritualistic worship for three days after a child is born in the family. Ramakrishna was born the next morning.

Ramakrishna was very fond of his mother. Towards the end of her life, Chandramani moved to Dakshineswar and stayed with her son. Lakshmi, the Master's niece, recalled:

> All through his life the Master had stomach trouble. When Grandma [Sri Ramakrishna's mother] was living in Dakshineswar, the Master would salute her every morning. Grandma was a large woman and very beautiful, but she was also old-fashioned and very shy. Even in front of her youngest son [Sri Ramakrishna] she would cover her face with a veil.

When he came she would ask him, 'How is your stomach?' The Master would reply, 'Not very good.' Grandma would then advise him: 'Don't take the prasad of Mother Kali. [It was very spicy food.] As long as your stomach is not all right your wife will cook plain soup and rice for you. Please eat only that.'

Sometimes the Master would get tired of eating invalid's food every day and would ask his mother to cook one or two dishes and season them as she used to do in Kamarpukur. So occasionally Grandma cooked for him and the Master enjoyed it.

After the death of her two older sons, Grandma became somewhat passive and withdrawn. Furthermore, she would not take her lunch until she had heard the noon whistle of the Alambazar Jute Mill. As soon as it sounded she would exclaim: "Oh! There is the whistle of heaven. That is the signal for offering food to Lakshmi and Narayana." A problem would arise on Sundays, however, when the jute mill was closed; no whistle was blown at noon and consequently she would not eat. This worried the Master very much, and he would lament: "Oh dear! My old mother will refuse her food today and she will be weak." Brother Hriday would say to the Master: "Don't be anxious, Uncle. When Grandma is hungry she will eat of her own accord." But the Master would reply: "Oh, no. I am her son. It is my duty to look after my old mother." With much coaxing the Master would persuade his mother to eat the prasad of Krishna.

One day Brother Hriday made a high-pitched sound by blowing through a pipe. He then said to Grandma: "There, Grandma, did you hear the whistle of heaven? Now please eat your food." But Grandma laughed and said: "Oh, no. You made the sound with your pipe." Everyone laughed.[4]

Chandramani passed away on 13 February 1877. When she was dying her body was taken to the bakul-tala ghat on the Ganges. M. one day said: "Holding the feet of his mother, the Master said with tears: 'Mother, who are you who held me in your womb?' The Master knew that he was an avatar, so he exclaimed in joy: 'You are not an ordinary woman.'"[5]

A few days later when the Holy Mother carried the Master's meal to his room, he said to her: "Please wait. Let me first cry for my mother in the Panchavati, and then I shall eat."[6] One cannot repay the debt one owes to one's mother. As a sannyasin, the Master could not perform any rituals for his mother, so he paid his tribute to her with his tears.

Days in Kamarpukur and Jayrambati

Those who have never visited Kamarpukur, the birthplace of the Master, are curious to know where Ramakrishna lived. Swami

Saradananda described in detail the parental home of the Master in *Sri Ramakrishna and His Divine Play*. In Kamarpukur the Master's room is 12'10" x 8'10"; it has one door and one window. It is a thatched hut, and the floor and walls are made of mud. It has been preserved as it was during the time of the Master.

The Master would generally leave Dakshineswar for Kamarpukur during the rainy season, because at that time the Ganges water was salty and not good for his stomach. Mathur would send money to pay the Master's expenses. Every day the Master would sit on the veranda of the Yogi Shiva temple and meet the villagers. He would inquire about their families and inspire them by talking about God. He was very fond of jilipis, which he would eat with puffed rice for breakfast.

Swami Subodhananda recalled:

> The Master married when he was twenty-four. Most of the time he was in a god-intoxicated mood and people considered him to be mad. One day he went to his father-in-law's house in Jayrambati. It is said that he went close to the house and then sat down outside of it. A passing villager thought he was insane. Later, the Holy Mother and others brought him into the house. After dinner the Master went to bed. Holy Mother finished her housework and then went to the bedroom, but she found no one in bed. Instead of the Master, she saw a blazing light. Holy Mother stood there with folded hands. When the sun rose, the Master emerged from that light and said to the Holy Mother, "You have appeared in this form — very good." Saying this, the Master bowed down to her. When she was eighteen, the Master worshipped her as the goddess Shodashi.[7]

The Master in Calcutta

In 1850 Ramkumar, Ramakrishna's elder brother, opened a Sanskrit school in the Jhamapukur area of Calcutta. He rented a cheap room with a tiled roof in a slum on Bechu Chatterjee Street and brought the Master there in 1852. The Master lived there for three years. As the Master was averse to a bread-winning education, Ramkumar engaged him in performing rituals in the homes of some of his clients. After performing worship, the Master would get some fruits and sweets, which he tied in a thin towel. On the way home he would sit in the shop of Nakur Bostom, a neighbour from his village. Nakur was a devout Vaishnava and was very fond of the Master. This shop was located close to M.'s house. Nakur later told M.: "Whenever the local people requested the young Master to sing some devotional songs, he would sing forgetting everything. Meanwhile, some young kids would unfold the Master's towel and eat those offered articles. But the Master would not get upset at all. He would smile and carry the towel home."[8] This slum does not exist anymore. Every afternoon the Master would sit in front of the Thanthania Kali temple, which still exists as it was.

The human mind is the fastest vehicle in the world. One can visit any place one likes through the mind. M. described an incident that took place one day when he was with the Master: "One day a man was showing pictures through a magic lantern on a sidewalk in Calcutta. He was shouting, 'Come, see Haridwar; see Badrika' — two famous holy places in the Himalayas. The Master was curious to see that show. He peeped into the box and seeing Badri Narayan, the deity of the Badri temple, he went into samadhi. After a while when he regained outer consciousness, he asked a devotee, 'Please give this man something.' The devotee paid six pice to that man. When the Master heard the amount the devotee had given, he said: 'What! This man showed us Badri Narayan, and you have given so little! He should be given one rupee.'

"The Master was not a human being. Wherever his mind was focussed he would experience God. His mind was like a dry matchstick, which could ignite by the slightest friction. Minds soaked in worldliness are like damp matchsticks. One may rub them a thousand times against the matchbox, but still they won't ignite."[9]

The Master at Dakshineswar

We have elaborately written about the Dakshineswar temple garden in the chapters, "The Stage for Ramakrishna's Divine Play" and "Dakshineswar: An Object of Meditation." Here we present some additional information so that the reader can more clearly visualize and feel the spiritual atmosphere that Ramakrishna created there more than 125 years ago.

Ramakrishna's room has 4 doors and 3 windows, and is located in one of the nicest spots of the temple complex. The room is 21 feet from east to west, and 19 feet from north to south. A statue of Buddha and the following pictures which Ramakrishna collected are still in his room: 1) Gopala and Radha; 2) Radha; 3) Durga; 4) Krishna-Kali; 5) Ramachandra with Sita, Lakshman, Vibhishan, and Hanuman; 6) Goddess Kali of Kalighat; 7) Buddha (a picture); 8) Buddha (an image); Gauranga and Nityananda with their followers; 10) Goddess Tara; 11) Brahma; 12) Vishnu; 13) Goddess Gayatri; 14) Dhruva; 15) Prahlad; 16) Ramachandra with Guhaka; 17) Ramachandra and Krishna merged into one form.

The Master had two cots, one for sleeping and the other for sitting. Both are still there as they were during his time. There are two bricks underneath each leg of the sleeping cot and one brick underneath each leg of the sitting cot. In his day there was no furniture in his room except a stool and a cabinet for keeping sweets and fruits. Once a day a maid or a devotee would sweep his room and clean it with water, and the bricks under the cots would keep the wooden legs from getting wet. In the evening Brinde would light the oil lamp, burn incense powder, and close the doors and windows so that the mosquitoes could not get in. During his first visit, M. saw the Master seated alone on his cot in the evening.

The Master would often pace back and forth on the bank of the Ganges at night. Sometimes he would watch the bore from the semicircular veranda on the western side of his room. He had tremendous faith in the purifying power of Ganges water, which he considered the liquid form of Brahman (*Ganga vari Brahma vari*). He told his disciples to sip Ganges water if they had any impure thoughts. He asked Girish, his bohemian devotee, to take a bath in the Ganges.

The Master would go to the pine grove, in the northwest corner of the garden, to answer the call of nature. Every morning he would brush his teeth with a twig and also scrape his tongue. He would wash his cloths in the goose pond, east of the Panchavati.

The Master received 6 dhotis (cloths) from the temple authorities every year. He had 2 dhotis for his everyday use. The devotees would supply him with his shirts. One set of clothes — a dhoti and shirt — he kept reserved for his Calcutta visits.

Ramakrishna's weight and height were not officially recorded. Swami Nirvanananda, however, in providing guidance to a sculptor who was preparing a marble image of Sri Ramakrishna installed in May 1951 at Ramakrishna's birthplace in Kamarpukur, calculated that the Master was 5 feet 9 1/4 inches tall. The swami made this calculation on the basis of the length of a coat of Sri Ramakrishna, now at Belur Math. This is the coat the Master wore in his studio picture taken at Radhabazar, Calcutta. By measuring the coat and calculating the relation of the coat to the figure, Swami Nirvanananda established Ramakrishna's height.[10]

So far as we know Ramakrishna was not ill very often. Occasionally he suffered from dysentery, fever, cold and cough; he finally succumbed to throat cancer.

Sometimes the Master would go for a walk in Shambhu Mallick's or Jadu Mallick's garden in Dakshineswar. M. recalled: "When the Master visited Jadu Mallick's garden, the caretaker of the garden would fan him. Seeing his devotion, the Master once went into samadhi. One day the caretaker invited the Master for lunch and he accepted. The Master went to his place accompanied by Rakhal Maharaj, me, and a young brahmin boy from Orissa (who was M.'s cook). Perhaps he would not have accepted if any rich man had invited him."[11]

The Master's samadhi was so unpredictable that he needed someone to always stay with him; for otherwise there was a chance of his having an accident. One day in an ecstatic mood, he had a vision of Jagannath. While trying to embrace Him, the Master fell down and broke his arm. M. also said, "While listening to the temple music (rasun chauki) being played at the nahabat, the Master would go into samadhi."[12] "The Master would merge into samadhi seeing a person closing an umbrella. It reminded him of withdrawing the mind from the world and giving it to God."[13] M. also recorded: "It was a winter morning, and the Master was sitting near the east door of his room, wrapped in his moleskin shawl. He looked at the sun and suddenly went into samadhi. His eyes stopped blinking and he lost all consciousness of the outer world. After a long time he came down to the plane of the sense world."[14]

Swami Ambikananda told the following incident, which he heard from his mother, Nistarini Ghosh, a devotee of the Master:

> The Master one day said to my mother, "Put on some jewellery like that of the Mother in the temple." My mother did what the Master told her. One day she went to Dakshineswar and saw the Master seated on his bed in samadhi. When she bowed down to him, her bangles made some noise. Immediately the Master was startled and his samadhi broke. He cried out: "What is this? Why are you making so much noise? The soul of a person who has left his body and merged into the Divine might not be able to return to his body. When I go into samadhi, I keep a thread between this body and the Cosmic Being, just as a very fine wire connects two things. If the connecting thread breaks by some noise I shall not be able return to this body." From then on, when my mother visited the Master, she would push the bangles up on her arms to keep them from jangling."[15]

The Master at Night

Ramakrishna slept only two or three hours at night. Sometimes he would walk around the garden and ask the night guard, "Can you chant the Lord's name a little?" In the early morning he would get up and pace in his room and chant the names of gods and goddesses. At that time he would use his yogic vision to observe the spiritual progress of his disciples, and then help them accordingly. At 3:00 a.m., when he would go towards the Panchavati, he would call Lakshmi and Holy Mother to get up and practise meditation.

The Master's Eating and Other Habits

Ramakrishna lived over 50 years depending wholly on God and without touching any money. As a result, God provided him with all he needed. Rasmani and Mathur arranged everything for him — his daily food, his clothing, his room. The temple officials regularly sent his allotted breakfast, lunch, and supper, which had all been offered to Kali and Krishna. For breakfast he had a little butter and rock candy from the Krishna temple and fruits and sweets from the Kali temple. One day Swami Brahmananda ate some butter and rock candy before the Master had eaten, and the Master scolded him.

When the Master first came to Dakshineswar, he cooked his own food on the bank of the Ganges, and Hriday helped him. Later he started taking Kali's cooked prasad, which he himself had offered to the Mother between 1:00 to 2:00 p.m. Later, during his days of sadhana, the Master could no longer perform the worship in the temple. Eventually he developed stomach problem and he tried to eat before noon. When Jadu Mallick heard about his difficulty, he engaged a cook for him. On 7 September 1884 the Master said: "Mallick noticed the late hours of my meals and arranged for a cook. He gave me one rupee for a month's expenses. That embarrassed me. I had to run to him whenever he sent for me. It would have been quite a different thing if I had gone to him of my own accord."[16] Then the Master improvised a humorous couplet: "Sudhamukhi's cooking no more, no more. When I ate, I cried and cried." He was a free soul and did not like to be obligated to anyone or to flatter rich people.

Later Holy Mother and some other women devotees would cook for the Master. Once during lunch the Master humorously said to Balaram: "Well, can you tell me why I married? What is the purpose of having a wife? I cannot even take care of the cloth on my body — it just drops off. Why then do I have a wife?"

Balaram smiled and kept quiet.

The Master: "Oh, I understand (*taking a little curry from the plate and showing it to Balaram*) — for this reason I married. Otherwise, who else would cook for me with such care? (*Balaram and the other devotees laughed.*) Truly speaking, who else would look after my food? They all left today — (*seeing that the devotees did not understand who had left*) along with Ramlal's aunt. Ramlal is going to be married, so everyone left for Kamarpukur today. I watched her departure impassively. It was truly as if someone else had left. Then I grew anxious when I thought about who would cook for me. You see, some kinds of food do not agree with my stomach, nor am I always conscious enough to eat. She (*the Holy Mother*) knows what kind of food suits me and makes various preparations accordingly. So I asked myself, who will cook for me?"[17]

Swami Premananda told a monk: "The Master could not wait long for his food after his bath. He always ate something after he bathed. That is why during the ritualistic worship, I offer the *naivedya* (food) after repeating the mantra for the bath. I follow his way of life. When he is pleased, all will be satisfied."[18] After lunch the Master would take a little rest.

The Master's supper was very simple. He ate a few pieces of luchi (fried bread) and a little farina pudding that had been offered to the Divine Mother at night. If he was hungry at night, he would eat some sweets and fruits from the cabinet in his room, or the Holy Mother would make some farina pudding for him. He would allow his disciples to eat a heavy meal at lunch but their supper would be light, because if one eats too much at night one cannot practise sadhana.

*　　　　*　　　　*

The Master smoked tobacco a few times a day, using a hubble-bubble that he kept in the southwest corner of his room. He sometimes offered a smoke to his visitors. After meals he would chew betel rolls. Holy Mother would prepare them for him, and his lips would become crimson from chewing them. Once the Master asked Gangadhar (later Swami Akhandananda) to have lunch at Dakshineswar. Gangadhar said: "When I returned to the Master's room [after eating] I found him waiting near the east door with a betel roll in his hand. Giving it to me, he said: 'Chew it. It is good to chew a couple of betel rolls after meals. It removes bad breadth.'"[19]

Swami Premananda recalled: "We saw how lovingly the Master would receive the devotees at Dakshineswar! He would ask, 'Do you want to chew a betel roll?' If the devotee said, 'No,' he would then ask, 'Would you like to smoke tobacco?' Thus, in so many ways he would take care of the devotees."[20]

Whenever Ramakrishna went to Calcutta his attendant always

carried his towel and spice bag, which contained fennel seeds, cloves, cubeb, caraway, and cardamom. Sometimes he would chew spices to bring his mind down to the sense plane. Quite often when he would come down from samadhi, he would say, "I shall smoke tobacco, or drink water, or I shall eat bitter squash curry." Those insignificant desires or habits would help him come down from samadhi.

The Master's Bathing

The Master would bathe in the Ganges at the chandni ghat, but if he had a cold he would have his bath from a bucket of water heated by the sun. He had a separate cloth (oil dhoti) for bathing. Either he or someone else would rub oil on his body before his bath. We do not have any record that he ever used soap, but he once told the Holy Mother to rub his body with *basan* (lentil powder), which cleanses the body.[21] The body is the temple of God, so the Master always kept it clean.

Once the Master went to hear a spiritual discourse and the speaker remarked: "Those who chant Rama's name become free from dirt." The Master had the faith of a child. He immediately pointed out, "Then why is there dirt on my body?" Krishnakishore explained, "The inner impurities go away and not the external dirt."[22]

How the Master's Beard Was Trimmed

During his second visit to the Master (28 February 1882), M. saw that he was about to have his beard trimmed on the southeast veranda of his room. The Master's skin was so soft and sensitive that he could not be shaved with a razor. The barber would simply trim his hair and beard with a scissors. M. later recalled: "When we first saw the Master, his beard had begun to turn grey. The barber would trim his hair and beard when they became long.... Before the barber started, the Master would tell him: 'Please wait. Let me think about God.' Thus he withdrew his mind from the body before having his hair and beard trimmed."[23]

Swami Ambikananda said: "When the Master was at the Cossipore garden house suffering from cancer, his beard grew long. For this reason the doctor could not see or touch his throat properly, so he suggested shaving that area. The Master asked Latu to bring a scissors and told him, 'I shall give you a signal when I have withdrawn my mind from the body, and then you trim my beard.' After seeing the signal, Latu began to trim it with a pair of dull scissors, but the Master did not feel anything at all."[24]

The Master in Different Moods

The Master could not bear any kind of hypocrisy or insincerity. He said:

In that state of God-intoxication I used to speak out my mind to all. I was no respecter of persons. Even to men of position I was not afraid to speak the truth. . . .

One day, in that state of divine intoxication, I went to the bathing-ghat on the Ganges at Baranagore. There I saw Jaya Mukherji repeating the name of God; but his mind was on something else. I went up and slapped him twice on the cheeks.

At one time Rani Rasmani was staying in the temple garden. She came to the shrine of the Divine Mother, as she frequently did when I worshipped Kali, and asked me to sing a song or two. On this occasion, while I was singing, I noticed she was sorting the flowers for worship absent-mindedly. At once I slapped her on the cheeks. She became quite embarrassed and sat there with folded hands.

Alarmed at this state of mind myself, I said to my cousin Haladhari: 'Just see my nature! How can I get rid of it?' After praying to the Divine Mother for some time with great yearning, I was able to shake off this habit.'[25]

Sometimes the Master would become angry like an ordinary human being. M. said: "One day Hriday went to buy some hay for some business affair. He told the temple manager that his uncle would perform the worship that day. When the Master found that the Mother's worship was not done, he hurriedly went to the temple and performed the worship with the help of Ramlal. When Hriday returned, the Master beat him. Hriday understood his mistake and said, 'Uncle, beat me more.' Then the Master said: 'Look, when I am angry, you keep quiet. And when you are angry, I shall keep quiet.'"[26]

The Master's life was established in truth. It was not possible for him to hide anything within. His mind and speech were united. Once he said: "Is it an easy matter to get rid of lust? I myself felt a queer sensation in my heart six months after I had begun my spiritual practice. Then I threw myself on the ground under a tree and wept bitterly. I said to the Divine Mother, 'Mother, if it comes to that, I shall certainly cut my throat with a knife!'"[27] The Master was the embodiment of purity. He said, "I have never enjoyed a woman, even in a dream."[28] He encouraged his devotees to overcome lust by citing his own experience. As long as one has a body one might feel lust, but one can transcend it by focussing the mind on God.

510 • How to Live With God

The Master would always help those who were sincere and sought his guidance. Sometimes we marvel at how skilful the Master was in using examples in his teachings. M. said: "One day the Master said to Thakur-da (Narayan Das Bandyopadhyay, a storyteller of Baranagore): 'Your teeth are not set properly. Now and then please come to Dakshineswar. I shall grind your teeth and set them properly.' The Master meant that Thakur-da's spiritual practices were not being done properly. He would be glad to make adjustments in them, just as an expert dentist fixes someone's denture."[29]

Grief for Keshab and Adhar

A knower of Brahman is not affected by disease, suffering, or grief. He remains unperturbed in happiness and misery, good and evil. Although he has a body, he transcends body-consciousness. The Master used to say that two persons lived inside him — the Divine Mother and a devotee. It was the devotee who had cancer. But he had the power and ability to move his mind back and forth at any time between the human and divine planes.

The Master was very fond of Keshab Sen. When Keshab died at the age of 45, the Master wept and remained in bed for three days covering himself with a chadar. He said, "My brain is boiling like hot water."[30] When Keshab's son visited Dakshineswar, the Master embraced him and wept. When our dearest one dies we cry, and so did the Master. M. said: "When the news of Adhar Sen's death reached the Master, I was in his room. He immediately went into samadhi. Regaining normal consciousness, he wept and said to the Divine Mother: 'Mother, you asked me to stay in the world with the devotees, cherishing devotion. Now look, how much pain I have.'"[31]

The Master and Holy Mother

People marry for happiness and peace and not for fighting and quarrelling. An ideal marriage consists of mutual love, respect, and understanding. Sri Ramakrishna and Sarada Devi demonstrated an ideal marriage in this age. They had a wonderful relationship. We have never come across any incident of bickering between them.

In March 1872, when Holy Mother first visited Dakshineswar, she had two concerns: First, she heard that her husband had become mad, and second, she feared he might reject her because he was a monk. But these misgivings disappeared when she arrived one night at Dakshineswar at 9:00 p.m.

As soon as the Master heard of the Holy Mother's arrival, he said: "O Hriday, I hope it is an auspicious time, because this is her first visit." This means that he was thinking of her welfare.

Second, upon seeing the Holy Mother, he greeted her, saying: "You have come. Very good!" This indicates that she was welcome.

Third, the Master told someone in the room, "Please spread a mat for her." There was no chair or sofa in the Master's room. The Holy Mother bowed down to the Master and sat on the mat.

Fourth, as soon as the Master heard that she had a fever, he became extremely concerned and arranged for her treatment and diet. He then said: "You have come so late! If Mathur were alive, he would take care of you nicely. My right hand has been broken [as it were, with his death]." (Mathur died in July 1871.) This indicates that the Master was apologizing to the Holy Mother because he could not serve her like Mathur, who had been wealthy and devoted to him.

Fifth, when the Holy Mother wanted to go to the nahabat to stay with Chandramani, the Master said: "No, no! It will be difficult for the doctor to treat you there. You sleep in my room."[32] The Master's behaviour and love overwhelmed the Holy Mother.

Then Hriday brought some puffed rice, which she ate, and then she lay down on the floor in the Master's room. Through all this, she realized that her husband was not mad and she was not rejected.

*   *   *

In the early days, when the Holy Mother lived in Dakshineswar, a maid would stay with her at night in the nahabat. One night there was torrential rain and the maid could not come, so the Master asked the Holy Mother to sleep in his room. When she arrived, the Master asked: "Where is your jewellery? Bring them here." The Holy Mother replied: "I can't go back now. It will be all right."[33] This little incident proves how much love and concern the Master had for his wife, though most of the time he was in an ecstatic state.

The Master and Swami Vivekananda

M. recalled: "We saw the Master talking to the Divine Mother in front of us. Swamiji was then 19 years old and was connected with the Brahmo Samaj. During one of his first visits, the Master said to him: 'Do you know Gauranga of Nadia? I am that Gauranga.' Swamiji then said to me privately, 'Is he mad?' Later Swamiji preached in America and said: 'Avatars are the Teachers of all teachers, the highest manifestations of God through men. We cannot see God except through them. As long as we are men, we must worship Him in man and as man. Talk as you may, try as you may, you cannot think of God except as a man.'"[34]

The Master loved Swami Vivekananda and made him his main disciple. M. recalled: "The Master scolded Swamiji twice: first at Dakshineswar and second at Cossipore. When Swamiji first began visiting Dakshineswar, he criticized Kali a lot. Finally the Master gravely said, 'Don't come here anymore.' Despite this scolding from the Master, Swamiji did not become upset. He immediately began preparing a smoke for the Master. Later in Cossipore the Master scolded Swamiji when the latter said something about the view of Tantra. The Master said, 'I have seen that those who practised those esoteric sadhanas in the name of religion, went astray.'"[35]

One day Swamiji came to visit the Master in Dakshineswar. His hair was beautiful and was nicely combed. The Master ruffled his hair and said, "My child, we have not come to this world for enjoyment."[36]

Swami Shuddhananda elaborated on this incident:

Vivekananda was then Narendranath; he was visiting Ramakrishna regularly at Dakshineswar. Pointing to Narendra's well-combed curly hair, the Master teased him about his foppishness. Narendra was also unsparing; he pointed out to the Master his varnished shoes, hubble-bubble, mattress, bolster, and so on. Then the Master told him, "Look here, the amount of austerity I practised for God-realization, if you can do one-sixteenth of that, I shall arrange for you to sleep on a costly bedstead with mattress upon mattress." Swamiji practised severe austerities in his life; and then when he returned from the West, his Western disciples presented him with a spring bed and mattress (which are still preserved in his room). While lying on that Western mattress and remembering those words of the Master, Swamiji would tell that incident to his disciples with tears.[37]

The Last Days of the Master

M. recalled: "The Master suffered from throat cancer for more than ten months. He had a terrible hemorrhage from his wound, but the devotees served him wholeheartedly. Holding the doctor's hand, he plaintively said, 'Please cure my disease.' But as soon as he felt a little better, he would talk about God. Finally he said, 'The Divine Mother will not keep this body anymore.'... The entire report of the Master's illness is in my diary. I recorded the amount of blood from each hemorrhage, the intensity of his pain, what he ate, and other things. Every day I carried that report to Dr. Mahendralal Sarkar."[38]

M. kept his diary with all the details about the Master's illness, but the last entry published in *The Gospel of Sri Ramakrishna* was for 24 April 1886. The previous day (23 April 1886) was Good Friday, which is a day of mourning for Christians. M. elaborately described what happened on that day, including the following incident:

> It was evening. A lamp was lighted in the Master's room. Amrita Basu, a Brahmo devotee, came in. A garland of jasmine lay in front of the Master on a plantain-leaf. There was perfect silence in the room. A great yogi seemed to be silently communing with God. Every now and then the Master lifted the garland a little, as if he wanted to put it around his neck.
> Amrita (*tenderly*): "Shall I put it around your neck?"
> Sri Ramakrishna accepted the garland.[39]

According to the Master's instruction, M. arrived the next day (24 April 1886) with his wife who was grief-stricken over the death of her son. M. recorded:

> That day the Master several times allowed M.'s wife the privilege of waiting on him. Her welfare seemed to occupy his attention a great deal. In the evening the Holy Mother came to the Master's room to feed him. M.'s wife accompanied her with a lamp. The Master tenderly asked her many questions about her household. He requested her to come again to the garden house and spend a few days with the Holy Mother, not forgetting to ask her to bring her baby daughter. When the Master had finished his meal M.'s wife removed the plates. He chatted with her a few minutes. [This is a wonderful scene for meditation.]
> About nine o'clock in the evening Sri Ramakrishna was seated in his room with the devotees. He had a garland of flowers around his neck. He told M. that he had requested his wife to spend a few days at the garden house with the Holy Mother. His kindness touched M.'s heart.
> M. was fanning him. The Master took the garland from his neck and said something to himself. Then in a very benign mood he gave the garland to M."[40]

Here M.'s entries for the *Gospel* end. The human aspect of Ramakrishna revealed in such incidents is very moving. Despite his terminal disease, he was thinking of others' welfare. The Master assuaged the grief of M.'s wife's heart and also blessed the recorder of his gospel with a garland.

It is not known why M. did not publish the entries from his diary through the last days of the Master. Swami Saradananda also did not write about the Master's last days at Cossipore. When he was requested to complete *Sri Ramakrishna and His Divine Play*, he humbly said: "Perhaps it will never be completed. I am not getting inspiration from within. The Master made me write whatever he wanted."[41]

Human desires are insatiable. We are hungry to know more about our beloved Master, but at the same time we are unable to fathom God's will. We will remain ever grateful to M. and Swami Saradananda for what they gave us about the Master. Moreover, the problem of our discontent was answered by the Master in the following conversation.

Sri Ramakrishna said about his intimate devotees, "All of you are part of this place [*meaning himself*]."

M: "That I have understood. But I am not fully satisfied."

Master: "You will never be fully satisfied."

M: "Sir, the amount of longing I had at the beginning still remains. I don't have full contentment."

Master: "None can have full contentment in God [because He is infinite]."[42]

29 Appendix

Centenary of the Ramakrishna Mission

An Avatar Comes with a Mission

In the Vishnu Purana it is said: "Those who do not perform their duties and do not practise religion, but say 'O Lord, O Lord,' are ignorant and are to be considered enemies of God, because God has to take human birth to show them how to practise religion." Hindus believe in the truth of this verse.

God comes in every age to fulfill the spiritual needs of that time. Rama, Krishna, Buddha, Jesus Christ, Muhammad, Chaitanya, Ramakrishna, and other divine incarnations and prophets have come one after another. Each of them came to fulfill a mission: Rama focussed on truthfulness and service; Krishna, unselfish action and devotion; Buddha, nonviolence, compassion, and other virtues; Jesus Christ, love and service; Muhammad, prayer and equality; Chaitanya, devotion and service; and Ramakrishna, God-realization, service to human beings, and the harmony of religions.

Buddhism was the first worldwide missionary religion. And it spread through love and friendship, not through force. Buddha taught his disciples: Be good and do good. Work out your own salvation. Sacrifice your life for the good of the many and the welfare of all. Hatred cannot be conquered by hatred; hatred can be conquered only by love.

When Buddha was on his deathbed, his disciple Ananda asked him: "Master, when you depart, who will teach us?" Buddha replied: "The truth and the rules of the Order which I have set forth and laid down for you all, let them, after I am gone, be a teacher unto you."[1]

Christ also empowered his disciples to continue his ministry through love, compassion, friendship, and humility. He said: "Preach as you go, saying, 'The kingdom of heaven is at hand.' Heal the sick, raise the dead, cleanse lepers, cast out demons. Freely you have received, freely you shall give."[2] According to the Bible, after Christ's resurrection the Holy Spirit descended upon his disciples, and with that power they carried his message to the masses.

Ramakrishna lived from 1836 to 1886. Like other avatars, he had a mission; and like other avatars, he came with a group of disciples whom he empowered to carry on that mission. Ramakrishna knew that his disciples would have to carry his teachings all over the world. Once, after coming down from samadhi, he told his wife, Sri Sarada Devi: "Listen, my dear, I went to the land of white people. Ah, how sincere is their devotion!" In 1902 Swami Turiyananda, speaking to some devotees in California, stated: "Once our Master told us that he had other disciples who spoke a different language, who had different customs, somewhere far away in the West. 'They also will worship me,' the Master said. 'They also are Mother's children.' You are those disciples."[3]

Compassion — Vision — Mission

One day in 1884 at Dakshineswar Ramakrishna was seated in his room, talking to his disciples about a famous statement of the Vaishnava religion taught by Chaitanya: "*Jivedayā nāme ruchi vaishnava sevan, Ihā vinā dharma nāi shuna Sanātan*" — "Listen O Sanatan, these are the foremost of all spiritual disciplines: compassion for all living beings, love of God's name, and service to devotees." Repeating the word *compassion*, Ramakrishna went into samadhi. After a while he returned to normal consciousness and said to the devotees: "How foolish it is to speak of compassion! Man is an insignificant worm crawling on the earth — and he is to show compassion to others! This is absurd. It must not be compassion but service to all. Recognize them as God's manifestations and serve them."[4]

Serve human beings as God. This was the very seed of the Ramakrishna Mission, planted in 1884 by Ramakrishna himself at Dakshineswar.

Ramakrishna died in 1886, and his disciples, led by Swami Vivekananda, established a monastery in Baranagore. Here they spent their time practising difficult austerities and remembering their blessed days with the Master.

In 1890 Vivekananda left the monastery to begin a period of wandering throughout India. It would be seven years before he returned. In 1893 some devotees in South India asked him to go to the West and represent Hinduism at the Parliament of Religions to be held in Chicago. Vivekananda had a vision that the Master was asking him to go to the West, and when Sarada Devi confirmed that she too had had a similar vision, Vivekananda went. He was the first Vedanta monk to go to America, carrying the message of Ramakrishna.

To Organize or Not to Organize

After reaching the United States in July 1893, Vivekananda observed the enormous power of organization that lay behind American life. Once he told his host, Emily Lyon of Chicago: "You know, I have had one of the greatest temptations of my life here." "Why, who is she, Swami?" Mrs. Lyon asked. "Oh, Mrs. Lyon," he laughed, "it isn't a lady. It's organization."[5]

Vedanta, the source of Hinduism, has never been an organized religion; it has always been the religion of free souls and mendicants. However, Vivekananda understood that an individual may be powerful, but it is not possible for one person to do everything on a large scale: A following is necessary in order to carry great ideas to posterity. He had the mission of his guru to fulfill; he could not do it alone.

But Vivekananda also understood the possible dangers of organization: politics, power struggles, corruption, and commercialism.

At Thousand Island Park, during the summer of 1895, he debated: "To organize or not to organize. If I organize, the spirit will diminish. If I do not organize, the message will not spread."[6] In the end, he was determined that his Master's great message should not be lost. Vivekananda knew that the only thing that would keep corruption out of organized work was purity of life. Two days after leaving Thousand Island Park, he wrote to a disciple:

> Neither numbers, nor powers, nor wealth, nor learning, nor eloquence, nor anything else will prevail, but purity, living the life, in one word, *anubhuti*, realization. Let there be a dozen such lion-souls in each country, lions who have broken their own bonds, who have touched the Infinite, whose whole souls are gone to Brahman, who care neither for wealth, nor power, nor fame, and these will be *enough* to shake the world.[7]

One year earlier, in November 1894, he had founded the Vedanta Society of New York, but its main activity was to publish his lectures. Now, in October 1895, he called for two of his brother disciples — Swami Saradananda and Swami Abhedananda — to come to the West and carry on the Vedanta work in London and New York.

Swami Saradananda taught Vedanta in America from 1896 to 1898, and then was called back to India. Swami Abhedananda remained in America for twenty-five years (1896-1921), fourteen of them as head of the Vedanta Society of New York. When Vivekananda sailed to the West for the second time in 1899, he took with him Swami Turiyananda. In April 1900, Vivekananda founded the Vedanta Society of San Francisco and asked Swami Turiyananda to take over that work and to establish a retreat centre in Northern California. Turiyananda was in America for three years (1899-1902). He was followed by Swami Trigunatitananda, who spent the last twelve years of his life (1903-1915) as head of the Vedanta Society in San Francisco.

The Bhagavad Gita tells us: "Whatever a great man does, that others follow; whatever he sets up as a standard, that the world follows."[8] These five disciples of Ramakrishna set high standards that have been upheld by generation after generation of Vedanta monks who have followed them. Through lectures, scriptural classes, and private instructions in spiritual practice, monks of the Ramakrishna Order in the West have always emphasized the divinity of the soul, the unity of existence, the universality of Truth, and the harmony of religions.

Birth of the Ramakrishna Mission

In 1897 Vivekananda returned to India. Upon receiving tremendous receptions everywhere, he said: "Friends, I am very pleased with your enthusiasm. It is marvellous. Only make it permanent; keep it up. Let not the fire die out."[9] He at last reached Calcutta. There he saw many of his brother monks, some of them for the first time since he left the monastery in 1890. After a few weeks, he went to Darjeeling for much-needed rest. Again, in Darjeeling, he considered how best to carry on the work. Still burning in his mind were the words of his Master, "Serve human beings as God."

Towards the end of April 1897, Vivekananda returned to Calcutta to give concrete form to Ramakrishna's teaching on practical Vedanta. The Ramakrishna Mission was officially founded on Saturday, 1 May 1897. Swamiji called for devotees to gather at 3:00 p.m. at Balaram Basu's home in Calcutta. Forty people came, both householder devotees and

519

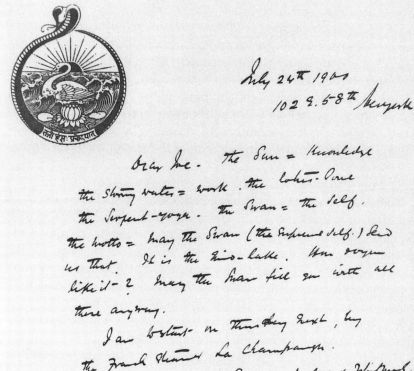

Vivekananda's description of the Ramakrishna Order emblem

monastics, and he said to them: "From my travels in various countries, I have come to the conclusion that without organization nothing great and permanent can be done. . . . This organization will bear the name of him in whose name we have become sannyasins; him, taking whom as your ideal you are leading the householder life in the field of activity — this *Samsara* [this world]; him whose holy name, and the influence of whose unique life and teachings, have within twelve years of his demise spread in such an unthought-of way both in the East and the West. Let this *Sangha* [organization] therefore be named the Ramakrishna Mission. We are but the servants of the Master. May you all help in this work!"[10]

Swamiji's proposal was welcomed with enthusiasm.

On 5 May Vivekananda again met with some householder devotees and brother monastics. At this time he declared: "This Association [Sangha] shall be known as the Ramakrishna Mission. The aim of the Sangha is to preach those truths which Sri Ramakrishna has, for the good of humanity, preached and demonstrated by practical application in his own life, and to help others put these truths into practice in their lives for their temporal, mental, and spiritual advancement."[11]

Vivekananda then talked about methods of work, training, establishment of arts and industries, and humanitarian work.

Vivekananda became the general president of the Mission, and he made Swami Brahmananda and Swami Yogananda president and vice-president respectively of the Calcutta centre; Narendranath Mitra was appointed secretary; Dr. Shashibhushan Ghosh and Sharat Chandra Sarkar, undersecretaries; and Sharat Chandra Chakrabarty, reader of scriptures.

Meetings were to be held every Sunday afternoon, and were to include readings and recitations from Vedanta scriptures as well as talks, expositions, and the reading of original papers.

Vivekananda wanted to establish an ideal society. He wanted to bring the best from the West and share it with India, and in turn to share India's spiritual treasures with the West. For this reason, he wanted Vedanta centres to be established in countries all over the world. This, he felt, would bring about a closer relationship between East and West.

Still, Vivekananda's ideas were not entirely accepted by all. His main opposition came from some of his own brother disciples. After the first meeting, on 1 May 1897, when the devotees had left, Swami Yogananda openly questioned Vivekananda's methods of work. The following conversation took place:

Yogananda: "You are doing these things by Western methods. Would you say that Sri Ramakrishna left us any such instructions?"

Vivekananda: "How do you know that these methods are not in keeping with his ideas? Sri Ramakrishna was the embodiment of infinite ideas: Do you want to shut him up in your own limits? I shall break those limits and scatter his ideas broadcast all over the world. He never instructed me to introduce worship of him, and so forth. The methods of spiritual practice, concentration and meditation, and the other higher ideals of religion that he taught — those we must realize and teach to all men. Infinite are the ideas and infinite are the paths that lead to the goal. I was not born to create a new sect in this world, too full of sects already. Blessed are we that we have found refuge at the feet of our Master. It is our duty to give the ideas entrusted to us freely to the whole world.

"Time and again I have received in this life marks of his grace. He himself is at my back and is making me do all these things in these ways. When I used to lie under a tree, exhausted, smitten with hunger; when I had not a strip of cloth even to tie my *kaupina* with; when I had resolved to travel round the world penniless — even then, through his grace, I received help in every way. Then again, when people in crowds jostled with one another in the streets of Chicago to have sight of this Vivekananda, I was able, through his blessings, to digest without difficulty all that honour, a hundredth part of which would have turned the head of any other man. By the will of the Lord, victory has been mine everywhere. Now I intend to do something for this country. Do you all give up doubts and misgivings and help me in my work; and you will see how, by his grace, wonders will be accomplished."

Yogananda: "Whatever you will, shall come about. We are always ready to follow your leading. I clearly see that the Master is working through you. Still, I confess, doubts do sometimes arise in the mind, for, as we saw it, his method of doing things was so different; and so I am led to ask myself whether we are not straying from Sri Ramakrishna's teachings."

Vivekananda: "The thing is this: Sri Ramakrishna is far greater than his disciples understand him to be. He is the embodiment of infinite spiritual ideas capable of development in infinite ways. Even if one can find a limit to the knowledge of Brahman, one cannot measure the unfathomable depths of our Master's mind! One gracious glance of his eyes can create a hundred thousand Vivekanandas at this instant! But if this time he chooses, instead, to work through me, making me his instrument, I can only bow to his will."[12]

Then Latu Maharaj (Swami Adbhutananda), a simple, unlettered mystic and a knower of God, objected to Vivekananda's methods. He asked: "Brother, why have you started all these activities? Won't these interfere with our meditation and prayer?"

Vivekananda at first joked light-heartedly with Latu Maharaj, saying: "How can you understand why I am introducing all these works. You are a dumbbell! At the sound of *ka*, you shed tears like Prahlada.* You are all devotees. What can you understand of this? You can only whine like babies. You think you can achieve liberation by crying, and that on the last day the Master will take you to heaven, and there you will enjoy life to your heart's content. And those who are studying the scriptures for knowledge, who are working to educate people in the path of righteousness, and serving the diseased and distressed will all go to hell because all these works are maya. What a grand idea! — that to do good to mankind is an unnecessary bother, and one cannot attain God through these activities. This is your view, isn't it? As if God-realization were very easy — you can call on God and here He comes. Does God appear before a man who merely puts His picture on an altar and throws a few flowers before Him? Tell me that."

Swami Adbhutananda was astonished. Then suddenly Vivekananda became grave and thundered: "Ah, what you call devotion is sentimental nonsense that only weakens a man. Who cares for that kind of devotion? I have no faith in that devotion which makes a man so self-centred, so busy with his own personal salvation, that his heart does not feel for others. . . . You know, one day I foolishly asked the Master for this kind of devotion and liberation, and he rebuked me and called me selfish and small-minded. Should I be misled by your words? I'll work as he has told me. . . . I will go into a thousand hells cheerfully if I can rouse my countrymen, immersed in tamas [inertia], to stand on their own feet and be *men* inspired with the spirit of karma yoga."[13]

The swami's voice became choked, tears streamed from his eyes, and he left the room. Later, when his brother disciples tried to console him, he told them: "When one attains bhakti, one's heart and nerves become so soft and delicate that they cannot bear even the touch of a flower! . . . I cannot think or talk of Sri Ramakrishna long, without being overwhelmed. So I am trying and trying always to keep down the rush of bhakti welling within me. I am trying to bind and bind myself with the iron chain of jnana, for still my work to my motherland is unfinished, and my message to the world not yet fully delivered. . . . Oh, I have work

*A devotee of Krishna who was reminded of Krishna by the first letter of Krishna's name.

to do! I am a slave of Ramakrishna, who left his work to be done by me, and will not give me rest till I have finished it!"[14]

The next day, Swami Adbhutananda went to Vivekananda and said: "Brother, what do I know? I am a fool. Please do not take my words to heart." After this dramatic incident, there were no more objections. Vivekananda's brother disciples saw clearly that the Master was indeed working through his beloved Narendra and that they must all sacrifice themselves for the good of the mission, for the welfare of all.

From the Minutes of the Ramakrishna Mission

The minutes of early meetings of the Ramakrishna Mission are a great treasure. One of the disciples of Ramakrishna would preside; another disciple or a devotee would speak; and there would be readings, and questions and answers. Sometimes M. (Mahendra Nath Gupta) would read portions of his diary, from which he was developing *The Gospel of Sri Ramakrishna*. Then there would be a closing song.

These meetings gave the disciples and devotees of Ramakrishna a chance to recall their happy experiences with the Master and to express their own understanding of his life and mission. Here are some extracts from the minutes of their meetings.

Third Meeting: 9 May 1897

Swami Brahmananda presided. About thirty members as well as some visitors were present. Swami Trigunatitananda read and explained a few verses from the Gita, bearing on the benefit of work as taught by Sri Krishna and exemplified by the teachings of Sri Ramakrishna.

Girish Chandra Ghosh then related his experiences with Sri Ramakrishna from the beginning of their association. . . . One night, Girish said, he was visiting a house of ill-fame with two friends when he suddenly felt an overpowering inclination to go to Dakshineswar. He then urged his companions to leave with him and hailed a carriage. Although the carriage was moving at a brisk pace, Girish told the driver to go even faster.

The night had far advanced and most people were asleep when the three of them staggered into Ramakrishna's room. To Girish's surprise, he received an extraordinary welcome. Grabbing him suddenly with his hands, Ramakrishna began to dance and sing with joy. A thought flashed through Girish's mind that indeed he was in the presence of an extraordinary man; for who else would give such a welcome to a fallen man like himself? His own father or mother would have shunned him in this condition. Yet here was one, honoured by hundreds as a saint, who thought it worthwhile to love and welcome him thus. If ever there were a purifier of errant souls, Girish thought, this is he.[15]

Fourth Meeting: 16 May 1897

Swami Brahmananda presided. More than fifty members were present. Sharat Chandra Chakrabarty read and commented on some verses of the Katha Upanishad, remarking that Sri Ramakrishna used to say, "Tucking the nondual knowledge in your pocket, do whatever you like." By this he had meant that the first requisite of life, either social or religious, is the knowledge of Brahman and that one should gain that knowledge before anything else.

Manomohan Mitra described his own meeting and experiences with Sri Ramakrishna. . . . On one occasion he had been very anxious to go to Dakshineswar, but the sky was cloudy, the night advancing, and the river was very rough. In spite of everything, he engaged a boat and went to Dakshineswar. As he entered Ramakrishna's room, the latter burst into tears and said, "You risked your life to see me."

Once Manomohan passed the night at Dakshineswar. It was quite late when Ramakrishna said to him, "What do you want?"

"I want to live with you. I don't want to go home."

"That is not right," Ramakrishna answered. "If you kill the mother fish, the little ones will all die. If you go away, who will look after your family?"[16]

Seventh Meeting: 6 June 1897

Swami Brahmananda presided. About sixty-five members were present. Swami Turiyananda read a hymn in praise of Sri Ramakrishna. He then explained a few verses from the Kena Upanishad.

Girish Chandra Ghosh spoke about the work of Swami Vivekananda, emphasizing that Swamiji was spreading the teachings of Ramakrishna without the least thought of making himself the originator of the ideas he was disseminating.

He continued as follows: "Vivekananda's deep love for the disciples of the Master reveals how deeply he loves and adores Sri Ramakrishna. This boundless love expressed itself one day, just before he was starting for Darjeeling, when he told me, 'I can lay down my life, even this very moment, in the service of the Master.' Through words and deeds he is striving to spread the teachings of the Master so that the entire world may benefit from the spiritual message of Sri Ramakrishna. I call that person ignorant who thinks Swami Vivekananda is separate or different from Sri Ramakrishna."[17]

Twenty-fifth Meeting: 24 October 1897

Swami Brahmananda presided. Brahmachari Prakashananda [later Swami Prakashananda, who became head of the San Francisco centre in 1915], commented on the Katha Upanishad. A question and answer session followed. [The respondent is most likely Girish Chandra Ghosh.]

Q: What was the need for Sri Ramakrishna's advent as an avatar?

A: Before Sri Ramakrishna came, religious ideals and practices were in a state of turmoil. For instance, if someone hides a key in a remote corner of a marketplace, how easily do you think it can be found? Similarly, prior to the advent of Ramakrishna it had become impossible to find the key to the realization of God in the welter of scriptures, sects, and creeds. Sri Ramakrishna's incarnation was needed to bring order and harmony to the various religions. It was he who said, "Every form of true faith in God is a true path to the one and only goal. All religions are true if they lead to God, and if one is sincere and earnest at heart, one can attain Him by following any religion."[18]

Thirty-fourth Meeting: 26 December 1897

Swami Brahmananda presided. Sharat Chandra Chakrabarty gave a talk on the eleventh book of the Bhagavata. A question and answer session followed.

Q: What were Sri Ramakrishna's instructions regarding meditation?

Swami Brahmananda: "Sri Ramakrishna asked everyone to meditate. If a regular habit of meditation is not formed and maintained, it is possible for one to fall from a higher spiritual state to a lower one. Once Sri Ramakrishna asked Tota Puri [his guru] why an illumined soul like him should still continue to meditate. Pointing to his shiny water pot, Tota Puri answered that his water pot would not remain clean and bright if it were not washed and polished regularly."[19]

Living Gods Everywhere

The Bhagavad Gita described the Cosmic God: "With His hands and feet everywhere, with eyes, heads, and faces on all sides, with ears on all sides, He dwells in the world, enveloping all."[20] Vivekananda experienced this and described it in a letter: "May I be born again and again, and suffer thousands of miseries, so that I may worship the only God that exists, the only God I believe in, the sum total of all souls. And above all, my God the wicked, my God the miserable, my God the poor of all races, of all species, is the special object of my worship."[21]

Gradually, Vivekananda's brother disciples began to accept the ideal of service to humanity to alleviate some of the pain and suffering in the world. Whenever there was any natural calamity, Ramakrishna monks and devotees would rush there to help people. Soon, Swami Akhandananda began relief work in Murshidabad. On 15 June 1897, Vivekananda wrote to him:

> I am getting detailed reports of you and becoming more and more delighted. It is that sort of work which can conquer the world. . . . Bravo! Accept a hundred thousand embraces and blessings from me. Work, work, work — I care for nothing else. Work, work, work, even unto death! Those who are weak must make themselves great workers, great heroes — never mind money, it will drop from the heavens. . . . If in the attempt to carry morsels of food to starving mouths, name and possession and all be doomed even, thrice blessed art thou! It is the heart, the heart, that conquers, not the brain.[22]

Margaret Noble (Sister Nivedita) came to India in January 1898. A few months later she and Swami Sadananda led an extensive plague relief drive in Calcutta, cleaning streets themselves, and teaching people how to boil water and to clean their living quarters. Nivedita also founded a school for girls, regarded today as one of the finest schools for girls in Calcutta.

To spread the message of Sri Ramakrishna and Vedanta, Vivekananda founded three magazines. Alasinga Perumal started publication of the *Brahmavadin* journal (now defunct) in Madras; Swami Swarupananda and Captain and Mrs. James Sevier started the *Prabuddha Bharata* journal in Mayavati; and Swami Trigunatitananda began publishing the Bengali journal *Udbodhan* in Calcutta.

And this was only the beginning. The work of the Ramakrishna Mission spread like wildfire and rapidly encircled the globe. By 1912, sixteen centres had been established. Today the official report of the Order lists 163 centres (December 2006) as well as hundreds of unaffiliated organizations dedicated to the ideals of Ramakrishna. The Mission focusses on spiritual, cultural, and educational activities; and it also works in the fields of relief and rehabilitation, health care, publishing, preaching, and rural and tribal development.

The Taittiriya Upanishad states: "Worship your mother as God, worship your father as God, worship your teacher as God, worship your guest as God." Vivekananda was not a mere preacher; he was a man of action. He gave a practical slant to this message of the Upanishad and taught that one should worship the sick, the illiterate, and the poor as God. In formal worship, particular deities require particular worship items: Mother Kali is worshipped with red flowers; Siva is worshipped with bel leaves; Vishnu is worshipped with tulsi leaves. In the Ramakrishna Mission, the sick are worshipped with medicine; the illiterate with education; the poor with food; and all are worshipped with spirituality.

A person becomes great through his or her sacrifice. Vivekananda told his monastic brothers and his disciples: "Remember, for the salvation of his soul and for the good and happiness of many, a sannyasin is born in the world. To sacrifice his own life for others; to alleviate the misery of millions rending the air with their cries; to wipe away tears from the eyes of widows; to console the hearts of bereaved mothers; to provide the ignorant and depressed masses with ways and means in the struggle for existence, and make them stand on their own feet; to broadcast the teachings of the scriptures to one and all without distinction for their spiritual and material welfare; to rouse the sleeping lion of Brahman in the hearts of all beings by the knowledge of Vedanta, a sannyasin is born in the world."[23]

Vivekananda's rousing call inspired the minds of future generations. That is the key to the continuity of the Ramakrishna Mission. He said: "Throw aside your meditation, throw away your salvation and such things! Put your whole heart and soul into the work to which I have consecrated myself. . . . I love you all ever so much, but I wish you would all die working for others."[24] This was not a curse. It was a great blessing from the founding father of the Order to his followers. What he meant was: Let ego and selfishness die. Be immortal.

30 Appendix

The Ramakrishna Order: Sources of Inspiration

Swami Vivekananda officially inaugurated the Ramakrishna Math and Mission on 1 May 1897 in Calcutta, and it now has (as of December 2006) 163 centres all over the world. Swamiji understood the problem of organizing, but at the same time he realized that no religion can function or spread without an organization. The only thing that can keep organized work from becoming corrupt, he felt, is purity of life.

No organization can function without some rules. Again, history tells us how too many rules and regulations inhibit religion. Before Buddha, the Hindu lawgivers and priests set rules and prescribed religious rites and rituals, and the people observed them mechanically. As a result, the Hindu religion was reduced to mere formalities.

The Scribes expanded the Code of Moses into thousands of detailed precepts designed to meet every circumstance, and as a result a pall of stagnation fell over Judaism. The religion of Christ also was organized by his disciples and followers. Then gradually doctrines, dogmas, rituals, ecclesiastical laws and rules restrained the spirit of Christianity and created hundreds of denominations.

What is lacking in religion today? It is love and freedom. Churches, temples, mosques, and synagogues are reverberating with prayers, music, sermons, and religious discourses, yet there is emptiness in the minds of people. Hunger for spirituality is innate in all human beings, and this hunger can be satisfied only by practising religion. Man has the power to transcend all limitations. We cannot change the world but we can change ourselves; and when we change ourselves the world begins to change. This is what Sri Ramakirshna taught and this, again, is at the core of the Ramakrishna movement.

'Sources of Inspiration' is a compilation of utterances and writings of the founders, followers, and admirers of the Ramakrishna Order.

The Beginning

Sri Ramakrishna was once seated in his room, talking about three salient disciplines of the Vaishnava religion: love of God's name, compassion for all living beings, and service to the devotees. Repeating the word compassion, he went into samadhi. After a while he returned to normal consciousness and said to the devotees: "How foolish to speak of compassion! Man is an insignificant worm crawling on the earth — and he is to show compassion to others! This is absurd. It must not be compassion, but service to all. Recognize them as God's manifestations and serve them." Only Narendra understood the implication of the Master's words.

Leaving the room, Narendra said to the others:

"What a wonderful light I have discovered in those words of the Master! How beautifully he has reconciled the ideal of bhakti with the knowledge of Vedanta, generally interpreted as dry, austere, and incompatible with human sentiments! What a grand, natural, and sweet synthesis! . . . Those following the paths of karma [action] and yoga [contemplation] are similarly benefited by these words of the Master. The embodied being cannot remain even for a minute without activity. All his activities should be directed to the service of man, the manifestation of God upon earth, and this will accelerate his progress towards the goal. If it be the will of God, I shall one day proclaim this noble truth before the world at large. I shall make it the common property of all — the wise and the foolish, the rich and the poor, the brahmin and the pariah."[1]

Sri Ramakrishna

[*In Cossipore, when Narendra said that his goal in life was to remain immersed in smadhi, Ramakrishna said to him*]: "Shame on you! You are asking for such an insignificant thing [samadhi], I thought that you would be like a big banyan tree, and that thousands of people would rest in your shade. But now I see that you are seeking your own liberation."[2]

[*Pointing to his young disciples, the Master said to Narendra*]: "I leave them in your care. Love them intensely and see that they practise spiritual disciplines even after my death, and that they do not return home."[3]

[*In Cossipore the senior Gopal bought twelve pieces of cloth and twelve rosaries of rudraksha beads to distribute among the monks. He dyed the cloths in the ochre colour himself. When the Master heard about it, he said to Gopal*]:

"You will attain a thousand times more virtue if you present those ochre cloths and rosaries to my children rather than giving them to the monks of Jagannath ghat. Where else will you find such all-renouncing monks? Each of them is equal to a thousand monks."[4]

[*At Cossipore Ramakrishna transmitted his spiritual power to Narendra, and said*]: "Today I have given you all and have become a fakir. By the force of the power transmitted by me, great things will be done by you; only after that will you go where you came from."[5]

Holy Mother

[*In 1890 Holy Mother visited Bodh Gaya. There she noticed how comfortably the members of a local monastery lived, with all their physical wants supplied. She later recalled*]:

"Ah, how much I wept, how often I prayed to the Master! That is why you see all these monasteries established by his grace. Immediately after his passing away, the children renounced the world and sought out a temporary shelter. But soon after, they began to wander about independently. I felt very sad and prayed to the Master: 'Oh Master, you came down to earth, had fun with a few companions, and then departed in a happy mood. Was that the end of everything? If so, what was the need of assuming a human body and going through all this suffering? I have seen many sadhus at Varanasi and Vrindaban who live on alms and seek shelter under trees. There is no dearth of sadhus like them. I cannot bear the sight of my children, who have renounced everything in your name, going from door to door for a morsel of food. I fervently pray to you that those who give up the world in your name may not lack simple food and clothes. Let them live together, with you and your teachings as their centre. Those who are afflicted with the sorrows of the world will come to them and obtain peace by listening to your teachings. That is the purpose of your advent, isn't it so? I cannot control myself when I see them drifting about helplessly.' Afterwards Naren slowly organized all this."[6]

"Love alone is the essential thing. Our organization is growing only through love. I am their mother. . . . They are my children and have taken shelter with Sri Ramakrishna. Wherever they go the Master will look after them."[7]

Swami Vivekananda

"This Math [monastery] is established to work out one's own liberation, and to train oneself to do good to the world in every way, along the lines laid down by Sri Bhagavan Ramakrishna. . . . For want of learning, religious orders become degraded. Therefore learning should always be cultivated. In the absence of renunciation and austerity, luxury takes possession of the organization; hence the spirit of renunciation and austerity should always be kept bright. Propagation of its ideas keeps the vitality of the Order strong. Henceforth you should never cease from preaching work."[8]

[On 9 December 1898 Belur Math was formally consecrated when Vivekananda installed the Master's relics in the shrine. Swamiji carried the casket of relics on his own shoulder, and on his way to the shrine he said to a disciple]:

"The Master once told me, 'I will go and live wherever you take me, carrying me on your shoulder, be it under a tree or in the humblest cottage.' With faith in that gracious promise I myself am now carrying him to the site of our future Math. Know for certain, my boy, that so long as his name inspires his followers with the ideal of purity, holiness, and charity for all men, even so long shall he, the Master, sanctify this place with his presence.

"It will be a centre in which will be recognized and practised a grand harmony of all creeds and faiths as exemplified in the life of Sri Ramakrishna, and religion in its universal aspect, alone, will be preached. And from this centre of universal toleration will go forth the shining message of goodwill, peace, and harmony to deluge the whole world."[9]

"The spiritual impact that has come here to Belur will last fifteen hundred years — and this will be a great university. Do not think I imagine it, I see it."[10]

"Here — here [pointing to the Belur Monastery], I left all my spiritual gems and jewels. You [monks] preserve them carefully. Just look after them. Those who will work with these treasures are coming — coming from a distant place. They will come after five or six generations. They will enjoy these spiritual treasures. Please preserve them. I sang only the āgamani [a special song related to the advent of Mother Uma]; you preserve my message."[11]

"Listen, Sri Ramakrishna came for the good of this world and gave his life for all human beings. I am also sacrificing my life for them, and all of

Belur Math from the Ganges

you will have to do the same. Whatever you see at present [in the Rama-krishna Mission] is just the beginning. As I shed the blood of my heart, know for certain that it will produce great heroes and many lionhearted souls who will work for the Lord, and they will overturn the world in the future."[12]

"This Math that we are building will harmonize all creeds, all stand-points. Just as Sri Ramakrishna held highly liberal views, this Math, too, will be a centre for propagating similar ideas. The blazing light of univer-sal harmony that will emanate from here will flood the whole world.

"The capable sannyasin children of Sri Ramakrishna, the teacher of the great synthesis of religions, will be honoured everywhere as the teachers of men. . . . The real self-sacrificing sannyasins of the Math will be the centre of the preservation and spread of religious ideas. . . . One spray from the full ocean of his spirituality, if realized, will make gods of men. Such a synthesis of universal ideas you will not find in the history of the world again."[13]

"To work with undaunted energy! What fear! Who is powerful enough to thwart you! We shall crush the stars to atoms, and unhinge the universe. Don't you know who we are? We are the servants of Sri Ramakrishna."[14]

Swami Brahmananda

"Swamiji did not utter these rules of the Order from the physical plane; he raised his mind to a higher realm and then gave dictation and Tarak-da [Swami Shivananda] wrote them down. He delineated them with a view to spreading the ideas and ideals of Sri Ramakrishna for the good of humanity. Everyone, whether man or woman, rich or poor, high or low, has an equal right to the spiritual heritage and service of Sri Ramakrishna. Blessed is he who serves the Master and follows his teach-ings! Accept those instructions of Swamiji with candid faith; practise them in your lives and then spread them in all directions. As a result you will see that the evil influence of the Kali [Dark Age] will diminish and the Golden Age will come in sight."[15]

"This Belur Math is like Kailash [the abode of Shiva]. Here the guru and the Ganges are present. Swamiji also left his body here. This is Vaikuntha [the abode of Vishnu]. . . . Tarak-da, I shall never be able to cut my attachment for Belur Math. Even after my death I shall watch Belur Math from above."[16]

Swami Shivananda

"From my little experience I tell you, children of Sri Ramakrishna, that our organization lasts as long as the spirit of God pervades its atmosphere. Love, catholicity, purity, and selflessness are the corner-stones of our organization. No man-made laws can save it from ruin when selfishness eats into its vitals. If you all try to become perfect — keeping intact your allegiance to this Math, which gives you every kind of facility for reaching that perfection — you will add a leaf to the life of the organization. Swamiji shed his blood for the Math. His spirit is still hovering over us. This Math is the visible body of Sri Rama-krishna. All those that have gone before us are still with us in spirit to help us in all possible ways. We must unfurl all sails so that we may take advantage of the divine wind that is ever blowing to take us to the destined goal."[17]

"The more there will be trials, tribulations, and adversities, the more the power of the Master's Order (*sangha shakti*) will be roused. All great achievements have to pass through many obstacles. The more we shall face opposition and adversity the more our love, faith and reliance on the Master will increase. This organization came into existence for setting in motion the religion of the age (*yuga-dharma*), and it is the Master who is working through each individual belonging to it. The activities of the Ramakrishna Mission will continue to progress for centuries; no one will be able to resist its course. These are the words of Swamiji himself, who was a *rishi* seeing the past, present, and future."[18]

"The love, affection, and respect which the members of the Order feel for one another constitute the life force of this organization. . . . After leaving the gross body, the Master now lives in this sangha. . . . It is to save all . . . that he came down as Sri Ramakrishna."[19]

Swami Premananda

"Elephants have two sets of teeth: one outside — the tusks — and another inside to chew food. The activities of our Mission are like the elephant's tusks. Whatever work you may do — managing hospitals or conducting relief work — unless you have character, all will be in vain. What is wanted is character, purity, steadfast devotion to God. If you have them, you will prosper; otherwise you will totally fail.

(*To the lay members*) "It is no good being only members of the Mission. You must build up your own character. You must make the whole world your own through love, so that people may find inspiration from your selflessness, renunciation, and purity. You must drive away all egotism and pride from your heart and consider yourselves as servants of the Lord and thus serve humanity.

"Our Master never sought name and fame, and so they have come to him in profusion. Swamiji often said in his later life that he was disgusted with name and fame. Be you all men of character. Grow into gods. Only then will the work of the Mission prosper. This is my earnest prayer to you all."[20]

"Don't think we are forming a sect in the name of Sri Ramakrishna. You will fall as soon as you introduce sectarianism in the Ramakrishna Mission. Nonsectarianism does not mean indifference to your own faith. Be liberal and at the same time have steadfast devotion to your ideal. Let the Hindus, Muslims, and Christians come to our monastery; I am ready to embrace them all and make them my own. To love all beings is the basis of the Ramakrishna Mission."[21]

Swami Adbhutananda

[About preaching, Sri Ramakrishna said: "It is very difficult to preach religion. It is not possible to do so without receiving a command from God." One day Swami Adbhutananda (Latu Maharaj) discussed the method of preaching by the Ramakrishna Order]:

"Can one preach religion simply by beating a drum? Is religion something external to us, something that one person speaks about and another person accepts? Religion is realization, and one cannot realize the truth through noise and fanfare. The more a preacher shouts, the more people's minds turn outward; and unless the mind is turned inward, God-realization is not possible.

"What an upsurge of religion there was here in Calcutta a few years ago! Preachers of the Salvation Army were found speaking on religion at almost every crossroads of the city. The Brahmo leaders used to preach their doctrines in their temples. The Vaishnavites would sing kirtan in their worship halls. Just think of all those meetings! One day Keshab Sen spoke on the New Dispensation in Beadon Square, the next day Reverend Kali Krishna Banerjee spoke on Christianity, and the third day Swami Krishnananda spoke on Hinduism. People gathered around them and listened. One preacher abused Hinduism and another defended it. What a storm of religious preaching! But what has come of all that? Where are they now? Those religious leaders tried to attract people through their preaching. Meanwhile, another group was devoting its time to silent meditation and prayer and directing its energies to the realization of God. And now don't you see multitudes gathering around this second group?

"Inevitably, if there is no substance inside, a person's words will sound hollow and carry no conviction. There must be renunciation, dispassion, and genuine love for God; only then will people believe you. The Lord's will works in this peculiar way. Look at Swami Vivekananda's life. After practising hard spiritual disciplines he got the command from the Master to preach, and people have accepted what he said. With one lecture Swamiji became world-famous."[22]

[*A monastic order needs some rules and guidelines to function but they are not applicable to those who are illumined souls. The following conversations took place between Swami Vivekananda and Swami Adbhutananda regarding some of the rules*]:

Swami Vivekananda made a rule at the Belur monastery that the monks must get up at 4:00 a.m. and, after washing quickly, sit down to meditate in the shrine room. The next morning a bell was rung and everyone was expected to rise. Swami Adbhutananda said later: "I did not like the rule, so without telling anyone I decided to leave the monastery. That morning, as I was leaving with my cloth and towel, Swamiji stopped me and asked, 'Where are you going?' I said. 'To Calcutta.' 'Why?' Then I told him: 'You have recently returned from the West and are introducing new rules and regulations. It will not be easy for me to abide by them. I do not have the degree of control over my mind that it will settle down to meditate when a bell is rung. Who knows when my mind might become absorbed? I have not yet reached that state. If you can do it, that is fine.'

"Then Swamiji said: 'All right. You may go.' But I had hardly reached the gate when he called me back and said: 'You don't have to observe this rule. You should do as you like. These rules are meant for the novices.' I said, 'I am glad you said that.'"

Another time Swami Adbhutananda said: "Swamiji wanted to see the monks strong and healthy, so he made a rule that everyone should do physical exercises with dumbbells. I was at the monastery then. I went to him and asked: 'Brother, what is this? Are we to do physical exercises at this age? That is impossible for me.' Swamiji broke into laughter and did not say anything."

Sometime in 1902, the last year of Swami Vivekananda's life, Swamiji told Latu Maharaj: "Leto, what do you think? This is just the beginning. The people of Europe and America are now starting to appreciate the greatness of our Master. After a few years they will accept his ideas. Now they are only a handful, but later hundreds will come. Then you will understand what this Vivekananda has done."

Latu Maharaj listened to Swamiji and then said quietly: "Brother, have you done anything new? Haven't you walked the same path that the other great teachers have travelled — Buddha, Shankara, and so on?"

Then Swamiji said: "You are right, my dear Plato. I have only followed in their footsteps." And Swamiji folded his hands and saluted the ancient teachers.[23]

Swami Yogananda

[*Regarding the advent of Sri Ramakrishna*] "There have always been various religious paths, countless scriptures, and holy places in every country. In spite of that why is there a decline in religion? Because in the course of time all ideals become lost. Therefore God incarnates Himself to explain the hidden mystery of religion and to show the ideal. . . . By the grace of the Master I have attained so much knowledge and devotion that I am unable to express it all."[24]

Swami Saradananda

"The Master came to make religion easy. People were being crushed under the weight of rules and regulations. To repeat the Lord's name or to worship Him, no special time and place is necessary. In whatever condition one may be, one can take His name. The Master never gave too much importance to these external observances. As to the means, adopt whichever suits you best. If you like God with form, that will also lead you to the goal. If you like God without form, well and good; stick to it and you will progress. If you doubt His very existence, then better put the question to Him thus: 'I do not know whether you exist or not, whether you are formless or have form. Do please grant that I may know your real nature.'"[25]

"Remember, the ideal and revelation that had been manifested through Sri Ramakrishna and voiced forth through Swami Vivekananda came as a divine dispensation for the present age and it is our solemn duty to realize them in our individual lives and instil them into others."[26]

"The Ramakrishna Order, to promote its spiritual culture and realize the doctrines of the time-honoured Vedanta Philosophy, has engaged itself since the very inception to serve the Lord by serving humanity to the best of its ability, remembering the imperative scriptural injunction to look upon man as nothing less than the Deity Himself (*Jivo Brahmaiva nāparah*). . . . Therefore, it will be readily understood that the Ramakrishna Mission has nothing to do whatsoever with any kind of political movement."[27]

Swami Ramakrishnananda

"In the beginning we had no thought of mission. We believed that all we had to do was to realize the ideal the Master had set before us, which meant living and serving humbly."[28]

"Whatever the Master makes me speak, I speak like a gramophone. I don't claim any personal credit from it. . . . Do you think it is we who are preaching his wonderful life and message? Far from it. The Master himself is doing it in mysterious ways. Wherever we go to preach about him we find that the field is already prepared. Some are blessed by him in dreams; some get spiritual initiation directly from him; some are attracted by the quality of his teachings, which clothe the highest truth in simple language and parables; and some are inspired by seeing and hearing his disciples."[29]

"Sri Ramakrishna, the divine incarnation of this age, realized and preached the harmony of religions. Buddha, Christ, Muhammad, and other world teachers — each proclaimed that the religion taught by him is the only way to salvation. The difference between Sri Ramakrishna and other prophets is that he himself preached no new religion, but practised all religions in his life and experienced the universal truth underlying them all. His message can be summed up in the sentence: 'As many faiths, so many paths.'"[30]

Swami Abhedananda

"The mission of Bhagavan Sri Ramakrishna was to show by his living example how a truly spiritual man, being dead to the world of senses, can live on the plane of God-consciousness; it was to prove that each individual soul is immortal and potentially divine.

"For the first time it was demonstrated that all religions were like so many paths leading to the same goal, that the realization of the same Almighty Being is the highest ideal of Christianity, Mohammedanism, Judaism, Zoroastrianism, Hinduism, as well as of all other religions of the world. Sri Ramakrishna's mission was to proclaim the eternal truth that God is one but has many aspects, and that the same one God is worshipped by different nations under various names and forms; that He is personal, impersonal, and beyond both; that He is with name and form and yet nameless and formless.

"His mission was to establish the worship of the Divine Mother and thus to elevate the ideal of womanhood into Divine Motherhood. His mission was to show by his own example that true spirituality can be transmitted and that salvation can be obtained through the grace of a Divine Incarnation. His mission was to declare before the world that psychic powers and the power of healing are obstacles in the path of the attainment of God-consciousness.

"The days of prophecy have passed before our eyes. The manifestations of the Divine powers of one who is worshipped today by thousands as the latest Incarnation of Divinity, we have witnessed with our eyes. Blessed are they who have seen him and touched his holy feet. May the glory of Sri Ramakrishna be felt by all nations of the earth, may his Divine power be manifested in the earnest and sincere souls of his devotees of all countries in all ages to come, is the prayer of his spiritual child and servant."[31]

Swami Turiyananda

"It is not so easy to speak about Sri Ramakrishna's philosophy. It seems to me that to encourage the followers of all religions, he declared, 'As many faiths, so many paths.' He made this statement after he himself had practised the disciplines of various religious paths and experienced that their paths lead to the same Truth.

"The ultimate Truth is one and nondual. It is called by various names: Brahman, Paramatman, Bhagavan [Lord], God, and so on. Whoever has realized that Truth has tried to express it according to his own temperament and understanding by giving it a particular name. But nobody has been able to express the *whole* truth. 'What he is, he is' — that is the final conclusion of those who have realized him.

"Hanuman said to Rama: 'O Lord, while I identify myself with the body I am your servant. When I consider myself as an individual soul, I am a part of you. And when I look upon myself as the Atman, I am one with you — this is my firm conviction.' Sri Ramakrishna referred to this statement as the best conclusion of different phases of spiritual experience.

"The Master used to experience a state beyond all thought and idea. That state transcends name and form, words and mind. There exists only One without a second, beyond the realm of prakriti [that is, beyond relativity]. Where is the doctrine of superimposition or the doctrine of no creation in that realm of Oneness? And yet again, all doctrines — whether of superimposition, or of no creation, or of transformation, etc. — originate from him.

"The *main thing* is we must see God. When we see him, everything else disappears. One experiences him as everything. Before we see him we have doubts and confusion, and all sorts of theories and controversies. But these cease to exist as soon as we see him. Then one experiences uninterrupted peace and bliss.

"Sri Ramakrishna's philosophy therefore is: In whatever way and at any cost we must attain God. The Master said, 'Tie the nondual knowledge in the corner of your cloth and then do as you please.' This means: Once you attain him, it does not matter which doctrine your temperament bids you to uphold. Liberation is assured when you know him."[32]

"Those who profess to be the children of Sri Ramakrishna must have yoga, bhakti, karma, jnana, nay, everything. For, Sri Ramakrishna stands for the synthesis and harmony of all religious paths. The spiritual growth of a person following a particular line was the rule in the past. But now one should have an all-round development combined with magnanimity of heart to love others."[33]

Swami Akhandananda

"Sri Ramakrishna one day cried aloud from the house-top for those young enthusiasts who were to come to him and pour forth their life's offerings on the altar of his service, and they came. But that cry has not ended there; it is still ringing through the air and shall continue for aeons. Many have come after that, many are still coming, and many more will come in the future.

"Remember what high hopes Swamiji cherished of you — the youth of the country. You fairest jasmines on earth, bring all that whiteness and fragrance you have and lay them on the altar of Sri Ramakrishna — of Humanity. All that is wanted of you today is that genuine feeling, that love and sympathy for the poor and the downtrodden which Sri Ramakrishna and Swami Vivekananda had in their heart of hearts.

"Read Swami Vivekananda's works and you will find them replete all through with this one behest to us — sacrifice the lesser for the greater; make your life an offering for the service of humanity and above all, of the poor and the ignorant of the country. It was to give effect to this cherished desire of his life that he inaugurated this movement known as the Ramakrishna Mission."[34]

"Our Master is living and moving in all as Narayana [God]. The seed of this *Religion of Service* was in him. Therefore you now see the tree and its branches. At Deoghar he said to Mathur Babu: 'Feed these poor people, give them clothing and oil [for anointing their heads in the scorching heat], or else I will not proceed to Varanasi [for pilgrimage].' That is how the wheel of this Religion of Service for this age started rolling."[35]

Swami Vijnanananda

"Sri Ramakrishna came to demonstrate the harmony of religions. Swamiji said, 'There should be a rule in our rule book that no one should criticize any religion or any followers of other religions.'"[36]

Swami Subodhananda

"Sometimes the Master would say, 'The Divine Mother Herself has come to visit the world in human form [*meaning himself*]; when people of all sects assemble here, this body will not last.'

"One day while walking in the Panchavati at Dakshineswar, the Master went into ecstasy. Then, facing the northwest, he pointed to himself and said, 'Look, the Mother is saying that the more a person thinks of me, the more quickly he will understand the highest truths of religion.' Again, pointing to the northwest, he said, 'I shall be born again in that direction; then many people will attain knowledge.'

"On another occasion the Master told me about himself: 'This body is a cage of flesh and bones, but the Mother is playing inside it. . . . He who was Rama and Krishna is living in this body.'

"It is better to live on rice and spinach at Belur Math than to have good food somewhere else.

"My last prayer is that the blessings of the Master be always on the Order."[37]

Swami Trigunatitananda

"All the prophets, sages, and incarnations of God are nothing else but messengers to bring the message from Heaven. Ramakrishna could explain beautifully that there is or can be not one messenger only, not one path only, not one incarnation of God, but many, so that the different types of minds could be satisfied."[38]

Swami Niranjanananda

[*Although there are no recorded statements by Swami Niranjanananda about the Ramakrishna Order, his austere life and selfless service remain a source of inspiration to future generations. Many years later, referring to the austerities of Niranjanananda and other disciples, Holy Mother recalled*]:

"What an austere life they led at the Baranagore monastery! Niranjan and others often starved themselves. They spent all their time in japa and meditation. One day they resolved among themselves: 'Well, we have renounced everything in the name of Sri Ramakrishna. Let us see if he will supply us with food if we simply depend on him. We will not tell anyone about our needs, nor will we go out for alms.' Saying so, they covered themselves with their chadars [shawls] and sat down for meditation. The whole day passed. It was late at night when they heard someone knocking at the door. Naren got up and said to one of his brother monks: 'Please open the door and see who is there. First, check if he has anything in his hand.' What a miracle! When the door was opened, they found that a man had come from Lala Babu's Krishna temple near the Ganges with various delicacies in his hand. They were overjoyed and became convinced of the protecting hand of Sri Ramakrishna. They then offered that food to the Master and partook of the prasad. Such things happened many times."[39]

Swami Advaitananda

[*An organization succeeds not because it is big or because it is long established, but because there are people in it who live it, sleep it, dream it, and build a future for it. Swami Advaitananda was one of them. He was eight years older than Ramakrishna and the oldest among all the monastic disciples of the Master. His love and dedicated service speak more than words about his love for the Ramakrishna Order.*]:

"In the early part of 1898, a plot of land was purchased at Belur on the bank of the Ganges for the permanent home of the Order, and Advaitananda was entrusted to make the land ready for construction. The site had previously been used as a dock for repairing boats and steamers, and the ground was uneven.

"Pioneering work is always difficult. Advaitananda worked every day until noon; then he took his bath in the Ganges and sitting under a tree he ate his lunch, which had been sent from the monastery. Apart from levelling the ground and doing other construction work, Advaitananda started a vegetable garden and a dairy farm. Swami Adbhutananda once recalled about the early days: 'Without Gopal-da the monks of Belur Math would not have had vegetables along with their rice. He worked so hard to produce various kinds of vegetables in the monastery garden.'

"Once Advaitananda went to visit Holy Mother in Calcutta. Mother was happy to see the old swami. In Dakshineswar he had been her devoted attendant. While eating prasad, Advaitananda inquired about Mother's rheumatic pain. She replied: 'That rheumatic pain is my constant companion. It will not leave me in this life. However, how are you?' 'I also suffer from rheumatic pain,' answered Advaitananda. 'But I work hard. I don't get much help from the boys. I am growing various kinds of vegetables — okra, eggplant, plantain, and so on — in the monastery garden. As a result, nowadays we seldom buy vegetables. Sometimes I send some vegetables to you.' Holy Mother: 'My son, you are an old-timer. Your life is different from the modern boys, who generally don't care for household matters. The monastery is like a family home, where you need food, clothing, and other necessities. Without these things how can you live there? So it is your duty to take care of the Master's children.'

"The young novitiates, who were educated in modern schools and colleges, could hardly rise to Advaitananda's standard of perfection regarding work, and for that reason they had a very hard time with him. Many of them received mild scoldings from the old swami, but they took his criticisms more as a token of his affection than as any indication of anger. One day he had a revelation, which he described later: 'The Master has shown me that it is he who is manifested through all. Then who is there to blame or whom to criticize?' After this experience Advaitananda ceased finding fault with anyone, however great might be the latter's errors. Turiyananda once said: 'We are much indebted to Gopal-da, because we learned the secret of work from him. He was organized and concentrated in everything he did. And he was very methodical in his habits. Until his last day he regularly practised meditation.'

"Humour breaks the barrier of age and eradicates monotony, sadness, and depression in life. For example, a sad countenance was an offense according to the rules of the Franciscan Order: The brothers were expected to turn a smiling face to God and to humanity. They were to make the Lord glad by their gaiety and not weary Him with whining and lamentation. The disciples of Sri Ramakrishna also did not care for a religion that was obsessed with fear or made life depressing. They learned from the Master that humour has its place in religion, and the bliss of God that they experienced was manifest in their lives. Advaitananda had a wonderful sense of humour and loved to tease the brothers. For example, he disliked tea while Swami Subodhananda loved it; so one day he said to Subodhananda: 'Look, don't drink tea. You will get blood dysentery.' But Subodhananda asserted emphatically, 'Gopal-da, each drop of tea produces a drop of blood.' 'All right, brother, drink more,' Advaitananda said jokingly. All laughed."[40]

Swami Shuddhananda

"Whether you believe in an impersonal or a personal God, whether you believe in Vishnu or Shakti or Muhammad or Buddha, Sri Ramakrishna's teachings apply equally to you. Not only that, he had a message even for an atheist. We hear that to an atheist he recommended prayer in the following form: 'O God, I do not know if Thou existest or not. If Thou art, reveal Thyself to me.'"[41]

"By Swamiji's grace and coming in close contact with him, this much I have understood that all of our actions — such as relief work, educational work, hospital work, or giving lectures and classes — are all worship of God, to spread His glory. The goal of every activity of the Mission is to manifest Sri Ramakrishna. Seeing our work, let the people be attracted to the Master and Swamiji and not to us. The goal of our lives is to manifest the glory of the Master and Swamiji, and the Ramakrishna Mission. Otherwise, whatever great work we may be involved in, it is neither Swamiji's work nor Ramakrishna's mission."[42]

Swami Virajananda

"What Swamiji wrote about the Ramakrishna Math is equally true of the Ramakrishna Mission: 'This organization is his [Sri Ramakrishna's] very body, and in this organization itself he is ever-present.' The true worship for the members of this organization consists in active participation in all its undertakings, and not in being mere believers in its goodness, and passive spectators of its successes and failures. Sri Ramakrishna is guiding and will ever guide his Mission. But he expects us to be willing partners in this divine lila (play). Our faith in Sri Ramakrishna and his Mission must be galvanized into active service for him in his diverse human forms. Short of this, mere love, admiration, or sympathy for organized activity will not lead us much beyond the traditional psychological attitudes and expressions of devotion for the Lord. . . . I cannot do better than conclude by putting you in mind of the inspiring words of Swamiji to his young disciples: 'I love you all ever so much, but I would wish to see you all die working for others.'"[43]

Swami Paramananda

"Sri Ramakrishna's greatest contribution to the modern world of religious thought was to bring into it a note of definiteness. Our present age of multiple theories and intellectual speculation had set the hearts of men adrift in regard to God and the ultimate realities. Here we find Sri Ramakrishna rising like a star of hope in the midst of chaos and confusion. His equipment and self-expression did not lie in erudition and intellectual cleverness but in direct vision and perception. When we approach him, he does not try to confuse our minds with theological doctrines and metaphysical implications. Instead, he gives us this unique and convincing statement: 'Yes, I have seen God and known Him, and furthermore, I can help you to see and know Him.'

"He demonstrated by his life and example that there is nothing but

Unity, that all men are the product of the same Substance whether it be called Brahma, Vishnu, Shiva, Kali, Allah, Jehovah, Father in Heaven, or in the terms of the monists, the Absolute, the One, the Eternal Brahman. . . . The mission of Sri Ramakrishna was not to create another new sect in the already overcrowded religious atmosphere of India and of the world at large. His rare gift to mankind cannot be overestimated. His mode of living, his simplicity of conduct, his naive, childlike parables, dynamic with the force of Truth, disarmed everyone completely.

"To unveil the illumined life of Sri Ramakrishna is to venture to portray the invisible spirit. May his passion for humility and service, sanctity and ecstasy of God, stimulate our minds so that they may reach out and attain the unattainable."[44]

Swami Achalananda

"The main foundations of the Ramakrishna Order are loyalty and love. Swami Shivananda said: 'The Master tied us together through love, and this vast organization has grown up through this cord of love. As long as this knot of love remains tight, the Order will continue smoothly.' I tell you from my personal experience that I left home not so much out of renunciation but by the attraction of Swamiji's and other direct disciples' pure, unearthly love; and I am still living hypnotized by their love.

"If we cannot maintain mutual love and respect, then in the near future the deadly, destructive result will definitely crop up. The activities of the Order should not be conducted through rigid rules and regulations, but rather through love and affection. Otherwise, discontent and disagreeableness among the monastic members will rise; moreover, a master-servant relationship will develop; work will turn into dry duty rather than worship; and karma-yoga will end in karma-bhoga [full of suffering]. . . . So, I fervently request the authorities of the Ramakrishna Math and Mission and the heads of the branch centres to conduct the activities of the Order with the Belur Math rules with love; and I request the monastic members to be respectful of the senior monks and do their respective duties thinking that all work belongs to the Master and Swamiji. That will make our lives blissful and our Order will be beautiful."[45]

Swami Atmananda

"There was a rule in the Belur Monastery. Swamiji set the rule that the monks should not have any personal belongings. Accordingly, whenever we received anything from anybody, we deposited it with the manager of the monastery. Once when I was at Rishikesh, a rich man gave me a water pot and a blanket. As soon as I returned to Belur Math, I gave those two things to the manager."[46]

Girish Chandra Ghosh

[*On 29 January 1910 Swami Vivekananda's birth anniversary was observed at Ramakrishna Advaita Ashrama in Varanasi. Girish was ill at the time, but he nonetheless wrote a long and valuable article,* Vivekanander Sadhan-phal ['The Result of Vivekananda's Sadhana'] *in Bengali and it was read at the meeting. Here are some excerpts from that article*]:

"Ramakrishna taught according to the temperament of each individual. For example, he advised some to renounce everything and devote their entire lives to realizing God; and again he told others to treat people as God and serve them. Both paths will lead to the same goal. Vivekananda attained perfection in each. The monks of the Ramakrishna Order are following their leader's ideal: The monks of the Ramakrishna Mission Home of Service worship the living gods in the hospital, and the monks of the Ramakrishna Advaita Ashrama worship the same God in the temple.

"Vedanta philosophy is based on same-sightedness. It is not a matter of study but realization. I know myself, so I should know that you and I are the same. This realization depends on sadhana. For that reason, Swami Vivekananda, the great disciple of Sri Ramakrishna, established these two centres [in Varanasi] on the basis of equality. Therefore, let us all say in one voice: 'Victory to Ramakrishna! Victory to Vivekananda!'"[47]

"Some people ask, 'What kind of monks are in the Ramakrishna Mission?' Some ridicule the monks, saying, 'Monks of the Kaliyuga!' Some say: 'Ramakrishna was a good man but we can't understand this type of monk. They wear shoes and clean clothes; they live in nice houses and have no restriction or discrimination about food. They are sannyasins in name only! All are swamis in ochre robes!' Let me say a few things to satisfy the curiosity of these critics.

"If you carefully investigate the area where those clean-clothed monks live, you will see that they are seated by the side of patients at midnight and thus helping the patients' relatives to get some rest. You will see that those monks are carrying food, which they prepared by begging money, to a patient living in a dilapidated house. During the plague epidemic in Calcutta, early in the morning you could see those monks in the company of sweepers, cleaning the narrow lanes in the slums that were overlooked by the municipal workers. You will see them teaching and helping poor, illiterate people and engaged in other philanthropic activities. If you go to Varanasi, you will see these clean-clothed monks at the Ganges ghat, picking up the helpless and dying people who were rejected by society, nursing them in their Ashrama, and thereby saving their lives. You will see the same thing in the Kankhal Ashrama. In the orphanage at Berhampore, you will see these monks rescuing orphaned children from the famine-stricken areas of Murshidabad and raising and educating them. O critics of these clean-clothed monks, you will see them wherever there is flood, famine, plague, and smallpox epidemic — from where even the wild monkeys run away."[48]

M. (Mahendra Nath Gupta)

"All activities of the Ramakrishna Mission are wonderful.... 'Renounce everything and hold onto God': this was the main message of the Master. And you (addressing the Ramakrishna monks) are the embodiments of that message."[49]

"An education for the purpose of attaining money, a house, a car, and name and fame is not true education according to the ideal and traditions of India. The Ramakrishna monks of Belur Math are imparting education according to our country's tradition. They are harmonizing spiritual education — faith in God, service to the guru and to the elderly, service to the poor and to society — with secular education. This education develops our culture and our character. Memorizing some books in order to pass an examination is not considered to be true education.

"Swami Vivekananda established this Ramakrishna Math. When some of his brother disciples asked, 'Why is it necessary to build this monastery?' Vivekananda replied: 'I have experienced the pains of hunger acutely because I had no food. That is the reason I have founded this monastery. In the future many young boys will come and they will at least get some food here.' In this Kaliyuga, people are totally dependent on food for their life. Their faces dry up if they miss one meal. Again, as a bird rests on a branch of a tree after becoming tired of flying, so monks who are tired after practising sadhana will be able to rest in this monastery. For these reasons Swamiji established this monastery.

"Again with this Ramakrishna Math in the centre, there will be the regeneration of India first and then of the world."[50]

(To a devotee) "Your problems will be solved if you have the company of the holy. Please visit the Ramakrishna Math at Belur. It is the Master who made this monastery. As a man goes to a hospital to cure his disease, so one must go to the monastery in order to cure the disease of ignorance. In this age, you will find no better hospital for curing this mental disease."[51]

Sister Devamata (Laura Glenn)

"I went to India as a member of the Order of Ramakrishna, a remarkable nonsectarian religious organization which in its methods and ideals strives to unite East and West, ancient and modern, action and meditation, philanthropy and self-help, broad catholicity and one-pointed devotion to a Chosen Ideal. It teaches that the form of faith is of minor importance; the vital concern is practice — living, not mere believing. It advocates inwardness and meditation as the preparatory means, service to mankind as the end."[52]

Sister Nivedita

"For the first time in the history of India an order of monks found themselves banded together, with their faces set primarily towards the evolution of new forms of civic duty. In Europe, where the attainment of the direct religious sense is so much rarer, and so much less understood than in the East, such labour ranks as devotional in the common acceptance. But in India, the head and front of the demand made on a monastic order is that it produce saints. And the value of the monk who, instead of devoting himself to maintaining the great tradition of the superconscious life, turns back to help society upwards, has not in the past been clearly understood.

"He [Swami Vivekananda] had defined the mission of the Order of Ramakrishna as that of realizing and exchanging the highest ideals of the East and of the West."[53]

(To Miss Josephine MacLeod) "You see, when we who understood Swamiji and remember him are dead, there will come a long period of obscurity and silence, for the work that he did. It will *seem* to be forgotten, until, suddenly, in 150 or 200 years, it will be found to have transformed the West."[54]

"To belong to a new sect does not often have the effect of opening a man's heart to all about him. Sects, as a rule, unite us to the few, but separate us from the many. . . . Sri Ramakrishna represents a synthesis in one person, of all the leaders [Shankara, Chaitanya, Nanak, Ramanuja, and Madhva]. It follows that the movements of his age will unify and organize the more provincial and fragmentary movements of the past.

"Ramakrishna Paramahamsa is the epitome of the whole. His was the great superconscious life which alone can witness to the infinitude of the current that bears us all oceanwards. He is the proof of the Power behind us, and the future before us."[55]

Josephine MacLeod

"I feel so grateful (for the 10,000 rupees which Betty sent as a donation to Belur Math). It establishes the right basis for all future generations. The day before Swamiji died he told them how great this place, Belur Math, was to be! They smiled incredulously. He said, 'The power of this place will last nine hundred years. Nothing can withstand it.'"[56]

"These little glimpses into the lives and purposes of these young monks [of Belur Math] show the lines along which the Order will grow.... These men have been lighted by the torch that Swamiji carried round the world.... Remember, Swamiji said, 'No fact in your life can equal your imagination, Alberta.'... You remember Swamiji saying 'Belur Math will be a great University with religious foundation,' so perhaps in yours and my lifetime we will see his prophecy come true.[57]

"I found myself laughing to think that a man called Ramakrishna, whom I had never seen, should be the magnet that had brought me to India, where I loved being! Why? Sometimes Eternity seems to enfold one! There being no why to that, or anything else — just Isness!

"Being here [Belur Math] on this beloved Ganges is a constant joy. Odd people turn up, some interesting, some not. Days go past without my going to the Math, or hardly seeing any of them, but I know one long prayer and worship service goes on to Ramakrishna as if he were the most beloved of living gurus. Day and night thinking of him! His tastes, his likes, his predilections — absorbing all the love and devotion of these thirty or forty monks. It's the youth and enthusiasm of it all that amazes me. It never grows stale to them."[58]

Christopher Isherwood

"The Ramakrishna Movement is unique because its Founder was unique.... Spiritual truth is eternal, but it has to be restated and redemonstrated in a human life in order that it may solve the varying problems of each succeeding epoch. Ramakrishna's teaching is our modern gospel. He lived and taught for us, not for the men of two thousand years ago; and the Ramakrishna Movement is responsible for the spreading of his gospel among us, here and now. For this reason alone, the Movement must be regarded as the most important of all existing religious movements, no matter how large or influential or venerable the others may be."[59]

Carl T. Jackson

"In a number of ways, the story of the Ramakrishna Movement in America is the story of the convergence of the right movement and the right time. . . . The appearance of Swami Vivekananda and other Asian representatives at the Parliament of Religions in 1893 marked the first time authentic Asian teachers presented their faiths directly to Western audiences. The appearance of Ramakrishna swamis in America in the 1890s inaugurated a new stage in the history of Eastern spirituality in the United States."[60]

References

Chapter 1
Various Forms of Ramakrishna

1. Swami Chetanananda, trans., *A Guide to Spiritual Life* (Vedanta Society : St. Louis, 1988), 115.
2. Swami Apurvananda, *Satprasange Vijnanananda* (Ramakrishna Math: Allahabad, 1953), 107-9.
3. M., *The Gospel of Sri Ramakrishna*, trans. by Swami Nikhilananda (Ramakrishna–Vivekananda Centre : New York, 1969), 559.
4. *Vedanta and the West*, 186:55.
5. *Udbodhan*, 64:655-56.
6. *Swami Dhireshananda's diary*, 53
7. Swami Vishuddhananda, *Satprasanga* (Ramakrishna Mission: Shillong, 1962), 1:30.
8. *Mayer Katha* (Udbodhan Office: Calcutta, 1965), 2:57-8.
9. Swami Saradananda, *Sri Ramakrishna and His Divine Play*, trans. by Swami Chetanananda (Vedanta Society: St. Louis, 2003), 501.
10. *Mayer Katha*, 2:51-53.
11. Krishna Chandra Sengupta, *Sri Sri Lakshmimani Devi* (Cuttack, 1943), 38.
12. Chandra Sekhar Chattopadhyay, *Sri Sri Latu Maharajer Smritikatha* (Udbodhan Office: Calcutta, 1953), 211.
13. Akshay Kumar Sen, *Sri Sri Ramakrishna Mahima* (Udbodhan Office: Calcutta, 1969), 122,130.
14. Mahendranath Datta, *Sri Sri Ramakrishner Anudhyan* (Mahendra Publishing: Calcutta, 1966), 29-30.
15. Swami Nirlepananda, *Ramakrishna-Sardamrita* (Karuna Prakashani: Calcutta, 1968), 19.
16. *Udbodhan*, 64:656.
17. Vaikunthanath Sanyal, *Sri Sri Ramakrishna Lilamrita* (Calcutta, 1936), 103-6.
18. *Divine Play*, 817.
19. *Gospel*, 92,261.
20. Ibid., 769.
21. Swami Jagannathananda, *Srima-Katha* (Udbodhan Office: Calcutta, 1941), 2:62-3, 1:44.
22. Ibid., 2:62.
23. Binod Behari Bandyopadhyay, *Sri Sri Ramakrishna: Jivan O Sadhana* (New Book Stall: Calcutta, 1949), 424.
24. *Divine Play*, 116.
25. Ibid., 168-69
26. *Gospel*, 593.
27. Ibid., 833.
28. Ibid., 359.
29. *Divine Play*, 232-33.
30. Ibid., 232-33.

31. *The Complete Works of Sister Nivedita* (Nivedita Girls' School: Calcutta, 1967), 1:120.
32. *Ramakrishna-Saradamrita*, 28.
33. Brahmachari Akshay Chaitanya, *Brahmananda Lilakatha* (Nava Bharat Publishers: Calcutta, 1962), 9.
34. *Divine Play*, 891-92.
35. *Ramakrishna-Saradamrita*, 22-23.
36. *Divine Play*, 171-72.
37. *Gospel*, 273.
38. *Lilamrita*, 145-46; *Divine Play*, 820-21.
39. *Divine Play*, 489-91.
40. Ibid., 100-01.
41. Ibid., 565.
42. *Bhakta Manomohan* (Udbodhan Office: Calcutta, 1944), 272.
43. *Divine Play*, 818.
44. Swami Chetanananda, *They lived with God* (Vedanta Society: St. Louis, 1989), 161-62.
45. *Lilamrita*, 336-37.
46. *Divine Play*, 435.
47. *Ramakrishna-Saradamrita*, 23.
48. *Udbodhan*, 57:58.
49. *Gospel*, 810.
50. Swami Nityatmananda, *Srima Darshan* (General Printers & Publishers: Calcutta, 1970), 7:20, 14:72.
51. *Manomohan*, 244.
52. Swami Jagadiswarananda, *Navajuger Mahapurush* (Orient Book Company: Calcutta, 1949), 394.
53. *Lakshmimani*, 49-50.
54. Ibid., 127-28.
55. *Dhireshananda's diary*, 53.
56. Sister Devamata, *Ramakrishna and His Disciples* (Ananda Ashrama: La Crescenta, 1928), 125-26.
57. Swami Jagadiswarananda, *Swami Vijnanananda* (Ramakrishna Math: Allahabad, 1947), 113-14.
58. Brahmachari Akshay Chaitanya, *Thakur Sri Ramakrishna* (Calcutta Book House: Calcutta, 1974), 516-17.
59. *Divine Play*, 297,298,300.
60. Ibid., 614.
61. His Eastern and Western Disciples, *The Life of Swami Vivekananda* (Advaita Ashrama: Calcutta, 1979), 1:141-42.

62. *Lilamrita*, 218-19.
63. Suresh Chandra Datta, *Sri Sri Ramakrishnadever Upadesh* (Haramohan Publishing: Calcutta, 1968), 10-11.
64. *Divine Play*, 408.
65. Ibid., 298.
66. Ibid., 505-6.
67. *Anudhyan*, 148-49.
68. *Gospel*, 687.
69. Ibid., 743.
70. Swami Prajnanananda, *Man O Manush* (Ramakrishna Vedanta Math: Calcutta, 1986), 3:32.
71. *Gospel*, 177.
72. *Divine Play*, 522-23.
73. Ibid., 680-82.
74. Ibid., 691.
75. Ibid., 91.
76. Akshay Kumar Sen, *Sri Sri Ramakrishna Punthi* (Udbodhan Office: Calcutta, 1949), 11.
77. *Divine Play*, 254.
78. Ibid., 579-80.
79. *Udbodhan*, 52:295-96.
80. Ibid., 49:530.
81. *Divine Play*, 228-29.
82. *Gospel*, 342.
83. *Ramakrishna and His Disciples*, 50.
84. *Mayer Katha*, 2: Intro.7.
85. *Udbodhan*, 49:530.
86. *Divine Play*, 228.
87. Ibid., 808-9.
88. Akshay Chaitanya, *Swami Saradanander Jivani* (Model Publishing House : Calcutta, 1955), 346-47.
89. Kamal Krishna Mitra, *Sri Ramakrishna O Antaranga Prasanga* (Dakshineswar, 1932), 52.
90. *Punthi*, 141.
91. *Divine* Play, 506-7.
92. Ibid., 335-36.
93. Ibid., 239-41.
94. *Gospel*, 830.
95. *Divine Play*, 667-68.
96. Ibid., 554-55.
97. *Udbodhan*, 27:49.
98. *Dhireshananda's diary*, 53-54.
99. *Swami Vijnanananda*, 220-23.
100. *Gospel*, 720.
101. Ibid., 831.

102. Ibid., 969.
103. Ibid., 841.
104. Ibid., 256.
105. *Divine Play*, 325.
106. Ibid., 356-58.
107. Ibid., 817.
108. *Gospel*, 825.
109. *Udbodhan*, 41:670-71.
110. *Srima Darshan*, 11:45.
111. *Divine Play*, 319.
112. *Antaranga Prasanga*, 2.
113. *Udbodhan*, 57:618.
114. *Divine Play*, 359.
115. Ibid., 359.
116. *Dhireshananda's diary*, 57.
117. *Gospel*, 832-33.
118. *Punthi*, 225.
119. Ibid., 204-5.
120. *Divine Play*, 623-25.
121. Ibid., 626 and *Lilamrita*, 100-01.
122. Ibid., 620.
123. *Ramakrishna-Saradamrita*, 5.
124. *Divine Play*, 237-38.
125. Ram Chandra Datta, *Sri Sri Ramakrishna Paramahamsadever Jivanvrittanta* (Yogodyana: Calcutta, 1950), 131.
126. *Ramchandra Mahatmya* (Yogodyana: Calcutta, 1905), 21-22.
127. *Navayuger Mahapurush*, 306.
128. Satya Charan Mitra, *Brahmananda Prashasti* (Baranagore, 1923), 17.
129. *Divine Play*, 803.
130. *Srima Darshan*, 1:53.
131. *Gospel*, 599-600.
132. *Divine Play*, 334-35.
133. *Satprasanga*, 2:134.
134. Suresh Chandra Datta, *Ramakrishna Paramahamsadever Jivani O Upadesh* (Calcutta, 1908), 71.
135. *Gospel*, 359.
136. *Divine Play*, 256-57.
137. Ibid., 362.
138. Rk. Upadesh, 114.
139. *Lilamrita*, 144.
140. *Jivani O Upadesh*, 77.
141. *Gospel*, 711 and Srima, *Sri Sri Ramakrishna Kathamrita* (Kathamrita Bhavan: Calcutta, 1957), 5:Appendix, 46.
142. *Kathamrita*, 5:Appendix, 46.
143. *Udbodhan*, 94:82.
144. *Punthi*, 606.
145. *They Lived*, 372.
146. Pranesh Kumar, *Mahatma Devendranath* (Calcutta, 1930), 115.
147. *Divine Play*, 451-52.
148. *Antaranga*, 35.
149. *Divine Play*, 929.
150. *Jivanvrittanta*, 176.
151. *Punthi*, 607-8.
152. Ibid., 608.
153. Swami Gambhirananda, *Sri Ramakrishna Bhaktamalika* (Udbodhan Office : Calcutta, 1964), 2:141.
154. *Gospel*, 885.
155. Ramakrishna Mission's Minute Book: 5th Meeting, 23 May 1897.
156. *Udbodhan*, 57:157.
157. *Bhaktamalika*, 2:279, *Punthi*, 262.
158. *Prabuddha Bharata*, 1925:522-23.
159. *They Lived*, 307-08.
160. *Mahatma Devendranath*, 55.
161. Swami Nikhilananda, *Holy Mother* (Ramakrishna-Vivekananda Centre: New York, 1962), 93-94.
162. Ibid., 96.
163. Ibid., 103-4.
164. *Life of SV*, 1:189.
165. *Belur Math Rule Book*, 14.
166. Swami Chetanananda, *God Lived with Them* (Vedanta Society: St. Louis, 1997), 102.
167. *They Lived*, 119.
168. Ibid., 153-54.
169. Swami Chetanananda, ed. & trans., *Ramakrishna as We Saw Him* (Vedanta Society: St. Louis, 1990), 30.
170. *They Lived*, 398.
171. *God Lived*, 326-27.
172. *Satprasange Vijnanananda*, 147.
173. *God Lived*, 212.
174. Ibid., 476.
175. Swami Apurvananda, *Shivananda Vani* (Udbodhan Office: Calcutta, 1964) 2:135.
176. *They Lived*, 132-33.
177. Ibid., 229.
178. Ibid., 187.
179. Ibid., 295,301.
180. Ibid., 15.
181. Ibid., 127.

182. Ibid., 83-84.
183. Ibid., 242.
184. Romain Rolland, *The Life of Rama-krishna* (Advaita Ashrama: Calcutta, 1931), 23.
185. *Gospel*, 301.
186. *Divine Play*, 437.
187. *They Lived*, 142.
188. Ibid., 69.
189. *Swami Vijnanananda*, 282-83.
190. Swami Abhedananda, *Amar Jivankatha* (Ramakrishna Vedanta Math: Calcutta, 1964), 48-49.
191. *Divine Play*, 440.
192. Ibid., 437-38.
193. *Rk. Upadesh*, 12.
194. *Mahatma Ramchandrer Vaktritavali* (Yogodyana: Calcutta, 1938), 2:501-2.
195. *Lilamrita*, 53.
196. *Gospel*, 725-26.
197. *Srima Darshan*, 1:333.
198. *They Lived*, 116.
199. Ibid., 318.
200. *God Lived*, 80.
201. *Gospel*, 285.
202. *Divine Play*, 321.
203. *God Lived*, 251.
204. *Divine Play*, 900.
205. *God Lived*, 518-19.
206. Swami Nikhilananda, *Vivekananda: The Yogas and Other Works* (Rama-krishna-Vivekananda Centre: New York, 1953), 708-09.
207. *Gospel*, 542.
208. Her Devotee-Children, *The Gospel of the Holy Mother Sri Sarada Devi* (Sri Rama-krishna Math: Chennai, 1984), 100.
209. Ottur Bala Bhatta, *Sri Ramakrishna Karnamritam* (Sri Ramakrishna Math: Chennai, 1975), 19.

Chapter 2
Ramakrishna: His Name and the Science of Japa

1. Romain Rolland, *The Life of Ramakrishna* (Advaita Ashrama: Calcutta, 1931), 314.
2. *Bhakta Manomohan* (Udbodhan Office: Calcutta, 1941), 58-59.

3. M., *The Gospel of Sri Ramakrishna*, trans. by Swami Nikhilananda (Ramakrishna-Vivekananda Centre: New York, 1969), 1027.
4. Swami Chetanananda, *They Lived with God* (Vedanta Society: St. Louis, 1989), 206-7.
5. *Udbodhan*, 38:501-2.
6. Swami Chetanananda, trans. *Spiritual Treasures* (Vedanta Society: St. Louis, 1992), 204-5.
7. *Mahapurushjir Patravali* (Udbodhan Office: Calcutta, 1953), 253.
8. Swami Chetanananda, trans., *A Guide to Spiritual Life* (Vedanta Society: St. Louis, 1988), 146-47.
9. Swami Virajananda, *Paramartha Prasanga* (Advaita Ashrama: Calcutta, 1949), 234.
10. *Gospel.*, 190.
11. *The Complete Works of Swami Vivekananda* (Advaita Ashrama: Calcutta, 1969), 7:407-8.
12. Vijay Krishna Chattopadhyay, *Ritambhara*, 241-46.
13. Swami Lokeswarananda, *Letters for Spiritual Seekers* (Advaita Ashrama: Calcutta, 1996), 196.
14. Jitendranath Sen, *Atmasamarpan Yoga*, 90-91.
15. Jaganmohan Tarkalankar, *Nitya-puja-paddhati*, 264.
16. Swami Saradananda, *Ramakrishna and His Divine Play*, trans. by Swami Chetanananda (Vedanta Society: St. Louis, 2003), 435.
17. Ibid., 435-36.
18. Gopinath Kaviraj, *Paramartha Prasange* (Pashyanti Prakashani: Calcutta, 1980), 3:52-53.
19. Swami Chetanananda, *God Lived with Them* (Vedanta Society: St. Louis, 1997), 98-99.
20. *Gospel.*, 1025
21. Akshay Kumar Sen, *Sri Sri Rama-krishna Mahima* (Udbodhan Office: Calcutta, 1969), 132-33.
22. Swami Chetanananda, *ed & trans.*, *Ramakrishna as We Saw Him* (Vedanta Society: St. Louis, 1990), 41.

23. Swami Nityatmananda, *Srima Darshan* (General Printers and Publishers: Calcutta, 1970), 2:151.
24. Swami Akhandananda, *Smritikatha* (Udbodhan Office: Calcutta, 1937), 41.
25. *Srima Darshan*, 7:178.
26. *Udbodhan*, 81:522.
27. Swami Apurvananda, *Shivananda Vani* (Udbodhan Office: Calcutta, 1964), 2:216.
28. Swami Basudevananada, *Astarage Alapan* (Calcutta, 1956), 1:131.
29. *Gospel.*, 138.
30. Ibid., 146.
31. Ibid., 181-82.
32. Ibid., 175.
33. Ibid., 551.
34. *Mayer Katha* (Udbodhan Office: Calcutta, 1965), 2:83,153,73.
35. Ibid., 115.
36. Srishchandra Matilal, *Bhakta Girishchandra* (Dey's Publishing: Calcutta, 2003), 47.
37. Swami Nirlepananda, *Ramakrishna-Saradamrita* (Karuna Prakashani: Calcutta, 1968), 16.
38. *Gospel*, 283.
39. Ibid., 943.
40. Ibid., 720.
41. Ibid., 831.
42. *Divine Play*, 194.
43. *Divine Play*, 649.
44. Ibid., 651.
45. Ibid., 437.
46. *They Lived*, 142.
47. *Divine Play*, 450.
48. *God Lived*, 360.
49. *Gospel*, 92.
50. Ibid., 459.
51. *They Lived*, 245-46.
52. *Ramakrishna Mahima*, 64.
53. *Srima Darshan*, 2:56.
54. *Gospel*, 368.
55. Ibid., 476.
56. *Srima Darshan*, 9:141-42.
57. *Ramakrishna Mahima*, 45.
58. *Thomas Merton: A Monk* (Sheed and Word, Inc.: New York, 1974), 88-89.

Chapter 3
How to Understand Ramakrishna

1. M., *The Gospel of Sri Ramakrishna*, trans. by Swami Nikhilananda (Ramakrishna-Vivekananda Centre: New York, 1969), 102.
2. Ibid., 283.
3. Ibid., 720.
4. Ibid., 943.
5. Ibid., 273.
6. Ibid., 942.
7. Ibid., 186.
8. Ibid., 174.
9. Gita, 10:12-13.
10. Swami Nityatmananda, *Srima Darshan* (General Printers and Publishers: Calcutta, 1970), 2:54.
11. *Gospel*, 128-29.
12. Ibid., 300-01.
13. Ibid., 358-59.
14. *Srima Darshan*, 11:36.
15. *Udbodhan*, 63:350.
16. *Gospel*, 825-26.
17. Swami Saradananda, *Ramakrishna and His Divine Play*, trans. by Swami Chetanananda (Vedanta Society: St. Louis, 2003), 480-81.
18. *Srima Darshan*, 3:207-8, 13:199-200; *Gospel*, 644.
19. *Gospel*, 711, 644, 647.
20. Ibid., 359.
21. Ibid., 564.
22. Ibid., 657.
23. Ibid., 548.
24. *Divine Play*, 231-32.
25. Ibid., 232.
26. *Gospel*, 894-95.
27. Ibid., 346.
28. Ram Chandra Datta, *Sri Sri Rama-krishna Paramahamsadever Jivan-vrittanta* (Yogodyana: Calcutta, 1950), 26.
29. *Gospel*, 231.
30. Ibid., 939.
31. *Srima Darshan*, 2:59.
32. Swami Siddhananda, *Satkatha* (Udbodhan Office: Calcutta, 1964), 239-40.
33. *Gospel*, 78.

34. Ibid., 425.
35. *Mayer Katha* (Udbodhan Office: Calcutta, 1965), 2:134.
36. *Gospel*, 234-35.
37. Ibid., 332.
38. Swami Vishuddhananda, *Satprasanga* (Ramakrishna Mission: Shillong, 1959), 2:134.
39. *Divine Play*, 809.
40. Swami Jagannathananda, *Srima-Katha*, (Udbodhan Office: Calcutta, 1941), 1:75-76.
41. *Srima Darshan*, 11:162,3:151.
42. *Divine Play*, 253-54.
43. Ibid., 565.
44. Ibid., 313.
45. Ibid., 627.
46. Ibid., 662.
47. Ibid., 598.
48. Akshay Kumar Sen, *Sri Sri Rama-krishna Mahima* (Udbodhan Office: Calcutta, 1969), 216-17.
49. Suresh Chandra Datta, *Ramakrishna Paramahamsadever Jivani O Upadesh* (Calcutta, 1908), 76-77.
50. *Gospel*, 650-51.
51. Ibid., 1009-10.
52. *Srima Darshan*, 2:153.
53. *Divine Play*, 723.
54. *Gospel*, 756-57.
55. Ibid., 880-81.
56. Suresh Chandra Datta, *Sri Sri Rama-krishnadever Upadesh* (Haramohan Publishing: Calcutta, 1968), 12.
57. *Divine Play*, 589.
58. Ibid., 728.
59. *Gospel*, 553.
60. Sharat Chandra Chakrabarty, *Sadhu Nag Mahashay* (Udbodhan Office: Calcutta, 1969), 41.
61. *Mahatma Ramchandrer Vaktritavali* (Yogodyana, 1938), 2:331.
62. *Divine Play*, 455.
63. *Ramakrishna Mission's Minute Book*, 15 August 1897.
64. Swami Chetanananda, *They Lived with God* (Vedanta Society: St. Louis, 1989), 389.
65. Ibid., 142.
66. Ibid., 103-4.
67. *Rk. Jivan O Upadesh*, 48-49.
68. *Satprasanga*, 1:79.
69. *Satkatha*, 15.
70. Chandra Sekhar Chattopadhyay, *Sri Sri Latu Maharajer Smritikatha* (Udbodhan Office: Calcutta, 1953), 232-33.
71. Jnanendra Nath Biswas, *Yogodyan Mahatmya* (Navabhava Library: Calcutta, 1941), 26-29.
72. *Srima Darshan*, 2:133.
73. *Divine Play*, 598.
74. *Satkatha*, 238.
75. Ibid., 9,3.
76. Swami Chetanananda, *God Lived with Them* (Vedanta Society: St. Louis, 1997), 360.
77. Ibid., 338.
78. *Divine Play*, 772.
79. Swami Chetanananda, *Vivekananda: East meets West* (Vedanta Society: St. Louis, 1995), x-xi.
80. *Talks with Swami Vivekananda* (Advaita Ashrama: Calcutta, 1990), 397-400.
81. Vaikunthanath Sanyal, *Sri Sri Rama-krishna Lilamrita* (Calcutta, 1936), 171-72.
82. *Gospel*, 282.
83. *Srima Darshan*, 11:162.

Chapter 4
Ramakrishna's Desires

1. Chandogya Upanishad, 6:2:3, Aiteraya Upanishad, 1:1:2-3, Taittiriya Upanishad, 2:6.
2. Yogavashishtha Ramayana, Upashama Chapter, 91:29.
3. Brihadaranyaka Upanishad, 4:4:5.
4. Amritabindu Upanishad, 18.
5. M., *The Gospel of Sri Ramakrishna*, trans. by Swami Nikhilananda (Ramarishna–Vivekananda Centre : New York, 1969), 680.
6. Shankaracharya, *Maniratnamala*, 5.
7. *Gospel*, 534.
8. Ibid., 660.
9. Ibid., 564.

10. Swami Saradananda, *Sri Ramakrishna and His Divine Play*, trans. by Swami Chetanananda (Vedanta Society: St. Louis, 2003), 404.
11. *Gospel*, 747.
12. Ibid., 810.
13. Ibid., 832.
14. Ibid., 770.
15. Ibid., 305.
16. *Divine Play*, 650.
17. *Gospel*, 332.
18. Ibid., 236.
19. Ibid., 562.
20. Ibid., 312
21. Ibid., 562.
22. Swami Nityatmananda, *Srima Darshan* (General Printers and Publishers: Calcutta, 1965), 3:176.
23. *Divine Play*, 581-82.
24. Swami Chetanananda, ed. & trans., *Ramakrishna as We Saw Him* (Vedanta Society: St. Louis, 1990), 46.
25. *Gospel*, 1027.
26. Ibid., 401.
27. Ibid., 113.
28. Ibid. 332.
29. Ibid. 437.
30. Suresh Chandra Datta, *Sri Sri Ramakrishnadever Upadesh* (Haramohan Publishing: Calcutta, 1968), 147.
31. *Divine Play*, 710-11.
32. Swami Chetanananda, *God Lived with Them* (Vedanta Society: St. Louis, 1997), 362.
33. *Divine Play*, 551.
34. Swami Nirlepananda, *Ramakrishna-Saradamrita* (Karuna Prakashani: Calcutta, 1968), 9-10.
35. Swami Gambhirananda, *Srima Saradadevi* (Udbodhan Office: Calcutta, 1968), 49.
36. *Gospel*, 559.
37. *Srima Saradadevi*, 48.
38. *Divine Play*, 555.
39. *They Lived*, 355.
40. *Divine Play*, 679.
41. *Gospel*, 549.
42. Ibid., 412.
43. Kamal Krishna Mitra, *Sri Ramakrishna O Antaranga Prasanga* (Dakshineswar, 1932), 13-14.
44. *Ramakrishna as We*, 407.
45. Ibid., 413.
46. *Gospel*, 1023-24.
47. *Antaranga Prasanga*, 15.
48. *Gospel*, 477.
49. Vaikunthanath Sanyal, *Sri Sri Ramakrishna Lilamrita* (Calcutta, 1936), 228.
50. *Gospel*, 1020.
51. Ibid., 694.
52. *Divine Play*, 495.
53. *Gospel*, 799.
54. *Divine Play*, 502-4.
55. *Gospel*, 970.
56. *Ramakrishna as We*, 427.
57. Ibid., 408.
58. Ibid., 50-51.
59. *Gospel*, 132.
60. *Divine Play*, 302.
61. *Gospel*, 332.
62. Ibid., 396-97.
63. *Divine Play*, 431.
64. *Gospel*, 745.
65. Ibid., 376.
66. Ibid., 938.
67. Ibid., 547.
68. Ibid., 379.
69. *Srima Darshan*, 3:178.
70. *Gospel*, 745.
71. *Rk Upadesh*, 201.
72. *Gospel*, 234.

Chapter 5
Ramakrishna and the People of Calcutta

1. Vaikunthanath Sanyal, *Sri Sri Ramakrishna Lilamrita* (Calcutta, 1936), 8.
2. Swami Saradananda, *Sri Ramakrishna and His Divine Play*, trans. by Swami Chetanananda (Vedanta Society: St. Louis, 2003), 486-87.
3. M., *The Gospel of Sri Ramakrishna*, trans. by Swami Nikhilananda (Ramakrishna–Vivekananda Centre : New York, 1969), 965.
4. Swami Nityatmananda, *Srima Darshan* (General Printers and Publishers: Calcutta, 1970), 2:79.
5. *Gospel*, 452.
6. Ibid., 86-87.

7. Ibid., 631.
8. Ibid., 483-84.
9. Ibid., 433
10. Swami Chetanananda, *Ramakrishna as We Saw Him* (Vedanta Society: St. Louis, 1990), 432.
11. Ibid., 331.
12. Ibid., 86-87.
13. *Gospel*, 400.
14. Ibid., 439.
15. *Divine Play*, 507.
16. Chandra Sekhar Chattopadhyay, *Sri Sri Latu Maharajer Smritikatha* (Udbodhan Office: Calcutta, 1953), 125.
17. *Gospel*, 281.
18. *Divine Play*, 866.
19. Ibid., 866.
20. *Gospel*, 549,179.
21. Ibid., 670.
22. Ibid., 1013-14.
23. Ibid., 80-81.
24. Ibid., 464-69.
25. Ibid., 1017.
26. Swami Chetanananda, *How a Shepherd Boy Became a Saint* (Vedanta Society: St. Louis, 2000), 128-29.
27. *Gospel*, 285.
28. Ibid., 751.
29. Ibid., 285.
30. *Shepherd Boy*, 34-5.
31. *Gospel*, 398.
32. Ibid., 695-96.
33. Ibid., 202.
34. Ibid., 757.
35. Ibid., 670.
36. Ibid., 874.
37. Ibid., 793.
38. Ibid., 179.
39. Ibid., 438-39.
40. *Divine Play*, 470.
41. *Gospel*, 434.
42. Ibid., 433-34.
43. Swami Virajananda, *Paramartha Prasanga* (Advaita Ashrama: Calcutta, 1949), 133.
44. *Gospel*, 224-25.
45. Ibid., 141.
46. Ibid., 540.
47. Ibid., 264.

48. Ibid., 296.
49. Ibid., 312.
50. *Rk as We*, 43.
51. *Gospel*, 118-19.
52. *Divine Play*, 237.
53. *Gospel*, 903.
54. Ibid., 915.
55. Ibid., 669-70.
56. Ibid., 1011.
57. *Divine Play*, 867.
58. Swami Prabhananda, *Sri Ramakrishner Antyalila* (Udbodhan Office: Calcutta, 1985), 1:120.
59. *Divine Play*, 866.
60. Swami Nikhilananda, *Holy Mother* (Ramakrishna-Vivekananda Centre: New York, 1962), 91.
61. *Mayer Katha*, (Udbodhan Office: Calcutta, 1969), 1:105.
62. Ibid., 2:207.
63. Swami Chetanananda, *They Lived with God* (Vedanta Society: St. Louis, 1989), 162-63.

Chapter 6
The Stage for Ramakrishna's Divine Play

1. Swami Saradananda, *Ramakrishna and His Divine Play*, trans. by Swami Chetanananda (Vedanta Society: St. Louis, 2003), 182-83.
2. *The Complete Works of Sister Nivedita* (Nivedita Girls' School: Calcutta, 1967), 1:191.
3. Swami Chetanananda, ed. & trans., *Ramakrishna as We Saw Him* (Vedanta Society: St. Louis, 1990), 475-77.
4. Swami Nityatmananda, *Srima Darshan* (General Printers and Publishers: Calcutta, 1970), 4:116-17.
5. Ibid., 6:90.
6. *Rk as We*, 478.
7. *Srima Darshan*, 4:200-201.
8. Ibid., 12:175.
9. Ibid., 6:91.
10. *Rk as We*, 479.
11. *Srima Darshan*, 12:174.
12. *Gospel*, 92.
13. *Rk as We*, 477.

14. *Srima Darshan*, 4:67.
15. Ibid., 1:340-41.
16. *Rk as We*, 477.
17. *Divine Play*, 487.
18. Swami Chetanananda, *They Lived with God* (Vedanta Society: St. Louis, 1989), 204.
19. *Rk as We*, 480.
20. *Srima Darshan*, 1:252.
21. *They Lived*, 182-83.
22. *Rk as We*, 484.
23. *Gospel*, 89.
24. *Srima Darshan*, 3:240,9:119.
25. *They Lived*, 17.
26. *Rk as We*, 483.
27. *Srima Darshan*, 3:236.
28. *Rk as We*, 483-84.
29. Ibid., 481.
30. *Srima Darshan*, 4:64.
31. *Rk as We*, 481.
32. *Srima Darshan*, 3:237, 5:113.
33. Ibid., 6:292.
34. *Gospel*, 504.
35. *Srima Darshan*, 8:22.
36. *Rk as We*, 482.
37. Ibid., 482.
38. Ibid., 482.
39. *Divine Play*, 274-75.
40. *They Lived*, 204.

Chapter 7
Dakshineswar: An Object of Meditation

1. Swami Chetanananda, *They Lived with God* (Vedanta Society: St. Louis, 1989), 11.
2. Ibid., 1.
3. Ibid., 1.
4. *Tattwamanjari*, 23:216-17.
5. Abani Mohan Gupta, *Swami Subodhananda*, 1:148-49.
6. His Eastern and Western Admirers, *Reminiscencess of Swami Vivekananda* (Advaita Ashrama: Calcutta, 1983), 278-79.
7. Swami Nirvanananda, *Devaloker Katha* (Udbodhan Office: Calcutta, 1997), 96-97.

Chapter 8
Christmas Vacation with Ramakrishna

1. M., *The Gospel of Sri Ramakrishna*, trans. by Swami Nikhilananda (Ramakrishna-Vivekananda Centre: New York, 1969), 331.
2. Ibid., 331-332.
3. Ibid., 338-39.
4. Ibid., 337-38.
5. Ibid., 334-40.
6. Ibid., 341.
7. Ibid., 341.
8. Ibid., 342.
9. Ibid., 343-44.
10. Ibid., 345-46.
11. Ibid., 346.
12. Ibid., 347.
13. Ibid., 348.
14. Ibid., 349.
15. Matthew, 21:13.
16. *Gospel*, 348-49.
17. Ibid., 349.
18. Ibid., 350.
19. Ibid., 351.
20. Ibid.,,352.
21. Ibid., 353.
22. Ibid., 353.
23. Ibid., 353.
24. Ibid., 353.
25. Ibid., 357.
26. Ibid., 358-60.
27. Ibid., 360.
28. Ibid., 362-63.
29. Ibid., 364.
30. Ibid., 365.
31. Ibid., 366.
32. Ibid., 370.
33. Ibid., 371.
34. Ibid., 371.
35. Ibid., 81-82.
36. Ibid., 372.
37. Ibid., 372.
38. Ibid., 373.
39. Ibid., 375.
40. Ibid., 375-77.
41. Ibid., 377.
42. Ibid., 378-79.
43. Ibid., 381-82.

Chapter 9
Ramakrishna in the Streets and Meadows

1. M., *The Gospel of Sri Ramakrishna*, trans. by Swami Nikhilananda (Ramakrishna –Vivekananda Centre : New York, 1969), 591.
2. Swami Chetanananda, *They Lived with God* (Vedanta Society: St. Louis, 1989), 202.
3. *The Complete Works of Swami Vivekananda* (Advaita Ashrama: Calcutta, 1968), 6:64.
4. *Gospel*, 367-68.
5. Ibid., 142.
6. Swami Saradananda, *Sri Ramakrishna and His Divine Play*, trans. by Swami Chetanananda (Vedanta Society: St. Louis, 2003), 167.
7. *Gospel*, 933.
8. *Divine Play*, 119.
9. Akshay Kumar Sen, *Sri Sri Ramakrishna Punthi* (Udbodhan Office: Calcutta, 1949), 24.
10. *Gospel*, 239-41.
11. Ibid., 131.
12. Ibid., 357.
13. Ibid., 379.
14. Ibid., 490-91.
15. Ibid., 1011.
16. *Divine Play*, 237-38.
17. *Gospel*, 536.
18. *Divine Play*, 502-4.
19. Swami Chetanananda, *ed & trans.*, *Ramakrishna as We Saw Him* (Vedanta Society: St. Louis, 1990), 34-35.
20. *Gospel*, 568.
21. Ibid., 797.
22. Ibid., 375.
23. Ibid., 405.
24. Swami Ishanananda, *Matri Sannidhey* (Udbodhan Office: Calcutta, 1969), 245.
25. *Gospel*, 293.
26. *Divine Play*, 519.
27. Ibid., 610.
28. *Gospel*, 119.
29. *Divine Play*, 612.
30. *Gospel*, 361-62.
31. Ibid., 129.
32. Ibid., 129-30.
33. Ibid., 549.
34. *Divine Play*, 620.
35. Ibid., 649.
36. Ibid., 584-86.
37. *Gospel*, 99-100.
38. Ibid., 110.
39. Ibid., 833.
40. Ibid., 133.
41. Ibid., 144.
42. Ibid., 154.
43. Ibid., 253.
44. Ibid., 356.
45. Ibid., 259-60.
46. Ibid., 261.
47. Ibid., 281.
48. Ibid., 286-87.
49. Ibid., 365-66.
50. Ibid., 366-67.
51. Ibid., 462.
52. Ibid., 463-64.
53. Ibid., 466.
54. Ibid., 471-72.
55. Ibid., 546-47.
56. Ibid., 550.
57. Ibid., 550-51,556-57.
58. Ibid., 637-38.
59. Ibid., 641-42.
60. Ibid., 724,730-32.
61. Ibid., 762.
62. Swami Akhandananda, *Smritikatha* (Udbodhan Office: Calcutta, 1937), 24.
63. *Gospel*, 738-39.
64. Ibid., 742.
65. Ibid., 815-20.
66. Ibid., 822-23.
67. Ibid., 825-26
68. *Rk as We*, 208-9.
69. *Gospel*, 391.
70. Ibid., 400-401.
71. Ibid., 1018-19.

Chapter 10
The Story of Rasik

1. Swami Vishuddhananda, *Satprasnaga* (Ramakrishna Mission: Shillong, 1959), 2: 50.
2. *Udobodhan*, 50:72.

3. M., *The Gospel of Sri Ramakrishna*, trans. by Swami Nikhilananda (Ramakrishna-Vivekananda Centre: New York, 1969), 291.
4. Swami Nikhilananda, *Vivekananda: The Yogas and Other Works*, (Ramakrishna-Vivekananda Centre: New York, 1953), 706.
5. *Gospel*, 587.
6. Swami Nityatmananda, *Srima Darshan* (General Printers and Publsihers: Calcutta, 1970), 7:168-71.
7. Swamis Vividishananda and Gambhirananda, trans., *For seekers of God* (Advaita Ashrama: Calcutta, 1975), 268.
8. *Shankarananda Galpakatha* (Ramakrishna-Shankarananda Sevasharama: Bamunmura, 1959), 38.
9. *Prabuddha Bharata*, 1958:113-14.

Chapter 11
Ramakrishna and the Bohemians

1. F. Max Müller, *Ramakrishna: His Life and Sayings* (Advaita Ashrama: Calcutta, 1951), 66-67.
2. *The Complete Works of Swami Vivekananda*(Advaita Ashrama: Calcutta, 1966), 4:419.
3. M., *The Gospel of Sri Ramakrishna*, trans. by Swami Nikhilananda, (Ramakrishna-Vivekananda Centre: New York, 1969), 679.
4. Swami Chetanananda, ed. & trans., *Ramakrishna as We Saw Him* (Vedanta Society: St. Louis, 1990), 207.
5. Ibid., 336.
6. Ibid., 338.
7. Swami Chetanananda, *They Lived with God* (Vedanta Society: St. Louis, 1989), 282.
8. Ibid., 110.
9. Ibid., 110.
10. Swami Chetanananda, *How a Shepherd Boy Became a Saint* (Vedanta Society: St. Louis, 2000), 44-45.
11. Swami Akhandananda, *Smriti Katha* (Udbodhan Office: Calcutta, 1937), 42-47.

Chapter 12
The Mysterious Kalpataru

1. Swami Saradananda, *Sri Ramakrishna and His Divine Play*, trans. by Swami Chetanananda (Vedanta Society: St. Louis, 2003), 509-10.
2. Ibid., 334.
3. Swami Chetanananda, ed. & trans. *Ramakrishna As We Saw Him* (Vedanta Society: St. Louis, 1990), 316.
4. *Divine Play*, 542.
5. *Mayer Katha* (Udbodhan Office: Calcutta, 1969), 1:90.
6. M., *The Gospel of Sri Ramakrishna*, trans. by Swami Nikhilananda (Ramakrishna-Vivekananda Centre: New York, 1969), 685.
7. *Gospel*, 820.

Chapter 13
The Gospel of Ramakrishna

1. M., *The Gospel of Sri Ramakrishna*, trans. by Swami Nikhilananda (Ramakrishna-Vivekananda Centre: New York, 1969), 675.
2. Brihadaranyaka Upanishad, 4:5:4.
3. *Gospel*, 433-34.
4. Suresh Chandra Datta, *Sri Sri Ramakrishnadever Upadesh* (Haramohan Publishing: Calcutta, 1968), 162.
5. *Vedanta for the Western World*, ed. by Christopher Isherwood (George Allen & Unwin Ltd.: London, 1961), 266.
6. *Udbodhan*, 37:359.
7. *Vedanta for the Western World*, 267.
8. Romain Rolland, *The Life of Ramakrishna* (Advaita Ashrama: Calcutta, 1931), 294-95.
9. Christopher Isherwood, *Ramakrishna and His Disciples* (Methuen & Co. Ltd.: London, 1965), 282.
10. Swami Nityatmananda, *Srima Darshan* (General Printers and Publishers: Calcutta, 1968) 6:106.
11. Ibid., 106.
12. Srima, *Sri Sri Ramakrishna Kathamrita* (Kathamrita Bhavan: Calcutta, 1957), 1:129 and *Gospel*, 266.

13. *Gospel*, vi.
14. Ibid, 83.
15. Ibid., 81-83.
16. Swami Abjajananda, *Swamijir Padaprante* (Ramakrishna Mission Saradapith: Belur Math, 1972), 37.

Chapter 14
The Centenary of The Gospel of Ramakrishna

1. Swami Jagannathananda, *Srima Katha* (Ramakrishna Math: Bhubaneswar, 1953), 2:146.
2. M., *The Gospel of Sri Ramakrishna*, trans. by Swami Nikhilananda (Ramakrishna–Vivekananda Centre: New York, 1969), 591.
3. Swami Nityatmananda, *Srima Darshan* (General Printers and Publishers: Calcutta, 1972), 9:18.
4. *Udbodhan*, 35:11.
5. Swami Nikhilananda, *Vivekananda: The Yogas and Other Works* (Ramakrishna-Vivekananda Centre: New York, 1953), 903.
6. *Gospel*, 338.
7. Swamis Vividishananda and Gambhirananda, trans., *For seekers of God* (Advaita Ashrama: Calcutta, 1975), 296.
8. *Gospel*, 1021-27.

Chapter 15
The Gospel of Ramakrishna According to Girish Chandra Sen

1. Brajendra Nath Bandyopadhyay and Sajanikanta Das, *Samasamayik Drishtite Sri Ramakrishna Paramahamsa* (General Printers and Publishers: Calcutta, 1968), 3.
2. Swami Chetanananda, *Ramakrishna as We Saw Him* (Vedanta Society: St. Louis, 1990), 287.
3. *Samasamayik*, 6-7.
4. Ibid., 7,53.
5. Ibid., 84-85.
6. Swami Saradananda, *Sri Ramakrishna and His Divine Play*, trans. by Swami

Chetanananda (Vedanta Society: St. Louis, 2003), 723-24.
7. *Adi Kathamrita*, ed. & comp. by Shyamal Basu (Ananya Prakashan: Calcutta, 1983), 23.
8. Ibid., 8.
9. Ibid., 63.
10. Ibid., 64.
11. Ibid., 64-65.
12. Ibid., 66-67.
13. Ibid., 69.
14. Ibid., 79.
15. Ibid., 83-84.
16. Ibid., 85.
17. Ibid., 87.
18. Ibid., 90.

Chapter 16
The Gospel of Ramakrishna According to Suresh Chandra Datta

1. Swami Chetanananda, *They Lived with God* (Vedanta Society: St. Louis, 1989), 232.
2. Ibid., 235.
3. Ibid., 236.
4. Suresh Chandra Datta, *Ramakrishna Paramahamsadever Jivani O Upadesh* (Calcutta, 1908), 1-82.
5. Ibid., 75-77.
6. Suresh Chandra Datta, comp. *Sri Sri Ramakrishnadever Upadesh* (Hara-mohan Publishing: Calcutta, 1968), 21-265.
7. Ibid., 21-208.

Chapter 17
The Gospel of Ramakrishna According to Ram Chandra Datta

1. Swami Chetanananda, *They lived with God* (Vedanta Society: St. Louis, 1989), 79-80.
2. Ibid., 80.
3. Ibid., 80-82.
4. Ibid., 83.
5. Ibid., 86.
6. Ibid., 86.
7. Ibid., 86.

8. Ram Chandra Datta, *Sri Sri Ramakrishna Paramahamsadever Jivanvrittanta* (Yogodyana: Calcutta, 1950), iii.
9. *They Lived*, 89.
10. Ram Chandra Datta, *Tattwasara*, ed. by Apurva Kumar Mukhopadhyay (Shashadhar Prakashani: Calcutta, 1983), i-ii.
11. Ram Chandra Datta, *Tattwa-prakashika* (Yogodyana: Calcutta, 1891), i-ii.

Chapter 18
The Gospel of Ramakrishna According to Mahendra Nath Gupta

1. Swami Chetanananda, *They Lived with God* (Vedanta Society: St. Louis, 1989), 191.
2. Ibid., 192.
3. Ibid., 192.
4. Ibid, 193.
5. M., *The Gospel of Sri Ramakrishna*, trans. by Swami Nikhilananda (Ramakrishna–Vivekananda Centre : New York, 1969), 77-78.
6. *They Lived*, 193.
7. *Gospel*, 79.
8. Ibid., 90.
9. Bhagavata, 10:31:9.
10. *Gospel*, 381.
11. *Prabuddha Bharata*, 1932:395.
12. *Gospel*, 92.
13. Ibid, 261.
14. Ibid., 718-19.
15. Swami Nityatmananda, *Srima Darshan* (General Printers and Publishers: Calcutta, 1972), 9:43.
16. Srima, *Sri Sri Ramakrishna Kathamrita* (Kathamrita Bhavan: Calcutta, 1971), 1:5.
17. Ibid., 1:5.
18. Swami Chetanananda, ed. & trans., *Ramakrishna as We Saw Him* (Vedanta Society: St. Louis, 1990), 321-23.
19. Ibid., 323.
20. Ibid., 323.
21. Ibid., 323.
22. *The Complete Works of Swami Vivekananda* (Advaita Ashrama: Calcutta, 1970), 5:140.

23. D. P. Gupta, ed. *Sri Sri Ramakrishna Kathamrita Centenary Memorial* (Srima Trust: Chandigarh, 1982), 85.
24. *Gospel*, 381.

Chapter 19
The Gospel of Ramakrishna According to Swami Brahmananda

1. Swami Chetanananda, *Ramakrishna as We Saw Him* (Vedanta Society: St. Louis, 1990), 125.
2. Swami Chetanananda, *God Lived with Them* (Vedanta Society: St. Louis, 1997), 189.
3. Swami Brahmananda, comp., *Words of the Master* (Udbodhan Office: Calcutta, 1982), i-ii.
4. Swami Prabhanada, *Brahmananda Charit* (Udbodhan Office: Calcutta, 1982), 230.

Chapter 20
After Ramakrishna's Passing Away By M.

1. M., *The Gospel of Sri Ramakrishna*, trans. by Swami Nikhilananda (Ramakrishna–Vivekananda Centre : New York, 1969), 679-80.
2. Ibid., 873.
3. Ibid., 808.

Chapter 21
Sri Ramakrishna and His Divine Play According to Swami Saradananda

1. Swami Chetanananda, *God Lived with Them* (Vedanta Society: St. Louis, 1997), 309.
2. Ibid., 314-15.
3. *Udbodhan*, 11:641.
4. Swami Saradananda, *Sri Ramakrishna and His Divine Play*, trans. by Swami Chetanananda (Vedanta Society: St. Louis, 2003), 381.
5. *God Lived*, 335.
6. Ibid., 335.

7. Ibid., 336.
8. Christopher Isherwood, *Ramakrishna and His Disciples* (Methuen & Co. Ltd.: London, 1965), 2.
9. *God Lived*, 336.
10. *Divine Play*, 380.
11. *God Lived*, 336-37.
12. Ibid., 337.
13. Swami Bhumananda, *Jeman Dekhiachi* (Udbodhan Office: Calcutta, 1928), 57-58.
14. *God Lived*, 337-38.
15. Ibid., 338.
16. *Divine Play*, 6-7.

Chapter 22
My Master According to Swami Vivekananda

1. Eastern and Western Disciples, *The Life of Swami Vivekananda* (Advaita Ashrama: Calcutta, 1979), 1:77.
2. *The Complete Works of Swami Vivekananda* (Advaita Ashrama: Calcutta, 1966), 4:179.
3. Ibid., 7:207.
4. Swamis Vividishananda and Gambhirananda, trans., *For seekers of God* (Advaita Ashrama: Calcutta, 1975), 97.
5. *Complete works of SV.*, 5:389-90.
6. Ibid., 8:79.
7. *Brahmavadin*, July 1907.
8. Swami Chetanananda, *God Lived with Them* (Vedanta Society: St. Louis, 1997), 54-55.
9. Swami Satprakashananda, *Sri Ramakrishna's Life and Message in the Present Age* (Vedanta Society: St. Louis, 1976), 7.
10. *Complete works of SV.*, 7:23-25.
11. Marie Louise Burke, *Swami Vivekananda in the West: New Discoveries* (Advaita Ashrama: Calcutta 1987), 5:230.
12. Swami Vivekananda, *My Master* (Udbodhan Office: Calcutta, 1962), v-viii.
13. *Complete works of SV.*, 2:288.
14. *New Discoveries*, 3:531-32.
15. Swami Nikhilananda, *Vivekananda: The Yogas and Other Works* (Ramakrishna-Vivekananda Centre: New York, 1953), 708.
16. Ibid., 708-09.
17. Ibid., 712.
18. Ibid., 712.
19. *My Master*, 74-77.
20. *New Discoveries*, 3:530.
21. Eastern and Western Disciples, *The Life of Swami Vivekananda* (Advaita Ashrama: Calcutta, 1974), 407.
22. *New Discoveries*, 6:28.
23. *Yogas and Other Works*, 903-4.
24. *New Discoveries*, 6:82.

Chapter 23
Disciples of Ramakrishna in the West

1. *The Middle Way*, November 1973, 104-6.
2. Bible, *The Acts*, 3:6.
3. Satyendra Nath Tagore, *Bauddha Dharma* (Calucutta, 1922), 38-39.
4. *Matthew*, 10:7,9,10,16,17,28.
5. Swami Saradananda, *Sri Ramakrishna and His Divine Play*, trans. by Swami Chetanananda (Vedanta Society: St. Louis, 2003), 547.
6. Swami Omkarananda, *Sri Ramakrishna, Swami Vivekananda O Dharmaprasanga* (Ramakrishna-Vivekananda Ashrama: Howrah, 1974), 92.
7. *The Complete Works of Swami Vivekananda* (Advaita Ashrama: Calcutta, 1970), 5:314.
8. Eastern and Western Disciples, *The Life of Swami Vivekananda*, (Advaita Ashrama: Calcutta, 1979), 1:448.
9. R. C. Majumdar, ed., *Swami Vivekananda Centenary Memorial Volume*, (Calcutta, 1963), 170.
10. *Complete Works of SV.*, 1:11.
11. *Prabuddha Bharata*, 1945:45.
12. *Vedanta Kesari*, 1993:29.
13. M., *The Gospel of Sri Ramakrishna*, trans. by Swami Nikhilananda (Ramakrishna–Vivekananda Centre : New York, 1969), 934.
14. Swami Chetanananda, *God Lived with Them* (Vedanta Society: St. Louis, 1997), 325.
15. Swami Atulananda, *With the Swamis in America* (Advaita Ashrama: Calcutta, 1946), 78-79.

16. Swami Asheshananda, *Glimpses of a Great Soul* (Vedanta Press: Hollywood, 1982), 23-24.
17. Swami Sambuddhananda, *Jeman Suniachi* (Ramakrishna Ashrama: Belanagar, 1970), 162, 170
18. Mary Le Page, *Swami Abhedananda in America* (Ramakrishna Vedanta Math: Calcutta, 1991), 107-8.
19. Swami Prajnanananda, *Man O Manush* (Ramakrishna Vedanta Math: Calcutta, 1959), 330-31.
20. Moni Bagchi, *Swami Abhedananda* (Ramakrishna Vedanta Math: Calcutta, 1968), 376
21. Swami Ritajananda, *Swami Turiyananda* (Ramakrishna Math: Madras, 1973), 46-47.
22. Ibid., 47.
23. Marie Louis Burke, *Swami Vivekananda in the West: New Discoveries* (Advaita Ashrama: Calcutta, 1987), 5:112.
24. *Swami Turiyananda*, 53.
25. Ibid., 52.
26. Ibid., 57.
27. Ibid., 55.
28. Ibid., 58.
29. *Vedanta and the West*, 1952: 135.
30. *Turiyananda*, 61-62.
31. *With the Swamis in America*, 97-98.
32. Ibid., 111-12.
33. *Prabuddha Bharata*, 1925:3-4.
34. Ibid., 1928:132.
35. Ibid., 1928:162.
36. Ibid., 1928:163.
37. Ibid., 1928:525.
38. *God Lived*, 512.
39. *Complete works of SV.*, 5:107.
40. Shankari Prasad Basu, ed., *Letters of Sister Nivedita* (Navabharat Publishers: Calcutta, 1982), 2:800.
41. Swami Mukteswarananda, *Smritikatha* (Calcutta, 1970), 55.

Chapter 24
Ramakrishna and the Renaissance of Art

1. M., *The Gospel of Sri Ramakrishna*, trans. by Swami Nikhilananda (Ramakrishna – Vivekananda Centre: New York, 1969), 778.
2. Svetasvatara Upanishad, 3:19.
3. *Encyclopaedia Britannica, 1948*, 2:441.
4. Ibid., 2:444.
5. Ibid., 2:445.
6. *Prabuddha Bharata*, 1943:580.
7. S. N. Dasgupta, *Fundamentals of Indian Art* (Bhratiya Vidya Bhavan: Bombay, 1960), 112.
8. *The Complete Works of Swami Vivekananda* (Advaita Ashrama: Calcutta, 1970), 5:259.
9. Swami Saradananda, *Sri Ramakrishna and His Divine Play*, trans. by Swami Chetanananda (Vedanta Society: St. Louis, 2003), 199.
10. Ibid., 498.
11. Ibid., 691-92.
12. Ibid., 734.
13. Swami Chetanananda, ed. & trans., *Ramakrishna as We Saw Him* (Vedanta Society: St. Louis, 1990), 44.
14. *Divine Play*, 136,141.
15. Edmund Fuller, ed., *2500 Anecdotes for All Occasions* (Doubleday & Company: New York, 1961), 207.
16. *Gospel*, 748.
17. Ibid., 667-68.
18. *Divine Play*, 629.
19. Ibid., 633-34.
20. *Vedanta and the West*, 186:56.
21. *2500 Anecdotes for All Occasions*, 227.
22. Romain Rolland, *The Life Of Ramakrishna* (Advaita Ashrama: Calcutta, 1931), 14.

Chapter 25
Ramakrishna and Monasticism

1. Swami Nikhilananda, trans., *Atmabodha* (Ramakrishna-Vivekananda Centre: New York, 1970), 207.
2. Swami Nikhilananda, trans. Bhagavad Gita (Ramakrishna-Vivekananda Centre: New York 1952), 51-52.
3. M., *The Gospel of Sri Ramakrishna*, trans. by Swami Nikhilananda (Ramakrishna–Vivekananda Centre : New York, 1969), 1009-10.

4. Sharat Chandra Chakrabarty, *Saint Durga Charan Nag* (Ramakrishna Math: Madras, 1951), 53.
5. *Gospel*, 549.
6. Ibid., 442.
7. Ibid., 580.
8. Ibid., 314.
9. Jabala Upanishad, 4.
10. Her Direct Disciples, *At Holy Mother's Feet* (Advaita Ashrama: Calcutta, 1963), 357.
11. *Gospel*, 747.
12. Swami Saradananda, *Sri Ramakrishna and His Divine Play*, trans. by Swami Chetanananda (Vedanta Society: St. Louis, 2003), 309-10.
13. Ibid., 310.
14. Ibid., 380.
15. *Gospel*, 832.
16. Ibid., 523.
17. *The Complete Works of Swami Vivekananda* (Advaita Ashrama: Calcutta, 1970), 3:447.
18. Swami Nikhilananda, *Vivekananda: Yogas and Other Works* (Ramakrishna-Vivekananda Centre: New York, 1953), 31.
19. *Complete Works of SV.*, 6:511-12.
20. *Gospel*, 195.
21. *Divine Play*, 592.
22. *Life of Sri Ramakrishna* (Advaita Ashrama: Calcutta 1943), 588.
23. *Divine Play*, 851.
24. Ibid., 852.
25. Ibid., 852.
26. *Complete Works of SV.*, 6:265-66.

Chapter 26
If Ramakrishna Were Alive Today

1. Swami Chetanananda, ed. & trans., *Ramakrishna as We Saw Him* (Vedanta Society: St. Louis, 1990), 54-55.
2. Kamal Krishna Mitra, *Sri Ramakrishna O Antaranga Prasanga* (Dakshineswar, 1932), 6-7,61-62.
3. *Rk as We*, 74.
4. Ibid., 190-91.
5. Swami Nityatmananda, *Srima Darshan* (General Printers and Publishers:

Calcutta, 1968), 3:207-08,13:199-200; M., *The Gospel of Sri Ramakrishna*, trans. by Swami Nikhilananda (Ramakrishna-Vivekananda Centre: New York, 1969), 644.
6. Katha Upanishad, 2:2:9.
7. *Rk as We*, 292-93.
8. *Srima Darshan*, 2:267-68.
9. *Udbodhan*, 49:70-71.
10. *Srima Darshan*, 3:30.
11. Swami Chetanananda, *God Lived with Them* (Vedanta Society: St. Louis, 1997), 399.
12. *Rk as We*, 56-57.
13. *Srima Darshan*, 11:90.
14. *Udbodhan*, 43:344.
15. *Srima Darshan*, 11:38.
16. *Gospel*, 91.
17. *Srima Darshan*, 2:56.
18. Swami Nirlepananda, *Ramakrishna-Vivekanander Jivanaloke* (Udbodhan Office: Calcutta, 1934), 258.
19. *Swami Vivekanander Vani O Rachana* (Udbodhan Office: Calcutta, 1964), 8:395.
20. Swamis Vividishananda and Gambhirananda, trans., *For Seekers of God* (Advaita Ashrama: Calcutta, 1975), 45.
21. Swami Abhedananda, *Patra Sankalan* (Ramakrishna Vedanta Math: Calcutta, 1943), 37.
22. *Rk as We*, 456.
23. *For seekers*, 237.
24. *Rk as We*, 461.
25. *Vedanta Kesari*, 1990:373-74.
26. Swami Chetanananda, *They lived with God* (Vedanta Society: St. Louis, 1989), 205
27. Ibid., 205.
28. *Ram Chandra Mahatmya* (Yogodyana: Calcutta, 1905), 64.
29. Swami Abjajananda, *Swamijir Padaprante* (Ramakrishna Mission Saradapith: Belur Math, 1972), 157.
30. *Bhakta Manomohan* (Udbodhan Office: Calcutta, 1944), 227.
31. *Vedanta and the West*, 187:58-59.
32. Swami Chetanananda, trans., *A Guide to Spiritual Life* (Vedanta Society: St. Louis, 1988), 78.

33. Brahmachari Akshay Chaitanya, *Swami Saradanander Jivani* (Model Publishing House: Calcutta, 1955), 340-41.
34. *Udbodhan*, 40:31.
35. John: 20:27-29.
36. Swami Chetanananda, trans., *Spiritual Treasures* (Vedanta Society: St. Louis, 1992), 98.
37. *Udbodhan*, 41:303.
38. *For seekers*, 61.
39. *Srima Darshan*, 9:170-71.
40. Swami Chetanananda, ed. & comp., *Matridarshan* (Udbodhan Office: Calcutta, 1987), 247.
41. Swami Omkareswarananda, *Swami Premananda* (Ramakrishna Sadhan Mandir: Deoghar, 1946), 2:52-53.
42. *They Lived*, 290.
43. *Udbodhan*, 53:609.
44. *Rk as We*, 369-70.
45. *Udbodhan*, 40:292-98.

Chapter 27
The Second Coming of Ramakrishna

1. M., *The Gospel of Sri Ramakrishna*, trans. by Swami Nikhilananda (Ramakrishna–Vivekananda Centre: New York, 1969), 829.
2. *The Complete Works of Swami Vivekananda* (Advaita Ashrama: Calcutta, 1964), 8:179.
3. *Mayer Katha* (Udbodhan Office: Calcutta, 1965), 2:10.
4. Swami Jagannathananda, *Srima Katha* (Ramakrishna Math: Bhubaneswar, 1953), 2:5.
5. Swami Basudevananda, *Astarage Alapan* (Calcutta, 1956), 1:148.
6. *Srima Katha*, 2:23-24.
7. *Swami Vivekanander Vani O Rachana* (Udbodhan Office: Calcutta, 1973), 9:251.
8. Swamis Vividishananda and Gambhirananda, trans. *For Seekers of God*, (Advaita Ashrama: Calcutta, 1975), 288.
9. Ibid., 7.
10. *Talks with Swami Vivekananda* (Advaita Ashrama: Calcutta, 1990), 128.
11. Ibid., 128.

12. Rulebook of Belur Math, 14-15.
13. Swami Apurvananda, comp. *Shivananda Vani* (Udbodhan Office: Calcutta 1964) 2:192-93.
14. *Vani O Rachana*, 7:243.
15. *Complete Works*, 5:31.
16. Her Devotee & Children, *The Gospel of the Holy Mother Sri Sarada Devi* (Ramakrishna Math: Madras, 1984), 167.
17. *For seekers*, 172.
18. Marie Louise Burke, *Swami Vivekananda in the West: New Discoveries* (Advaita Ashrama: Calcutta, 1987), 6:17.
19. *Gospel*, 798-99.
20. Ibid., 359.
21. Ibid., 829.
22. Swami Chetanananda, trans., *A Guide to Spiritual Life* (Vedanta Society: St. Louis, 1988), 136-37.
23. *Udbodhan*, 25:726-27.
24. Swami Apurvananda, *Satprasange Swami Vijnanananda* (Ramakrishna Math: Allahabad,1953), 157-58.
25. M., *The Gospel of Ramakrishna*, revised by Swami Abhedananda (The Beacon Press: Boston, 1947), 418.
26. *Talks with*, 103.
27. Swami Saradananda, *Sri Ramakrishna and His Divine Play*, trans. by Swami Chetanananda (Vedanta Society: St. Louis, 2003), 649.
28. *Rk as We*, 31.
29. *Gospel of Holy Mother*, 77.
30. *Divine Play*, 360.
31. *Udbodhan*, 29:723.
32. Swami Bhumananda, *Jeman Dekhiachi* (Udbodhan Office: Calcutta, 1928), 417.
33. *Udbodhan*, 45:223.
34. Krishna Chandra Sengupta, *Sri Sri Lakshmimani Devi* (Cuttack, 1943), 41.
35. *Complete Works of SV*, 5:131-32.
36. *Gospel*, 943.
37. *Mayer Katha*, 2:171-72.
38. Ibid, 2:87-88.
39. Brahmachari Akshay Chaitanya, *Sri Sri Saradadevi* (Calcutta Book House: Calcutta, 1972), 30.
40. Ashutosh Mitra, *Srima* (Calcutta, 1944), 84.

41. Upendra Nath Bhattacharya, *Banglar Baul O Baul Gan* (Orient Book Company: Calcutta, 1957), 46.
42. *Gospel*, 397.
43. Ibid., 832.
44. *Udbodhan*, 25:725.
45. *Gospel*, 422.
46. *Talks With*, 128-29.
47. Ibid., 129-30.
48. *Udbodhan*, 25:731.
49. *Gospel*, 140-41.
50. *Yogas and Other Works*, 386.
51. *Gospel*, 322
52. *Complete Works of SV*, 5:35.
53. *Talks with*, 402.
54. Swami Chetanananda, *How a Shepherd Boy Became a Saint* (Vedanta Society: St. Louis, 2000), 89.

Chapter 28
Some Glimpses of Ramakrishna

1. *The Complete Works of Sister Nivedita* (Nivedita Girls' School: Calcutta, 1967), 137.
2. *Mundaka Upanishad*, 2:1:4.
3. Swami Jagannathananda, *Srima-Katha* (Udbodhan Office: Calcutta, 1941), 1:78.
4. Swami Chetanananda, *They Lived with God* (Vedanta Society: St. Louis, 2006), 80.
5. Swami Nityatmananda, *Srima Darshan* (General Printers and Publishers: Calcutta, 1966), 4:64.
6. Swami Purnatmananda, ed. *Sri Sri Mayer Padaprante* (Udbodhan Office: Calcutta, 1995), 2:433.
7. Swami Chetanananda, ed. *Swami Subodhanander Smritikatha* (Udbodhan Office: Calcutta, 2005), 249.
8. *Srima Darshan*, 3:72,79.
9. Swami Jagannathananda, *Srima-Katha* (Ramakrishna Math: Bhubaneswar, 1953), 2:16.
10. Swami Chetanananda, ed. *Ramakrishna as We Saw Him* (Vedanta Society: St. Louis, 1990), 458.
11. *Srima-Katha*, 2:75-76.
12. Ibid., 2:120
13. Ibid., 2:242
14. M., *The Gospel of Sri Ramakrishna*, trans.

Swami Nikhilananda (Ramakrishna-Vivekananda Centre: New York, 1969), 348.
15. *Swami Dhireshananda's Diary*, 75.
16. *Gospel*, 518.
17. Swami Saradananda, *Sri Ramakrishna and His Divine Play*, trans. Swami Chetanananda (Vedanta Society: St. Louis, 2003), 465.
18. *Sri Ramakrishna Puja Paddhati* (Udbodhan Office: Calcutta), 62.
19. *Rk as We*, 232.
20. Swami Chetanananda, *God Lived with Them* (Vedanta Society: St. Louis, 1997), 187.
21. *Srima-Katha*, 1:251.
22. Ibid., 1:276.
23. Ibid., 1:116,15.
24. *Dhireshananda's Diary*, 67.
25. *Gospel*, 118-19.
26. *Srima-Katha*, 2:149.
27. *Gospel*, 739.
28. Ibid., 832.
29. *Srima Darshan*, 1:323.
30. *Srima-Katha*, 1:156.
31. Ibid., 2:242.
32. Swami Gambhirananda, *Srima Sarada Devi* (Udbodhan Office: Calcutta, 1968), 58-59.
33. *Srima-Katha*, 1:176.
34. Ibid., 1:230 and *Sri Sri Ramakrishna Kathamrita* (Udbodhan Office: Calcutta, 1999), 1088-89.
35. *Srima-Katha*, 1:196.
36. Ibid., 1:25.
37. *God Lived*, 63.
38. *Srima-Katha*, 2:160, 163, 221.
39. *Gospel*, 973.
40. Ibid., 973-74.
41. *God Lived*, 338.
42. Swami Prabhananda, *Sri Ramakrishner Antyalila* (Udbodhan Office: Calcutta, 1987), 2:211.

Chapter 29
Centenary of the Ramakrishna Mission

1. *The Middle Way* (Journal of the Buddhist Society: London, November 1973), 105-6.

2. *Matthew*, 10:7-8.
3. Swami Atulananda, *With the Swamis in America* (Advaita Ashrama: Calcutta, 1946), 103.
4. Swami Chetanananda, *God Lived with Them* (Vedanta Society: St. Louis, 1997), 35.
5. His Eastern and Western Admirers, *Reminiscences of Swami Vivekananda* (Advaita Ashrama: Calcutta, 1983), 133.
6. *Prabuddha Bharata*, 1978:125.
7. *Letters of Swami Vivekananda* (Advaita Ashrama: Calcutta, 1981), 247.
8. Bhagavad Gita, 3:21.
9. *The Complete Works of Swami Vivekananda* (Advaita Ashrama: Calcutta, 1970), 3:205.
10. His Eastern and Western Disciples, *The Life of Swami Vivekananda* (Advaita Ashrama: 1981), 2:247.
11. Ibid., 2:247.
12. Ibid., 2:249-50.
13. Swami Chetanananda, *Swami Adbhutananda: Teachings and Reminiscences* (Vedanta Society: St. Louis, 1980), 79-80; Swami Nikhilananda, *Vivekananda: The Yogas and Other Works* (Ramakrishna-Vivekananda Centre: New York, 1953), 128.
14. *Life of Vivekananda*, 2:253.
15. *Vedanta and the West*, 185:11-14.
16. Ibid., 185:15-17.
17. Ibid., 186:49-50.
18. Ibid., 187:60.
19. Ibid., 187:63.
20. Bhagavad Gita, 13:13.
21. *Letters of Vivekananda*, 350.
22. Ibid., 342.
23. *Yogas and Other Works*, 124.
24. *Complete Works of SV*, 5:382-83.

Chapter 30
The Ramakrishna Order: Sources of Inspiration

1. Swami Chetanananda, *God Lived with Them* (Vedanta Society: St. Louis, 1997), 35.
2. Swami Nikhilananda, *Vivekananda: The Yogas and Other Works* (Ramakrishna-Vivekananda Centre: New York, 1953), 31.
3. Ibid., 31.
4. *God Lived with Them*, 519-20.
5. His Eastern and Western Disciples, *The Life of Swami Vivekananda* (Advaita Ashrama: Calcutta, 1979), 1:182.
6. Swami Nikhilananda, *Holy Mother* (Ramakrishna-Vivekananda Centre: New York, 1962), 241.
7. Ibid., 251-52.
8. *Rules and Regulations of the Ramakrishna Math*, Belur Math, 1-2.
9. *God Lived with Them*, 57.
10. His Eastern and Western Admirers, *Reminiscences of Swami Vivekananda* (Advaita Ashrama: Calcutta, 1983), 243.
11. Swami Mukteswarananda, *Smriti Katha* (Calcutta, 1971), 55.
12. Swami Gambhirananda, *Yuganayak Vivekananda* (Udbodhan Office: Calcutta, 1966), 3:228.
13. *The Complete Works of Swami Vivekananda* (Advaita Ashrama: Calcutta, 1969), 7:115, 261-62.
14. Ibid., (1968), 6:275.
15. *God Lived with Them*, 96-97.
16. Ibid., 113.
17. Ibid., 163.
18. Swamis Vividishananda and Gambhirananda, *For Seekers of God* (Advaita Ashrama: Calcutta, 1975), 200; Swami Apurvananda, *Shivananda Vani* (Udbodhan Office: Calcutta, 1955), 152-53.
19. *For Seekers of God*, 203, 210.
20. *God Lived with Them*, 215.
21. Swami Omkareswarananda, *Premananda* (Ramakrishna Sadhan Mandir: Deoghar, 1946), 2:98.
22. Swami Chetanananda, *Swami Adbhutananda: Teachings and Reminiscences* (Vedanta Society: St. Louis, 1880), 128-29.
23. Ibid., 87-89.
24. *God Lived with Them*, 239-40.
25. Ibid., 346.
26. The Ramakrishna Math and Mission Convention (1926), 65.

27. Brahmachari Prakash, *Swami Sarada-nanda* (Basumati Sahitya Mandir: Calcutta, 1936), 300.

28. Sister Devamata, *Days in an Indian Monastery* (Ananda Ashrama: La Crescenta, 1927), 255.

29. *God Lived with Them*, 297.

30. Ibid., 298-99.

31. *The Religions of the World* (Ramakrishna Mission Institute of Culture: Calcutta, 1987), 121-22.

32. Swami Chetanananda, tr. & ed. *Spiritual Treasures* (Vedanta Society: St. Louis, 1992), 195-97.

33. *Prabuddha Bharata*, 1936:112.

34. *Convention 1926*, 85, 48, 47.

35. Swami Niramayananda, *The Call of the Spirit* (Ramakrishna Math: Madras, 1984), 44.

36. Swami Jagadiswarananda, *Swami Vijnanananda* (Ramakrishna Math: Allahabad, 1947), 106.

37. *God Lived with Them*, 538, 555.

38. Swami Chetanananda, ed. & tr., *Ramakrishna as We Saw Him* (Vedanta Society: St. Louis, 1990), 262.

39. *Sri Sri Mayer Katha* (Udbodhan Office: Calcutta, 1969), 1:100-01.

40. Swami Chetanananda, *God Lived with Them* (Vedanta Society: St. Louis, 1997), 522-26.

41. *Prabuddha Bharata*, 1921:90.

42. Swami Abjajananda, *Swamijir Padaprante* (Ramakrishna Mission Saradapith: Belur Math, 1972), 35.

43. *Prabuddha Bharata*, 1945:123-25.

44. *The Religions of the World*, 2:585-89.

45. *Swamijir Padaprante*, 330-31.

46. Swami Jagadiswarananda, *Navayuger Mahapurush* (Ramakrishna Ashrama: Raghunathpur, 1951), 2:350.

47. Girish Chandra Ghosh, *Thakur Sri Ramakrishna O Swami Vivekananda*, ed. by Sankari Prasad Basu and Bimal Chandra Ghosh (Mandal Book House: Calcutta, 1981), 38-40.

48. Ibid., 57.

49. Swami Nityatmananda, *Srima Darshan* (General Printers & Publishers: Calcutta, 1973), 13:117-18.

50. Ibid., 7:88-90.

51. Ibid., 2:252.

52. *Days in an Indian Monastery*, 1

53. *The Complete Works of Sister Nivedita* (Sister Nivedita Girls' School: Calcutta, 1967), 1:40, 42.

54. Sankari Prasad Basu, ed., *Letters of Sister Nivedita* (Navabharat Publishers: Calcutta, 1982), 2:800.

55. *Sister Nivedita's Lectures and Writings* (Sister Nivedita Girls' School: Calcutta, 1975), 128, 132

56. Pravrajika Prabuddhaprana, *The Life of Josephine MacLeod* (Sarada Math: Calcutta, 1990), 165

57. *Reminiscences of Swami Vivekananda*, 427.

58. Linda Prugh, *Josephine MacLeod and Vivekananda's Mission* (Ramakrishna Math: Chennai, 2001), 361, 363.

59. Swami Gambhirananda, *History of the Ramakrishna Math and Mission* (Advaita Ashrama: Calcutta, 1957), ix.

60. Carl T. Jackson, *Vedanta for the West* (Indiana University Press: Indianapolis, 1994), 1, 15.

Index

Rk = Ramakrishna. SV = Swami Vivekananda. Page numbers followed by "n" indicate a footnote. Page numbers for illustrations are in italics.

Abhedananda, Swami (Kali): devoted student of Vedanta, 389; met President McKinley, Thomas Edison, William James, 421; on Rk as gods and goddesses, 83; on Rk elevating womankind, 538; on Rk's future return, 489; Rk, vision of, 77, 423; teaching in West, 421-4

Abhayananda, Swami, 404n

Achalananda, Swami, on love/respect among Rk monks, 545

Adbhutananda, Swami (Latu): abhorrence of rules, 536; on disciples' squabbles, 141; dispute with SV, 522; on Kalipada's vision of Rk, 81; on preaching at God's command, 535; on religion as realization, 190; on Rk and caste restrictions, 126; weeping for Rk, 462

Advaitananda, Swami (Brother Gopal): brought ochre cloths to Rk, 454, 530; Rk as Gadadhar (Vishnu), vision of, 32; Rk, vision of, 72; serving brother monks, 542-3; treats Rk's throat at Cossipore, 89

Aghoremani. *See* Gopal-ma

Akhandananda, Swami, 540

Ambikananda, Swami, 15

Ananda (Buddha's attendant), 413

art: brief explication of, 434; Christ's influence on, 435; Indian, explication of, 436; Rk as painter, sculptor, 437

Arupananda, Swami, 492

Atmananda, Swami, 545; on SV's rule against monks' possessions, 546

Atul (Girish's brother): Rk blessed on Kalpataru Day, 71; vision of Rk as half Krishna, half Radha, 39

Atulananda, Swami (Gurudas): took responsibility for Shanti Ashrama, 427

avatar: characteristics of, 494; cultural renewal and, 315; description, 118; eternal recurrence, SV on, 481; has harmless desires, 148; hidden nature of, 20-1; imparts religion, 318; messenger for era, 319; missions of, 515; on name and form, 95; recognition of, 114, 115-20; signs of, 65